THE BURROUGHS CYCLOPÆDIA

For my girls

THE
BURROUGHS
CYCLOPÆDIA

Characters, Places, Fauna, Flora, Technologies,
Languages, Ideas and Terminologies Found
in the Works of Edgar Rice Burroughs

by CLARK A. BRADY

McFarland & Company, Inc., Publishers
Jefferson, North Carolina, and London

The present work is a reprint of the library bound edition of
The Burroughs Cyclopædia : Characters, Places, Fauna, Flora,
Technologies, Languages, Ideas and Terminologies Found in
the Works of Edgar Rice Burroughs, *first published in 1996 by
McFarland.*

LIBRARY OF CONGRESS CATALOGUING-IN-PUBLICATION DATA

Brady, Clark A., 1963–
    The Burroughs cyclopædia : characters, places, fauna, flora, tech-
nologies, languages, ideas and terminologies found in the works of
Edgar Rice Burroughs / by Clark A. Brady.
        p.   cm.
    Includes bibliographical references and index.

    ISBN 0-7864-2123-1 (softcover : 50# alk. paper)

    1. Burroughs, Edgar Rice, 1875–1950 — Encyclopedias.   2. Popular
literature — United States — Encyclopedias.   3. Fantastic fiction,
American — Encyclopedias.   4. Adventure stories, American —
Encyclopedias.   5. Science fiction, American — Encyclopedias.
I. Burroughs, Edgar Rice, 1875–1950.   II. Title.
PS3503.U687Z58   2005
813'.52 — dc20   96-32787

British Library cataloguing data are available

Cover ©2005 Pictures Now!

Manufactured in the United States of America

*McFarland & Company, Inc., Publishers
  Box 611, Jefferson, North Carolina 28640
  www.mcfarlandpub.com*

CONTENTS

For the convenience of the reader, this cyclopædia is alphabetized word-by-word.

PREFACE

Edgar Rice Burroughs was not satisfied with creating characters and events to move around in the world that we know; instead, his rich imagination created new worlds and filled them with peoples, cultures, technologies, beings, plants, languages, wars and cities just earthly enough to allow the reader to relate to them, yet alien and fantastic enough to thrill and delight. With several notable exceptions (and several other infamous ones), all of his books were set in an integrated and largely self-consistent universe. The Tarzan and Pellucidar books certainly take place in the same universe, and the presence of the enigmatic Jason Gridley links them to the Mars and Venus books; John Carter and Barsoom are a part of the Moon series, and Tarzan appears in *The Eternal Savage*, whose main character is the sister of the hero of *The Mad King*; these adventurous siblings hail from Beatrice, Nebraska, which was also the home of James Torrance of "The Efficiency Expert." Central to all of these connections is Burroughs himself, who appears as narrator in the vast majority of his books and as an actual character within the main text of several (most notably *The Eternal Savage*, *The People That Time Forgot*, *Pirates of Venus* and *Tarzan at the Earth's Core*).

The Burroughs universe is so complex (giving an impression of being nearly as much so as our own real one, which it often intersects) as to demand a thorough reference to its countless otherworldly characters, places, terms and ideas, and I have attempted to fill that need. In writing this book I imagined myself a typical modern person with no prior exposure to Burroughs' works, and I set out to define every unfamiliar term that such a person would encounter in all of Burroughs' narrative fiction. Thus the reader will find not only things drawn entirely from Burroughs' mind, but also real-world terms, which would have been familiar to the reading public of the first half of the twentieth century but perhaps not to the modern reader. Many brand names, celebrities, placenames, song titles, and other terms that were once household words are now every bit as alien to the average reader as anything from Barsoom. I also included foreign words, animals, plants, places, and other items I did not think the average reader would know. In doing this I tried to err on the side of inclusiveness, so a very well-read person with a long memory for minutiæ may find many such entries superfluous, but the average reader should find them helpful. If there was any doubt about an entry, it went in.

I also included entries on real-world people and places which, though familiar, have an interesting or surprising or unusual connection to the Burroughs fictional universe. I think most people would find it amusing or intriguing to know that Tarzan had met Haile Selassie and been considered a political enemy by Stalin, so I have included entries on these and others like them. Also included are cross-references to the modern names of places and in some cases things which had different names in Burroughs' heyday.

A few explanatory words may assist the reader in using the book. First, I should note that Burroughs nearly always used the nineteenth century literary device of claiming that all of the events of his books were absolutely true and that he was merely the narrator of them. In keeping with this practice, the entries herein (with only a few exceptions) are written as if the stories are all true and the events happened just as Burroughs described them. I have also included the Burroughs narrator's remarks about how individual stories came to him.

Entries are alphabetized word by word (rather than letter by letter), with a hyphen always treated as a word break; thus A-Kor comes before Aanthor, for example. Each entry includes at least one textual citation where the term in question may be found. These citations identify Burroughs' books using abbreviations, which are listed in the Abbreviations Used section following this preface.

Obviously, any work of this nature is finite in scope, and there are many terms which could have been defined but were not. These fall into three categories. The first included things which were sufficiently obvious that I did not feel they needed any kind of explanation or cross-reference of any kind; there was no need to describe a lion or elephant, for instance. The second category includes terms from excluded works, such as nonfiction writings, letters, poems, plays, fragments, and the like; it was for this reason, for instance, that "The Scientists Revolt" was not included. (If in doubt about whether a work is included, look up its title; each title has a separate entry itself.) The third category of omissions consists of things I simply overlooked. At each stage of the preparation I found a few things that I had missed, and I am sure that sharp-eyed enthusiasts will find others. If anyone finding such omissions (or outright errors, for that matter) will kindly alert me to them via a letter to the publisher, I will research and verify them for inclusion in any future editions.

I know that I am not alone in clinging to the totally irrational but very comfortable delusion that somewhere, in some alternate universe perhaps, Tarzan still swings through his beloved Africa, David Innes struggles to carve a civilization out of a savage and unyielding world, and John Carter's fighting smile continues to strike fear into the hearts of his enemies. Perhaps it is the little boy in me that wants it so—the same little boy who memorized all of the ape-words and used to stand out in the field behind his house trying to astrally project himself to Barsoom. It is to that little boy, and to millions of others like him, that I dedicate this book.

Several people deserve mention as being particularly helpful in preparing this book. Special thanks go to Faye Mahan of the St. John the Baptist Parish Library's interlibrary loan department, for digging up copies of the more obscure works that I did not own copies of; to Randy DeSoto, director of that library, for help in finding reference sources for a number of the more elusive terms; to the reference staffs of the Louisiana State University Library and the University of New Orleans Library; to Sandra A. Galfas of Edgar Rice Burroughs, Inc., who referred me to a very important source I had completely overlooked; to Dr. Lee Shiflett of the Library School at Louisiana State University, who steered me to the right publisher; and most of all to my beloved wife, who not only typed the entire book from my dictation but also put up with long nights at the library and endless talk about nothing else but the book for the first few months of our married life. To these and all the others who gave technical, intellectual or moral support I give my heartfelt thanks.

ABBREVIATIONS USED

In all dictionaries it is customary to abbreviate the name of the language from which a given word is derived, and this cyclopædia is no different. The following abbreviations are used:

Amt	Amtorian	*Min*	Minunian
Apa	Apache	*Pal*	The language of Pal-ul-don
Ape	The Tongue of the Great Apes	*Pell*	Pellucidarian
Ara	Arabic	*Sp*	Spanish
Bar	The Tongue of Barsoom	*Swa*	Swahili
Cpk	Caspakian	*Uni*	The Unisan language of Poloda
Fr	French	*Van*	The Tongue of Va-nah
Ger	German	*WA*	The pidgin trade language of West
Kap	The Kapar language of Poloda		Africa
Lat	Latin		

In order to keep references to books simple, I have devised a simple alphanumeric abbreviation for each book. In any reference the abbreviation for the book will be followed by a semicolon and the number of the chapter or chapters in which the term is found. (I have omitted page numbers because they differ among various editions, while chapters do not.) Occasionally references will occur in which a colon follows the book abbreviation, then a number, then a semicolon and another number. This form is used in those novels which have "books" within the whole novel, and those books are subdivided into chapters. For example, M10:3;4 translates into *Llana of Gathol* (the 10th book of the Mars series), book 3, chapter 4. The title abbreviations are as follows:

Adventure Stories		The Resurrection of Jimber-Jaw	J
The Monster Men	Q	The Lost Continent	LC
The Land of Hidden Men	HM		
The Rider	R	**Apache Novels**	**(A)**
The Lad and the Lion	LL	The War Chief	A1
The Maneater	ME	Apache Devil	A2

5

Beyond the Farthest Star	(B)	**Moon Series**	(MM)
Adventure on Poloda	B1	The Moon Maid	MM1
Tangor Returns	B2	The Moon Men	MM2
		The Red Hawk	MM3
Caspak Series	(C)		
The Land That Time Forgot	C1	**The Mucker Series**	(K)
The People That Time Forgot	C2	The Mucker	K1
Out of Time's Abyss	C3	Return of the Mucker	K2
		The Oakdale Affair	K3
The Cave Girl	(CG)		
The Cave Girl	CG1	**Pellucidar Series**	(P)
The Cave Man	CG2	At the Earth's Core	P1
		Pellucidar	P2
Contemporary Dramas		Tanar of Pellucidar	P3
The Girl from Hollywood	GH	*Tarzan at the Earth's Core	P4
The Girl from Farris's	GF	Back to the Stone Age	P5
The Efficiency Expert	EE	Land of Terror	P6
		Savage Pellucidar	P7
The Eternal Savage	(E)		
The Eternal Lover	E1		
Sweetheart Primeval	E2	**Pirate Blood**	PB
Historical Novels		**Tarzan Series**	(T)
The Outlaw of Torn	OT	Tarzan of the Apes	T1
I Am a Barbarian	I	The Return of Tarzan	T2
		The Beasts of Tarzan	T3
The Mad King	(MK)	The Son of Tarzan	T4
The Mad King	MK1	Tarzan and the Jewels of Opar	T5
Barney Custer of Beatrice	MK2	Jungle Tales of Tarzan	T6
		Tarzan the Untamed	T7
Mars Series	(M)	Tarzan the Terrible	T8
A Princess of Mars	M1	Tarzan and the Golden Lion	T9
The Gods of Mars	M2	Tarzan and the Ant Men	T10
The Warlord of Mars	M3	Tarzan, Lord of the Jungle	T11
Thuvia, Maid of Mars	M4	Tarzan and the Lost Empire	T12
The Chessmen of Mars	M5	*Tarzan at the Earth's Core	T13
The Master Mind of Mars	M6	Tarzan the Invincible	T14
A Fighting Man of Mars	M7	Tarzan Triumphant	T15
Swords of Mars	M8	Tarzan and the City of Gold	T16
Synthetic Men of Mars	M9	Tarzan and the Lion Man	T17
Llana of Gathol	M10	Tarzan and the Leopard Men	T18
John Carter the Giant of Mars	M11A	Tarzan's Quest	T19
Skeleton Men of Jupiter	M11B	Tarzan and the Forbidden City	T20

*This book is designated both T13 and P4.

Tarzan the Magnificent	T21	**Venus Series**	(V)
Tarzan and the Foreign Legion	T22	Pirates of Venus	V1
Tarzan and the Madman	T23	Lost on Venus	V2
Tarzan and the Castaways	T24	Carson of Venus	V3
Tarzan and the Champion	T24A	Escape on Venus	V4
Tarzan and the Jungle Murders	T24B	The Wizard of Venus	V5
The Official Guide of the			
Tarzan Clans of America	TC	**Western Novels**	
		The Bandit of Hell's Bend	HB
Tarzan Twins Novels	(TT)	The Deputy Sheriff of	
Tarzan and the Tarzan Twins	TT1	Comanche County	D
Tarzan and the Tarzan Twins			
with Jad-bal-ja the Golden			
Lion	TT2		

ALPHABETICAL LISTING BY ABBREVIATION

A (1–2)	Apache Novels	LC	The Lost Continent
B (1–2)	Beyond the Farthest Star	LL	The Lad and the Lion
C (1–3)	Caspak Series	M (1–11)	Mars Series
CG (1–2)	The Cave Girl	ME	The Maneater
D	The Deputy Sheriff of	MK (1–2)	The Mad King
	Comanche County	MM (1–3)	Moon Series
E (1–2)	The Eternal Savage	OT	The Outlaw of Torn
EE	The Efficiency Expert	P (1–7)	Pellucidar Series
GF	The Girl from Farris's	PB	Pirate Blood
GH	The Girl from Hollywood	Q	The Monster Men
HB	The Bandit of Hell's Bend	R	The Rider
HM	The Land of Hidden Men	T (1–24)	Tarzan Series
I	I Am a Barbarian	TC	Tarzan Clans
J	The Resurrection of	TT (1–2)	Tarzan Twins Novels
	Jimber-Jaw	V (1–5)	Venus Series
K (1–3)	The Mucker Series		

THE CYCLOPÆDIA

a (*Cpk*) Silent (C1;9).

a (*Pal*) Light (T8;2).

A-Kor The keeper of the **Towers of Jetan** in **Manator** on **Barsoom**. He was the son of O-Tar, **Jeddak** of Manator, by **Haja**, a slave who had been a **Gatholian** princess, and was thus **Gahan's** cousin. He and his father despised one another. He was kind to **Tara of Helium** while she was imprisoned in the towers, but spoke unkindly of his father once too often and was himself imprisoned, leaving **E-Med** as **Dwar** of the Towers. He was later freed by **Tasor**, went to join **U-Thor** in his siege on Manator, and was made Jeddak after the overthrow of O-Tar (M5;11,20,22).

A-lur "City of Light" (*Pal*). The capital city of the **Ho-don** of **Pal-ul-don**. It was a large city of limestone, cut out from the limestone hills and outcroppings over many centuries, each building being roughly in the shape of the original piece of stone from which it was cut. The waste limestone cut from the interiors was used to make walls and pave roads. As with the cliff dwellings of the **Waz-don**, the buildings were all of great age, laboriously cut out over time, and were covered with carvings from top to bottom, inside and out (T8;2,8).

A-Sor The name by which **Tasor** of **Gathol** was known in **Manator** as a member of the Jeddak's guard (M5;18).

Aanthor An ancient ruined city of Barsoom, where **Astok**, Prince of **Dusar**, planned to trap both **Thuvia** and **Carthoris**. His plans were foiled, however, when **Thar Ban**, a green **Jed** of **Torquas**, captured Thuvia and was pursued by Carthoris (M4;4). The city lies west-southwest of **Helium**, on the southeast side of the **Highlands of Torquas**, at 50 degrees south, 40 degrees east.

Aarab *see* **Arab**

aasvogel "Carrion-bird" (*Ger*). A vulture (T7;6).

ab (*Pal*) Boy (T8;4).

Ab el-Ghrennem A sheik of the Sahara who led his men into the **Ituri Forest** to assist the film crew of *The Lion Man* in 1932 (for pay, of course). He and his men believed the movie script to be real and, as it involved a treasure map, stole both the map and the leading lady from the safari (T17;2,9,12). He was killed in an ambush when he and his men tried to enter the real **Valley of Diamonds** (T17;21).

Ab-on "Boy-ten" (*Pal*). The warrior left by **Om-at** as acting **gund** of **Kor-ul-ja** while he was away (T8;4).

abaca (*Musa textilis*) A plant of the Philippines, related to the banana, whose fibers can be used to make ropes, etc. (P7: 3;4).

abalu (*Ape*) Brother (TC).

Abbas One of the black slaves of the **Arab** tribe **el-Harb**, a loyal and trustworthy man (T11;2).

Abd el Aziz The Arab of the raider tribe **el-Harb** whose fortunately placed **beyt** saved the life of **Tollog**, the tribal sheik's brother, when **Tantor** tossed him aside to save Tarzan from the Arabs in 1921 (T11;2). Later, he led a group of the raiders (at **Ibn-jad's** command) to raid **Nimmr**, but was totally defeated (T11;20–23).

9

Abdul Tarzan's young Arab guide and interpreter while he was in **Sidi Aissa** in 1910, while working for the French War Office. The young man was loyal and tried to help Tarzan stay out of trouble, with little success. Failing that, he fought with the ape-man against the Arabs who had been paid by **Nikolas Rokoff** to kill him, the two eventually escaping with the help of a friendly **ouled-nail**. He left town that night with Tarzan and **Kadour-ben-Saden**, and helped the former fight their pursuers on the road to **Bou Saada**. It was he who taught Tarzan to speak Arabic (T2;7–9). Another Abdul was **Bertrade de Montfort's** white palfrey, which she rode to and from **Stuteville** in the spring of 1262 (OT;9).

Abdul Kamak A young Arab of **Amor ben Khatour's** following, who lusted after **Meriem** after her recapture by the sheik about five years after her initial escape from him. He saw Meriem looking at the picture of herself and the news clipping explaining her abduction, both of which she had stolen from **Sven Malbihn**. He took them from her, then fled the sheik after avowing his hatred for the old man; he then made his way to Paris and informed General **Armand Jacot** of the whereabouts of his daughter **Jeanne**, Meriem's real identity (T4;23,27).

Abdul Mourak An **Abyssinian** general of the early 20th century, who in 1913 led an expedition to track down and punish **Achmet Zek**, the Arab raider, who had had the effrontery to conduct a raid in Abyssinia some months before. In the **Belgian Congo**, they encountered Lt. **Albert Werper**, who convinced Abdul Mourak that his force could not defeat Achmet Zek's. The general turned back, giving Werper a free ride toward Abyssinia (T5;15). Eventually, however, Werper grew fearful of his captors and traded the location of Tarzan's gold for his freedom. Mourak's party was met at the burial site by Achmet Zek's band and, true to Werper's prediction, was defeated, leaving only Mourak himself and a small number of his men to escape (T5;18). They later captured Jane, but the party was attacked soon afterward by a group of hunger-crazed lions and destroyed; only Jane escaped through Tarzan's intervention (T5;23–24).

Abdullah abu Nejm An Arab enemy of Tarzan's who captured him in 1938 while he

was suffering from **aphasia** and sold him to an animal trapper to sell to a circus. He was accidentally brought on board the *Saigon* and took part in a mutiny (T24;1–7), and was for his part in it kicked out of camp with the other mutineers by Tarzan after the *Saigon* wrecked on **Uxmal** (T24;11,16). He was killed by **de Groote** after attempting to raid the castaways' camp (T24;19–22).

Abraham, son of Abraham The Prophet of Paul in the southern settlement of the land of **Midian** in the **Ghenzi Mountains** of Africa. He was a a hideous, cruel old fanatic who, like his forefathers, ordained severe penalties (i.e., death) for the most minor of sins (i.e., smiling) (T15;2,6). He tried to execute **Lady Barbara Collis** on two separate occasions, but she was saved — once by her own ingenuity and once by **Dr. Lafayette Smith** (T15;9,11–12).

absinthe A strong, chartreuse-colored liqueur flavored with wormwood. From that ingredient the drink gained a high content of thujone, a psychoactive drug, which made it addictive and extremely popular until it was banned (France was one of the last countries to do so, in 1915). Tarzan indulged heavily in it when he first came to civilization (T2;3).

abu (*Ape*) Knee (T22;9).

Abu Batn A Bedouin sheik of the 1920s who allied himself with the **Zveri** expedition of communist agitators in 1928 when they came to cause trouble in northeast Africa, mostly because it was a good way to get a lot of loot easily (T14;1–2). He later betrayed Zveri while the Russian was at **Opar**, abducting **Zora Drinov** and La of Opar and heading north, setting fire to the camp as he left (T14;8). He was later killed by **Wayne Colt** when he tried to molest Zora (T14;11).

Abul Mukarram *see* **Mukarram, Abul**

Abyssinia Nation of northeast Africa which is today called **Ethiopia**. It was ruled from 1889 to 1913 by **Menelek II**, who sent a punitive expedition led by **Abdul Mourak** to punish **Achmet Zek** for raiding within Abyssinia (T5;15). Southern Abyssinia was also the location of the **Valley of the Sepulcher** (T11;1–2), of **Onthar** and **Thenar** (T15,T21), and of **Alemtejo** (T23). Abyssinia was also the powerful African nation that ruled all of Africa, as well as parts of Europe and the Arabian peninsula, in the early 22nd century of *The Lost Continent*. Its capital was at **Adis Abeba**. It had 20th century weaponry, but apparently had lost motor vehicle technology (LC;8).

accumulator A device in a Barsoomian flier's engine that collects up magnetic force from the planet's magnetic field and drives a flier engine with it (M7;2).

Ace The large bay stallion caught and broken by **Tom Billings** in the **Galu** country of **Caspak** late in the summer of 1917 while he was searching for the lost **Ajor** (C2;7).

Achmet ben Houdin An Arab marauder of **Algeria** whose band was destroyed by the **French Foreign Legion** when **Jack Clayton** was about seven years old. The Arab himself met his death on the guillotine for several murders, as did several of his followers. It was in revenge for ben Houdin's death that Captain **Armand Jacot's** daughter, **Jeanne**, was stolen by ben Houdin's uncle, **Amor ben Khatour** (T4;5).

Achmet din Taieb An Arab, cousin to **Kadour ben Saden**, who told that sheik's daughter that **Tarzan** had been captured by a neighboring tribe, which information allowed her to rescue the ape-man (T2;10).

Achmet Zek An Arab ivory and slave raider of the **Belgian Congo** in the early 20th century, who had constantly fought with the Belgians but accepted the renegade **Albert Werper** into his service after the latter had killed his superior in an unprovoked attack. He eventually grew to trust the Belgian, and used him to kidnap **Jane Clayton** in a move to get ransom from Tarzan, who had sharply curtailed Zek's once-profitable raiding activities. While Werper followed the ape-man on a mission to **Opar**, Zek attacked the **Greystoke** bungalow, killing all the **Waziri** guards there (except for **Mugambi**, whom they left for dead but was not) and kidnapping Jane (T5;1–6). Eventually, Werper returned and told Zek about the gold the Waziri had brought from Opar and buried, but did not tell him of the jewels he had stolen from Tarzan. When the Arab discovered his lieutenant's deception, Werper fled (T5;10,15). Soon after, Jane was "rescued" by the ape **Taglat** and the enraged Zek set out to dig up the gold lest someone steal it as well. His party

destroyed the **Abyssinian** detachment of **Abdul Mourak**, whom Werper had led to the gold, and Zek himself set off in pursuit of Werper, whom he had spotted among the Abyssinians. He was soon afterward shot and killed by Werper (T5;16–19).

acid A special acid is fired at enemy lantars during naval engagements in **Middle Anlap**. It is designed to dissolve the T-ray protective coating which each ship is given, and to produce a discoloration in the armor as well so that T-ray gunners can aim at the unprotected spots of the armor (V4;45).

ack-ack (WW II slang) Anti-aircraft fire (T22;2).

ad (*Amt*) City (V4;31).

ad (*Bar*) The Barsoomian "foot," measuring about 9.745 English feet. It is divided into ten smaller units called **sofads**. Two hundred ads make up one **haad**, the Barsoomian mile (M4;6)(M7;2).

ad (*Pal*) The number three (T8).

adad (*Pal*) The number six (T8).

adadad (*Pal*) The number nine (T8).

adaden (*Pal*) The number seven (T8).

Adams, Bert A man from Boston, a guest at **Cory Blaine's** dude ranch (D;3).

Adams, Frank Johnny **Lafitte's** high school and college rival (a friendly one, but...) in football, scholarship and love. Lafitte was good at all of them, but Adams was always just a little bit better. After the great **Glenora** oil strike of the 1920s, his family became rich; he eventually became engaged to **Daisy Juke**, but broke it off because of her drinking (PB;1,12).

Adams, Henry A small-town attorney of **Glenora**, California, in the early 20th century, father of **Frank Adams**. After the great Glenora oil strike of the 1920s, he became quite rich (PB;1).

addax (*Addax nasomaculatus*) A kind of antelope of the Sahara which has ringed, spiral horns more than 40 inches long. The animal stands about three feet at the shoulder and is of a yellowish-white color with a brown mane and a black patch on its forehead (B1;6).

aden (*Pal*) The number four (T8).

adenaden (*Pal*) The number eight (T8).

Adendrohahkis The king of Trohana-dalmakus, a city of Minunia, when Tarzan came there in 1918. He was very favorably inclined toward Tarzan because the ape-man had saved his son, **Komodoflorensal**, from being devoured by a **Zertalacolol** (T10;6).

Adenen (*Pal*) The number five (T8;4).

Adis Abeba The capital of the Abyssinian Empire of the early 22nd century (LC;8).

Admiral Jason Gridley's nickname for Burroughs, because of a yachting cap the author was fond of wearing at the beach (P3).

Adrian, Gilbert (1903–1959) A Hollywood clothing designer of the 1930's who married Janet Gaynor (B1;5).

adu (*Ape*) Lose (TC).

"Adventure on Poloda" The title of the first novella in *Beyond the Farthest Star* (abbreviated B1), in which **Tangor**, an earthly pilot of World War II, is mysteriously transported to the country of Unis on the distant world of **Poloda**, and adopts that country and world as his own, joining them in the bloody war in which their planet, like ours, was locked at the time.

Adventurer's Club Birmingham, Alabama, club for which **Robert Jones** had worked as a servant prior to World War I (P4;3).

Aedis Flumen The main tributary of the Tiberis Flumen of the **Wiramwazi** (T12).

Aegyptus The Roman name for Egypt, where **Marcus Crispus Sanguinarius** was stationed with his cohort until he fled south to escape Nerva's wrath (T12;10).

aero-sub A type of 22nd century naval vessel capable of travel either in or under water or in the air, held aloft by **gravity screens**. Early models were beset by a host of problems, later corrected (LC;1).

Afars and Issas A French territory on the east coast of Africa, today the country of Djibouti, known in Tarzan's time as French Somaliland (T14;1).

afi (*WA*) A river (T4;21).

afrit In **Arab** lore, a type of evil spirit, similar to a djinn (T11;1).

Aggie Germanicus Caesar's nickname for his wife, Agrippina (I;2).

Ago XXV The king of the lost city of **Xuja** in the 1850s, when Queen **Xanila** first arrived there as the captive of a lost Arab raiding party (T7;19).

Agricola, Gnaeus Julius Roman general (A.D. 37–93) and governor of Britain from A.D. 78 until his death at the hands of the agents of **Domitian**. He subdued Britain completely, Romanizing the **Britons** by showing them the luxuries of civilization, and built a set of fortresses to keep back the **Picts** and Scots. He was also the first to conclusively prove Britain an island by circumnavigating it (A1;1).

Agrippa Posthumus The brother of Agrippina, a madman who was assassinated by order of Augustus (I;1).

Agrippina (13 B.C.–A.D. 33) Wife of Germanicus Caesar and mother of **Caligula**, a haughty Roman matron described by **Britannicus Caligulae Servus** as a bitch (I;1). She was the daughter of **Julia**, thus granddaughter of Augustus Caesar (I;2). She plotted against **Tiberius**, who in A.D. 30 banished her to the island of Pandateria, where she died three years later by starving herself to death (I;13–15). She hated Britannicus, and until her exile caused him no end of trouble (I;1–4).

Agrippina Minor (A.D. 15–59) Caligula's younger sister (I;4), who was later the mother of the emperor Nero and the wife of her uncle **Claudius**, whom she eventually poisoned so that Nero could have the throne. She herself was killed by Nero when she opposed his second marriage.

ah (*Pell*) Old (P5;13).

Ah Ara, Ma Rahna "Old White, the Killer" (*Pell*). A huge rogue **tandor** of Pellucidar, a very intelligent beast with a white patch on one jowl, from which he derived his name. **Wilhelm von Horst** came upon the beast caught in a stake-trap set by the **Mammoth Men** of Ja-ru and helped it escape, a kindness the great beast did not forget (P5;12–13). Later, it rescued him from the **Little Canyon** of the Mammoth Men (P5;17) and again, from the pursuit of the **Ganaks** (P5;20–21).

Ah Cuitok Tutul Xiu A Mayan warrior-king who founded the city of **Uxmal** in the **Yucatan** in A.D. 1004 (T24;1).

Ah-gilak "Old Man" (*Pell*). The name given by **Ghak the Hairy One** to the old man whose name was not **Dolly Dorcas**, the only survivor of the wreck of a Cape Cod whaler of that name in the Arctic Ocean. He and other crew members drifted about in the Arctic Ocean in a lifeboat, eventually sailing into **Pellucidar**, but by that time the crew had eaten one another, and "Ah-gilak" was the only one left alive. He wandered about Pellucidar, learning its language and ways, and was eventually captured by the cannibalistic **Sabertooth Men**, among whom he lived (acquiring more of a taste for human flesh, thanks to them) until he escaped with **Hodon the Fleet One** and **O-aa** in 1931 and went back to **Sari** with them afterward (P7:1;7)(P7:2;1). At the time, he was 126, having been born on March 29, 1805 (apparently, **David Innes** had lost all track of time; he calculated the old man's age as 153!) (P7:2;2). He later designed and built the clipper ship *John Tyler* for the Pellucidarian navy, skippering it on its maiden voyage to rescue Innes and O-aa from the land of the **Xexots** (P7:3;4,7)(P7:4;1–5,7–9,11–12).

ah kin mai In the Mayan language, "high priest" (T24;1).

Ahm The **Bo-lu** of **Caspak** taken prisoner by the crew of the **U-33** in August of 1916, after he and his savage band had attacked the U-boat and been repulsed. Through him, they began to learn the language and facts of life of Caspak (C1;6).

Ahrens Bugler of "D" Company of the U.S. Cavalry, who shot the Apache medicine man **Nakay-do-klunni** at the battle of Cibicu Creek in September of 1881 (A1;14).

A'ht Meriem's way of pronouncing the name **Akut**, because it had sounded that way to her when she first heard it (T4;14).

Aht A Niocene warrior of the tribe of **Nu**; he was the son of **Tha** and brother of **Nat-ul** (E1;9).

ailette (*Fr*) A shoulder-ornament worn on a suit of armor, the prototype of the modern epaulet (OT;15).

Air School The academy for the International Peace Fleet, from which **Julian** 5th graduated (at the age of 16) in 2016 (MM1;1).

air that runs away The **Va-ga** term for the fierce windstorms of **Va-nah**, which they believed to be created by a beast-god called **Zo-al** (MM1;5).

aircraft, Barsoomian *see* **fliers**

aircraft, Polodan The airplanes of **Poloda** are constructed of a very light, rigid, practically indestructible plastic of enormous strength. The wings are hollow and the fuselage double-walled, and after these portions of the plane are sealed in construction all of the air is drawn out of them, creating a vacuum which gives the plane a great deal of extra lifting power. Pursuit aircraft are equipped with four guns: two rotating ones in a rear turret, one facing straight down, and one fired forward through the propellor shaft. These planes have a ceiling of over fifteen miles (due to their construction and Poloda's thick atmosphere) and can fly at speeds of 500 to 600 miles per hour, powered by **broadcast power** from their home base (B1;5–8)(B2;9).

Airedale A large breed of terrier, primarily used as a hunting dog (C1;1).

Aisle of Hope The central aisle in the **Temple of Reward** in **Helium** on Barsoom (M2;17).

Ajax The name given to the great ape **Akut** when taken to London as a performing ape by **Alexis Paulvitch** (T4;1–3).

Ajor The **Galu** woman of **Caspak** whom **Tom Billings** saved from both a huge panther and a band of **Alus** soon after wrecking his seaplane while looking for **Bowen Tyler** late in the summer of 1917. They were very attracted to one another, and she taught him the language of Caspak. She traveled north with him toward her country, saving him from the **Band-lu** on one occasion (C2;2–4), and fell in love with him, though it was some time before his pride let him realize that he loved her (C2;6). She was a **cos-ata-lo**, and had been captured by a **Wieroo** (after fleeing the warrior **Du-seen**, with whom she refused to mate), but escaped from him in the distant south, where she had met Tyler (C2;2,5). She and Billings became separated in the village of the eastern **Kro-lu**, where Du-seen had come to recruit Kro-lu for his expedition against

Ajor's father, Jor (C2;6). Billings finally caught up with her after searching the Galu country for some time, barely saving her from Du-seen. He was in turn rescued by the forces of Jor and the *Toreador* crew, coordinated by Bowen Tyler. She and Billings were mated, and since the future of Galus and Caspak depended upon Ajor and cos-ata-lo like her, Jor insisted she must stay in Caspak — and Billings with her (C2;7). Two weeks later, however, John Bradley and the recaptured U-33 arrived, "kidnapped" Ajor and Billings (who didn't resist much), and headed back to California with the *Toreador*, which had not yet left the area (C3;5).

Akamen A noble of **Ashair** into whose care **Atan Thome** and **Lal Taask** were placed when they warned Queen **Atka** of Tarzan's coming in November of 1936 (T20;13). Akamen conspired with the outsiders to kill Atka so he could become king, but was double-crossed by Thome and sentenced to a cage in the temple for life (T20;19,22). He was later killed while trying to escape with Tarzan and the others (T20;29).

Akmed din Soulef The Arab of Sidi Aissa who played host to **Nikolas Rokoff** when the Russian came there to kill Tarzan in 1910 (T2;8).

Akut The strongest ape of the tribe native to "**Jungle Island**," who challenged Tarzan after the latter killed their king, **Molak**. Tarzan easily defeated him, getting him to surrender, and thus gained his respect and, eventually, his friendship, especially after he saved Akut from being killed by a panther. Akut and several of his bulls accompanied Tarzan in **Mugambi**'s boat to the mainland and up the **Ugambi** River in pursuit of **Nikolas Rokoff**, but only Akut himself was intelligent enough to figure out how to use a paddle by watching Tarzan and Mugambi. Eventually, though, he was able to teach a few of the others (T3;4-7). He and his apes rescued Tarzan from a cannibal tribe and pursued Rokoff all the way down the Ugambi to the ocean after they thought Tarzan had been killed by a crocodile (T3;10,15). They later helped him to rescue Jane from **Schneider** and the *Cowrie* mutineers, and when Tarzan left them again on "Jungle Island," Akut sadly stood and watched his ship leave (T3;21).

Ten years later, when the scientific research ship *Marjorie W.* stopped to make tests on the island, Akut came to the beach and looked into the face of each white man, looking for his beloved Tarzan. Unfortunately, **Alexis Paulvitch** was among the crew, having just been rescued from the Ugambi region. He claimed Akut as his own, naming him **Ajax** and taking him aboard. Akut of course complied, thinking he would be taken to Tarzan, and so came to London as a performing ape. He performed at a music hall for a few weeks, until during one show he entered **Jack Clayton**'s box (in a part of the performance where the ape entered the boxes to look for Tarzan) and immediately recognized Tarzan in the boy, snuggling up to him and refusing to go back onto the stage. Fortunately for all involved, Tarzan arrived at that point to pick up the boy, who had gone to the show against his mother's expressed wishes, and Akut recognized Tarzan, telling him that he had come to live with him. Tarzan asked Akut to remain with his trainer until he returned for him, and as the ape refused to perform on stage anymore after seeing Tarzan, Paulvitch (whom Tarzan did not recognize, so changed was he after his ten years of abuse in Africa) eventually sold Akut to Tarzan for a ridiculous sum and promised to send him back to "Jungle Island." In the meantime, however, Jack was secretly visiting the unusually intelligent Akut almost daily, and had actually managed to learn a little of the **Tongue of the Great Apes** from him by the time Tarzan bought him. The ape-man wanted Akut to live with them, but Jane refused, so Jack planned to escort the ape to Dover instead of going off to school as he was supposed to. This gave Paulvitch an opportunity for revenge against Tarzan through the person of his son, but when he tried to harm the boy, Akut burst his restraints and killed Paulvitch (T4;1-3). Jack then disguised Akut as a wheelchair-bound old lady with a heavy veil and took him back to Africa on a steamer, fearing that the English authorities would kill Akut for the murder of Paulvitch. The ape hid in their cabin the whole way so that none might penetrate his disguise. Once in Africa, Akut killed a man who tried to rob Jack, and the frightened lad led Akut into the jungle (having lost the money by which he could have returned to England) to escape legal prosecution for the second murder (T4;4).

Akut taught the boy jungle life over the

next year, training him to fight, track, and get food, though the boy could never adjust to eating many of the things the old ape found toothsome. Later, after his savage pleasure in killing became apparent, the ape named Jack "Korak," meaning "the killer," since he could not say "Jack" (T4;6–8). He stayed with the boy as friend and teacher, and after Korak rescued Meriem from the Arabs, he eventually accepted her too. A few years later, after Korak killed a king ape who had abducted Meriem, Akut became king of the tribe (because Korak did not wish to himself), but remained Korak's friend and ally ever after. Eventually, he was again reunited with both Korak and Tarzan (T4;10–11,27).

al (*Amt*) "No" or "without" (V2;5).

Al-tan The chief of the eastern Kro-lu of Caspak, who was **batu** and thus receptive to **Du-seen's** plan for the Kro-lu to aid him in his conquest of the land of the Galus, which Al-tan would otherwise never see (C2;5). His party was fought off by a Galu force with the help of the *Toreador* crew, and when he got back to the Kro-lu country, he and the survivors of his party were killed for their sins against Caspakian tradition (C2;7).

ala (*Ape*) Rise (TC).

Alabama Southern state, birthplace of Robert Jones (P4;3).

Alahanpandjang A Sumatran city of the mountains near the west coast of the island (T22;27).

alalus A creature born without the ability to speak. The massive **Zertalacolols** of **Minunia** were alalus (T10;2–3).

Alam A Sumatran youth of the village of Tiang Umar who often brought food to Sing Tai and Corrie van der Meer while they were hiding from the Japanese in a cave in the spring of 1944. He was forced by the Japanese to reveal the hiding place to them, however, or see his whole village killed (T22;1).

Alaska The warship that rescued and helped repair the disabled *Lotus* after the crew of the *Halfmoon* left it stranded after abducting Barbara Harding from it in 1913 (K1;15).

Alauddin Shah The chief of a Sumatran coastal village from whom Sarina got a boat

and provisions for Tarzan and his "foreign legion" to escape the island with in the spring of 1944 (T22;29).

albargan "No-hair-man" (*Amt*). The **Nobargan** word for a human — hairless indeed compared to the hairy **Kloonobargan** (V2;5).

Albion Poetic name for Britain, mythologically derived from the name of a giant who ruled the island in prehistoric times (A1;1).

Albus A famous racehorse of the **Blue Stables** of early 1st century Rome (I;8).

Alchise One of the **Apache** scouts of Captain Crawford's command in 1880s Arizona, who took a message from **Shoz-dijiji** to **General Crook** on March 29th, 1886 (A2;9).

alcohol Although Tarzan drank a great deal shortly after his first contact with civilization (T2;1–3), he afterward foreswore it altogether, and coffee became his only vice (T9;5).

Aldea The nearest Arizona town with a telegraph office and train station to **Hendersville** and the **Bar-Y Ranch** in the 1880s (HB;8).

Alemtejo A lost Portuguese colony high in the **Ruturi Mountains of Abyssinia**, built on a 3000 foot plateau in the early 1500s by Portuguese colonists led by **Christoforo Da Gama** (brother of **Vasco Da Gama**) and named for the Portuguese district from which he hailed. By the 20th century, Alemtejo was inhabited by a mixed race of Portuguese and **Bantu** blood, and their language and religion were mixed as well. The religion retained many of the symbols of Christianity (such as the rosary and the sign of the cross), but worshipped tribal gods with human sacrifice. They also had an incredibly rich gold mine which they tapped often, even though it lay near **Galla** territory and the Gallas would attack any of them who came to mine it. Alemtejo was protected at its front by a gorge closed with a palisade and inhabited by hungry lions (T23;8,10,14).

Alemtejo, Guardians of The dozens of hungry lions kept trapped by a gate in a box canyon below **Alemtejo** (T23;8).

Alexandria The great Egyptian city founded by Alexander the Great in the 4th century B.C.; it was the intellectual center of the world until 31 B.C., and still an important port and center of learning for centuries thereafter (T15).

Alexis III King of Margoth in the late 19th and early 20th centuries, father of Princess Mary (R;5).

Alextar The younger brother of Nemone, Queen of Cathne in the 1920s; at the age of ten he was judged insane and locked in the temple, and Nemone, at the age of twelve, was made queen. After her death in October of 1930, he was again placed on the throne by public demand (T16;11,19). He turned out, however, to be a weak and spineless ruler, and fell under the influence of Tomos, who became the virtual ruler of the city. After the people rebelled in the face of his unfair treatment of Tarzan upon the ape-man's return to Cathne in 1935, Alextar killed Tomos and then committed suicide, leaving Thudos king (T21;18–19).

Algeria Modern north African nation, a French colony until 1962, to which Tarzan was sent in 1910 as an agent of the French War Office (T2;7). It was in Algeria that Burroughs, on a lion hunt in 1913, met David Innes, who had returned at the wrong angle from Pellucidar and ended up there instead of America, where he really wished to come up. It was also the place (obviously) from which he returned to Pellucidar, laying a telegraph line behind him with the upper-earth end hidden beneath a cairn in the Sahara near his point of departure (P1;15).

Algiers The capital of the French colony of Algeria, from which Tarzan embarked on a ship to Cape Town for his second mission for the French War Department, registered incognito as John Caldwell of London (T2;11).

Algiers-and-Club The hotel at which Cogden Nestor stayed awaiting Burroughs' arrival in the summer of 1915 (P2).

Ali The Sultan of the village of Gallas who fought the Alemtejo of Ethiopia, and who captured Rand (the false Tarzan) and Sandra Pickerall in 1938. He was himself captured by the Alemtejo a few days later (T23; 20,22).

Ali ben Ahmed One of the Arab warriors sent by Nikolas Rokoff to assassinate Tarzan in Algeria of 1910. Ali captured Tarzan alive instead and returned him to the douar of his tribe, where Rokoff waited (T2;10).

Ali ben Kadin Amor ben Khatour's half-brother, whose mother had been a negro slave. He was old and hideous, with a skin disease, and the sheik gave Meriem to him as a wife after recapturing her when she was 16. She was saved from him, however, by Korak, who killed the old half-caste (T4;25).

Ali es Hadji An Arab sheik of northwest Africa whose tribe contained the first land-based people the amnesiac Prince Michael ever remembered seeing (LL;8). He eventually accepted Michael, now known as Aziz, into his tribe (LL;24).

All-Around Magazine Magazine in whose February 1916 issue *Beyond Thirty* (a.k.a. *The Lost Continent*) was first published.

All-Story Cavalier Weekly The magazine in which *The Mucker* (1914) and *The Beasts of Tarzan* (May-June 1914) were originally published.

All-Story Magazine Periodical in which *A Princess of Mars* (February-July 1912), *Tarzan of the Apes* (October 1912), *The Gods of Mars* (January-May 1913), *The Cave Girl* (summer 1913), *The Monster Men* (November 1913), *The Warlord of Mars* (December 1913–March 1914), *At the Earth's Core* (April 1914), and *Pellucidar* (1915) were originally published.

All-Story Weekly The magazine in which *The Eternal Lover* (March 7, 1914), *Sweetheart Primeval* (1914), *Thuvia, Maid of Mars* (April 1916), *The Return of the Mucker* (1916), *The Cave Man* (spring 1917), *The Rider* (1918), *Tarzan the Untamed* (Part II)(1920), and *Tarzan the Terrible* (1921) were originally published.

Allaban The Korsar city of Pellucidar in which Stellara was born (P3;3).

Allah In the Muslim religion, practiced by most Arabs and many African blacks, the name of the One God (T2;7).

Allara A Pellucidarian woman of the island of Amiocap, stolen from her home by

The Cid, chief of Korsar, just after she had become pregnant by Fedol, her mate. The Cid thought, however, that the child born later was his and accepted the girl, Stellara, as his daughter, only Allara knowing the truth: that Stellara had a birthmark exactly like her true father's, thus proving paternity. Allara died years later in Korsar and never returned home (P3;2–3).

allegiance, oath of The Caspakian oath of allegiance consists of kneeling before the new friend or master, dropping one's weapon, and covering one's eyes with his hands. This bonds a man as a friend or follower. To accept such an offer, one takes the gesturer's hands from his eyes, then returns his weapon. To refuse, one walks away, and upon getting out of sight is an enemy again (C2;4).

Allen, Slick A cowboy of Rancho del Ganado in the early 1920s. He was one of those rare birds: a good horseman who did not love horses (GH;1). He was fired from the Rancho for kicking a horse — an unpardonable crime there (GH;2). He hung around the area afterward, however, to make contact with Guy Evans, for Allen was a bootlegger and drug dealer (in cahoots with Wilson Crumb) who forced Evans to sell his hootch, or else be framed for stealing the whole shipment from a government warehouse (GH;7). Later, after an argument with Crumb over an overdue payment, Crumb tipped off the police, and Allen was convicted of possession and sent to jail (GH;12). A year later, he was released from prison and went to kill Crumb, but Guy Evans beat him to it. To revenge himself upon Custer Pennington (whom he hated and had had framed for bootlegging almost a year before), he planted evidence to frame him again for Crumb's murder. He did not confess his part in the crime until he finally realized that Shannon Burke was his daughter (whether legitimate or not, we are not told), which awakened a spark of paternal protectiveness in him (GH;21–23,27,34–37).

alley, Oo-oh The "streets" of the Wieroo city of Oo-oh are actually narrow, winding blind alleys that go at most for a few dozen buildings and then stop, mostly because the Wieroos can fly and so have no need for long, continuous thoroughfares. The alleys, like the whole city, occur on many vertical levels (C3;2).

allosaurus, Caspak The allosaurus of Caspak is beautifully colored, with large, irregularly-shaped black and yellow spots about a foot in diameter, with red outlines about an inch wide. The underside of its body and tail are greenish white (C1;5).

Alope The first wife of the 19th century Apache war chief Go-yat-thlay. She bore him three children, all of whom were killed with her by Mexicans at Kas-ki-yeh, prompting Go-yat-thlay (more popularly known by the name the Mexicans called him, Geronimo) to swear revenge against the Mexicans (A1;1,6).

alphabet The original means by which Tarzan taught himself to read was a child's illustrated alphabet book brought to Africa years before by the Claytons for the education of their then-unborn child, who would be old enough to need them before they returned to England. Tarzan discovered the book and taught himself to read after realizing that the "bugs," as he called the letters, were always in the same combinations under the same pictures in all the books, like "b-o-y" appearing under a boy's picture. After many years of study, he discovered the use of the dictionary and its by-then-familiar alphabetical structure (T1;6–7). Tarzan had a different spoken name for each letter of the alphabet, including a classification of male and female for upper or lower case letters (T6;4).

Althides The under-officer of Cathne in whose charge Tarzan was placed when he was imprisoned there in October of 1930. He was much impressed with Tarzan's bow, the like of which the Cathneans had never seen, and Tarzan promised to make him one (T16;5).

altimeter, Barsoomian The Barsoomian altimeter is optical, working on the principle of automatic adjusting of the device's focus on the ground (which would certainly work better on nearly cloudless Barsoom than on Earth). It is usually wired into the controls so that a cruising altitude may be set (M9;2).

Alu "Silent man" (Cpk). The most primitive human race of Caspak. Alus are very hairy and apelike and have no speech or weapons (C1;9).

Alvarez, John The first officer of the Pan-American aero-sub Coldwater on the fateful voyage that carried her beyond the line of 30 degrees longitude; he was about 40 at the time, and a good and trustworthy officer. He shot out the instruments on the *Coldwater's* bridge when it seemed inevitable that the line of 30 degrees would be crossed, so as to save Lt. Jefferson Turck from disgrace and court-martial (LC;1). He was imprisoned by Porfirio Jones and returned to Pan-America, but made such an impassioned case at his trial that the tide of public opinion, long growing against the "beyond thirty" policy, finally broke down the government's resistance and diplomatic relations resumed with China (LC;9).

Alzo A Vepajan girl of the city of Kooaad on Amtor, who was the woman of Olthar, son of Duran (V1;4–5).

am (*Pell*) River (P4;14–15).

amak A unit of Minunian troops, consisting of 1000 men in four units called novands. An amak is commanded by an officer called a kamak (T10;13).

Amar The name given to Dian the Beautiful when she was a slave to Ul-van of Ruva (P6;24–25).

Amaryllia A notorious brothel-keeper of early 1st century Rome (I;9).

Amat A Sumatran collaborator with the Japanese occupation troops of World War II, who in the spring of 1944 reported the position of Tarzan and his "foreign legion" to the Japanese on two separate occasions (T22; 10–11,20,22).

Amazing Stories The magazine in which "John Carter and the Giant of Mars" (January 1941), "The City of Mummies" (March 1941), "Black Pirates of Barsoom" (June 1941), "Yellow Men of Mars" (August 1941), "Invisible Men of Mars" (October 1941), "The Return to Pellucidar" (1942), "Men of the Bronze Age" (1942), "Tiger Girl" (1942), "Skeleton Men of Jupiter" (February 1943), and "Savage Pellucidar" (1963) were originally published. In addition, the magazine reprinted all three Caspak novels in 1927.

Amazing Stories Annual for 1927 The magazine in which *The Master Mind of Mars* was originally published.

Amazons A fierce people of Greek mythology whose women were larger and stronger than men and were the warriors, and whose men were small and frail and employed with domestic duties. There were three different Amazonian civilizations mentioned in Burroughs' works: the Zertalacolols of Minuni (T10;2–5), the Oog of Pellucidar (P6;2–3), and the Samary of Amtor (V3;2–3).

amba (*Ape*) Fall (TC).

ambad (*Amt*) Psychologist. It is one of the five ruling classes of the city of Havatoo, who live in a section named for their profession (V2;13–14).

Ambad Lat "Psychologist Avenue" (*Amt*). One of the five main avenues of the Amtorian city of Havatoo, leading from Tag Kum Voo Klambad (The Gate of the Psychologists) to the central hub of the city on the waterfront (V2;13).

Ambat A korgan kantum (warrior physicist) of Havatoo on Amtor who was swept downriver from his city, captured by Thorists, and eventually ended up in Falsa, a warlike nation of 20th century Middle Anlap (V4;44).

am'dan (*Ara*) The plural of amood, meaning "column"; this can mean any roof support from the mighty pillar of a palace down to a humble tent pole (T11;8).

Amdar A Pellucidarian village not terribly far from Basti (P5;6).

Amhara The region of Abyssinia from which the Amhara ruling class comes. The Amhara, like the Tigreans, are of Semitic origin (T16;1).

Amharic The official language of Ethiopia, language of the Amhara ruling class (T15;7).

Amhor A small cattle-raising principality on Barsoom, lying north of the Toonolian Marshes and east of Duhor, its hereditary enemy. Jal Had, the ruling Prince of Amhor, attacked Duhor (while the latter city was at war with Helium) because of the Jeddak of Duhor's refusal to give his daughter, Valla Dia, in marriage to Jal Had. This, of course, touched off another long and bloody war (M6;4). It is not a very populous country, nor very technologically advanced, although it is far from backward, being far more advanced than Kaol, Jahar, or Phundahl. One of the most interesting features of the city was a menagerie containing almost every type of beast on Barsoom, including specimens of the various humanoid races and even a Kaldane. This menagerie was part of the palace grounds, but was open to the public during the day (M9;24).

Amiocap The Island of Love, a dumbbell-shaped island in the **Korsar Az** of Pellucidar inhabited by a blond-haired, peace-loving people. The island itself is tropical, and its two halves are dotted with inlets and coves and connected by a narrow, low strip of land so that, at a distance, it looks like two islands rather than one (P3;3).

Amlot The capital city of the Amtorian nation of **Korva**. It lay southwest of **Sanara**, the largest seaport of Korva, and was the largest city known on Amtor apart from Havatoo (V3;4,9).

Amoeba Men of Amtor *see* **Vooyorgan**

Amor ben Khatour An Arab sheik of early 20th century **Algeria** whose nephew, **Achmet ben Houdin**, was captured as a marauder by a detail of the French Foreign Legion under Captain **Armand Jacot**. Ben Khatour tried to bribe the Frenchman into letting ben Houdin escape, but was kicked out of camp instead, and later abducted Jacot's daughter, **Jeanne**, in revenge for ben Houdin's execution by the French colonial government (T4;5). Many years later, he was killed by a runaway elephant (T4;25).

Amoz A large and powerful tribe of Pellucidar, dwelling in the cliffs above the **Darel Az** (P1;4). They were ruled in **David Innes'** time by **Jubal the Ugly One** until he was killed by Innes, after which they were ruled by **Dacor the Strong One**, brother of **Dian the Beautiful**. Amoz was one of the first two member nations of the **Empire of Pellucidar** (the other being **Sari**, where Dacor's uncle **Ghak the Hairy One** was king)(P1; 14–15).

Amoz The flagship of the navy of the Empire of Pellucidar (P2;14).

Amtor The name given to their planet by the inhabitants of Venus. It is a large, watery world with two separate cloud envelopes to filter out the heat of the sun and so make the planet habitable. It is a world populated by various races, including some very unusual ones, but there is apparently only a single language spoken by all (V1;4).

Amtorian (language) Like Barsoom, Amtor has only one language (in the advanced southern hemisphere, that is). It is written with an alphabet of 24 characters, each of which (including the five vowels) has only one pronunciation. It has no verb conjugation of any kind, and all alterations to word meanings are formed by prefix or agglutination — there are no suffixes (V1;4).

Amundsen, Roald Norwegian explorer (1872–1928) who was the first person to reach the South Pole (a short time before the British explorer **Scott**), and who flew over the North Pole in the dirigible *Norge* in May of 1926, "definitely disproving" the theory of a polar entrance to the inner world of the Earth (P4;1).

An (*Amt*) Bird (V3;1).

An (*Pal*) Spear (T8;4).

An-tak The withered, emaciated **Galu** prisoner in **The Blue Place of Seven Skulls** in **Oo-oh**, who had gone mad from hunger and loneliness in the year or so he had been there, and who in September of 1916 told **John Bradley** that there was a way out that he had not been able to find. Bradley found it, but while he was exploring it the old man died, and so could not escape. He was the brother of **Co-tan**, whom Bradley rescued and fell in love with (C3;3–4).

An-un "Spear-eye" (*Pal*). A **Waz-don** warrior of the **Kor-ul-ja** in **Pal-ul-don**, father of **Pan-at-lee**, who was sent (with his two sons) by the **gund**, **Es-sat**, to spy on the **Kor-ul-lul** people and was almost killed by them. Their deaths would have left Pan-at-lee protectorless, which was what Es-sat wanted (T8;4).

Anatok The mighty **Jed of Gooli**— the biggest braggart and coward of the whole ridiculous Gooli tribe (M9;20–22).

ancestors The religion of Barsoom is primarily a form of ancestor worship, the ancestors being believed to give minor, though often important, aid to their living descendants. These ancestors are conceived of as living in the **Temple of Issus** or the **Valley Dor**, both at the south pole.

"The Ancient Dead" The first book of *Llana of Gathol*, originally titled "The City of Mummies."

Andereya The native bearer for the **Old Timer** who was left to guard **Kali Bwana** in the hunter's camp, but was killed by the **Leopard Men** (T18;5,18).

Anderssen, Sven The cook of the *Kincaid*, the steamship which **Nikolas Rokoff** chartered to kidnap Tarzan, Jane, and baby Jack to Africa. Anderssen was a tall, dirty man whose command of English did not extend very far beyond the expression, "ay tank it blow purty soon purty hard," at least as far as anyone could tell; actually, he spoke English, French, and the West Coast trade dialect as well, and helped Jane to escape from the *Kincaid* with a baby he thought hers, fleeing up the **Ugambi** river with her to escape Rokoff's wrath. As far as anyone could tell, he helped Jane because she had been kind to the Swede, who, under his unpleasant exterior, had a good heart. Jane did not realize how good a man he really was until he showed genuine concern at Jane's discovery that the only baby on the *Kincaid* was not hers, though Rokoff thought it was. After a fairly long pursuit, Rokoff caught up with the fleeing pair, mortally wounded Anderssen, and left him to die. Tarzan found him in his last few minutes of life, and he directed the ape-man to Rokoff's trail and confirmed Tarzan's suspicion that the Russian had indeed abducted Jane (T3;2, 9–10,12).

Andoo A mountainous country of the continent of **Noobol** in **Strabol**, Amtor's tropical zone (V2;11).

Andover The university attended by **David Innes** at the very beginning of the 20th century (P1;1).

Andresy Fictional name of a scholarly sort of revolutionary of an unnamed European country of the 1920s, the brains of his revolutionary party (LL;3–11). He came up with many plots over the years, and planned several assassinations (LL;13–23), but was eventually executed himself after trying to rebel against **Sarnya** (LL;25).

Andrews, Roy Chapman (1884–1960) American naturalist and explorer, who explored Alaska, Korea, China, Burma, Tibet and Mongolia and discovered much about ancient life, both human and non-human, including the famous dinosaur egg find in the Gobi Desert. He once said that all adventures are the result of incompetence and inefficiency (V5;1).

androde In the language of the **Xexots** of Pellucidar, "bronze" (P7:3;3).

Andua A **Waziri** warrior whom **Jack Clayton** taught to both fly and repair airplanes (T10;2).

Angan (*Amt*) Singular of **Klangan** (V1;8).

Angkor Thom The ruined city surrounding the ancient temple of **Angkor Wat** (HM;1).

Angkor Wat A huge **Khmer** temple complex in central **Cambodia**, lost for hundreds of years in the jungle until it was rediscovered early in the 20th century (HM;1).

Angola Present day country in which Tarzan grew up, then a colony of Portugal called **Portuguese West Africa** (T1;1, 13,21).

Angora goats The type of goats owned by **Julian 8th** on his farm in the **Teivos** of Chicago, from which the family got fleece, milk and meat (MM2;2).

Angustus the Ephesian An epileptic young man of the House of **Onesiphorus** in **Ephesus**, who was converted to Pauline Christianity by **Paul of Tarsus** himself. He was an extreme fanatic, and after Paul's martyrdom at Rome conceived the paranoid delusion that he would be next and so fled to **Alexandria**, thence up the **Nile** into Africa, taking with him only a Germanic slave girl he had either purchased or converted in **Rhodes** (T15). They settled in a remote area in the **Ghenzi Mountains** of Africa and founded the awful, inbred **Midianite** race (T15;2).

Animas Valley A large valley of southern **Arizona**, leading down to **Guadalupe Pass** near the Mexican border (A1;20).

Anlap "Birdland" (*Amt*). A vast continent lying northwest of **Vepaja** on Amtor, partly in **Trabol**, partly in **Strabol**, and mostly in the northern hemisphere. It is divided into three areas by mountain ranges: **Northern**

Anlap, Middle Anlap, and Southern Anlap. Each is very different from the other areas and is treated separately herein (V3;4)(V4;31,44).

Anlap, Middle The area of the Amtorian continent of Anlap lying in Strabol, bounded on the south by the Mountains of the Clouds and on the north by another, equally impassable range. It is the most technologically advanced area of Amtor (aside from Havatoo), having all of the advancements of the southern hemisphere plus a few Havatooite ideas like radio and anti-T-ray solutions. Warfare is carried on here with lantars, huge nuclear-powered landships on tank treads bristling with both T-ray and explosive armament. The area is pretty much cut off from most of Amtor, but its people know of Noobol, Havatoo and the Thorists at least (V4;43–55).

Anlap, Northern That portion of Anlap lying entirely in the northern hemisphere of Amtor and separated from Middle Anlap by a range of barrier mountains. The area is home to several semi-humanoid races and many humans, and like the rest of Amtor's northern hemisphere was only at an iron age stage of development, with no guns, motors or advanced medicine. Even the language is different from that of the southern hemisphere (V4;4).

Anlap, Southern The portion of Anlap lying in Trabol (and partly in Strabol), occupied entirely by the kingdom of Korva and bounded on the north by the impassable Mountains of the Clouds (V3;4) (V4;55).

Annamese A southeast Asian people enslaved in ancient times by the Khmers (HM;6).

Anne of Cleves The fourth wife of the gorilla-king Henry VIII, who was married to him at the same time as the other five, unlike her historical namesake (T17;20).

Annette The Princess Sborov's French maid on her ill-fated African trip in 1934 (T19;3). She was a sweet, naive girl who was strongly attracted to Neal Brown (and vice versa). She was also the first to find evidence of Prince Sborov's guilt in his wife's murder (the unburned sleeve end of a coat he had burned when her blood spattered it) (T19;11–12,15). She was abducted by Ydeni the Kavuru on the night after the princess' murder and taken to the Kavuru village (T19;17,19–20). She was later rescued by Tarzan and Neal Brown and got one-sixth of the Kavuru immortality pills taken from the village, enough to assure her of a long life as a young and beautiful woman (T19;30–31).

Anoos A Thorist spy among the prisoners aboard the *Sofal* with Carson Napier in 1929. He tried to betray the prisoners to the captain, but was found out by the others and killed during the night by Zog (V1;9).

Anoroc A large island in the Lural Az of Pellucidar, inhabited by the Anoroc tribe of Mezops, ruled in David Innes' time by Ja. The Anoroc people's greatest enemies were the Mezops of Luana (P1;10) until the Luanians joined the empire in 1914, after which they became friendly economic competitors (P2;15).

anotar "Birdship" (*Amt*). Term coined by Duare of Vepaja for the airplane built by Carson Napier in the super-scientific city of Havatoo. It was built of light, strong synthetic materials and was powered by a noiseless, vibrationless lor engine, the whole having an expected lifetime of 50 years before any maintenance, overhaul or refueling was needed (V3;1).

ant bear, giant A huge Pellucidarian animal, similar to the South American ant bear, which feeds on the giant ants of Pellucidar (P6;21).

Ant Men *see* Minuni

antelope, Polodan A creature with long, sharp horns that looks something like an earthly addax (B1;6).

antelope, royal (*Neotragus pygmaeus*) A small antelope of west Africa which stands about ten inches tall at the flank (T10;5).

Antioch The Roman capital of the province of Syria, where Germanicus Caesar died (I;6).

Antium A city of Latium in Roman Italy which lay just a little south of Rome itself (I;15).

Antonia The sister of Tiberius Caesar and mother of Germanicus. She died in A.D. 38, probably poisoned by order of Caligula (I;16).

Antoninus Builder of a wall across Scotland to keep the **Picts** and **Scots** from coming south in the 2nd century A.D. (A1;1).

Antos One of the two planets of **Omos** closest to **Poloda** in its weird shared orbit, to which the leaders of **Unis** considered staging a mass migration to escape the **Kapars** and their war (B2;1).

ants, giant One of the most amazing and peculiar species of Pellucidar is a kind of giant ant which lives in the area south of **Azar** along the shores of the **Korsar Az**, building enormous ant mounds as large as hills. These creatures are as large as men and far stronger, and carry out agriculture in symmetrically planted fields between their hills. They also take men and other animals prisoner, force-feeding them until they are fat enough to be eaten by the queen ant and her children (P6;19–20).

aoponato The **Minunian** number 800^3+19, the number given to **Komodoflorensal** while he was a quarry slave in **Veltopismakus** (T10;11).

aopontando The **Minunian** number 800^3+21, the number given to **Tarzan** while he was a quarry slave in **Veltopismakus** (T10;12).

Apache **Custer Pennington**'s absolutely fearless bay stallion (GH;1).

Apache Devil The name given to **Shozdijiji**, the Black Bear, during his solo raids in **Sonora** and **Chihuahua** early in 1882 (A1;18).

Apache Devil The name of the second and final book in Burroughs' Apache series, abbreviated A2. It is the continuation of the story of **Shoz-dijiji** begun in *The War Chief*, and chronicles his adventures from 1884 to 1886, as **Geronimo** made his last stand against the white men. Eventually, the Apaches surrendered, bringing an end to their way of life forever and leaving Shoz-dijiji alone and friendless except for **Wichita Billings**, the white girl he was in love with.

Apaches Indians of **Arizona** who killed Jim Powell and trapped John Carter in a cave, where he apparently died from inhalation of poisonous fumes, but was astrally transported to Mars instead (M1;1). The Apaches were also the central figures of Burroughs' Apache novels, *The War Chief* (A1) and *Apache Devil* (A2).

ape, great A species of African ape, now almost extinct, related to the **gorilla** but more savage and intelligent (T4;8). It was among this species that Tarzan of the Apes grew up, originally considering them his own kind. The males of the great apes (called bulls) are among the fearsome monsters of the jungle and often burst into uncontrollable rages for no apparent reason, attacking any ape that comes within their grasp, often with fatal results (T1;4). The apes reach maturity at about nine or ten, clinging to their mothers for the first year or so of life but able to find their own food in only a few months. The apes eat mostly bugs, fruit, leaves, and small game, but also engage periodically in an act of ritual **cannibalism** called the **Dum-dum**. The tribes are composed of some 50 or 60 individuals, including children, and are nomadic, usually ranging an area of about 1000 to 1500 square miles in the African jungles (T1;5). They are closely related to the **yeti** of Asia (T6;10).

ape, white The Barsoomian ape. The great white ape of Barsoom is an awe-inspiring sight—15 feet tall and heavily muscled, females being only a little smaller. They stand upright and have six limbs, as do the **green men**. They are of a dead white color and have only a single shock of white hair on top of their heads; they are otherwise hairless. Their eyes are frontally located, while "their ears [are] high set, but more laterally located than those of the [green] Martians, while their snouts and teeth were strikingly like those of our African **gorilla**. Altogether they were not unlovely when viewed in comparison with the green Martians" (M1;6). These creatures are very fierce but also highly intelligent; they use some tools, such as the large stone cudgel used by many of them. Some tribes are even more intelligent, being able to fashion bands of fur from hides, which they wear across their breasts in imitation of green men's harnesses. These tribes are also larger, numbering several dozen individuals to the tribe (M4;11). They are sacred to the **Therns**, who believe them to be one of the four primordial creature types of Barsoom, and also believe them to be the repositories of lost Thern souls (M2;4). See also **Plant Men**. The creatures are sometimes captured young and trained to put on performances (M6;9). In "John Carter and the Giant of Mars" they were erroneously said to be eight feet tall (M11A;2).

apes, great, tongue of The extremely limited, but practically universal, language used by the great apes of Africa, which, similarly to the **Tongue of Barsoom**, can be understood to some extent by most of the African and Eurasian animals. The monkeys chatter in a very simple form of it, the gorillas and chimpanzees use a more advanced form, and the great apes speak a very advanced form, though it is still primitive and incomplete by human standards (T1;6) (T4;10). The Oparians, after millennia of associating with the great apes and even occasionally mating with them, have become apelike themselves and speak the language of the great apes on an everyday basis, calling it "the language of the **First Men**" (T2;20). It is also the language of the **Sagoths** of Pellucidar (T13;4).

aphasia Loss of the ability to speak, usually as the result of a brain lesion (T24;1).

apodyterium (*Lat*) The dressing room of a public bath (T12;8).

Aponius Saturninus A Roman patrician who was tricked into paying nine million sesterces for 13 gladiators in one of **Caligula's** auctions (I;18).

Apostle Title held by the elders of the **Midianites** of the **Ghenzi Mountains** of Africa (T15;2).

Appius Applosus The commander of the **Colosseum** guards of **Castra Sanguinarius**, the lost Roman city, after **Maximus Praeclarus** was arrested in August of 1923. He was a good friend of Praeclarus', however, and fetched the latter's hidden set of dungeon keys to him so he could escape (T12;15).

applause, Minunian The "ant men" of **Minunia** applaud by rubbing their palms together in a circular motion (T10;5).

Apple Gran'ma'am Rhonda Terry's intentional mispronunciation of **Ab el-Ghrennem's** name (T17;15).

Apponius A noble Roman whom **Caligula** had executed in A.D. 39 after losing a wager to him (I;19).

apron The only clothing worn by the adult **Xexots** of Pellucidar (of both sexes) was a decorated apron-like garment of leather hanging from the waist down. They also wore jewelry, and the men leather helmets; children went entirely naked (P7:2;4).

Apronius The Roman commander of the forces on the lower Rhine during **Caligula's** reign. He was the brother-in-law of **Gaetulicus** (I;18).

apsaras Among the ancient **Khmers** of **Cambodia**, a temple dancing girl (HM;4–5).

apt "An arctic monster [of Barsoom]. A huge, white-furred creature with six limbs, four of which, short and heavy, carry it over the snow and ice; the other two, which grow forward from its shoulders on either side of its long, powerful neck, terminate in white, hairless hands with which it seizes and holds its prey. Its head and mouth are similar in appearance to those of a hippopotamus, except that from the sides of the lower jawbone two mighty horns curve slightly downward toward the front. Its two huge eyes extend in two vast oval patches from the centre of the top of the cranium down either side of the head to below the roots of the horns, so that these weapons really grow out from the lower part of the eyes, which are composed of several thousand ocelli each. Each ocellus is furnished with its own lid, and the apt can, at will, close as many of the facets of his huge eyes as he chooses" (M4). One might also note that apts are incredibly fierce, attacking even when not hungry. The largest specimens stand about eight feet tall. They lair in the **Carrion Caves** and roam both the polar wastes inside the barrier and those outside. They are sacred to some **Okarians** (M3;7–9).

Ara (*Ape*) The lightning (T1;9).

ara (*Pell*) White (P5;13).

Arabic Tarzan's third human language, the Arabic dialect of North Africa, was taught to him by his interpreter, **Abdul**, while he was an agent of the French government in Algeria in 1910 (T2;9).

Arabs Nomadic, desert-dwelling people of North Africa and the Middle East, encountered by Tarzan many times on both friendly and unfriendly terms, as the Arabs' wanderings sometimes took them south to the jungles for ivory, gold and slaves, and Tarzan's wanderings sometimes took him to the deserts of North Africa. They are primarily an equestrian people, riding either horses or camels depending on terrain and availability, and live primarily in tents, which can be packed up and moved at a moment's notice. Tarzan had a great respect for Arabs; being civilized, yet adventurous, they appealed to him more than did staid Europeans. Even though his first encounter with a large group of Arabs was as an enemy (they had been hired by Nikolas Rokoff to kill him), he had known enough examples of noble Arabs (like Abdul and Kadour ben Saden) to outweigh the bad examples (like the Arabs who attacked the Waziri for ivory and slaves) (T2;7-8, 16-17).

Arad The name of Tarzan's spear (possibly derived from **Ara**, the lightning) (T7;5).

Ararat Mountain of the Middle East, the location of which is uncertain (although it may possibly be the mountain now possessing that name in Turkey) upon which Noah's Ark was supposed to have grounded after the deluge (A2;7).

Arbok A huge, vicious Barsoomian "tree reptile" appearing only in **"John Carter and the Giant of Mars"**—apparently, a creature so vicious that even John Carter feared it (M11A;1).

archer The word-example for the letter "a" in the illustrated alphabet Tarzan learned to read from. He identified **Kulonga**, the black cannibal who killed **Kala**, with the archer of his beloved book after seeing him use his bow; this gave Tarzan the idea of using the bow as a weapon (T1;6,9).

architecture, Barsoomian There are various interesting points of Barsoomian architecture, of which only a few may be listed here. One is the complete absence of stairways, which are replaced in Barsoomian buildings by ramps. In ancient times, ladders were often used (M7;3), and cities of that period had huge, wheel-shaped gates (M4;6). In ancient buildings, beds were suspended from the ceiling by chains, but in modern times a flat platform covered with silks and furs serves the purpose (M1). The ancient cities were built in blocks; buildings ran along the streets, with an open courtyard in the center

of each block (M1;16). Modern architecture is very ornate, to the point that a strong and agile man can climb the outside of a 1000 foot tall building with relative ease (M1;23). The architecture of **Manator** was of a middle period — no landing stages on the roofs (because no aviation), and defenses geared to bow-and-arrow technology. The buildings were even more ornate than those of the rest of Barsoom, and public buildings were designed so that **thoats** might be ridden through them (M5;11). Barsoomian architecture is dominated by domes, towers and minarets which "only in recent ages have been giving way slowly to the flat landing-stages of an aerial world" (M7;9). The architecture of **Invak** was very peculiar — a horizontal, one-story, enclosed city broken periodically by open courtyards in which trees grew. The entire city roof was covered with vines, so that the whole was practically invisible (M10:4;3).

architecture, Euroban There are two known forms of Euroban architecture.

Morgor: The Morgor method of building can hardly be termed architecture, as the buildings are all rectangular, laid out in exactly square blocks in a perfectly rectangular city, and are made totally without ornament, composed entirely of a brown volcanic stone. There are no tapestries, carvings, statuary, or other embellishments, and the only relief from complete monotony is the fact that the buildings are of different sizes (M11B;3).

Savator: Some of the Savators of **Eurobus** build cylindrical houses of one room divided by partitions. The outsides of these buildings are plastered with **Sands of Invisibility**, and their locations are marked by **umpalla** plants (M11B;9).

architecture, Minunian The cities of Minunia were made up of collections of domes built from stones and wood mortared with asphalt that were very large, most domes being about a hundred feet tall and two hundred wide, with some thirty or more levels inside. The halls were about three feet wide and eighteen inches tall, and each dome had a central air shaft ten feet wide running from the ground to the top of the building for ventilation. Floors above the first were broken by windows, but there were only four entrances to each dome, at each of the four cardinal points. Interior areas were illuminated by large, slow-burning, smokeless **candles**. An exact description of construction methods appears in (T10;6).

architecture, Va-nah There are two basic forms of architecture in Va-nah.

U-ga: The architecture of the U-gas of Va-nah, as exemplified by that of the **Laytheans,** was strange and beautiful. Their cities were built in the craters of extinct volcanoes, especially those whose depths passed all the way through the crust to the outer lunar surface. The cities were built in tiers, row upon row being built upon one another, always with a park or cultivated area upon the roofs of the innermost houses of a tier, these cultivated areas being where crops were grown or Va-gas grazed. The innermost buildings (those nearest the crater wall at the bottom) were used as prisons and storerooms, as they were buried deep within the city and never saw the light of day. Broad stairways connected the levels, with the palace of the **jemadar** occupying the very top level all by itself (in a huge ring shape). The buildings were beautifully ornamented and carved and the terraces gorgeously landscaped with gardens, pools, and artificial streams and waterfalls which could be used for fire control. Unless one was flying, access to the city was only possible through one single long tunnel to a nearby crater (MM1;11–14).

Kalkar: The **Kalkar** cities were essentially similar to those of the U-gas, but lacked ornamentation and landscaping, and were generally smaller and more crowded (MM1;9–11).

The Arcturus Adventure A book detailing the New York Zoological Society's first oceanographic expedition, with 77 illustrations from colored plates, photographs, and maps, written by Charles William Beebe and published in 1926 (T24;7).

Arden, Elizabeth (1884–1966) The assumed name of Florence Nightingale Graham, a nurse and cosmetics designer of the early 20th century (B1;5).

Argo *(Ape)* Fire (T22;15).

Argonne The World War I battle in France during which **Julian 1st** received the American flag that he passed to his descendants, and which they treasured, then revered, and later worshipped. Under the Kalkars, it was treason punishable by death to own such a flag (MM2;3)(MM3;1). The Argonne was also the area to which Jack Clay-

ton (a.k.a. **Korak**) was sent to fight the war (T8;21).

Argosy Magazine in which *Tarzan and the City of Gold* (March 12–April 16, 1932), *Pirates of Venus* (1932), *Lost on Venus* (1933), *Back to the Stone Age* (1937), *Tarzan and the Forbidden City* (March-April 1938), *Carson of Venus* (1938), *Synthetic Men of Mars* (January 7–February 11, 1939), and *Tarzan and the Castaways* (1941) originally appeared.

Argosy All-Story The magazine in which *Tarzan and the Golden Lion* (1922) and *Tarzan and the Ant Men* (1924) were originally published.

Argosy All-Story Weekly The magazine in which *The Efficiency Expert* (October 8–29, 1921), *The Moon Maid* (May 5–June 2, 1923), *The Bandit of Hell's Bend* (Autumn 1924), *The Moon Men* (February-March 1925), *The Red Hawk* (September 1925), *The War Chief* (1927), and *Apache Devil* (1928) were originally published.

Argus The hundred-eyed watchman for the goddess Hera in Greek mythology, who was the personification of watchfulness since only a few of his eyes at a time were closed in sleep. He was set as a guard by jealous Hera over the transformed Io after Zeus' liaison with the unfortunate girl (R;5).

Arizona State in which John Carter and Jim Powell struck gold. Powell was killed by Apaches, and Carter was apparently killed by poisonous fumes in a cave. There his body lay, undiscovered, for ten years, until he reanimated it in 1876 after apparently dying on Mars (M1;1). The **Julian** tribe could have settled in Arizona, but chose instead to stay in the California desert where they could pressure the **Kalkars** (MM3;1). Arizona was also the state where **Jefferson Turck** was born in 2116 (LC;1), and in which several of Burroughs' westerns took place.

Ark The nickname of Professor **Archimedes Q. Porter** during his youth in the 1840s and 50s, when he first befriended **Mr. Philander** (T1;16).

Armenia Region of western Asia lying between the Caucasus Mountains and Asia Minor (modern Turkey). It is the site of the headwaters of the Tigris and Euphrates rivers and of Mount **Ararat** (J;2).

armor, Kalkar The Kalkars returned to the use of armor during the three hundred years that they were being pushed back across the face of the world, because as both sides lost firearm technology and returned to the use of sword and bow, it again became advantageous to them. The Julians, however, disdained the use of armor, preferring to use skill in combat instead (MM3;3).

arquebus Variant of harquebus (P4;14).

Arrow The ship on which Professor Archimedes Q. Porter and his party were traveling after recovering a buried Spanish treasure when the crew mutinied to possess the loot and left them at the same place the *Fuwalda* mutineers had left John and Alice Clayton more than 20 years before, choosing the place partly because of the presence of the Clayton cabin (T1;13-14). The crew buried the treasure to hide it from a nearby French cruiser and then headed out to sea, but no one on board knew anything of navigation and so they drifted aimlessly, having run out of food and water, until they were again found by the aforementioned cruiser. The surviving mutineers told their story to the crew of the cruiser, thus allowing the Porter party to be rescued (T1;17,19).

arrows, poisoned The arrows which were used by the Mbonga tribe of West African cannibals were poisoned, killing by only the slightest prick. Tarzan saw the advantages of such arrows and constantly stole a supply of them from the terrified natives (T1;9-12).

Artol An Amtorian warrior of Japal who was a slave among the Myposans when Carson Napier came to their city late in 1930 (V4;8-9).

Artolian Hills A fairly high, snow-clad mountain range of Barsoom's northern hemisphere, on the western slopes of which lies Duhor (M6;4).

as (*Pal*) "Sun" or "day" (T8;12).

Ashair The Forbidden City, a mostly underwater walled city in the center of the sacred Lake Horus of Tuen-baka in Northern Rhodesia. No one who sees it is ever allowed to leave again. The city was built 3000 years ago by ancient Egyptians who had contact with their parent nation at least as recently as Roman times but became cut off thereafter, probably for religious reasons or because of the fall of Egypt (T20;12-13,16-18,21). It was at war with its sister city of Thobos, on the opposite side of Lake Horus, and had been for some time. The war did not get "hot," however, until after the Ashairians sank the Thobotian galley carrying the god Chon and the Father of Diamonds on their annual tour of the lake, losing both. The Ashairians yet claimed to possess the stone, and the war continued until Thobos conquered Ashair, with Tarzan's assistance, in 1936 (T20;13-14, 19-23, 27,30-32).

Ashikaga A ruling house of medieval Japan in the 1500s (K1;9).

Asiaticus, Valerius One of the Roman nobles attached to the royal family of Rome in Caligula's day (I;21).

askari Any African tribesman recruited by a white safari to act as a mercenary soldier (T3;11).

Asoka The Lascar keeper of the animals (including Tarzan and the English prisoners) aboard the tramp steamer *Saigon* while it was under command of mutineers in 1938. He was overpowered by Tarzan and his keys stolen (T24;7-8).

Aspar The officer of Castrum Mare who relieved Mallius Lepus when Erich von Harben first arrived there in 1923 (T12;6).

Asprenas One of the Roman senators involved in the plot to assassinate the emperor Caligula in 41 AD (I;21).

assassination The great fear of all Barsoomians, as the practice is very widespread on Barsoom. Most guards and bars on that planet are intended against assassins rather than thieves, which are practically unknown there. See also gorthan.

assassin's guild On Barsoom, an association of assassins designed to regulate the profession (designed by the assassins themselves, that is, not by any government). The assassin's guild of Zodanga was the most powerful on the planet, and so it was the one targeted for destruction by John Carter (M8;1).

Astok The Prince of Dusar on Barsoom, who was infatuated with Thuvia of Ptarth and tried to claim her, first by words and then by abduction (M4;1–2). He later tried to get Vas Kor to kill her (so no one could blame him or Dusar for her disappearance) because he didn't have the strength to do it himself (M4;13).

Astura A Roman town near Antium (I;15).

at (*Pal*) Tail (T8;2).

At the Earth's Core The first book in the Pellucidar series, abbreviated P1. The events within transpired in the years 1903 to 1913 and were narrated to Burroughs personally by David Innes in 1913, to be published as a book in 1914. It concerns Innes' adventures in Pellucidar, the land inside the hollow Earth, after he and the inventor Abner Perry entered it in a mechanical digging machine. There they found a savage world where ice age men and mammals still exist unchanged, with a few species of dinosaur and some even weirder monsters thrown in for good measure. They found this world dominated by the hideous Mahars, and set out to free Pellucidarian humanity from them.

ata (*Amt*) The letter "a" (V4;31).

ata (*Cpk*) The Caspakian word for the Mystery of Life; it can mean "life," "eggs" or "reproduction," and describes the bathing ritual of Caspakian females (C1;8)(C2;3).

Ata-voo-med-ro "A-1,000,003" (*Amt*). The Vooyorgan of Amtor who first greeted Carson Napier and Duare after their forced landing in Voo-ad in early October of 1931 (V4;31).

atan (*Ape*) Male (TC).

Ateja The beautiful daughter of the Arab sheik Ibn-jab of the tribe el-Harb, of whom Zeyd, a young warrior of the tribe, was enamored. She helped him escape Ibn-jad's wrath and they were later reunited, thanks to Tarzan (T11;1,8,24).

Atewy One of the chief lieutenants of sheik Ab el-Ghrennem when he came to the Ituri Forest with the B.O. Pictures film crew in 1932. He was the only one of the Arabs who understood English (T17;2). He was killed with the other Arabs in an ambush upon trying to enter the Valley of Diamonds (T17;21).

ath (*Amt*) Look (V4;46).

Athapascan A group of related Indian tribes, including the Apache and Navaho, spread out over territory reaching from Alaska and Canada down to Mexico (A1;1).

athgan "Lookman" (*Amt*). The Amtorian word for "scout"; by extension, also a scout ship or scout lantar (V4;46).

athgan 975 The armored scout lantar aboard which Carson Napier and Ero Shan took service in the Falsan navy in 1931, in order to search for Duare more effectively (V4;46).

Athne The City of Ivory, lying in the valley of Thenar in the Ethiopian Highlands due east of the volcano Xarator. The Athneans keep elephants in particular, but also goats and sheep, and they also grow fruits, vegetables, and hay. They have traded since time immemorial with a certain band of shiftas for salt, slaves, and steel. Once a year, they also trade with the Cathneans for gold and hay, but the rest of the time are at war with them (T16;3–4). In 1935 there was a revolution in Athne, and the king, Zygo, was overthrown in favor of a revolutionary government, many of the nobles being killed in the process. Later, however, after Tarzan's appraisal of the conditions there, the Cathneans came to Athne to oust the revolutionary government and replace the rightful one, so they would have foes worthy of fighting (T21; 20,24–25).

atis (*Cpk*) The woolly rhinoceros (C1;6).

Atka The Queen of Ashair when Tarzan and the Gregory expedition came there in 1936. She was in her thirties at the time, and though a handsome woman had a cold, haughty appearance and temperament. She was very religious, though, and did not take lightly any affront to Brulor or the Father of Diamonds, locking "defilers of the temple" in cages forever. She was overthrown by King Herat of Thobos in November of 1936 and her city conquered (T20;13,18,32).

Atlantis The lost continent, sunk beneath the Atlantic Ocean in a mighty cataclysm over 10,000 years ago. Atlantis was home to a mighty empire of which Opar was an outpost, but the descendants of the builders of that city had degenerated to such a low level by the time Tarzan arrived that they did not even remember the name of their country, and only spoke its language for ceremonial purposes, like the Catholic Church now uses **Latin** (T2;20).

atmosphere, Polodan The atmosphere of **Poloda** is extremely thick and maintains its thickness to a great altitude due to the pressure exerted upon it from above by the atmosphere belt of **Omos**. Above 100 miles high it blends into the atmosphere belt and loses its distinctive character (B1;6,8).

atmosphere belt The dwarf star **Omos** is surrounded by an atmosphere belt 7200 miles in diameter which orbits in tandem with the system's eleven coorbital planets at a distance of one million miles from the star. It is probably very tenuous and unbreathable, but is thick enough to exert considerable pressure on the atmosphere of **Poloda**, keeping it dense to a high altitude. Polodan scientists believe it is possible to traverse the belt in specially-equipped aircraft (B1;8)(B2;10).

atmosphere plant The plant which maintains the atmosphere of Barsoom. It is a huge square building almost two miles on a side and two hundred feet tall. The walls are more than 150 feet thick, and the single entrance is closed by three 20 foot thick doors, one behind the other. The delicate instruments on the roof extract the indescribably beautiful ninth solar ray from sunlight, and are protected by a five foot thick plexiglass roof. The ninth ray is stored in huge reservoirs which constitute 75 percent of the building, and which can hold 1000 years' supply of the ray, which is electrically treated, then pumped by a huge **radium** pump (which has 19 alternate pumps, each of the 20 being used for one day, then resting for 19) to five air centers on Barsoom, there to be released as atmosphere. Practically everyone knows how the plant works, but only two people at a time know the secret of entering the building — a sequence of nine sounds which, when thought, open the doors of the plant. The two men are citizens of all Barsoom, having no country, and each wears a beautiful ornament as large as a dinner plate and covered with diamonds, in the center of which sparkles a one inch wide **gem of nine rays**. This ornament labels them as keepers of the plant and allows them safe passage anywhere, even among the green men, though they do not trust the latter unless they must.

John Carter came to the atmosphere plant accidentally after escaping from **Warhoon** and read the nine secret thought-sounds from the plant keeper's mind. They enabled him to escape the plant keeper, who wished to kill him because of his knowledge of the plant (for the good of Barsoom). They also enabled him to open the doors when, nearly ten years later, the plant broke down (M1;20,27). In **Okar**, each city has its own atmosphere plant (M3;9).

atom gun An imaginary Barsoomian weapon appearing only in "**John Carter and the Giant of Mars**." Its effect is deadly, and it leaves a tiny, bloody hole in its target. It also uses shells and is silent (M11A;1).

Ator A continent and country west of **Anlap** on Amtor, with whom the **Korvans** had the disastrous war which made possible the rise of **Mephis** and the **Zani** party. Because of this, Atorians were hated, feared and destroyed in Zani controlled Korva. The reason given for this persecution was that Atorians had large ears, which trait would contaminate the blood of the pure "master race" of Korva (V3;7–9).

atrium An open courtyard occupying the center of a typical Roman house (I;4).

Attica The beautiful Belgian slave-girl whom **Britannicus Caligulae Servus** saved from two ruffians, almost at the cost of his own life (I;7–11), and whom he loved for many years, even though she would not choose between him and **Numidius**, one of his best friends (I;12–16). She eventually married him and bore him a son, **Numerius Tiber Britannicus** (I;19–21), but was killed later by **Caligula**, out of jealousy over the girl's beauty; this was the final straw that prompted Britannicus to participate in the mad emperor's assassination (I;21).

aud (*Ara*) Salt (T17;12).

Aumale A town along the road from **Bouira** to **Bou Saada**, in which Tarzan stopped for the night while traveling that way in 1910. There he saw **Lieutenant Gernois**, on whom he was spying for the French War Office, conversing secretly with a suspicious man (T2;7).

Auris One of the five continents of **Poloda**. It lies north of **Kapara** across the Mandan Ocean (B2;2).

aurochs (*Bos primigenius*) A type of prehistoric cattle still common in modern Pellucidar (P2;8).

Austria European nation (formerly the Austro-Hungarian Empire) of eastern Europe, one of the chief aggressor nations of the First World War. Lutha was, demographically speaking, a part of it, and lay just between it and Serbia to the south (MK2;1).

automobiles, Amtorian The only automobiles on Amtor were found in the scientifically advanced city of Havatoo in Strabolian Noobol. They are powerful wheeled vehicles, powered by broadcast power. A dial on the dashboard selects for the proper frequency, and traffic patterns are controlled from the power station (see traffic, Amtorian) by interrupting the power to cars at intersections intermittently (V2;13).

automobiles, Polodan Passenger automobiles of Unis on Poloda are all made exactly alike to save labor and time and seat four people (six uncomfortably). They are driven by broadcast power and have nearly unlimited range (B1;4).

Avalon A sight-seeing boat which carried tourists from Los Angeles to Santa Catalina in the 1920s (T17).

Avan The chief of the village of Clovi in the Mountains of the Thipdars in Pellucidar. Tarzan saved his son Ovan from a ryth (P4;11).

Ave Maria "Hail Mary" (*Lat*). A Catholic prayer to the Blessed Mother (T22;10).

Avenue of Ancestors The chief avenue of Helium on Barsoom, leading from the Gate of Jeddaks to the Temple of Reward. Major parades and processions are held along this thoroughfare, which is five miles long (M2;16).

Avenue of Gates The street which follows the wall of Manator all the way around the city. Most of the city's inns are found on it (M5;16). See also Klootag Lat (V2;15).

Avenue of Jeddaks An important thoroughfare of ancient Horz on Barsoom (M10:1;12).

Avenue of Quays The seafront avenue of ancient Aanthor on Barsoom, where Thar Ban captured Thuvia (M4;4). It was also the name of the seafront avenue of ancient Horz (M10:1;12).

Avenue of the Green Thoat Street of Zodanga on Barsoom in which John Carter killed the assassin, Uldak (M8;5).

Avenue of Warriors A street of Zodanga on Barsoom, the address of the restaurant frequented by Rapas the Ulsio (M8;8). See also Korgan Lat (V2;15).

ax An Amtorian month, comprised of 20 Amtorian days — a total of 22 days, 11 hours Earth time (V3;4).

axe, battle The only battle axes used on Barsoom are the two-bladed affairs used in Manator (M5;16).

axe, hand A weapon used, albeit rarely, by green Barsoomians (M1;14). It was also used by the phantom bowmen of Lothar (M4;5).

Axuch One of the slaves of the family of Dilecta, beloved of the officer Maximus Praeclarus in the lost Roman city of Castra Sanguinarius when Tarzan came there in 1923 (T12;9).

ay (*Bar*) The number one (M9;11).

Ay-Mad "One-Man" (*Bar*). The name taken by the third Jed of Morbus when he proclaimed himself Jeddak (M9;11).

Aychuykak The Mayan war god (T24;13).

aytan (*Bar*) One hundred (M9;4).

az (*Pell*) Sea (P1;4).

Azar A wooded country of Pellucidar east of the valley of the Jukans, inhabited by giants seven or eight feet tall with rather pronounced canine teeth. The Azarians are man-eaters, keeping humans to be fattened for slaughter and considering them a rare delicacy. They are very low on the scale of development, inhabiting a log palisade enclosure with no roof and no huts within. They have only stone knives, wooden clubs, and grass ropes as weapons (P6;17–18).

azdyryth "Sea sloth" (*Pell*). The fearsome ichthyosaur of Pellucidar, which will eat almost anything (P1;4).

Aziz "Beloved" (*Ara*). The Arabic name given to the amnesiac Prince Michael by the gorgeous Nakhla when she taught him to speak her language (LL;12–16).

aztarag "Sea tiger" (*Pell*). A fierce aquatic dinosaur of Pellucidar (P7:2;2).

B.O. Pictures The Hollywood motion picture company which came to make *The Lion Man* in the Ituri Forest of Africa in 1932 (T17;1).

B-24 Liberator A type of American bomber aircraft of the Second World War (T22;2).

baba (*Swa*) Father (T10;1).

Babangos A light-skinned tribe of black African **cannibals** with fine features and high intelligence who eat men because they like the taste, and not for any religious or magical reason. They hunt man as they would any other beast, preferring to take their prey alive. They then break the limbs of their victims in several places and soak them in a river for three days to make them tender (T24A).

baboons Relatives of the apes; more primitive than the latter, but more advanced than **Manu**, the monkey. They are very fierce and vicious, but usually neutral toward humans and apes, though they speak a limited version of the **Tongue of the Great Apes**. **Korak** befriended a tribe of them after rescuing their chief from the cage-trap of **Sven Malbihn** and **Carl Jenssen**, though he did so more in revenge against the men than in friendship for the baboons. Later, he led that tribe in a raid against the village of **Kovudoo** to rescue **Meriem** (T4;12,15).

Back Bay Fashionable area of Boston, Massachusetts, home to various bluebloods, including the aristocratic **Smith-Jones** family (CG1;1).

Back to the Stone Age The fifth book of the Pellucidar series, abbreviated P5. The events of the story took place in 1927 and 1928 and were communicated to Burroughs by **Abner Perry** via the **Gridley Wave** in 1929, to be written up as a novel and published by Burroughs in 1936 under the title *Seven Worlds to Conquer*. It is the story of Lt. Wilhelm von Horst, of the O-220 expedition to Pellucidar, who became separated from his fellows and was left behind when the dirigible departed. It is the story of his search first for his fellows, and later for a barbaric little slave girl he had fallen in love with, and who

kept getting stolen from him — when she wasn't running away herself, that is.

backers The descendants of the followers of Sir **Bohun**, who inhabited the **City of the Sepulcher** in the **Valley of the Sepulcher** in southern **Abyssinia**. They held that they had reached the tomb of Christ (hence the name of their valley and city) and, having liberated it from the **Saracens**, could now return to England; thus, they wore their crosses on their backs, showing that they had finished their crusade, unlike the "**fronters**" of **Nimmr**, who held their crusade to be unfinished and so wore their crosses on their breasts (T11;12).

"The Bad Hombre" The ballad eternally sung by **Texas Pete** of the **Bar-Y Ranch** in 1880s Arizona (HB;1,3).

Bad men A tribe of stone-age savages of the south Pacific, the enemies of **Nadara's** people. They were almost apelike, of a very low order of development, and were **cannibals** (CG2;4).

Bagalla An east African **cannibal** tribe (TT1;3).

Bagego A tribe of African natives living on the outer slopes of the **Wiramwazi Mountains** who often carried on trade with the lost Roman outposts within the mountain range, the inhabitants of which they believed to be some sort of bloodthirsty ghosts (T12;1).

Bagesu A tribe of northeast Africa whose members are often employed as porters by white **safaris** (T15;4).

Baggs, John The best-known miser of **Oakdale**, Illinois, who was murdered and robbed on the night of **Abigail Prim's** disappearance in 1917 by **Dopey Charlie** and **The General**, two murderous bums of **Sky Pilot's** gang (K3;2,9).

Baian Gulf An Italian bay about two miles wide across which the Emperor **Caligula** built a bridge of boats so he could "conquer King Neptune" (I;17).

Baine, Jerrold One of the actors in B.O. Pictures' 1932 film *The Lion Man*. He was killed in a **Bansuto** ambush just as the company was leaving Bansuto country (T17; 2–3,7).

Bakla The sole waitress at **Peter's Inn** in early 20th century **Karlova** (R;4), who saved

Prince Boris from execution as The Rider by riding to Sovgrad to explain the switch (R;16–17).

bal (*Pal*) "Gold" or "golden" (T8;18).

Bal Tab A green Barsoomian warrior trapped in the menagerie of Jal Had, Prince of Amhor, next to Vor Daj/Tor-dur-bar. He came up with the plan the group used to escape the zoo, and helped Vor Daj rescue Janai as well, killing Jal Had in the process with a metal goad taken from the menagerie. He was later killed by gunfire from an Amhorian patrol boat while the party was fleeing the city (M9;26–28).

Bal Zak The captain of Ras Thavas' flier, *Vosar*. His father was a noble whom Gor Hajus had refused to slay, and Bal Zak repaid his debt of gratitude by helping Ulysses Paxton, Gor Hajus and their friends when they stowed away to Toonol by not revealing their hiding place aboard the *Vosar* (M6;7–8).

Balal A young Himean of the tribe of Garb whom Tanar the Fleet One saved from a giant codon (P3;10).

Balando One of the Waziri warriors who went with Muviro to the Kavuru country in search of Buira. Balando was one of the few Waziri to remain alive after the Kavuru attack (T19;25).

Baldwin, Dr. The local doctor of the Ganado area of southern California in the early 1920s (GH;16).

Baldy One of the horses of Rancho del Ganado in the early 1920s (GH;1). Another Baldy was a fairly gentle horse of Cory Blaine's early 20th century dude ranch in Arizona, whom Bruce Marvel bought after the horse proved what a fast, sure animal it was (D;3,5–6).

ballet, Mahar The Mahars of Pellucidar had a sort of dance which apparently took the place of music for the deaf creatures. It consisted of elaborate wing, tail and head movements performed by a group of twenty or so Mahars (P1;6).

ballista A siege engine in the form of a giant crossbow which fires spear-sized missiles (T12;19)(I;16).

ballochute A safety device invented by Carson Napier after he retired to Korva in

1932. It consists of a balloon made of tarel and compressed into a tube. When activated, it is ejected and a tiny piece of lor is annihilated inside it, generating sufficient heat to instantly inflate the balloon and keep it inflated for some time. The user can then either slowly descend, remain aloft for awhile, or pull a ripcord and descend quickly (V5;2).

Balmen A sailing ship of Halmstad, Sweden, bound for Spain from Brazil, which Bowen Tyler stopped for provisions in the mid–Atlantic in June of 1916. It was soon afterward sunk by a U-boat before reaching Madrid (C1;3).

Baltimore American city of Maryland where Professor Archimedes Q. Porter and his daughter Jane originally lived (T1;18).

Baltoo The jong of the Amtorian country of Andoo on the continent of Noobol (V2;11).

balu (*Ape*) A baby or small child (T6;3).

balu-den "Baby tree" (*Ape*). Branch or stick (TC).

Balza "Golden Girl." The name was either a mistake on Burroughs' part or a cognate — it was supposed to be in the language of the Great Apes, but clearly uses Pal-ul-don roots in an ape-type construction (see Bal; Za).

In any case, Balza was a seemingly pure human born to one of the gorillas of London in the Valley of Diamonds, one of the few who managed to survive without being destroyed for long enough to learn English and flee to the territory of the hybrids at the valley's south end. She was the mate of Malb'yat, but when Tarzan defeated him she became Tarzan's by the customs of the strange creatures, and helped him escape the valley. He gave her to the crew of *The Lion Man* to take care of, and she became a civilized girl (well, almost) in no time at all, becoming the leading lady of *The Lion Man* and a starlet within a year. No one thereafter could have ever guessed her origin as a wild woman of Africa (T17;29–33).

Balzo Jan The brother of Balzo Moro, shot down behind Kapar lines in January of 1940 and thought dead until he came back with Tangor a few weeks later (B1;10).

Balzo Moro The young woman who was the first person to see Tangor (and vice versa) when he mysteriously appeared in the

Polodan city of Orvis in the country of Unis in September of 1939 (B1;1–2).

Ban-tor An enemy of Ptang, warrior of Xaxak the Dator of Kamtol on Barsoom. When John Carter bested him in swordplay, he did not take it as well as did the others, but instead became angry at Carter, becoming his first active enemy in the Valley of the First-Born. He sneaked into John Carter's room there and traded swords with him, giving him a shorter sword so as to disadvantage him in his duels the next day, then placing large bets against him. In punishment, he was commanded by Doxus to fight John Carter, who cut an "x" on Ban-tor's forehead with his sword — a badge of dishonor Ban-tor would wear forever (M10:2;7–9).

Banat The Pangan yorkokor (colonel) who arrested Carson Napier and Ero Shan in Hor after the defeat of the Falsan navy in 1931. He later befriended them, getting captured by and escaping from the Hangors with them (V4;48–53).

Banatoff The last ruling house of the tiny Slavic kingdom of Margoth (R;7).

band (Ape) Elbow (TC).

band (Cpk) Spear (C1;9).

Band-lu "Spear-man" (Cpk). The next highest Caspakian race of humanity above the Sto-lu. The Band-lus are of late Paleolithic development and have well-made stone weapons, fairly organized communities, simple clothing, ornamentation, primitive art, fireplaces, and a fairly complex language. They are not bad to look upon, resembling the lower humanoid types, but not as ugly. After a while a Band-lu may develop into a Kro-lu. Band-lus usually wear a loincloth of snakeskin cured with the head on, and depending in front to the knees (C1;9).

Bandar Az A Pellucidarian ocean, identical to the Lural Az and the Sojar Az (P6;20).

The Bandit of Hell's Bend Burroughs' first western novel, written in 1923 and published a year later in Argosy All-Story Weekly from September 13th to October 18th, 1924. The story is set in Arizona in the 1880s, and the characters and ranch are based on Burroughs' father's Bar-Y Ranch in Idaho, upon which Burroughs worked as a cowboy in 1891 and 1898. In the story, the beautiful young

Diana Henders inherits the Bar-Y Ranch from her dead father, and a pair of unscrupulous businessmen from back East team up with her foreman to swindle her out of the ranch. Help comes in the person of Bull, the former foreman, whom the swindlers have tried to frame as the notorious criminal of the title. It is abbreviated HB.

Bandolian The emperor of the Morgors of Eurobus, an incredibly cruel and monstrous tyrant who kept his people's loyalty by generations of inbred fear, obedience training, and military regimentation (M11B;3–4).

Bangali A British outpost of Northern Rhodesia at which Lt. Cecil Giles-Burton's father was resident commissioner, and at which city he planned to drop off the Brown plans to his father (T24B;3).

Bangalo A peaceful east African tribe, ruled in the 1920s by Kabariga (T15;1).

Banos One of the ten other planets of the star Omos sharing Poloda's weird orbit (B1).

Bansuto A tribe of African savages who attacked the B.O. Pictures' safari with poisoned arrows after warning them to stay out of their territory and being ignored by Tom Orman, the director. They are ritual cannibals; that is, they eat only brave, strong or wise enemies in the belief that they will absorb those qualities in the process (T17;3,8).

Bantango A cannibal tribe of the Ethiopian Highlands (T21;13).

banth The fierce Barsoomian lion. It is hairless except for a large, bristly mane around its thick neck. It has a long, muscular body and ten legs. Its mouth reaches behind its ears, which are very small, and it has three rows of needle-like teeth, much as does a calot. It has huge, protruding green eyes and its body is a tawny yellow color. The beast favors hunting in the hills surrounding the dead sea bottoms, and is used by more than one evil group as a method of torture (throwing people to the banths, etc.). The Therns are one of these groups, keeping an enormous number of banths in their citadels as guards and sources of amusement (M2;3). The creatures are incredibly fierce, enjoy the taste of human flesh, and emit a low, eerie moan when hunting. They are used by the Lotharians as war beasts as well as for cleanup of enemy bodies; they also revere them as sacred animals (M4;4–6).

Bantoom The city of the Kaldanes of Barsoom. It lies in a fertile, well-watered valley a good distance southwest of **Gathol**. In Bantoom a forest grows and cultivation is carried out by the Kaldanes, mounted on their **rykors**. It is less a city than a collection of farms, each of which has an enclosed compound in the center. In the center of each compound is a tower that looks like a **silo**, which is the entrance to an underground maze of passages, the main ones being large enough to admit humans, but the peripheral ones being only about a foot in diameter, just large enough for Kaldanes. Each set of burrows is inhabited by a **king** Kaldane and his swarm, and the swarms get along well most of the time (M5;5–6).

Bantor Han The gunner who survived with **Tangor** the latter's first engagement with the **Kapars** in January of 1940. Like all modern **Unisans**, he was somewhat agoraphobic after living underground his whole life (B1;6).

Bantu A group of related east African tribes sharing common blood and closely related languages (T12;1).

bar (*Amt*) Hair (V1;14).

bar (*Bar*) The number eight (M9;4).

bar (*Pal*) Battle (T8;3).

Bar Comas The green Jeddak of **Warhoon** on late 19th century Barsoom. He attacked the **jed**, Dak Kova, in response to an insult, made a mistake, and was killed. Dak Kova, older and far more vicious, survived (barely) to become the new jeddak (M1;18).

Bar-Y Ranch The name of both the Burroughs family ranch in Idaho and the **Henders** family ranch in **Arizona** (HB;1).

Bara (*Ape*) Any deer or antelope — one of Tarzan's favorite meals (T1;9).

barbarians The black **Bagego** subjects of the Romans of **Castra Sanguinarius** and **Castrum Mare** in the **Wiramwazi Mountains** of Africa (T12;6).

Barney Custer of Beatrice The original title of the second part of *The Mad King*, now usually published as the second part of a two-part novel. This second book (abbreviated

MK2) takes place in time after *The Eternal Savage* (E1 and E2), which in turn follows *The Mad King* (MK1).

Barnum, Phineas Taylor (1810–1891) American showman and entrepreneur whose animal and freak-show based carnival was possibly the most famous of all time (ME;11).

Barnut, Lieutenant A Chicago police officer of the early 20th century (GF;1).

barranco (*Sp*) A ravine or gorge (GH;2).

Barren Hills, the A chain of volcanic hills of central Africa during the **Niocene Era** (E1;9).

Barry Mason Compton's chauffeur (EE).

Barsoom The name given by its inhabitants to the planet Mars. Barsoom is a dying world, covered mostly with deserts and arid wastes which were once sea bottoms, interspersed with hilly country where there is a little water. The history of civilization on the planet goes back about a million years to the **Orovars**, an ancient white-skinned human race who dominated the world when its oceans still rolled across its surface. In later days, the black and yellow human races developed technologies and cultures, but all of their lifestyles were eventually doomed to die as the seas receded, leaving the barbarian **green Barsoomians**, who flourished in the wastes, to multiply and become a threat to the civilized humanoid races. As the seas receded, the cities of the ancients expanded to follow them down the slopes of the continents until, eventually, the green men drove the ancients from their cities (M4;6–7)(M7;3). During the last years, many members of the black, yellow and white races cooperated to save Barsoom from extinction while the rest of the members of those races fled to the far corners of the planet to escape being butchered by the green men. Members of the three races who worked to save the planet interbred for hundreds of generations, eventually producing the race of **red men**, the dominant race of modern Barsoom (M1). It was during this time that the **atmosphere plant** and **canals** were invented and built, the former from a design perfected by the **yellow men**. The universal **tongue of** Barsoom was probably developed during this period, and today is spoken or understood (at least partially) by all of Barsoom's creatures. In modern times, the canals and atmosphere plant are maintained by the red men, who have also brought their science to a higher degree than that possessed by the ancients. Indeed, most of the modern inventions of Barsoom — firearms, fliers, etc. — were invented by the red race and adopted by others (M1). The cities of the red men dot the landscape, built along the canals or in the few wetlands left on the planet, and are all walled and mostly autonomous, except for those which are part of a larger empire. Almost every city has some canal land to itself.

The remnants of the ancient races who chose flight survive until the present day, hidden in their remote sanctuaries at the poles or in hidden valleys. The yellow race fortified itself in the land of Okar behind Barsoom's north polar ice barrier, built hothouse cities in the frozen north, and adopted a policy of insularity, destroying or enslaving all who came into their land (M3;9). The black race, possibly the proudest of the three ancient races, withdrew to the Valley Dor at the south pole and turned to a parasitic existence of piracy, stealing what they needed from the "lesser" races of the planet (see First-Born). The most important white remnant also established itself in the Valley Dor and in the nearby Mountains of Otz, and founded a religion which they foisted upon the rest of Barsoom so that they, like the blacks, could live off their "lesser" cousins, the red race, and the green men who had driven them into exile (see Therns).

Almost all Barsoomians are warlike, a legacy handed down from eon to eon since the recession of the seas began. They all have common customs, perhaps coming down from the same source as their common language. These customs include their similarities of dress, fighting techniques, etc., which vary only slightly from place to place.

Except in the Kaolian Forest and the Toonolian Marshes, there are very few wild species of lower animals left on Barsoom, and owing to the spectacular hardships offered by life on the planet, it is no wonder that most of the remaining types are very dangerous (see banth; calot; thoat).

For most of Barsoom's modern history, the inhabitants were almost constantly at war, until the Earthman John Carter helped to begin a new era of cooperation among many of the red nations, and even the yellow, white and black races, who had been so hostile to the red race and each other for so long. Even some of the tribes of the savage green men began to participate in this new understanding, thanks in large part to Tars Tarkas, Jeddak of Thark and a great friend of John Carter's.

In 1967, after 22 years of work (based on that begun in the late 1920s by Jason Gridley of Earth and Ulysses Paxton, an Earthman on Barsoom [P3][M7]), a full scientific language was developed and the exchange of Earthly and Barsoomian science begun, culminating in the construction of the Barsoom, which left Earth for Barsoom on Christmas Day, 2025. The ship, unfortunately, was sabotaged and landed inside the moon instead, precipitating the events that were eventually to lead to the Lunarian invasion and subsequent breaking off of communication with Barsoom, the latter tragedy being accomplished by the actions of a powerful fundamentalist religious group. This group, which preached against all scientific progress (especially in space), had lobbied in Washington so successfully that all communication with Barsoom was suspended and therefore, Barsoomians could not help when the Earth was invaded by the Kalkars (MM1;1) (MM2;1).

Barsoom The name of the first Earth-Mars space vessel, designed by Lt. Commander Orthis of the International Peace Fleet and constructed under the supervision of Captain Julian 5th in 2024 and 2025. It was launched on December 25, 2025. Lt. Commander Orthis sabotaged the ship, however, in vengeance against Julian (who had bested him throughout his life), and the ship made a forced landing inside the moon, passing into its hollow interior through a crater.

The ship possessed **buoyancy tanks** filled with the **eighth ray** of the sun and each inner planet, as well as those of **Jupiter** and the Earth's moon. The primary engines collected and exhausted the eighth ray of either Earth or Mars, driving the ship at 1200 miles per hour, and the auxiliary engine could collect the eighth ray of any body and exhaust it, propelling the ship at up to 600 miles per hour if the main engine should fail. It was manned by a crew of five: Julian 5th in command, with Lt. Commander Orthis, lieutenants West and Jay, and Ensign Norton. It carried provisions for the five men for 15 years. The sabotage wrought by Orthis was the opening of the lunar eighth ray tank and the destruction of the auxiliary engine, so that the moon's gravity would draw the ship toward it, and there would be no way of collecting the moon's eighth ray to propel the ship back away from it, as the auxiliary engine could have done (MM1;1-2). After many years of labor Ensign Norton, who had absorbed much of Orthis' technical knowledge through his long association with the mad genius, was able to repair the ship, and in 2036 it returned to Earth without Orthis (who had joined the Kalkars, the ruling race of the world inside the moon) (MM1;14).

Barsoom, tongue of The universal language of Barsoom, dating back to the time of the Orovars.

Bartolo The scruffy Mexican right-hand man of Slick Allen, who handled the transportation of his bootleg whiskey to Guy Evans (GH;20-21).

Barunda The Dyak headman of Rajah Muda Saffir's expedition to carry off Virginia Maxon. He was defeated by Bulan, surrendered, and guided him in pursuit of his hated master. When he met up with the traitorous Ninaka, who had left the rajah behind, he again turned coat; losing Bulan and his remaining monsters in the jungle, the two Dyaks fled into the interior with both Virginia and the "treasure" chest. Barunda was later murdered by Ninaka after the girl escaped and the two quarreled over division of the spoils (Q;9-11,13).

Basembo A tribe of east Africa whose lands later became British possessions (T14;2).

basilica A type of ancient Roman building, rectangular in shape and divided by columns so as to form a nave with two aisles on the sides, used as a kind of meeting hall (I;5).

Basilica Julia A basilica of ancient Rome built in honor of Julius Caesar (I;5).

Bass, Abner J. A New York multi-millionaire of the early 20th century; a rather affable man in spite of his position, quite unlike his social-climbing wife. He paid for Hemmington Main's trip to Europe to save his daughter from being forced to marry a titled European (R;1).

Bass, Gwendolyn The attractive daughter of early 20th century millionaire Abner J. Bass, who was in love with Hemmington Main, a poor newspaper reporter. Her social-climbing mother planned otherwise for her, however — she wished to marry the sole heir to the Bass millions into a noble European family. She was followed to Europe by Main when her mother took her there to make a match (R;1) and was "abducted" by the infamous brigand The Rider masquerading as Prince Boris, while the real Prince Boris, masquerading as The Rider, abducted Princess Mary of Margoth, mistaking her and her maid for the Basses on the basis of Main's inadequate description. Boris and Main had planned to abduct Gwen so Main could marry her. Thanks to Mrs. Bass, Gwen was almost forced to marry the brigand in royal clothing, but Main arrived on the scene and saved her by shooting him (R;5-7, 10-11). The incident shocked some sense into Mrs. Bass, who, after everything had been sorted out, gave her consent for Gwendolyn to marry Main. They did so soon afterward in Demia, with Prince Boris (the real one) as best man and Gwen's old school chum, Princess Mary, as maid of honor (R;14-17).

Basti A Pellucidarian tribe and village on the continent to the west of Korsar. Basti was carved into a cliff, and the villagers practiced deceit as a way of life. In addition, they were slave-takers and cannibals — all in all, a thoroughly dislikable sort (P5;5-7).

basto A large Amtorian omnivore, standing as tall as a man at the shoulder and weighing up to 1200 pounds. The top of its head resembles an American bison's, with short, thick horns. It has a broad snout like that of a boar and four tusks. A basto is blue in color and has an elephantine hide with thick, curly hair on its head but none elsewhere except at the tip of the tail. Three quarters of the creature's weight is carried by its short, stocky front legs (with broad, three-toed feet), as its body is sort of ham-shaped, sloping down from the shoulder to the rump and up underneath, so that its hind legs are longer than its front and its hind feet smaller. It is very short-tempered, but not difficult to kill for one who knows how, and its meat is delicious (V1;7).

bat, Barsoomian   A creature mentioned only in "John Carter and the Giant of Mars" (M11A;2).

Batando   The wise old chief of the Galla village where Fejjuan (né Ulala) was born, abducted from as a child, and returned to many years later (T11;10).

Batavia   Former name of Jakarta, the capital of Indonesia (T24;2).

baths, Laythean   The U-gas of Laythe in Va-nah enjoyed cold baths, using no soap but instead rubbing the skin with rough fiber gloves until it glowed. The Laytheans loved the water, and the large public baths in the city were a popular pastime. There men, women and children bathed, swam and dived together (MM1;11).

Baths of Caesar   The richest and most exclusive public baths of Castrum Mare, frequented only by the richest of patricians (T12;8).

Batoro   The Bantu tribe to which Gabula, Erich von Harben's faithful servant, belonged (T12;4).

Battak   A cannibal tribe of Indonesia who ate their old people in the belief that they would thus be immortal, their spirits living on in the bodies of the young (T22;16,25).

Battel   An English town of east Sussex, near which a battle was fought between Henry III and his barons in May of 1264 (OT;15).

"The Battle for Teeka"   The tenth short story in the collection *Jungle Tales of Tarzan*, in which Tarzan rescued his ape-friend Teeka from a renegade bull ape who had abducted her and almost killed her baby Gazan in the bargain. The story is abbreviated T6:10.

Battling Dago Pete   An almost unbeatable turn-of-the-century New York prizefighter who met his match in Billy Byrne, the mucker from Chicago (K1;17).

batu   "Finished" (*Cpk*). The Caspakian term used to describe an individual who is no longer capable of evolutionary progress, and is thus stuck at whatever stage (Bo-lu, Band-lu, or whatever) he had achieved; usually the same as his mother's, but occasionally one step higher (C2;5).

Bauli   A Roman town on one side of the Baian Gulf, across from Puteoli (1;17).

Baynes, The Honorable Morrison   A young, handsome, rich Englishman who visited Tarzan and Jane on their African estate about a year after Meriem came to live with them, and quickly developed a strong attraction to the girl, which she returned by a teenage fascination. He originally considered asking her hand in marriage, but after hearing her speak to a group of baboons, and later being told of her life in the wild, he decided to "honor" her by making her his mistress, because he certainly could not marry someone of such a low social level (T4;16–17). After it became apparent to Tarzan what Baynes had in mind, he asked the Englishman to leave his estate, turning him into a martyr in Meriem's eyes (the situation was not properly explained to her, so she did not understand Baynes' dishonorable intentions toward her). This made his secret return to abduct her with "Mr. Hanson's" help much easier, but "Hanson" double-crossed Baynes and took the girl for himself. This, however, finally made Baynes realize that he really did love Meriem, and so he set out to track down "Hanson" and rescue or revenge her. After overtaking them, Baynes shot "Hanson" (actually Korak's enemy Sven Malbihn) and was himself shot. After directing Korak in pursuit of Meriem, Baynes later died of his wounds (T4;19–27).

bayonet, Spanish   A yucca or agave plant of the American Southwest (A1;6).

Be-don-ko-he   A large Apache tribe of 19th century Arizona, which Go-yat-thlay (a.k.a. Geronimo) joined after he married one of its daughters, Alope. He became its war chief, and after the murder of Mangas Colorado in 1863, its full chief. It was thus the tribe in which Shoz-dijiji grew up (A1;1). It joined the other five Apache tribes on the warpath on several occasions (A1;3–6,14–15) throughout the 1870s, but eventually settled down at Geronimo's insistence (A1;19).

Bean, Norman   Pseudonym used by Burroughs for some of his early work.

The Beasts of Tarzan   The third book in the Tarzan series, published in 1914. The events of the book took place late in 1912, just after the rainy season in west Africa, and were narrated to Burroughs by Tarzan himself, whom the author first met in 1911. The story concerns the abduction of Tarzan's young son Jack by Nikolas Rokoff and Alexis Paulvitch in revenge against Tarzan after Rokoff's escape from a French prison. They furthermore marooned Tarzan on an island off the coast of Africa, and the ape-man not only had to escape the island, but also track down and rescue Jane and his son before any harm befell them; Tarzan led a tribe of great apes and a trained panther in the pursuit. The abbreviation of the book is T3.

Beatrice A town of Gage County, on the Blue River of Nebraska, home of Barney Custer and his sister Victoria (MK1;1), and also of James Torrance, Jr. (EE;2).

Beatrice Corn Mills, Inc. The early 20th century business of which James Torrance, Sr., was president and general manager (EE;2).

Beauchamp One of the three knights who were the first such that Norman of Torn ever saw, when they came to his "father's" castle in 1255. Beauchamp was killed by the young Norman after attempting to defend Paul of Merely against him (OT;5).

Bedouin The Arabs of north Africa (T11;1).

Beduw *see* Bedouin

Beebe, Charles William (1877–1962) A zoologist and member of the New York Zoological Society, who wrote several books about their expeditions, including *The Arcturus Adventure* in 1926 (T24;7).

beled (*Ara*) The home camp of a family, often at an oasis (T11;1).

Beled el-Guad The home oasis of the Fendy el-Guad, an Arab clan of the early 20th century (T11;1).

Belgae The Celts of Belgium, who defeated the tribe of Britannicus Caligulae Servus and sold them into slavery in Germany after Britannicus' father tried to conquer them in A.D. 16 (I;1).

Belgian Congo The name of the Congo Free State from 1909 to 1960, at which time it became the Republic of Zaire (T1;21).

Belgium The European country whose officers treated the people of Mbonga so badly

that they were forced to leave the Congo Free State and flee west to the area where Tarzan grew up, Portuguese West Africa (T1;9,21).

Belik, Colonel Abu Commander of the Abyssinian outpost along the upper Rhine where Lt. Jefferson Turck was captured in the summer of 2137. He was a cultured and civilized man who treated Turck well, seeing that he was also a civilized person. He had been commander of the guards of his emperor's palace until he was disgraced by false rumors and sent to the frontier (LC;8).

Bellows, "Doc" The fat, jovial coroner for early 20th century Commanche County, New Mexico (D;2).

Bellus A famous racehorse of the Green Stables in early 1st century Rome (I;8).

Belter's Canyon The next canyon east of Cottonwood Canyon in 1880s Arizona (HB;2).

Belthar The man-eating pet lion of Nemone, Queen of Cathne, when Tarzan came to that lost city in October of 1930. Nemone suffered from the peculiar delusion that her and Belthar's lives were linked, so that if one died, the other would also. Indeed, when Belthar was killed by Jad-bal-ja, who had followed Tarzan to Onthar, Nemone killed herself as well (T16;10,16,19).

ben (*Pal*) Great (T8;2).

Ben A man-eating lion, title character of "The Maneater." He was captured in a lion pit in central Africa after his mate was killed by Scott Taylor, but he was freed by Richard Gordon, whom he afterward remembered and was friendly toward. Tracking his mate's killer, he killed Bill Gootch, but failed to get Taylor and was later caught by animal trappers and sold to a traveling circus, where he received his name. Later, he escaped in Scottsville, Virginia, due to a derailment of the circus train, and appeared on the scene just in time to save Gordon from Taylor by killing the latter. Gordon afterward bought him from the circus and donated him to a New York zoo (ME;4–11).

"Ben, King of Beasts" Original title of "The Maneater."

Ben Saada An Arab of the tribe of sheik Ali-es-Hadji, who was the first person to see the amnesiac **Prince Michael** and his lion (LL;8). He was a scoundrel who wanted **Nakhla** for himself. When she rebuffed him, he took to spying on her, caught her with Michael, and later lied to him, telling him she had married someone else. Nakhla still would have none of him, however, and so he took it upon himself to abduct her. He lost her to marauders, but himself escaped (LL;14–20).

benat Plural of **bint** (T17;2).

Beng Kher The king of the lost Khmer city of **Pnom Dhek** when **Gordon King** stumbled upon it in the mid–1920s (HM;5). He opposed his daughter's love for King and would have had him executed, but King escaped with the princess' help. It wasn't that Beng Kher disliked King, but rather that he insisted on his daughter marrying the Prince **Bharata Rahon** (HM;12–13). Later, he launched an invasion against **Lodidhapura** after King had become a hero and officer of that city, and in the retreat was traitorously stabbed and thrown from his elephant by Bharata Rahon, who wished to become ruler of Pnom Dhek immediately. Unfortunately for his plans, Gordon King saw his action and saved Beng Kher, who afterward blessed King and proclaimed him King of Pnom Dhek upon his death, which came soon afterward from complications of the stab wound (HM;15–16).

Benguela current A current which flows northward along the west coast of Africa, past **Jungle Island** (T3;16).

Benham, Samuel A rich older man with an important family whom **Abigail Prim's** stepmother wished her to marry in 1917 Oakdale, Illinois. He had become rich purely through luck, and had no imagination and little intelligence (K3;1–2).

Benito One of the **vaqueros** of the **El Orobo Ranch** in 1916 Mexico, who was sent with **Bridge** to get the payroll from **Cuivaca** (K2;9).

Benson A member of the crew of the British tug which rescued **Bowen Tyler** and **Lys La Rue** from the English Channel and captured the submarine U-33 on June 4, 1916. He was a socialist and hated all Americans, which led him to become a German agent even though he hated them, too. He sabotaged the U-33's compass, destroyed its wireless and navigational instruments, betrayed

the ship to the Germans, and even tried to kill Tyler once, but was finally found out by Lys and shot, confessing his acts as he died. Because of his extensive sabotage, the U-33 ended up at **Caprona** in the south Pacific (C1;3–4).

Beny Salem Fendy el-Guad An Arab clan of which Sheik **Ibn Jad** of the tribe **el-Harb** was a member (T11;1).

Beppo A large and dangerous gypsy dancing bear (usually led by a steel collar and chain) who belonged to the gypsy girl **Giova** and her father. In 1917, they lived in the neighborhood of the old **Squibbs** house south of **Oakdale**, Illinois, and Beppo was the "thing" that so terrified "**The Oskaloosa Kid**" and the hobo band of the **Sky Pilot** on the night of "**The Oakdale Affair.**" He was brought by Giova in her flight with **Bridge** and his friends and saved them from the attack of the Sky Pilot and his band, but went mad in the process and had to be killed by **Detective Burton's** men (K3;3–5,8,10).

Berengaria The betrothed (later wife) of **Richard I** of England, who was insulted by the King of **Cyprus**, triggering Richard to invade that island to conquer it on his way to the **Third Crusade** (T11;12).

Berger, Sam A notorious womanizer of the late 1920s whom **Jerry Jerome** shot and left for dead when Berger tried to seduce Jerome's girlfriend. He recovered, refused to press charges, and was later shot dead by a girl he had wronged (T18;23).

berkelium Heavy radioactive element (atomic number 97) which on Earth does not occur in nature. It apparently does on Amtor, however, and in a more stable form. When exposed to **vik-ro** (neptunium) it undergoes a chain reaction to emit the disintegrative T-ray, at least on Amtor (V1;8).

Berlin The capital of unified Germany, near the river **Elbe** in the northeastern part of the country. It was the site of the **Abyssinian** frontier city of **New Gondar** in the 22nd century of *The Lost Continent* (LC;6,8).

bernoose Head covering worn by the **Arabs**, composed of a piece of cloth tied around the head at the brow and hanging about the shoulders like a cloak. It keeps the head cool and the hair free of sand, and often has a piece covering the lower face to keep sand and dust from the nose and mouth (T2;7).

Bert The husband of **Victoria Custer's** friend **Margaret**. He was also **Barney Custer's** business partner — they owned a corn mill which **Captain Ernst Maenck** blew up in August of 1914 in an attempt to kill Barney (MK2;1).

Bertram, Sir The Keeper of the Gate of Nimmr on the day when Tarzan arrived there in search of **James Hunter Blake** in February of 1921 (T11;19).

Betete A tribe of cannibalistic African pygmies of the Congo region, who held **Kali Bwana** prisoner for **Bobolo**, a neighboring chief, in 1931. They planned to eat her, but she was saved by Tarzan and the **Old Timer** (T18;15,18–19).

Bethelda One of the pure human descendants of **Orthis** who were persecuted by **Or-tis 16th**; she was, in fact, the daughter of **Or-tis 15th**. She fled into the hills near the **Kalkar** capital and was saved from capture by **Julian 20th**, who had himself just escaped from the Kalkars. Even though he knew she was an Or-tis, he found himself falling in love with the beautiful and sweet girl, who probably hated the Kalkars more than he did because she had lived so long among them. Even so, he at first tried to convince himself that she was an enemy, to no avail. He brought her to the camp of the **Nipons**, who knew and loved her, and while he was out hunting, **Raban** and his men came and kidnapped her, and Julian rode in pursuit. He rescued her from Raban and the two were married, she bearing him **Julian 21st** around 2432 (MM3;7,10).

Bettilinus, Capito The father of **Cassius Bettilinus**, whom **Caligula** had executed when he objected to his son's execution (I;20).

Bettilinus, Cassius A Roman senator executed by **Caligula** for no particular reason (I;20).

Beverly, May The madam of **The Beverly Club** (GF;5).

Beverly Club A house of prostitution on the south side of early 20th century **Chicago** (GF;1).

Beverly Hills Posh suburb of Los Angeles, home of **Pat Morgan** in the 1930s (J;4).

Beyond the Farthest Star A two part novel, actually two novellas put together. The first, "Adventure on Poloda," is abbreviated B1, and the second, "Tangor Returns," is abbreviated B2. Burroughs probably intended the series to be a multi-part saga, but his death in 1950 stopped the mysterious typewriter messages from Tangor, so that no one has ever found out how the American airman managed to activate it all the way from Poloda in the first place. John Carter–like, Tangor was a warrior who was mysteriously transported to another world after his apparent death, this time in World War II. He never found out how he got there, but he found on Poloda another world at war, a world which he adopted and went to war for. The events of B1 took place from September 1939 to January 1940, and those of B2 from January to autumn of 1940.

Beyond Thirty The original title of *The Lost Continent*, referring to the fact that the lands lying east of 30 degrees longitude were forbidden to the citizens of 22nd century Pan-America, where the story takes place. It also refers to the fact that the hero of the story, **Lt. Jefferson Turck**, is forced beyond that line by a series of accidents to an unplanned voyage of discovery (LC).

beyt (*Ara*) House (T11;1).

beyt es-sh'ar "House of hair" (*Ara*). A type of camel-hair tent favored by the Bedouin (T11;1).

Bharata Rahon A prince of **Pnom Dhek**, lost city of **Cambodia**, who wished to marry **Fou-tan**, prompting her to run away when her father consented to the match (HM;5). When she returned, her father still insisted upon her marrying him (HM;12–13), and she would have had to had not Bharata Rahon become impatient for the throne and assassinated Beng Kher with only one witness — **Gordon King**, who led a force of warriors into Pnom Dhek by a secret route and killed Bharata Rahon (HM;15–16).

Bi-er-le A runner of the **Cho-ko-nen** tribe of Apaches of mid-19th century New Mexico, who was sent by **Cochise** to tell the **Be-don-ko-he** of the murder of **Mangas Colorado** at Fort McKane in 1863 (A1;1).

The Big Bwana One of the names by which Tarzan was known in central Africa, especially in his role as champion of fair play (T4;21).

Big Fist The warrior of **Nadara**'s tribe who claimed its kingship after **Flatfoot**'s death, and held it because **Thandar** was not interested. When Thandar later killed him after he struck Nadara, Thandar was made king of the tribe (CG2;1–2).

Big Jon The father of **Corrie van der Meer**'s friend **Sarina**. "Big Jon" was a man of contradictions; he was a bloody pirate of the South Seas during the 1920s and 1930s who was nonetheless kind to his wife and daughter. He was also a well-educated man and made sure that his daughter was educated as well. Eventually, one of his many murders caught up with him and he was hanged in 1938, leaving Sarina alone in the world but well able to fend for herself (T22;23).

Big Little Books The series of children's book from Whitman Publishing in which several adaptations of Tarzan stories appeared in the late 1930s, and in which "**John Carter and the Giant of Mars**" was originally published in 1941.

Big Smoke The nickname of John A. Johnson (1878–1946), who held the world heavyweight title from 1908 to 1915 (K1;17).

Bill One of the **Arrow** mutineers (T1;17). Another Bill was the mechanic of **Beatrice**, Nebraska, whom **Ernst Maenck** hired to drive him to **Lincoln** (MK2;1). Yet another Bill was the driver of the stagecoach which was robbed by the **Black Coyote** while **Mary Donovan** was aboard (HB;2).

Billah (*Ara*) A negative ejaculation, as in the expression, "Billah, no!" (T11;1).

billian A hardwood of the South Pacific (CG2;11).

Billings The captain of the *Fuwalda*. He was a brutish man who beat and threatened his crew to keep them in line, and eventually paid the price for his behavior when his crew mutinied and killed him. Even though **Lord Greystoke** had warned him of the impending mutiny, he had refused to listen (T1;1–2). Billings was also the assumed name under which **Jack Clayton** traveled from Dover to Africa with his "invalid grandmother," the

heavily veiled, disguised, wheelchair-riding **Akut**, who after boarding their ship stayed hidden in their cabin for the whole trip so no one could guess he was an ape (T4;4).

Billings, Jefferson A rough-and-ready rancher of late 19th century **Arizona**, the father of **Wichita Billings**. He was a hardheaded man of strong opinions who hated Indians with a passion, especially after the death of his best friend, ostensibly at **Apache** hands (A2;3). He himself was killed in 1886 by "**Dirty**" **Cheetim**, who scalped him to make it look as though an Apache had done it (A2;18).

Billings, Thomas The late **Bowen Tyler, Sr.**'s secretary, a man who was "force, energy, initiative and good judgment combined and personified." After Mr. Tyler's death, he arranged the expedition to rescue **Bowen Tyler, Jr.**, from **Caspak** and led it himself. He had been a poor cowboy, but was "discovered" by Mr. Tyler and given an education at the same college Bowen, Jr., had attended, so that the young men became the best of friends (C2;1). Upon arrival at **Caprona**, he passed over the cliffs alone in a seaplane, and was wrecked in its eastern area after an aerial battle with a huge pterodactyl. Soon afterward, he saved a **Galu** girl named **Ajor** from a huge panther, and later from a group of **Alus**, and together they set out for the Galu country, through which Billings would have to pass in order to circle Caspak's central sea and return to the *Toreador*. On the way, she taught him the language of Caspak. They were captured by and escaped from the **Band-lu**, then passed through many dangers to the **Kro-lu** country, where they found out about a plot hatched by the renegade Galu **Du-seen** to conquer the Galu country with the help of some unwise Kro-lu. Here Billings realized that Ajor loved him and he her, but here they were separated by Du-seen's plotting (C2;2–6). Billings searched for Ajor for some time before finding her in the Galu country and rescuing her just as Du-seen was about to kill her. They were both rescued in turn a few minutes later by the arrival of a force of Galus and the men from the *Toreador*, coordinated by Bowen Tyler. Since Ajor was **cos-ata-lo** her father, chief **Jor** of the Galus, would not let her leave Caspak, and so Billings remained there with her when the others left for home (C2;7). Two weeks later, though, **John Bradley** arrived in the recaptured U-33, "captured" Billings and Ajor, met the *Toreador* outside Caprona, and returned to California (C3;5).

Billings, Wichita A young white girl whose father owned an Arizona border ranch in Cochise County in the late 1800s, and who was saved from rape at a ruffian's hands by **Shoz-dijiji** in 1879 (A1;10). They afterward became friends, and she provided Shoz-dijiji with a horse and food when he was cut off from his tribe later that year after the battle of **Cibicu Creek**, in return for which she bound him to promise not to kill whites when not at war with them, at least for awhile (A1;15–16). Later, he saved her from an Apache raid and took her back to his tribe for a time, until the hostile Apaches left the area. It was during this period that the two fell in love with each other, although Wichita did not realize it until after Shoz-dijiji had brought her home and left (A1;19–20). They met again three years later quite by accident, but just in time for him to save her from "Dirty" Cheetim again (A2;3,5). They did not see each other again for some time, and when they did it was a nightmare, for Cheetim had killed Wichita's father and framed Shoz-dijiji for it (A2;13). The matter was finally cleared up late in 1886, when Cheetim abducted Wichita once more and told her the truth just before Shoz-dijiji caught up with him and killed him. In the end, she gave up her prejudice against Indians in the face of her love for Shoz-dijiji, but one must wonder whether he ever told her of his true origins or not (A2;18–19).

Billy The stable boy for **Dick Gordon** of New York (ME;2).

Bince, Harold The fiancé of Elizabeth Compton in 1910s Chicago, and the assistant manager of her father's company, the International Machine Company (EE;5–6). He was an inveterate gambler (EE;9) and was systematically embezzling a thousand dollars a week (a huge sum in 1920) from the company, and thus tried any means possible to get rid of James Torrance, Jr. (EE;16–20). He eventually murdered Mr. Compton before he could read the accountant's reports and so discover Bince's crime (EE;24). Torrance's trial aggravated the overwhelming guilt he already felt, and when he was revealed as the murderer, he jumped to his death from the

fourth-floor window of the courtroom (EE;28).

bint (*Ara*) Girl (T11;2).

Bird An American cavalryman killed at the battle of Cibicu Creek in 1881 (A1;14).

bird, Ladan A strange creature of Ladan which was presented to Umka the Masena to eat while he was imprisoned with John Carter. It had wings, four legs, and the scales of a fish, but also had a beak and a comb, giving it a birdlike appearance (M8;17).

birds, Barsoomian Barsoomian birds are rare, gorgeously feathered, and voiceless (M9;3). See also **feathers; malagor.**

Birmingham American city of Alabama from which **Robert Jones** hailed (T13;3).

birth control Because of the Serum of Longevity, birth control became necessary in Vepaja. Only enough births to replace those citizens who died were allowed (V1;5). Birth control is also used in Kamtol to keep the population at 200,000 because that is the maximum number the valley can support (M10;2).

Bismark An expensive restaurant of early 20th century Chicago (GF;8).

Bison-men of Pellucidar *see* Ganaks

Bivaspe A river of northern Sonora (A2;14).

Black Coyote A notorious bandit of Hendersville, Arizona, in the 1880s who daringly robbed stagecoaches with only one accomplice, the Mexican Gregorio. He was marked by the wearing of two black silk handkerchiefs, one about his neck and one about his face, and for some time everyone thought the bandit was Bull of the Bar-Y Ranch, mostly because Hal Colby, the real Black Coyote, started a rumor to that effect and planted false evidence to back it up. The resourceful Bull later caught him, though, and was cleared (HB;2–13,17).

Black Guard, the A crack regiment of the Karlovan army (R;3).

black men of Pellucidar The members of the race inhabiting the Floating Islands of Pellucidar, and possibly other areas as well, are black with a coppery tint and are just as advanced as the white Pellucidarians. They can also use their homing instinct even at sea, even to the extent of finding one of the Floating Islands after it had moved. They are for the most part very arrogant, but treat their white-skinned slaves well and do not overwork or mistreat them (P6;21,24).

Black Michael A sailor of the *Fuwalda* whose life **Lord Greystoke** saved by ruining **Captain Billings'** shot at the sailor. For his kindness Greystoke and his wife were only put ashore by Black Michael after the crew mutinied, instead of being killed as most of the mutineers wished (T1;1–2).

Black Mountains A small group of very rough mountains in **Lutha**, part of the **Dinaric Alps**. They lie south of **Blentz** and are inhabited chiefly by brigands (MK1;6).

black people with long tails The **Man-apes** of Pellucidar (P3;4).

Black Pirates of Barsoom Popularly supposed to come from the nearer moon, they actually hail from the cavern of **Omean** near the south pole (M2;8), and also from a colony in a large, deep rift in the northern hemisphere, wherein lies the city of **Kamtol** (M10:2). They descend upon the peoples of Barsoom from time to time, stealing ships, weapons, ammunition, food and (especially) young women. Their chief prey are the **Therns**, whom they attack semi-annually and derive most of their sustenance from, just as the Therns derive theirs from the outer world. The Black Pirates are men of six feet and above, well-built and handsome, and their skin is the color of polished ebony. Their eyes are very white and large, but slightly narrow, and they have jet-black hair. They are incredibly good fighters, but have no other useful skills except engineering and airmanship (M2;6). See also **First-Born**.

"The Black Pirates of Barsoom" The title of the second novella comprising *Llana of Gathol*, which originally appeared in *Amazing Stories* magazine in June of 1941.

Black River Station A postal station on the Black River in the **Fort Apache Indian Reservation**. Below the station, the Black River joins the White to form the Salt River, which flows into the Gila at Phoenix (A1;15).

The Black Wolf A brigand of mid–13th century Derbyshire, the first man killed in public by **Norman of Torn** in 1256 (OT;6).

Blagh The **Oparian** warrior who first saw the **Waziri** entering the valley of Opar when they returned for more gold for Tarzan in the summer of 1917 (T9;6).

Blaine, Cory An early 20th century entrepreneur who opened one of the first **dude ranches** in **Porico County, Arizona**. He was in love with **Kay White**, and tried to win her heart. Unfortunately, he was also the leader of a notorious criminal band of the time (D;2–6) and had her kidnapped as part of an elaborate plot to win her by "saving" her from the bandits. **Buck Mason** caught on, however, and foiled the plot, saving Kay and killing Blaine in a shoot-out (D;14–22).

Blake, James Hunter A rich young American who, on his safari in Africa in 1921, had a falling out with his companion, **Wilbur Stimbol**, which caused them to split their safari and go their separate ways. Blake later wandered some distance away from his safari to take photos of wildlife, but his guide was killed by a bolt of lightning during a freak electrical storm and Blake, having not paid attention to the way he had come, was thoroughly lost. He wandered around until he stumbled upon the entrance of the hidden **Valley of the Sepulcher** (T11;4–7), where he was accepted as a knight of **Nimmr** and fell in love with **Guinalda**, the Princess of Nimmr. He was forced to fight for his honor with the arrogant **Sir Malud**, who also wished to marry the princess (T11;11–12,14). He won that combat, and also won honors in the **Great Tourney** for that year, afterward saving the princess from **King Bohun**, who tried to kidnap her (T11;18–19). He later decided to stay in Nimmr, giving up the outside world for the woman he loved (T11;24).

Blanche A bleached blonde, one of **Scott Taylor's** friends in early 20th century New York. She was **James Kelley's** live-in girlfriend and did not approve of the plan to kill **Richard Gordon**, and so told **Virginia Scott** about the plan to save Kelley from the electric chair (ME;2–3).

Blanco A large **Ethiopian** who was the cook of the brigantine *Halfmoon*. He participated in **Billy Byrne** and **Henri Theriere's** plan to doublecross the skipper and **Larry Divine** (K1;4).

blat (*Ape*) Nose (T1;4).

Blazes Bull's favorite pony of the Bar-Y Ranch in 1880s Arizona, a blaze-faced chestnut with white hind feet (HB;1).

Blentz A grim castle and town of **Lutha,** lying some distance north of **Lustadt,** ruled in the early 20th century by **Prince Peter of Blentz.** Blentz was more than 300 years old and contained a good number of secret passages, some known to its rulers and others unknown (MK1;1,4–5).

Blentz, Prince Peter of The uncle of young **King Leopold of Lutha,** who rushed the boy off to his castle right after the old king's death in 1902, announcing that the boy had been stricken with mental illness and that he, Prince Peter, had been named regent until the boy should recover. In September of 1912, however, the "Mad King" escaped just as Prince Peter brought in a new doctor who was to have poisoned him (MK1;1). After reports of the killing of **Barney Custer** (whom many had mistaken for Leopold) reached him, he tried to have himself crowned King of Lutha, only to be stopped by Custer posing as Leopold. He accused Custer of being an impostor at that time and tried to have the real king (whom he found and captured shortly thereafter) killed in order to produce his body as evidence against Custer, but the American saved Leopold and placed him on the throne of Lutha, exposing Peter's treachery (MK1; 8–12).

He was not out of the way for long, however — he later conspired with **Count Zellerndorf,** the **Austrian** ambassador to Lutha. Zellerndorf would intercede with Leopold to gain a pardon for Peter, in return for which Peter would maneuver the weak King Leopold into an alliance with Austria. After this plan succeeded, Peter was again able to make Leopold a prisoner (MK2;2,5–6), but his plans were once again foiled by Barney Custer, who rescued the king (MK2;12–13). Later, acting as King of Lutha in his own right, Custer had Peter tried, and he was convicted of treason and hanged (MK2;15–16).

Blessed Mary The mother of Jesus Christ, revered by Catholics in particular, who pray to her to intercede with **God** on their behalf (T22;10).

Blk One of the banished priests of **Opar,** who found a place to build a temple for the renegades in the summer of 1920 (TT2;3).

blood pump One of the many medical inventions of **Ras Thavas,** the Master Mind of Mars, was a special pump with which to draw out the blood of a patient and replace it with a preserving fluid. This causes the patient to go into suspended animation and reduces the risks of operation, and also can be used to keep a person in suspended animation for centuries, if need be. To wake up the patient, his blood is warmed to body temperature, a few drops of a special reagent are added, and the pump is used to replace the blood in the body (M6;1–2).

Bloom An alias quickly adopted by **"Gunner" Patrick** when captured by **Dominic Capietro** and **Leon Stabutch** upon returning to his camp (which they had taken) on the slopes of the **Ghenzi Mountains** of Africa in 1929. He did this to hide his affiliation with Tarzan, whom it was obvious that the two men wished dead (T15; 13).

Bluber, Adolph A short, fat, big-necked, rich German, who helped finance **Flora Hawkes'** 1917 expedition to steal the gold of **Opar.** He was the expedition's treasurer, chosen for his stinginess, but that same stinginess got them in trouble when he hired too few porters, causing great unrest (T9; 3,5,10) and eventual rebellion, and almost got the white members of the expedition killed. They were later escorted safely to the coast by native warriors at Tarzan's command (T9;15, 17–19).

Blue The **Wieroos** of Caspak use the color blue to signify murder (C3;3). See **colors, Wieroo.** Blue was also the name of one of the horses of **Cory Blaine's** dude ranch in early 20th century **Arizona** (D;15).

Blue Book Magazine The magazine in which *Jungle Tales of Tarzan* (September 1916–August 1917), *The Land That Time Forgot* (1918), *The People That Time Forgot* (1918), *Out of Time's Abyss* (1918), *The Oakdale Affair* (1918), *Tarzan, Lord of the Jungle* (1927), *Tarzan and the Lost Empire* (1928), *Tanar of Pellucidar* (1929), *Tarzan at the Earth's Core* (September 1929–March 1930), *A Fighting Man of Mars* (April-September 1930), *Tarzan the Invincible* (October 1930–April 1931), *The Land of Hidden Men* (1931), *Tarzan Triumphant* (October 1931–March 1932), *Swords of Mars* (November 1934–April 1935),

"Tarzan and the Champion" (1941), and *Beyond the Farthest Star* (January 1942) originally appeared.

Blue Place of Seven Skulls A Wieroo prison—a square, blue building marked by seven skull-topped pillars of varying heights (C3;2). See also **colors, Wieroo.**

Blue Room The ballroom of the transoceanic liner *Harding,* in which Burroughs met **Julian 3rd** on June 10, 1967, and where the events comprising *The Moon Maid* (MM1) were narrated.

Blue Stables One of the four officially sanctioned horse racing syndicates of ancient Rome (1;8).

Blug A Neanderthal-type Pellucidarian warrior of **Kali,** to whom **Oose,** King of Kali, tried to give his daughter **O-aa** in 1931. The girl refused and **Hodon the Fleet One** defended her, making an enemy of Blug in the process (P7:1;5). Hodon killed him soon afterward, however, and Oose then agreed to the match of Hodon and O-aa (P7:2;1).

bo (*Ape*) Flat (TC).

bo (*Cpk*) Club (C1;9).

Bo-lu "Club-man" (*Cpk*). A primitive human race of **Caspak,** next above the **Alus.** Bo-lus are sub–Neanderthal in development, use only clubs as weapons, and speak a very limited version of the language of Caspak. After a time, a Bo-lu may develop into a **Sto-lu** (C1;9).

Boat-builders A coastal tribe of **Niocene** Africa, more advanced than the tribe of **Nu;** they possessed the arts of pottery making and, of course, canoe making (E2;4).

Bobbydoklinny White man's mispronunciation of the **Apache** name Nakay-doklunni (A1;15).

Bobolo A native chief of early 20th century Africa who was friendly to the **Old Timer** (T18;4). He was also a **Leopard Man** and kidnapped **Kali Bwana** for himself when the power of the Leopard Men fell, keeping her prisoner in the village of **Rebega** the pygmy (T18;9–15). Later, he was arrested by the authorities for his crimes as a Leopard Man (T18;23).

boche (WW I Slang) A deprecatory term for a German person, particularly a German soldier (T7;1).

Bodkin, Paul One of the Negro guards of the entrance to the **Valley of the Sepulcher,** who was on duty when **James Hunter Blake** blundered into the valley in 1921 (T11;7).

Boers Dutch inhabitants of **South Africa,** among whom **Lt. Obergatz** hoped to find help and support (T8;17).

Boes, Lieutenant de The Belgian officer who went to rescue the **Morton** mission at the time of the **Wakanda** revolt (ME).

Bohar the Bloody One of the chief lieutenants of **The Cid,** chief of the **Korsars** of Pellucidar. He was a surly, ugly pirate, his already ugly face made more hideous by a sword-scar that ran from above his left eye (which had been blinded by the wound) to below his mouth. He had few teeth, and his upper lip was curled up by the scar. Because of an altercation he had had with The Cid over **Tanar,** he hated the young **Sarian** with a passion (P3;1–2). Later, he showed up by accident on **Amiocap** and kidnapped **Stellara** from her father's village, but was killed by Tanar when the young warrior came to rescue her (P3;7,9).

Bohun, Humphrey V de, Earl of Essex An important noble of 13th century England. He was for a time the ally of the king and fought against **de Montfort,** but at various times before that fluctuated between the camps of each side. He was present at the **Battle of Lewes** (May 13, 1264) on the baron's side (OT;12,16).

Bohun, King The king of the **City of the Sepulcher** at the north end of the **Valley of the Sepulcher,** having the same name as all of his predecessors back to the time of **Richard I** of England. He and his men kidnapped the Princess **Guinalda** of **Nimmr** at the end of the **Great Tourney** in 1921, but James Blake stole her back before Bohun could get her within his city (T11;12,18–19).

Bohun, Sir The knight of **Richard I** of England who founded the **City of the Sepulcher** in the **Valley of the Sepulcher** (T11;12). See also **Gobred, Sir.**

Bokhara (Also Bukhara) City of the Uzbek S.S.R. (modern Uzbekistan) in which

Peter Zveri had assembled a fleet of 200 assorted aircraft for his overthrow of Abyssinia (T14;13).

bol (*Amt*) Country (V1;4).

Boleyn, Anne The second wife of the gorilla king Henry VIII, who unlike her namesake was married to him concurrently with every other wife (T17;18).

Bolgani (*Ape*) The gorilla: a beast as mighty as the Great Apes but hostile to their kind. Tarzan's first major battle was fought with Bolgani when the ape-man was but a boy of ten, and resulted in the death of the gorilla and the maiming of the boy. He bore the scars of the encounter on his shoulder, neck and chest for the rest of his life (T1;6). The dominant race of the Valley of the Palace of Diamonds referred to themselves as Bolgani, but were actually a mix of gorilla, great ape and human, just as the inhabitants of Opar were a human race tinged with ape blood. These Bolgani were taller, more erect, and far more advanced than ordinary gorillas; they walked upright, wore clothes and jewelry, and even made tools, weapons and buildings. They were the enemies of the Oparians, however, and sometimes conducted raids into the neighboring valley of Opar, perhaps to improve the stock of their subhuman slaves (T9;8–9). They were overthrown when Tarzan incited the aforementioned Gomangani to revolt, killing most of the Bolgani, whom the Gomangani outnumbered five to one. The few survivors returned to Opar with La as her bodyguards (T9;16).

Boloon The pirate of Tsao Ming's crew who was captured by head hunters a few days before Thandar's arrival on their island. After his escape, he told Thandar of the girl he had seen among those savages — none other than Nadara (CG2;10).

Bolt Head A headland marking the eastern side of Plymouth Bay in southwest England (LC;3).

Bolton The captain of the English yacht *Naiad*, which was taken as a prize by Wilhelm Schmidt and his crew of *Saigon* mutineers late in 1938 (T24;6).

Bolton, Lieutenant Commander The commander of the British submarine which saved Tarzan and his "foreign legion" from

an armed Japanese merchant ship while they were headed for Australia in a native proa (T22;30).

Bolton-Chilton, Francis An English pilot and friend of Colin Randolph's who was captured and enslaved by the Gallas in Abyssinia after bailing out of Randolph's plane in 1936. He was held for two years before being captured by the Alemtejo and taken to their city. He escaped from there with Tarzan, who had come in search of Sandra Pickerall, and while searching for a way off the plateau they met the false Tarzan, who turned out to be Randolph. Under Bolton-Chilton's prodding, Randolph's memory returned and they flew back to civilization (T23;17,21,30–33).

boma (*Swa*) A temporary barricade made from thorn bushes, branches and the like, just high enough and thorny enough to keep out lions and other predatory animals. The safaris of the white men also used bomas, having been taught to do so by their African guides (T2;16).

bomb, radio a fiendish device of World War III (MM1).

bomb, time An explosive device set to go off after a certain amount of time by means of an attached clock; a device Alexis Paulvitch learned to make as a Nihilist in Petrograd, and used to blow up the steamship *Kincaid* while Tarzan, Jane, and Akut and his apes were aboard (T3;18–19).

bone saw One of the many medical inventions of Ras Thavas, the Master Mind of Mars, was a bone saw — a circular saw at the end of a flexible tube that can cut bone with ease (M6;1).

Bonga The African outpost of Northern Rhodesia in which the Gregory safari of 1936 was gathered (T20;2).

Boris, Prince The handsome, roguish young Crown Prince of Karlova, to whom Princess Mary of Margoth was to be married on the eve of World War I to seal the breach between their two countries (R;1). Boris was a young rake, however, who did not wish to marry at all, and certainly not an enemy princess for political reasons, and so conceived of a practical joke to avoid the marriage. He would trade places with the notorious bandit,

The Rider, whom he had captured, and let the boorish brigand pass for him in his first presentation to the Margoth princess, who had never seen him nor a picture of him. The Rider, Boris hoped, would so repel the royal family of Margoth by his uncouth manners and ugly appearance that the wedding would be called off (R;1–4). Meanwhile, he (as The Rider) plotted with **Hemmington Main**, the young American he had met in **Demia**, to kidnap **Gwendolyn Bass** from her mother so Gwen and Hemmington could marry. Due to a mixup, however, the ersatz bandit captured instead Princess Mary, who was fleeing from marriage to the ersatz prince (R;5–7). The princess, upon finding that "The Rider" thought her Gwendolyn Bass, played along, and in the strange events that followed the two fell in love in spite of themselves. They remained so even though Boris would not reveal his true identity to her, especially after he knew she was the princess, for fear that she would be insulted when she realized the trick he had played on her and her country. The truth was found out in spite of him, the princess of course forgave him, and the two were married, allying their countries (R;8–17).

Borson   A mesa southwest of **Amlot** on Amtor, near which lay the farm of **Lodas** (V3;12).

bos   A genus of large, hairy prehistoric cattle (P1;6). See also **thag; aurochs.**

Bou Saada   A French outpost town in the **Petit Sahara**, to the east of **Sidi-bel-Abbes**, to which **Lt. Gernois** was transferred late in 1910, forcing Tarzan (who was spying on him for the French government) to follow (T2;7).

Bouira   A French outpost town in **Algeria**, where the railway from **Sidi-bel-Abbes** ends (or at least did in 1910) (T2;7).

Bovar   The son of **Hamlar**, chief of the **Tandarites** of Pellucidar, when **Dian the Beautiful** was captured and enslaved there in 1931. He became infatuated with her and planned to steal her for himself, but when he threatened her he was killed by three **tarags** she had befriended from among the village pets (P7:3;3,5–6).

bow, long   Upon Barsoom, bows were used extensively in ancient times, but in modern times only by the **phantom bowmen** of **Lothar** (M4;5). On Earth, the **Kalkars**

returned to the use of the long bow after losing the ability to make guns and ammunition after centuries of attrition (MM3;6–7).

bow, short   A weapon used by the tribe of **Julian** in the post–**Kalkar** 25th century American West (MM3;3,6).

bow, Tarzan's   Tarzan's third weapon of proficiency was the bow and arrows, which he first stole from **Kulonga** the **cannibal**, **Kala**'s murderer, after seeing how easily the native's poisoned arrows brought death to his victims. Later, he began stealing the weapons from the village of **Mbonga**'s people, and much later learned to make them himself (T1;9–10)(T3;4). Eventually, he developed a short, powerful bow; short for ease of transport through the trees, and so powerful none but Tarzan could draw it (T16;1).

Bradley, John   The mate of the British tug which both rescued **Bowen Tyler** and captured the **U-33** in the English Channel on June 4, 1916. He was Tyler's best and most trusted man, and the second in command of the captured **U-boat**. On September 4, 1916, he led an expedition from "**Fort Dinosaur**" to circle the inner cliffs of **Caspak** to find if there was any place in which they might be scaled (C1;2–6). The expedition did not return until the 15th, but it returned without Bradley, who had been carried off by a **Wieroo** the night before (C3;1–2). He was taken to the Wieroo island, **Oo-oh**, to be examined in an attempt to discover the secret of the **cos-ata-lu**. He escaped, rescuing the beautiful **Co-tan** in the process (C3;3–4). They lived for about a year in the wilds outside the city of Oo-oh, until finally Bradley captured two Wieroos and forced them to carry him and Co-tan to the mainland. Once there, he rejoined the others and helped them to recapture the U-33, which had returned to the island for more fuel after being lost for quite some time. On it, he and Co-tan returned to **California** (C3;5).

Brady   An American Irishman, one of the "allied" crew of the captured **U-33** when it ended up in **Caspak** in July of 1916. He accompanied the ill-fated **Bradley** expedition which left "**Fort Dinosaur**" on September 4th and returned short three members (C1;5–6)(C3;1).

Brady's Livery Stable   A businessplace of the west side of turn-of-the-century **Chicago** (K1;3).

Brahma In the Hindu religion, the Creator; first person of the Trinity of Godhead (HM;14).

Brazos The pony Bridge was given to Cuivaca to pick up the payroll there; he in turn gave the pony to Billy Byrne to get away on (K2;10–11).

breasts, Barsoomian It is unclear whether Barsoomian women nurse their children, considering that they are hatched nearly fully formed and grow up completely in an extremely short period. Perhaps the breast is a vestigial structure from a time when it served a more utilitarian purpose (M1).

breasts, Caspak The female breast is almost nonexistent in the female Alus, and only rudimentary among the Bo-lu and Sto-lu, but it is fairly developed in the women of the Band-lu, more so among the Kro-lu, and very well among the Galus (C2;3).

Brebisch A close friend of Ben Saada's (LL;18).

Brently, Mister The first officer of the liner upon which Tarzan was traveling from Algiers to Cape Town in 1910 when Nikolas Rokoff and Alexis Paulvitch threw him overboard (T2;13).

Bridge (short for "The Unabridged," for his large vocabulary) The educated hobo Billy Byrne hitched up with in 1915 Iowa while fleeing wrongful imprisonment for the murder of Old Man Schneider. Bridge was fond of quoting Service, Kipling and Knibbs, and found in Byrne an appreciative audience (K2;2–3). They passed through Kansas City, where Bridge saved Byrne from capture by Detective Flannagan, and then together saved a farmer's wife from being robbed and killed by two hobos. In thanks, she gave them train fare to El Paso, where they crossed into Mexico, Byrne there joining the band of a Mexican bandito while Bridge went to work at the El Orobo Ranch as a bookkeeper (K2; 3–9). He got in trouble after helping Byrne escape from Pancho Villa's men, but Byrne rescued him and they escaped together (K2; 11–12). Bridge was forced back into danger, however, by having to warn Anthony Harding about the coming Pesita attack on his ranch, against which Bridge himself led the defense. After Byrne's return, the party fled to the border with Pesita's men in hot pursuit,

and Bridge was wounded when the party was forced to make a stand less than ten miles from the border. He recovered in an American army hospital after their rescue, and promised to visit Byrne and Barbara Harding (whom he was secretly in love with) in New York (K2;15,17).

Whether he ever got there or not we are not told, but in 1917 he turned up in Oakdale, Illinois, where he met and befriended a youth who falsely called himself "The Oskaloosa Kid" and claimed to have burglarized a home (K3;3). Bridge, who had met the real Oskaloosa Kid, knew better, but unaccountably felt drawn to the boy (despite his unmanliness and possible criminality), and protected him from both discovery by the law and murder by hobos (K3;4–7). They escaped south after various adventures to the little town of Payson, where they were caught, first by the hobo band of the Sky Pilot, then by Detective Burton and his men. A lynch mob soon formed to hang both Bridge and the "Kid" for the supposed murder and robbery of Abigail Prim, only daughter of an Oakdale banker, but the mob was foiled (and Bridge's inexplicable attachment to the boy explained) when the "Oskaloosa Kid" revealed himself to be none other than Abigail Prim in disguise, fleeing a forced marriage to an old man she despised. Bridge at last had found in Abigail his **"Penelope,"** a woman who loved him, and was revealed by Burton to the Prims as the prodigal son of a rich Virginia family. We may assume that the two were married thereafter (K3;8–10).

Bridge of Gold The gold-plated bridge across the river of Onthar into the city of Cathne, seven miles below the ford for the road to Athne (T16;4).

brigantine A type of two-masted sailing ship, square-rigged on the foremast but fore-and-aft rigged on the mainmast (K1;2).

Brighton A small town near Chicago, in the southwest part of Macoupin County, site of a grisly murder known to Brady (C3;1). It is a very small town even today (GF;1).

Brit Nickname given to Britannicus Caligulae Servus by his master, Caligula, and used thereafter (I;1).

Britannicus Caligulae Servus Personal slave to the Emperor Caligula, from whose memoirs the novel *I Am a Barbarian* was translated and adapted. He was born in A.D. 6 in Britain, crossed to Belgium with his father in A.D. 16, and was there captured by the Belgae. They sold him into slavery in Germany, from where he was captured by Germanicus Caesar and given to Germanicus' son, Caligula, then four years of age (I;1). It was due to the fact that Caligula would not let Britannicus out of his sight that the young barbarian learned to read and write, since he had to sit through Caligula's classes with him (I;4). As they both grew to manhood, Britannicus kept a fairly complete journal, detailing both his own life as the mad emperor's slave and, in the process, necessarily that of Caligula himself. Britannicus had a long, drawn-out love affair with a female slave named Attica that began in A.D. 23 and did not culminate in their marriage until A.D. 40 (I;7–20). Eventually, his loathing for Caligula grew to the point where it could no longer be contained, and it exploded on January 24, A.D. 41, when Caligula killed Attica for no real reason except jealousy, and was in turn killed by Britannicus, who joined in the on-going conspiracy to kill the madman (I;21). Britannicus is portrayed in his own memoirs as an intelligent and sensitive man of a quick wit and good humor, but somewhat indecisive and of no great courage. The same things frightened him as would frighten any man not made of iron, and perhaps his worst fault was that he, who so many times could have taken the life of Caligula and so prevented the perpetration of any further death and destruction, did not do so because of a mixture of fear and misplaced morality.

British East Africa The present-day nation of Kenya, in Tarzan's time a British colony (T5;15). It was the site of Tarzan's second African estate, several days' march north of Kilimanjaro (T7;2).

British Royal Air Forces Branch of the British Armed Forces in which Lt. Harold Percy Smith-Oldwick flew a scout plane in World War I (T7;11).

British West Africa British colony in west Africa to which John Clayton, Lord Greystoke was sent to investigate the mistreatment of blacks by the officers of another (unnamed for the sake of diplomacy) European power. He of course never reached his post, because he was set ashore following a mutiny on his ship (T1;1).

Broadcast power Electrical power broadcast by radio waves through the air. It is picked up and used by any device equipped with the proper receiver. The Amtorian city of Havatoo makes extensive use of it to power automobiles and other devices. For traffic usage, the power is broadcast on separate frequencies — one for cars bound to or from the outer wall, another for transverse avenues, and another for vehicles outside the city (see also **automobiles, Amtorian; traffic, Amtorian**) (V2;13). The country of Unis on Poloda has a very extensive broadcast power system, with stations broadcasting solar-derived energy that can apparently be picked up anywhere on the planet, considering that the Polodans even use the power to run their airplanes. Although it is not explicitly stated, it is obvious that the Kapars have a similar system. See also **automobiles, Unisan** (B1;4) (B2;9).

Broadway Besides the famous one in New York, there was also a street by this name in Payson, Illinois (K3;9).

Brokol A country of about 50,000 awful creatures, lying about 40 klookob inland from Japal in Amtor's northern hemisphere. The Brokol people are of a disgusting green color and are entirely hairless (lacking even eyebrows or lashes). Brokols talk very little; to them, the worst insult possible is "You talk too much." They are a sort of plant-people; Brokol females bring forth large nuts (laying them like eggs) which are planted and grow into large trees from which one or two baby Brokols grow, starting at about an inch long and growing to about 15 inches long, at which point they become very active and eventually fall off the tree, leaving a knob of flesh on their heads which remains there for life (V4; 24–25). They have white blood. Guypals eat many young Brokols off of the trees, and insect pests account for many more, so that only about one in a thousand live to maturity. So many are produced, however, that the race continues to thrive. Brokols do not eat meat, but do drink warm blood (V4;28).

brontotherium An ancestral rhinoceros of the Oligocene, to which the **sadok** of Pellucidar is similar (P1;15).

Bronx A mixed drink made with a jigger and a half of gin and a half jigger each of French vermouth, Italian vermouth, and orange juice (R;5).

bronze An alloy of copper and tin, useful both for weapons and tools and for decoration. It is not as hard as iron, but is far harder than most stones, and is more easily worked and holds an edge better as well (P7:2;4).

Brooklyn A borough of New York City, famous for the distinctive accent of its inhabitants (T22;2). It was the city from which Betty Caldwell, whom the Brokols of Amtor knew as Loto-el-ho-ganja, originally came (V4;28–29).

Brophy A boxer of 1910s Chicago with whom Jimmy Torrance got a job as a sparring partner. His job was to let himself be beaten up without knocking Brophy around too hard, so that the press would pick Brophy as the favorite. Then, he and his managers would bet heavily on his opponent in the next prizefight and Brophy would take a dive, thus becoming very rich in about ten seconds. This would have worked had not Brophy been unnecessarily rough with Torrance in front of Elizabeth Compton, which prompted the young man to punch Brophy's lights out in front of reporters, ruining both Brophy's reputation and the scam (EE;12).

Brosnov A small Serbian town near that country's border with Lutha (MK2;9).

brother The title by which the citizens of Kalkar-occupied America were required to address one another (MM2;2).

Brother of Issus One of the titles held by Matai Shang, the leader of the Therns of Barsoom (M2;7).

Brouke, Billy A friend of Reece's, party crasher extraordinaire in 1933 Hollywood (T17;33).

Brown A big game hunter who was a guest at Tarzan's bungalow in 1913 at the same time as Barney Custer and Edgar Rice Burroughs were (E1;4).

Brown, Horace An American inventor of Chicago who in 1939 developed an electronic device which could disrupt the ignition system of any internal combustion engine at a range of 3000 feet. He intended to sell his device only to the British and American governments, but he was murdered in London by Joseph Campbell and the Russian Zubanev and his plans were stolen (T24B;2).

Brown, Mr. The manager of the company where June Lathrop got her first regular job (GF;5). Another Mr. Brown was the manager of a sash, door and blind factory where Jimmy Torrance applied for a job (EE;4).

Brown, Neal An American pilot who convinced the Princess Sborov to finance his expedition into the African interior in search of a witch doctor who supposedly possessed the secret of a longevity potion (T19;1). He was an excellent pilot who was able to land the Sborov plane in the treetops of the jungle without seriously injuring anyone, and, besides Jane, was the only member of the party with any woodcraft at all. In addition, he really was a nice guy (T19;3–12). He fell in love with Annette, the princess' maid, and insisted on going with Tarzan into the Kavuru village to rescue her after learning that she was there (T19;15–19,26). It was his skills as a pilot that got them into the village — he flew an abandoned plane over the temple so that he and Tarzan could parachute in. At adventure's end he got one-sixth of the immortality pills captured from the Kavuru in the end (T19;29–31).

Brown Derby A famous Hollywood restaurant, a hang-out of movie stars and movie people (T17;33).

Brulor The god of Ashair, who was also called the Father of Diamonds (not to be confused with the stone, the Father of Diamonds, which lay in a case in his temple) (T20;17). His "earthly form" was that of an old man, whom we must assume was a god in the same sense as the pharaohs of ancient Egypt were; that is, in a mystical sense, for Brulor was certainly a very real and very human old man (T20;18) who was also an alcoholic (T20;23). He was killed by Herkuf (whom he had had condemned to a temple cage several years before) when he and Tarzan came to rescue their friends from the temple after having earlier escaped themselves (T20;29).

Brulor, Temple of The temple of the Father of Diamonds in Ashair, lying beneath the waters of Lake Horus both on and below the lake bottom. Those who would have profaned the temple (i.e., stolen the Father of Diamonds) were locked up in small cages within sight of the stone's casket and left there indefinitely, always within reach of the treasure they would have stolen (T20;18). The temple was built atop an "air geyser" which had been capped in ancient times by the Ashairians. The temple has air locks which work by allowing air under pressure from this geyser into the lock, forcing the water out. By this means, air is also kept in the temple proper (T20;26).

Bruma   The high priest of Ogar in the Jukan village of Meeza in Pellucidar, who wished to sacrifice Dian the Beautiful to Ogar against the wishes of Meeza, who wished to keep her (P6;10).

Brun   The chief of the Pellucidarian village of Lo-har and the father of La-ja, Wilhelm von Horst's beloved (P5;17). While searching for her, Brun was captured by David Innes and his small army, who were themselves searching for von Horst and needed a guide to Lo-har — a position they forced Brun to fill (P5;21–22).

Brus   Henry III of England's gardener at Westminster Palace in the mid 1200s (OT;3).

Brute-men   A strange species of Pellucidarian primate, standing about seven feet tall with a gorilla-like physiognomy and a sheeplike face and eyes. They are hairy and tailless, have white skins, and stand upright. They speak a very simple version of the common tongue of Pellucidar and actually cultivate plants on top of the buttes and mesas of Indiana (Hooja's island) upon which they live. They are very peaceful, almost never fight, and will never kill except in self-defense or hunting. Their favored weapon is the lasso (P2;8).

Bryan, Hiram   A hunter of early 20th century Porico County, Arizona. He was a surly fellow who owned four good "liondogs" (D;4) and was a member of Cory Blaine's gang who helped him kidnap Kay White. He was killed in a gunfight with "Bruce Marvel," who was on Kay's trail (D;6,14–17).

Brynilda, Princess   The wife of Prince Gobred of Nimmr when James Hunter

Blake stumbled upon the lost city in 1921 (T11;14).

bu   (*Ape*) "He" or "male" (T6:4).

bu   (*Pal*) The moon (T8;2).

Bu-lot   "Moon-Face" (*Pal*). A Ho-don nobleman, son of chief Mo-sar, to whom King Ko-tan wished to give his daughter O-lo-a in marriage to appease Mo-sar's ambition (T8;2). At a banquet the night before the wedding, Bu-lot killed Ko-tan while in a drunken rage, thus touching off a civil war. While trying to abduct O-lo-a from the palace soon afterward, he was killed by Tarzan (T8;15).

Bu-lur   "Moon-City" (*Pal*). The city of the Waz-ho-don of Pal-ul-don, built in cliffs where the main river of the land passes through the encircling mountains to empty into the outer morass (T8;19).

Bubonovitch, Staff Sergeant Joe "Datbum"   The assistant engineer and waist gunner of the *Lovely Lady*, a B-24 bomber sent on a reconnaissance mission over Japanese-held Sumatra in the spring of 1944 along with Colonel John Clayton. He was a very educated man, a Columbia graduate who worked for the New York Museum of Natural History before the war, and was fond of teasing "Shrimp" Rosetti by using scientific terminology (T22;2–3). After months of hardship, he survived to be rescued by a British submarine and sent home unharmed (T22;30).

Bucharest   The capital of Romania (R; 10).

buckboard   A light, open carriage without springs (D;3).

Buckingham   A warrior of Grabritin who killed King Wettin so he might be king by taking Wettin's woman as his own (LC;4).

Buckingham, Duke of   The gorilla who captured Rhonda Terry at the foot of Omwamwi Falls and took her to see Henry VIII in the Valley of Diamonds. He later captured Naomi Madison for himself, but was caught and killed by Tarzan soon afterwards (T17; 18,21,23).

buckler   Few Barsoomians use shields, but the Okarians use a cup-shaped buckler to defend against their hooked swords (M3;9).

Buckskin   Wichita Billings' favorite horse (A1;15).

Bud   One of the cowhands on **Cory Blaine's** dude ranch of early 20th century Arizona. He was a friendly sort of fellow (D;4).

Bududreen   The Malay first mate of **Professor Arthur Maxon's** schooner ***Ithaca***, who conspired to deliver **Virginia Maxon** to **Rajah Muda Saffir**—and keep the Professor's "treasure" chest himself. He was drowned in a storm with all of his men while trying to kidnap Virginia (Q;1,5,8–9).

bugs   Tarzan's original conception of printed letters, which he knew of from the books in his dead father's cottage, was that they were little bugs somehow stuck to the pages. He soon learned, from careful scrutiny, that there were only a certain number of "bugs" and that they went together in certain ways (T1;6–7).

Buira   The daughter of **Muviro**, acting chief of the **Waziri**. She was stolen from him by the **Kavuru** in 1934, prompting Muviro to take ten Waziri and set out to find her. She was eventually found unharmed in the Kavuru village and rescued by Tarzan and **Neal Brown** (T19;2,31).

Buiroo   A cannibalistic African tribe of **Northern Rhodesia** who captured and planned to eat **Helen Gregory** in October of 1936 (T20;7). Three years later, Tarzan himself fell into their hands, but of course escaped as well (T24B;4).

Bukawai   A black witch-doctor of early 20th century **Angola** who lived in a cave north of the village of **Mbonga**. He was supposed to be a black magician who spoke with devils, and it was believed by the natives that his two pet hyenas were actually devils in disguise. He suffered from a disease that was causing his face to rot away and was thus an outcast, but **Momaya**, a woman of the tribe of Mbonga, braved this fearsome apparition in order to have him cast a magic spell for her to get back her son **Tibo**, whom Tarzan had abducted to be his own child. The magic was not needed, however, as Tarzan let the child go back to his mother before the spell could be cast, earning Bukawai's anger against both Tarzan and Momaya (T6:5). A few months later, he came to Mbonga's village to collect

the pay that he had never earned, and when Momaya would not pay, he kidnapped Tibo to his cave to hold for ransom; he was foiled by Tarzan, who rescued the boy and brought him home again (T6:6). One day soon after, Bukawai found Tarzan unconscious after being hit by a falling tree branch during a storm. He bound him and carried him to his cave to be eaten by his hyenas, but Tarzan managed to turn the tables, and it was Bukawai that the hyenas feasted on that day (T6:7).

Bukena   A tribe of central Africa whose territory lay nearest to that of the mysterious **Kavuru**. Because of that proximity, they were deathly afraid of the strange white savages, and would not help Tarzan to find them (T19;2,4). The Kavuru spoke the Bukena dialect (T19;8).

Bukula   A black porter of the **Zveri** expedition to central Africa in 1928, who was taken into virtual slavery by **Abu Batn**, Zveri's **Arab** confederate, when Batn and his band fled north with **La of Opar** and **Zora Drinov**. He later helped the Arab **Ibn Dammuk** to kidnap La from Abu Batn in return for the promise of his freedom (T14;10).

bula   In Tarzan's adolescent letter-pronunciation system, the capital letter "G"; a "male" G, as opposed to **mula**, a "female" (lower case) "g" (T6:4).

Bulabantu   An under-chief of the village of **Mbonga** when Tarzan was growing up. He wandered into a gathering of the tribe of **Kerchak** once, but was spared from instant death by Tarzan, who respected the man's courage (T6:12).

Bulala   A native cook for a white **safari** in Africa of 1920 who was captured and imprisoned by the **Bagalla** tribe along with the "**Tarzan Twins.**" He escaped with them when they found the chance (TT1;5–11).

Bulamutumumo   Tarzan's adolescent pronunciation of the word "**God**," which he had seen in his father's books but did not know the pronunciation or meaning of. In Tarzan's letter-naming system, the name literally means "male G—female o—female d." Tarzan was quite mystified with the concept of God, thinking at first that he was the moon, then a native witch-doctor; he eventually arrived at the theologically sound idea that God was unknowable and undetectable by direct observation (T6:4).

Bulan The name given to **Number Thirteen** (**Professor Arthur Maxon**'s most perfect synthetic man) by the **Dyak** head hunters of **Borneo** in recognition of his great, godlike power and the appearance of his white skin shining like the moon (in the Dyak tongue, Bulan) when he first attacked them. "Number Thirteen" liked the name and kept it (Q;9). He fought his way with his band of synthetic men through the Bornean interior until he finally found and rescued **Virginia Maxon** from the Dyaks. After she had fallen in love with him, they were found by Maxon and his party, including the faithful **Sing Lee**, who told Bulan's true story: Sing had found him, a hopeless amnesiac, washed up on the shore of Maxon's island and substituted him for the half-formed Number Thirteen so that Virginia could marry a real man and not a monster, as Professor Maxon had planned. Eventually, his memory returned, and he was revealed as **Townsend J. Harper, Jr.**, heir to the Harper Railroad fortune, who had followed Virginia to the island to meet her but suffered an accident upon arrival and lost his memory. The two were married a few days later in **Singapore** (Q; 10–17).

Bulando A **Waziri** warrior who went with **Muviro** to rescue his daughter from the mysterious **Kavuru** in 1934 (T19;25).

Bulf An important **Korsar** of Pellucidar who wished **Stellara**, the "daughter" of **The Cid**, as his wife. He was killed in 1926 by **Tanar the Fleet One** when he tried to rape the girl (P3;12,16).

Buliso The **Bagego** clan by which Tarzan was captured in the **Wiramwazi Mountains** in 1923. Their clan totem was **Timba**, the black cow (T12;5).

bull (American slang) A policeman (GF;1).

Bull The tall, dark foreman of the **Bar-Y Ranch** in 1880s **Arizona**, who had a little problem holding his liquor, and so rarely drank — "... and, when not in liquor, rarely spoke." He was tricked into getting drunk and going to town to make a fool of himself one night when **Elias Henders** was there, and so was demoted from foreman. This was only the beginning of **Hal Colby**'s plan to frame

him as the notorious **Black Coyote, The Bandit of Hell's Bend**, and frame him he did, always sending him to out-of-the-way places on the days Colby would rob so as to remove any alibi Bull might have (HB;1–3). Bull was very much in love with **Diana Henders**, who did not realize she loved him until the night Colby led a lynch mob to hang Bull as the Black Coyote, and she saved him (HB;4–13). He thereafter kept a watch on her from a distance, and helped her to outwit the evil **Maurice Corson** and his cronies, who tried to trick her out of the ranch, then steal it outright. Eventually, Bull was able to steal documents proving Diana's sole right to the property, which forced the conspirators to attempt a daring coup by stealing both the papers and Diana in order to close the deal. Bull captured and later killed Colby, the real Black Coyote, and rescued Diana in time to stop the Corson deal from being completed. Of course, he and Diana were married thereafter (HB;11–19).

Bulland, Sir The marshall of the **City of the Sepulcher** in the early part of the 20th century, who was shot dead by the **Arab** raiders of **Ibn-Jad** when they invaded the Valley of the Sepulcher in 1921 (T11;17).

bullets, Barsoomian Barsoomian bullets are made of an opaque, brittle, glasslike substance that shatters on impact to expose a pellet of their **radium** powder within, which, when exposed to sunlight, results in a terrific explosion. For this reason, the powder must be prepared in artificial light, and the morning after a night battle bullets all over the battlefield explode as soon as dawn's first light touches them (M1;13).

bullets, Kalkar The **Kalkars** were taught to make bullets by **Orthis** but lost the technology after his death, and so conserved their ammunition by not wasting bullets on things like firing squads (MM1;13–14)(MM2;6). See also The Butcher.

bullets, Unisan The **Unisans** of **Poloda** used both "**dum-dum**" and exploding bullets in their guns (B1;6).

Bull's Eye **Buck Mason**'s horse, a blue roan with a saucer-sized white mark around its right eye (D;1).

Bulvik The fictional name of a revolutionary of an unnamed European country of the 1920s. He was shot to death by General Sarnya when he tried to assassinate him a few years after the old king's death (LL;3–5).

bund (*Ape*) Dead (TC).

Bund The largest and strongest of the Samary of Houtomai, who "really should" have been jong of the tribe, at least according to her mate Lula. She had a deep scar on the left side of her face (V3;2–3).

bundolo (*Ape*) Kill (T17;14).

Bungalo The east African homeland of the **Bangalo** people, which lay near the **Ghenzi Mountains** (T15;1).

Bunny Hazel Tennington's nickname for her husband, **Lord Tennington** (T19;1).

buoyancy tanks The tanks aboard a Barsoomian flier in which the **eighth ray** of Barsoom is contained, allowing the ship to defy the gravity of the planet. If one of these tanks is ruptured, the ship will begin to list, and if too many are damaged, the ship cannot remain aloft. The rays can also be directed to raise, lower or hold steady the ship (M1;13). See also **flier, Barsoomian**.

bur (*Ape*) Cold (TC).

Bureau of Communications The government office for which Burroughs worked in the 1960s, during and after **World War III** (MM2;1).

Burgh, John de One of the English barons who rebelled against **Henry III**. He was present at the **Battle of Lewes** on May 13, 1264 (OT;16).

Burgova A small Austrian town near the Serbian border, beyond which **Barney Custer** was not allowed to pass when he tried to get to **Lutha** by that way late in the summer of 1914, after the outbreak of World War I (MK2;1).

Buried people *see* **Coropies**

Burke, Mrs. George (Charity) A widow from the Midwest who moved into the area of the **Rancho del Ganado** in April of 1922. She was the mother of actress and de facto drug pusher **Gaza de Lure**, who had bought a little farm for her. Mrs. Burke died of a heart attack in the last week of July of that same year (GH;4–5,13).

Burke, Shannon The real name of actress **Gaza de Lure** (GH;10). It was the name the **Penningtons** of **Rancho del Ganado** knew her by when she stayed there after the death of her mother in July of 1922. There, under the influence of clean living and the Penningtons, she gradually broke the morphine habit, recovered her health, fell in love with **Custer Pennington**, and vowed never to return to Hollywood (GH;13–18). Her problems followed her, however, first in the person of **Slick Allen**, the supplier of the "junk" **Wilson Crumb** had gotten her addicted to. Allen framed Custer for transporting whiskey, for which the innocent young man was incarcerated (GH;20–29). Later, trouble followed in the person of Wilson Crumb himself, who came to Rancho del Ganado to make a movie, tried to get Shannon back, then tried to seduce **Eva Pennington**—all of which put both Shannon and Custer under suspicion when Crumb was murdered that night (GH;31–35). After Custer's conviction, she worked ferociously to get a confession out of **Guy Evans** (the real killer), and finally broke through his madness sufficiently to do so, saving both Custer and, in the long run, Guy. Even though her whole sordid past was revealed in the course of the murder trial, the Penningtons accepted her as a changed woman and, we must assume, Custer married her (GH;36–37).

Burket's Coal-Yard A self-explanatory business on **Ella Street** in turn-of-the-century **Beatrice, Nebraska** (MK1;6).

Burlinghame, Captain Cecil A retired naval officer who commanded **John Alden Smith-Jones'** 1911 expedition to find his castaway son in the South Pacific, where he had been lost almost a year before (CG1;11).

Burnham, Lieutenant The navigator of the *Lovely Lady*, the **B-24 Liberator** that carried RAF Colonel **John Clayton** as an observer on a reconnaissance mission over Japanese-held **Sumatra** in the spring of 1944. When the plane was shot down and the crew forced to bail out, Burnham's parachute failed to open and he fell to his death (T22;2).

Burroughs, Edgar Rice Edgar Rice Burroughs, as he appears in his own stories, was a sort of human crossroads; many tales of interesting events fell into his hands. He was the chosen method of communication between Earth and the worlds of Mars, Venus and Pellucidar. It was he who brought the amazing adventures of Tarzan of the Apes to public attention, and he to whom the story of Tangor of Poloda was mysteriously revealed. Even if we accept Burroughs at his word as to the veracity of these tales and their authorship by other than himself, we cannot deny that the unmistakable stamp of his literary style appears on every tale, whether written by him or merely adapted from another's manuscript. The stories that were certainly written by his own hands from other's notes (as in the case of the Tarzan books) or from his own imagination (*The Lost Continent*) bear his stamp no more or less than those completely written by his adventurous acquaintances and merely "edited" by him.

Be that as it may, the "fictional" Burroughs had a much longer life than did his real-life counterpart. According to the foreword of *A Princess of Mars*, he was born in 1855 rather than the real Burroughs' 1875, and aged only very slowly, though certainly not so slowly as his "Uncle Jack" Carter. The narrator of *The Moon Men* could not have been the same man, even given enormous longevity — after all, he was still young enough to go polar bear hunting in 1969 (MM2;1). Perhaps this "second Burroughs" was the first's son. Who can tell?

Burton, Dick A well-known private detective of early 20th century Chicago, who was hired by Jonas Prim in 1917 to investigate his daughter's disappearance and the theft of her jewels. On the way, he solved the Baggs murder case and caught Hettie Penning, who explained the Paynter murder, clearing Abigail Prim (K3;6–7,9–10).

busso (*Ape*) Fly (TC).

Busuli A Waziri warrior of Africa whom Tarzan planned to kill for his weapons after the ape-man's return to the jungle in 1910, only to find that his new-found social conscience prohibited him from doing so. He instead saved the warrior from a lion, thus earning his friendship and that of his whole tribe; they adopted Tarzan as one of their own, teaching him their language and giving him food and weapons (T2;14–15). Busuli was afterward Tarzan's lieutenant, leading the party that first went with him to Opar, and also the party that searched for him when the Waziri thought him lost (T2;19,22,25–26). He was

Tarzan's right-hand-man ever after, leading the Waziri with Tarzan back to Opar in 1913 (T5;4), and back again without the ape-man after he was lost in an earthquake. They buried the gold they brought back near Tarzan's bungalow upon their return, and went to track the Arabs who had killed the Waziri guards and kidnapped Jane in their absence (T5;9). They later returned, reburied the gold that the Arabs had since found, and destroyed the tribe of raiders completely (T5;18,24).

Butch The tail gunner of the B-24 Liberator *Lovely Lady* on her ill-fated reconnaissance mission to Japanese-occupied Sumatra in the spring of 1944. He was killed by anti-aircraft fire (T22;2).

The Butcher In Kalkar-occupied 22nd century America, an executioner. The Kalkars wished to conserve the precious ammunition which they no longer knew how to make, so condemned criminals had their throats slit by a man known as The Butcher (MM2;6,11).

Buto (*Ape*) The rhinoceros (T5;11).

Butts A rude, bowlegged cowhand of Cory Blaine's dude ranch in early 20th century Arizona and a member of Blaine's gang as well. He was killed by Buck Mason in a shoot-out (D;3,6,22).

Butzow, Lieutenant Otto The noble and fair officer of the Luthanian Royal Horse Guard who first captured Barney Custer in October of 1912 and "returned" him to Blentz on orders from Prince Peter to capture and return the "Mad King," Leopold of Lutha (MK1;3). He was greatly impressed later by the "king's" courage and character, and sided with him against Peter, helping him to stop the evil prince's coronation on November 3, 1912. He later helped Custer attempt a rescue of the true king and rode into battle under him against the forces of Prince Peter. At that time he became convinced that if Custer were not the true king, then he should be because of his courage, dignity and ability. Later, he and Custer successfully rescued the real Leopold, who, after he was securely on the throne, promptly forgot all Custer had done for him and, jealous of the respect given him by the people and nobles and the love given him by Emma von der Tann, ordered him executed. Butzow, however, warned Custer, helped him escape, and returned to Nebraska with him (MK1;8–12).

In 1913, he went to the Greystoke estate in Africa with Custer and his sister, Victoria (E1;2), and in 1914 returned to Lutha to serve the House von der Tann when World War I broke out, at great personal risk (MK2;1). Later, he again helped Barney Custer (again masquerading as Leopold) to save the real king from execution at Blentz (MK2;11,13), and after Custer took Leopold's place for good, Butzow was made Prince of Blentz and a general in the Luthanian army (MK2;16).

Buulaoo One of the young children of M'ganwazam, the chief of the Waganwazam, when Tarzan stopped in their village in pursuit of Nikolas Rokoff late in the summer of 1912. Buulaoo overheard Tambudza, one of his father's wives, helping Tarzan in direct opposition to the chief's wishes, and tattled (T3;11).

Bwana "Master" (*Swa*). The title given many white hunters by their native employees. It was the title by which Meriem first came to know Tarzan, because the natives always used it when speaking to or about him (T4;14).

b'wang (*Ape*) Hand (TC).

b'yat (*Ape*) Head (T17;30).

Byea One of the Vepajan women captured aboard the Thorist ship *Sovong* in 1929 and later rescued by Carson Napier and the *Sofal*. It was Byea who told Napier that Vilor was a Thorist spy (V1;13).

Byrne, Billy A "mucker" of Chicago's west side during the early part of the 20th century who, while fleeing a wrongful murder rap, was "shanghaied" onto the brigantine *Halfmoon* in San Francisco and forced to participate in the kidnapping of heiress Barbara Harding from her father's yacht, *Lotus* (K1;1–4). After the abduction, though, his character began to change, influenced by Barbara's courage and character and the qualities of Henri Theriere, the gentleman-turned-scoundrel-turned-gentleman second mate of the *Halfmoon* (K1;5–8). After the ship was wrecked in a storm on the island of Yoka, inhabited by the descendants of Japanese samurai, Byrne really began to change, particularly after the girl was abducted by the Yokese and Byrne and Theriere rescued her. Months

spent together with Barbara on the island completed the transformation, and Billy Byrne became a new man; he was changed so much that, although he loved Barbara, he spurned her love because he did not want her seen with a "mucker" after their rescue (K1;8–18).

He went to New York afterward and became a great heavyweight boxer with his name in all the papers, at which point she contacted him again, and again he spurned her for her own sake (K1;18). He returned to Chicago to stand trial for the murder of Schneider (for which he had been framed) and was convicted, much to his chagrin (K2;1). He escaped thereafter, making his way to Kansas City with an educated hobo called Bridge (K2;2–4). While fleeing the police, he saved a Kansas farm woman from being robbed and murdered by two hobos, and she paid Byrne's and Bridge's train fare to El Paso in thanks for his kindness. They then crossed the border, where Byrne was induced to join with the forces of Pesita, a Mexican bandito. Byrne, thinking he was serving in the legitimate Mexican army, helped rob a bank which was held by Pancho Villa (K2;5–10). He was later captured for the crime and brought to the El Orobo Ranch for a night, where he again met up with Barbara. She helped him escape, but was herself abducted by Indians in the employ of Grayson, the ranch manager, who wanted her for himself. Byrne rescued her from them, and they (Byrne, Barbara, Bridge, and Mr. Harding) fled toward the border, pursued by Pesita's men the whole way. Trapped and surrounded, Byrne realized that only the U.S. Cavalry (stationed ten miles away on the border) could save them, and went to fetch them himself. After their rescue, he finally claimed Barbara for his own and, freed from legal trouble by the real murderer's confession, he went to New York with Barbara and married her with her father's blessings (K2;12–17).

b'zan (*Ape*) Hair (TC).

b'zee (*Ape*) Foot (TC).

Cadj The high priest of the lost city of Opar, whom La, the high priestess, was supposed by custom to mate with. He hated her, however, because she refused to mate with him and instead openly avowed her love for Tarzan, who had defiled the temples of Opar more than once (T5;14). Eventually she was forced to mate with him, but he knew she hated him, so when **Esteban Miranda** came to Opar in the guise of Tarzan to steal its gold, Cadj took a party of priests and warriors to hunt him down and kill him. Soon afterward, he plotted with the princess **Oah** to overthrow La, but she escaped with Tarzan. When they returned with an army of **Gomangani** and **Bolgani** to replace La on her throne, Cadj was killed by **Jad-bal-ja** while he was trying to kill Tarzan (T9;6–8,16).

Caecilius Metellus The best friend of **Cassius Hasta**, Prince of **Castrum Mare**, who was captured by the soldiers of **Castra Sanguinarius** and imprisoned in August of 1923 in the same dungeon as Tarzan, Cassius Hasta, and **Maximus Praeclarus**. It was through him that the latter three were informed of the happenings in Castrum Mare, including the knowledge that **Erich von Harben** was there. Metellus escaped with the other three and returned to Castrum Mare (T12;13–23).

Caelian Hill One of the seven hills of Rome (I;7).

Caesar Family name of the great general Julius Caesar and of the first few emperors of Rome. The name became so associated with the position that Roman emperors were afterward referred to as Caesar, although none of them were of the family (T12;8). It is also worth noting that the German "kaiser" and the Russian "czar" are also derived from the name.

Caesonia (Full name Milonia Caesonia) A.D. 10–41) The daughter of the Roman senator **Helvidius Pius**, to whom **Attica** was a slave. Many years later she became one of Caligula's mistresses and he married her in A.D. 39. She bore him his only child, **Julia**, and was assassinated with him on January 24, 41 A.D. (I;7,17,19–21).

Cafe Maure A coffee house with music and dancing girls popular in **Algeria** (T2;7).

Cage, "Uncle" Billy An old layabout of early 20th century **Comanche County** (D;2).

Caius One of **Agrippina's** brothers, a sickly boy who died young and mad (I;1).

Caius Caesar The son of **Germanicus Caesar** and **Agrippina**, better known as

Caligula. He was the grandnephew of **Tiberius Caesar** and the third Emperor of Rome, from A.D. 37 to 41.

Caius Caetronius One of the officers under **Germanicus** in his German campaign of A.D. 16 (I;1).

Cajon Pass The main pass through the mountains to the Los Angeles area. See also **Pass of the Ancients** (MM3;2).

Caldwell, John The assumed name taken by Tarzan on his second mission for the French War Department, during which he was thrown overboard by **Nikolas Rokoff** and **Alexis Paulvitch**. It was as John Caldwell that **Hazel Strong** met him, and as Caldwell that she told **Jane Porter** of his loss at sea. Jane knew his true identity, however, from the picture Hazel had taken of him on the cruise (T2;11–13).

Caledonia The Roman name for Scotland (A1;1).

Calhoun One of **David Innes'** troublemaking classmates at **Andover** around the turn of the century (P1;1).

California American state, home to **Carson Napier** (V1;1).

caligae (*Lat*) The sandal-like footwear of Roman soldiers; often translated as "boots" (T12,6)(I;1).

Caligula "Little Boots" (*Lat*). Nickname given to **Caius Caesar** (A.D. 12–41) while he was mascot to his father's army in Germany. The name refers to the miniature legionnaire's outfit he used to wear. The child was spoiled and selfish and would never let his slave **Britannicus** out of his sight without throwing a temper tantrum (I;1–4).

To attempt in this small synopsis to explain his character would be utter foolishness; suffice to say that the normal excesses which his family was known to practice were multiplied a thousandfold in the young Caligula when he became mad after a violent epileptic seizure in A.D. 38. Many of these mad excesses are recorded in the book *I Am a Barbarian* and many others are a matter of historical record. After two years and some months of the most brutal and appallingly tyrannical reign the world has ever known, Caligula was assassinated by the members of his own **Praetorian Guard** on January 24, A.D. 41 (I;13–21).

Callwell, Betty A young Brooklyn woman who disappeared from her home in 1906 and was somehow mysteriously transported to Amtor, where she became **Loto-el-ho-ganja**, goddess of the **Brokols**. It was not until September 24, 1931, that she regained her memory (with **Carson Napier's** help) and, just as mysteriously as she had come, returned to Brooklyn as a corpse (V4;29).

calot A green Barsoomian's "hound." The beast is "about the size of a Shetland pony and has ten short legs. The head bears a slight resemblance to that of a frog, except that the jaws are equipped with three rows of long, sharp tusks" (M4). They are incredibly fierce creatures and are also the fastest land animals on Barsoom. "Calot" is also used as a deprecatory term among Barsoomians.

calot tree A Barsoomian tree of the Forest of **Kaol**, about the size of a large sagebrush, with a set of strong jaws at the end of each branch. It is of course carnivorous, and can drag down even large predators (M3;5).

Calumet Avenue Chicago address of June Lathrop when she worked for **John Secor and Company** (GF;9).

cambon In the Minunian language, the ratel (T10;20).

Cambrian The first geological period of the Paleozoic Era. It lasted from 600 million to 500 million years ago and its best known life forms were the trilobites.

el Camino Corto "The Short Road" (*Sp*). One of the trails of the **Rancho del Ganado** (GH;2).

el Camino Largo "The Long Road" (*Sp*). A trail of early 20th century **Rancho del Ganado** which intersected the Sycamore Canyon Trail (GH;1).

camp In the terminology of the **Grubitten** people of the 22nd century of *The Lost Continent*, a village or city (LC;3).

Camp of the Lions The ruined city of London, infested in the early 22nd century of *The Lost Continent* by lions, probably descended from 20th century zoo animals (LC;4).

Camp Saigon The camp of the survivors of the wreck of the tramp steamer *Saigon*,

minus the mutineers (who were cast out by Tarzan) (T24;11,20).

Campbell, Joseph (Alias "Joe the Pooch") A criminal of Chicago, who after finding out about **Horace Brown's** ignition disruptor in 1939 flew to London (where Brown was staying while demonstrating his device to the British), befriended the Russian **Zubanev**, murdered Brown, took his plans, and headed to Rome to sell them to Italy's Fascist government. En route, the British agent **Lt. Cecil Giles-Burton** stole them from him and headed for **Cape Town** with them, prompting Campbell and Zubanev to pursue. Campbell shot Burton down over **Northern Rhodesia**, then happened upon him later after they both joined the **Ramsgate** safari (Campbell taking the alias "Smith"). After he recognized Burton, he killed both him and Zubanev and took the plans for himself, but was caught by Tarzan (who played detective to solve the murder) and arrested in **Bangali**, and the plans returned to the British government (T24B;2–7).

Campnee, Sieur Ralph de A French knight who joined **Norman of Torn's** outlaw band in order to prey upon the English and became one of his captains (OT;12).

Campus Martius A district of ancient Rome lying near the **Tiber**, site of a huge collection of monuments, theaters, temples and baths (I;5).

canals, Barsoomian The celebrated Martian canals are actually huge underground conduits running from the polar icecaps to the cities of the planet. Along these conduits the whole way lie narrow, walled farm districts where all of the livestock and crops of the mighty red nations are raised. The water is brought directly to the roots of the plants via a vast network of tiny pipes so as to prevent waste through evaporation, and the crops thus raised are always controlled and always perfect. All strains of crops were perfected millennia ago, and all destructive diseases, insects and birds were long ago eradicated (M1;21). In these cultivated districts huge fruit trees are raised, and trees for wood as well. The dark lines seen from Earth are these cultivated districts. A well paved concrete highway follows the full length of each canal, and crossroads are far from uncommon. It is these crossroads that the **green men**

use in crossing the canals during migrations (M1;16).

Canapa The **Polodan** name for the globular cluster NGC 7006, roughly 220,000 light years from Earth and 230,000 light years from Poloda (B1;2).

Canary A fine medieval wine (OT;8).

Canby, the honorable Patricia The real name of **Fraulein Bertha Kircher**, an English spy who posed as a German spy in **German** and **British East Africa** during the first part of World War I. She married **Lt. Harold Percy Smith-Oldwick** in 1915 (T7;24).

Canda An island of Pellucidar in the **Lural Az**, off the coast of **Kali** in the north (P7:2;2).

Canda the Graceful One The daughter of **Goork**, King of **Thuria**, stolen by **Dacor the Strong One** to be his mate (P1;15)(P2;6).

candles, Minunian The beehive-like cities of the **Minunians** were lit by ingenious candles which provided light at the same time as they burned by consuming carbon dioxide. They thus returned oxygen to the air, making the enclosed cities livable (T10;12). See also **Lighting**.

Canler, Robert An acquaintance of **Professor Archimedes Q. Porter**'s who loaned him $10,000 for his trip to Africa, fully expecting the Professor to be unable to pay it back so Canler could claim Jane, the Professor's beautiful daughter, as his wife. Tarzan rescued Professor Porter's treasure, allowing him to pay Canler back, and then throttled Canler until he promised to leave Jane alone (T1;18,27–28).

cannibalism The eating of the flesh of one's own species, practiced in many places for many different reasons. The **Therns** and the **First Born** of Barsoom both engaged in the practice, though neither considered it such because only the flesh of "lower orders" was consumed. The Therns ate the flesh of outer-world Barsoomians, and the blacks ate both the outer-worlders and the Therns (M2;8–9). The people of **U-gor**, a province of **Jahar**, on the other hand, had descended to cannibalism out of necessity to feed their hungry multitudes (M7;14), as had the people of **Punos**, a country destroyed by the **Kapars** of **Poloda**. The Punosians managed to maintain a dignity, even in starvation: they would not eat each other or the friendly **Unisans**, only the detested Kapars (B1;9).

The **Va-gas** of **Va-nah** also engage in cannibalism out of necessity, because they are carnivorous and the flesh of almost all other creatures of Va-nah is poisonous. They eat both the flesh of enemy Va-gas and that of the fallen wounded of their own side, killing the latter as soon as they fall. They eat only males, however, saving females for reproductive purposes. The females of the U-gas, however, they will eat (MM1;4). The U-gas in turn eat the Va-gas, who although closely related are technically of a different species, run about on all fours, and are dangerous enemies anyway (MM1;7).

Other creatures engage in cannibalism for ritual purposes or to extract some magical benefit from the act. The **great apes** of Africa engage in ritual cannibalism during their **Dum-dum** ritual, but do not ever eat the dead of their own tribe, only that of enemies (T1;7–8).

The west African blacks of the tribe of **Mbonga** were cannibals of the worst sort, savages who filed their teeth into points and ate anyone unlucky enough to fall into their hands. They executed a Dum-dum–like dance of death about the doomed victim, poking and prodding him with spears until he slowly bled to death, then they cooked and ate him (T1;9–11). The **Manyuema** of central Africa were of the same type (T2;15–17) as were many other tribes encountered by Tarzan in his long career.

Pellucidar also has its share of cannibalistic tribes, most notably the **Bastians** (P5;5).

cannon, T-ray Amtorian T-ray cannons are usually about 15 feet long and eight inches in diameter, with a bore about half an inch in diameter. A crank in the breech opens a shutter within the weapon, exposing element 93 (**vik-ro**, or **neptunium**) to a charge of element 97 (**berkelium**), releasing the deadly T-ray which dissolves everything in its path. Some materials are more resistant to the T-ray than others, and the gun barrel is made of these, so the beam tends to follow the path of least resistance (down the bore). Even so, the cannon will eventually be ruined by the rays and fall apart. Naval guns are usually locked with a key that the gunnery officer carries, and ships are plated with an armor of the

T-ray resistant metal to protect them, otherwise the first shot would win the battle (V1;8,13).

canoe, Himean   The canoes built by the islanders of **Hime** in the **Korsar Az** of **Pellucidar** were similar in construction to Eskimo kayaks, with watertight compartments fore and aft and a hide covering which could lace about the body of the paddler, making the canoe practically unsinkable (P3;10).

cap-a-pie   (*Fr*) "From head to foot" (OT; 15).

Cape Cod   An American seafaring center of Massachusetts, whence came the old man whose name was not **Dolly Dorcas** (P7:1;7).

Cape Farewell   The cape forming the southernmost point in **Greenland** (C1;1).

Cape Santang   A prominence of eastern **Borneo** lying just north of the equator (Q;1).

Cape Town   The largest city of South Africa, to which Tarzan was bound on a liner from **Algiers** when **Nikolas Rokoff** and **Alexis Paulvitch** sneaked up behind him and heaved him into the Atlantic, thus returning him to the African jungle (T2;11–12).

Cape Verde Islands   A group of islands which lie off the west coast of Africa between 15 and 18 degrees north latitude. It was in these islands that **Professor Archimedes Q. Porter** found the buried treasure which the crew of the *Arrow* mutinied to steal from him (T1;18).

Capell, Colonel   The commanding officer of the Second Rhodesian Infantry during **World War I**, to whom Tarzan gave aid in the African campaign of that war (T7;3).

Capena Gate   The gate by which the Appian Way left ancient Rome (I;9).

Capietro, Dominic   An Italian communist, leader of a band of **Shiftas** in east Africa during the late 1920s, whose men captured **Leon Stabutch** after his safari deserted him. Capietro befriended the Russian, but was later killed by him in a drunken quarrel over who was to keep **Jezebel**, the beautiful blond **Midianite** girl Capietro's men had captured (T15;7,20).

Capri   An island off the coast of Italy where lay the palace to which the Emperor

Tiberius retired in A.D. 26, to rule Rome from there for the last 11 years of his life (I;14).

Caprona   A large and isolated island of the South Pacific, lying somewhere in the uncharted waters of the southernmost part of that ocean. It is ringed entirely with steep cliffs about 1300 feet high, falling off to a bowl-shaped valley heated by volcanic action to tropical temperatures despite the Antarctic waters without. Its cliffs are highly magnetic, attracting nearby compasses to point to them rather than north. These cliffs are so steep that they rise straight up from the ocean floor for hundreds of fathoms, so that Caprona stands in deep water all the way up to its cliffs all the way around and has no shelf, shoals or beaches approaching it as other islands do. The only break in its cliffs is the mouth of the river that drains its great central lake, and as that empties into the ocean below the surface, it is navigable only by submarine, and that carefully. Caprona is actually a monstrously huge volcanic caldera, which accounts both for the sharp cliffs inside and out and the heat of its water, heated by volcanic vents from below to almost 90 degrees Fahrenheit. **Bowen Tyler** theorized that Caprona once lay on a mighty landmass (the continent of Mu?) which sank in ancient times, leaving only Caprona sticking out above the waters. This would explain its great diversity of fauna, unusual in a true island so distant from a continental landmass (C1;4–5).

Caproni   An Italian explorer of the South Pacific, who discovered the "mini-continent" or large island of **Caspak** in the far South Pacific and named it **Caprona** after himself. He got into political difficulties upon his return to Italy and is scarcely mentioned even by his contemporaries (C1;4).

Captain   One of **Diana Henders'** favorite horses (HB;4).

Captains That Go Before   A Mayan title for the gods (T24;13).

"The Capture of Tarzan"   The second short story in the collection *Jungle Tales of Tarzan*, which concerns Tarzan's capture by a native pit trap while trying to keep **Tantor** from falling into it in 1906. The story is abbreviated T6:2.

Caraftap   A **Minunian** quarry-slave of **Veltopismakus** who wanted to mate with the slave girl **Talaskar** but was spurned by her. He threatened her in front of Tarzan, who of course took action to protect the girl. Caraftap was a bully, and every slave was glad when Tarzan bested him in combat. Later, he saw Tarzan and **Komodoflorensal** free in Veltopismakus and informed **Kalfastoban**, but was killed by Tarzan soon afterward (T10; 11–12,17–18).

Carb A warrior of the village of **Clovi** in Pellucidar when Tarzan came there in 1927 (T13;11).

carborundum Not the earthly silicon carbide abrasive, but rather an immensely hard Barsoomian substance of which city walls are sometimes made (M1;24); it is probably some sort of polymer or crystalline polycarbide. It is used in an aluminum alloy called carborundum aluminum which is light, strong and "almost impenetrable," and is used extensively in the construction of Barsoomian fighting ships (M2;8).

Carl A new "servant" of the **Greystoke** household in 1912, actually a plant placed by **Nikolas Rokoff** so he could kidnap Tarzan's infant son, Jack (T3;1). Another Carl was the headwaiter at **Feinheimer's Cabaret** in Chicago for many years (EE;26).

Carlotta The old nanny of the **Princess Mary of Margoth** who had filled the child's head with awful stories of the "horrible" **Karlovans**. She was mistaken for **Mrs. Bass** by **Prince Boris** (posing as **The Rider**) when he abducted the princess as **Gwendolyn Bass** by mistake (R;1,7).

Carlyn The fictional name of a revolutionary of an unnamed country in the 1920s, a military man who had been cashiered from the army because of a gambling debt. As part of the plot the revolutionaries hatched with **Prince Ferdinand**, he was reinstated in the military without loss of rank and later used his position within the palace to assassinate **King Otto** (LL;3,7,9,17). He was soon afterward double-crossed by Ferdinand and transferred to the frontier with **General Sarnya**. Carlyn was a cad who paid court to the widow of **William Wesl**, the man he had framed for the king's assassination, then murdered. He got his just desserts when the woman figured him out and shot him (LL;19,21,23).

Carn The village of the island of **Hime**

from which came **Jude**, the scoundrel who kidnapped **Stellara** from **Tanar the Fleet One** in 1925 (P3;12).

Carnegie, Hattie (1886–1956) A fashion designer of the 1910s through the 1940s (B1;5).

carpentum (*Lat*) A two-wheeled carriage (I;3).

Carr, Colonel The commander of Fort Apache during the **Apache** uprising of 1881 (A1;15).

Carranza, Venustiano Mexican revolutionary leader (1859–1920) and president of Mexico from 1914 to 1920. He was a conservative revolutionary and was opposed to men like **Pancho Villa** and **Emiliano Zapata**, who also wanted the presidency and mounted a military campaign against Carranza in 1914 (K2;6).

Carrion Caves The only passage through the ice barrier to the frozen land of **Okar** on Barsoom. When the **yellow men** fled north to escape the **green men**, a mighty battle was fought there, and the yellow men won. To discourage pursuit all the thousands of dead were piled in the caves so that the stench of their decay would warn off invaders. Since that time, all the dead of Okar and all of its garbage as well have been brought to the caves and dumped, so as to add to the incredible stench. The caves are a connected series of 27 wide but low chambers, carved in ancient times by a subterranean arctic river flowing south, and their crampedness tends to concentrate the stench. The caves are also the lairing place of the apts (M3;8). The Carrion Caves were eventually cleansed by the order of **Talu** when he became ruler of Okar, so as to make contact with other nations easier (M3;16).

carruca (*Lat*) Cart (I;2).

Carruthers An English tutor of **Prince Ferdinand** in the early 20th century (LL;3).

Carruthers, Dr. An excellent Los Angeles surgeon who performed the operation that saved **Eva Pennington's** life after her attempted suicide in August of 1923 (GH;34).

Carson, Judge John A rich old magistrate of **Virginia**, known to Burroughs. He was **Carson Napier's** great-grandfather and left him a considerable fortune (V1;1).

Carson, Mrs. The manager of the typist and stenographer's employment agency which got June Lathrop her job in Ogden Secor's office (GF;7).

Carson of Venus The title taken by Carson Napier (after the Amtorian form, "so-and-so of such-and-such") after his arrival in Sanara in 1930. He used the Earth word "Venus," so the Amtorians had no idea what place he actually meant (V3;5).

Carson of Venus The third book of the Venus series, abbreviated V3. The events within took place in 1930 and 1931 and were communicated telepathically to Burroughs in the latter year and published a few years later. In it, Carson and Duare, having escaped from the super-scientific city of Havatoo (where Duare had falsely been condemned to death for espionage) in Carson's newly-built anotar, encounter various adventures before finally arriving in the land of Anlap, where Carson becomes involved in a war. He is first a scout and later a secret agent, and finds Duare's father, Mintep, a prisoner of the evil Zani party.

Carter, John The hero of the Mars series, an ageless fighting man who could recall no childhood and has always looked about 30 years old. The last earthly war in which he fought was the American Civil War, fighting for Virginia. He was mysteriously transported to Mars after his apparent death in a cave in Arizona on March 4, 1866 (M1;2), and his known adventures on Mars cover a period of some 75 years.

His nephew, Edgar Rice Burroughs, described him as "a splendid specimen of manhood, standing a good two inches over six feet, broad of shoulder and narrow of hip, with the carriage of a trained fighting man. His features were regular and clear cut, his hair black and closely cropped, while his eyes were of a steel gray, reflecting a strong and loyal character, filled with fire and initiative. His manners were perfect, and his courtliness was that of a typical Southern gentleman of the highest type." Like many fighting men, he was somewhat tongue-tied in the presence of the fairer sex, and when he fell in love with the incomparable Dejah Thoris, it was forever and without reservation. Carter is brave to the point of recklessness and finds no greater joy in life than fighting. He has an excellent sense of humor, and often laughs in the face of danger.

After his marriage to Dejah Thoris, he became a prince of the House of Tardos Mors, Jeddak of Helium, and after the events of *The Warlord of Mars*, he received that title from the jeddaks of five empires. It was he who brought several "lost" Martian races out of hiding, including the yellow and black races (M2)(M3), and he who helped to first establish communication between Earth and Mars (MM1;1).

After his initial transportation to Mars, he lived there for ten earthly years, apparently died, then returned to Earth in his original earthly body, leaving no trace behind on the Red Planet. On March 4, 1886 (ten years after his return to Earth), he again seemed to die, returning then to his beloved Barsoom (as Mars is called by its inhabitants) for more adventures, leaving behind his seemingly dead body in a specially designed, ventilated tomb closed with a door that could only be opened from the inside (M1). In 1898 he returned to Earth for three months after learning the secret of going between the worlds at will, and later, with the help of Kar Komak the bowman, he learned to transport inanimate matter as well, returning periodically to visit his nephew with a new story to tell.

Although he can read the minds of Barsoomians (as they can each other's), they cannot read his.

After becoming Warlord of Barsoom, he decided to begin a war against the practice of assassination, and especially against the powerful assassin's guild of Zodanga. This personal mission led him to permanently neutralize many assassins of that city, and then to go in pursuit of guild officials who had kidnapped Dejah Thoris and taken her to Thuria. He followed, eventually rescued his wife, and returned with her to Helium (M8).

A few years later, he went with Vor Daj of Helium to find Ras Thavas, the Master Mind of Barsoom, when Dejah Thoris had broken her back in an aviation accident (M9;1). He and Vor Daj were captured and enslaved by the hormads, synthetic humans of Ras Thavas' creation, but succeeded in escaping their city and returning Ras Thavas to Helium in time to save the princess. He later returned to rescue Vor Daj and destroy the horror from Vat Room #4 (M9;2–15,28–31).

A few years later, on a pleasure flight to

explore **Horz** (the ancient Barsoomian seat of learning), John Carter was captured by the ancient **Orovars** inhabiting that city and sentenced to death, but escaped with the help of **Pan Dan Chee**, an Orovar warrior. In the escape, they also discovered **Llana of Gathol**, Carter's granddaughter, and rescued her (M10:1). After escaping Horz on foot following the loss of Carter's flier, they miscalculated their direction and ended up at the rift of **Kamtol**, in which they were enslaved and Carter forced to fight in the games of the **First Born**, who ruled the valley. After destroying the **nerve-index machine** which would have been able to kill them, they stole a flier and escaped (M10:2). They soon reached Gathol, but found it besieged. John Carter, still in disguise as a **Black Pirate**, was caught and arrested by Gatholian herdsmen, during which period Llana, Pan Dan Chee and **Jad-Han** were captured by the **Panar** invaders, prompting John Carter to disguise himself again and infiltrate **Hin Abtol's** navy (M10:3;1–5). He later made his way to **Pankor** (city of the Panars) and rescued Llana by stealing back his own flier from Hin Abtol (M10:3;13). While heading south to Helium, he and Llana stopped in the hidden forest of **Invak** to look for food and were captured by the invisible Invakians, who imprisoned them. He eventually got hold of some of the **invisibility pills** himself and escaped, finally reaching Helium in time to dispatch its navy to destroy Hin Abtol's (M10:4).

About a year later, he was kidnapped by the **Morgors**, hideous skeleton men from **Jupiter**, in order that they might pick his brain about Barsoom's defenses in order to invade it. He eventually escaped the creatures, freeing Dejah Thoris (who had been brought along in order to enforce his cooperation) in the process, and made his way back to Barsoom to head off the invasion (M11B). It is unknown whether the Morgors ever invaded Barsoom or not, but if they did they were certainly repulsed, because Barsoom was in constant communication with Earth from the 1950s until around 2030, and it is known that John Carter was alive at least until that time (MM1;1).

Carthoris   The son of John Carter and Dejah Thoris. He was hatched in 1876, soon after his father saved Barsoom by opening the **atmosphere plant**, and like all Barsoomians

(growing as they do in the egg) was already a young man and a skillful fighter by the time ten years had gone by. On a routine air scouting mission for **Helium** near the south pole, he decided to look for the **Valley Dor**, developed engine trouble, and was captured by the **First Born**. After being forced to fight in their games for a while, he met his father (who had just returned to Barsoom) and the two escaped **Omean** together and eventually returned to Helium. There, he had to rescue his father from the death sentence of **Zat Arrras**, then lead the expedition to rescue his mother from the First Born (M2). He was made acting **Jeddak of Helium** during the absence of **Tardos Mors** and **Mors Kajak** (M3;1).

He later fell in love with **Thuvia of Ptarth** and went to rescue her from **Astok**, Prince of **Dusar**, although she was promised to **Kulan Tith of Kaol**. He and she rediscovered the lost city of **Lothar** and befriended **Kar Komak** the bowman. Later, after seeing Carthoris and Thuvia's love for one another, Kulan Tith renounced his claim to her, and they were married (M4).

Casa Grande   "Big House" (*Sp*). A Mexican trading town of 19th century **Sonora** (A1;6).

Casas Grandes   "Big Houses" (*Sp*). A Mexican town of **Chihuahua** south of which the **Be-don-ko-he Apaches** camped in 1880 after fleeing American soldiers (A1;11).

Case, Jeb   The farmer outside of **Oakdale**, Illinois at whose home the "Oskaloosa Kid" bought food for himself, **Bridge** and "Abigail Prim" the morning after the latter's disappearance (K3;6).

Case, Miranda   The wife of Illinois farmer Jeb Case (K3;6).

Case, Willie   The son of **Oakdale** farmer Jeb Case, to whom the "Oskaloosa Kid" blurted out the story of his supposed crime. Willie repeated the story to **Burton**, the **Chicago** detective, and later found and tracked **Bridge** and the "Kid" and reported their whereabouts to Burton — twice (K3;6–10).

Caspak   The inner country of **Caprona** is a tropical land ringed by almost unscaleable cliffs and dominated by a large, hot central lake which is fed by both warm and cold streams and drained by a large river in the south which flows beneath the barrier cliffs into the Pacific. Caspak utterly teems with life (both prehistoric and modern forms), all in constant battle for survival like nowhere else on Earth — more savage than even Pellucidar (C1;5–6).

Caspak, biology of The creatures of Caspak each recapitulate phylogeny in their own lives, coming up **cor sva jo** (from the beginning) as tiny, wriggling, tadpole-like creatures borne live by Caspakian females of all species in the **ata** ritual, conducted every day in stagnant-looking pools all over Caspak. These "tadpoles" make their way into the central sea of Caspak, where they slowly grow and develop over time, eventually emerging onto land and slowly developing (if they survive) into the kind of creature that spawned them. In the case of humans, there is a slow progression from **Ho-lu** (*Ape*) to **Alu** (ape-man) to **Bo-lu** (club-man, a sort of primitive humanoid), to the tool-using **Sto-lu**, then the smarter and more organized **Band-lu**, the neolithic **Kro-lu**, and finally the metalworking **Galu**. Some humans progress even further, becoming the winged **Wieroo** (C2;3). Among the Galus and Wieroos are born **cos-ata-lu**, live births, but these are the only Caspakian examples of the process (C2;5). At least, such births are rare among the Galus — all Wieroos are now cos-ata-lu, but must mate with **cos-ata-lo** Galus to accomplish their births, as there are no female Wieroos. No Wieroos come up cor sva jo any more, although it was only recently that this change came about (C3;3).

Caspak, language of All the higher life forms of Caspak speak the same language, as could be expected. The higher types merely fill out the tongue with a larger vocabulary and more strict grammar than do the lower (C1;8).

cassava *see* manioc

Cassidy, Professor A New York–based trainer of boxers who gave **Billy Byrne** his first real job in 1915 (K1;17).

Cassiu A Roman thug killed by **Britannicus** in defense of **Attica**. Tibur was arrested and convicted for his murder until Britannicus confessed (I;7–10).

Cassius Chaerea A tribune of the Emperor **Caligula**'s guard who was at the center

of the plot which claimed the tyrant's life in A.D. 41 (I;21).

Cassius Hasta A nephew of **Validus Augustus**, the "Emperor of the East" in the lost Roman outpost of **Castrum Mare** in the 1920s. The Emperor accused him of treason and supposedly banished him, actually sending him on a dangerous mission to **Castra Sanguinarius**, where he was captured and imprisoned. He later returned in triumph with a body of troops (including Tarzan's **Waziri**) and was proclaimed "Emperor of the East" in Castrum Mare (T12;8,13,22–23).

Cassius Longinus The first husband of **Caligula**'s sister **Drusilla**, whose marriage Caligula dissolved to give her to **Lepidus** (I;16).

Castra Sanguinarius The more western of the two lost Roman outposts deep within the **Wiramwazi Mountains** of Africa, at the forested end of the valley. It was the eternal foe of **Castrum Mare** and was a corrupt, crime-ridden place usually ruled by cruel emperors like **Sublatus**. Castra Sanguinarius was supported by its gold mines and its raids on the outer world, to which it controlled the only way from the valley (T12;6,8–10).

Castro y Pensilo, Don Piedro de A Spanish nobleman with a price on his head who joined **Norman of Torn**'s mid–13th century force of bandits and became one of his captains (OT;12).

Castrol, Miss Ogden Secor's nurse at St. Luke's Hospital after he was injured in a robbery of his office (GF;9).

Castrum Mare The more eastern of the two lost Roman outposts deep within the **Wiramwazi Mountains** of Africa, built on an island in the **Mare Orientis** at the eastern end of the valley. The inhabitants of Castrum Mare are the eternal foes of those of **Castra Sanguinarius**. The city was founded in the Roman year 935 (A.D. 200) by **Honus Hasta**, a patrician of Castra Sanguinarius who was disgusted with the high crime rate there and wished to make a change. Its primary products were fish, snails, paper and iron, which it traded to Castra Sanguinarius for gold and slaves (T12;6,8,10).

Cat-men of Ladan *see* **Masenas**

Catherine of Aragon The first wife of King Henry VIII, both in England of the 1500s and Africa of the 1930s (T17;18).

Cathne The City of Gold, lying in the valley of Onthar 16 miles south of the volcano Xarator in the Ethiopian Highlands. The Cathneans raise lions for war and sport, and also mine gold and produce hay, fruits and vegetables, which they trade once a year with the Athneans for salt, steel and cloth. The rest of the time, the two cities are at war. There are about 500 adult male lions in Cathne, 300 of which are owned by the queen and the rest by the Lion Men, Cathne's hereditary nobles. The Cathneans are often cruel and relish blood sport, taking the heads of Athneans as trophies equally with those of beasts (T16; 3–5,11). They and the Athneans both seem to be of Greek descent.

Catiline conspiracy A conspiracy hatched by Lucius Sergius Catilina (108–62 B.C.) to overthrow the Roman government after he lost the consular election to Cicero. The plot was discovered, the conspirators proclaimed public enemies, and Catilina himself fell in battle a year later (I;4).

cattle, Polodan The cattle of Poloda have uncloven hooves and no horns at all; when threatened, they bite and kick like an Earthly horse does. They are kept for meat and milk (B1;6).

The Cave Girl A two-part novel, originally published as *The Cave Girl* in 1913 and *The Cave Man* in 1917. The stories originally took place in 1911 and came to Burroughs in 1912, one to be published almost immediately and the other to be held for several years. In the original *Cave Girl* (Part I of the combined novel, abbreviated CG1), "Waldo Emerson Smith-Jones," a Bostonian aristocrat, is shipwrecked on an uncharted island and, in the process of surviving, builds up a powerful physique that he had always had the potential for but never developed. He fights to win Nadara, the beautiful savage of the title, whom he has fallen in love with.

The Cave Man The second part of *The Cave Girl* (abbreviated CG2), originally published in 1917. It tells of the further adventures of "Waldo Emerson Smith-Jones" (now called Thandar) and his mate Nadara. Thandar becomes king of Nadara's tribe, but they

are separated when Nadara is abducted and an earthquake delays pursuit, all of this happening only a few weeks before the arrival of Smith-Jones' father to rescue him.

cayuse (American West) A horse (HB;1).

celibacy All unmarried red Barsoomian men are required to pay a rather high celibacy tax. Those too poor to pay it are shipped off to work on the farms along with convicts, prisoners of war, and delinquent debtors (M1;20).

cell 3-17 The cell in the pits of Morbus from which a secret passage led out to an island in the Toonolian Marshes, enabling John Carter and Ras Thavas to flee the city (M9;15).

Celsus, Cornelius A great Roman physician of the 1st century A.D. (I;9).

centipedes, Euroban The riding animals of the Morgors of Eurobus are like huge, hoofed centipedes with sharp-toothed, fishlike heads. The segments of their bodies are each about 18 inches long, and they are incredibly ugly. They are long enough for ten or twelve Morgors to ride on at the same time (M11B;3).

Central Laboratories The self-explanatory title of an institution of Havatoo on Amtor, which is responsible for (among many other things) the "fitness testing" of those brought to Havatoo. It is also their seat of government (V2;14–15). See also **Sera Tartum.**

Centurion In the military organization of ancient Rome, an officer commanding 100 men (T12;6).

Certus A famous race horse of early 1st century Rome, whose sire was Princeps (I;8).

cetacean A mammal exclusively adapted to aquatic life, such as a dolphin or a whale (P1;7).

Cha-ja-la (*Apa*) The magical spirit dance (A1;14).

Chab Xib Chac "The Red Man" who led a rebellion against the Cocom family of tyrants in Mexico of 1451 and murdered them all (T24;1).

Chac Tutul Xiu The king of the lost Mayan colony of Uxmal, a direct descendant of Ah Cuitok Tutul Xiu, who with many of his "followers, nobles, warriors, women, and slaves" went to the west coast of Mexico, set out into the Pacific in large dugout canoes in 1452, and was never heard from again (T24;1).

Chal-az A warrior of the Kro-lu of Caspak whom **Tom Billings** saved from the **Band-lu** late in the summer of 1917, and who told Billings and **Ajor** of **Du-seen**'s plan to conspire with the Kro-lu to conquer the land of the **Galus**. He later helped Billings escape the treachery of **Al-tan** (chief of the Kro-lu) and his ally Du-seen when they would have killed Billings. After Al-tan and his followers went with Du-seen to invade the Galu country, Chal-az was made chief and had Al-tan and his men put to death on their return. Soon afterward, he advanced to Galu status himself, leaving a good man as chief behind him (C2;5–7).

Chal Yip Xiu The **Ah Kin Mai** (high priest) of **Chichen Itza** on **Uxmal** when Tarzan was shipwrecked there in 1938 (T24;13).

Chamber of Mystery A death chamber within the **Golden Cliffs** of **Otz** on Barsoom. Banths or other monsters were released into the interior through secret panels while the room's occupants were turned in another direction, and the latter were tormented by mocking voices through hidden speakers. With the help of a hand mirror, John Carter and **Tars Tarkas** escaped its confines (M2;3).

Chamber of Reptiles Although reptiles are nearly extinct upon Barsoom, there was a roomful of horribly venomous serpents and lizards along the secret tunnel from the **Mountains of Otz** to the **Temple of the Sun** (M3;3).

Chamber of the Dead A long-disused chamber of the ancient **Temple of the Sun** in **Opar**. La, the high priestess of Opar, hid Tarzan there after he saved her life because she knew that no Oparian other than herself would dare enter the chamber, which was believed to be a chapel where the spirits of the dead came to offer sacrifice to the sun. It was believed that they would sacrifice any living man or woman they found within, except the high priestess. La, however, being highly intelligent and privy to the secrets of the

temple, knew that the story was untrue and so was unafraid to hide Tarzan there (T2; 20,22).

Chams A Southeast Asian people enslaved by the **Khmers** of medieval Cambodia (HM;6).

Chand A Lascar sailor and mutineer of the tramp steamer *Saigon* when it carried Tarzan across the Pacific as a captive wild man late in 1938 (T24;3).

Chand Kabi The old **Hindu** who taught the young **Carson Napier** many things, among them telepathy and the projection of psychic images (V1;1).

Charicles The physician to the Emperor **Tiberius** at the time of his death in A.D. 37 (I;15).

chariot, Barsoomian The green Barsoomian chariot is large and commodious and is usually drawn by a zitidar. It is three-wheeled, has tires, and is almost noiseless (M1;7). Similar chariots, though smaller, were used by the **Manatorians** (M5;11).

Charlie One of the cowboys of the **Crazy "B" Ranch** (A2;18).

Charlotte A friend of **Ruth Morton Scott**'s (ME;1).

Charnel Isles Small islets in the river **Iss** beneath the **Golden Cliffs** of **Otz** on Barsoom. They were home to gibbering maniacs, those who had turned away from **The Pilgrimage** at the last moment and had descended to **cannibalism** to survive. Many of the islets are solid masses of bones, picked clean over many ages (M3;1).

Charpentier, Lieutenant One of the officers of the French steamer which rescued the **Porter** party, who led a search party into the jungle to search for **Jane Porter** after she was carried off by the ape **Terkoz**. He also led a force of sailors to the village of **Mbonga** to search for his close friend **Lt. Paul d'Arnot** and massacred all of the savages, but did not find d'Arnot, as he had already been rescued by Tarzan (T1;19,22).

Chatti The German tribe to whom the surviving members of **Britannicus**' tribe were sold after being defeated by the **Belgae**. The Chatti were themselves later defeated by a Roman force under command of **Germanicus**

Caesar and the slaves passed into his custody (I;1).

Che   The Mayan god of forests, with whom **Thak Chan**, the Mayan **Tarzan** rescued on **Uxmal** in 1938, identified the ape-man. Later, all of the people of **Chichen Itza** accepted him as such (T24;13,24). Another **Che** was the Khmer peasant of **Lodidhapura** who first found the delirious **Gordon King** when he stumbled into that country in the mid-1920s (HM;3).

Cheeracow   White man's mispronunciation of **Chihuicahui**, the Mexican name for the **Cho-kon-en** tribe of **Apaches** (A1;15).

Cheese it!   (American slang) "Cut it out!" or "stop it!" (D;3).

Cheetim, "Dirty"   A ranch hand who was fired by **Wichita Billings'** father and later returned to rape her in 1879 but was shot by **Shoz-dijiji** in the attempt (A1;10). He survived to open up a tavern and brothel known as the **Hog Ranch** some two years later, thus becoming a prime factor in the corruption of local Indians and a great troublemaker in the bargain, trying on several occasions to steal both **Wichita Billings'** cattle and the young lady herself, for which latter offense he was tortured to death by **Shoz-dijiji** (A2;2,5, 16–19).

chemical fuel   The fuel of the launch used by **Lt. Jefferson Turck** and his men in 2137 was apparently not derived from petroleum (LC;3).

Chemungo   The son of **Mpingu**, chief of the **Buiroos**, who captured **Helen Gregory** after she escaped from **Atan Thome** in October of 1936 (T20;7). Three years later he ambushed and wounded Tarzan himself, capturing him, but of course Tarzan escaped (T24B;4).

The Chessmen of Mars   The fifth book in the Mars series, narrated to Burroughs by John Carter in a visit to Earth about 1919 or 1920. The events took place around 1915, and the book was published in 1922. In the book **Tara of Helium**, John Carter's daughter was swept away by a rare Barsoomian hurricane while flying in her personal **flier** and was captured by the hideous **Kaldanes**. She escaped with the help of a rogue Kaldane, met up with **Gahan of Gathol** (disguised as a **panthan**),

and was captured by the people of **Manator**, who play **jetan** (Barsoomian chess) with live people. The rules of the game are appendicized at the end of the book, abbreviated M5.

Chi   Neal Brown's nickname, since he came from **Chicago** (T19;12).

Chi-e-a-hen   One of the **Apache** tribes (A1;3).

Chicago   Birthplace of Edgar Rice Burroughs and original home of the **Julian** family, at least from **Julian 3rd** to **Julian 10th** (MM1;1). Under the **Kalkars** it was the center of a **teivos**, and **Julian 9th** played in its ruins as a child (MM2;2).

Chicago Press Club   A turn-of-the-century social organization for newshounds (R;5).

Chicago Saloon   One of the five drinking establishments of **Hendersville, Arizona** in the 1880s (HB;10).

Chichen Itza   The **Mayan** city on the lost island of **Uxmal** in the South Pacific, named for an ancient Mayan city in Mexico. Like any ancient Mayan city, it featured paved streets and a central stepped pyramid (T24;12–13).

Chidin-bi-kungua   "The House of Spirits" (*Apa*). The **Apache** concept of the afterlife (A1;4).

chief   The most powerful piece in a game of Barsoomian jetan. It moves three spaces in any direction — straight, diagonal or any combination — and may not be taken by any piece except the opposing chief, or else the game ends in a draw (M5).

Chief   A famous **Santa Fe** passenger train which ran from **Chicago** to Los Angeles; until it was replaced by the Super Chief, it was the most luxurious train in the world (T17;33).

Chief of Chiefs   The title of the leader of the confederation of the tribes of **Julian** in the American West of the 25th century (MM3;1).

chieftain   Besides the usual meaning, when a Barsoomian woman uses the term "my chieftain" to a man, she is calling him her beloved; i.e., it is a term of endearment. See **princess**.

Chigo-na-ay   (*Apa*) The sun (A1;1).

Chih-hen-ne An Apache tribe of Sonora and Chihuahua (A1;3).

Chihuahua Northern Mexican state lying primarily along the southern border of west Texas and New Mexico (K2;7)(A1;3). Chihuahua was also the Mexican name of an older Apache of the late 1800s who spoke against war in the pow-wow at Geronimo's camp on May 16, 1885 (A2;6).

Chihuicahui The Mexican name for the Cho-kon-en Apaches (A1;1).

chil-jilt (*Apa*) Night (A1;2).

Child's An American restaurant chain of the early 20th century which was apparently especially known for pancakes (M6;10).

China One of the three great powers of the early 22nd century of *The Lost Continent* was a very civilized and progressive Chinese empire which ruled Asia and the Pacific islands as far east as 175 degrees west longitude and was determined to pacify and civilize barbaric Europe as well. Its capital was at Peking, and in 2137 it had cities as far west as Moscow. After the arrival of Lt. Jefferson Turck and (coincidentally) a Pan-American peace delegation (sent as a result of the work of John Alvarez), the Chinese became allies of Pan-America (LC;9).

Chinnereth The supposedly bottomless lake in the center of the hidden land of Midian in the Ghenzi Mountains of Africa, used by the Midianites for their usually-fatal "purifications" of sinners (T15;6).

Chiricahua Mountains A small mountain range of southern Arizona which lies south of the San Simon Valley (A1;20).

chirurgeon (Archaic) A physician (T11; 18).

Chita Short for Wichita, as in Billings (A1;15).

Cho-kon-en A large Apache tribe of mid–19th century New Mexico whose chief was the famous Cochise. They were also known as the Chihuicahui (a Mexican name)(A1;1,3).

Chon The "true god" of Tuen-baka, who resided at Thobos, and to whom the Father of Diamonds originally belonged before it was stolen by the Ashairians (T20;23). Like

Brulor, he was also an old man. He had been attacked and his galley sunk by the Ashairians and was thought dead by all but his secret followers while he searched for the true Father of Diamonds on the lake floor; when he found it, he returned to Thobos (T20;31–32).

Chon, Temple of The Temple of Chon, living god of Thobos, was a beautiful cave complex lit by openings in the limestone cliffs overlooking Ashair at the lower end of Lake Horus. In this temple he lived, unknown to the Thobotians, while searching for the Father of Diamonds, which lay lost somewhere on the lake bed (T20;27,30–32).

Chowambi The chief of the tribe of Waziri when they fled south to escape the Arabs in the mid–1800s. It was he who settled them in the location they occupied when first encountered by Tarzan, and he who first encountered the city of Opar while searching for a better location for their village. Chowambi was the father of Waziri, the chief when Tarzan joined the tribe (T2;15).

Christian The Abyssinians of the 22nd century of *The Lost Continent* were, like their ancestors, Christians (LC;8).

Christiania The former name of Oslo, the capital of Norway, in which Sven Anderssen lived (T3;10).

chuck wagon (American Wesst) The wagon accompanying a cattle drive in which the provisions are carried (D;3).

Chuldrup A Lascar mutineer of the tramp steamer *Saigon* in 1938, who was ordered into the jungle to reconnoiter by Wilhelm Schmidt after they had been shipwrecked and driven out of Tarzan's camp. He was killed by one of the tigers Tarzan had rescued from the ship (T24;16).

Chulk A great ape of Africa, a member of the tribe Tarzan joined while amnesiac in 1913. Chulk agreed to come with Tarzan on his search for Jane, whom the ape-man had felt a tinge of recollection for upon seeing her as a prisoner of Achmet Zek, the Arab raider. He wandered away from Tarzan after the abortive rescue and stole Mugambi's pouch from him while he slept, thus gaining possession of the jewels of Opar. Later, he led the great apes to rescue Tarzan and Albert Werper but was shot and killed during the operation, allowing Werper to regain possession of the jewels (T5;16,19,22–23).

Chung   The Chinese cook of the Crazy "B" Ranch (A2;18).

church, secret   The Julian 8th family and their friends kept up a secret church in the woods outside Chicago, an ancient (now buried) edifice to which they went on the first Sunday of every month for an interdenominational worship service. Julian 9th and Juana St. John were married in the church, a ceremony as much in violation of Kalkar law as the church itself was. Eventually, the Kash Guard found the church and destroyed it (MM2;6–8).

churl   (Archaic) A peasant, or a rude and boorish person (OT;5).

Cibicu Creek   Site of a major battle between American cavalry and a great force of Apaches in September of 1878 (A1;14).

Cicero   A suburb of Chicago from which "Shrimp" Rosetti hailed (T22;2).

Cicero, Marcus Tullius   (106–43 B.C.) Probably the greatest Roman orator; he was a senator, consul, and politically active citizen and wrote on various philosophical subjects in a clear prose style which set the standard for Latin prose. He stepped on Octavian's toes at a later time, however, and was executed (I;4).

The Cid   The chief of the fierce Korsar sea raiders of Pellucidar, a very intelligent and very brutal man who maintained his position by craft and force of arms and led his people on raids personally. The name "The Cid" was not a name as such but actually a title, taken from that given to Rodrigo Diaz de Bivar, the Spanish national hero. The name, coupled with the customs, dress, architecture and ships of the Korsars proved to David Innes their origin on the outer Earth (P3;1–2,13).

Cingetorix   A Briton chieftain and king of Kent in the 1st century B.C., great-grandfather of Britannicus Caligulae Servus (I;1).

Circeii   A Roman city north of Antium where Tiberius suffered an abdominal attack a few days before his death (I;15).

Circle G   The ranch owned by "Ole" Gunderstrom in early 20th century New Mexico (D;2).

Circle Terrace   A street of Hollywood (GH;27).

Circus Flaminius   A Roman theater (I;5).

Cit Coh Xiu   Ruler of the lost Mayan colony of Uxmal in the mid–20th century. He was a direct descendant of Chac Tutul Xiu, who first colonized the island in 1453 (T24;1).

Citadel of Horz   A walled, almost impregnable city within the city of Horz, within which the last Orovars live. No aliens are permitted within its walls, being killed outside instead (M10:1;4).

cities, Amtorian   The following is a list of the cities of Amtor (city-states are in bold). See individual entries.

Amlot	Japal	Maltor	Tolan
Hangor	Kapdor	Mypos	Torlac
Havatoo	Kooaad	Onar	Voo-ad
Hor	Kormor	Pandar	
Houtomai	Ladja	Sanara	

cities, Barsoomian   The following is a list of the cities of Barsoom (city-states are in bold). See individual entries.

Aanthor	Helium	Korvas	**Ptarth**
Amhor	Horz	Lothar	**Raxar**
Bantoom	Illall	Manataj	**Thark**
Duhor	**Invak**	Manator	Thurd
Dusar	Jahar	Manatos	**TJanath**
Exum	Kadabra	Marentina	**Toonol**
Gathol	Kamtol	Morbus	Torquas
Ghasta	Kaol	**Onvak**	Warhoon
Gooli	**Kobol**	Pankor	Xanator
Hastor	Korad	**Phundahl**	Zodanga
			Zor

cities, lost   The following is a list of lost cities (on Earth). See individual entries.

A-lur	Lodidhapura
Alemtejo	Mandalamakus
Ashair	Nimmr
Athne	Oo-oh
Cathne	Opar
Castra Sanguinarius	Pnom Dhek
Castrum Mare	Thobos
Chichen Itza	Trohanadalmakus
City of the Sepulcher	Tu-lur
Geryeh	Uxmal
Ja-lur	Veltopismakus
Kavuru	Xuja

cities, Pellucidarian   The following is a list of Pellucidarian cities. See individual entries.

Allaban	Garb	Korsar	Pheli
Amdar	Gef	Lar	Phutra
Amoz	Go-hal	Liba	Sari
Basti	Gombul	Lo-har	Suvi
Carn	Greenwich	Lolo-lolo	Tanga-tanga
Clovi	Julok	Oog	Thuria
Gamba	Kali	Paraht	Zoram

cities, Unisan The cities of Unis on Poloda were built largely underground, with buildings which could go up and down like elevators very quickly. Between attacks they were up in the sunlight on the surface, but when the first sign of attack came they quickly dropped into shafts in the ground leaving only their bombproof roofs showing. After many years of war, construction of completely underground structures had instead become the rule, and all buildings, highways, etc. were completely buried, leaving the surface as a beautiful, well-kept garden (B1;1–4).

cities, Va-nah The cities of Va-nah, the world within the moon, were always built in the bowls of craters, terraced from the floor of the crater to the rim and thus becoming more vertical as one ascended toward the rim. Farming takes place on the roofs of the next terrace down, and many buildings (those near the rim and near the bottom) are thus completely buried beneath other buildings and are totally inaccessible to light and air and are reached only by corridors (MM1;10).

City of Human Skulls The city of Oo-oh, habitation of the Wieroos of Caspak (C3;2).

City of Menofra The name to which Menofra proposed changing "Athne" after a revolution put her husband in charge there (T21;23).

"The City of Mummies" The original title of "The Ancient Dead," the first novelette comprising *Llana of Gathol*, when it appeared in *Amazing Stories* magazine in March of 1941.

City of Phoros The name to which the Erythra proposed changing "Athne" after their revolution — the only reason they did not was because Menofra insisted it be called "The City of Menofra" (T21;23).

City of the Sepulcher The city built by Sir Bohun at the north end of the Valley of the Sepulcher to protect the supposed site of the Sepulcher of Christ and keep the follow-

ers of Sir Gobred from returning north out of the valley. Since that time it and Nimmr have been at war, though the sole practice of that war was the Great Tournament held on the first Sunday of Lent every year. The city was sacked in February of 1921 by the Arab raiders of the tribe el-Harb while most of its warriors were away at the Great Tourney (T11;12,17).

Clan of Lions In the lost city of Cathne, the clan to which all nobles born to the title belong. They are called this because each is descended from a warrior who led the king's lions to victory in battle (T16;8,10).

Clan Torn The band of Norman of Torn, eventually numbering 1000 men, which preyed upon the rich and noble of mid–13th century Derbyshire (OT;6).

Clare, Gilbert de An English nobleman of the mid–13th century who was allied to Simon de Montfort, Earl of Leicester (OT; 2,4).

Claremont A small but excellent California college attended by Carson Napier in the 1920s (V1;1).

Clarinda The false name given by Skipper Simms to his ship, the *Halfmoon*, while attempting to take the yacht *Lotus* in 1914 (K1;4).

Clark, Price One of the two Clark brothers at whose Mexican ranch Billy Byrne, Bridge and the Hardings withstood Pesita's final assault in March of 1916 (K2;17).

Clark, Westcott One of the two Clark brothers of early 20th century Mexico (K2; 17). See also **Clark, Price**.

Claude, Father An old priest of a hamlet near Torn in mid–13th century Derbyshire, who became the good friend of Norman of Torn in 1256 and taught the young man about chivalry, fair play and Christian ideals. This made him as hated by de Vac as he was loved by everyone else (for his wit and good nature), because he was jeopardizing the old man's plans by keeping Norman from becoming a complete scoundrel (OT;6,8). After knowing Norman for some time, he began to suspect the truth about the young man's birth and eventually arranged a meeting between him and Simon de Montfort to let the noble know of his suspicions. Unfortunately, he was murdered on the eve of the meeting by de Vac, who of course could not let the truth come out lest his revenge be spoiled. So died Norman of Torn's best friend and advisor; he was buried at Leicester after being found the next day by de Montfort (OT;13–15).

Claudius Caesar   (Full name Tiberius Claudius Drusus Nero Germanicus)(10 B.C.–54 A.D.) The nephew of Emperor Tiberius Caesar, a stutterer who was thought to be an idiot, but was actually quite shrewd. Britannicus appears to have pierced his front, as he considered Claudius' "idiocy" to have been a careful deception calculated to preserve himself from the dagger (I;1,6).

Claudius Taurus   The best-known professional gladiator of the lost Roman city of Castrum Mare in the early 1920s (T12;21).

Clayton, Jack   Tarzan's son by his wife, the former Jane Porter of Baltimore. When he was less than a year old, he was kidnapped by Nikolas Rokoff and Alexis Paulvitch with the intent to make Tarzan suffer slowly by worrying about his son's fate forever while stranded on an island and powerless to help him. Rokoff planned to give the baby to a tribe of African cannibals to be raised as one of their own (T3;1–4) but was double-crossed by Paulvitch, who changed the baby for another in the hopes that he could later ransom it to Tarzan's family. Paulvitch was in turn double-crossed by his partner in the deal, who ransomed the child to Tarzan's lawyers a few days after Paulvitch and Rokoff left for Africa (T3;21).

Ten years later, Jack was already as large and strong as a strong grown man, and was terribly interested in Africa and wild animals, an interest his mother did her best to discourage for fear he would run off into the jungle to be like his father. This misguided concern of course only encouraged the boy's interest, and he once even disobeyed her to go to see a trained great ape called Ajax at a music hall. The ape was actually Akut, Tarzan's friend from Jungle Island, who had allowed himself to be taken to England by the newly rescued "Michael Sabrov" (actually Alexis Paulvitch) in order to find Tarzan. In one of his music hall performances, he saw Jack and recognized Tarzan in him, coming into his box and snuggling up to him. "Ajax's" trainer demanded he leave the box, but the ape refused and it took Tarzan's arrival (to

fetch the disobedient boy) to break up the altercation. Tarzan then told Jack the story of his life, hitherto kept from him, after the boy realized that Tarzan had actually spoken with Akut. Afterwards, the boy secretly visited the ape often in an attempt to learn his language, and succeeded to a small degree.

It was about this time that Tarzan succeeded in buying the ape (who had refused to go back on stage again after seeing Tarzan) and extracting Paulvitch's promise to send him back to his home on Jungle Island. The boy was supposed to return to boarding school about this time, but instead sneaked away to Paulvitch's to escort Akut to Dover, planning to arrive at school about a week late. The Russian, anxious for revenge against Tarzan, tried to kill the boy and would have done so had not Akut burst his bonds and saved him. Jack then disguised the ape as an old invalid woman (complete with veils and wheelchair) and took him back to Africa, but in the process of getting the disguised ape off the ship and into a boat to get to the shore, his roll of money fell out of his pocket, unbeknownst to him. Later that night an American criminal who had been on the ship and seen Jack's money broke into his room to rob him, but was killed by the protective Akut, after which the boy became convinced that both he and the ape would be hanged as murderers. Having no money, their only recourse (he thought) was flight into the jungle (T4; 2–4).

Hoping to make his way back to civilization, Jack headed north and west, intending to circle around the outpost they had left and head back to another coastal town. During this month of travel, he became more proficient in the **Tongue of the Great Apes** and more versed in jungle lore. He came to hate the black Africans after being attacked by a tribe of them, at which time Jack killed his first man. Not much later, he encountered the safari of **Sven Malbihn** and **Carl Jenssen** and approached them, only to be shot at by the nervous Malbihn and the superstitious natives. This incident drove the boy further from civilization and into the interior to seek out the great apes, whom he felt would be friendlier. Eventually the boy became a great ape-man like his father, mighty in the ways of the jungle and named by Akut **Korak**, which means "killer." After their rejection by the great apes the two lived alone in the jungle, seeking no one out for company until they discovered Meriem, who joined them in their jungle life (T4;6–10). Eventually, after several adventures, Jack was rediscovered by Tarzan and brought home again, where he married Meriem (T4;27).

When World War I broke out, he enlisted and was sent to the Argonne, but was given leave to go and seek out his father and mother when they disappeared, eventually tracking them to Pal-ul-don, where he saved them by demonstrating the "divine power" of his Enfield rifle against the evil Lu-don and his followers (T8;2–12,24–25). Years later, he taught Tarzan to fly an airplane, a skill he himself had learned in the armed forces (T10;2).

There is a problem with the chronology of Jack Clayton's life, however. He was born around the beginning of 1912, which would have made him ten around 1922 — long after the end of World War I. Perhaps there were actually two "Jack Claytons" — that is, two sons of Tarzan — whom Burroughs took literary license to combine into one. The first would have to have been born before Tarzan's discovery by the Europeans at age 20 (in 1909), possibly of a native woman. This would have made the first son a half-breed and illegitimate and thus unacceptable to Burroughs' early 20th century readership. Another possibility is that the first meeting of Tarzan and Jane took place much earlier than Burroughs tells us, perhaps in their mid-teens, which would allow the first son to be theirs, but still born out of wedlock and thus equally unacceptable to early 20th century audiences. Unfortunately, we may never know.

Clayton, Jack, Jr. The son of Korak and Meriem; Tarzan's grandson (T10;1).

Clayton, Jane Even after her marriage to Tarzan, Jane's adventures were not over. They lived happily for almost two years and Jane bore Tarzan a son named Jack, but their happiness was shattered in 1912 when Nikolas Rokoff escaped from prison and kidnapped Jack, then lured Tarzan into a trap as well. Jane, realizing too late that the summons her husband had received (from the disguised Alexis Paulvitch) was a trap, followed just in time to be captured herself and taken to Africa with Tarzan and the baby. She escaped the ship with the help of Sven Anderssen, the ship's Swedish cook, and with a baby Anderssen at first thought hers. They fled up the Ugambi River with Rokoff in hot pursuit; Jane soon realized that the baby she had rescued from the Kincaid (who was the only baby on the ship) was not hers, but she loved and cared for it anyway until it died on the day Rokoff caught up with and recaptured her at the village of the Waganwazam, to whom Rokoff had planned to give the baby to raise as a cannibal. After it died, he decided to give Jane to the chief, M'Ganwazam, as a wife after he had had her first. She escaped from him, however, just before Tarzan arrived to save her. She then fled downriver in a dugout, coming onto the Kincaid while its crew was on shore and the watchmen drunk in the forecastle, into which she locked them, thus commandeering the vessel and preventing the pursuing Rokoff from boarding. Tarzan arrived soon afterward, and they escaped the explosion of the Kincaid together, but she became the victim of a kidnap plot by Schneider, first mate of the Kincaid. Tarzan saved her again, and they commandeered the Cowrie (a mutiny ship which had arrived at the island secretly and was assisting Schneider) and returned to England, where they found out that Paulvitch had double-crossed Rokoff and switched another baby for Jack, whom he had planned to hold for ransom in England. Paulvitch's confederate there had in turn betrayed him and collected a ransom for the child, who had been safe at home all along (T3;1–2,9–21).

For the next ten years (see Clayton, Jack for problems with this chronology), she did her best to discourage Jack's interest in Africa for fear he would want to live there as his father had, but her efforts were to no avail — Africa and wild animals were his only loves. After he ran away to Africa and was presumed dead, Jane was understandably crushed, but eventually recovered and she and Tarzan returned to his African estates to live, there adopting Meriem a few years later without realizing that the "Korak" of whom the girl continuously spoke was her son. She loved Meriem as a daughter and re-civilized the girl in about a year, but her happiness was complete when Jack was found, married Meriem, and moved back to England with them (T4;2,14–18,27).

In 1913, she was kidnapped by Arab slave raiders while Tarzan was away at Opar. Tarzan, rendered amnesiac by a concussion, took a long time to come for her, and when he did come he brought with him the ape Taglat, who took Jane for himself and carried her off into the jungle. He was killed by a lion, but Jane soon afterward fell into the clutches of the traitorous Albert Werper, who intended to hold her for ransom. She was later taken from him by Abdul Mourak, but rescued by a recovered Tarzan and taken home (T5;6, 16–17,23–24).

In the autumn of 1914, she was kidnapped by a detachment of German troops under Hauptmann Fritz Schneider, and Tarzan's bungalow was burned and destroyed. For some time Tarzan thought her dead, but eventually found out otherwise (T7) and tracked her and Lt. Obergatz, who had taken custody of her from Schneider, southward into the lost land of Pal-ul-don. Here she had been captured and imprisoned by the Ho-don in their city of A-lur, where both the high priest Lu-don and the king Ko-tan wished to marry her, thinking her to be a goddess because she had obviously been born without a tail (they believed their gods to be so). When civil war broke out in A-lur, Jane was kidnapped by the pretender Mo-sar but soon escaped into the forest and set herself up in a tree house until Tarzan came to save her and brought her back to his bungalow and her family (T8;17–21,24–25)(T9;1–2).

When Tarzan was trapped in the Valley of the Temple of Diamonds in 1917, Jane set out with a group of Waziri to find him but was abducted by the traitorous Luvini, the head man of the Flora Hawkes expedition, who had betrayed his white employers and tried to kill them. She escaped, though, and was found and rescued by Tarzan a few hours later (T9;17,20–21).

Jane did not take direct part in any of Tarzan's adventures after that until 1934, when a private plane on which she was returning to Nairobi from London was lost in a storm and made a forced landing near the country of the Kavuru, a strange race of white savages. Jane, with the woodcraft she had learned from Tarzan, was the only thing holding the little party of survivors together until she was abducted by a Kavuru warrior and taken to their temple (T19;1–21). While there, the priest-king of the Kavuru fell in love with her (or at least lust) and revealed to her the Kavuru's secret of immortality as the price of her love. She of course resisted him, and was saved

eventually by Tarzan, returning home with the immortality pellets so they could be young again and stay that way ever after (T19;24, 27–31). See also Porter, Jane.

Clayton, John (Jr.) Tarzan's English name (T3;1).

Clayton, John (Sr.) A young British nobleman, Lord Greystoke, who was sent to British West Africa by his government in 1888 to investigate mistreatment of black British subjects there by the officers of a friendly (unnamed for diplomatic reasons) European power. He never reached his post because he and his wife, the former Alice Rutherford, were put ashore following a mutiny on his ship (the *Fuwalda*) in unexplored west African territory about 1500 miles north of Cape Town in Portuguese West Africa. He built a cottage there for his wife and himself, finishing it in one month but gradually adding to it for the next year until the day his wife died, because he himself was killed by the king ape Kerchak the very next day. His remains were discovered and finally buried by his nephew William Clayton and the Porter party 20 years later, at which time his diary was found and his story first made known to the world (T1;1–4,13,17).

Clayton, Mrs. A friend of Ruth Morton Scott's in early 20th century Scottsville, Virginia. It is not known whether there was any relation, however distant, between herself and John Clayton, Lord Greystoke (ME;1).

Clayton, William Cecil Tarzan's cousin, the son of his father's younger brother, who inherited Tarzan's rightful title in his absence. He was stranded by mutineers (along with Professor and Jane Porter and the Professor's secretary and maid) on the African coast at the same place as his uncle had been left more than 20 years before, probably because of the very visible Clayton cottage that the mutineers had discovered. Soon after their arrival, the somewhat senile Professor Porter wandered off into the jungle and Clayton was forced to pursue. He was soon lost, but was rescued by Tarzan and brought back to the cottage (T1;13–15). After Tarzan rescued Jane from Terkoz, Clayton became jealous of his cousin (whom he of course did not know was such) and began to insinuate nasty things about him to Jane, whom he was in love with. Jane of course defended him, but after the

French rescue cruiser had waited a week at Jane's insistence, she was forced to give up her vigil and return with the others to civilization (T1;22,24). Clayton wanted to marry her then, but she was to marry Robert Canler instead, so he would forgive her father's debt. After Tarzan's "persuasion" of Canler to revoke his suit, Clayton chanced to ask Jane to marry him before Tarzan did, and in her confused state of conflict between primal passion and the need for security and social comfort she said yes, regretting it an hour later when Tarzan proposed to her. She decided not to break her promise to Clayton, and soon afterward Tarzan received a telegram notifying him that he had been proven the real Lord Greystoke, but because his taking Clayton's title, money and lands (although they rightfully belonged to Tarzan) would rob Jane of them as well, Tarzan decided to tell no one (T1;28).

A few minutes later, Clayton found the crumpled telegram which Tarzan had discarded and immediately recognized its significance. Becoming fearful, he tried to push Jane into marrying him immediately, but she did not acquiesce, putting the wedding off until after their planned cruise around Africa on the *Lady Alice*, Lord Tennington's yacht, should be completed (T2;12). When the yacht was wrecked off the coast of Portuguese West Africa, he was in the same lifeboat with Jane and "Mr. Thuran," the disguised Nikolas Rokoff, and was without food or water for over a week when they became separated from the other three lifeboats. They built a crude shelter and lived near the beach for two months. During that period a lion once attacked them, and after Clayton shrank in fear from it, Jane realized that she could never marry a lesser man than Tarzan, and told Clayton so in no uncertain terms (T2;18,21).

He died about two months after Jane's abduction by the Oparians, of a jungle fever which "Mr. Thuran" had abandoned him in the midst of. Tarzan and Jane found him a few hours before he died, after their return from Opar, and he told Jane the truth about Tarzan by giving her the crumpled telegram, which he had saved, thus proving himself an honorable man before he died. He was buried beside Tarzan's cottage, next to the grave of his uncle (T2;24–26).

Clinker The agent of Larry Divine, who found a ship and crew of cutthroats for Divine to abduct Barbara Harding with (K1;2,10).

clock, Barsoomian The clocks of Barsoom have four concentric circles marked on their faces. Between the innermost and next to innermost circles are marked the zodes, between the latter circle and the penultimate are marked the xats, and between the penultimate and last are marked the tals. The clocks have three hands of different length and color (M10:4;11). Wrist chronometers in ornate bracelets are common all over Barsoom and have been for millennia, even in backward places like Manator (M3;3)(M5;22).

clothes, Tarzan's Tarzan began to wear the clothes and accoutrements of the black warriors he had killed, out of the desire to be like other humans (as his picture books had taught him he was) rather than like the apes. He became proud of being a man and wore his clothes to show all the jungle-folk that he was one, and not an ape. He learned to shave for the same reason, because he feared the growth of hair on his face meant he was turning into an ape (T1;13).

clothes, Unisan To conserve material and labor all Unisans were allowed three suits of clothes, two for ordinary wear and one for work. They were skin-tight and made of an indestructible plastic resembling metallic sequins. The clothes were colored according to the social group the wearer belongs to, as follows: Fighting men wore blue, police red with black boots, scientists black with white boots, messengers wear yellow, workers brown, unmarried women gold with red boots, married women silver, and widows purple. The clothes were sold and resold as the wearer's status changed (B1;1–5).

Cloud People An Amtorian race inhabiting the Mountains of the Clouds on Anlap. They have paper-thin skin of the color of a corpse that would dry out in anything less than 100 percent humidity, so they protect themselves by completely covering up in fur if they have to go down out of the clouds. They have no pores and so cannot sweat, panting instead; they are entirely hairless and have great, bulging eyes and tiny noses, making them extremely hideous. They are not evil, however, wishing mostly to just be left alone, and they do understand gratitude and honor (V4;55).

Clovi One of the tribes of the Mountains of the Thipdars in Pellucidar. The village of Clovi is not very far from the village of Zoram, and the men of the two tribes frequently steal each other's women for wives (P4;7).

club, Pal-ul-don The Ho-don and Waz-don of Pal-ul-don used a heavy club which served the functions of both weapon and shield. It was also balanced for throwing (T8;21).

Cluros The farther moon of Barsoom, called **Deimos** by Earthmen. It orbits Mars at a distance of about 14,500 miles and circles the planet in "something like thirty and one quarter hours." It is usually conceived of poetically as a male and married to **Thuria**, the nearer moon (M1).

Cluvius A consul of Rome at the time of Caligula's assassination (I;21).

Co-si-to Chief of the Chi-e-a-hen Apaches in the late 1800s (A1;3).

Co-tan The beautiful Galu cos-ata-lo of Caspak whom **John Bradley** rescued from Oo-oh in September of 1916. They lived in the woods of the uninhabited part of the **Wieroo** island for almost a year before managing to capture two Wieroos and force them to carry them back to the mainland. It was not until after all of this time that Bradley realized that he loved the girl as much as she evidently loved him, and after they rescued Bradley's friends from the Germans of the U-33 (who had returned for more fuel) and recaptured the sub, they were married and set out for California along with the *Toreador* (C3;2–5).

Cobarth, Baron von A nameless German nobleman with a price on his head who joined **Norman of Torn**'s mid–13th century bandit force and became one of its captains (OT;12).

cobbler's pretty daughter A bright, loyal young lady friend of **Hilda de Groot**, whose name is unknown. She went around with **Count Max Lomsk** until he was exiled, then married **William Wesl**, the bookkeeper-cum-revolutionary at whose home **Prince Ferdinand** met with Hilda for years, and who was framed for the assassination of **King Otto**. She was smart enough to figure out that Carlyn had framed and killed her husband, so

when he tried to get cozy with her later, she pretended to get cozy with him just long enough to get him alone and kill him (LL;7,9, 15–23).

Coblich The Luthanian Minister of War under the regency of **Prince Peter of Blentz**, from 1902 to 1912. He was the prince's most trusted creature, and carried out much of his dirty work for him, such as the kidnapping of the "Mad King" Leopold from the Tafelberg Sanatorium in November of 1910 and his attempted murder soon afterward (MK1;1, 9–11). He returned to Lutha with Prince Peter in August of 1914, but was arrested after **Barney Custer** became king of Lutha and committed suicide soon after (MK2;2–3,16).

Coburn The navigator of the first warship on which **Jefferson Turck** served (LC;1).

cochino (*Sp*) Pig (K2;13).

Cochise (1815?–1874) A great chief of the Cho-kon-en Apaches who led a series of very successful raids against white settlers and wars against American troops in the 1860s and 70s. He rose to become war chief of all of the Apaches, then died of a fever in June of 1874, leaving **Go-yat-thlay** (**Geronimo**) as the new war chief (A1;1,3).

Cocom The tyrant ruling house of Mayapan in the Yucutan, lineal descendants of **Ah Cuitok Tutul Xiu**, who had founded the original city of **Uxmal** in A.D. 1004. The entire family was destroyed in 1451 by **Chab Xib Chac**, "the Red Man" (T24;1).

Cocos Islands "Big Jon's" name for the Keeling Islands (T22;29).

codon A giant wolf of the Pleistocene, often a solitary rather than a pack hunter (P3; 10).

coffee Black coffee, especially late at night, was Tarzan's only vice (T9;5).

coins *see* **money**

Colby, Hal A very handsome, cultured young cowpoke of the **Bar-Y Ranch** in 1880s Arizona who tricked **Bull** into going into town drunk while **Elias Henders** (the ranch owner) was there, and so got Bull demoted from foreman and himself promoted to that position. He then set out wooing **Diana Henders** with the intent of getting both the beautiful girl and her property. He was also the notorious Bandit of Hell's Bend, the Black Coyote, and used his position as foreman to arrange for very damaging circumstantial evidence to fall upon Bull, whom he almost succeeded in getting lynched (HB;1–13). When the beautiful, seductive Lillian Manill came to the ranch in an attempt to swindle her cousin Diana out of it, she seduced Colby and got him to help her and her partners until the whole scheme was revealed by Bull, who had found them out (HB;9–16). Later, Colby was captured as the Black Coyote by Bull, but was sprung by his accomplice, the crooked sheriff Gum Smith. He then took the abducted Diana Henders from his gang for his own lustful purposes, but was found and killed by Bull to save the girl (HB;17–19).

Colby, Orrin The minister of the secret church in the woods near Chicago in Kalkar-occupied 22nd century America. He was a blacksmith, but his great-grandfather had been a Methodist minister, and so he was the closest thing to a clergyman the group had. It was he who performed the marriage ceremony of Julian 9th and Juana St. John. He was killed in the first battle of the revolution (MM2;7,11).

Colchester An English city of eastern Essex near which the castle de Tany lay in medieval times (OT;15).

Coldwater An aero-sub of the SS-96 class commanded by Lt. Jefferson Turck in 2137, at that time an aging and unreliable craft that should have been scrapped years before. Her gravity screen generators went out during a storm while patrolling the line of 30 degrees west longitude, stranding the ship on the stormy ocean. After its engines were sabotaged, it was then swept east over the forbidden 30 degree line. It was subsequently repaired and headed home, abandoning Lt. Turck in mid-ocean in a launch (LC;1).

Cole Codoveg A Briton king or chieftain of the third century A.D., from whom Carson Napier was descended on his mother's side (V4;6).

Colfax A Saxon castle of England, built by Ethelwulf in the mid 800s A.D. (OT;9).

Coll A hideous old hag in the service of Peter of Colfax in the mid–13th century (OT;9).

collars, golden *see* mating, Barsoomian

College Inn A Chicago restaurant patronized by Danny "Gunner" Patrick in the 1920s (T15;23).

Collier Quay A wharf of early 20th century Singapore (PB;11).

Collis, Lady Barbara The daughter of the first Earl of Whimsey, an intrepid aviatrix of the 1920s and 30s who attempted to cross Africa by plane in 1929 but was forced to bail out over the Ghenzi Mountains, landing in the hidden land of Midian, where she was at first considered an angel from God until she began to oppose the hideous religious practices of the Midianites. She was then branded a blasphemer and would have been executed if not for the timely arrival of Dr. Lafayette Smith, who saved both Lady Barbara and her Midianite friend Jezebel from crucifixion and burning, only to fall into the hands of the North Midianites. They were rescued soon afterward by Tarzan, and Lady Barbara and Dr. Smith seemed to be on the verge of a relationship; at least she promised to teach him to shoot straight when they got back to England (T15;1–2,6,9–12,14–19,26).

Cologne A great industrial city on the Rhine, completely obliterated by the time Lt. Jefferson Turck visited its site in the summer of 2137 (LC;6).

Colombia South American nation, original home of the wizards Woora and Mafka, and from which they brought the Great Emerald of the Zuli (at least, this was Lord's theory) (T21;5).

Colonial Office The British department to which John Clayton, Lord Greystoke was attached. In this service he was sent to British West Africa, but never reached his destination nor returned to England (T1;1).

colors, Karlovan The colors of the tiny nation of Karlova were black and yellow (R;6).

colors, Unisan *see* clothes, Unisan

colors, Wieroo When a Wieroo of Caspak has committed a certain number of murders without being caught, he is given a robe with a yellow slash on it. More murders add more slashes until the entire robe is of yellow, after which the Wieroo is given a robe with a red slash on it. Still more murders add red slashes until the robe becomes entirely red, at which time he is given a curved knife as a weapon and symbol. Wieroos with yellow on their robes are considered very important, but individuals with completely red robes are more important still, and if one kills such a Wieroo he is tortured to death immediately, no matter how high ranking he is. Still more murders will earn an individual a white robe with a blue slash which is added to as before, but only He Who Speaks for Luata has a completely blue robe.

Blue is the color of murder, and every time a murder is committed in a room, a certain portion of that room is painted blue. When a room becomes completely blue it is shunned, and if every room in a house becomes completely blue the outside is painted blue as well and the building is used as a prison, torture chamber, etc., or else shunned altogether. There are many such places in Oo-oh. Skulls of people who have been murdered are painted blue when displayed, but those of known murderers are only streaked with blue (C3;3).

Colosseum The large, open arena of the lost Roman city of **Castra Sanguinarius**, modeled after the much larger one at Rome (T12;8).

Colossus The nickname of a very tall man of 1st century Rome whom **Caligula** had dragged through the streets and killed out of jealousy for his size (I;17).

Colt, Wayne Ostensibly, a wealthy American turned communist who went to Africa in 1928 to back the **Zveri** expedition. Actually, he was a U.S. government agent sent to spy on Zveri. He was one of the two members of the party brave enough to enter **Opar**, the others all fleeing at the hideous screams of its watchers. In a sense, they were rightfully afraid, since Colt was captured and would have been sacrificed had he not been released by the priestess **Nao**, who had become infatuated with him. Weeks later, he caught up with Zora Drinov, whom he found himself falling in love with, and saved her from **Abu Batn** by killing the **Arab**. They were again separated soon afterward when Zora was abducted by To-yat the great ape. Colt, blindly seeking her trail in the jungle, was eventually overcome by fatigue and fever and was only saved because of the arrival of **La** of Opar and **Jad-bal-ja**. Eventually, he was exposed as an American agent just in time to be befriended by Tarzan. He and Zora were also finally reunited after the girl killed Zveri to save Colt (T14;9-17).

Colt .45 A .45 caliber handgun popular from the late 1800s up until World War II for its stopping power, dependability and deadliness (T13;3)(D;2).

Columbia The American university from which **Joe "Datbum" Bubonovitch** had received his degree (T22;3).

Columbus A New Mexico town of Luna County, near the Mexican border, which **Pancho Villa** and his men raided on March 9, 1916, spurring the U.S. 13th Cavalry to pursue him into Mexico. They did not catch him (K2;17).

Columbus Blackie One of the hobos who tried to rob the "Oskaloosa Kid" of the loot from the **Prim** house in 1917 Oakdale, Illinois. He and his gang later attempted to rob and kill the "Kid" and his friends (**Bridge**, "Abigail Prim" and Giova), but Blackie was killed when Giova's bear **Beppo** went mad and attacked the bums (K3;1,10).

Comanche A large Indian tribe of the American West whose territory lay to the east of that of their hereditary enemies, the Apaches, and stretched from Colorado to New Mexico, including much of Texas. They were efficient raiders, but after ruinous wars with the whites and an epidemic of smallpox the tribe was decimated and the remainder moved to a reservation in Oklahoma in 1875 (A1;3).

Comanche County Fictional county of New Mexico, site of the events of *The Deputy Sheriff of Comanche County* (D).

combat, aerial, Polodan Combat between **Polodan** fighter aircraft tends to take place at an altitude of about 12 miles above sea level (B1;6,8).

compass, Barsoomian *see* **destination compass**

compensatory adjustment of masses The name **Fal Sivas** of **Zodanga** gave to the peculiar relationship existing between Barsoom and **Thuria** but not between other planets and their satellites. Any object traveling to Thuria would grow smaller until it had the same proportion to that world that it originally had to Barsoom, and objects travelling away from Thuria would get larger in proportion. Thus, Thuria seems to be an entire full-sized planet to anyone landing there (M8;12).

Compton, Elizabeth An attractive young socialite of 1910s Chicago, daughter of industrialist Mason Compton, who kept running into Jimmy Torrance at his menial jobs, often in places she herself was not supposed to be, and was thus very shocked when she found out that her father had employed him as an efficiency expert. She threatened to reveal him but was stopped by the knowledge Torrance had of her activities. She testified against him to the police after her father's death, but after the truth became known she apologized to him and made him general manager of her late father's company (EE; 5–7,11–14,20,25,28).

Compton, Mason The president and general manager of the International Machine Company of early 20th century Chicago and father of Elizabeth Compton. He hired Jimmy Torrance as his efficiency expert, a move which resulted in the discovery of Harold Bince's embezzlement and Compton's murder by Bince to cover up his misdeeds (EE;6,17–21,24).

concrete An artificial building material used in the construction of buildings on both Earth and Barsoom for many centuries. It was apparently even known to the ancient Atlanteans, because much of Opar is made of it (T2;19).

Conde, Roger de The alias adopted by Norman of Torn when he introduced himself to Bertrade de Montfort, so as not to frighten her with his reputation. It was as Roger de Conde that she fell in love with and pledged to marry him, but he could not accept her dedication until he told her the truth about himself two years later (OT;7,11,18).

Condon An American criminal who traveled to Africa on the same ship as Jack Clayton and Akut. He saw the large bundle of money that the boy carried and tried to steal it from him in his hotel, only to be killed by the enraged Akut (T4;4).

Congo Free State The African country (today the Republic of Zaire) which was taken

over by the Belgians under Leopold II, annexed, and claimed as the Belgian Congo in 1909. It was the original home of the tribe of Mbonga until it was forced to flee the exploitation and abuse of the Belgians and moved to the area of Portuguese West Africa where Tarzan grew up (T1;9,21).

Congo River A major river of west Africa, which lent its name to several African nations of the early 20th century. It flows from the interior of the present-day Republic of Zaire (in Tarzan's time, the Belgian Congo) to the Atlantic Ocean (T5;1).

Connecticut The American state in which David Innes was born (P1).

Constans, King The king of the tiny eastern European nation of Karlova in the first part of the 20th century, a bullet-headed individual whose son was the handsome Prince Boris (R;2).

Constantine, Father The French priest whose mission in Africa was the first European outpost Tarzan ever saw. d'Arnot brought him there during their journey back to civilization (T1;25).

controlling destination compass *see* destination compass

Cooper, Charity The maiden name of Mrs. George Burke (GH;10).

coovra In the language of Nadara's people, a snake (CG2;8).

Coppington English town, site of a supposedly haunted castle of the 1800s (C3;1).

cor *(Cpk)* From (C2;3).

cor sva jo "From the beginning" *(Cpk)*. The Caspakian expression for the way most animals (including humans) come to be, by developing from the tiny "tadpoles" produced in Caspakian females' ata ritual. Since the more primitive types occupy the south and the more advanced the north, the expression also means "from the south" (of Caspak) (C2;3).

Corbett, James John (Gentleman Jim) (1866–1933) American prizefighter from San Francisco, who knocked out the great John L. Sullivan in the 21st round to become the first World Heavyweight Champion under the Marquis of Queensbury rules. He was undefeated until 1897, when Bob Fitzimmons took his title (K1;18).

Coripies The Buried People of the island of Amiocap in Pellucidar, a horrible underground race of carrion eaters who occasionally attack a living thing for food. Coripies stand about five feet tall and are humanoid in form but not in features. Their feet are enormous and flat, with short, stubby, nailless webbed toes. Their arms are short and three-fingered with heavy claws. The creatures' heads are utterly repulsive, having holes for ears and a nose, loose, flabby lips, great fangs, and sealed eyes; these two great bulges roll about under the skin with no way of opening. The creatures are entirely hairless and as pallid as corpses, but are also enormously strong and very vicious. Their only diversions are sleeping and eating, particularly warm-blooded animals. In fact, they will eat anything warm-blooded as a break from their diet of fish, toads and carrion, including other coripies (P3;5,7–8).

Cornell University Ivy League college known especially for its science department, at which **Professor Arthur Maxon** taught biology in the 1920s until he quit to pursue his artificial life experiments (Q;1).

Cornwall The long, thin peninsula which makes up the southwest portion of England (LC;2).

Coronado, Francisco Vasquez de (1510–1554) Spanish explorer of Mexico and the southwestern U.S. who explored much of New Mexico, Arizona and the Colorado valley (A1;1).

corphal An evil spirit of Barsoomian mythology, in which the superstitious **Manatorians** still believe. A corphal was supposed to enter the bodies of the lowest of criminals to work its evil: it commanded evil spirits, and caused hallucinations in its victims to control their minds. A corphal could not be killed by a normal man, but a **jeddak** could slay one with impunity. Ghek the **Kaldane** and **Tara of Helium** were both accused of corphalism in Manator because of Ghek's appearance and actions (M5;13).

Corrigan, Dennis A man of the Teivos of Chicago in Kalkar-occupied 22nd century America. He was a member of a secret church group there, who had been sentenced to the mines for ten years for the crime of reading. He was freed from the mines (along with everyone else there) by Julian 9th and joined his rebellion, but was killed in battle soon afterward (MM2;4,7,11).

cors (*Pell*) Plains (P4;8).

Corson, Maurice B. John Manill's attorney in New York, who took care of his end of the **Henders-Manill** holdings while Manill was away in Europe. He was friends with Jefferson Wainright (Senior and Junior) and was in cahoots with them to swindle **Diana Henders** out of the **Bar-Y Ranch** and the Henders' mine. Corson went to work on her when he came out to see the property with **Lillian Manill** after the deaths of John Manill and **Elias Henders** in the 1880s. He knew that Lillian Manill had no claim to the property but hid that fact from Diana in order to fool her into a deal, and later to steal the property from her entirely. He was found out by **Bull**, who stole the real documents (showing Diana's complete ownership) from him and gave them to her. Not to be foiled, he arranged for her abduction in order to push the deal through, but was again found out by Bull and run out of town at gunpoint (HB;5,9–19).

Cortoran, Professor A 22nd century anthropologist who theorized that the reason for the English reversion to savagery was that after the **Great War** a mass exodus of the surviving English took place. They went across to Europe, expecting to find better land than their war-devastated country, and left behind only mentally defective or insane persons. The descendants of these abandonees, though sane and intelligent, were primitive and had no clear concept of their history and origins because they had had no one to teach them. Lt. **Jefferson Turck** had a similar theory in which the abandonees were children (LC;4).

Coruna The pirate ship of The Portuguese (PB;13).

cos (*Cpk*) "No" or "not" (C2;4).

cos-ata-lo "Not-egg-woman" (*Cpk*). The feminine form of **cos-ata-lu**. Cos-ata-los are rare among the **Galus** but nonexistent among the **Wieroos**, and so the latter abduct almost every baby cos-ata-lo born in order to perpetuate their species (C2;5).

cos-ata-lu "Not-egg-man" (*Cpk*). A Caspakian Galu or Wieroo born alive as a full member of his group, not forced to come cor sva jo. The feminine form is cos-ata-lo, and all such females can bear live young — the only Caspakian creature known to be capable of doing so. According to Galu religious thought, only a person who has completed seven cycles can be cos-ata-lu. The Wieroos steal almost every single female baby born this way from the Galus, so as to use them to try to produce female Wieroos. The reason for this was that both the Galus and Wieroos believed that the race that could eventually reproduce itself consistently, male and female, would become the dominant race of Caspak (C2;5).

coslupak "No man's land" (*Cpk*). The uninhabited areas between the territories of the different levels of humanity in Caspak (C2;4).

cosmology, Amtorian The Amtorians of the southern hemisphere conceive of their planet as a disk with upturned edges floating in a sea of magma, with the equatorial regions at the center of the disk and the polar regions at the outer circumference. This belief means that Amtorian maps are totally inaccurate and disproportionate to the point of being almost completely useless. It is believed that the outer cloud envelope is surrounded by fire (which occasionally breaks through when a break occurs in both cloud envelopes simultaneously). When a break occurs in the surface of Amtor, a volcano forms from the molten mass below. The fact that the "inner" border of the temperate zone is longer in circumference than the "outer" border is explained away by a peculiar bit of nonsense called the Relativity of Distance which insists that since all circles are of 1000 degrees (in Amtorian measure), all distances must be the same and are only different to human perceptions (V1;4).

cosmology, Julian The primitive Julian tribe of the post–Kalkar 25th century American West believed in a flat Earth that had been made by The Flag, which they worshipped (MM3;2).

cosmology, Mahar Like the Laytheans of Va-nah, the Mahars of Pellucidar thought of the universe as made entirely of solid rock, broken only by the cavity that is Pellucidar (P2;1).

cosmology, Minunian The Ant-men of Minuni believed that the Great Thorn Forest extended to the end of creation at the foot of the "blue dome" of the sky (T10;13).

cosmology, Pellucidarian The Gilaks of Pellucidar believed their world to be a flat disk surrounded by a high wall, floating on a flaming sea called Molop Az. The flaming rock of this sea was believed to be the source of volcanic lava. The dead buried in the ground were believed to be taken to Molop Az by tiny demons, and so most Pellucidarians preferred to hang their honored dead in trees so that the birds might bring them piece by piece to the Dead World, Pellucidar's "moon" (P1;10).

cosmology, Phundahlian The people of the city of Phundahl on Barsoom believe that they live on a flat planet created by their god, Tur, and thrown out into space from his home in the sun. They further believe that this happened 100,000 years ago (even though recorded Barsoomian history goes back farther) and that there are no other habitable worlds than Barsoom, despite proof to the contrary (M6;10).

cosmology, Va-nah The U-gas of Va-nah believed that the entire universe was composed of rock except for Va-nah, a habitable hole in the eternal stone. They did, however, concede that there might be other inhabited cavities to which the hoos (craters) might lead by way of long tunnels (MM1;6).

Cosoom The Barsoomian name for the planet Venus (M6;2). See also Amtor.

cottage, Tarzan's The cottage built by Tarzan's father, John Clayton, was later found and taken over by Tarzan. The nobleman built the original structure, a log cabin coated with clay, in about a month, but added to it for a year, eventually giving it a strong, thick door, very strong window gratings, a wooden floor and walls, and a cleverly fashioned wooden door lock that the great apes could not operate. After Kerchak killed Lord Greystoke, he accidentally closed the door in his retreat from the cottage, thus springing the lock and preventing the entry of the great apes for many years (T1;3–4). Tarzan was very curious about the cottage, and eventually (at the age of ten) figured out the trick of opening the lock and gained access to the building, where he discovered (among other things) his long-dead father's hunting knife and the books the Greystokes had brought along on their trip for their as-yet-unborn child's education, which indeed served that very purpose years later when the boy taught himself to read (T1;6–7). Tarzan moved into the cottage when he was about 20, but gave it up soon after for the **Porter** party to inhabit when they were stranded there by the mutiny of the crew of their ship, the *Arrow*, early in 1909. At this time they found a message from Tarzan claiming ownership of the cabin and warning them to steal nothing from it. They also found and buried the remains of Lord and Lady Greystoke (T1;13–17). After Tarzan was thrown off of his ship by **Nikolas Rokoff** in 1910, he returned to his cottage for a while, and later the survivors of the *Lady Alice* wreck landed nearby. Tarzan and Jane were married in it, and **William Clayton** buried beside it, next to his uncle's grave (T2;14,21, 25–26).

Cottonwood Canyon   A canyon lying some 20 miles from the **Bar-Y** ranch house in 1880s **Arizona**, named for a single cottonwood tree which grew at its mouth (HB;2).

coude   (*Fr*) Elbow; specifically, the elbow protector of a suit of plate armor (OT;15).

Coude, Count Raoul de   A French nobleman "high in the official family of the French Minister of War" whom **Nikolas Rokoff** and **Alexis Paulvitch** tried to frame for cheating at cards, but was saved by Tarzan, who had seen Rokoff drop some cards secretly in the unsuspecting nobleman's pocket. In this way Tarzan won the friendship of the count and the enmity of Rokoff and Paulvitch, who were attempting (while in disguise) to besmirch the honor of the count in order to blackmail him into giving them French naval secrets (for sale to the Russians) in return for their confession about the card game. He was later manipulated by Rokoff into catching the countess and Tarzan in a seeming tryst and challenged Tarzan to a duel. The ape-man let de Coude shoot him, inflicting two wounds, but refused to shoot back at the innocent count, instead giving him Rokoff's confession to read. Afterward, they became the best of friends, and de Coude got Tarzan a job as an agent with the French War Office, a post Tarzan was only too happy to accept because it sent him back to Africa (T2;4–7).

Coude, Countess Olga de   A Russian noblewoman married in her late teens to the French **Count de Coude**, a man 20 years older than she. She was a beautiful and intelligent young woman of 20 when, returning from America on a passenger liner, she caught sight of the handsome and sexy Tarzan and decided to befriend him, especially after he saved both her and her husband from the plots of her brother, **Nikolas Rokoff**. The latter was trying to frame them for honor-destroying incidents that he could use to blackmail the count into giving him French military secrets to sell to the Russians. Rokoff tried to make it look as if the count had cheated at cards, then tried to make it look as though the countess were having an affair with Rokoff's valet, **Alexis Paulvitch**. Tarzan foiled both of these plans, however, earning the countess' friendship and gratitude and Rokoff's hatred and enmity. She was later manipulated by Rokoff into a seeming tryst with Tarzan in which they were discovered by the count, who then challenged Tarzan to a duel. After the incident was over and the situation explained to the count, she paid Rokoff 20,000 francs to leave France and never return, which money he used to go to **Algeria** and attempt several times to have Tarzan killed (T2;1–6,9).

Council of the Seven Jeds   The ruling body of **Morbus**, city of the **hormads**. The jeds were all exceptionally intelligent hormads who had forced **Ras Thavas** to transfer their brains into handsome human bodies. They ruled the city and Ras Thavas with an iron hand, planning the conquest of all Barsoom with their enormous hormad army. Eventually, amid considerable internal strife, the third jed declared himself **Jeddak** of Morbus after conquering the whole island outside the city itself. He took the name **Ay-mad**, captured the city by night with the help of **Vor Daj/Tor-dur-bar**, and imprisoned the remaining six jeds (M9;5, 11–12).

Council of Three   The actual **Bolgani** rulers of the **Valley of the Palace of Diamonds**, a group of three Bolgani who made all decisions and "interpreted the commands" of the **Emperor Numa** (T9;13).

Council Ring   The great circular table belonging to the tribe of **Julian** around which the chiefs and warriors gathered to eat (MM3;1).

countries, Amtorian The following is a list of the countries of Amtor (city-states are in bold). See individual entries.

Andoo	**Hangor**	**Maltor**	Thora
Ator	**Havatoo**	Morov	Tonglap
Brokol	**Japal**	Mypos	**Torlac**
Falsa	**Kapdor**	Panga	**Vepaja**
Gavo	**Korva**	Samary	Vodaro
			Voo-ad

countries, Barsoomian The following is a list of the countries of Barsoom (city-states are in bold). See individual entries.

Amhor	**Invak**	**Okar**	Raxar
Duhor	Jahar	Onvak	Tjanath
Dusar	**Kaol**	Panar	**Toonol**
Gathol	**Kobol**	**Phundahl**	U-gor
Helium	**Manator**	**Ptarth**	

Court of Mystery The inner courtyard of **Professor Arthur Maxon**'s compound on his tiny island off of **Borneo**. It was christened by **Dr. Van Horn**, Maxon's assistant (Q;2).

cow, Polodan *see* cattle, Polodan

Cowrie A schooner carrying a cargo of pearls from the South Seas to Europe, whose crew (led by **Gust the Swede, Momulla the Maori**, and the "arch fiend," **Kai Shang of Fachan**) mutinied in the South Atlantic for the cargo and stopped off at **Jungle Island** to hide from a passing war ship in the last part of 1912, while Tarzan and the survivors of the *Kincaid* explosion were marooned there. With the help of **Schneider** (first mate of the *Kincaid*) the *Cowrie* mutineers kidnapped Jane, only to be caught and destroyed by Tarzan and the apes of **Akut**. Tarzan and **Mugambi** then commandeered the ship and headed back to Europe (T3; 20–21).

Coxey's Army A large group of unemployed men who, led by Jacob Sechler Coxey (1854–1951), marched to **Washington, D.C.**, in 1893 to demonstrate in favor of legislation to reduce unemployment (K3;1).

Coyote One of the warrior chiefs under Julian 20th in the post–**Kalkar** 25th century American West (MM3;1).

Coyote Canyon A small canyon east of **Hell's Bend Pass** near Hendersville, Arizona, in the 1880s (HB;14).

Coyote Springs A spring at the head of **Horse Camp Canyon** on the Rancho del Ganado (GH;24).

Cramer The supervisor of the west ranch portion of the **Bar-Y Ranch** in 1880s Arizona (HB;12).

Cranmer The gorilla of London in the Valley of Diamonds who insisted on bringing the captured **Rhonda Terry** to God, since she was an Englishwoman (well, American, close enough for a gorilla) (T17;18).

Crater Mountain A long-extinct Arizona volcano near **Corey Blaine**'s dude ranch (D;11).

Crawford, Captain Emmett One of the few American cavalry officers of the Old West who understood any of the **Apache** tongue or made any effort to understand and help the Apaches. He was greatly respected by them for it, and when **Geronimo** surrendered to **General Crook** on January 11, 1886, it was through Crawford that they parleyed. Later that same day, he was accidentally shot by a Mexican soldier in **Captain Santa Anna Perez**'s detachment and died instantly (A2; 4,8).

Crawford's Indian Scouts A detachment of **Cho-kon-en** and White Mountain Apaches, led by U.S. Cavalry **Captain Emmett Crawford**, who went to war against Geronimo in the spring of 1885 because they had given up rebellion and felt that the white men were cracking down on reservation Indians because of Geronimo (A2;6).

Crazy "B" Ranch The **Arizona** ranch owned by **Jefferson Billings**, passed to his daughter **Wichita** after his death in 1886 (A2;1–5).

Crazy J A ranch near the Bar-Y in 1880s Arizona (HB;2).

Crecy, Count of *see* Valois, Henri de la, Count of Crecy

Crecy, Countess of *see* Valois, Eugenie Marie Celeste de la, Countess of Crecy

Cretaceous The third and last period of the Mesozoic Era, lasting from 135 million years ago until 63 million years ago. It is probably the most publicly well-known era of prehistory, since the great dinosaurs were at their peak of power during this time. The mighty tyrannosaurus roamed the scene, as did triceratops, trachodons, and pterodactyls. The period ended with the mass extinction of the dinosaurs (P1).

cri de guerre (*Fr*) War cry (T11;18).

Crook, Major-General George U.S. Army general who negotiated a treaty with Geronimo in the late 1870s, and who commanded **Fort San Carlos** and its attendant Indian reservation. He chased down Geronimo when the old chief went out again in 1885 to 1886 and negotiated a new treaty with him in March of 1886, but was relieved of duty in the area after Geronimo and his warriors escaped in the night a few days later (A2;1–2,8–10).

Crossroads Inn An inn and restaurant with a rather bad reputation, lying north of Oakdale, Illinois, in 1917 (K3;10).

Crouch, Dr. The physician of the British yacht *Naiad*, captured by **Wilhelm Schmidt** and the mutineers of the *Saigon* late in 1938 (T24;6).

Crowell, Dora An extremely intelligent guest at **Corey Blaine's** dude ranch who wore an elaborate getup "that would have turned Tom Mix green with envy." She had been a schoolmate of **Olga Gunderstrom's** in Philadelphia and was the person who had summoned Olga to the ranch to help her forget her father's death (D;3,10,15).

Crowhop A somewhat ungentle horse of **Corey Blaine's** early 20th century dude ranch (D;3).

Crown Prince Nobbler **Bowen Tyler's** prize Airedale terrier, who was with him when he was captured by a German U-boat and so subsequently accompanied him to Caspak. He became very attached to **Lys La Rue** and was often left to guard her in Caspak. He disappeared thanks to **Kho the Stolu** on October 6, 1916 (C1;1–10). The dog eventually ended up in the hands of **Du-seen** the renegade Galu and served him well until he met up with **Tom Billings** (whom he had known since he was a puppy) late in the summer of 1917, when Billings came to rescue Tyler. The dog at that point immediately attached himself to Billings and attacked Duseen when he tried to reclaim him. He stuck with Billings until they met up with the Galus, who had in the meantime been joined by Tyler, and "**Nobs**" happily rejoined his master (C2;6–7).

Croydon Airdrome A small airport in the London suburb of Croydon where **Princess Sborov** kept her airplane (T19;1).

crucifix An heirloom of the **Samuels** family given to one of **Moses Samuels'** ancestors during **World War III** by a Catholic nun who nursed him back to health after he was wounded. It was a very fine work carved from the tusk of an elephant and was given to **Julian 9th** for **Juana** by Samuels as a wedding present because he had no heirs and wished to give it to those he loved the most. The **Kash Guard**, however, broke in and found the figure, using it as proof of Samuels' forbidden practice of religion and crushing it beneath his heel. Later, Julian found the pieces and repaired it almost as good as new (MM2;8).

Crumb The hobo accomplice of **Dink**, who would have stolen food from the eloquent **Bridge** had not **Billy Byrne** happened by. Later, Crumb and Dink phoned the police to get the reward placed on Byrne's head for the supposed murder of **Schneider**, and in the process robbed the wife of the farmer at whose home they made the call. They were again foiled by Byrne, however, and arrested soon afterward (K2;2,5).

Crumb, Wilson A famous motion picture actor/director of 1920s Hollywood whom **Eva Pennington** met and invited down to the Pennington ranch in 1922. He was actually a drug pusher as well, and had trapped the girl **Gaza de Lure** by getting her addicted to cocaine. He had her do the actual peddling from his house while he was busy at the studio, thus giving her the monetary means to eventually escape him. Crumb was true to his name — he tipped off the police, landing his supplier **Slick Allen** in jail for possession rather than pay him a large debt (GH;4–12) and seduced **Grace Evans** as he had Gaza, by tricking her into cocaine use and playing on her ambitions. Later, by threat of revealing her brother **Guy** as a bootlegger, he manipulated her into becoming his kept woman, and still later he threw her against a table during an argument, resulting in injuries that killed her; he thus turned Guy into a vengeance-seeker (GH;10, 27–28,30).

When he came to the Pennington ranch to film a movie in August of 1923, he recognized **Shannon Burke** as Gaza and tried to force her back to him, but was foiled by Shannon and **Custer Pennington.** Later, he tried to seduce Eva Pennington; to keep her from reporting his behavior he threatened to turn in **Guy Evans** (Eva's fiancé). The hurt, confused girl went home, reported him anyway, then attempted suicide. Crumb was murdered that night by Guy Evans for the murder of his sister, but even in death caused anguish — Evans went mad upon finding his beloved Eva "dead," and Custer would have been hanged for the murder had not Evans recovered his sanity in time to confess (GH;32–37).

Crump, Tom A notorious ivory poacher whom Tarzan chased out of Africa in the mid–1930s, but who came back in 1938 to try to track down Tarzan for the bounty that had been placed on his head by **Timothy Pickerall** for the abduction of his daughter, supposedly perpetrated by Tarzan (T23;2). He tried to track the girl down for a reward as well, and succeeded in doing so all the way to the **Ruturi** region, where he was captured by the **Galla** enemies of **Alemtejo** (T23;17,20). He and **Minsky** escaped during a battle between the villages, met up with the false Tarzan, and traveled with him until they happened upon the gold mine of Alemtejo, where they promptly loaded themselves down with more gold than they could carry in their exhausted state (T23;25–26). Crump killed Minsky soon afterward to get his gold, then died of dehydration within sight of a stream (T23;29).

Crusade, Third The third attempt by European Christianity to retake Palestine from the Moslems. It was on this crusade that the ancestors of the inhabitants of the **Valley of the Sepulcher** were embarked when they were shipwrecked in Africa in 1191 (T11;12).

cuirass The breastplate of a suit of armor, which can also be worn alone (T12;6).

cuisse (*Fr*) The thigh protector in a suit of full plate armor (OT;15).

Cuivaca A small Mexican town in Chihuahua, where Francisco "Pancho" Villa kept considerable funds in 1916 until Billy Byrne removed them. The **El Orobo Ranch** lay north of it (K2;8,10,12).

Cullinan A huge diamond found in South Africa in 1905, which weighed 3,106 carats (1.37 pounds) before cutting and was pronounced by crystallographers to be a fragment of a far larger stone which was never found. The stone was cut into 105 gems for a total of 1,063 carats, the largest of which is the Star of Africa (at 530.2 carats, the largest known cut diamond), which is set in the British Royal Scepter (T21;1).

Cullis, Margaret The wife of Captain Cullis of **Fort Thomas, Arizona.** She taught **Wichita Billings** proper English in 1879 (A1;18).

culture vats The vats in which **Ras Thavas** grew his **hormads** out of a culture of human tissue. Most hormads, though deformed, are able to function, but those who are too grossly deformed to even function as humans are chopped into tiny pieces and re-added to the culture, each piece becoming a full hormad in only nine days. Hormad parts severed in battle are also thrown into special culture vats, where they can grow new limbs, heads or even complete bodies. The culture vats are also used to grow synthetic food (M9;4,7).

Culver City A suburb of Los Angeles which lies about 15 miles southeast of **Tarzana** (T22;28).

Curtiss, Glenn (1878–1930) American aviation pioneer who improved on the early designs and built the first airplanes and seaplanes for general use by the U.S. military after 1912 (C1;1).

Curtiss, William A young gentleman of turn-of-the-century **Beatrice, Nebraska,** who was in love with **Victoria Custer.** He was the one living man who most closely matched her "dream man" and so she felt something for him, but that was utterly eclipsed when she had a vision of that "dream man," Nu, actually appearing in the flesh. In that vision, Curtiss began to feel a murderous hatred for Nu, a feeling powerful enough to change his personality so much that the dog **Terkoz** sensed it and hated Curtiss, eventually killing him when he tried to kill Nu (E1;2,4,8–9,13). Of course, this only happened in Victoria's vision, but even after awakening she would have nothing to do with Curtiss, who was perhaps a reincarnation of the ancient **Tur**, who had coveted **Nat-ul** 100,000 years ago (E2;15).

Custer, Bernard (Barney) An American gentleman farmer of **Beatrice**, Nebraska, whose mother had been a **Luthanian** princess. He came to see her home country for himself in 1912, only to be mistaken for **Leopold II**, the "Mad King" of Lutha, whom he strongly resembled, and thereby propelled into intrigue against **Prince Peter of Blentz**, Leopold's regent, who had been trying to kill him when Leopold escaped from Blentz, thus setting the stage for Custer's adventure (MK1; 1–4). Custer eventually succeeded in convincing a few people that he was not the king, and eventually rescued the real King Leopold from Prince Peter just before he was to have been killed. Leopold was thus replaced on his throne, but felt jealousy toward Custer because the nobles and people had come to admire him for his courage and nobility (apparent when Custer led the **Royal Horse Guard of Lutha** into battle against Prince Peter's forces), but especially because the king's betrothed, **Princess Emma von der Tann**, was in love with Custer. This jealousy caused Leopold to order the arrest and execution of Custer, who was thus forced to flee into **Austria** (MK1;8–12).

A few months later he went to the estate of **Lord Greystoke** (a.k.a. **Tarzan**) in Africa with his sister **Victoria** to hunt and forget Princess Emma, and it was there that he met Burroughs and told him his story. He figured largely in his sister's vision of **Nu** of the **Niocene** when they discovered the 100,000-year-old remains of a cave man (E1;4–9)(E2; 15).

In August of 1914 he became the victim of an assassination plot by Prince Peter and Captain **Ernst Maenck**, who came to Beatrice to fling bombs at Custer and almost got him twice. To protect his family and get to the bottom of the trouble, Custer pursued Maenck to Lutha by way of Austria, having several adventures along the way (like being mistaken for a **Serbian** spy and sentenced to death). Quick thinking and rapid reflexes saved him, and he made his way to Lutha, where a fortuitous set of circumstances allowed him to again impersonate Leopold and drive the invading Austrian army out of Lutha with Serbian help (MK2;1–11). Later, the real

Leopold was killed by Maenck (who had mistaken him for Custer), and so Custer, being the closest in line to the throne by virtue of his mother's blood, and being the logical choice for his great leadership ability (and the fact that no one would be the wiser for the switch except a few nobles), became King of Lutha and married Princess Emma (MK2; 12–16).

Custer, Victoria The younger sister of Barney Custer; a slender, graceful girl with "large, dreamy eyes" who was afraid only of mice and earthquakes, and nothing else. Why she was afraid of mice we do not know, but the earthquake fear was apparently because she had died in a tremendous upheaval 100,000 years before as **Nat-ul**, a fate she unconsciously remembered. She also remembered **Nu**, and since coming to womanhood had dreamed of him constantly, refusing to even be courted by others. As the time for Nu's reawakening approached, and as he grew physically nearer after his awakening, the visions grew stronger until she finally heeded the call within her and went to Nu, becoming almost entirely possessed by her Nat-ul personality and even remembering her ancient language (E1;2,4–7)(E2;14). After Nu rescued her from the **Arabs**, she went into a cave with him and somehow time traveled back to the Niocene, becoming Nat-ul and reliving their adventures in that long-ago time. She finally awakened again in the present after "dying" in an earthquake to the realization that everything after the earthquake had "freed" Nu had been a vision. She also realized that she was finally at peace after all of her years of haunting dreams, especially after finding the remains of Nu in the very cave from which he had come forth in her vision (E1; 12–13)(E2;1–15).

cutlass A curved sword similar to a scimitar, favored by European pirates of the 16th and 17th centuries (P3;1).

Cuyhenga A street of Hollywood, which runs north-south and crosses Hollywood Boulevard (GH;11).

cycads Palm-like trees which dominated the forests of the **Triassic** and **Jurassic** periods (P1;2).

cycle A level of eminence among the **Therns** of Barsoom. The tenth cycle is the level at which one becomes a **Holy Thern** (M2;4)(M3;3). Also, a calendric period used by the **Galus** of **Caspak**, equivalent to our century (C2;5).

Cyprus An island kingdom in the eastern Mediterranean, homeland of the women who were the female ancestors of the people of the **Valley of the Sepulcher.** They were taken from that island by the soldiers of the **Third Crusade** when **Richard I** stopped there on his way to the crusade to conquer the island in response to an insult its king had made to **Richard's** betrothed, **Berengaria** (T11;12).

da In the **Kapar** tongue, the pronoun "I" (B2;4).

Dacor the Strong One A mighty warrior of **Amoz** in Pellucidar, brother of **Dian the Beautiful.** He was made King of Amoz after **David Innes** killed **Jubal the Ugly One** and afterward swore allegiance to Innes and his newly-formed **Empire of Pellucidar** (P1;4,14–15).

Dag A Niocene warrior of the tribe of **Nu** who swore to seek out and rescue **Nat-ul** and **Nu, Son of Nu,** whom he had passed his manhood ordeal with (E2;9).

dagger On Barsoom, a weapon generally used only by women and sometimes assassins.

dahl (*Apa*) Coming (A2;6).

Daimon A demon that the **Athneans** believed killed unwary night travellers (T21;21).

daimyo The Japanese term for a feudal lord served by **samurais** (K1;9).

Daj A Pellucidarian warrior of **Lo-har** who killed **Frug,** Chief of **Basti** when the two were imprisoned together in the **Little Canyon** of the Mammoth Men of **Ja-ru.** He later guided **von Horst** to Lo-har after **La-ja** had abandoned him (P5;17,21–22).

dak (*Pal*) Fat (T8;2).

Dak-at "Fat Tail" (*Pal*). Chief of a rebellious **Ho-don** village which was subdued by **Ta-den** and his men. Dak-at was taken as a prisoner (T8;2).

Dak Kova A jed of the **Warhoons** on Barsoom. He killed the old **jeddak, Bar Comas,** and became jeddak of the horde shortly after John Carter was captured by them in 1866 (M1;18).

Dak-lot "Fat Face" (*Pal*). A **Ho-don** palace guard of **A-lur** who dared to try to touch the person of Tarzan, the self-appointed **Dor-ul-Otho** (T8;8).

dako (*Ape*) Thick (TC).

dako-zan "Thick-skin" (*Ape*). Meat (T24;13).

Dalfastomalo A Minunian nobleman of **Veltopismakus** who wagered with **Zoanthrohago** that his shrinking process would not last for the 39 moons that Zoanthrohago claimed it would (T10;9).

dan (*Amt*) The letter "D" (V4;32).

dan (*Pal*) Rock (T8;4).

dan-do (*Ape*) "Stop" or "cut it out!" (T20;31).

dan-sopu (*Ape*) Nut (TC).

Dan-voo-med "D-1,000,000" (*Amt*). The **Vooyorgan** guard who divided right before **Carson Napier's** and **Duare's** eyes — the first time they saw the process (V4;32).

Dance of Barsoom A stately and beautiful court dance of Barsoom. Before a youth attends a formal Barsoomian dance, he must learn this dance, the dance of his country, and that of his city. The music is provided by the dancers themselves on **monochords** strapped to each dancer's left forearm, and never changes — nor do the steps and figures. In John Carter's words, "the Dance of Barsoom is a wondrous epic of motion and harmony — there is no grotesque posturing, no vulgar or suggestive movements. It has been described as the interpretation of the highest ideals of a world that aspired to grace and beauty and chastity in woman, and strength and dignity and loyalty in man" (M5;1).

Dance of Death A method of ritual torture and execution meted out to the prisoners of the **Band-lu** of **Caspak**— what it exactly involves, we are not told (C2;3,5).

dancing-water The vile alcoholic beverage prepared and consumed by the **Ganaks** of Pellucidar, so called because it befuddles their minds and causes them to dance about (P5;20).

Dangar A Pellucidarian warrior of **Sari** whom **Wilhelm von Horst** met while they were both paralyzed victims in a **trodon** lair.

Having nothing to do but talk, Dangar taught von Horst the Pellucidarian language and they became friends. Later, when von Horst overcame his paralysis, he escaped with the still-paralyzed Dangar and stayed with him until he recovered. Later, Dangar led an expedition with David Innes to find von Horst (P5; 1–4,22).

Dango (*Ape*) The hyena (T1;9).

Danlot The lotokor (general) commanding the land fleet of Falsa when Carson Napier passed through Middle Anlap late in 1931 (V4;44).

dano (*Ape*) Bone (TC).

Danul Tangor's second servant while in Kapara as a spy in the summer of 1940. Danul was highly recommended by Lotar Canl (B2;8).

Danus The 500-year-old head librarian of Kooaad, who taught Carson Napier the Amtorian language and some details of Amtorian life when he first arrived there in 1929 (V1;4).

dar (*Bar*) A military unit consisting of 1000 men, analogous to an Earthly regiment (M7;1)(M10;3;4).

Dar Tarus A soldier of the guard of Xaxa, Jeddara of Phundahl on Barsoom. He was a very handsome man who was slain by one of Xaxa's assassins so that Sag Or, one of her favorite nobles, could have his brain transferred to Dar Tarus' body and woo the latter's girlfriend, Kara Vasa. Dar Tarus' brain was placed in the noble's healthy, though ugly body, and he was about to kill Ras Thavas in revenge when Ulysses Paxton appeared, slaying him to save the old surgeon's life. Later, Paxton resurrected him to aid Paxton in his abduction of Xaxa. The Barsoomian, anxious for revenge against the old woman, readily acquiesced. To Ras Thavas, Dar Tarus was subject #378-J-493811-A. Dar Tarus was eventually restored by Paxton to his own body and made Jeddak of Phundahl by command of the Great Tur. He also married Kara Vasa (M6;1–2,7,13–14).

darel (*Pell*) Shallow (P1;4).

Darel Az "Shallow Sea" (*Pell*). A shallow bay or inlet of the Lural Az in Pellucidar (P1;4).

Dareyem One of the followers of Ibn Dammuk who helped him to abduct La of Opar from Abu Batn in 1928 (T14;10).

Dark Swamp A treacherous morass of central Africa during the Niocene Era (E1;9).

d'Arnot, Lieutenant Paul Tarzan's first human friend, a French sailor from the cruiser that came to rescue the Porter party. While searching for Jane Porter in the jungle, he was captured by the savages of Mbonga's tribe who tortured him with the idea of eating him, but he was rescued by Tarzan and nursed back to health. During his convalescence he taught the ape-man to speak French. He was given up for dead by his own people, who left for civilization, but he and Tarzan journeyed on foot to a European outpost that d'Arnot knew and eventually got back to France. D'Arnot used the time to teach Tarzan of human manners, customs and language, including English (T1;19–25). It was also he who arranged to have Tarzan fingerprinted, proving that he was the Greystoke heir, whose fingerprints had been made in his father's diary. He let Tarzan live at his house in Paris, taught him to drive, and even helped him to buy a car (T1;26–28).

When Tarzan returned to Paris, he lived with d'Arnot, who again gave him money, helped him escape a plot by Nikolas Rokoff, and was generally a good friend. It was his ship that again rescued the Porters and their friends from the shipwreck of the *Lady Alice* in 1911 (T2;3–6,26). In 1912, Tarzan was visiting d'Arnot in Paris when he found out that Rokoff had escaped from the French prison where he had been incarcerated (T3;1). By the time ten years more had gone by, d'Arnot had progressed all the way to the rank of admiral (T24;27).

Many years later (in 1936) d'Arnot was once again engaged in an adventure with Tarzan, at this time being referred to as a captain (?). In any case, he convinced Tarzan to help Helen Gregory and her father to find Brian Gregory, who had been lost while looking for the Forbidden City of Ashair two years earlier and was presumed to be imprisoned there (T20;1–4). Tarzan led a small safari there, which d'Arnot accompanied since he had fallen in love with Helen Gregory. They were captured together and imprisoned in Ashair, but eventually escaped with the help of Tarzan and King Herat of Thobos

(Ashair's enemy), whom Tarzan had won as an ally. The party was escorted out of **Tuenbaka** with honors, and d'Arnot won Helen (T20;9,12,17–24,29–32).

Daroz One of the tribes of the **Mountains of the Thipdars** in Pellucidar, whose warriors often steal wives from **Clovi** and **Zoram**, and vice versa (P4;7).

darseen A small reptile; the Barsoomian chameleon (M4).

Darus An aged priest of **Opar** who remained loyal to La when Oah overthrew her for the second time in 1928 (T14;6).

dator Among the **First Born** of Barsoom, a prince — the strongest, most intelligent, and best trained of a race possessing all of those qualities to a high degree (M2;7).

David Elizabeth Compton's chauffeur, upon whom she relied to protect her when she did things she was not supposed to do. He was "a big young fellow" whom Elizabeth described as "a sort of Rock of Ages and Gibraltar all in one" (EE;11).

David I The name taken by **David Innes** as **Emperor of Pellucidar**.

Davis A sharpshooter for the Los Angeles Police Department in the 1920s (PB;9).

Davis, Staff Sergeant Bill One of the waist-gunners of the bomber *Lovely Lady*, brought down in the spring of 1944 while on a reconnaissance mission over **Japanese**-held Sumatra. He bailed out safely but was lost from the others, captured by the Japanese along with **Douglas** (the radioman), and rescued by Tarzan a few weeks later. He was one of the "legionnaires" who survived to reach Sydney (T22;8,26,30).

day, Amtorian The Amtorian day is 26 hours, 56 minutes, 4 seconds long and is divided into 20 equal segments called **te** (V1; 10). Twenty days make an **ax**, or Amtorian month (V3;4).

De-klu-gie The chief of the **Ned-ni** Apache after **Shoz-dijiji** killed **Juh** (A2;1).

Dead World A small planetoid which orbits the Pellucidarian sun in exactly the same time it takes the Earth to rotate, so that it seems to hover exactly above one area, the **Land of the Awful Shadow**. The Dead World

is believed by Pellucidarians to be the site of their afterworld, so the honored dead are placed in trees to be taken piece by piece to the Dead World by the birds, instead of down to **Molop Az** by the little **demons** as those buried in the ground are (P1;10). The Dead World has vegetation, water and landforms of its own, and its rotation allowed **David Innes** to bring time to Pellucidar by observation of its rotating landmarks. He believed it to be only a mile above the surface of Pellucidar, but it would have actually had to be about 70 or 80 miles in diameter and orbit at about 500 to 1000 miles above the surface to account for the size of the shadow observed on the ground (P2;6,15).

Dearborn Avenue The site of **Farris'** brothel on the south side of early 20th century Chicago (GF;9).

The Death A name for several different forms of ritual execution on Barsoom. In **Lothar**, "The Death" means being fed to the banth-god **Komal**, either secretly or in public (M4;8). In **Tjanath**, "The Death" consists of being lowered into a deep, mysterious pit in a cage which, after descending a certain distance, has its bottom pulled out, precipitating its contents into the river **Syl**, which runs beneath Tjanath. From the moaning, shrieking echoes of the river, the superstitious Tjanathians have conjectured horrible tortures, but the reality is just as bad — a monster-filled cavern first, then farther downriver the horrible city of **Ghasta** (M7;7).

The Death was also the name of the plague (probably a man-made bacteriological weapon) which spread across England in the 1930s of *The Lost Continent*, forcing mass evacuations to the continent in pursuit of the Germans who had conquered England and released the weapon. By August of 1937, the country was almost completely deserted and civilization had collapsed (LC;5).

death-tree The burning-stake of the Ganaks of Pellucidar, a small tree stripped entirely of its branches and set in the ground upright (P5;20).

debt On Barsoom, delinquent debtors are sent to work in mines or on farms, performing hard labor far from home that no free man would willingly do (M1;20). It was because of **Professor Archimedes Q. Porter**'s debt to **Robert Canler** that Porter's daughter, **Jane**, was to be forced to marry Canler (T1;18,27–28).

degree, Amtorian The Amtorians divide the circle into 1000 degrees, so each is equal to 21 minutes, 36 seconds of arc in terrestrial measure (V1;4). See **Hita.**

Deimos *see* **Cluros**

Dejah Thoris The daughter of **Mors Kajak, Jed** of **Lesser Helium;** granddaughter of **Tardos Mors, Jeddak** of **Helium;** wife of **John Carter** of **Virginia;** she was certainly the most alluring creature on at least two worlds. Often called "incomparable," her beauty has been the cause of wars on Barsoom just as Helen's was on Earth. Like others of her race, Dejah Thoris has copper-colored skin and coal-black hair.

On an 1866 mission to chart atmospheric phenomena, her battleship was brought down in a sneak attack by the **green men** of **Thark.** She was captured, but helped to escape by John Carter, who had fallen in love with her. After a series of adventures, they were married and had at least two children, **Carthoris** and **Tara,** both of whom had adventures of their own. After the loss of Carthoris in the south, while John Carter was missing and presumed dead (and long before the birth of Tara), Dejah Thoris was pressured by **Zat Arras** to marry, and escaped only by taking **The Pilgrimage.** She was captured en route by the **Black Pirates** and taken to **Issus** as a slave. When it looked as though the fall of Issus was imminent, Dejah was locked in the **Temple of the Sun** with **Thuvia** of **Ptarth** and **Phaidor,** who tried to kill Dejah out of jealousy, but was foiled by Thuvia (M2). Before her year of imprisonment was up, however, she was kidnapped by **Matai Shang** and taken to **Kaol,** then **Okar,** but was found and rescued by John Carter (M3).

Many years later, while John Carter was waging his secret war against the **assassins' guild** of **Zodanga,** she was kidnapped by **Ur Jan,** leader of the guild, to ensure that John Carter would not trouble the guild anymore. She was taken in **Gar Nal's interplanetary flier** to **Thuria,** forcing her husband to follow in the similar ship built by **Fal Sivas.** On Thuria she was imprisoned by the **Tarids** along with her abductors and rescuers (M8; 10–16). They all eventually escaped after declaring a truce, but Gar Nal betrayed them

and kidnapped Dejah Thoris back to Barsoom. She was found and rescued by John Carter (M8;21–24). Years later, her back was broken in an aviation accident, forcing John Carter to seek out the missing **Ras Thavas,** the only surgeon with enough skill to mend it. He was of course found and Dejah Thoris healed (M9;1,29). Her last known adventure was her abduction by the **Morgors,** the hideous **Skeleton Men** of **Jupiter,** to force John Carter to divulge information on Barsoom's defenses so the Morgors could conquer it. John Carter of course rescued her and took her back to Barsoom (M11B;5–6,9).

Delcarte One of the three sailors of the aero-sub *Coldwater* who were abandoned in a power boat with **Lt. Jefferson Turck** around 20 degrees west longitude in 2137. After Turck's capture by the **Abyssinians,** Delcarte and **Taylor** were found by **Pan-American** ships at the mouth of the **Rhine,** thanks to **John Alvarez's** work to lift the 30 degree ban (LC;1–2,7–9).

Delgadito A great **Apache** warrior of the early 19th century (A1;2).

Delmonico's An expensive restaurant of late 19th century New York (HB;11).

demesne A manor house and its lands (I;4).

Demia Capital city of the tiny eastern European country of **Margoth** (R;4).

Deming The county seat of Luna County, New Mexico (D;16).

demons, Pellucidarian Little demons are thought to inhabit the **Molop Az,** the flaming sea upon which the flat Pellucidar is believed to float. These little demons take buried corpses to Molop Az bit by bit, which is what the primitive Pellucidarians believe is the cause of decomposition. Because of this, only dead enemies are buried in Pellucidar—dead friends are placed in trees so the birds might carry them piece by piece to the **Dead World** (P1;10).

Dempsey, Jack (1895–1983) A famous heavyweight boxer of the early 20th century, described as "Sir Dempsey, a Knight of the Squared Circle" by **James Hunter Blake** to **Prince Gobred** of **Nimmr** (T11;14).

den (*Pal*) Tree (T8;2).

denarius (*Lat*) A silver Roman coin of some small value still in use in **Castra Sanguinarius** and **Castrum Mare**; a Roman penny. The plural is "denarii" (T12;9)(I;5).

depilatory salve, Amtorian A greasy Amtorian concoction which "looked like vaseline and smelled like the devil" and would remove hair in one minute and retard its regrowth for some time. Used six days in succession, it destroys the ability of the treated area to ever again grow hair. The Amtorians are beardless, but the salve is used for brain surgery and also to permanently remove the hair of career criminals to brand them as such (V1;5).

The Deputy Sheriff of Comanche County One of Burroughs' four pure westerns, abbreviated D. It is set in early 20th century **New Mexico** and is the story of the title character, **Buck Mason**, who is unjustly accused of the murder of his sweetheart and must go undercover to investigate and find the true murderers. The trail takes him to a **dude ranch** run by the gang leader, which he infiltrates disguised as an easterner.

Derby The most important city of Derbyshire in central England, near which lay the old Saxon castle purchased by **Sir Jules de Vac** to hide out in with his charge, the kidnapped **Prince Richard** (OT;5).

dermatitis Generic name for a skin disease, an aggravated form of which was suffered by **Lodivarman**, the "leper" king of **Lodidhapura**, brought on by an allergic reaction to the mushrooms he craved (HM;14).

desert Tarzan often travelled to and through deserts, such as the **Sahara**, in his adventures, but his greatest desert challenge was the crossing of a high, waterless, lifeless plateau in western **Tanganyika** in the winter of 1915 in order to reach the good hunting-land beyond. The area was extremely arid, cut by deep gorges; it was almost entirely lifeless, and Tarzan almost died in the crossing, which took several days (T7;7). Later, he returned to the waste in search of the downed plane of Lt. **Smith-Oldwick**, and discovered that at the southernmost end of one of the gorges (at a great distance below the surrounding plateau) lay a fertile valley forested with slightly unusual vegetation and inhabited by slightly different versions of various jungle animals.

In the valley lay **Xuja**, a walled city of great antiquity inhabited by maniacs (T7;17–23).

Desquerc, Monsieur The fingerprint expert of the Paris police force who proved that Tarzan was the true son of **John Clayton, Lord Greystoke**, by examining his adult fingerprints in comparison to those he had made as a baby in his father's diary (T1;26, 28).

Dessent, Era A sexy platinum blond cast by **Abe Potkin** to play Jane in **Prominent Pictures'** 1933 film *Tarzan of the Apes* (T17;33).

destination compass A device installed on Barsoomian fliers consisting of two circular maps of Barsoom, each representing a hemisphere, with a moveable pointer. Once the pointer is set to any point on either map, the arrow on a third dial will point straight to the destination and remain pointing there, so that all one must do to navigate is keep the arrow pointed directly ahead (M1). See also **destination compass, controlling**.

destination compass, controlling An improvement of the **destination compass** invented by **Carthoris**. This improved device could automatically fly the ship to its destination and even land it. The prototype was sabotaged shortly after its invention by the evil **Vas Kor** so that it might carry Carthoris to **Aanthor** rather than to his desired destination (M4;1,3). Despite this unfortuitous beginning, the improved compass later became standard equipment on **Heliumetic fliers**. In "John Carter and the Giant of Mars," the device was incorrectly called a "gyro-compass" (M11A;2).

Devil of Torn, the *see* **Norman the Devil**

Devonport The first English city in which Lt. **Jefferson Turck** and his men landed in 2137 after being abandoned by their ship. They found it a complete and utter ruin, so overgrown as to be invisible (LC;2).

Dexter A close friend of **Townsend Harper, Jr.**'s who was an alumnus of **Cornell** and knew both **Professor** and **Virginia Maxon** by sight (Q;1).

dhow (*Ara*) A type of small sailing ship (T24;1).

Dhung The younger son of **Scurv**, the chief of the **Himean** village of **Garb** in

Pellucidar. Dhung was a horrible little brat, like all of his race (P3;11).

La Diablesa "The She-Devil" (*Sp*). The absolutely gorgeous consort of **The Vulture**, a pirate of the south seas in the 1920s. She was a Frenchwoman who had been married off to an old man with an important family by her father, but on a cruise of the South Seas (to help her husband's asthma) the yacht was attacked by The Vulture and his men and all but she perished. She was taken by The Vulture, and had been with him for two years when **Johnny Lafitte** arrived. She fell in love with him and vice versa, but there was The Vulture to consider. Finally, though, she killed him and she and Lafitte married and moved to Paris, far from any pirates (PB;8–11,13).

diadet   The beast of burden and sole mount of the **Minunians**, a species of antelope similar to the **Royal Antelope** of west Africa but slightly larger, standing about fifteen inches tall at the flank. In battle, they were quite formidable when guided by Minunian warriors (T10;6).

diadetax   The **diadet**-mounted cavalry of **Minuni** (T10;7).

dialects, 25th century   By the 25th century wide separation and poor communication had made the various dialects of English spoken in post–**Kalkar** North America so different as to be almost unintelligible to members of other groups. There was, however, a common trade language as well (MM3; 1,6).

Diamond Head   A large volcanic mountain on the island of **Oahu** in Hawaii (B1).

Dian the Beautiful   The daughter of the King of **Amoz** in Pellucidar, whom **David Innes** fell in love with some time after being enslaved alongside her by the **Sagoths** soon after his arrival in Pellucidar. She taught him the language of Pellucidar but not enough of its customs to keep him out of trouble, especially with her. Later, she was abducted by **Hooja the Sly One** but escaped him, made her way home, and was later saved by Innes from the suit of **Jubal the Ugly One**. For all of this time she pretended to hate Innes because of his ignorant affront to her soon after she had taught him her language — he had saved her from another man but had neither taken her as his mate nor released her,

and his inaction had bound her to him as a slave by Pellucidarian custom. Finally, Innes forced his affection on her, giving her the proof of his love she wanted, and she accepted him as her mate (P1;4–5,14–15). She was later captured by the **Mahars**, taken from them by Hooja, and again rescued by Innes (P2;5, 10–11,14–15).

Years later, when rumor reached **Sari** that Innes had been killed on his way back from locating the lost **Wilhelm von Horst**, Dian set forth with an expedition to find him, but was ambushed by **Do-gad**, nephew of the King of **Suvi**, who wished her for himself. In fleeing from him, she was captured by the mad **Jukans**, rescued by Innes, recaptured by Do-gad, then fell into the hands of the maneating **Azarians**. After escaping them, they were captured by the **Ko-vans** and enslaved, but finally, after escaping them, Dian killed Do-gad and was rescued by a ship of the Pellucidarian navy (P6;10–11,17–18,26–28).

Her last known adventure occurred in 1931, soon after she and Innes returned to Sari. While he was away in the north preventing a war between **Kali** and Suvi, **Abner Perry** invented a hot gas balloon which Dian insisted on testing. When the balloon broke free of its tether, she was carried south across the **Nameless Strait** to land in the country of the yellow-skinned **Xexots**, who proclaimed her a **Noada** (a daughter of their god **Pu**) and set her up as a virtual prisoner in their city of **Lolo-lolo**. She made an enemy of the high priest by reducing the amount of money the people were forced to tithe, and even gave back much of it; because of this he had his priests spread lies and tales among the people to cause them to rise up against her, but she narrowly escaped with the help of **Gamba**, the go-sha (king) of Lolo-lolo (P7:1;3–7)(P7:2; 1–7). They sailed out across the Nameless Strait in a crude canoe, were carried into the **Korsar Az** by the current, and landed on the island of **Tandar**, where Dian was enslaved but eventually escaped, and was saved by a Sarian regiment under command of **Hodon the Fleet One** aboard the EPS *Lo-har* seeking O-aa. She was later transferred to the EPS *John Tyler* and sailed back to Sari (P7:3;1–7)(P7:4; 7–12).

diary, Greystoke   John Clayton, Lord Greystoke kept a personal diary locked in a strongbox. The diary was kept in French and later served as a means of confirming the story of Tarzan as well as helping in the ape-man's self-education. It was read to him (finally) by Lt. Paul d'Arnot, his first human friend, while the two were travelling from the cottage back toward civilization, and gave d'Arnot the truth about Tarzan, although the ape-man did not himself believe the story at first. Tarzan's identity was finally proven by comparing his adult fingerprints with those impressed in the Clayton diary by the Clayton baby (T1;1,3,11, 25–28).

Diaz, Father Pedro A 16th century Portuguese priest who built castles in Abyssinia as part of Portugal's planned colonization of the area (T23;8).

Dick The black-haired English-born "Tarzan Twin," quieter than "Doc" but otherwise resembling him very closely in both looks and manner. He was distantly related to Tarzan on his father's side (TT1).

dictionary One of the books in the deserted **Greystoke cottage**, found by Tarzan and used by him to learn to read. From age 10 to 15 he learned to read the words in the alphabet books and the primers, by 16 he could understand the primers almost completely, and by 17 he discovered the dictionary, arranged in the by-now-familiar alphabetical order, and learned to read most other common words from it (T1;7) (T6:4).

Dietz One of the German crew members of the U-33 on its cruise to **Caspak** in 1916-17. He was killed by the engineer, Olson, when the Germans betrayed their truce and tried to take the English prisoner early in 1917 (C3;5).

Dieu et mon droit "God and my right" (*Fr*). Motto of the British royalty and the inscription above the door of the ancient secret church of Chicago in Kalkar-occupied 22nd century America (MM2;6).

dijiji (*Apa*) Black (A1;2).

Dilecta A beautiful young patrician girl of Castra Sanguinarius who was the beloved of the officer Maximus Praeclarus. Tarzan saved her from being raped by Fastus, son of the Emperor, shortly after his arrival in the city in 1923. Later, she was saved from being forced to marry Fastus by his death in a Tarzan-inspired slave revolt (T12;9,18–19).

Dimmie The nickname used by **Prince Boris** of Karlova at Peter's Inn in order to remain incognito (R;4).

dimorphodon A small, extinct flying reptile, still common in Pellucidar (P4;7).

Dinaric Alps The main mountain range of Yugoslavia, in which lay the tiny country of Lutha (MK1;1).

Dink An early 20th century hobo who, with his pal Crumb, tried to steal food from the eloquent Bridge in southern Iowa, but was beaten up by Billy Byrne for his trouble. He later called the police to turn in the fugitive Byrne for the $500 reward, robbing in the process the farmer's wife at whose home he made the call, but was again foiled by Byrne (K2;2,5).

Dinosaur I The first balloon in Pellucidar, built by **Abner Perry** from dinosaur peritonea in 1931 and filled with hot, light natural gas from a spring. By accident, it carried **Dian the Beautiful** out over the **Nameless Strait** and down into the land of the **Xexots** on the other side (after being punctured by a curious thipdar)(P7:1;3–7)(P7:2;1–4).

Dinosaur II The second balloon **Abner Perry** made in Pellucidar (see *Dinosaur I*), with the same construction techniques as the first, but with a ripcord for descent this time. **David Innes** went up in it in search of **Dian the Beautiful**, who had been carried off in the *Dinosaur I*. Innes hoped that the second balloon would be taken by the same prevailing winds as the first and swept to the same locale (P7:2;7).

dinotherium An elephantine creature of the Miocene with a short trunk, downward-curving tusks coming from the lower jaw, and small ears like a pig's. It stood about ten feet at the shoulder and was about 20 feet long (P4;3). See also **maj**.

Diocletian (A.D. 245–313) The Roman Emperor who reorganized the administration of the Roman Empire and set up the two-Caesar system which eventually led to the splitting of the empire into eastern and western halves (R;7).

Dion Splendidus A senator of Castra Sanguinarius, father of Dilecta. After the death of Sublatus in the revolution started by Tarzan in August of 1923, Splendidus was declared Emperor (T12;9,11,20).

Dirty Eddie One of the hobos who tried to rob the "Oskaloosa Kid" of the proceeds from his "robbery" of the Prim house in 1917 Oakdale, Illinois. He had earned his sobriquet by his foul language. He was with the gang when they caught up with the "Kid" and his friends, and was mauled by Beppo badly enough to land him in the hospital (K3;1,10).

disarmament All of the world's nations disarmed after World War III ended in 1967, and in the next 70 years almost every weapon on Earth was destroyed; even the International Peace Fleet was eventually cut in half. It was this pitiful state that the Kalkars found upon invading Earth, making their conquest of the planet a simple matter (MM1)(MM2;1).

disintegration rifle A Barsoomian weapon invented in the early 20th century by Phor Tak of Jahar. It caused metal to disintegrate by disrupting the nuclear forces holding it together and could thus destroy all the metal parts of a flier, sending it crashing to earth as a dissolving wreck. A protective pigment, colored a ghastly blue, was also developed. This pigment could protect metal against the ray, rendering it harmless. Later, Phor Tak developed cartridges for the rifle which would enable it to disintegrate wood or flesh, but of course the Jaharians knew nothing of these, since they had chased Phor Tak out of Jahar in the meantime (M7;5,11). See also **rifle, electronic**.

Divine, Lawrence Cortwrite A "friend" of Barbara Harding's who agreed to pay a huge sum of money to the captain and crew of the brigantine *Halfmoon* in order to have the girl kidnapped in an elaborate ploy to force her to marry him, both for her looks and her money. The plan backfired, however, and she quickly found out that he was behind it; thus he lost her forever. What the *Halfmoon* crew did with him later (after their shipwreck on Yoka island) is unknown, but considering that he now could not pay them, he was probably killed (K1;2–10).

Djelfa A city of Algeria, far to the south of which the Arab tribe of Kadour ben Saden lived in the early 20th century (T2;7).

Djibouti A tiny nation on the east coast of Africa, bordered by Ethiopia and Somalia, and known in Tarzan's time as French Somaliland, later Afars and Issas (T14;1).

Djor Kantos The son of Kantos Kan of Barsoom. At the time of the invasion of the land of the First Born he was a padwar attached to the 5th Utan of Helium (M2;21). Later, he was betrothed to Tara of Helium, but both secretly loved someone else. He eventually married Olvia Marthis, a princess of Hastor (M5;22).

Djup An Amtorian cannibal savage of Northern Anlap who tried to take Duare for his mate, but made the mistake of trying to climb into the moving anotar and fell to his death when she looped it (V4;39).

do In the adolescent Tarzan's letter naming system, the letter "B" (T6:4).

Do-gad The nephew of the King of Suvi in Pellucidar. He pestered Dian the Beautiful nonstop to marry him when the rumor reached Sari in 1929 that David Innes had been killed by the warrior women of Oog. She expelled him from Sari, but he later waylaid her expedition to find Innes and, when she escaped that ambush, chased her halfway across the continent to the land of the Jukans. He later caught her again, but both of them were taken soon afterward to the floating island of Ko-va. After they escaped from there, Dian finally succeeded in getting rid of Do-gad by killing him (P6;11,26–28).

Doarty, Officer A plainclothes policeman of Chicago's south side who developed a personal vendetta against "Abe" Farris after the latter removed certain privileges previously enjoyed by Doarty. It was to further this vendetta that Doarty arranged for Maggie Lynch to testify against Farris in court. It was Doarty who remembered Maggie later when, as June Lathrop, she worked for John Secor and Company. Doarty told Mr. Stickler, the office manager, about her, resulting in a great deal of trouble for the poor girl. It was also Doarty who arrested her in Goliath, Idaho almost three years later (GF;1,8,13).

Dobbs, Henry The captain of the *Sally Corwith*, the sailing ship which met Waldo Emerson Smith-Jones on his island in 1911. Dobbs carried a letter to Waldo's mother with him and mailed it to her from San Francisco as soon as he arrived there (CG1;6)(CG2;6).

Doble steam car The steam-driven automobile produced from 1924 to 1932 by Abner Doble. It was eventually pushed off the market, probably by the oil companies (J;2).

Doc The nickname of the blond, American-born "Tarzan Twin," who was more open and friendly than his cousin **Dick**, but otherwise resembled him strongly in both looks and manner (TT1).

Dodson A small train-junction town in Missouri (K2;5).

dogface (WW II slang) A private soldier in the army (T22;8).

Dogman An **Arab** of the band of **Abu Batn** who tried to grab **La** of **Opar** to kidnap her from the **Zveri** expedition in 1928 and was killed by La for his pains (T14;8).

Dolly Dorcas The name of a Cape Cod whaling ship that was wrecked in the Arctic in 1845. Her survivors, confined to a lifeboat lost among the icebergs with an erratic compass (as one might expect that far north), descended to **cannibalism** to survive, and so only one was left when the boat reached **Pellucidar** after passing through the polar opening. This survivor was an old man who could not remember his name (but was sure it was not Dolly Dorcas) and who told his story to **Hodon the Fleet One** and **O-aa** of **Kali** when they were prisoners of the **Sabertooth Men** with him in 1931 (P7:1;7).

Dolphin The steam yacht of **Henri de la Valois**, Count of **Crecy**, on which he and his wife were honeymooning when they were wrecked in the South Pacific around 1892 (CG1;11).

Domnia One of the countries of **Ladan**, inhabited by the same white-skinned, blue-haired humanoid race as the **Tarids** belong to (M8;20).

don (*Pal*) Man (T8;2).

Dongo The black headman of the **Shifta** tribe of raiders led by **Dominic Capietro** in Africa of the late 1920s, who was killed by Tarzan while trying to capture him (T15;7, 23).

Doningham, Duke of A British noble at whose castle a young woman was reputedly abducted by a ghost (T19;19).

Donovan, Mary A fat old Irish "widdy lady" who was on a stagecoach robbed at

Hell's Bend in Hendersville, Arizona, in the 1880s. She spoke in a thick brogue and was incredibly spunky, daring to grab a gun and shoot at the bandits when the men aboard would not. She was the owner of the **Donovan House** and the matron of the whole town, a good friend of **Diana Henders'** and a loyal supporter of **Bull**. She eventually warmed up to her persistent suitor, **Wildcat Bob**, and married him the day after he was shot while guarding **Hal Colby**, the captured **Black Coyote** (HB;2–4,10,13–15,18–19).

Donovan, Timothy The late husband of Mary Donovan (HB;3).

Donovan House The only hotel of Hendersville, Arizona, in the 1880s (HB;3).

Donuk A small continent of Amtor lying some distance due west of **Anlap**, mostly in **Strabol**. Its countries are in a medieval stage of development (V5;4).

door, Wieroo **Wieroo** doors are made of thin strips of wood glued to a hide or wood framework in a patchwork pattern running both vertically and horizontally, like a quilt; sometimes different "patches" are painted different colors. The whole is painted with a thick varnish and one side is fastened to a wooden pole set in holes in the ceiling and floor so as to form a hinge upon which the door can turn. The latch is a circle of metal set off-center so as to be able to be turned into a slot in the frame when the door is closed (C3;2).

Dooth The **Oparian** priest who stopped **Cadj** from sacrificing Tarzan when they found him drugged in the **Hawkes'** camp in the summer of 1917. His action was not based on love for Tarzan, but rather respect for the laws of Opar, which state that only the high priestess (i.e., **La**) may offer up a sacrifice to the **Flaming God** (T9;7). He was later made high priest, but was corrupted by the words of **Oah** into helping her to overthrow La and become high priestess, with Dooth as her mate and consort. He and Oah were later killed by the loyal followers of La (T14;4,17).

Dopey Charlie One of the hobos who pursued the "Oskaloosa Kid" for the goods he had "stolen" from the **Prim** house in 1917 **Oakdale, Illinois**. He was very pale and had clammy hands. He tried to kill the "Kid," but failed. Later, it was he and **The General** who ended up in the Squibbs house upstairs with the "Kid" and Bridge after coming into the house in pursuit of them and being cut off by the chained "thing" below (see Beppo). He and The General were sent on their way the next morning by a threat and an automatic pistol, and were caught later that day (with the loot from the Baggs murder/robbery, which they had committed apart from their usual gang) by detective Burton and sent to the gallows (K3;1,3–7,9).

dor (*Pal*) Son (T8;8).

Dor, Valley The sacred valley near the south pole of Barsoom, lying south of the ice wastelands and north of the Lost Sea of Korus. Long thought to be a material heaven, it was shown by John Carter to be instead a place of death where the hideous plant men killed pilgrims so the Therns could have treasure and meat. The valley is surrounded by the Golden Cliffs of the Mountains of Otz, and despite its horror is a very beautiful place with grass, trees and flowers in abundance — one of the last few forests left on dying Barsoom (M2).

Dor-ul-Otho "Son of God" (*Pal*). The title claimed by Tarzan when he came to seek Jane in A-lur, the capital of the Ho-don of Pal-ul-don. His contention was primarily based on the fact that he had no tail, and the tailed Ho-don conceived of their god as having none. The claim was disputed by the high priest Lu-don but was eventually "proven" by the intervention of Korak and the "divine power" of his Enfield (T8;8,11–13,18–25).

Doran The second son of Jantor, Jong of Japal when Carson Napier came there early in 1931 (V4;19).

Dorf A young German air force officer who was one of the mates of the dirigible O-220 on its mission to Pellucidar in 1927 (P4;2).

Doria The beautiful daughter of Thudos, the Cathnean noble who was head of the faction which wished to place Prince Alextar on the throne in Nemone's place. Doria was beloved by Gemnon, the Cathnean noble who befriended Tarzan in October of 1930. Tarzan later saved Doria from Nemone's jealousy by hiding her at the house of the mine foreman Niaka until after the queen's death (T16; 13,19).

Dorsky, Michael One of the communist conspirators of the Zveri expedition to rob Opar in 1928. He was killed by Tantor when he menaced Tarzan (T14;5,15).

Dotar Sojat John Carter's green Barsoomian name, formed from the surnames of the first two chieftains he killed (M1;14). See also O Mad. He often used the name as an alias when disguised as a red man (M9;2), including the time he was captured by the First Born of Kamtol, who would have killed him had they known his true identity (M10:2;11).

douar (*Ara*) Village (T2;8).

doughboy (American slang) An infantryman of the First or Second World War (T22;8).

Douglas, Staff Sergeant Carter The radioman of the bomber *Lovely Lady*, shot down while on a reconnaissance mission over Japanese-held Sumatra in the spring of 1944. He bailed out safely but was lost from the others, captured by the Japanese along with Davis (the waist gunner), and rescued by Tarzan a few weeks later. He was one of the crew members who survived to reach home unhurt (T22;8,26,30).

Doval An incredibly handsome young man of the village of Paraht on the island of Amiocap in Pellucidar who fell in love (or at least lust) with Stellara and tried to win her. She would have none of him, however, and instead tricked him into the arms of Letari, who was chasing Tanar (P3;6–7).

Dowie, John Alexander (1847–1907) Scottish-born American founder of a fundamentalist religious sect whose tabernacle he built in Zion City, on the shores of Lake Michigan near Chicago. He was ousted by his own followers in 1906 after various scandals (A1;1).

Downes, Frank The British telegraph operator employed by Burroughs in 1914 to communicate with David Innes via his telegraph line to Pellucidar in the Sahara Desert (P2).

Downs, Lorna Movie star of the 1930s whom "Jimber-Jaw" believed was his beloved Lilami until he found out what she was really like (J;4–5).

Doxus Jeddak of the First Born of Barsoom at Kamtol. He was a ruthless tyrant who controlled his populace by fear of his nerve-index machine, with which he could kill any Kamtolian he chose no matter where they might be. All prisoners captured immediately belonged to Doxus and had to be bought from him by a person who wished one as a slave. He was cruel and sadistic, and probably a bit mad. After seeing John Carter's swordsmanship, Doxus bought him back from Xaxak so that Carter might secretly teach him all of his tricks of swordsmanship. Carter's coaching pleased Doxus so much that he was given the freedom of the city, allowing him to further his plans of escape (M10:2;5, 9–10).

drachma A Greek coin also used in Onthar and Thenar (T16;8).

Drake The name of the captain of the airship which rescued Burroughs from the Arctic Ocean in March of 1969 (MM2;1).

Drinov, Zora Ostensibly, a Russian communist who came to Africa with **Peter Zveri** in 1928 to foment rebellion and cause a war between France and Italy. She was kidnapped from her camp by the **Arab Abu Batn** and his men and taken north along with La of Opar, but later escaped with the help of **Wayne Colt**, with whom she began to fall in love. After she and Colt were separated, she was again saved by Tarzan and returned to the Zveri expedition, where she was in turn able to save Tarzan. After the ape-man utterly demolished Zveri's plans, Zveri tried to kill Colt, but was shot in the back by Zora, who then revealed to all that she was actually the daughter of an unnamed Russian noble whom Zveri had murdered. She and Colt were thus reunited (T14;8–14,17).

Drontoff, Stefan A Serbian spy of World War I Austria for whom **Barney Custer** was mistaken in September of 1914 and taken before the firing squad, narrowly escaping with his life (MK2;2–3).

Drovan The chief of the Ganak tribe of Pellucidar who captured **Wilhelm von Horst** early in 1928 and was killed by him shortly thereafter (P5;19).

drum, earthen The strange construction built by the **great apes** for use in their **Dumdum** ritual. It is sounded by being hit by small branches and gives off a loud, dull, booming noise (T1;7).

drunkenness Drunken officers are not tolerated on Barsoomian flying ships, and are usually "helped" to "fall" overboard by the men, often in full view of the other officers (M10:3;6).

Drusilla The younger sister of **Caligula**, born when he was five years old. In A.D. 38 he decided to marry her, as he had been infatuated with her and sexually active with her for some time, and considered her (as a fellow Julian and therefore divine) to be his only fitting wife. She died of a fever later that year (I;2,16).

Drusus Caesar Older brother of Caligula, who was arrested for plotting against Tiberius in A.D. 31 and died in prison three years later (I;3,15). Another Drusus was Nero Claudius Drusus Caesar, the son of Tiberius, who was poisoned in A.D. 31 by his own wife and her lover, **Sejanus** (I;6,15).

Dry Spring Gulch A descriptively-named place of southern **Arizona** where **Kay White** was kidnapped to fulfill **Cory Blaine's** plan to win her heart (D;14–15).

du (*Amt*) "Letter" (of the alphabet) (V4; 31).

Du-seen A powerful warrior of the **Galus** of **Caspak** in the early 20th century who wanted **Ajor** as his mate and the chieftainship of the Galus for himself. He had a considerable following among the newer Galus, and even made a deal with the **Wieroos** to deliver all **cos-ata-lo** to them at birth. It was because of him that Ajor fled south in the summer of 1917 and met **Tom Billings**. After she left he made another plan with the chief of the eastern **Kro-lu, Al-tan**, to invade the land of the Galus and make Du-seen chief. He accomplished this plan by convincing Al-tan and his men (most of whom were **batu**) that they would become Galus by doing so. Only a few of the Kro-lu fell for this story, and after Du-seen's force was repelled by the Galus with help from the *Toreador* crew and Du-seen killed, the remainder of the force returned to the Kro-lu country and were there put to death by their own people for their crime against the laws of Caspak (C2;5–7).

Dua The Vadjong of the Brokols of Amtor was always named Dua (V4;25). See also **Duma**.

Duare   The gorgeous daughter of Mintep, Jong of Vepaja on Amtor, whom Carson Napier fell in love with while living in the house of Mintep. She was abducted by Thorist Klangan and taken hostage along with Napier, but was rescued from them by him and eventually avowed her love for him (after several heroics enacted in her behalf) even though it was a sin for her to do so (V1;5–8, 11–14). After escaping the Thorist city of Kapdor together they fled inland to a dense and tangled forest in which they wandered aimlessly for some time until they were captured by Skor, the mad Jong of Morov. Duare escaped without Napier, but was recaptured by Skor and taken to Kormor, his capital, where he began to work on her to get her to accept him as her mate (V2;2–11). Napier eventually rescued her, only to have her suspected as a spy from Kormor by the inhabitants of his adopted city, Havatoo, and sentenced to death, forcing her to flee the city with Napier (V2;18–21).

They flew to the neighboring continent of Anlap and the country of Korva, where they landed in the city of Sanara, then under siege by the totalitarian Zani party which had taken over Korva. While Napier was on a secret mission for Sanara in Amlot, the capital of Korva, the acting jong Muso was trying to take Duare for his own (V3;1–6). Napier arrived in time, however, and took Duare with him to Amlot to save her father Mintep, who was a prisoner in the Gap Kum Rov of Amlot. He lost her in the scuffle, though, and she (assuming him dead) returned with her father to Vepaja to face charges that she had mated with Napier before she was 20 (V3;12–17). Napier pursued and arrived in time to rescue her, a feat he was able to accomplish primarily because nobody really wanted Duare executed, and so there were no guards to stop her, since she had been placed under house arrest (V3;20). They escaped together in Napier's anotar, but en route to Korva encountered a terrific hurricane which threw them off course and into the uncharted northern hemisphere of Amtor, where they were captured by and escaped from the hideous Myposan fish-men (V4;1–17).

Later, Duare had to rescue Napier from being killed by the hideous Brokols by scaring them with the anotar. They then headed for Anlap again, but were captured in the northern portion of that continent by the Vooyorgan of Voo-ad and made into living museum exhibits. Thanks to Duare, they were again able to escape when a mutant Vooyorgan fell in love with her and freed her, then abducted her in the anotar. After several harrowing adventures, Duare was finally able to recover control of the plane from the creature and get back her pistol and the antidote to the paralysis Napier was still bound by. She returned and freed him and Ero Shan of Havatoo, who was also there, and he told her that the Sanjong of Havatoo had reversed its decision on her and she was free to return there (V4;29–42).

They flew south and were then shot down in a war in Middle Anlap, were separated for some time, and were reunited as slaves in brutal Hangor. After escaping from there they returned to Korva, where she could finally live peacefully with Napier. Although he had other adventures, she stayed put thereafter (V4;43–55).

Il Duce   "The Leader" (Italian). Title held by Benito Mussolini as the head of state of Italy after 1922 (LL;15).

dude ranch   A ranch where inexperienced riders (usually from the cities of the east) can learn to ride and enjoy a pseudo-western lifestyle as a vacation (D;3).

Dufranne, Captain   The commander of the French cruiser which rescued the Porter party from where they had been stranded by the Arrow mutineers at the site of Tarzan's cottage in Portuguese West Africa (T1;19). His ship also rescued the crew of the Lady Alice from their shipwreck at the same site two years later (T2;26).

Duhor   A city-state of Barsoom lying against one of the planet's few remaining mountain ranges, the snow-clad Artolian Hills. Duhor is a beautiful country and, until recent times, one unfriendly to Helium. Its chief enemy, however, is Amhor, which lies east of Duhor. Valla Dia, the love of Ulysses Paxton, was a princess of Duhor—the daughter of its jeddak, Kor San—and after his marriage to her, Paxton became a prince (M6;4) (M9;1–2).

duklij   (Apa) Turquoise (A1;4).

Dum-dum   The ritual of the great apes of Africa, enacted for a specific event such as a victory in battle against another ape tribe, the defeat of an enemy, the accession of a new leader, etc. It is a simple, primitive ritual, similar to the ones no doubt practiced by the common ancestors of apes and men millions of years ago. The Dum-dum occurs in a natural amphitheater hidden deep in the jungle, usually a hollow or clearing of some kind, where the apes have built a strange earthen drum. The corpse of the enemy whose death the Dum-dum celebrates is placed near this and the male apes form a circle around it. The females and young form another, larger circle beyond, and three old females sit around the drum in the center. They beat upon it with small branches and the males dance a war-dance around it, shouting fierce cries and leaping into the air for half an hour or so, then pick up branches and attack the corpse until it is beaten to a pulp. The frenzied bulls then descend upon the corpse and tear it to bits, each ape devouring all he can get. The ceremony is very sacred and very secret, and Tarzan was the only human ever to observe or participate in one and survive (T1;7).

dum-dum bullet A hollow-point bullet which expands on contact with a target, thus transferring all of its kinetic energy to the target. This uses the energy of the bullet more efficiently and does more damage than a conventional bullet, which may pass entirely through a living body without giving up all of its energy (B1;6).

Duma The jong of the Brokols of Amtor. The jongs of Brokol were always named Duma, and were indeed all pretty much alike (V4;24–25).

dur (*Bar*) The number one million (M9;4).

Dur Ajmad A kinsman of Vanuma, Princess of Amhor, who was poisoned by her husband, Jal Had. Dur Ajmad aspired to be the prince and was much more popular than Jal Had, especially with the army. After Jal Had killed Vanuma, Dur Ajmad had all the reason he needed to invade the palace and claim the princeship. The fact that Jal Had was murdered shortly thereafter made the coup even easier (M9;26–27).

Dur-dan An intelligent hormad of Barsoom, loyal to Ras Thavas, who helped him and John Carter to build a boat in which to escape Morbus (M9;15).

Duran The Amtorian warrior of Vepaja who first captured Carson Napier when he landed in Kooaad via parachute upon his arrival on Amtor (V1;3–4).

Durg The Gorbus of Pellucidar whom Wilhelm von Horst saved from a zarith, and who was thus grateful and advocated setting von Horst and La-ja free. He was a murderer of four men in his outer-Earthly life (his father, two brothers and a policeman) and told the two humans about the Gorbuses and their hideous life (P5;8–10).

Durham English city on the Thames below London, site of a bishopric (OT;5). Also, a famous brand of cigarette tobacco (A2;16).

durian An edible Sumatran fruit with a prickly skin. The interior smells spoiled but tastes good, and the seeds can also be eaten (T22;3).

Duro (*Ape*) The hippopotamus (T6;5).

Dusar A city of Barsoom lying at 15 degrees north latitude, 20 degrees east longitude. It is a powerful and modern country with many canals to itself, but ruled by evil men — specifically Nutus and his son Astok (M4). It is famous for its delicious honey (M7;16).

Dusar A ship of Hin Abtol's fleet which John Carter, posing as a Panar officer, was placed in command of. It was not really a very old ship as the Panar ships went, but was so incredibly dirty that its fuel lines were clogged and it would not fly. John Carter fixed that, cleaning up and repairing the ship until it was serviceable again. He recruited a crew for it, but they mutinied and put Carter and the loyal Gor-don out in the frozen north, keeping Tan Hadron and Fo-nar to fly the ship (M10:3;5–10).

Dutton, Pelham A white hunter who came to Africa on safari in 1938 with the millionaire Timothy Pickerall and fell in love with Pickerall's daughter Sandra, rendering him frantic when she was abducted by the false Tarzan. He went with the real Tarzan on her trail to Alemtejo but was captured by their Galla enemies and enslaved. He later escaped with Sandra and the false Tarzan but was killed by the great apes of Mal-gash, whom they had unwittingly enraged (T23;2, 11–15,20,24).

dwar (*Bar*) In the Barsoomian armed forces, an officer corresponding to a captain in the Earthly army. The term is used on ships as well, but corresponds to the same rank as it does in the army (M2;21). Dwar is also the name of a jetan piece with a move of three spaces straight in any direction or combination (M5).

Dyak A member of a headhunting tribe of Borneo (Q;1).

dyal A flightless, carnivorous bird of Pellucidar, similar to the Phororhacos of the Miocene, but much larger, standing about eight feet tall. Its flesh is considered very tasty by Pellucidarians (P4;6). Some tribes use the dyal as a riding animal, and what it lacks in comfort it makes up for in speed (P6;4).

Dyaus The god of Athne, the City of Ivory; he was the patron god of elephants and appeared as an elephant himself (T21;23–24).

dyrodor One of the most peculiar creatures of Pellucidar, a stegosaurus-like beast that has somehow gained the ability of flight, or more exactly, gliding. Its huge, awkward-looking bulk, combined with its great speed and tiny gliding plates (evolved, no doubt, from the stegosaurus' back plates) suggest that the creature's body is perhaps a huge gas bag, making it a sort of "natural dirigible" which can only fly downhill. The dyrodor is 70 feet long and 25 feet tall at the rump (P4;10,12).

dyryth The giant ground sloth of Pellucidar, a creature as large as an elephant and just as powerfully built, with the characteristic long, curved foreclaws of its family and a sort of rudimentary trunk coming from its lower jaw. It is a fierce and ill-tempered creature which bends down trees to eat the foliage at their tops, but fortunately for the human inhabitants of Pellucidar, it is an immensely slow-moving one (P1;2).

dzonot The sacred well of Mayan sacrifice into which a victim was thrown at dawn and, if he managed to keep afloat until noon, was taken out and given highest honors, becoming practically a god on Earth. The dzonot of Chichen Itza on Uxmal was an obsidian-sided well filled with water up to about 70 feet of its top, located in the bottom of the crater of an extinct volcano (T24;23–24).

e (*Pal*) Where (T8;15).

E-Med The man who replaced A-Kor as Dwar of the Towers of Jetan in Manator on Barsoom. His promotion was short-lived: He attempted to touch Tara of Helium, and she stabbed him to death (M5;13).

E-Thas A chief of Manator on Barsoom, major-domo of the palace of O-Tar, Jeddak of Manator. He was one of O-Tar's favorites and was thus intensely disliked by those chiefs who had gained their positions by merit (M5;20).

Earle, Dr. The Compton family doctor in 1910s Chicago (EE;6).

earth gods The explanation that Thak Chan, the Maya of Uxmal, had for the two orang-utans that accompanied Tarzan when he rescued the Maya late in 1938 (T24;13).

East Camp One of the two "camps" (villages) found by Lt. Jefferson Turck on the Isle of Wight in 2137 (LC;3).

East Tower The building of Tjanath on Barsoom in which Tavia was imprisoned upon returning to the city with Tan Hadron after he rescued her from the green men (M7;5).

ecca (*Cpk*) The eohippus (C2;5).

ed (*Pal*) The number 70 (T8).

Eddie The assistant director of Prominent Pictures' 1933 movie *Tarzan of the Apes* (T17;33). Another Eddie was a number of Cory Blaine's gang in early 20th century Arizona. He had a harelip and was captured alive by Buck Mason when Mason rescued Kay White, giving proof to Mason's allegations about the gang (D6;10–11,19–23).

Eddie the Dip A young hoodlum of early 20th century Chicago, an acquaintance of Maggie Lynch's. He was really a good-hearted man, and when Maggie was down and out, he hocked his own jewelry to help her, though she did not know it. Once in a good position, she paid him back as quickly as possible (GF;5–7).

Edward The squire of James Hunter Blake after he became Sir James of Nimmr (T11;14).

Edward I King of England from 1272 to 1307, who was a fine general in the Crusades and a much better king than his father, Henry III. Among other accomplishments, he reformed English law and conquered Wales. He was the older brother of the lost **Prince Richard** and was probably the jealous king who wiped his brother's heroic story from English history (OT;1,5,19).

Edward the Confessor The last Saxon King of England, who ruled from 1004 to 1066 and left his kingdom in the hands of **Harold the Dane** when he died (OT;3).

Edwild A former serf who became a captain of **Norman of Torn's** mid–13th century bandit force (OT;10).

Ee-ah! (*Min*) Bravo! (T10;12).

"The Efficiency Expert" A novella originally appearing in *Argosy All-Story Weekly* as a four-part serial from October 8th to 29th, 1921, but not appearing in book form until 1966, published then by **House of Greystoke**. In the story, **James Torrance, Jr.**, struggles to get a decent job in **Chicago** of the late 1910s, eventually finding friends, a good job, and a frame-up for murder. It is abbreviated EE.

eggs All Barsoomian creatures are oviparous, and the eggs of the humanoid species take five years to hatch. They are a bit larger than goose eggs when laid and grow during the incubation period to a diameter of about two and a half feet. They have hard shells and are snowy white in color (M1).

eho (*Ape*) Much (TC).

eho-dan (*Ape*) Hand (TC).

eho-kut (*Ape*) Hollow (TC).

eho-lul (*Ape*) Wet (TC).

eho-nala (*Ape*) Top (TC).

eighth ray The eighth ray, or Ray of Propulsion, was first discovered and used on Barsoom, and later on Earth with Barsoomian assistance. It is this ray which propels light outward from its source. The solar eighth ray propels light from the sun to the planets, and the eighth ray of each planet causes the light to be propelled (reflected) back into space. When confined in **buoyancy tanks**, the eighth ray will lift enormous weights from the surface of its planet. It is by this principle that Barsoomian **fliers** operate (M1;21)(MM1;1).

el (*Amt*) More (V4;24).

el (*Pal*) "Grace" or "graceful" (T8).

el (*Uni*) High (B1;3).

el Adrea (*Ara*) The black lion of north Africa, a beast every bit as fierce as his jungle cousin (T2;8).

el Djebel The horse of the beautiful **Nakhla** (LL;8).

el-Engleys (*Ara*) An Englishman or Englishmen (T11;8).

el-fil (*Ara*) The elephant (T11;1).

el-Guad The clan name of most of the members of the tribe **el-Harb** of **Arab** raiders (T11;1).

El-habash (*Ara*) The Arabic name for the area of **Abyssinia** inhabited primarily by the Galla people, from which the slave **Fejjuan** had been stolen as a boy by the **el-Harb** (T11;1).

el-Harb "The War" (*Ara*). An **Arab** tribe of raiders who frequented early 20th century northeastern Africa of the subsaharan region, raiding for slaves and ivory. They searched for and found the lost **Valley of the Sepulcher** in 1921, sacking the **City of the Sepulcher**, but were afterward defeated at **Nimmr** and fled the valley, only to be defeated by the **Waziri** of Tarzan and given over to the **Gallas**, who probably sold them into slavery (T11;1–2, 15–17,20–24).

el-Howwara A great rock in the plain of **Medain Salih**, said in **Arab** legend to be the site of a great stone tower full of cursed treasure and guarded by an **afrit** (T11;1).

el-Lazzary The name given by **Fahd** to his ancient **matchlock** musket (T11;1).

eland, Pellucidarian A creature similar in size and shape to the African eland, but with back-curving horns ending in sharp points on a level with its eyes and about a foot in front of them. It has a striped coat like a zebra's (P1;15).

elasmosaurus A type of aquatic dinosaur much like the plesiosaur (P7:2;3). See **ta-ho-az**.

Elbe A river of northern Germany, along which **Berlin** is built (LC;6).

Elders   The Midianite social rank below Apostles and above common people (T15;1).

Eleanor see Roosevelt, Eleanor

Eleanor de Montfort, Princess   The sister of Henry III of England and wife of Simon de Montfort, Earl of Leicester (OT;9).

Eleanor of Provence   The wife of Henry III of England (OT;3).

element 93 see neptunium; Vik-ro

element 97 see berkelium

element 105 see hahnium; yor-san

Elephant Country   The area of the lower Thames in the 22nd century England of *The Lost Continent* (LC;4).

Elephant Men   The nobles of Athne, equivalent to the Lion Men of Cathne. Like the latter, they are all descendants of those warriors of the past who led the king's war animals into victory, and as such are the only Athneans permitted (and required) to keep elephants (T1;20).

elevator, Amlotian   In the Amtorian city of Amlot, guests in hotels are carried up to their rooms in a chairlike contraption strapped to the back of a burly porter (V3;8).

Elija, son of Noah   The Prophet of Paul in the northern settlement of the land of Midian in the Ghenzi Mountains of Africa. Though not quite as twisted as his southern counterpart Abraham, he would still have put Dr. Lafayette Smith through a trial by ordeal had Smith not tricked him into shooting himself through the head with the pistol he had confiscated from the American (T15;2,19).

Elite   A little restaurant on Broadway Avenue in 1917 Payson, Illinois (K3;9).

Eljanhai   "High-seven-elect" (*Uni*). The ruler of Unis, elected from the Janhai by its members for a six-year term. No one can serve two consecutive terms (B1;3).

Elkomoelhago   The King of Veltopismakus in Minuni while Tarzan was there. His daughter Janzara was coveted as a mate by Komodoflorensal of Trohanadalmakus. Elkomoelhago was a pompous fool as well as a despot, who claimed all good things about his city as his own accomplishments and blamed all bad things on his cabinet, most of whom he had appointed to positions they were not suited for (T10;6,10).

Ella Street   A somewhat dingy thoroughfare of turn-of-the-century Beatrice, Nebraska (MK1;6).

ellat   (*Amt*) Might (V4;9).

Ellie   One of the two Samary men of Houtomai who shared Lula's cave when Carson Napier came there in 1930 (V3;3).

Ellsworth, Lincoln   (1880–1951)   An American explorer of the arctic regions who accompanied Roald Amundsen on the *Norge* expedition over the North Pole in 1926 (P4;1).

Em-Tar   A warrior of Hin Abtol, Jeddak of the Panars of Barsoom. He was a Kobolian by birth and was impressed into service by the Panars. He gave John Carter information regarding Llana of Gathol's capture when Carter was disguised as one of Em-Tar's fellow soldiers (M10:3;4).

Emanuel   The steamship that Jack Clayton would have returned to London on from Africa had he not lost his money while disembarking from the ship he had arrived on (T4;4).

embalming, Barsoomian   Most Barsoomians burn their dead, but the inhabitants of Manator have them carefully embalmed and then pose them in their homes in the attitude of life. Another kind of embalming is given to valorous enemies who die on the Fields of Jetan— their bones are carefully removed and their bodies immersed (hanging by the hair) for one year in a special concoction that will cause them to slowly shrink and harden into a statuette-like form that is then placed on a shelf in the Gate of Enemies (M5;15). The Manatorians probably kept their tradition of embalming from the ancient Orovars, who embalmed their dead well enough to allow them to retain the semblance of life for hundreds of thousands of years (M10:1;5).

Emilio, Count de Gropello   A mid-13th century nobleman chased out of Italy by a quarrel with the pope. He became one of Norman of Torn's captains (OT;10).

Emperor of Ganado   A large, surly bull of the Rancho del Ganado in the early 1920s (GH;2).

Emperor of the East The title taken by the rulers of Castrum Mare, the lost Roman outpost in the Wiramwazi Mountains (T12;6).

Emperor of the West The title taken by the rulers of Castra Sanguinarius (T12;9).

en (*Pal*) The number one (T8).

"The End of Bukawai" The seventh short story in the collection *Jungle Tales of Tarzan*, in which the evil witch doctor Bukawai finally meets his fate when he tries to revenge himself upon Tarzan for making a fool out of him. The events of the story took place in 1908 and the story is abbreviated T6:7.

Endar The Klootogan of Pandar in Gavo when Carson Napier came there in 1932 while lost over Donuk. He was the son of the Vootogan Tovar (V5;4).

enen (*Pal*) The number two (T8).

Enfield A type of British military rifle favored by Jack Clayton (T8;5).

Enggano An island off the southwestern coast of Sumatra (T22;29).

England The name given by God to the Valley of Diamonds to reflect the society he created there (T17;20).

English Tarzan's nationality by birth and his second human language, which he actually learned to read and write by himself before he met any men, but of course had no idea of how to speak. Because of Lt. Paul d'Arnot's mistake of teaching him to speak French before English, Tarzan always spoke the language of his own country with a French accent thereafter (T1;23,27–28)(T2;7).

Ennia The wife of Macro the Prefect, she was one of Caligula's mistresses and later committed suicide with her husband at Caligula's command (I;17).

ental A Minunian military unit consisting of ten men commanded by a vental. Five entals make an entex of 50 men (T10;13).

entex A Minunian military unit of 50 men, divided into five entals of ten men each. Five entex in turn make up a novand of 250 men. An entex is commanded by an officer called a ventex (T10;13).

Eocene The second epoch of the Tertiary period, lasting from about 58 million to 36 million years ago, when many of the ancestors of modern animals first appeared, such as eohippus and moeritherium, the ancestor of the elephant.

Eohippus The "dawn horse" of the Eocene, a dog-sized animal with four toes (P1;15). See also orthopi; ecca.

Ephesus An ancient Ionian Greek city of Asia Minor which Paul of Tarsus visited early in his missionary career and there converted Angustus the Ephesian (T15).

Epris A huge Polodan continent on which the country Kapara lies (B1;8).

EPS The prefix for Pellucidarian ship names (e.g., "EPS Sari"). It stands for "Empire of Pellucidar Ship" (P7:1;2).

equilibrimotor A personal flying device popular in some Barsoomian cities, notably Toonol. It consists of a life jacket–like device filled with enough of the eighth ray to counter the force of gravity, and is propelled by a small radium motor in the back with controls in the front. Two small wings projecting from the top of the belt may be manipulated like airplane flaps to control ascent and descent (M6;8). Hin Abtol used thousands of equilibrimotors to land his troops in Gathol (M10:3;3)(M10:4;13).

Ergos The capital of Kapara on Poloda. It lies about 11,000 miles from Orvis, the capital of Unis (B1;8).

Erith English city, upon the site of which Lt. Jefferson Turck rescued Victory on July 6, 2137 (LC;4).

Eritrea The region of northern Abyssinia where Dominic Capietro was stationed with the Italian army while spreading discord and mutiny among the Fascist troops (T15;7).

Ero Shan A korgan sentar (warrior biologist) of the scientifically advanced city of Havatoo on Amtor. It was Ero Shan who, with his men, saved Carson Napier and Nalte from the Kloozangan and took them to Havatoo, where he became Napier's good friend and helped him and Nalte adjust to life there. It was in Ero Shan's house that Napier lived during his stay in Havatoo in 1930. He later mated with Nalte (V2;13–17,20–21).

In 1931, he built another **anotar** from Napier's plans (left behind after the latter's escape from Havatoo) and set out to explore, but was caught in the same hurricane which drove Napier and **Duare** to the northern hemisphere. He eventually was forced to land near **Voo-ad**, was taken in by their duplicity (as many others had been), and was paralyzed as a living museum exhibit for some months before Napier and Duare (mostly Duare) arrived to save him. He flew south with them, intending to build a new anotar in **Korva** to fly home with, but the party was shot down in a war in **Middle Anlap** and he and Napier impressed into military service and later enslaved. They eventually escaped and made it through to **Southern Anlap** and Napier's adopted country of Korva (V4;33–55).

They then built another anotar for Ero Shan to return to Havatoo in, but while testing it were knocked far off course by a freak drop in the cloud cover coupled with an instrument malfunction and ended up in distant **Donuk**, where they landed in the medieval country of **Gavo** and were taken to be wizards. In order to get the anotar back, they had to defeat the wizard **Morgas** and free the valley from his domination. Afterward, they returned to Korva and (we must presume) Ero Shan to Nalte in Havatoo (V5;1–11).

Eros A famous race horse of the **Blue Stables** of early 1st century Rome (I;8).

Erot A young officer of **Cathne** who was made a noble by Queen **Nemone** when she took a fancy to him. She would not marry him, however, because he was not of noble blood. **M'Duze**, the old hag who controlled many of Nemone's actions, liked Erot and wished that Nemone would forego tradition and marry him anyway — this Nemone would not do, especially after meeting Tarzan. Because of this Erot hated Tarzan and plotted against him, but was undone when he tried to rape the beautiful **Doria**, **Gemnon's** sweetheart, and was killed by Tarzan for it (T16;7, 11,13–15,18).

ersite A heavy Barsoomian building stone similar to marble. It is very expensive and can be polished to a high luster, and can also be carved (M4;1).

Erythra The organization which overthrew Zygo, King of **Athne**, and placed **Phoros** on the throne (T21;20).

es (*Pal*) Rough (T8;2).

es-a-da-ded (*Apa*) A drum made of a buckskin stretched over a hoop (A1;3).

Es-sat "Rough Skin" (*Pal*). The chief of the Waz-don tribe of Kor-ul-ja in Pal-ul-don. Out of jealousy he drove Om-at away from the tribe, but Om-at eventually returned and killed Es-sat, thus becoming chief (T8; 2–3).

"Escape on Mars" The title of the third book of *Llana of Gathol*, originally titled "Yellow Men of Mars."

Escape on Venus The fourth Venus novel (abbreviated V4), the events of which took place primarily in 1931 but were not sent to Burroughs telepathically for some years afterward — why, only **Carson Napier** knows. In any case, the novel is actually a series of four connected novelettes, which begin when Napier rescues **Duare** from death by her own father's command. On the way back to **Korva** (where Napier was now a tanjong) they are blown off course by a terrible hurricane and end up in the unexplored northern hemisphere of Venus, where they encounter all sorts of hideous humanoid monstrosities before finding their way back to **Southern Anlap**, where Korva lies.

Eshbaal A goatherd of the north **Midianites** from whose herd **Dr. Lafayette Smith** stole a goat for food, thus attracting the attention of the north Midianites and precipitating their ire upon himself, **Lady Barbara Collis**, and **Jezebel** (T15;15).

Esmerelda The 280 pound black woman who was **Professor Archimedes Q. Porter's** maid and was stranded with him on the African coast in 1909 along with Porter's daughter and secretary and Tarzan's cousin, **William Clayton**. Esmerelda was no consolation whatever to Jane, as she was incredibly superstitious and afraid of everything. She also had a strong tendency toward malapropism. She was rescued along with the party by the French navy and returned to **Baltimore**, then went with them afterward to **Wisconsin** (T1;13–14,22,24,27). She later accompanied the Porters on their cruise on the *Lady Alice*, which was wrecked not five miles north of where they were marooned before (T2;18,22). She stayed with Jane when she married Tarzan, and when **Jack Clayton** was kidnapped and recovered in 1911, Esmerelda identified the baby in the Claytons' absence (T3;21).

Esteban A Mexican who was associated with "General" Pesita and with Jose in 1916. He was hired by Grayson to kidnap Barbara Harding, then decided to keep her for himself (K2;13–14).

et (*Pal*) The number 80 (T8).

eta (*Ape*) Little (TC).

eta-gogo (*Ape*) Whisper (TC).

eta-koho (*Ape*) Warm (TC).

eta-nala (*Ape*) Low (TC).

Etamps A town near Paris, outside of which Tarzan and the Count de Coude had their duel in 1910 over Tarzan's seeming affair with the Countess de Coude (T2;6).

etarad (*Ape*) Arrow (probably a Tarzan coinage) (TC).

The Eternal Lover The original title of the first part of *The Eternal Savage*, abbreviated El.

The Eternal Savage A two-part novel originally published as *The Eternal Lover* (Part I) and *Sweetheart Primeval* (Part II). Today they are usually collected into one volume. The first part took place early in 1913 and was observed firsthand by Burroughs as a guest on Tarzan's estate in Africa at the time when the events of the story took place. It is the story of Victoria Custer of Beatrice, Nebraska, sister of Barney Custer, hero of *The Mad King*, and takes place between MK1 and MK2. In the story, Victoria meets up with her soul-mate, Nu, a caveman of the "Niocene" period who, kept in suspended animation by mysterious gases, awoke in our own time. The two somehow return together to the Niocene and relive their lives there as Nu and Nat-ul, until Victoria finally returns to the present upon Nat-ul's death and finds a real surprise.

Ethelwulf Second Saxon King of England, who succeeded his father Egbert and ruled from 839 to 858 (OT;9).

Etherealists One of the two philosophical schools of Lothar on Barsoom. Etherealists are led by Tario, the Jeddak of Lothar, and believe that there is no matter, only mind; to make anything happen, therefore, one must merely imagine it to be so and be joined by others in the conviction. They hold that eating is unnecessary, and exist entirely without food. This fact is used by the Realists as proof that all Etherealists are only disembodied minds with imaginary bodies (M4;7).

Ethiopia The present-day name of Abyssinia (T5;15).

etiquette, Barsoomian Most Barsoomian etiquette (though certainly not all) either applies to or touches on combat. A few customs: In single combat a warrior may only defend himself with the same weapon he is attacked with or a lesser one. Men do not kill women, nor women men (except in self-defense). No *man* lies; if he does not wish to speak the truth, he remains silent. The Barsoomian man only asks personal questions of his mother and lover, but no other women. He must fight for and win a woman before calling her his (see Princess)(M1;10–14).

Eugene City of Oregon, site of the University of Oregon (T22;11).

Eugenie Bay The large bay of Nadara's island near which the crew of the *Priscilla* found the Countess of Crecy's jewels, forgotten there by Nadara in her flight from Waldo Emerson Smith-Jones late in 1911. Because of this, the crew named the bay for the countess (CG2;6).

Eurobus The name given to the planet Jupiter by its inhabitants. Its inner, rocky part is 30,000 miles in circumference, and that core is surrounded by a 20 mile thick breathable atmosphere topped by an incredibly dense unbreathable atmosphere a few thousand miles thick. The planet's immense gravity is countered by its fast spin so that its gravity is about the same as Barsoom's. The inner world is the inhabited portion of the planet and is very volcanically active, the light and heat of the whole planet being provided by enormous volcanoes a hundred miles in diameter which constantly belch forth flames thousands of feet into the air. There is a chain of these monumental volcanoes all along the planet's equator, while others dot its surface. Like Earth, the planet possesses all sorts of different terrain, including mountains, jungles, deserts and immense, totally unnavigable oceans (unnavigable because of their incredible roughness, to be expected on such a geologically unstable world). Most of the land area is replete with jungle, and nearly all the plants of that jungle are carnivorous. The planet has at least two intelligent life forms and innumerable lower forms and is totally ruled by the warlike **Morgors**, who kidnapped John Carter in 1941 in order to pick his brain about Barsoom's defenses as a prelude to invasion. He escaped, of course, but it is unknown whether the Morgors ever invaded Barsoom or not (M11B;3–9).

Evans, Grace The girlfriend of **Custer Pennington** of **Rancho del Ganado**. She was a beautiful young thing with aspirations to movie stardom, and went to Hollywood in April of 1922 to achieve those aspirations. Once there she fell under the influence of **Wilson Crumb**, who after **Gaza de Lure's** defection got Grace addicted to cocaine, then morphine, then took her as his kept woman. During this period she wrote home less and less (principally because of shame) and died in April of 1923 after a fight with Crumb; her skull was fractured when he threw her against a table, and this injury was further complicated by morphine withdrawal (obviously, she could not get a "fix" in her condition) (GH; 1–10,27–30).

Evans, Guy Thackeray Grace Evans' brother, a bootlegger in 1920s **California** who was a good friend of the **Penningtons**. He was in love with **Eva Pennington** and had aspirations to being an author, but was forced into bootlegging by **Slick Allen** by a combination of threat and the promise of great financial gain (GH;2,6–9). When **Custer Pennington** was arrested in September of 1922 after being framed for bootlegging by Allen, Evans wanted to confess the crime but was talked out of it by Custer, who did not want to see his sister Eva crushed by the truth. All the while Custer was in prison (for six months) Evans tortured himself mentally because Custer was his best friend, and this experience was even worse than jail would have been. On the day Custer was released he went to see Grace, and his report of her situation prompted Evans to go the next day, just in time to speak to her before she died. He then set out to kill **Wilson Crumb** (guided only by a photograph), and when the director came to make a picture in **Ganado**, Evans killed him. He soon afterward found Eva, apparently dead after her attempted suicide, and went mad. He was brought to a sanitorium in Los Angeles and did not recover until months later, when he found out Eva was alive. He then recovered completely and confessed to Crumb's murder, freeing Custer (who was the main suspect). He was acquitted for the murder himself by reason of temporary insanity (GH;26–37).

Evans, Mae The mother of **Guy** and **Grace Evans** (GH;2).

Evans, Porky The owner of the barn in which "**Ark**" **Porter** beat up "**Skinny**" **Philander** around 1850, and reminded him of the incident some 60 years later (T1;16).

The Evening National A New York newspaper of the early 20th century owned by a former schoolmate of **Barney Custer's** (MK2;1).

Everitt The cashier at the **International Machine Company** in 1910s **Chicago** (EE;16).

Evodius One of the most trusted of the Emperor **Tiberius'** freedmen, who was crucified after seeing **Caligula** murder Tiberius (I;15).

Examiner A Hollywood newspaper of the 1930s (T17;33).

Exum The city that serves as the modern Barsoomian Greenwich. It lies directly south of **Horz** at zero degrees latitude and zero degrees longitude (M9;2).

Eyad One of the lieutenants of Sheik **Ab el-Ghrennem** when he kidnapped **Naomi Madison** and **Rhonda Terry** from the safari of ***The Lion Man*** crew in 1932. He was the only member of the band to escape destruction in the **Valley of Diamonds**, mostly because he had been left behind to guard their horses (T17;11,16,21).

eyebrows The Apache women plucked their eyebrows to make themselves more beautiful but, unlike their white sisters, plucked out their eyelashes as well (A1;6).

F-30-L One of the laboratories of **Ras Thavas'** medical complex at the **Tower of Thavas** (M6;5).

Fachan Chinese city from which the "arch fiend" **Kai Shang** hailed (T3;20).

Factor, Max Cosmetician and cosmetics magnate of the early 20th century (B1;5).

Fadan One of the officers of **Morgas**, the wizard of **Gavo**, when **Carson Napier** came there in 1932 (V5;7).

Fahd An Arab raider of the tribe **el-Harb** who shot at an elephant one day in 1921 and brought down **Tarzan** by accident, thus making him a prisoner of the Arabs. Fahd planned to kill Sheik **Ibn-Jad** so the sheik's brother **Tollog** would become the new sheik and give **Ateja**, Ibn-Jad's daughter, to him. He used the **matchlock** of **Zeyd**, his rival for Ateja, to shoot at Ibn-Jad, thus framing Zeyd. Fahd was also the only one of his tribe who could communicate with **Wilbur Stimbol** (in French) and so was the only one who knew of the lost American's wealth and the reward he promised for his safe return to civilization, a reward Fahd planned to keep for himself. After the sack of the **City of the Sepulcher**, Fahd abducted **Princess Guinalda** of **Nimmr** from her previous abductors and escaped into the forest with Stimbol, but was robbed of her by the king ape **Toyat**. The troublemaking Fahd was finally killed by Zeyd, who had come with Tarzan's **Waziri** to look for Tarzan (T11;1–2,8,21–23).

Fairbanks, Douglas (1883–1939) Screen name of Douglas Elton Ulman, an actor who became famous in swashbuckling roles. He married **Mary Pickford** and was one of the founders of United Artists (GH).

fal (*Amt*) Kill (V1;12).

Fal Sivas A scientist of **Zodanga** on Barsoom, inventor of the **mechanical brain** and the **interplanetary flier**. He hired John Carter as a bodyguard and assassin while the latter was working undercover in Zodanga, giving Carter a perfect cover for his spying activities and allowing him to discover the plot to kidnap **Dejah Thoris**. Fal Sivas was suspicious and sadistic, given to examining the brains of slaves (especially beautiful female ones) with his equipment in order to perfect the functioning of his mechanical brain. He was in close competition with **Gar Nal**, also of Zodanga, to build an interplanetary flier first. Fal Sivas became absolutely livid when Gar Nal launched his first. Soon afterward John Carter caught him again experimenting on the brains of living girls and stopped him, prompting the inventor to order him killed, so Carter had to subdue and bind him and steal his ship in order to pursue Gar Nal. Fal

Sivas eventually recalled the ship, commanding it to take no orders from anyone else but him, planning thus to strand John Carter on Barsoom while Dejah Thoris was on **Thuria**. While this was going on, Fal Sivas planned to hide in the house of Gar Nal, to whom he had promised the secret of the mechanical brain. Luckily for John Carter, Gar Nal double-crossed Fal Sivas by keeping Dejah Thoris prisoner in his house instead of on Thuria (M8;2–11,13,24).

Falsa A nation of **Middle Anlap** on Amtor, almost as technologically advanced as **Havatoo**. When **Carson Napier** arrived there in 1931, Falsa was engaged in a war with the nearby nation of **Panga** over grazing land, a war they had been fighting since 1921. The Falsans are militaristic (though not in the extreme) and consider women only as necessary evils (V4;45).

faltar (Contraction from **fal notar**, "kill ship")(*Amt*) A pirate ship (V3;19).

faltargan "Pirate ship man" (*Amt*). A pirate (V3;19).

Fantastic Adventures The magazine in which *Escape on Venus* first appeared as a serial in 1941 and 1942.

Farias, Manuel A Sonoran woodchopper shot in the summer of 1885 by an **Apache** of **Geronimo**'s band (A2;6).

faro A card game popular in the late 1800s (HB;1).

Farris, Abraham (**Abe**) A saloon and brothel keeper of early 20th century **Chicago** who got in trouble with the law after **Doarty** discovered that he had held **Maggie Lynch** prisoner in his brothel (GF;1–2).

Farris's A bar and brothel on **Dearborn Avenue** on the south side of **Chicago** in the early 1900s (GF;1).

fasces (*Lat*) The emblem carried at public gatherings to represent a particular official's authority. Each fasces was a bundle of rods surrounding an axe with a projecting blade (I).

Fash The king of **Suvi** in Pellucidar, uncle of **Do-gad**. He withdrew Suvi from the empire in 1931 to make war upon **Kali** and captured it, making himself its king and then luring **David Innes** there to destroy him in an ambush. He was later defeated and Innes and his warriors saved by Ghak the Hairy One, who brought an expeditionary force in answer to a command Innes had sent before marching to Kali (P7:1;2–3,7).

Fastus The son of Sublatus, emperor of Castra Sanguinarius. He was a shifty and reprehensible character who attempted to force himself on a young patrician girl named Dilecta (beloved of the officer Maximus Praeclarus) but was stopped by Tarzan. A thoroughly disliked person, he was killed by barbarians after Tarzan fostered a revolution in the city in August of 1923 (T12;9,20).

Father of Diamonds The legendary sacred gem of Ashair, which both Brian Gregory and Atan Thome were searching for — Thome with murderous means. The Father of Diamonds had originally been housed with the god Chon at Thobos, but was lost when the Ashairians sank the galley carrying both god and stone on a tour of Lake Horus. The Ashairians claimed to have captured the stone, but it lay on the lake bed for quite some time — all they actually had was a lump of coal, indeed the "Father of Diamonds." The priest Herkuf found the true stone again in 1936 while crossing the lake bottom with Tarzan to Ashair, and returned it to Chon. Question: Was the real Father of Diamonds a gem, or another lump of coal? We are not told (T20;2,23,29–32).

Father of Therns One of the titles held by Matai Shang, the Holy Hekkador of the Holy Therns of Barsoom (M2;7).

fauna, Amtorian The following is a list of the animals mentioned in the Venus books. See individual entries.

basto	lizard,	tharban
gantor	flying	tongzan
guypal	mistal	vere
kazar	rotik	zaldar
klangan	snakes	zangan
kloonobargan	targo	zorat

fauna, Barsoomian The following is a list of the animals mentioned in the Mars books. See individual entries.

ape,	calot	marsupial	sith
white	darseen	orluk	sorak
apt	fish	plant	spider
arbok	insects,	men	thoat
banth	giant	reptiles	ulsio
bat	malagor	rykor	zitidar
birds	mammal	silian	

fauna, Pellucidarian The following is a list of the animals mentioned in the Pellucidar books. See individual entries.

ant bear, giant	gyor	ta-ho-az
ant, Giant	hydrophidian	tandor
aurochs	jalok	tandoraz
azdyryth	lidi	tarag
aztarag	maj	thag
codon	orthopi	thipdar
dimorphodon	rat	tola
dyal	ryth	trachodon
dyrodor	sadok	trodon
dyryth	sithic	tylosaurus
eland	snakes	whale
gorobor	ta-ho	zarith

Favonia The beautiful daughter of Septimus Favonius of Castrum Mare whom Erich von Harben fell in love with at first sight. She was also coveted by Fulvus Fupus, however, and he used his influence with Emperor Validus Augustus to have von Harben imprisoned. With the fall of Augustus (and Fupus), however, order was restored and Favonia freed to love von Harben (T12;8,13,23). She eventually married him and moved with him to his father's mission in the Urambi country (T13;1).

feathers The few birds of Barsoom are very brightly and variously colored, and both the red and green races use their feathers for ornamentation (M1;21).

Federated Kingdoms of Pellucidar see Federated Tribes of Pellucidar

Federated Tribes of Pellucidar The organization upon which the Empire of Pellucidar was based (P2;2).

Fedol A great tandor hunter of Amiocap in Pellucidar, father of the girl Stellara. His wife Allara was stolen by the Korsars just after she had conceived, so that Fedol did not meet his daughter until almost two decades later. He was the chief of the village of Paraht and received Stellara and Tanar the Fleet One in peace there after seeing the birthmark that proved her his daughter (P3;3,5–6).

Feinheimer's Cabaret A basement restaurant of 1910s Chicago frequented by a "social goulash" of society people, businessmen and underworld figures. "The Lizard" got Jimmy Torrance a job waiting tables there when the latter was destitute (EE;9).

Fejjuan A black Galla slave of the tribe

el-Harb who had been stolen from his people in his youth. His real name was Ulala, and when he was sent by the Arabs to negotiate with the Galla for guides, he happened upon his own village and left the Arabs for good, returning only to lead them into a trap in the Valley of the Sepulcher (T11;10–13).

felucca A small, swift vessel propelled both by oars and by lateen sails. Most of the early ships of the navy of the Empire of Pellucidar were feluccas (P2;14).

fence (American slang) A dealer in stolen goods, through whom a criminal may dispose of such goods for cash (K1;1).

fendy (*Ara*) Clan or extended family (T11;1).

Ferdinand, Prince The son of King Otto. Ferdinand was a horrible and arrogant brat who grew up to be a horrible and arrogant adult. He struck up a friendship with the gardener's daughter Hilda de Groot which blossomed into love, and he kept her in an expensive apartment, promising to marry her after he became king; however, he married instead Princess Marie of a neighboring rich country. Ferdinand was so ambitious to become king that he cooperated with revolutionaries who killed his father to put him on the throne, but he double-crossed them and so they killed him as well, leaving General Sarnya in control of the government (LL; 3–7,9–13,17–19,23).

Fernando One of the great ape servants of Alemtejo who helped the false Tarzan abduct Sandra Pickerall in 1938 but misstepped on the way back to the city and fell to his death (T23;7–8).

Ferrath The Luthanian hospital attendant of the sanatorium at Tafelberg who betrayed the "Mad King" Leopold's presence there to Prince Peter of Blentz (MK1;7,9).

Ferus "Wild" (*Lat*). A famous racehorse of the Green Stables of early 1st century Rome (I;8).

Festivitas The mother of Maximus Praeclarus (T12;11).

Fibs An Arizonian who held the government beef contract for Fort Apache and was killed in the Apache siege of the fort in September of 1881 (A1;15).

Field of the Lions The great grassy plain lying north and west of Cathne in the valley of Onthar. It is named for the large, specially-bred lions of Onthar that roam there, kept by the men of Cathne (T16;4).

Fielder, Colonel Kendall J. An American military man of the 1940s, a friend of Captain Jerry Lucas' (and Burroughs'), who was an accomplished sleight-of-hand artist (T22;25).

Fields of Jetan An arena styled in the manner of a huge jetan board, upon which the Manatorians play their deadly version of the game (M5;15).

1580 Panizo Circle Shannon Burke's Hollywood address, known only to herself and her mother (GH;10).

"The Fight for the Balu" The third short story in *Jungle Tales of Tarzan*, in which Tarzan rescues the infant child of Teeka and Taug from a leopard. The events took place in 1907, and the story is abbreviated T6:3.

A Fighting Man of Mars The seventh book in the Mars series, originally published as a six-part serial in *Blue Book Magazine* from May to September of 1930. The events in it took place about 1926 and were sent as a communication to Earth via Gridley Wave by Ulysses Paxton in 1927 or 1928. The novel is one of the most interesting and exciting of the Mars series and concerns Tan Hadron of Hastor, a Heliumetic warrior who must rescue the woman he loves from the Jeddak of Jahar, who has developed a super-weapon with which he intends to conquer Barsoom. The book is abbreviated M7.

fighting potato A very loosely translated Barsoomian epithet for the usa, owing to its heavy usage by the military (M5;3).

Fink, Abe The real name of Abelard Furnois (T13;8).

Fire God To the Tarids of Ladan, the sun, to which they sacrifice prisoners. Ulvas, their jeddak, was supposed to be his son (M8;18). See also The Flaming God.

Fire Goddess see Loto-el-ho-ganja (V4; 26).

firemaker A small Barsoomian appliance used for starting fires in the field (M8;24).

Firg A lesser priest of **Opar** who was the keeper of the few functional keys of that ruined city. He was killed by the priestess **Nao** in order to free **Wayne Colt** in 1928 (T14;10).

First-Born The name the **Black Pirates of Barsoom** call themselves, from their belief that one of the four primordial creatures of Barsoom was a black man, and that he first of any creature burst his shell to come into the world (see **Tree of Life**). In any case, they are an immensely old race, one of the three original races of Barsoom (see **red men**), who fled to the south polar regions to escape the assaults of the savage **green men** (it is interesting to note that, in modern times, they were far better and fiercer fighters than the green men, according to John Carter). They built a huge city in the cavern of the buried sea of **Omean**, including huge pumps with which to pump out the water and so prevent the cavern's flooding. Later, they turned to a life of piracy because, like the **Therns**, they apparently felt that the "lesser" races of Barsoom owed them a living by virtue of their seniority, if nothing else. They preyed upon and deceived the Therns in the same way that that race deceived the rest of Barsoom, and were in turn deceived by their goddess-queen, **Issus**. The First-Born are a race of non-producers, and every one of them is some sort of noble. The men do nothing but fight and the women do absolutely nothing at all, each member of the race having slaves to do everything for them (M2;6–11).

A small colony of the First-Born had been established in the **Rift of Kamtol** in Barsoom's northern hemisphere at some time in the distant past, eventually separating from the main nation over time. They banded together every once in a while for a very big raid, but otherwise remained separate, even to the point of having their own **jeddak**. These First-Born were a bit more cosmopolitan than those of **Dor** and apparently made more frequent raids (M10:2).

First Men The name by which the Oparians call the **great apes**, whom they associate with, speak the language of, and sometimes mate with, although such mating is forbidden and punishable by banishment (T2; 20).

fish, Barsoomian Obviously, fish are a rare commodity on the almost-waterless world of Barsoom, but they inhabit the rivers **Iss** and **Syl** and the lost seas of **Korus** and **Omean**. **Tan Hadron** and **Nur An** caught fish and ate them raw while in the cavern of the Syl, knowing from history that they were edible (M7;7).

fish-men of Amtor see **Myposans** (V4;3)

Fishkill-on-the-Hudson A small resort town in **New York** (D;9).

Fitt The young **Korsar** chosen by **David Innes** to accompany himself and **Ja** of **Anoroc** as a guide to the land of the Korsars in return for the promise of his freedom. He later served as their guard while they were prisoners in the city of **Korsar** itself (P3;13).

Fitz-John, John One of the English barons who rebelled against **Henry III** in 1264 and fought against him at the Battle of **Lewes** on May 13th of that year (OT;16).

The Flag Specifically, The Flag of Argon, the **American flag** that **Julian 1st** carried in the battle of the **Argonne** in World War I, the same flag that **Julian 7th** and **8th** hid in their mantelpiece, the same flag that **Julian 9th** and his descendants carried into battle against the Kalkars. Over the years their reverence for it became awe, then worship. By the time of **Julian 20th**, The Flag had ceased to be a symbol for God (as **Julian 10th** had conceived of it) and had instead become a god itself; the Tribe of Julian believed that it had created the world, made the winds blow, etc. Although some of them may have doubted this idea, the only one to vocalize his doubt was the highly intelligent **Rain Cloud**, Julian 20th's younger brother (MM3;1–2).

flag, American In Kalkar-occupied America it was death to possess one of these, but **Julian 8th** still kept the one that came back from the **Argonne** with the body of Julian 1st. **Julian 9th** later carried it into battle against the Kalkars in 2122, then gave it to his wife, **Juana St. John**, to pass to his descendants (see **The Flag**) (MM2;3,11).

flak (WW II Slang) Anti-aircraft fire. It is an acronym from the German "Flieger Abwehr Kanone," meaning "aircraft defense gun" (T22;2).

The Flaming God The sun, worshipped by the **Oparians** in their ancient Atlantean tongue. The Flaming God is offered human sacrifice by the hand of the high priestess only, and the blood of the victim is collected by the priests and priestesses in golden cups and drunk. The victims are sacrificed at noon, just as the sun appears above the hole in the temple's roof placed there for that purpose (T2; 19–20).

Flammarion, Nicolas Camille (1842–1925) A French astronomer who especially studied the moon and Mars. He believed that Mars was inhabited by intelligent beings (M11B;1).

Flannagan, Detective Sergeant The **Chicago** policeman who almost caught **Billy Byrne** in **Kansas City**, but lost him, then was tipped off by a hobo as to Byrne's presence in **Shawnee, Kansas.** He missed him there thanks to **Mrs. Shorter**, but caught up with him in **El Paso**, where Byrne escaped by crossing the border (K2;4–6).

flashlight Barsoomian flashlights are small **radium** torches that can be turned on and off at will (M3;3).

Flatfoot The chief of the people of **Nadara**'s island in the early 20th century. Like **Korth**, he was a huge brute and an impulse killer who was hated and feared by his whole tribe. He went after Nadara when he heard that Korth was dead, but was himself followed by **Waldo Emerson Smith-Jones** and killed, though the American almost died in the attempt (CG1;4,9–11).

Flaubert, Monsieur The Count de **Coude**'s second in his duel with Tarzan outside **Etamps** in 1910 (T2;6).

Fletching A small town of southeastern England nine miles from **Lewes**, site of the baronial army's camp in their 1264 uprising against King **Henry III** (OT;15).

flier Barsoomian fliers, from the smallest one-man patrol ships (measuring about 16 feet long, two feet wide and three inches thick, and tapering to a point at either end) to the largest battleships (big enough for a thousand men) are all held aloft by the **eighth ray**, contained in **buoyancy** tanks within the ship's hull. If one of these tanks is ruptured the ship will begin to list, and if too many are damaged the ship cannot remain aloft. The rays can be directed to raise, lower, or hold stationary the ship. The ships are driven for-

ward or backward by propellers that at the time of John Carter's arrival on Barsoom were driven by compact, powerful **radium** motors. These fliers could attain top speeds of 150 to 200 miles per hour, the fastest being small **Heliumetic** fliers built with a certain trick of gearing which can be adapted to other fliers by those who know how (M1)(M2;13).

A new type of engine was invented by a virtually unknown **padwar** in the navy of Helium sometime during the first quarter of the 20th century. This engine is extremely powerful and apparently fuelless, being driven by the magnetic field of Barsoom. Its exact design is a secret, but basically consists of a propeller shaft supported by bearing armatures connected by switches to a device called an **accumulator** which soaks up the magnetic force and transmits it to the armatures, causing the shaft to turn by magnetism. The greater the number of armatures on the shaft, the faster it goes, and the magnetic force to the armatures is controlled by the throttle — the farther back it is pulled, the more armature switches are closed and the faster the motor turns. Since the engine derives its power from the planet's magnetic field, it is seemingly fuelless, and the power it can generate is limited only by the strength of its construction. The first ships built with these engines could attain a speed of about 300 miles per hour, and later versions achieved a speed of 400 miles per hour (M7;2)(M9;1).

The great battleships of Barsoom are armored above and below and are bristling with big guns, not to mention bomb bays in the keel. It is customary in Barsoomian naval warfare that should a ship wish to surrender, her commander must voluntarily jump from the prow of the ship as a signal. If the remaining ships of a fleet wish to surrender together, the fleet commander must take the awful plunge to his death (M1;26). Most battleships carry many smaller fliers on board: Five ten-man cruisers, ten five-man scouts, and a hundred one-man scouts is within normal equipment range (M2;19).

The street-fliers of most of Barsoom are the same as regular fliers, but built for city needs, having a ceiling of only about 100 feet and a top speed of about 60 miles per hour (M9;24). Traffic flows smoothly, as at intersections east-west traffic must rise above north-south, being forced to do so by ramps on either side of the intersection. Passing slower vehicles takes place vertically, and to turn one rises above both lanes, then settles into line when possible. Freight and passenger vehicles fly at a higher level (M4;2).

There are few fliers in **Phundahl** or **Too- nol**, almost none in **Kaol**, and none at all in **Manator, Lothar** or any other ancient (lost) cities. The fliers of **Jahar, Tjanath**, and **Pan- kor** are all primitive and of obsolete design. In **Okar**, there are no standard fliers, but there is a strange sort of ground flier with huge, balloon-like tires filled with just enough eighth ray to give the car traction. They are driven by propellers and roll along the moss-covered streets of Okarian cities smoothly and silently (M3;9). After the advent of technical communication with Barsoom, flier technology became known on Earth as well, and by the 1970s Barsoomian-type fliers could be seen all over the Earth (MM1;1). In addition to their large planetary and interplanetary fliers, the **Morgors** of **Eurobus** also had small ground fliers much like those on Barsoom (M11B;6).

Flier is also the name given to a **jetan** piece having a move of three spaces diagonally in any direction or combination. It can also jump intervening pieces. In ancient times this piece was called an **odwar** (M5;16).

flier, interplanetary The first inter-planetary flier on Barsoom was completed in 1930 by **Fal Sivas of Zodanga** and was cigar-shaped, attaining its greatest width just behind the nose and gradually tapering off toward the rear. It was controlled by a me-chanical brain and could fly from Barsoom to either of its two moons at about 500 miles per hour, directed by the mechanical brain under control of its pilot's thoughts. A similar flier, controlled directly by a human pilot, was built around the same time by **Gar Nal** of Zo-danga, a rival of Fal Sivas.

The interplanetary ships of the **Morgors** of **Eurobus** use the **eighth ray** of the various planets they pass near, but also use gravita-tional forces and cosmic rays to propel their cigar-shaped ships (with fins and rudders at the back) along at a maximum interplanetary speed of 23 miles per second, fast enough to travel from Barsoom to Eurobus in only 18 days. They can cruise within an atmosphere at 600 miles per hour. These ships are equipped with weird weapons unknown to Barsoomian science and have magnetizable

hulls so that **sands of invisibility** can be sprayed on them and will adhere, rendering the ships invisible. It was with a fleet of such ships that they hoped to conquer Barsoom (M11B;1–3).

Even after the repulsion of the Morgor in-vasion, the people of Barsoom could not copy the Morgor technology, and soon afterward communication was established with Earth, allowing the scientists of Earth and Barsoom to cooperate in developing interplanetary fliers. The first, built by the Barsoomians and launched in 2015, did not have any means of negating the gravity of the sun or other plan-ets (other than Earth and Barsoom) and was lost in space, saved by its crew's efforts from a collision with the sun but consigned to oblivion in the void, headed outward at 1000 miles per hour. The Earth scientist **Orthis** later succeeded in isolating the eighth rays of the sun, Mercury, Venus, the Moon, and Jupiter, and an Earth-built ship, the *Barsoom*, was launched in 2025, provided with **buoy-ancy tanks** filled with the eighth rays of all the aforementioned bodies and three kinds of engines: Atmospheric, deep space impulse en-gines (driven by the eighth rays of Earth and Barsoom to a top speed of 1200 miles per hour) and auxiliary engines which could iso-late the eighth ray of any heavenly body and use it to propel the ship at up to 600 miles per hour. This engine would be used in the event of a breakdown of the primary engine, as it could be used to escape any planet. The *Bar-soom* never reached its destination, however, as it was sabotaged by its designer in an act of revenge and landed inside the moon after passing through a crater into its interior (MM1;1–2).

Orthis later became the ruler of the **Kalkars**, the dominant race of **Va-nah** (the world inside the moon), and showed them how to construct space fliers, a fleet of a thou-sand of which he led to Earth, conquering the disarmed planet easily. After Orthis' death, the Kalkars used the fleet to transport about seven million Kalkars per year to Earth until all the ships were lost or broke down and left to rust, since the lazy and ignorant Kalkars did not know how to fix them (MM2;1–3).

Floating Islands of Pellucidar Their name is self-explanatory. They float in the **Bandar Az** of Pellucidar, drifting in a slow current which sometimes takes them far out to sea and sometimes close to land. They are inhabited by Pellucidar's black race and float because each island is actually a huge patch of a cactus-like plant with a common root system, holding together a big clump of dirt formed from dead and decomposed plants. Vines, grass and several other types of small plants grow in this dirt, holding the island together even tighter. The cactus-like plant is edible, both its bulk and its fruit, and can be tapped for fresh water (P6;23).

Floran A Barsoomian warrior of **Gathol**, later a slave in **Manator**, who volunteered to be on **Gahan of Gathol's** jetan team in order to win **Tara of Helium** from the Manatorians. He survived the escape from the **Fields of Jetan** to reach the camp of **U-Thor** and assisted **Val Dor** in the repair of Tara's **flier**, which they then used to fly to Gathol to raise an invasion force (M5;16,22).

Flory, James A bandit of medieval **Derbyshire**, formerly a follower of **The Black Wolf**, who became one of **Norman of Torn's** men after the latter bested Flory and his brother **John** in combat in 1256. He later became one of Norman's captains (OT;6,10).

Flory, John One of the bandits of **The Black Wolf's** band in medieval **Derbyshire**, who was wounded by **Norman of Torn** in 1256 and afterward became one of the first five men in his band. He later became one of Norman's captains, but was killed by **de Vac** (so he could take Flory's place) in May of 1264 (OT;6,10,18).

flumen (*Lat*) River (T12;6).

Flying Death A guided missile invented by **Phor Tak** of Barsoom. It could be attuned to detect and travel to any substance, exploding upon collision with that substance (such as the blue protective pigment of a **Jaharian flier**). The Flying Death would be coated with the compound of invisibility to make it undetectable to its target until it was too late. The only working model was disintegrated by **Tan Hadron** (M7;10,17).

flying wings A flying device, one of the few scientifically advanced devices left in **Laythe**, the last city of the **U-gas of Va-nah**. The wings were strapped to the arms of the flier and provided steering and propulsion, while lift was provided by a lighter-than-air gas (probably the **eighth ray** of the moon in

actuality, considering the small size of the bag) in a bag strapped to the flier's back. **Nah-ee-lah** was flying above Laythe in such a contrivance when a freak windstorm carried her away and deposited her in the hands of the **Va-gas** (MM1;6). See also **Equilibrimotor**.

Fo-nar A panthan from **Jahar** who was the sole warrior aboard **Hin Abtol's** ship *Dusar* when John Carter took over as its **dwar**. He helped Carter clean up the ship and recruit a crew for it, and Carter made him the ship's first **padwar**. When the crew later mutinied, Fo-nar was kept by the mutineers as pilot, but he was rescued after the defeat of Hin Abtol's fleet (M10:3;5–10)(M10:4;13).

Fodil One of the followers of **Ibn Dammuk** who helped him abduct **La of Opar** from the camp of **Abu Batn** in 1928 (T14;10).

Folar An officer of the *Nojo Ganja*, the pirate ship which picked up **Carson Napier** from the sea between **Anlap** and **Vepaja** in 1930. Folar picked a fight with Napier almost immediately, but Napier made a fool of him and thus an enemy of him. Later, Napier was forced to kill Folar when the pirate attacked him again with a pistol (V3;19–20).

Foley, Annie The maiden name of the one-quarter Cherokee mother of **Andrew Macduff**, later known as **Shoz-dijiji**. She was killed by **Apaches** in **Arizona** shortly after his birth in 1863 (A1;1).

food, synthetic The culture vats of Ras Thavas could also be used to grow synthetic food for either human or **hormad** consumption (M9;4).

Fooge One of the woman warriors of **Oog** who took **David Innes** prisoner in 1929 (P6;2).

Foola One of the husbands of **Gluck**, chief of the gender-reversed **Oog** tribe of Pellucidar who captured **David Innes** in 1929 (P6;3).

"For Liberty!" The battle cry of the **Soldiers of Liberty** (V1;10).

forandus The hardest and lightest metal known to Barsoomian science (M7;11). See also **harbenite**.

Forbidden City The hidden underwater city of **Ashair** (T20;1).

Foreign Legion   The nickname given by the Dutch guerrillas of Japanese-occupied Sumatra to the little group that was to attempt to steal a boat and reach Australia in the spring of 1944, owing to its mixed national and racial character. It was made up of Tarzan (an Englishman living in Africa), AAF Captain Jerry Lucas (an American with Cherokee blood), AAF Staff Sergeant Joe "Datbum" Bubonovitch (an American of Russian extraction), AAF Staff Sergeant Tony "Shrimp" Rosetti (an Italian-American), Tak van der Boss (a Dutch army reserve officer), Corrie van der Meer (the daughter of a murdered Dutch planter), and Sarina (the rough-and-ready daughter of a Dutch pirate and an Indonesian woman). The group later added Sing Tai, Corrie van der Meer's faithful Chinese servant (who had been in hiding until Tarzan found him) and staff sergeants Bill Davis and Carter Douglas, who had been captured by the Japanese and rescued by Tarzan. All of the group survived to reach Australia except for van der Boss and Sing Tai (T22;26,30).

Forest of Death   A dank, dark climax forest of Pellucidar lying a good distance from Lo-har, between it and Basti. The forest is so full and dark at ground level that only mushrooms and a few stunted green plants grow on its floor and almost no animals live there except for the horrible Gorbuses and a few predatory reptiles (P5;8).

Forest of Lost Men   Another name by which the men of Invak call the Forest of Invak (M10:4;3).

Formosa   Former name of the island of Taiwan (K1;15).

Fort Apache   U.S. Cavalry outpost with an Indian reservation attached, site of a siege laid by the Apaches after the Battle of Cibicu Creek in September of 1881 (A1;15).

Fort Bowie   A U.S. Cavalry outpost in 19th century Arizona (A2;6).

Fort Dinosaur   The name given by the U-33 crew to the fortress they built in Caspak two miles inland from the central lake alongside the northwest stream. It was 135 feet square with stone walls three feet thick at the bottom and 18 inches thick at the top, 15 feet high. It had wooden buildings within (C1;6).

Fort McKane   American cavalry outpost of Arizona where Mangas Colorado was trapped and killed in the summer of 1863 (A1;1).

Fort Marion   Military outpost of Florida at which Geronimo, Na-chi-ta and all of their renegades (except Shoz-dijiji) were imprisoned in September of 1906. They eventually grew sick in the humid climate and had to be moved to Fort Sill, Oklahoma (A2;14).

Fort Thomas   U.S. Cavalry outpost on the Gila River, about 50 miles due south of Fort Apache (A1;15).

Fortis   "Powerful" (*Lat*). A famous racehorse of early 1st century Rome, sire of Spatium (I;8).

Fosh-bal-soj   The Wieroo of Caspak who captured John Bradley on September 15, 1916, and carried him off to Oo-oh as a prisoner, only to have Bradley kill him soon after their arrival there (C3;2).

fosse   (*Fr*) Moat (V5;6).

Foster   The first officer of the *Lotus*, Anthony Harding's steam yacht (K1;4).

Fou-tan   The daughter of Beng Kher, king of the lost Khmer city of Pnom Dhek. She fled that city to escape an unwanted marriage to Prince Bharata Rahon and was captured by the warriors of Lodivarman of Lodidhapura and made a dancing girl in their temple. With the help of the American Gordon King, she escaped that city and returned to her own, falling in love with King in the process. She attempted to get her father to agree to her marrying King, but to no avail — in a fury, he ordered King executed and Fou-tan returned his favor by helping him escape, but duty would not let her leave again. Later, Bharata Rahon mortally wounded Beng Kher in secret and left him for dead, then tried to force Fou-tan to marry him. She was rescued by King again and taken to her dying father, who blessed their marriage, making King a king — that of Pnom Dhek (HM;5, 8-17).

Four-F   The fourth classification in the American selective service, reserved for those who are not physically fit enough to take into the army for one reason or another (T22;4).

1421 Vista del Paso The Hollywood address of Wilson Crumb, from which he and Gaza de Lure sold drugs (GH;5).

Francois A "servant" of the Countess de Coude's in Paris, whom Alexis Paulvitch invented on the telephone in order to lure Tarzan to the de Coude home late one evening so the count could find Tarzan and the countess in a compromising position (T2;5).

Frank A. Munsey Co. The company which published the popular *Argosy* family of magazines in the first part of the 20th century, including *All-Story, All-Story Weekly*, etc.

Frecoult, Monsieur Jules The alias adopted by Albert Werper when he infiltrated Tarzan's estate in the guise of a big game hunter to kidnap Jane for Achmet Zek to hold for ransom (T5;2).

Freetown The capital of Sierra Leone, a British colony of west Africa. Freetown was a fairly important port of 19th century Africa (T1;1).

French The first human language Tarzan learned to speak. It was taught to him by Lt. Paul d'Arnot rather than English because the lieutenant could more easily teach his own native language. Of course, this caused innumerable problems, given Tarzan's knowledge of written English, and rendered his learning of both French and English more difficult later (T1;23,27–28).

French Somaliland A tiny French colony on the Red Sea, today known as Djibouti. In 1928, a bit of trouble was caused by communist agitators there (T14;1).

Frenjy (*Ara*) A Frenchman or Frenchmen (T11;8).

Friedrich A Luthanian brigand of the band of Yellow Franz who captured Barney Custer in the Black Mountains after he escaped from Blentz in October of 1910 (MK1;6). Another Friedrich was a servant of the house from which Barney Custer stole a car to escape with the Princess von der Tann from Captain Maenck's forces in September of 1914 (MK2;8).

Friedrichschafen A German manufacturing center which was home in the early 20th century to several airship-building factories. It was here that the great dirigible O-220 was built early in 1927 (T13;1).

friendship ritual The friendship ritual of the primitive people of Nadara's island consisted of each taking a handful of grass, giving it to the other, and then rubbing the handful given one by the other on one's own forehead. This simple ceremony constituted an unbreakable bond (CG2;9).

frigidarium (*Lat*) The large, cold pool of a Roman public bath (T12;8).

Frink A Kapar agent in the city of Pud in Auris who gave Tangor and Morga Sagra a Kaparan plane with which to enter Kapara when Tangor "defected" to the Kapars in 1940 (B2;2).

Frisco (American slang) San Francisco (D).

Fritz The servant of House Von der Tann who was planted among the servants of Blentz in order to help the "Mad King" Leopold escape in September of 1910. After the escape, all of the servants were replaced and Fritz gave up his position to Joseph, another Von der Tann plant (MK1;4).

Fronteras A small Mexican town of Sonora (A2;14).

fronters In the parlance of the inhabitants of the Valley of the Sepulcher, the people of Nimmr, descendants of the followers of Sir Gobred, who held that the crusaders had not yet reached the Holy Land and must therefore continue to wear their crosses upon their breasts until the crusade was finished (T11;12). See also backers.

Frug The chief of the Pellucidarian cliff-village of Basti when Lt. Wilhelm von Horst was enslaved there in 1927. They later met again as prisoners of the Gorbuses and escaped together, but Frug afterward abducted von Horst's sweetheart, La-ja, while the German slept. Frug was killed by Daj of Lo-har in the Little Canyon of the Mammoth Men of Ja-ru (P5;5,10–11,17).

Führer "Leader" (*Ger*). The title taken by Adolf Hitler, dictator of Germany from 1933 to 1945 under the Nazi party (T24;3).

Fulad An area north of Tagwara, to whose sultan Sheik Ibn Aswad planned to sell Victoria Custer after he abducted her from Tarzan's estate in 1912 (E1;8).

Fulm, John de, Earl of Buckingham
One of the sycophantic courtiers of **Henry III** of England. He was a foreigner by birth, but was one of Henry's favorites. He captured **Norman of Torn** and **Joan de Tany** near London in the summer of 1263, but Norman escaped with the girl, returning the next day to avenge her by killing de Fulm (OT;1,13–14).

Fulvus Fupus A short, dark, greasy-looking patrician of **Castrum Mare** who was often a guest of **Septimus Favonius'** and was in love with his daughter, though she certainly did not return the favor. He took an instant disliking to the noble **Erich von Harben** and vice versa. By manipulating the emotions of **Validus Augustus** he had himself declared heir to that emperor, then used his clout to have von Harben sent to the games. He took over as emperor after the assassination of Validus, but fled when **Cassius Hasta,** the true heir, returned to Castrum Mare (T12;8,13,21–23).

fun A Chinese coin of very small value (CG2;10).

funeral, Apache The Apaches afforded very elaborate burials to their chiefs, at least to well-loved ones like **Cochise.** A large grave was dug at least six feet deep, with walls of stone built up from the bottom to a height of three feet. The corpse was then dressed in his finest clothes and laid with all of his weapons and cherished possessions on a layer of blankets in the bottom of the grave. A layer of poles was then placed atop the stone walls and more blankets placed atop these, then the whole was covered with dirt and stones. The second blankets kept dirt from falling on the corpse, and the stones prevented coyotes from digging up the body. Afterward, a few of the chief's horses were killed to provide mounts for his spirit and the immediate family destroyed all of their possessions to show mourning. The rest of the tribe would then destroy all food on hand and go hungry for 48 hours in respect for the dead chief (A1;3).

funeral, Cathnean Cathneans who cannot afford to pay for a funeral are stripped and thrown into the street for the stray lions to eat. Those who can afford a funeral (and those who cannot but are diseased) are thrown into the volcano **Xarator.** Many Cathneans who can afford a funeral have their corpses fed to the lions anyway, as the Cath-neans worship them and it is an honor to be eaten by one (T16;11).

funeral, Wieroo The Wieroo of Caspak dispose of their dead by cutting off the head and wings; the wings are saved and the skull is used for building, but the body is dropped down a pit into the river which runs below the city into Caspak's warm central sea, without ceremony. Garbage is disposed of in a similar fashion (C3;3).

fungus, Lunar The outer surface of the Earth's moon holds only an extremely tenuous atmosphere if any, but a species of fungus lives there, its entire life cycle taking place in one sidereal month. The fungus blooms as the sun touches it, grows at a very rapid rate (observable by the naked eye) into an angular, grotesque plant with broad, thick leaves of many colors, sometimes hundreds of feet in height. As the shadow of the lunar night touches it, the plant dies and crumbles into powder immediately. There may be other life forms which feed on the plant, but that is not a proven fact (MM1;1).

Funston An American cavalry officer in charge of the 13th Cavalry who, in March of 1916, chased **Pancho Villa** into Mexico after his raid on **Columbus, New Mexico.** He failed to catch him, but did catch and defeat "General" **Pesita**'s little army (K2;17).

fur (*Pal*) The number 30 (T8).

Furnois, Abelard A Hollywood film director of the 1920s who was born **Abe Fink** (T13;8).

Furnois, Cynthia One of **Jason Gridley**'s girlfriends, the daughter of Hollywood film director **Abelard Furnois.** She was a beautiful but haughty girl, and a "rotten little snob" to boot (T13;8).

Furp The go-sha (king) of the **Xexot** city of **Tanga-tanga** in Pellucidar when **O-aa** was "Noada" there in 1931. He was not sure whether O-aa was really a goddess, but believed in playing it safe. After **David Innes'** appearance as **Pu** and his subsequent tax reforms, Furp plotted against him, only to be met by a mob of Innes' loyal followers, since Innes had anticipated Furp's actions. Furp then ran off with his loyal followers to **Lololo** to seek the friendship of the new go-sha there (P7:2;7)(P7:3;1–6).

Fuwalda The sailing ship that Lord and Lady Greystoke chartered to take them from Freetown to his post in British West Africa. It was a one hundred ton barkentine run by a brutal captain with a crew of cutthroats. As on many ships before, brutal treatment led to mutiny, but the Greystokes, having tried to help the men, were put ashore rather than being killed. Sometime in the next two months the *Fuwalda* was wrecked and her wreckage washed up on St. Helena, so the search for the missing Greystokes was abandoned, the navy assuming they had been lost at sea (T1;1–2).

ga (*Ape*) Red (T6:4).

ga (*Cpk*) Rope; specifically, the heavy rawhide lasso used by the Galus of Caspak (C2;6). See also honda.

Ga-un One of the great apes of the tribe of Ungo who accidentally stumbled upon the Temple of Chon in November of 1936. Ga-un, confused, would have killed Helen Gregory had not Tarzan intervened (T20;31–32). In 1938, Tarzan ran into Ga-un again near the Ruturi Mountains (T23;8).

Ga-va-go The chief of the No-vans, the tribe of Va-gas of Va-nah who captured Julian 5th and Orthis in 2025. Not knowing whether they were edible or not, Ga-va-go commanded that they be taught the tongue of Va-nah so he could ask them himself. When Julian 5th told him that they were poisonous, Ga-va-go asked what humans ate, if not each other. When Julian 5th answered him truthfully, Ga-va-go demanded to be led to Julian's country, where there was plenty of meat for everyone. Orthis promised to do this, thus earning himself the friendship of Ga-va-go, who gave Nah-ee-lah to him. Of course, Julian had something to say about that (MM1; 5–7).

Gabriel A powerful archangel of Judeo-Christian mythology who is said to be the being who will announce the Judgment Day by blowing on his trumpet, the sound of which will raise the dead from their graves (T15;2).

Gabula Erich von Harben's black body servant on his expedition to the Wiramwazi Mountains in 1923. Gabula fled along with the others when the expedition got too close to the area that they considered haunted by evil ghosts, but he returned later, willing to face what he believed to be certain death to fulfill his oath to von Harben. When he did so, he brought with him food and a rifle and helped von Harben descend into the deep valley he had discovered, where the two lost Roman cities lay. He was left free when von Harben was imprisoned for suspicion of treachery and succeeded in assassinating Validus Augustus at the commencement of his yearly games in August, fleeing into the city with von Harben in the confusion that followed (T12;2,4,21).

Gaetulicus, Cornelius Lentulus An extremely popular Roman general who commanded the legions in Germany; he conspired with Lepidus and Caligula's sisters against the emperor and was caught and executed in A.D. 39 (I;18).

Gahan The Jed of Gathol, a perfect prototype of his people: Vain in the area of personal appearance (but not overbearingly so) but very valiant in war. He met Tara of Helium at one of her father's court functions and offended her by an avowal of love, sending her into a tantrum during which she took off in her personal flier and was blown away by a rare Barsoomian windstorm. Gahan pursued her through the storm, eventually catching up to her at Bantoom, where he rescued her (with the help of Ghek) from the clutches of the king Kaldane, Luud. After drifting in Tara's disabled flier for a few days, they landed near Manator, where he was captured, freed by Ghek, and entered the jetan games of Manator to win Tara's freedom. He and she were eventually married and had a daughter, Llana (M5) (M10).

Gal-lan-tin A white bounty hunter of the 1840s who made quite a bit of money by presenting "Apache" scalps (actually those of Mexicans that he had killed in an Apache-like manner) to the governor of Chihuahua, who had offered a reward of $30 per scalp out of anger over the continued killing of Mexican soldiers by "Apaches" (actually Gal-lan-tin and his men). Gal-lan-tin was finally killed by the Yuma while fleeing to California (A1;8).

Galerius (Died A.D. 311) The adopted son and successor of the Roman emperor Diocletian (R;7).

Galla An African people who make up about 40 percent of the population of Ethiopia. They live chiefly in the area called el-Habbash by the Arabs; many Gallas knew of the location and secret entrance to the Valley of the Sepulcher but would not go there because all who did never returned (T11;1, 10–12).

Galla Galla The immensely fat old chief of the Bagalla tribe who captured the "Tarzan Twins" in 1920 (TT1;6).

galley, Ashairian The galleys of Ashair were similar to those of their ancient Egyptian ancestors and were used to war on Thobos, travel about Lake Horus, and travel down the river to the outside world (to a limited extent) (T20;12–13).

Galu "Rope-man" (*Cpk*). The highest type of human life in Caspak, totally human and usually very comely in appearance. They wear simple clothing of well-tanned hides with a leopard tail as a badge and live in well-organized communities which are walled and consist of stone buildings. Galus have a complex language, work iron, gold and precious stones, and use a lasso as their weapon of distinction. Galus are at the apex of development in Caspak (discounting the alternate Wieroo line) and are the only race which produces cos-ata-lu of both sexes (C1;9) (C2;2,5–7).

galul (*Ape*) Blood (TC).

Galveston A port on an island of southeast Texas. Billy Byrne planned to take Barbara Harding there to live until he found out that he had been exonerated from blame in the murder of Schneider (K2;17).

Gama, Christoforo da The king of Alemtejo in the 1930s, who claimed that Rand (the false Tarzan) was a god because he had fallen from the sky; Gama sent Rand out to get a goddess. His people took to the belief, however, and accepted both Rand and Sandra Pickerall (whom he had abducted) as deities. Da Gama fell from power in 1938 when the real Tarzan came to Alemtejo and was proclaimed as the true god. Da Gama denied it and the people overthrew him, forcing him to flee. He was a direct descendant of the first Christoforo da Gama, brother of the Portuguese navigator Vasco da Gama, who was defeated with his musketeers by the Muslims and (according to history) executed, but

actually escaped south and founded Alemtejo in the Ethiopian Highlands (T23;4, 12,21).

Gama, Vasco da (1469?–1524) Portuguese explorer who first circumnavigated Africa in 1491. His brother Christoforo da Gama founded Alemtejo in the Ethiopian Highlands (T23;12).

Gamba The Jukan village most distant from the village of Meeza (P6;9).

Gamba The go-sha (king) of the Xexot city of Lolo-lolo in Pellucidar when Dian the Beautiful came there via balloon in 1931. He was a bit of a bronze age atheist and did not believe in the priests or their religion, even after the arrival of the "Noada" Dian. He definitely reveled in her pulchritude, however, and helped her in her plan to break the power of Hor and the priesthood. The plan backfired, though, and Gamba barely escaped the city alive with Dian after the people turned against him thanks to Hor's rumors and lies. He was enslaved on the island of Tandar with Dian soon afterward when they landed there after being swept out into the Korsar Az by a storm. They escaped and were rescued by Hodon the Fleet One and his troops, who had come looking for O-aa. Gamba later settled in Sari (P7:2;5–7)(P7:3;1,3,5–7)(P7:4;12).

gamboge A bright yellow-orange pigment obtained from the gum resin of a tree of Southeast Asia (HM;9).

games, Barsoomian Among the green Barsoomians, "Great Games" are held yearly for all horde members. These games are like those of the ancient Romans at their worst — there are gladiatorial fights, people are thrown to wild beasts, and other such fare makes up the bulk of the bloodbath. The victors of each contest are pitted against one another, and the single winner of the day, whether man or beast, is released (M1;19).

The **red men** of Manator have "Great Games" in the form of jetan for the settlement of quarrels, punishment of criminals or traitors, execution of troublemakers, and for allowing slaves and prisoners to win their freedom (M5;13). Tjanath also holds games for the execution of prisoners, but it can be many years between those games (M7;5).

Among the **First-Born**, the games are different. They are held monthly, and serve a fourfold purpose: To exterminate those who saw **Issus** a year since; to kill those men captured by the blacks from the outer world and the domain of the **Therns**, so they can be eaten; to entertain the population; and to test sinful men of the First-Born in trial by combat with a beast or slave (M2;11).

The First-Born of **Kamtol** hold games which are different from all other Barsoomian games, being more like Earthly boxing matches in that they are played for disarming or first blood, and seldom to the death. The games are played by slaves and bet upon, bringing the owner of a good fighter a great deal of profit in winnings (M10:2;7).

Gamfor A huge Amtorian man who had been a farmer under **Vepajan** rule but was under the **Thorists** a sailor. He hated the Thorists and took part in **Carson Napier's** mutiny aboard the *Sofal* (V1;9).

gams (American slang) Legs, especially a woman's (T22;14).

gan (*Amt*) Man (V1;14).

Gan Had A Toonolian warrior of Barsoom who was a prisoner of the **hormads** at the same time as John Carter and **Vor Daj** were. He later became one of Vor Daj/**Tor-dur-bar's** lieutenants while the latter was an odwar in **Morbus**, but deserted Vor Daj when he wished to return to Morbus after **Janai** (M9;4,16,19).

Gan-ho An assassin recruited as part of the crew of the *Dusar*, the ship John Carter stole from the **Panars** of Barsoom. Gan-ho rebelled upon being told that the ship was going to **Pankor** to rescue **Llana of Gathol**, and John Carter was forced to kill him in order to maintain discipline (M10:3;8).

Gan Hor The dwar of the utan of **Gatholian** herdsmen who captured John Carter while he was disguised as a **Black Pirate** during the siege of Gathol by the **Panars**. When he found out who their prisoner actually was he would have had **Kor-an** killed for John Carter's mistreatment had the Warlord allowed it. It was Gan Hor who filled Carter in on Gathol's situation (M10:3;3).

Ganado The little village below the **Rancho del Ganado** in early 20th century southern **California** (GH;22).

Ganak The Bison-Men of Pellucidar, a race inhabiting a forested, rocky area not very

far from **Ja-ru**. Ganaks are squat, powerfully built, and very hairy and have horns like a bison's growing out of the sides of their foreheads. They also have bison tails, emit bison noises, eat grass and chew cud. Ganaks are very primitive, use few tools, and are not terribly bright, but they do make a liquor they call "**dancing-water**" (P5;20).

Ganale Dorya A river of **Ethiopia**, one of the tributaries of the **Wabi Shebelle**; it is possibly equivalent to or near the **Neubari** (T20;32).

gando (*Ape*) Win (TC).

ganfal "Man-kill" (*Amt*). Criminal (V1;8).

Gangor A ship captain of **Japal** on Amtor who conspired with **Myposan** prisoners to rid himself of the soldiers who had seen him hide while others fended off a Myposan attack. He later led a revolution against **Jantor, Jong of Japal**, but was killed by Jantor's son, **Kandar** (V4;9,19–23).

ganja (*Amt*) Woman (V3;5).

Ganjo The **rokor** in command of the **Athgan 975** when **Carson Napier** and **Ero Shan** came aboard it in 1931 (V4;46).

gantor An Amtorian animal of Southern **Anlap**. It is larger than an African elephant and has elephantine feet with three-part hooves. Its head is like a bull's and is equipped with a single horn in its forehead (like a rhinoceros' but a foot long) and a very large mouth with powerful teeth. Its coat is short and colored light yellow with white splotches like those of a pinto. The gantor has a short neck covered by a heavy, dark mane and its tail is like a bull's. Gantors are used as mounts and beasts of burden in **Korva** (V3;5).

Gantry, Bill The guide and hunter for the 1938 safari of Timothy Pickerall and **Pelham Dutton**. Gantry summoned his acquaintance Tom Crump, the notorious ivory poacher, for help when Pickerall's daughter **Sandra** was kidnapped by **Rand**. Gantry got scared and turned back when the party reached cannibal country, but was caught and eaten by the **Waruturi** (T23;2,13).

Gantun Gur An assassin of **Amhor** who was captured by the **hormads** and taken to **Ras Thavas**. The master mind destroyed his brain and moved into his body the brain of Tor-dur-bar, an unusually intelligent hormad who had befriended Vor Daj and sworn loyalty to Ras Thavas. From that time on, Tor-dur-bar took a human name as well as body, being called Tun-gan, a transposition of the syllables of "Gantun." Later, when he was picked up by an Amhorian cruiser, Tun-gan took Gantun Gur's own name and position, since everyone believed him to be the real assassin anyway (M9;8–9,23).

gap (*Amt*) Prison (V3;7).

Gap kum Rov "Prison of Death" (*Amt*). The Korvan equivalent of the Bastille or the Tower of London, in which political prisoners of Korva were kept, especially during the Zani period (V3;7,10).

Gapth The Kalkar warrior who captured Julian 5th while he was attempting to escape the Kalkar city into which he and Nah-ee-lah had blundered (MM1;10).

Gar Nal An inventor of Zodanga on Barsoom, a worse fiend than his rival, Fal Sivas. Like the latter, Gar Nal invented an interplanetary flier, and he and Fal Sivas were in the habit of stealing each other's secrets in order to perfect his own ship first. Gar Nal was an ally of the assassin's guild of Zodanga and had paid to have Fal Sivas assassinated when John Carter entered the latter's household in disguise as a bodyguard. Gar Nal later helped Ur Jan kidnap Dejah Thoris by flying her to Thuria in exchange for part of her ransom, but was there captured by the Tarids and forced to cooperate with John Carter to escape. He betrayed him soon afterward, abducting Dejah Thoris back to Barsoom and planning to hide her from John Carter there, meanwhile promising to hide Fal Sivas in return for the secret of his mechanical brain. All of his treacheries were discovered, though, and Ur Jan ran him through (M8;3,11,18–24).

Gara Lo One of the friends of Ero Shan (V2;16).

Garb The cliff village of the island of Hime in the Korsar Az of Pellucidar to which Tanar the Fleet One first came in his search for his abducted mate Stellara (P3;10).

Garcia, Jesus A Mexican Indian-fighter who was killed in a raid by Geronimo in the summer of 1877 (A1;5).

Garden of the Gods A park of Colorado which features strange and beautiful erosion formations of sandstone (E1;2).

Garfield, James Abram (1831–1881) President of the United States from 1880 to 1881. He was shot by Charles Guiteau in the summer of 1881 and died a few months later of an infection of the wound (A2;3).

Garfield Park A city park of Chicago (T22;11).

Garobus The Euroban name for the planet Mars (M11B;3).

Garrigan One of Hemmington Main's reporter friends (R;5).

Gartolas, Hill of A hill of Minuni which lies to the west of Trohanadalmakus, midway between it and Veltopismakus (T10;7).

Gary A city of Indiana which was the farthest west any railroad line connecting to Washington, D.C., ran after the Kalkars got through making a mess of everything (MM2;2).

Gascony A region of southwestern France inhabited by a people of mixed Basque descent (OT;3).

gash (*Ape*) Tooth (T13;4).

Gate of Enemies The west and largest gate of Manator on Barsoom, 50 feet thick and very tall and wide. It is lined with shelf-like niches in which are placed the mummified and shrunken bodies of the most valiant enemies who died in Manator's games of jetan. Each body is about a foot tall, but its hair is of the same length as in life, falling down to the tiny mummy's feet or even longer. It was at this gate that U-Thor assembled his siege army (M5;11,16).

Gate of Jeddaks The most important gate of Helium (M2;16).

Gate of the Physicists *see* Tag kum voo Klookantum (V2;16).

Gate of the Psychologists *see* Tag kum voo Klambad (V2;13).

Gate of Triumph The gate of the Circus Maximus in Rome through which the winning charioteer in a race drove after collecting the palm leaf representing victory (I).

Gatewood, Lieutenant Charles B. An American officer of the 6th Cavalry who was always fair and honest in his dealings with the Apaches and was well-respected by them for it. It was he who parleyed with **Geronimo** at **Skeleton Canyon** and got him to surrender on September 4, 1886 (A2;8,14).

Gathol The oldest inhabited city on Barsoom. It was built on an island in **Throxeus** and, as the ocean receded, followed it down the slopes, so that the modern city is built onto and into a mountain. Its rough, almost vertical topography makes the landing of hostile airships difficult, and the salt marsh which surrounds the city makes land attack equally difficult. The mountain of Gathol is honeycombed with diamond mines from which a seemingly endless supply of the gems is mined. This makes Gathol one of the richest of cities, yet it has remained free since the time of the seas because of its natural protections and the valor and skills of its warriors. It is an ally of **Helium**, but not a possession.

Gathol's territory extends from the equator to 10 degrees north latitude and from 10 degrees to 20 degrees west longitude, containing about a million square **haads** where the herds of **thoats** and **zitidars** are grazed. Most of the area is fine grazing land with no natural protection, and this fact (combined with the sheer size of the herds) makes it necessary that Gatholian herdsmen, farmers and ranchers be good fighters. The necessity of capturing slaves for work in the diamond mines (work no Gatholian will do) also necessitates good warriors and military force. The Gatholians are kind masters, however, allowing hard-working slaves to go free after only a few years, often as little as one year. Each male Gatholian must give an hour of labor per day to the city, but his own slave may do the work for him and thus pay six years of his "labor tax" in a single year.

The Gatholians are vain, vying with each other for the splendidness of their trappings during peacetime, but during war their harness is the plainest on Barsoom. The present **Jed** of Gathol is **Gahan**, and he is a perfect example of this fair and noble city's inhabitants (M5;1).

To the west of Gathol lies a rough and treacherous land, and beyond that **Manator**. Since Gathol is the closest country to that lost civilization (Manator's eastern border is at 30 degrees west longitude), it was the primary

source of slaves for the Manatorians until its alliance with that power (M5;13,22).

In the late 1930s Gathol was besieged by **Hin Abtol**, Jeddak of the **Panars**, because of the refusal of Gahan to give his daughter **Llana of Gathol** to Hin Abtol as wife; the siege was lifted with the assistance of the navy of **Helium** under the command of John Carter, Gahan's father-in-law (M10:3;2/4;13).

Gatlin, Bill A stagecoach driver of 1880s **Hendersville, Arizona** (HB;2–3).

Gato Mgungu An African chief whose tribe had dwindled over the years until his people filled but a single village; while this "normal" power had waned, however, his power as chief of the feared **Leopard Men** had waxed until he had followers in every village within a hundred miles — men sworn to obey Gato Mgungu to the death. This power was broken by the **Utenga** war party led by Tarzan and **Orando** in 1931 and Mgungu found himself trapped with the survivors in the **Temple of the Leopard God** with no food and no way to get off the island. We must presume that he died in the situation (T18;6,11,14).

Gault, Gerald The guide of the Romanoff safari to **Northern Rhodesia** in 1939. Gault was domineering, sarcastic, and hated by everybody (T24B;5).

Gavo An Amtorian country on the continent of **Donuk** which is at a medieval level of technology and is feudalistic in its political organization (V5;4).

Gay, Charlie An animal trainer of the 1930s who worked for B.O. Pictures (T17;13).

Gayat "Redhead" (*Ape*). A great bull ape whom Tarzan had saved from a lion when Gayat was a child, and so refused to obey his king's command to kill the ape-man when they met again in 1921 (T11;3). They later met again in the arena of **Castra Sanguinarius** and he helped Tarzan escape that lost Roman city (T12;17). When **Zu-tho** broke off from **Toyat's** tribe to form his own, his lifelong friend Gayat went with him, and they were together when Zu-tho rescued Tarzan from the **Betete pygmies** in 1931 (T18;21).

Gaz A great warrior of **Lo-har** who wished to mate with **La-ja** until she was abducted by a **Bastian**. Fear of him led La-ja to try to lose **von Horst** or scare him away, but he succeeded in finding her anyway and killed the awful 300-pound man-mountain Gaz (P5;8,22).

Gazan "Redskin" (*Ape*). The son of Teeka of the tribe of Kerchak. Tarzan rescued him from peril on several occasions (T6:3, 4,10).

ged (*Pal*) The number 40 (T8).

Geeka Meriem's hideous doll, the abused child's only playmate while among the **Arabs** of **Amor ben Khatour**. Its head was made from crudely chipped ivory, its arms and legs from wood, and its body from a rat skin stuffed with grass. It was made for the child by a kindly disposed slave named Geeka (for whom she named the doll), and she showered all of the affection her childish nature craved upon the ugly thing, never letting it out of her sight and telling all of her troubles to it. She kept it around for years afterward, even after blossoming into an early womanhood, and carried it on her back by a leather thong. It was by this doll that she was later recognized by the brother of the slave who had made it, who had himself escaped the Sheik shortly after Meriem had. He and his people abducted the girl and took her back to the Sheik for a reward, since he was not as kind as his brother had been (T4;5,10–11).

Geela One of the husbands of **Gluck**, chief of **Oog** (P6,3).

Gef One of the tribes of the Pellucidarian continent west of **Korsar**. Gef, like **Oog**, was a tribe of large, bearded women and their puny mates (P6;2).

Gefasto The **Chief of Warriors** of the **Minunian** city of **Veltopismakus** while Tarzan was imprisoned there. He was a young rake who was elevated to his position by **Elkomoelhago** because the king thought he would be pliable, but Gefasto proved himself a great leader instead (T10;10).

Geier "Vulture" (*Ger*). The German cruiser/raider of **World War I** sunk in the South Pacific in July of 1916 by **Bowen Tyler** in the captured **U-33** (C1;3).

Gemba A trusted black slave of **Thudos**, the powerful **Cathnean** noble, while Tarzan was in the city in October of 1930 (T16;16). He was in 1935 enslaved in post-revolutionary **Athne**, but escaped and took news of the

situation there to **Thudos**, who was now king of **Cathne** (T21;23–25).

Gemnon A young noble of **Cathne**, assistant officer to **Tomos**, who first interviewed Tarzan when he arrived in the City of Gold in October of 1930. Gemnon became a good friend to Tarzan during his stay there and helped him understand and survive the intrigues of the city until he was imprisoned and ordered executed — fortunately for Gemnon, **Nemone** committed suicide and he was freed (T16;5,10–19).

Gemonian Steps The site of the ignominious executions of a great many Romans, who were pushed down the steep, high stairway to their deaths (I;5).

The General One of the hobos who tried to rob the "**Oskaloosa Kid**" of his loot from the **Prim** house in 1917. He and **Dopey Charlie** hung out together and were cut off from the rest of the hobos and forced into hiding with **Bridge** and the "Kid" by the "thing" in the **Squibbs** house while searching for the "Kid" inside of it (see **Beppo**). He was later caught with Dopey Charlie and the loot from the **Baggs** murder/robbery (which they had committed) by **Detective Burton** and sent to the gallows for it (K3;1,4,7,9).

George III (1760–1820) The British king whose unfair treatment of the American colonies (actually, his parliament's treatment) led to the American Revolution (T22;2).

George V (1865–1936) The British king (1910–1936) whom "**Big Bill**" **Thompson** threatened to "biff … on the snoot" if he dared come to **Chicago** (T22;2).

Georgetown The port of British Guiana to which **Bowen Tyler** planned to take the captured U-33 after discovering how lost the ship really was (C1;3).

Gerard, Captain The officer of the French Foreign Legion who befriended Tarzan while the latter was in **Sidi-bel-Abbes** spying on **Lt. Gernois**. He invited Tarzan to travel with him and Gernois to **Bou Saada** when they were transferred there (T2;7).

gerlat (*Amt*) River (V2;19).

Gerlat kum Rov "River of Death" (*Amt*). The mighty river (comparable in size to the Mississippi) which drains most of the

Amtorian continent of Noobol. Both Hava-too and Kormor lie on its banks (V2;17).

gerloo (*Amt*) Water (V4;9).

German One of the many languages Tarzan spoke fluently (T7;2).

German East Africa The former name (from 1885 to 1920) of the area today known as Tanzania, in which several of Tarzan's adventures took place (T3;11).

Germania (*Lat*) The Roman name for Germany (T12;6).

Germanicus Caesar (15 B.C.–A.D. 59) A Roman **patrician** and general, nephew and adopted son of the Emperor **Tiberius** and father of **Caligula**. He is described by **Britannicus** as fair and just, though not very strong or bright. He died (possibly poisoned) in Syria on October 9, A.D. 19 (I;1–6).

Gernois, Lieutenant The officer of the French Foreign Legion in **Algeria** who was suspected of selling military secrets to a foreign power, and whom Tarzan was assigned to spy on for the French War Office. It turned out that Gernois had been blackmailed for the secrets by **Nikolas Rokoff**, who also demanded money and Gernois' compliance in Rokoff's plot to kill Tarzan. When Gernois saw the ape-man alive again after the plot, he committed suicide (T2;7–11).

Geronimo The name by which the Apache chief **Go-yat-thlay** was better known. It was given to him by the Mexicans after his raids on **Sonora** in the early 1870s, raids chiefly conducted in revenge against the Mexicans, who had killed his wife **Alope** and his children. Geronimo was the adoptive father of **Shoz-di-jiji** and war chief of all the Apaches throughout the 1870s. In 1884, he went on the warpath again after the American Army confiscated his herds (which he had in turn stolen from the Mexicans) and for two years he led his people on raids throughout Mexico and **Arizona**, outwitting the armies of two "civilized" nations for the entire time, until he finally surrendered to **General Miles** at **Skeleton Canyon**, Arizona, on September 4, 1886, and was sent to **Fort Pickens, Florida**, as a prisoner. Later, he was transferred to **Fort Sill, Oklahoma**, where he died in 1909 (A1;2–6)(A2;14–15).

Geryeh A ruined city of **Arab** legend which lies about one day's march north of **Tebuk**. According to legend, a great treasure rolls out of the city and runs around the desert outside every Friday (the Muslim holy day) (T11;1).

Ghak the Hairy One The king of **Sari** in Pellucidar and **Dian the Beautiful**'s uncle. He was a prisoner of the **Sagoths** with her when **David Innes** and **Abner Perry** were also captured in 1903. He escaped with them later, led them back to Sari, and later swore allegiance to Innes as emperor of Pellucidar along with his nephew **Dacor the Strong One**, king of **Amoz** (P1;4,12–15), becoming one of the Empire's greatest generals (P2;14–15)(P7:1;7).

Ghasta A small, walled city with archaic and gloomy architecture built of black volcanic rock in the forest of the **Valley Hohr** near **Tjanath** on Barsoom. It is almost deserted except for about 600 people living in or near the palace, and the ancient method of surface irrigation (no longer used anywhere else for fear of evaporation) is still used in its fields. The city is ruled by **Ghron**, the mad **jed**, and is a city of horror — passers-by, those who have come down the river **Syl** either on the pilgrimage or after being condemned to **The Death** in Tjanath, are enticed into the city by smiling girls and promised food and hospitality, only to find a choice of slavery or torture from which there is no escape (at least until **Tan Hadron** and **Nur An** arrived). The art and customs of the city, conceived as they were by Ghron, are utterly bizarre — there are tapestries depicting weird creatures and dancing trees, and food is served out of goblets and drink from plates, just to name a few examples (M7;7–8).

Ghek A **Kaldane** of Barsoom, third foreman of the fields of **Luud**. In reward for his capture of **Tara of Helium**, he was promoted to an underground post, that of tending to the Princess' fattening up for eating; unfortunately for him, she refused to be fattened. In the meantime, Ghek had become entranced by Tara's singing, a thing he had never heard before. He refused to tell Luud of it because, since all Kaldanes have the same likes and dislikes, he knew Luud would take her for himself if he heard her. He later helped **Gahan** of **Gathol** rescue her from the clutches of Luud because she had awakened emotions and love of life within him and he wished to escape **Bantoom** for good. In the process, Ghek killed Luud, stole his royal **rykor**, and escaped with Tara and Gahan (M5;5–8). He was captured with Tara in **Manator**, northeast of Bantoom, and assisted Gahan and Tara to escape by means of his Kaldane powers. Later, he brought **Val Dor** and **Floran** to Tara's **flier**, enabling them to repair it and reach Gathol, which then invaded Manator with the help of Helium and rescued Gahan and Tara. Ghek moved to Helium to live with his single rykor (M5;12,14,22).

Ghenzi Mountains   A mountain range of central Africa (possibly a part of the **Ruwenzori** of Uganda) within which **Lady Barbara Collis** was forced in 1929 to bail out of her airplane when it ran out of gas. In the middle of the mountain range, in an extinct volcanic caldera five miles in diameter, lay the land of **Midian** (T15;2).

ghrazzu   (*Ara*) A raid (T11;2).

ghrol   (*Ara*) An evil spirit (T14;5).

Ghron   The mad Jed of **Ghasta** on Barsoom, an enormous man covered with shaggy black hair like an Earthly ape's. He has a broad, flat face with eyes very far apart, and is totally and sadistically insane. Everything around him must be uncoordinated and disproportionate (like his furniture and tableware) and he seems to find it all beautiful. Visitors to Ghasta are given a choice of one of three fates. Be grilled on a fire for Ghron's amusement; be hopelessly maimed and crippled to then dance for Ghron's amusement; or become a slave, required to watch or inflict the other two kinds of tortures (M7;8).

Gian-na-tah   The best friend of **Shoz-dijiji** when he was a boy. They underwent their manhood ritual at the same time and later became warriors at the same time. Gian-na-tah's one bad fault was his weakness for the white man's liquor, and this caused many arguments between him and Shoz-dijiji after the **Apaches** had settled down in the early 1880s. Gian-na-tah was one of the small group of Apaches who went out with **Geronimo** in 1885 and died in May of 1886 while holding a pass against the American Cavalry so his fellows could escape (A1;4–5,11)(A2; 2–4,9–11).

gibbon   A type of very long-armed bipedal anthropoid ape of India, Indochina, and the Malay Archipelago. The gibbon is the smallest of the anthropoid apes, standing about two feet tall, and is very gentle and easily tamed (T22;3).

gibbon, black *see* **siamang** (T22;3)

Gila   A river which, after beginning in New Mexico, cuts westward across southern Arizona and empties into the Colorado near the Gulf of California (A1;2).

gilak   "Man" (*Pell*). The human race of Pellucidar, similar in most respects to humans of the outer Earth but different in a few important respects. They are an attractive people (more so than the average outer-Earth person) and possess several adaptations to life under the eternal sun of Pellucidar. For instance, a gilak can find his way home from any point in Pellucidar, flawlessly and by the most direct route, as long as he is on land (P1;3–5). Also, gilaks can "save up" sleep as humans of the outer world store energy in fat, sleeping a great deal when possible and going without, if necessary, for long periods of time thereafter (P3;2).

Gilbert Islands   A small chain of islands at the southeast end of Micronesia that lies on the equator just west of the International Date Line (T22;23).

Giles   The servant whom **Bertrade de Montfort** sent with a message to **Norman of Torn** at Battel (OT;18).

Giles-Burton, Lieutenant Cecil   A RAF pilot and British agent who in 1939 restole the plans for **Horace Brown's** ignition disruptor from Joseph Campbell and Zubanev in Rome, then headed for **Cape Town**, but was brought down over **Northern Rhodesia**. He was lost for some time but eventually stumbled upon the safari of his friends **Lord** and **Lady Ramsgate**. In only a few days with them, he made three enemies, then was murdered one night by Campbell, who had entered the safari under an alias (T24B;1–7).

Giles-Burton, Colonel Gerald   The British resident commissioner at **Bangali**, whose son, **Lt. Cecil Giles-Burton**, was to have delivered the secret **Brown** plans to him at Bangali in 1939 after recovering them from Rome. His son was murdered by **Joseph Campbell** en route, but Tarzan caught the murderer and delivered him to Colonel Giles-Burton (T24B;3,7).

gill, artificial A device used by the priests of Ashair to go out into Lake Horus. It extracts oxygen from water by an efficient chemical process so its wearer can breathe underwater almost indefinitely. Physically, the gill is a large, backpack-contained device with vents for water to pass in and out and a tube leading into a helmet worn atop a waterproof suit. The chemical used in the gill was accidentally discovered by an Ashairian alchemist who later died after successfully inventing gunpowder, then hitting it very hard with a hammer in order to transmute it into gold (T20;20,26).

Gimla (*Ape*) The crocodile (T6:5).

Gimlet A horse of the Bar-Y Ranch of 1880s Arizona—a dejected, droopy-looking animal until one spurred him, at which point he showed the derivation of his name. He would begin to spin about, then bolt off for a hundred yards or so, then spin about again, and continue in this manner until his rider was thrown—he would never buck, however (HB;11).

Gimmel Gora Kapar woman who befriended the traitor Morga Sagra soon after her arrival in Kapara in the spring of 1940. She was actually a Zabo agent assigned to spy on Sagra (B2;5–6).

Giova A gypsy girl, owner of Beppo the dancing bear, whose father (a renegade gypsy) died of an epileptic fit in the old Squibbs house outside of Oakdale, Illinois, on the night of the "Oakdale Affair" in 1917. Giova, Bridge, "The Oskaloosa Kid," and "Abigail Prim" cooperated to help each other after the latter three discovered her secret while fleeing Detective Burton the next morning. After her father's body was found and autopsied and her companions cleared of wrongdoing, she was herself set free (after her arrest by Burton) and went to work for the Penning family of Payson (K3;3,8,10).

"The Girl from Farris's" A novelette which first appeared as a 26-part serial in the *Tacoma Tribune* newspaper starting on February 24, 1920. It concerns the fall and rise of June Lathrop (a.k.a. Maggie Lynch), a supposed prostitute who works her way up from the gutter, and that of Ogden Secor, the man she loves. It is abbreviated GF.

The Girl from Hollywood Burroughs' only major work of contemporary realism, set in rural southern California of 1922. It is the saga of the Evans and Pennington families and how they are both almost destroyed by the bootlegger Slick Allen and his dopepusher friend Wilson Crumb through a series of sleazy blackmail plots, frame-ups, and seductions. The book is abbreviated GH.

gladius hispanus (*Lat*) The two-edged Roman short sword used by the imperial legions (T12;6).

Glenora Johnny Lafitte's hometown in Los Angeles County, California, a poor town in which oil was struck in the 1920s, making it a boom town. It lay about 20 miles northeast of the Pacific coast, just inland from the San Fernando Valley (PB;1–2).

gloresta A beautiful flowering tree of Barsoom which grows in the depressions of hills where most of the moisture of that arid planet is found (M9;3).

gluck (*Ara*) A negative interjection (T11;1).

Gluck The female chief of the gender-reversed Pellucidarian tribe of Oog, where David Innes was enslaved in 1929 (P6;2).

Gluf A Pellucidarian warrior of the tribe of Pheli whom Jason Gridley shot dead to protect Jana (P4;7).

Gluh In the tongue of Niocene Africa, the mammoth (E1;10).

Glula One of the husbands of Gluck, chief of Oog (P6;3).

Gnaeus Domitius Ahenobarbus A Roman patrician, probably mad, who married Caligula's sister Agrippina Minor when she was 13. It was from this union that Nero, later Emperor of Rome, was born (I;14).

go (*Ape*) Black (T4;10).

go (*Pal*) Clear (T8).

Go-hal A Pellucidarian tribe and village lying not very far from Basti (P5;7).

Go-lat "Black nose" (*Ape*). The king of a band of great apes that Tarzan joined during a Dum-dum in the winter of 1915, somewhere in northwest Tanganyika (T7;8).

Go-pi An Apache warrior killed in a trap set by white soldiers in the late 1850s (A1;2).

go-sha In the language of the Xexots of Pellucidar, "king" (P7:2;5).

Go-yad "Black head" (*Ape*). A great bull ape of the tribe of Toyat who tried to abduct the Princess Guinalda of Nimmr after Arab raiders had fled out of the Valley of the Sepulcher with her (T11;22). He later helped Tarzan escape the arena of Castra Sanguinarius when the two met there in August of 1923 (T12;17).

Go-yat-thlay "The Yawner" (*Apa*). (1829–1909) An Apache warrior, war chief of the Be-don-ko-he tribe of 1860s Arizona, who became the full chief of that tribe when Mangas Colorado was killed in 1863. He led his tribe on the warpath thereafter against the white Americans and the Mexicans many times during the 1860s to 1880s and became famous by the name the Mexicans called him —Geronimo. He eventually became war chief of all of the Apaches (as Cochise had been) and almost continually warred until his final "retirement" in 1886 (A1;1–6,19–20).

gob (American slang) A sailor (T22;29).

Gobi Desert A large, high-altitude desert of central Asia (chiefly Mongolia). It is one of the reported habitations of the yeti (T6:10).

Gobred The Prince of Nimmr when James Hunter Blake arrived there early in 1921. He accepted Blake as a Knight of Nimmr because the young man told the Nimmrites that he was already a Knight Templar, but Gobred was very skeptical of the American's obvious ignorance of knightly matters (T11;11).

Gobred, Sir A knight of Richard I of England and bastard son of Henry II, whose ship was lost on the way to the Third Crusade and shipwrecked on the African coast. After wandering inland for awhile, he and his men found the Valley of the Sepulcher, where the followers of another knight, Sir Bohun, claimed the tomb of Christ lay. Sir Gobred knew that it was not the true valley, and so he built the city of Nimmr to keep Bohun's men from returning to England. In return, Bohun built the City of the Sepulcher to keep Gobred's men from pushing forward on what Bohun had declared an unnecessary search for the Holy Land. Gobred made himself Prince of Nimmr, and all of his lineal

descendants who ruled the city took his name and title (T11;12,23).

Gobu "Black male" (*Ape*). A great ape who was killed by Esteban Miranda while posing as Tarzan for the purpose of ruining his reputation in the jungle. The ploy worked, at least on the tribe of Pagth, of which Gobu was a member (T9;4).

God The god of the Valley of Diamonds was in actuality an English biologist born in 1833 who had graduated from Oxford in 1855 and learned the secret of the genetic code by 1858. He learned how to genetically engineer animals by injecting human genetic matter into their gametes, then went to Africa and began his experiments on gorillas, so that generation by generation they acquired more and more human characteristics. He then gave them the English culture, a set of historical names, laws and a government, and set himself up as God of the valley. As he grew older he discovered how to inject himself with young body cell genes in order to keep himself young, and the process worked; unfortunately for him, he was using young gorilla genes and began to take on some gorilla traits, such as coloration, hairiness, and heavy claws. To remedy this he planned to use the body cells of Tarzan and Rhonda Terry, both young humans, to rejuvenate himself. This would have been fine except that God had discovered that the process was facilitated if he ate the donor afterward. After Tarzan helped him escape his burning castle, though, he let Tarzan and Rhonda Terry go in gratitude (T17;24–30).

Another God was Rand, the false Tarzan who had "fallen from the sky" to Alemtejo in 1936. He was proclaimed so by Christoforo da Gama, King of Alemtejo, because he thought he could control the religion of Alemtejo through Rand. The people accepted him as God, and he eventually came to half-believe it himself and kidnapped Sandra Pickerall to be his goddess. When she told him that he was not God he was glad, since he did not want to be (T23;4,7,10,14,16).

God, Servants of The great apes of Alemtejo, who cooperated with and obeyed some of that city's inhabitants (T23;7–8,16).

"The God of Tarzan" The fourth story in the collection *Jungle Tales of Tarzan*, abbreviated T6:4. In it, Tarzan searches for God, whose existence he had learned of through his father's books. The events of the story took place in 1907.

Godensky, Sergei A professional photographer who accompanied the Ramsgate safari to Northern Rhodesia in 1939. Godensky was a quick-tempered man who would as soon kill a man as kiss him (T24B;5).

gods Burroughs' books, featuring as they do a plethora of strange cultures, also feature a variety of strange religions. Below is a list of the gods and god-concepts, both "real" and false, that have appeared in the books. Each has its own separate entry.

Allah	Jad-Ben-Otho
Ancestors	Jehovah
Aychuykak	Kavandavanda
Blessed Mary	Kibuka
Brulor	Leopard God
Bulamutumumo	Loto-el-ho-Ganja
Che	Luata
Chon	Mulungu
Dor-ul-Otho	Munango-Keewati
Dyaus	Noada
Fire God	Ogar
The Flag	Parrots
The Flaming God	Pu
God	Siva
Huitz-Hok	Therns
Hun Ahau	Thoos
Hunab Kuh	Tur
Isis	Usen
Issus	Walumbe
Itzamna	Zo-al

The Gods of Mars The second book of the Mars series, abbreviated M2, it was originally published in *All-Story Magazine* as a five-part serial from January through May of 1913. The events took place in 1886-87 and were written down by John Carter while visiting Earth in 1898. In it, he finds himself again upon Mars, this time in the mysterious Valley Dor, the Barsoomian heaven — or hell, as it turns out. He eventually escapes, but falls into the clutches of the dreaded Black Pirates of Barsoom.

Gofoloso The Chief of Chiefs of the Minunian city of Veltopismakus while Tarzan was a prisoner there. He was one of the few brave members of Elkomoelhago's cabinet (T10;10).

gogo (*Ape*) Talk (TC).

Gojam A region of Abyssinia lying south of Lake Tana (T16;1).

Golato The huge head man of the Kali Bwana expedition in 1931. He attempted to rape his mistress (the only white in the safari) and was shot in the arm for his pains. The next day he and his men packed up and went, leaving Kali Bwana alone in the jungle (T18; 1,3).

gold A heavy, soft yellow metal, fairly common on Barsoom and Ladan, but not so on Earth. The Waziri tribe had the first gold jewelry that Tarzan had ever seen worn by African natives (not counting those trinkets gained by trading with the Europeans), and he decided to get himself some after the Waziri offered to show him whence they had gotten it — the lost city of Opar, from which Tarzan stole about four tons of gold in the form of ancient Atlantean ingots, thus making him a very rich man upon his return to England (T2;15,22,26).

Goldeen, Ben The production manager for Prominent Pictures' 1933 film *Tarzan of the Apes*. He unknowingly rejected the real Tarzan to play himself and instead hired Cyril Wayne, an adagio dancer (T17;33).

Golden Cliffs *see* Otz, Mountains of

Goldie One of the whores at "Dirty" Cheetim's Hog Ranch in 1880s San Carlos, Arizona (A2;2).

golf According to Carson Napier, a mental disorder (V2;6).

Goliath A small town in southwestern Idaho, formerly a division headquarters of the Short Line railroad (GF;10).

Goloba The black head man of the ill-fated Stabutch expedition of 1929, who deserted his master and ran away with all of his men when the safari was attacked by shiftas (T15;4).

gom (*Ape*) Run (TC).

gom-lul (*Ape*) River (TC).

Gomangani "Great black ape" (*Ape*). The Negro (T4;10). The subhuman blacks of the Valley of the Palace of Diamonds were also called Gomangani (T9;9). See also Tarmangani.

Gombul A primitive village of Pellucidar (P10;2).

Gompth The **Kapar** agent in **Gorvas** on **Poloda** who got **Tangor** and **Morga Sagra** into **Kapara** in the spring of 1940 (B2;2).

Gonfal An enormous (6000+ carat) diamond with strange hypnotic powers which belonged to the **Kaji** Amazons of **Ethiopia**. Despite the fact that they attributed all of their powers and those of their wizard **Mafka** to the Gonfal, they seemed to exhibit no particular reverence for it and even apparently allowed outsiders to see and handle it; it was, however, well protected in an ancient castle (which may have been built by the Portuguese in the 1530s or earlier; in any case, it was definitely of European style). In reality, Mafka kept the Gonfal close to him at all times and visitors were only allowed to handle a clever fake Mafka had created through alchemy. Tarzan later gave the diamond to **Gonfala** so she could be rich in civilization (T21;1–2, 9,25).

Gonfala The queen of the **Kaji** Amazons of **Ethiopia**, considered to be the living personification of the **Gonfal**. She was an incredibly beautiful woman, but also apparently schizophrenic — soft and feminine one moment, and a she-devil the next. This apparent "split personality" was actually caused by **Mafka** taking over her through the power of the Gonfal to do his bidding when necessary. Gonfala was actually the daughter of **Lord** and **Lady Montford** and fell very much in love with **Stanley Wood** and vice versa. She helped him escape the Kaji, and after the death of Mafka they went to Tarzan's estate with him, planning to then travel to London and marry. On the way there, however, she was abducted by **Spike** and **Troll**, the hunters who had previously stolen the Gonfal, because they believed her presence to be necessary for the stone to function. They took her to the **Ethiopian Highlands**, where they stumbled into **Thenar** and were imprisoned by revolutionaries. After the counter-revolution Gonfala was released and allowed to return safely to London (T21;2–3,8–14,17,22–25).

Goob One of the baboons recruited by **Korak** for his attack on the village of **Kovudoo** to rescue **Meriem** (T4;15).

Good Friday Massacre On a Good Friday in the early 1920s the old king was murdered, touching off riots that left seven peasants dead at the hands of the army (LL;3).

Goofo A functionary in the "palace" of **Meeza**, king of the village of the **Jukans** of **Pellucidar** in which **David Innes** was "entertained" in 1929. Like every other Jukan, Goofo was an erratic semi-maniac who imagined himself to be the only sane person in the village. He was killed a few weeks after Innes' arrival by his assistant **Noak**, who then took his place (P6; 7–8).

Gooli The village of the Goolians on the island of **Ompt** in the **Toonolian Marshes** of **Barsoom**, which the silly Goolians believe to be the largest city in the world. They are a primitive form of humanoid with long, powerful legs for leaping and long tails for balance, and the females are pouched like kangaroos. The Goolians are incredibly self-important and believe themselves to be the most advanced, most intelligent, fiercest, etc. people on Barsoom although they are only savages who live in grass huts and arrant cowards as well, refusing to fight any foe unless the odds are 10 to 1 in their favor; otherwise, they give up. Even the mighty treasure that they brag of is only a chest half full of sea shells — since no one else would want such a thing, it was a safe treasure to possess. The Goolians wear very simple harness and use **dagger**, spear and **short sword**. To top off all of their other bad qualities, they are lazy as well. **Vor Daj** called them "the most useless race of people … ever encountered" (M9; 20–22).

Goork The King of **Thuria** in Pellucidar and father-in-law of **Dacor the Strong One**. He eventually swore allegiance to **David Innes** and the **Empire of Pellucidar** (P2;6,15).

Goose Island Kid A lightweight prizefighter whom **Billy Byrne** hung out with in turn-of-the-century **Chicago** and from whom he learned to fight with science (K1; 1,14,17).

Gootch, William One of **Scott Taylor's** shady friends, who went with him on his trip to Africa to get rid of **Richard Gordon** and was killed by the title character of the story (ME;2,6).

gor (*Ape*) Growl (TC).

Gor-Don A padwar of the **Panars** of Barsoom who was rescued twice by **John Carter**: Once from a ship the *Dusar* had disabled, and once from being "helped" to "fall" overboard by two members of the ship's cutthroat crew. He swore to help John Carter in gratitude for his life and was put out on the ice with Carter when the crew finally mutinied. Gor-Don later sneaked Carter into Pankor by pretending that the Warlord was his slave (M10:3; 10–11).

Gor Hajus A noted gorthan of Toonol on Barsoom. He was an honorable man who never accepted a contract on a woman or a faultless man and never struck a blow from behind, always giving his victims a fair fight instead. He was loyal to his friends, which got him in trouble when Vobis Kan, Jeddak of Toonol, asked him to slay a noble who had once done Gor Hajus a good turn. The assassin of course refused the contract, which Vobis Kan incorrectly assumed meant that there was a contract out on him. Gor Hajus was executed and his body purchased by Ras Thavas, and he was later resurrected by Ulysses Paxton to aid the Earthman in his abduction of Xaxa, the Jeddara of Phundahl. When Dar Tarus was made Jeddak of Phundahl, Gor Hajus stayed on as his personal bodyguard and assistant voice of The Great Tur (M6;6,14).

Gorbuses A peculiar and eerie tribe of Pellucidarian humanoids who inhabit the Forest of Death near Basti. Gorbuses are as pale as corpses and have white hair and pink eyes, long fangs in both upper and lower jaws, and strong nails. The tribe numbers several hundred males, a few score females, and about a dozen children, and inhabits a series of dark caves in a cliff in the forest. In addition to their other bad qualities, they are cannibals, but they do not enjoy their meals, only eating to survive and thus avoid dying and ending up in a worse place. This is because all of the gorbuses were former sinners from the outer crust, mostly heinous murderers, who had somehow been reincarnated in Pellucidar. Just how remains a mystery, since the gorbuses could remember nothing of their former lives except the murder which had condemned them to gorbushood (P5;10).

Gordon, Richard The son of Robert Gordon of New York, described as "rich, indolent and bored," who ran off to Africa to recover the papers which would prove Virginia Scott's right to inherit the Scott fortune, thus putting himself in danger from the designs of Scott Taylor. He found the papers in a buried strong box in the ruins of the Morton mission with little trouble and encountered Virginia on his way back, at which time she warned him about Taylor. He fell in love with her and later came to visit her in Virginia, where Taylor tried to get him again and failed, thanks to a jammed automatic pistol and the chance arrival of Ben, King of Beasts, whom Gordon had released from a lion pit while in Africa and befriended. Gordon later married Virginia and donated the lion to a New York zoo (ME;2,5,7–11).

Gordon, Robert The best friend of Jefferson Scott, Jr., who went with Scott on the safari that bagged Scott a wife. Gordon carried the Morton fortune to America with him for safekeeping when he left, at the request of Reverend Morton. He died about two years before Jefferson Scott, Sr., did (ME;1).

Gore A white ape of Barsoom with a red man's brain, who was the guard of Pew Mogel and was killed by John Carter (M11A;7).

Gorgo (Ape) The buffalo (T6:8).

Gorgum The Morgor officer on Eurobus who questioned John Carter as to how his friends had escaped, but would not accept the truth because his mind was so arrogantly closed (M11B;7).

gorilephant Esmerelda's malapropism for "gorilla" (T1;18).

Goro (Ape) The moon (T5;3).

gorobor (Pell) The riding animal of the Horibs of Pellucidar. It is a swift, ten foot long anomodont reptile analogous to the periosaurus of the Triassic. The gorobor is considered the swiftest animal in Pellucidar, and even burdened with a Horib rider the creature's movement is nothing less than phenomenal (P4;13).

Gorph A short, middle-aged warrior of the Mammoth Men of Pellucidar who was assigned to guard Von Horst while he was their prisoner early in 1928 (P5;13).

gorthan (Bar) Assassin. The profession is not entirely without honor on Barsoom, where some assassins are actually heroes in the minds of the masses and assassination is so prevalent that guilds have been organized for regulatory purposes among the members of the class. All locks and guards on Barsoom are intended to keep out assassins, as thievery is practically unknown there. Indeed, assassination is the third most common cause of death on Barsoom, after war and accident. In the 1930s John Carter began a years-long campaign to wipe out the practice or at least make it more scarce (M8;1).

Gorvas A city on the continent of **Karis** on **Poloda**, mostly unaffected by the **Kapar** war because it is cold and poor in resources, having nothing that the Kapars want. It was here that **Tangor** and **Morga Sagra** got a Kapar plane with which to fly into **Kapara** in the spring of 1940 (B2;2).

Gosoda The Apache name for a pass through the **Sierra Madre** in **Sonora**, south of Casa Grande (A2;13).

Gozan "Blackskin" (*Ape*). A **great ape** of the tribe of **Kerchak** while Tarzan was growing up (T6:12).

Gozava Sola's mother, **Tars Tarkas'** forbidden lover. They loved and had Sola in secret, but Gozava's end came when **Sarkoja** exposed her to **Tal Hajus** while Tars Tarkas was away, resulting in Gozava's death by torture (M1;15).

Gr-gr-gr The king of the **brute-men** of **Indiana** in Pellucidar who captured **David Innes** when he came to the island in 1913 (P2;8).

Grabritin (Derived from "Great Britain") The name given to England by the powerful barbarian nation residing at London who were descended from either the mentally incompetent or children who were left behind when the tide of war had at last receded from the devastated country (LC;4). See also **Grubitten**.

Gracial A Mexican bootlegger of southern **California** who was killed by **Bartolo** in an argument in 1922 (GH;25).

graduation exercises, Morgor The Morgors of **Eurobus** train their youth only in military skills since the race has no art, science or any other study but war. The graduation exercise consists of a battle between the Morgor graduating class and a group of slaves and criminals which the students outnumber two to one. Those Morgors who survive are

inducted into the warrior caste, the highest Morgor caste. John Carter led a revolt against the Morgors during their graduation exercises (to which he had been condemned) and, with help and superior strategy, killed the entire class of 40 Morgors (M11B;4,8).

Graecinus, Julius A Roman senator whom **Caligula** executed for daring to disobey him (I;17).

Graham, Mary The not-very-pretty unmarried secretary to **Chicago** inventor **Horace Brown**, who at a party in 1939 blabbed about Brown's new invention to **Joe "The Pooch" Campbell**, a man who was actually paying attention to her. Alas, Campbell was a man with connections to certain spies... (T24B;2).

grama Any of several species of pasture grass of the genus *Bouteloua* native to the American West (A1;3).

Grampian Hills A mountain range which bisects Scotland into northern and southern portions. It is geologically related to the Appalachians of eastern North America (A1;1).

grampus A type of large dolphin best known for the "wheezing" or "huffing" sound of its respiration when at the surface of the water (I;2).

Gran Avenoo Billy Byrne's pronunciation of his home street, **Grand Avenue**, which the quick-thinking **Bridge** told **"General" Pesita** was the name of a German colony from which Billy came, thus explaining his awful command of English and clearing him of being a "**gringo**." It must be remembered that at the time, the Germans were supplying Mexican revolutionaries with arms (K2;7).

Grand Avenue A street of the west side of **Chicago**, site of **Kelly's Feed Store** and home of **Billy Byrne** around the turn of the century (K1;2).

Grand Hunt In **Cathne**, a hunt with a man as the quarry and two or more lions as hunting animals (T16;14).

Grant Park A Chicago park on Michigan Avenue (GF).

grass, Barsoomian Barsoomian grass is of a scarlet color (M1).

grass, Pellucidarian Pellucidarian grass is flowering — each blade is tipped by a tiny, five-pointed blossom (P1;7).

Grauman's Chinese Theater A famous Hollywood film theater where new movies are often premiered, and where the footprints or handprints of movie stars are often impressed in wet cement in front of the building to immortalize them (T17;33).

gravitation screen The device which allowed the aero-subs of the early 22nd century of *The Lost Continent* to remain aloft. Their generators were at first poorly designed and subject to frequent problems (LC;1).

Grayson The manager of the El Orobo Ranch in Mexico during the revolutions. He was a wolf who paid some Indians to abduct **Barbara Harding** for him but was double-crossed by them and forced to flee for his life when **Billy Byrne** found out (K2;9,13–15).

greasewood (*Sarcobatus vermiculatus*) A prickly shrub native to salt deserts in the American West and Mexico (HB;19).

Great Chief's Blanket One of the insignia of rank of the **Chief of Chiefs** of the tribe of **Julian** in the post–Kalkar 25th century American West (MM3;1).

Great Emerald of the Zuli, the A companion to the **Gonfal** of the **Kaji**, stolen by the wizard **Woora** when he split off from the tribe with his followers, the **Zuli**, years ago. Each stone is powerful in its own right, but they are far more powerful together, so the Kaji and Zuli constantly fought to try to capture the other stone. Tarzan took the emerald from the Zuli after he killed Woora in 1935, and used it to keep them off his trail. Later, after rescuing **Stanley Wood** and his companions, Tarzan gave it to **Gonfala** to finance her acceptance into European society. The emerald was then stolen by **Spike** and **Troll**, but lost by them in the **Bantango** country, picked up by the Bantango, reclaimed by Tarzan, and returned to Gonfala (T21;3,6–15,25).

Great Feud The name given by the tribes of **Julian** to the war between the descendants of **Julian 5th** and his followers (mostly Americans) and the descendants of **Orthis** and his followers (mostly Kalkars and half-breeds). It was ended by the marriage of Julian 20th to Bethelda, the pure human daughter of **Or-tis 15th**, and her brother's voluntary oath of fealty to Julian (MM3;1, 9–10).

Great Jed U-Thor, the Jed of Manatos (M5;13).

Great Lake of Japal A huge freshwater lake of **Northern Anlap**, some 500 miles in length, which empties into the sea through a narrow channel about four **klookob** from **Mypos** (V4;5).

Great Nagoola A creature of the mythology of the people of **Nadara**'s island in the south Pacific. Nagoola was supposed to be an immense panther trapped in ancient times beneath two mountains by mighty warriors; occasionally, he growls and struggles to escape, causing the rumbling of earthquakes (CG2;3).

Great Plaza The large central plaza of the Barsoomian city of **Kamtol** (M10:2;11).

Great Power *see* **Guardian of the North**

Great Rift Valley *see* **Rift Valley, Great**

Great Secret The formula for the chemical by which the **Mahars** of Pellucidar artificially fertilize their eggs, kept only in a single book in the basement of the library of the Mahar city of **Phutra** lest eager Mahar scientists experiment with the formula and induce overpopulation. **David Innes** stole the book in 1903 after killing its guards and hid it in a secret cave near **Amoz**, but was later blackmailed into returning it to them in exchange for his and **Dian**'s lives (P1;11,14) (P2;4–5).

Great Thorn Forest An almost impenetrable thicket into which only the smallest animals can venture, lying somewhere to the north of the Ugogo River in present-day Tanzania or Zaire about 200 miles from Tarzan's estate. Beyond the ring-shaped thicket (which is only about 20 miles wide) lies a series of bowl-shaped valleys (the remnants of extinct volcanoes) surrounded by rocky, forested hills which blend into the Great Thorn Forest. In this area lies the land of **Minuni** (T10;2).

Great Tourney The main expression of the war between **Nimmr** and the **City of the Sepulcher**, held every year on the first Sunday of **Lent**, with the two cities taking turns hosting the event. The winner of the tournament each year took five maidens from the loser's city, to be given in honorable marriage to knights of the winning side. This practice kept bloodlines moving back and forth so as to prevent inbreeding and also kept the cities from drifting too far apart in language, manners or customs (T11;12,16).

The Great Tur   A 50-foot tall statue of Tur, the god of **Phundahl**, in the temple of the Jeddak of Phundahl on Barsoom. The statue is of a squatting man and contains a remarkably well-hidden secret door in the back which opens into the statue's hollow interior. Inside is a set of controls for the eyes of the statue (which can move and greatly magnify images), the ears (powerful microphones), and the voice (an amplifier system). Through this statue the jeddaks of Phundahl were accustomed to speak to their credulous believers until **Hora San** fell from the statue's head (on the inside) and died before revealing the secret of the statue to his daughter, **Xaxa**. Ulysses Paxton discovered the secret room by accident while attempting to hide from Xaxa's guards in the temple and later used the secret equipment to frighten the superstitious Phundahlians into giving Xaxa up to him. After **Dar Tarus** became Jeddak, the voice of the Great Tur was provided by **Hovan Du** and **Gor Hajus** (M6;11–14).

Great War Game   A yearly event in Havatoo which involves two teams of 100 men each and one queen (who rides in a car) for each team. The sides contend until all of one team has fallen, and the side who captured the other team's queen most often during the game is the winner. Many men die in the game, and it is nearly impossible to escape unwounded. It is played because the **Klambad** (psychologists) of Havatoo realized that the people needed some controlled outlet for the pent-up aggression that is natural to man (V2;16).

Great White Father   Apache term for the president of the United States (A1;1).

Greater East Asia Co-prosperity Sphere   A pseudo-communistic Japanese propaganda device of **World War II**, designed to get natives of the European Pacific colonies to rise up, overthrow their European masters, and cooperate with the Japanese (T22;1).

gree-ah   (*Ape*) "Like" or "love" (TC).

Green, Barbara   One of Jason Gridley's girlfriends, the daughter of a Los Angeles realtor. She was of the nouveau riche and was, according to Burroughs' description, something like a 1920s version of a "valley girl" (T13;8).

Green, John   A realtor of the 1920s, originally from **Texas**, who had made it big and moved to Hollywood with his wife and his daughter, **Barbara**, whom he often shocked with his utter ignorance of table manners (T13;8).

green men of Barsoom   The rulers of the dead sea bottoms of Barsoom, an incredibly fierce and immensely warlike race. Adult males stand some 13 to 15 feet in height, are muscular in a wiry way, and are of a dark olive green color. Adult females are about 10 to 12 feet tall and are of a lighter shade of green. The males are the military strategists, warriors and lawmakers, while the females prepare food, make weapons, heal the wounded, teach the young to fight, and serve as reserve troops.

Burroughs describes the green men thus: "[They have] two legs and two arms, with an intermediary pair of limbs which could be used at will either as arms or legs. Their eyes were set at the extreme sides of their heads ... and protruded ... such ... that they could be directed forward or back ... independently of each other. The ears, which were slightly above the eyes and closer together, were small, cup-shaped antennae ... their noses were but longitudinal slits in the center of their faces ... there was no hair on their bodies ... the iris of the eyes is blood red ... the pupil is dark. The eyeball ... is very white, as are the teeth ... the lower tusks curve upward to sharp points ... [their] whiteness ... is not that of ivory, but of the snowiest and most gleaming of china" (M1;3).

Befitting their horrible appearance, the green men have equally horrible mannerisms. Their children are selected at random from all those hatched in a year from the group incubator and raised without love. Their sense of humor is sadistic—to a green man, the sight of a creature writhing in pain constitutes a side-splitting joke. Their basic social division is the horde, numbering some ten to thirty thousand members on the average, but this is subdivided into smaller groups of about four to twelve hundred members which wander about the horde's territory. These separate groups are each ruled by a chieftain or jed. The green men are communistic and all property is owned in common by the community except for a few weapons and personal effects. Even of those an individual may own only as many as he needs.

Their awful characteristics notwithstanding, John Carter of Earth first found acceptance on Barsoom among these monsters, and made at least three friends among them. Under his influence and that of the great Tars Tarkas (Carter's friend) several of the hordes called truces (they usually warred continuously among themselves) and began to move toward peaceful coexistence with each other and the red Barsoomians (M1).

Green Stables One of the four officially sanctioned racehorse syndicates of ancient Rome (I;8).

greenhouse Each city of Okar on Barsoom has a huge dome which acts as a greenhouse to warm the city (M3;9).

Greenland The Earth's largest island, an eternally glaciated landmass in the Atlantic east of North America. Burroughs spent the summer of 1916 there and found Bowen Tyler's manuscript of *The Land That Time Forgot* washed ashore in a thermos bottle (C1;1).

Greenwich The name given by David Innes to the spot where the iron mole entered Pellucidar for the second time, from which spot he first recorded magnetic north in Pellucidar and began the first map of it. He later made it the site of his royal observatory (P2;1,15).

Gregorio A Mexican outlaw of 1880s Arizona whom Bull had once saved from hostile Apaches. He was the accomplice of the notorious Black Coyote, but after urging by Bull (coupled with the fact that the Coyote and his cronies were cheating Gregorio out of his share) he decided to go straight, help Bull catch the Coyote, and confess the names of his accomplices (HB;2-3,15-19).

Gregory, Brian An American adventurer of the 1930s who bore a fair resemblance to Tarzan. After getting directions to the Forbidden City of Ashair in 1934 he disappeared, prompting his father and sister to go in search

of him two years later. **Paul d'Arnot** met him as a prisoner in Ashair and they escaped with the help of Tarzan and **Helen Gregory**. Although Gregory's lust for the **Father of Diamonds** almost got him killed, he eventually gave up on it and left **Tuen-baka** in honor with the others (T20;1,18-24,29-32).

Gregory, Helen The 19-year-old sister of Brian Gregory who set out with her father in 1936 to locate her missing brother. She was blond, beautiful and vivacious, especially to Tarzan's friend **Paul d'Arnot**. She was kidnapped by **Atan Thome** before her safari left Loango and was held hostage by him in case he needed to stop Brian Gregory (whom he thought Tarzan to be). She escaped from him and was found by Tarzan, only to be captured by the soldiers of **Ashair** as they approached the city. After a harrowing series of narrow escapes she was reunited with her family and was escorted with honors out of **Tuen-baka** by the people of **Thobos**, who were happy to get their god and treasure back (T20;1-4, 7-8,14,17-32).

Gregory, Mister The father of **Brian** and **Helen** Gregory; we are never told his first name. He came to Africa in October of 1936 to search for his son and made friends with **Paul d'Arnot** in Loango. D'Arnot got Tarzan to accompany the Gregorys into the interior, and when they got to **Tuen-baka** they befriended **Thetan**, a noble of **Thobos** whose life Tarzan saved. Thetan brought them to Thobos, where (to his chagrin) they were imprisoned. Tarzan won their freedom, but Gregory was later captured by the minions of **Chon**, who planned to sacrifice him for divinatory purposes, a fate which he escaped by mere seconds. He was soon after reunited with his children and escorted out of Tuenbaka in style by the now-friendly Thobotians (T20;1-4,14,17-32).

Gregovitch, General Demitrius The Minister of War for **Karlova** in the late 19th and early 20th centuries (R;3).

Gregovitch, Nicholas The son of General **Demitrius Gregovitch** of Karlova, an officer in the **Black Guard**, and a close friend of **Prince Boris'** (R;3).

Grey, John de A loyalist baron of medieval England whose estate **Norman of Torn** sacked in June of 1262 (OT;9).

Greystoke British title (a viscounty) held by Tarzan (T1;1).

Greystoke, Viscount An early Viscount Greystoke was a Saxon nobleman at the time of Henry III who was killed in a duel with the young **Norman of Torn** in 1255. It must be assumed that this man was Tarzan's ancestor (OT;5).

Greystoke Diary *see* Diary, Greystoke

Gridley, Jason A young Californian radio bug (B.S. from Stanford), described by Burroughs as "scandalously good looking." It was he who discovered the **Gridley Wave**, a previously unused form of electromagnetic radiation with the penetrating power necessary to communicate with either Pellucidar or Mars. In the early 1920s Gridley established a home and lab in **Tarzana** near Burroughs' ranch and the two became good friends. Burroughs was present when the 23-year-old inventor received the urgent message (in 1926) from **Abner Perry** in Pellucidar, intended for Burroughs' ears, summoning aid to Pellucidar to rescue the imprisoned **David Innes** of whom Gridley had read as a teenager (P3).

Gridley organized an expedition and recruited Tarzan to head it. They left for Pellucidar in June of 1927 in a specially constructed dirigible, the O-220. Due to a collision with a thipdar in midair, his scout plane (which had been brought aboard the dirigible) was downed. He was lost in Pellucidar, fell in love with a native girl, was captured by the horrible **Horibs**, and eventually escaped, making his way back to the O-220 after encountering Tarzan (P4;1–2,5,14–17). He originally intended to set out for **Sari** to begin a search for the missing Lt. **Von Horst**, but was eventually persuaded to return to the outer crust with his new wife **Jana**, the **Red Flower of Zoram**, who settled with him in Tarzana (P5;1,22).

Gridley Wave A powerful and previously unknown form of radio wave discovered in the early 1920s by **Jason Gridley**, with which communication was first established with Pellucidar in 1926 and Barsoom in 1927. Other than as the medium of communication between Earth and Pellucidar (and to a lesser extent Barsoom) the discovery was practically ignored until the 1940s, when it finally came to public attention (P3)(M7)(MM1;1).

Grift One of **Gum Smith's** men who helped kidnap **Diana Henders** for **Maurice Corson** and his friends (HB;18).

Grimaldi race Archaic term for Cro-Magnon man (C1;8).

Grimsby, Willie One of Jack Clayton's boyhood friends in London (T4;2).

Gringo (Mexican slang) Deprecatory term for a white person (an "Anglo"), especially an American (K2;6).

Gron The wife of **Tur** of the Boat-Builders, who resented Tur's capture of **Nat-ul** and wished her dead. When Tur forsook her to take Nat-ul as a mate, Gron evolved a plan to free **Nu, son of Nu** from the torture that her tribe had planned for him — not from any affection for Nu, but to rob Tur of his pleasure in torturing Nu and also to make him jealous by thinking she had run off with Nu. Later, she really did fall in love with the good and noble Nu and saved his life by killing Tur, but then killed herself when she saw Nu with his true love, Nat-ul (E2;4,7–14).

Groot, Hans de The son of **Martin de Groot**, brother of **Hilda**, and playmate of **Prince Michael**. When he grew up he joined the army and was eventually assigned to a post in the capital, where the revolutionary **Carlyn** courted him as a friend because of his hatred for his sister's boyfriend, **Prince Ferdinand**. Hans joined the revolutionary faction of the army after Ferdinand became king and committed suicide after Hilda was killed with Ferdinand in a coup that Hans had helped to execute (LL;1,3,7,11,21–23).

Groot, Hilda de The extremely pretty young daughter of **Martin de Groot**, who was loved by **Prince Ferdinand** and took advantage of the situation, allowing him to support her in the best of styles until the time they should marry — after he became the king. Her father and brother of course strongly disapproved, knowing what would happen; he eventually married another woman, but kept Hilda as a mistress, a move that resulted in her being killed along with Ferdinand when the army took over on **Friday the 13th** (LL;3, 7,11–23).

Groot, Martin de The head gardener in the royal palace of an unnamed European country in the early 20th century. He was

Dutch by extraction and was discharged by King Otto after his daughter was found with Prince Ferdinand. He then began his own business, at which he became much more prosperous than he ever had been as a palace gardener (LL;3,7,11).

Groote, Hans de The first mate of the *Saigon* when it carried Tarzan across the Pacific as a captive "wild man." He was a good-looking young Dutchman who abhorred the treatment afforded Tarzan by Fritz Krause and fell in love with Janette Laon (despite her past) after the wreck of the *Saigon* on Uxmal. They were married by Bolton aboard the *Naiad* after it rescued them six weeks later (T24;2,7–11,15–21,24).

Grotius The second-in-command of the Dutch outlaw band that captured Corrie van der Meer in Japanese-occupied Sumatra in the spring of 1944 (T22;16).

Grubitten (Derived from "Great Britain.") The name given by the primitive inhabitants of the Isle of Wight in 2137 to their island — they knew of no other land (LC;3). See also Grubritten; Grabritin.

Grubritten (Derived from "Great Britain.") The name by which some of the natives of 22nd century England in *The Lost Continent* called their country (LC;3). See also Grabritin.

Grum The elder daughter of Gorph the Mammoth Man. She was a short, squat girl (built just like her father) with an ugly face who could not get a husband and so continued to live in Gorph's cave until such time as she could. Von Horst fought the warrior Horg for her and won, so the unlucky victim was forced to marry her (P5;15).

Grunge The boyfriend of Gimmel Gora, who was also a Zabo agent and spied on Morga Sagra. He also coveted her, though, and tried to get her by framing Tangor in order to remove him, since he thought Sagra was Tangor's woman. Like most Kapars, Grunge was "arrogant, supercilious, stupid, and rude" (B2;5–7).

gryf A huge monster of Pal-ul-don, descended from the triceratops of the Cretaceous. The gryf has evolved considerably from its ancestor, however. It is omnivorous, has teeth in its beaked jaws, and its feet are equipped with talons rather than pads, five on

each front leg and three on each rear. Its face is yellow with blue bands around the eyes, its crest red on top and yellow beneath, and its belly is also yellow; its body and legs are of a dirty slate blue. All bony protuberances are yellow except for those along the spine, which are red.

The gryf has several unique evolutionary adaptations. It is far more intelligent than its ancestor, understanding loyalty and training, and is very persistent in its pursuit of prey. It gives off almost no body odor and moves very silently in spite of its great bulk.

The Tor-o-dons have a method of subduing the beast which allows them to ride on the back of one whenever they so choose. Tarzan learned the method and rode the creatures on three separate occasions while in Pal-ul-don (T8;8,22,25).

gu (*Ape*) Belly (TC).

gu-e-ho A word in the language of Vanah which, depending on the notes in which its syllables are sung, can have many meanings; this particular word has at least 27 separate and distinct meanings (MM1;5).

Guadalupe Island A small Mexican island far off the western coast of Baja California on which Carson Napier built and launched the giant rocket torpedo with which he intended to fly to Mars (V1;1).

Guadalupe Pass A valley of southern Arizona which leads across the border into Mexico (A1;20).

The Guard The elite force of the Royal Guard of the tiny eastern European nation of Margoth (R;9).

Guardian of the North A monstrously huge black steel shaft resting directly over the north magnetic pole of Barsoom. The huge electromagnet was controlled from within the palace of the Jeddak of Jeddaks of Okar in Kadabra and was turned on whenever a flier approached, dragging it to its inevitable destruction against the shaft. The survivors of a wreck were then enslaved and the dead and dying fed to the apts. This Guardian destroyed every exploratory vessel since time immemorial, making exploration of Okar impossible for outworlders. It was also by its power that the fleet of Tardos Mors and Mors Kajak (with which they were searching for Carthoris) was destroyed and its warriors captured. The Guardian was destroyed when Talu became ruler of Okar (M3;9,16).

Guaymas A seaport in **Sonora** (V1;1).

gudgeon The socket into which a hinge pin or axle fits (Q;11).

gugu (*Ape*) Front (TC).

guilder A unit of currency (formerly a silver coin) used in the Netherlands (OT;3).

Guinalda The Princess of **Nimmr**, the beautiful young daughter of **Gobred**, Prince of Nimmr, who was fascinated by the handsome young **James Hunter Blake**, who stumbled upon the lost city early in 1921. Due to a vicious rumor started by **Sir Malud**, she was angry at Blake for a time, but found out the truth when he saved her from being abducted by **King Bohun** of the City of the Sepulcher. After this rescue, she was abducted by (in rapid succession) **Ibn-jad** and his raiders, the **Arab Fahd**, and the king ape **Toyat**. She was rescued from the latter by Tarzan's lion **Jad-bal-ja** and brought home by Tarzan (T1; 11,16–23).

Guiteau, Charles (1840–1882) A disappointed office-seeker who shot president James Garfield in the summer of 1881 (A2;3).

Gulf of Torquas An ancient gulf of **Throxeus**, mightiest ocean of ancient Barsoom, which lies west of the city of **Torquas** amidst the present-day **Highlands of Torquas** (M7;3).

Gulm The leader of the group of renegade Oparians (followers of **Cadj**) who were expelled from Opar in 1917 after the death of Cadj and who kidnapped **Gretchen von Harben** in 1920 to be their new high priestess. Gulm was killed by **Jad-bal-ja** (who had been tracking the "Tarzan Twins") when he tried to sacrifice **Dick** (TT2;3–7,12).

gumado (*Ape*) Sick (TC).

Gum's Place — Liquors and Cigars The most profitable saloon in 1880s Hendersville, Arizona— it was owned by **Gum Smith**, the sheriff (HB;1).

gun control The primary reason for the **Kalkars** being able to conquer the Earth was the fact that stringent gun and weapon control laws had been enacted in the days since the close of **World War III**, so that there were no weapons with which the citizens of Earth might defend themselves. Even the military had been reduced to nothing by shortsighted fools (MM2;1).

gun-ju-le (*Apa*) "Be good" (A1;2).

gund (*Pal*) Chief (T8;3).

gund-bar "Chief-battle" (*Pal*). A personal mortal combat held to determine the chieftainship of a **Waz-don** tribe (T8;3).

Gunderstrom, Olaf (Ole) A cantankerous old miser of early 20th century **Comanche County, New Mexico** who feuded with **Buck Mason** and his father over the placement of a fence for 20 years until his violent death about two years after that of Mason's father. He was killed by **Cory Blaine**, a criminal and cattle rustler he acted as a fence for and was trying to double-cross. Unfortunately, the blame fell on Mason until he found the real murderers (D;1–2,23).

Gunderstrom, Olga The pretty young daughter of **Olaf Gunderstrom**, whom he had sent to **Philadelphia** for an education about six years before his death. She and **Buck Mason** had grown up together and been sweethearts, but she bore him a violent hatred after he supposedly murdered her father, creating a gap in his affections that **Kay White** filled (D;1,8,14–23).

Gung One of the woman warriors of the gender-reversed Pellucidarian tribe of **Oog** who tried to beat **David Innes** while he was enslaved there in 1929 and ended up beaten herself. She was later killed by **Gluck** (P6;3).

guns, anti-aircraft, Polodan These rather formidable weapons fire a 1000 pound shell some 12 to 15 miles into the air, where it detonates and sends shrapnel more than 500 yards in all directions. Other guns shoot out wire nets supported by parachutes which are intended to entangle aircraft and foul propellers (B1;8).

Gunto A bull ape of the tribe of **Kerchak** who cruelly bit his lazy mate **Tana**. He was eventually killed by **Taug** in defense of Tarzan (T1;12)(T6:1,12).

Gunung Tebor A trading post of 1920s Borneo (Q;13).

Gupingu The aged witch doctor of the **Bukena** tribe when Tarzan was their prisoner in 1934. He believed that Tarzan was one of the Kavuru and that if the tribe killed him the Kavuru would wipe them out. When the warriors voted to kill Tarzan anyway, Gupingu freed him so he would tell the "other Kavuru" to leave Gupingu and his daughters alone. Tarzan also tricked him into telling him how to get to the Kavuru country (T19;6–8).

Gur Tus Dwar of the 10th Utan of the Heliumetic forces which invaded the land of the **First Born** on Barsoom. He was a very valiant warrior (M2;21).

Gura The daughter of Scurv, chief of the Himean village of Garb in Pellucidar. **Tanar the Fleet One** was the first man she had ever met who was not an utter and complete brute, and so perhaps it was inevitable that she fall in love with him and help him escape from her father. She traveled to **Korsar** as one of their prisoners, escaped with Tanar, **David Innes, Ja** of Anoroc, and **Stellara**, and moved to Sari (P3;11,13–14,17).

Gurrul The head of the **Zabo**, the secret police of **Kapara** on **Poloda**, when **Tangor** came to Kapara as a **Unisan** spy in 1940. He had "a cruel mouth and close set eyes" and enjoyed shouting at and tormenting people (B2;2–3).

guru (*Pal*) Terrible (T8;3).

Gust The Swedish leader of the mutineers of the *Cowrie* in 1912 who, though unpopular with the others, was not killed because he was the only mutineer who could navigate the ship. This changed when **Kai Shang** and **Momulla**, two other mutineers, encountered **Schneider** (navigator of the *Kincaid*) marooned on **Jungle Island** and recruited him to replace Gust. When they came to kill him, however, he fled to Tarzan and told him of their plans in time for him to save Jane and capture the *Cowrie* (T3;20–21).

gustatio (*Lat*) Appetizer (I;6).

Guva One of the women of the **Mammoth Men** of Ja-ru. She was struck by **Trog** when she refused one of his commands (P5; 13).

Guy The right-hand man to **Peter of Colfax**. Guy was in charge of both of Colfax's expeditions to capture **Bertrade de Montfort** in the spring of 1262 and was killed by **Norman of Torn** in the second attempt (OT;9–10).

Guy, Sir James Hunter **Blake's** first opponent in the **Great Tourney** of the **Valley of the Sepulcher** for 1921. He was a noble knight whom Blake defeated but administered first aid to afterward and so saved his life. Because of his kindness, Sir Guy later helped him escape from the clutches of the evil **King Bohun** (T11;16,18,22).

Guypal A large, vicious Amtorian bird of prey native to **Northern Anlap**. Guypals attack in flocks of 10 or 12 which can kill even an armed man, and they love to eat **Myposan** and **Brokol** infants (V4;11,28).

gyan "Friend" (*Amt*). The title used by the **Thorists** to address one another (V2;1). See also **Brother; Ongyan**.

gyor The Pellucidarian triceratops (P4;11).

Gyor Cors "Gyor plains" (*Pell*). The great plain inhabited by the **gyors** of Pellucidar; it lies just south of the **Mountains of the Thipdars** (P4;8).

gyro-compass An incorrect name for the Barsoomian **destination compass** used in "John Carter and the Giant of Mars" (M11A;2).

haad The Barsoomian "mile," equal to about 1,949 English feet (594 meters). A haad is subdivided into 200 **ads**, and 100 haads make a **karad**, or Barsoomian degree, at the equator (M4;6)(M7;2).

habet "He has" (*Lat*). Customary abbreviation of the idiomatic expression (used by spectators in reference to a wounded gladiator) "hoc habet," literally "he has that"—in other words, "he has that [hit]" or "he is wounded" (T12;14).

Habush (*Ara*) An inhabitant of el-Habash (T11;2).

Had Urtur Odwar of the first Umak of **Hastor** on Barsoom and commander of the largest warship Hastor ever contributed to the navy of **Helium** (it accommodated his entire umak and 500 fighting ships). Had Urtur married a princess of **Gathol** and was the father of **Tan Hadron** (M7;1).

Hafim The Galla slave of **Cathne** whom Tarzan saved from a **Grand Hunt** by letting him out of the woods near the mountains when he visited the **City of Gold** in 1930 (T16;15).

Hagar A formerly great city of Unis on Poloda, utterly destroyed by the Kapars in a century of war. It lay on the east coast of the Bay of Hagar (B1;6).

Hagar, Bay of An enormous gulf, 1200 miles long, in the west coast of the Polodan continent occupied by Unis (B1;6).

Hagenbeck, Carl (1844–1913) A well-known German circus owner and animal trainer who toured the whole world with his animal acts (T4;2).

Haglion The commander of the Morgor ship which abducted John Carter in 1941. He was a typical Morgor — cruel, sarcastic, and unimaginative (M11B;3).

hahnium A highly unstable radioactive element, atomic number 105. Its most stable Earthly isotope has a half-life of only 40 seconds, but the Amtorians can produce a more stable form which they call yor-san and use in their nuclear reactors (V1;8).

hai (*Uni*) Elect (B1;3).

Haile Selassie (1892–1975) Last Emperor of Abyssinia, from 1930 to 1974. Born Ras Tafari Makonnen, he was effective ruler of Ethiopia from 1916 to 1930 and Emperor thereafter. He was deposed in 1974 and died of natural causes in 1975 (T14;13).

Haj Alt The Prince of Tjanath on Barsoom, son of Haj Osis. He tried to take Tavia as his slave but was foiled by Tan Hadron, who attacked him and forced him to flee (M7;11).

Haj Osis The Jed of Tjanath on Barsoom, father of Kal Tavan and grandfather of Tavia. He became so suspicious because of the activities of Tul Axtar of Jahar that he almost went mad from fear for his country and imprisoned all visitors to the city as Jaharian spies (M7;5).

Haja of Gathol A princess of Gathol, Gahan's aunt, who vanished long ago while returning from a visit to a neighboring country. She had been stolen and taken as a slave to Manator, where the jeddak, O-Tar, took her as his own and had a son named A-Kor by her. Later, fearing her power among the Gatholian slaves, O-Tar sent her to Manatos, where U-Thor freed and married her (M5;14).

Hajan The Jong of Panga on Amtor when the fleet of Falsa rolled into the Pangan capital, Hor, in 1931. Hajan had actually allowed the Falsans to take the city in order to implement a surprise plan against them — while the Falsans were celebrating that night, the Pangans captured the entire fleet and either imprisoned or killed most of the Falsan warriors (V4;47).

Hajellan One of the followers of Ibn Dammuk who assisted him in the abduction of La of Opar from Abu Batn in 1928. He was later killed by Jad-bal-ja at La's command (T14;10–12).

Haka Gera The woman of the Kapar scientist Horthal Wend. She was a rather stupid woman, but a good housekeeper and manager (B2;6).

Hal Vas The son of Vas Kor of Dusar on Barsoom, dwar of the road for a Dusarian canal in the southern hemisphere. He helped his father to recruit warriors from his district for the war against Helium and unwittingly recruited Carthoris (M4;11).

Hala The woman of Zurts in Pellucidar who was assigned to help O-aa of Kali when she was a guest in their country early in 1932 (P7:4;7).

Halfmoon The brigantine aboard which Billy Byrne was shanghaied to Asia in 1913. Its captain and crew then set out to kidnap Barbara Harding, but were afterwards wrecked in a typhoon on a remote Pacific island (K1;2–8).

Hall of Chiefs A large hall in the palace of the Jeddak of Manator on Barsoom which is lined with the embalmed bodies of the former jeddaks of Manator, each sitting upon an embalmed thoat in full battle regalia. Jeddaks of Manator sometimes closed the doors at the ends of the hall and conferred with their dead predecessors, in spirit at least (M5;15).

Halmstad A port at the mouth of the Nissan River in southern Sweden (C1;3).

Halsted Street One of the streets bordering Chicago's west side (K1;1).

Hamadalban A Minunian warrior of Veltopismakus through whose quarters one had to pass to reach those of Kalfastoban (T10;17).

Hamar A loyal slave of Fou-tan's in Pnom Dhek who carried her messages to Gordon King while he was her father's "guest" in the palace after returning her to the city (HM;12).

Hamas The major-domo of Fal Sivas' establishment in Zodanga on Barsoom. He became jealous of John Carter's position in Fal Sivas' eyes and tried to get him in trouble with the inventor (M8;3,8).

Hamlar The chief of the people of Tandar who captured and enslaved Dian the Beautiful in 1931 (P7:3;3).

Han Du The first friend John Carter made among the Savator prisoners who had been condemned to die with him in the next Morgor graduation exercises. After Carter defeated the bully Pho Lar, Han Du thanked him and shook his hand. Han Du was an exceptional fighter who escaped the city of the Morgors with John Carter after killing the graduating class they were pitted against, then took Carter across a vast area of wilderness to his invisible city and gave him his hospitality (M11B;7–9).

Handon Gar A top Unisan secret agent in Kapara on Poloda who was missing from 1938 to 1940. Tangor found him in a Kapar prison camp in the spring of 1940 planning an escape with Tunzo Bor, but circumstances convinced him that Tangor was a traitor to Unis and told everyone so after his escape and return to Unis. He was very sorry when he found out the truth and hastened to repair the damage he had caused. He later accompanied Tangor on his flight to Tonos, the outcome of which must forever remain a mystery (B2;1,4–5,10).

Hangor A city-state of Amtor which lies about 500 miles from Panga, inhabited by criminals and outcasts from all over Middle Anlap who subsist by bandit activity. During Panga's war with Falsa, the Hangorites stole nearly all of Panga's herds. The city is poorly built, filthy and destitute-looking (V4;45–49).

Hank A farmhand of the Billings ranch in 1880s New Mexico (A1;10).

Hannah The Pennington family cook at Rancho del Ganado (GH;13).

Hanson, Mister The name taken by Sven Malbihn when he disguised himself by shaving off his beard and came to Tarzan's estate in order to abduct Meriem (T4;18).

Hara Es A woman of the Amtorian city of Havatoo in whose charge Nalte kum Andoo was placed while awaiting the results of her "entrance examination" there in 1930 (V2;13).

harbenite The lightest, strongest metal known, as light as cork but stronger than steel. It is probably the same metal as the Barsoomian **forandus** but was discovered on Earth in the Wiramwazi Mountains of Africa by the explorer Erich von Harben, who found the local natives making boats of it. Its first practical refined application was in the building of the great dirigible, the O-220, early in 1927 (T13;1).

Harber, Mack A courier for the Henders' Mine who was shot and wounded by the Black Coyote during a stagecoach robbery at Hell's Bend Pass. On his first trip on the stage again after his recovery, he was shot again and died (HB;2–4,13).

Harding A transoceanic passenger airship of the late 1960s, motivated by broadcast power from Chicago to Paris. It was in the Blue Room of the *Harding* that Burroughs met Julian 3rd on Mars Day (June 10, 1967) and was told the events comprising *The Moon Maid* (MM1).

Harding, Anthony The millionaire father of Barbara Harding, who in 1914 came in search of his abducted daughter to Yoka, was captured by the samurai who inhabited the island, and was rescued by Billy Byrne (K1; 3–4,15–16). In the winter of 1916, Harding and Barbara went to his Mexican ranch, El Orobo, for a vacation and were attacked by banditos. After they were rescued from this situation by Byrne, Harding realized that Byrne was really a good man and that Barbara really loved him, and so welcomed Byrne as his son-in-law (K2;9–17).

Harding, Barbara The beautiful daughter of millionaire Anthony Harding who was in 1914 abducted from her father's yacht by the crew of the *Halfmoon* in the employ of Larry Divine, who had hatched the scheme in order to get her for himself. At first she and Billy Byrne hated one another for what the other represented, but as each began to impress the other with his/her courage and character, that feeling began to change. After the

Halfmoon was wrecked on the uncharted island of Yoka, Barbara was abducted by the degenerate descendants of Japanese samurai and rescued by Byrne, who then completely fell for her. They were forced to hide for several months thereafter awaiting rescue, and during this period she realized that she also loved him, particularly after he unselfishly went forth to save her father from the samurai even though he knew that Mr. Harding would never consent to Byrne's marrying his daughter (K1;3–17).

Byrne was left for dead on the island, and Barbara did not hear of him again until he was also rescued and turned up again in the New York newspapers as a heavyweight prizefighter. At this point, he spurned her "for her own good," believing that he was no good for her, and demanded that she marry Billy Mallory, to whom she had been engaged. She did not marry Mallory, however, and got her father to take her to his El Orobo ranch in Mexico, where she first met up with Byrne's friend Bridge, and later, after his capture for robbing Pancho Villa's bank, with Byrne himself. She released him, but was herself captured immediately afterward by Indians in the employ of Grayson, the ranch manager, who wished to keep her for immoral purposes. Byrne rescued her from the Indians and then he, she, her father and Bridge headed for the border in flight from the bandito force of Pesita. They were soon rescued by the U.S. 13th Cavalry (in Mexico to pursue Pancho Villa) and she and Byrne, who now recognized his own worth, returned to New York and were married (K1;18)(K2;9, 13–17).

hareem (*Ara*) The women's quarters of an Arab dwelling (T11;1).

Harkas Don   The son of Harkas Yen. Don became Tangor's best friend on Poloda (B1;2–11).

Harkas Yamoda   The beautiful daughter of Harkas Yen. She was captured in a Kapar raid in January of 1940 but jumped from the plane and was badly hurt. She was rescued by Tangor and rushed to a hospital in time to save her. Later, she and Tangor began to fall in love with one another (B1;2,11)(B2; 1,10).

Harkas Yen   The elderly psychiatrist of the Unisan city of Orvis on Poloda into whose care Tangor was placed after his unusual arrival on that world. Harkas Yen examined Tangor and taught him the language of Unis (B1;2).

Harlem Hurricane   A heavyweight boxer of the early 20th century, the sparring partner of Battling Dago Pete (K1;17).

harness   The only form of clothing worn on Barsoom is a leather harness worn about the body which is often encrusted with gems and precious metals and is used to support weapons and a pocket pouch. Women wear even less harness than men, going almost totally nude, and both sexes wear metal armlets, decorations, etc., including insignia of their city, house, etc. (M1).

Harold   (1022–1066) The last Saxon king of England, who ruled for only ten months in 1066 before being defeated by William the Conqueror (OT;5).

Harper, Townsend J., Jr.   Heir to the Harper Railroad fortune of the 1920s, who followed Virginia Maxon to Borneo to meet her but suffered an accident and lost his memory, waking up in the place of Number Thirteen, a synthetically created humanoid. After many adventures in search of Virginia (see Bulan) he found and won her, eventually regaining his memory and marrying her (Q;17).

harquebus   An archaic type of firearm of the 1400s and 1500s with a smooth, cylindrical bore and a heavy barrel and stock. The weapon was muzzle-loaded with shot or stones and touched off by a matchlock. Early harquebuses had to be fired from a rest, but later versions (of roughly .60 to .80 caliber) could be shoulder fired. Harquebuses of this type were used by the Korsars of Pellucidar, indicating that they had come from the outer world in the early 1500s (P3).

Hartford   The Connecticut home town of David Innes and Abner Perry before they came to Pellucidar (P7:1;7).

Hasan   An Arab sentry of the tribe el-Harb who fired upon Tantor and missed when the elephant came to save Tarzan from the Arabs in 1921 (T11;2).

Hash-ka-ai-la   Chief of the Apaches who inhabited the White Mountains of Arizona in the late 1800s (A1;3).

Hastor A city of the Empire of Helium on Barsoom which lies southwest of Helium proper. It was in this city that the rescue ships for **Dejah Thoris** were secretly equipped with water propellers so they might navigate **Omean** (M2;18). Hastor was also the home city of **Tan Hadron** (M7).

hatab lil nar (*Ara*) "Fuel for hellfire" (T17;12).

Hatcher and Holland John Bell Hatcher (1861–1904) and William Jacob Holland (1848–1932); turn-of-the-century paleontologists who worked to restore the diplodocus (C2;2).

hatchet One of the preferred weapons of the **Sagoths** of Pellucidar, used both in hand and as a throwing weapon (P1;3).

hauberk The part of a suit of plate armor which serves to protect the shoulders and neck (OT;15).

hauptmann (*Ger*) A military (not naval) captain (T7;1).

Havatoo The most scientifically advanced city of Amtor, a semicircular walled city of gleaming white about five miles in diameter which lies along the **Gerlat kum Rov** across from **Kormor**, the city of the living dead. Havatoo has six sections divided by five major avenues (the **avenues of the Psychologists, Biologists, Physicists, Chemists and Warriors**) which run from the wall to the hub of the city. A semicircular park containing a civic center and the seat of government (the **Central Laboratories**, or **Sera Tartum**) lies at the center of the waterfront. Many other minor streets run from wall to hub, and there are many transverse streets (parallel to the city wall) as well.

Havatoo is a planned city whose people are divided into six classes; the five professional classes mentioned above and the **yorgan**, or workers. Citizens are tested to see which class they are best suited for and trained for it. They live in whatever section of the city has been designated for their class; each of the five "upper classes" has its own district between the hub of the city and the **Yorgan Lat**, which runs parallel to the outer wall about halfway between the hub and the wall. The yorgan live in the large district between the Yorgan Lat and the city wall, except for the outermost semicircle of the city (against the wall) which

is the district of shops, markets and factories (V2;13).

Havatoo Lat "Havatoo Avenue" (*Amt*). One of the most important "spoke" streets of the Amtorian city of Havatoo (V2;16).

Hawkes, Flora An attractive and greedy young woman of pre–1920s London who conceived of a plan to rob the treasure vaults of **Opar** by substituting a look-alike for Tarzan. She had been a maid in Tarzan's London townhouse for years and in that time had learned of Opar's location, thus becoming the only white person other than Tarzan and **Jane** to know it. When her expedition to rob Opar began to hit trouble due to lack of food, she was elected boss and continued to act as such until the whites were betrayed by their headman **Luvini**, who would have murdered them all had they not escaped. After doing so, they met up with Jane and the **Waziri** and so came under their protection, but Flora was kidnapped by **Esteban Miranda** and left to die, which she certainly would have had not Tarzan saved her. She confessed the plot, was forgiven, and came back to work for them (T9;3, 5,10,15–20).

Hazim A fendy friendly to the fendy el-Guad (T11;1).

He Who Speaks for Luata The title held by the king of the **Wieroos** of Caspak. The creature who held the title in the early 20th century was killed by **John Bradley** on September 15, 1916 in his escape from **Oo-oh** (C3;2,4).

headdress, Barsoomian The ancient **Orovar** warriors of Barsoom wore a headdress in addition to their **harness**. It consisted of a leather band running around the head above the brows, attached to which were two bands going over the top of the head, one from side to side and the other from front to back. They were highly ornamented with carving, jewels, and precious metals and bore a sort of badge device in the front. The badge of **Horz** was a gold spearhead, point up, carved and inlaid with the city's symbol in red and black (M10;1;2).

headdress, Oparian Oparian priestesses wear a sort of cap made from circular and oval pieces of gold welded together, from which hang two long chains of oval pieces which fall to the wearer's waist, one such chain on either side of the head (T2;20).

healing, Barsoomian Among the green men, healing is performed by the women, and their skill and the strength of the ointments and drugs they prepare can heal wounds in minutes that would require days of recuperation to heal on Earth (M1;15).

Heinz One of the German crew members of the U-33 on its cruise to Caspak in 1916 and 1917 (C3;5).

hejra (*Ara*) A small tent (T11;1).

Hekkador, Holy The chief title held by Matai Shang, leader of all Therns on Barsoom (M2;7).

heliotrope A soft, rosy shade of purple (V2;5).

Helium The most powerful, most technologically advanced, and richest empire on Barsoom. Under the rule of Tardos Mors it spread its influence over the whole of Barsoom during the days of John Carter, eventually ruling much of the planet and carrying on alliances with another large portion. Helium proper consists of two cities; Greater Helium, marked by a vivid scarlet tower almost a mile high, and (75 miles to the southeast) Lesser Helium, marked by a yellow tower of the same height (M1;23). The two cities are linked by a pneumatic subway system so that the trip may be made in only a few seconds. The streets of both cities are filled with ground fliers and, at a higher altitude, great passenger liners to distant regions embark and disembark. The wealth and high technology of Helium give the inhabitants of the cities a standard of living unavailable anywhere on Earth. As elsewhere on Barsoom, the citizenry is always armed and slaves (mostly prisoners of war) and machines do most of the menial labor (M4;2).

Culturally, the Heliumites are considered the highest of Barsoomian peoples. Her women are the most beautiful and her navy the mightiest — in fact, the only reason that Than Kosis of Zodanga was able to threaten her in the late 19th century was that the navy was spread about the planet searching for Dejah Thoris, Princess of Helium, who is worshipped by her people and family (M1). By the mid–20th century, the Heliumetic navy was absolutely supreme and could only be threatened by enemies with new and secret weapons (M7;15)(M11B;1).

Helium Forest A landform appearing only in "John Carter and the Giant of Mars," described as a "lonely" timber forest near Helium — obviously, an impossibility on arid Barsoom (M11A;1).

Hell Creek Site in Montana where one of the earliest and best finds of Tyrannosaurus rex bones was made (C3;1).

hellhounds A large and vicious pack of wild dogs living in the Teivos of Chicago in Kalkar-occupied 22nd century America. They were a pack of cunning and vicious brutes with a great deal of collie and Airedale blood whom the humans could not kill because weapons were forbidden to them. Julian 9th saved Juana St. John, his future mate, from a small pack of them by killing several with his bare hands (MM2;2–3). Later, all wild dogs came to be called hellhounds (MM3;2).

Hell's Bend Pass A treacherous, narrow gap in the hills of Hendersville, Arizona, in the late 1880s, through which the North Pass Road went, and at which the notorious bandit, the Black Coyote, was wont to commit robberies (HB;3).

helmets, Barsoomian Helmets are practically unknown on modern Barsoom but were used by the ancient Orovars (M10:1;5).

Helvetians A Celtic people who occupied what is now called Switzerland (I;4).

Helvidius Pius A Roman senator of the 1st century A.D. to whom Attica, later wife of Britannicus Caligulae Servus, was a slave. He was the father of Milonia Caesonia, later wife to the emperor Caligula (I;7).

Hemmy The nickname of Hemmington Main (R;1).

Henders, Diana The beautiful young daughter of Elias Henders, born in New York and educated by her father both in formal knowledge and Western ranch life. She was musically talented and very vivacious and was loved and respected by all the ranch hands for these traits and also for her good sense and horsemanship. She was the target of various men who wooed her for her money, among them Hal Colby and Jefferson Wainright, Jr., both of whom she thought she might marry until they both proved their unworthiness — Wainright by his cowardice and Colby by his perfidy. After her father's death, Jefferson Wainright, Sr., and Maurice Corson (her cousin's New York attorney) both tried to fool her into selling her property to Wainright (who had a deal with Corson) for a fraction of its worth, but the clever Diana would not bite. Even when they tried to steal it from her outright she outwitted them (with Bull's help) and they were forced to take drastic steps — namely, abducting her to get her out of the way. She was rescued by Bull, however, and after the conspirators were run out of town she and Bull were married (HB).

Henders, Elias The owner of the Bar-Y Ranch in Arizona together with his school chum John Manill. Henders was an Oxford man, originally from Kentucky, and was very solicitous of his daughter Diana, whom he had fathered when already middle-aged. When he died (killed by Apache renegades in the 1880s) he left Manill and the 19-year-old Diana as owners of his ranch and gold mine (HB;1–6).

Henders, Sir John An Oxford-educated Englishman who settled in Kentucky, establishing the American branch of his family (HB;2).

Henders' Mine The gold mine on the Bar-Y Ranch property in 1880s Arizona (HB;2).

Henders' Mine Road A road of 1880s Hendersville, Arizona, which led up from the mine to North Pass Trail (HB;2).

Hendersville The small town south of the Bar-Y Ranch in 1880s Arizona, containing a "general store, restaurant, Chinese laundry, blacksmith shop, hotel, newspaper office and five saloons" (HB;1).

Hendersville Tribune The sole newspaper of late 1880s Hendersville, Arizona (HB;1).

Henrietta Street London street on which Paul d'Arnot ran into Samuel T. Philander in 1910 and thus found out about Jane Porter's postponement of her marriage to William Clayton and their plans to take a yacht cruise around Africa, which information he forwarded to Tarzan in a letter (T2;9).

Henry "One-Punch" Mullargan's auto mechanic in New York (T24A).

Henry III (1207–1272) King of England from 1216 to 1272. He was the son of King John and assumed the throne at the age of eight, proving to be a futile and unfit king throughout his whole reign, which was marked by civil wars led by his brother-in-law Simon de Montfort, Earl of Leicester, whom he had accused of treason in a quarrel in 1243. He allowed his wife to influence him into gathering various foreign favorites about him, thus making himself unpopular with his own barons. On the day of his quarrel with de Montfort in 1243, he insulted and spit upon his swordmaster, Jules de Vac, who afterward vowed revenge upon him and kidnapped his younger son Richard, raising the boy as the outlaw Norman of Torn who afterward preyed for years upon the king and his barons. The plan was for Norman to be captured and hanged so that Henry would have unwittingly executed his own son, but the plan was eventually revealed and the young prince accepted by Henry and proclaimed a prince a few days after Henry's defeat at the hands of the barons, thanks in part to Norman (OT;1–6,18–19).

Henry VIII The gorilla king of the city of London in the Valley of Diamonds who, like his historical namesake, defied church authority and had multiple wives — unlike the original, he had seven wives all at the same time. He plotted against his God ceaselessly and planned to make himself God when the original died. He was killed by a lion while attempting to flee from God with Rhonda Terry (T17;18–29).

Hentig, Captain An American cavalry officer of D Troop killed by an Apache scout at the Battle of Cibicu Creek (A1;14).

Herat The King of Thobos when Tarzan and the Gregory safari came there in 1936. He was "a large man with a black spade beard and a smooth upper lip" who imprisoned Tarzan, Mr. Gregory and Lavac when they came there with Thetan, but later released them after Tarzan won their freedom — all but Magra, who he planned to keep for himself. He befriended them after Tarzan helped him get back the Father of Diamonds and conquer Ashair, and he had them escorted out of Tuen-Baka in style (T20;14,19–23, 30–32).

Heris The fifth continent of **Poloda**, which lies west of **Auris** and east of **Unis**. Nothing is known of its condition or inhabitants (B1).

Herkuf A priest of **Brulor** in **Ashair** who made an enemy of his god and was indefinitely imprisoned for it. He helped the **Gregorys** and **Paul d'Arnot** escape Ashair by leading them out through a secret passage known only to the priests after they let him out of his cage, then later helped the group sneak back into Ashair to steal both the **Father of Diamonds** and Brulor for the king of **Thobos**, since Herkuf had decided the stone really belonged to Thobos and Brulor was a false god. While trekking across the lake bottom to Thobos, Herkuf found the real Father of Diamonds and returned it to **Chon** (who was also found alive) and thus earned many blessings for himself (T20;23–32).

Herlak The soldier of **Havatoo** assigned by **Ero Shan** to care for **Carson Napier** while they awaited the results of Napier's "entrance examination" late in 1929 (V2;14).

Herman A **Luthanian** brigand of **Yellow Franz**'s band who captured **Barney Custer** in the **Black Mountains** of Lutha after Custer's escape from **Blentz** in October of 1911 (MK1; 5–6).

Hermosilla A town of northern Mexico (A1;5).

Herod Agrippa (10 B.C.–A.D. 44) A Jewish king whom **Caligula** befriended while with **Tiberius** at **Capri** in the A.D. 30s (I;15).

Herog XVI The king of the lost city of **Xuja** when Lt. **Smith-Oldwick** and **Bertha Kircher** were captured there in the winter of 1915 (T7;19).

Herschel Island The Arctic island off the coast of the Yukon near which Burroughs went polar bear hunting in March of 1969, bringing him to meet **Julian 3rd** again after two years (MM2;1).

het (*Pal*) The number 50 (T8).

Hickam An American air force base in Honolulu, Hawaii (T22;25).

Hicks The young cowboy who helped "Dirty" **Cheetim** capture **Wichita Billings** early in 1884, but regretted it after he sobered up (A2;5).

Hiero I (?–467 B.C.) A tyrant of Syracuse reputed to have built a magnificent galley that was basically a floating palace (I;5).

high place The **Wieroo** term for a temple (C3;2).

Highest Most High The preferred term of reverence used when addressing the **Pom Da**, leader of the **Kapars** of Poloda (B2;5).

Highlands of Torquas Once a Barsoomian continent, now a mountainous highland area ruled by the **green men of Torquas**, who defend it with artillery. In a hidden valley deep within these highlands lies **Lothar** (M4;4–5).

hijab (*Ara*) A protective amulet (T11;21).

hikiee (Hawaiian) A large Hawaiian couch (B1).

Hilmore, Larry The owner of a gymnasium in early 20th century downtown Chicago (K1;1).

Hime An island not far from **Amiocap** in the **Korsar Az** of Pellucidar. If Amiocap was the Island of Love, certainly Hime was the Island of Hate, since the inhabitants of that island practiced cruelty and harshness as a way of life, mating for life to people they hated and raising as well children they hated, who in turn hated them and everyone else (P3;7,11).

Hin Abtol Jeddak of the **Panars** of Barsoom and self-styled **Jeddak of Jeddaks** of the north, as he claimed to have conquered **Okar** and reduced it to vassalage, a dubious claim in view of the cowardice of the Panars and the fact that nothing was heard about such a thing anywhere else on Barsoom. Hin Abtol was a swaggering jackass with an overinflated idea of himself and the strength and bravery of his people and no sense of diplomacy at all. He came in one of his ancient ships to **Gathol** to brag about his planned conquest of Barsoom, saying to **Gahan** that he would allow Gathol to remain free after the conquest and would demand only "a little tribute" from the city. He also decided to "honor" **Llana of Gathol** by marrying her, notwithstanding the fact that he already had seven wives. Soon afterward he abducted her, massacring her guards in the process, but lost her after she sabotaged his ship near **Horz**. Marooned, he stole John Carter's **flier** to return home, claiming to his people that he had taken it in battle. He returned later to lay siege to Gathol and abduct Llana back to **Pankor**, his capital, from which John Carter rescued her. **Hin Abtol** was a tyrant hated by all his people, especially for his horrible policy of freezing captured fighting men alive until he needed their services. He was finally defeated when John Carter, protected by one of the invisibility spheres of **Invak**, abducted him, thus protecting Gathol from further attack until the navy of **Helium** arrived to destroy Hin Abtol's (M10:1; 10–11/3;3,11–13/4;13).

Hindle One of the two honorable crew members of the U-33 who, because of his disgust at **Von Schoenvorts'** breaking his word and betraying the English in **Caspak**, helped them to overthrow the captain and his men and recapture the U-33 (C3;5).

Hines, Lieutenant The navigator of the dirigible O-220 on its expedition to Pellucidar in 1927. He taught the art of aerial navigation to Tarzan and **Jason Gridley** against the possibility of his being lost on the mission (T13;2).

hipponocerous Esmerelda's malapropism for (one might think) a hippopotamus or rhinoceros (T1;22).

Hiram The Old-Timer's first name (T18; 20).

Hirfa The wife of Sheik **Ibn-Jad** of the tribe el-Harb (T11;1).

Hirohito (1901–1989) The Emperor of Japan from 1926 until his death. For the first part of his reign he was a god-emperor who was manipulated by his advisors into starting World War II in the Pacific, but after his defeat he renounced his godhood (at the insistence of the Allied powers) and ended his reign as little more than a figurehead (T22;13).

Histah (*Ape*) The snake (T1;6).

Hita (*Amt*) An Amtorian "degree" of arc, equal to 1/1000 of a circle, or 21 minutes, 36 seconds of arc by Earthly measure (V2;11).

Hitler, Adolf (1889–1945) Dictator of Nazi Germany from 1933 to 1945, who rebuilt a Germany devastated by over a decade of recession and led it to conquer most of Europe until his forces were defeated by the Allied nations in **World War II** (T22;27).

ho (*Amt*) Than (V4;24).

ho (*Ape*) Many (TC).

ho (*Cpk*) Beast (C2;2).

ho (*Pal*) White (T8;2).

Ho-den A tribe of great apes who lived in the Forest of **Alemtejo** when Tarzan came there in 1938 (T23;18).

Ho-don "White man" (*Pal*). The dominant race of Pal-ul-don, basically similar to a normal Caucasian human but with a prehensile tail, long thumbs and opposable big toes. Their hair is black and distributed like a normal human's. The Ho-don have a higher technology than do the **Waz-don**, but are intellectually equal to them (T8;2).

Ho-lu "Beast-Man" (*Cpk*). The lowest type of humanoid life in **Caspak** are the Ho-lus, or anthropoid apes, who rank below even the ape-like **Alus** (C2;2).

Ho Ran Kim The Jeddak of the **Orovars** of **Horz** in the 20th century on Barsoom, the last remnants of a dead race. His policy, like that of countless jeddaks before him, was to maintain the secrecy of Horz by killing all who came within its walls (M10:1;2–5).

ho-wala "Many nests" (*Ape*). Village (this is probably another Tarzan coinage) (TC).

hoddentin (*Apa*) A sacred powder made from the pollen of cattails and thrown about by the **Apaches** as an offering to the spirits (A1;2–3).

Hodon, the Fleet One A young Pellucidarian warrior of **Sari**, one of **David Innes'** most trusted runners, who brought Innes' message to **Oose of Kali** in 1931 but was captured by **Fash of Suvi**, who had taken Kali by surprise and conquered it. He escaped from Kali too late to stop Innes and his men from walking into Fash's trap, but did rescue him with the help of **O-aa**, the beautiful compulsive liar who was Oose's daughter and whom Hodon fell for. They were captured soon after by the **Sabertooth Men**, escaped, and were rescued by the Imperial Army, under command of **Ghak the Hairy One**, which was headed for Sari. They were stopped before getting there by a meeting with Oose and his men, at which time Hodon was forced to kill **Blug**, a Kalian who wanted to mate with

O-aa. During the fight, she ran away because she thought Hodon would be killed. It was some time before he heard she had been picked up by a derelict ship and remained aboard when the warriors quit the vessel, but when he heard this he set out on the EPS *Lohar* to search for her. The ship was swept into the **Korsar Az** and rescued **Dian the Beautiful** from **Tandar**, then sailed around until it encountered the EPS *John Tyler*, which had news of O-aa, whom Hodon then followed to the **Zurts** country, where they were reunited. Afterward, they returned to Sari (P7:1; 2–7/2;1,6/3;7/4;7–12).

Hodson, Captain   The Chief of Police for **Tarzana, California**, in the late 1920s (V1;1).

Hoesin   The chief of a **Sumatran** village who helped guide the **Van der Meer** family to safety while they were fleeing the **Japanese** in February of 1942, then double-crossed them by telling their pursuers where they had gone (T22;1).

Hoffmeyer   The agent of **Pthav**, the **Kalkar** coal merchant, who once charged **Julian 8th** five milk goats for one hundred pounds of coal. He was torn to pieces by a mob at the beginning of the revolution against the Kalkars (MM2;2,11).

Hog Ranch   "Dirty" **Cheetim**'s saloon and brothel, opened in **San Carlos, Arizona**, around 1880 (A2;2).

hogan   (*Apa*) Hut (A1;1).

hohotan   (*Ape*) Tribe (TC).

Hohr, Valley   An extinct volcanic crater of **Barsoom** which lies in the midst of impassable volcanic country. The river **Syl** runs through the bottom of it and waters a beautiful forest in which lies the lost city of **Ghasta**. It has remained undiscovered for millennia, though it is very near **Tjanath**, because of the impassability of the terrain and the isolationist policies of Ghasta's mad **jed, Ghron** (M7;8–9).

Hokal   An Amtorian officer of **Kapdor** who captured **Carson Napier** on the orders of **Ongyan Moosko** and ordered him to die in the **Room of Seven Doors** (V2;1).

Holden, Harriet   Elizabeth Compton's friend, who was with her on Christmas Eve at

Feinheimer's Cabaret when **Steve Murray** tried to paw Elizabeth and was decked by **Jimmy Torrance**. She slipped Torrance her address as she left the restaurant, suggesting that her father could find him a better job. After meeting him several times, she became infatuated with him and continued to believe in him when he was framed for the murder of Elizabeth's father **Mason Compton**—enough so to convince her father to have his lawyer defend Torrance. After he was proved innocent, she married him (EE;6,10–14,23,26–28).

Holliday   A small **Kansas** town near Shawnee (K2;5).

Hollis, Jimmy   Second in command of Tom Billings' expedition to rescue **Bowen Tyler, Jr.**, from **Caspak** in the summer of 1917 (C2;1).

Hollywood   City near Los Angeles, California, home of the American film industry and many of its stars (T13;8)(GH).

Hollywood Boulevard   The main thoroughfare of **Hollywood, California** (GH;11).

Hollywood Drug Store   A 1920s business on **Hollywood Boulevard** near **Cuyhenga** (GH;11).

Holy Hekkador *see* Hekkador

Holy Horus *see* Lake Horus (T20;24).

Holy Stairs   The stairs cut into the cliff above **London** in the **Valley of Diamonds**, leading up to the **Golden Gates**, the palace of God (T17;24).

Holy Therns *see* Therns

Homo sapiens   "Wise Man" (*Lat*). The species name for a human being. **Carson Napier** used it as an alias while acting as a spy in **Amlot** in 1930 (V3;6).

Honan   An Amtorian of **Vepaja** who was captured by the **Klangan** in 1929 while trying to protect **Duare** from them and later took part in **Carson Napier**'s mutiny against the **Thorists** on their ship *Sofal* (V1;8–10).

honda   (*Cpk*) An oval weight made of gold which serves as the locus about which a **Galu** of **Caspak** braids his **lasso**. The weight serves not only as a throwing weight for the rope, but also as a weapon; it can be thrown with great force at a victim's head, then drawn back by the rope if it misses (C2;6).

honey, Amtorian Amtorian honey suggests candied violets to the taste (V1;3).

honey, Barsoomian The Barsoomian city of **Dusar** produces a famous and delicious honey (M7;16).

Honolulu The capital of **Hawaii**, which lies on the island of **Oahu**. **Waldo Emerson Smith-Jones** married **Nadara** there (CG2;13).

Honus Hasta A patrician of **Castra Sanguinarius** who, in the Roman year 953 (A.D. 200), revolted against the emperor of that city and founded **Castrum Mare** on the island in the middle of **Mare Orientis** at the east end of the valley. Honus Hasta was considered a tyrant because of his harsh laws, but perhaps they were in a way wise ones—the punishment for any crime was death, not only that of the criminal but also of his whole family, so that criminal tendencies could not be passed on to descendants. As a result, modern Castrum Mare has very few (if any) criminals (T12;8).

hoo "Hole" (*Van*). Any crater of the moon's outer surface which penetrates into **Va-nah** is a hoo. Some **U-gas** believed that the hoos might lead to other inhabited rock-cavities, such as they conceived Va-nah to be (see cosmology, Va-nah). The hoos were used as the basis of telling time by the U-gas, who observed the light of the sun through the craters and used the cycle of light and dark (the sidereal month) as the basis for their measurement of time (see ula)(MM1;6).

Hooft The leader of an outlaw band of Japanese-occupied **Sumatra** who captured **Tarzan** in the spring of 1944 and went looking for him when he escaped, only to find **Corrie van der Meer**, who escaped from Hooft as well (T22;14–17).

Hooja the Sly One A Pellucidarian warrior of **Sari** who wished to mate with **Dian the Beautiful** and let her know in no uncertain terms, but was completely ignored by her until he succeeded in escaping from the Sagoths, who had captured both of them. He then took her with him, much against her will. He was later recaptured and escaped with **David Innes**, **Abner Perry** and **Ghak the Hairy One**, only to betray them in an attempt to cause Innes' death. It was Hooja who somehow substituted a **Mahar** for Dian when Innes wished to take her to the outer Earth on his

mission for supplies in 1913 (P1;4–5,11–15). The persistent Hooja later abducted her again and took her to the island where he was building a great army to help the Mahars destroy the **Empire of Pellucidar**. This army, and Hooja with it, was destroyed in the Battle of the Unfriendly Isles, Pellucidar's first serious naval engagement (P2;5–6,13–14).

hook The Brokols of **Amtor's** northern hemisphere use a long, barbed hook in battle to draw an opponent into reach, where a sword held in the other hand can dispatch the victim. If the Brokol hits his opponent in the spine or the base of the brain, the hook alone is enough to kill (V4;24).

Hoosiers Nickname given to inhabitants of the state of **Indiana**. The name was also given to the followers of **Hooja the Sly One** in Pellucidar by **Abner Perry**, who even went as far as to name Hooja's island "Indiana" to complete the joke (P2;11).

hooves Almost all **Euroban** land animals have hooves, these being necessary because of the vast areas of unbroken lava on the planet and the prevalence of sharp lava fragments in its soil (M11B;3).

hop (American slang) Archaic term for the narcotic **morphine** (K3;1).

Hor The high priest of **Pu** at **Lolo-lolo** in the land of the **Xexots** in Pellucidar. Like all of the priests, he was greedy and corrupt and used the religion to control people. When **Dian the Beautiful** dared to use her powers as **Noada** to change the status quo, Hor stirred the people to rebellion against her and the **go-sha**, **Gamba**, by lies and rumors, and she barely escaped the city alive with Gamba's help (P7:2;5–7).

Hor The nearly impregnable capital city of **Panga**, a peaceful Amtorian nation of Middle Anlap (V4;44–45).

Hor Kai Lan A prince of ancient **Horz** eons ago, brother of the **jeddak** of his time, who was hypnotized and placed into suspended animation by the madman **Lum Tar O** and lay in the **pits** beneath the city until awakened by Lum Tar O's death at the hands of **John Carter**. Carter had earlier removed Hor Kai Lan's weapons from his body in the mistaken impression that he was dead, and Hor Kai Lan was very upset about the matter when he awoke. Like the others victimized by the evil psychic, he refused to believe that Throxeus was gone until he saw it for himself, then died and turned to dust as the millennia caught up with him (M10:1;8–12).

Hor Vastus A padwar in the navy of Helium on Barsoom who was with the fleet of Zat Arrras when John Carter and the escapees from Omean were found. He threw his sword at John Carter's feet (see **throwing one's sword**) and was put in charge of recruiting men for the secret mission to Omean (M2; 16–18).

Hora San The Jeddak of Phundahl and high priest of Tur on Barsoom, the father of Xaxa. He was the last one to know the secret of the Great Tur and died one hundred Barsoomian years before Ulysses Paxton's arrival in a fall from the head of the statue. His body remained there undiscovered until Paxton and Gor Hajus accidentally discovered the secret room in the statue while fleeing Xaxa's guards (M6;12).

Horg The Mammoth-Man of Pellucidar whom the ugly Grum wanted for a mate. Unfortunately for her, Horg could only be forced to take her if someone fought him for her and won. The problem was, Horg was the biggest, strongest man of the tribe. Von Horst fought Horg for Grum and defeated him, thus forcing him to marry her (P5;14–15).

Horibs The Snake Men of Pellucidar, who inhabit the area known as the Gyor Cors as well as the Phelian Swamp. They are humanoid in conformation, having three-toed feet, five-fingered hands, a reptilian head with pointed ears and two short horns. Their faces, hands and bellies are covered with tinier scales than other parts of their bodies and are of the same dead white color as a snake's underbelly; their only garment is a heavy apron-like affair made of the hide of a plated dinosaur and is intended to cover the soft underbelly. Horibs are intelligent and fairly well-developed, using gorobors as mounts and lances shod with bone when attacking. They are practically emotionless, however, and have no love, loyalty or any other sort of human sensibility. Horibs, like chameleons, change color for display or camouflage. They are semi-aquatic and build nests in river banks as crocodiles do (P4;13–15).

Horjan The brother of Lodas, the farmer who smuggled Carson Napier into Amlot to spy on the Zanis in 1930. Horjan was none too happy about having his house used as Napier's base of operations while in Amlot and let it be known in no uncertain terms, even going so far as to turn him in to the Zani guards. Napier escaped before the guards arrived, but Horjan later saw him impersonating a Zani and informed on him (V3; 6–7,12).

hormads The Synthetic Men of Barsoom, created at Morbus in the Toonolian Marshes by Ras Thavas. They are grown in culture vats from living human tissue and are grossly misshapen, having all of their anatomical parts in correct number but not correct proportion or placement. They are alive on a cellular level and are thus impossible to kill except by fire or acid and impossible to stop except by complete dismemberment. Even then they do not die, but instead are merely returned to the culture vats to regrow — a new body for a severed head, for instance, or a new head for a headless body. The regeneration in the vats takes nine days. Hormads are none too bright, except for very rare ones like Tor-dur-bar and the Seven Jeds (M9;3–7). In "John Carter and the Giant of Mars," Pew Mogel, a hormad, was said to have learned all of Ras Thavas' secrets, including brain transplantation and the making of synthetic men (M11A;6).

Horn Cape Horn, southernmost point of the South American continent (C1;3).

Horsan the Dane One of the captains of Norman of Torn's mid–13th century English bandit army (OT;12).

horse, Polodan The horses of Poloda have three-toed feet and a little horn in their foreheads. They are used as saddle animals, beasts of burden, and sometimes food (B1;6).

Horse Camp Canyon One of the canyons of the Rancho del Ganado (GH;18).

Horsecamp Butte A landmark of southern Arizona near Cory Blaine's early 20th century dude ranch (D;15).

horses Although the horse trade in Kalkar-occupied 22nd century America was controlled by the Kalkar government, some skilled horse trainers were given leave to hold and train the animals, though the government reserved the right to impound the herds at any time. Julian 9th decided to raise horses on his farm and was given permission to do so by the Teivos against the will of General Or-tis (MM2;8).

horses, Nipon The "horses" of the Nipons of post–Kalkar 25th century California were actually burros (MM3;6).

horses, Pellucidarian *see* orthopi

Horta (*Ape*) The boar — one of Tarzan's favorite meals (T1;8).

Hortan Gur The jeddak of the green Barsoomian horde of Torquas. Thar Ban gave Thuvia to him, but Carthoris wounded him and stole the girl while the green men were retreating before the Lotharians (M4;5).

Horthal Gyl The son of the Kapar scientist Horthal Wend. Gyl was 14 in the summer of 1940 and was precocious and egotistical, a loudmouthed little know-it-all who hated his father for his sentimentality and "weakness" — in short, he was a perfect Kapar. He hung around with Grunge and wanted to be a Zabo agent, beginning his career by turning in his father, and later Morga Sagra (B2;6,8,10).

Horthal Wend The Kapar scientist who invented the power amplifier. He was an intelligent and kindly man whom Tangor instantly liked, but was taken away by the Zabo one night and never seen nor heard from again after his son Horthal Gyl turned him in for expressing disapproval of the Zabo (B2;5–8).

Horur The Morgor officer on Eurobus who sentenced John Carter to death after his friends' escape (M11B;7).

Horus An Egyptian god known for the rescue of his dead father Osiris from the evil Set. The Ashairians apparently had a slightly different concept of the god, and offered him human sacrifice (T20;24).

Horz An ancient ruin of Barsoom, once a great center of learning and culture, through which Barsoom's prime meridian runs (M4; 12). It is probably the oldest of the ruins and was once the greatest city on the planet. It was built on what is now a plateau and, like many Barsoomian ruins, shows a long line of less ancient buildings down the slope, built to follow the ocean as it receded. Horz has been inhabited for countless ages by the remnants of the Orovar race who built it. They live in the impregnable Citadel of Horz and kill all who come to the city and discover them, thus maintaining their security in hiding throughout the ages since the death of the oceans. John Carter stumbled into Horz in 1940 and was condemned to death by this custom, but escaped with the help of the Orovar warrior he had stopped in the city to save, Pan Dan Chee. He did this by passing through the pits of the city, and in the process discovered his granddaughter Llana of Gathol, who was hiding there from Hin Abtol, from whom she had escaped after he had abducted her (M10:1; 1–5,10).

Hot Springs A town of Sierra County, New Mexico, which lies on the Rio Grande. It is today named Truth or Consequences (after the popular game show) but in the 1870s was the site of an army campsite (A1;7).

hotan (*Ape*) Clan (TC).

Hotel du Petit Sahara The hotel in which Tarzan stayed while in Bou Saada in 1910 (T2;8).

Hotel Grossat A hotel in Aumale, Algeria, where Tarzan spent the night once in 1910 while traveling from Sidi-bel-Abbes to Bou Saada (T2;7).

Hotel Raleigh, Richmond The hotel in which John Carter spent the summer of 1898 preparing the manuscripts for the second, third and fourth Mars books (M2).

Hotel Royal The grandest hotel of early 20th century Demia (R;7).

hotels, Barsoomian *see* inns, Barsoomian

hour, Korvan In the Amtorian nation of Korva, the day is divided into 36 periods rather than 20 as in Vepaja. Each period is thus about 40 minutes long (V3;8).

houri An angel-like female being of Muslim mythology. When men go to heaven they are given the incredibly beautiful houris to attend to their needs there for all eternity (T11;20).

House of the Gods The domed temple of the city of Lolo-lolo in the land of the Xexots in Pellucidar (P7:2;4).

House of the Janhai The capitol building of Unis (B1;5).

houses, Barsoomian Red Barsoomian houses are elevated hydraulically on huge metal poles to a height of about 40 or 50 feet at night. This is not to prevent against theft (which is practically unknown on Barsoom) but rather against assassination, which is rampant. A wireless transmitter (rather like an Earthly garage door opener) can raise or lower the house from without at the owner's discretion (M1).

Houtomai A large cave village of the Samary of Noobol on Amtor which lay in a narrow canyon of the hill country near the Gerlat kum Rov (V3;2–3).

Hovan Du A Barsoomian warrior from Ptarth whose brain had been grafted by Ras Thavas to that of a white ape and the composite returned to the ape's skull. The human half of the brain was almost completely dominant, and Ulysses Paxton resurrected and recruited Hovan Du for his mission to kidnap Xaxa, promising to restore him to a human body at the end of the mission. In the meantime, his ape abilities came in handy several times, and after his restoration he became the voice of the Great Tur for Dar Tarus (M6; 13–14).

How to Be a Detective The book Willie Case consulted for help after realizing that the "Oskaloosa Kid" he had spoken with was wanted for murder and grand larceny (K3;7).

Howard One of Henry VIII's loyal gorillas (T17;29).

Howard, Catherine The fifth wife of the gorilla king Henry VIII who, unlike her historical namesake, was married to him at the same time as the others were (T17; 20).

Howwara *see* el-Howwara

HRH the Rider The original title of *The Rider* when it was published in *All-Story Weekly* in 1918.

hual A Minunian unit of linear measurement which equals about three inches (T10;15).

Hud A Niocene warrior of the tribe of Nu who coveted Nat-ul and abducted her when she would not consent to be his mate. She later tricked him and killed him with her knife (E2;2–3).

Hudson New York river on which John Carter owned a cottage from 1877 to 1886, after which it passed to his nephew Burroughs (M1).

Hudson, Edith *see* Little Eva (EE;19).

Huerta, Victoriano (1854–1916) Mexican soldier and politician who seized power in 1913 but resigned and went into exile in Europe and the United States in July of 1914. He died in El Paso, while in U.S. custody, for trying to incite a revolution in Mexico (K2;7).

Hugo The sentry of a Sumatran outlaw band whom Tarzan killed while escaping them in the spring of 1944 (T22;14).

huh (*Ape*) Yes (T1;12).

Huitz-Hok The Mayan god of hills and valleys (T24;13).

hul (*Ape*) Star (TC).

Hun Ahau The Mayan god of Metnal, their underworld (T24;13).

Hunab Kuh The Mayan creator god (T24;13).

Huntington, Shirley A good friend of Johnny Lafitte's in 1920s Glenora, California. She was in love with Frank Adams, who in turn loved Daisy Juke (PB).

hussar A light cavalryman (LC;8).

hut, hanging In the Valley of the Palace of Diamonds, the Gomangani inhabited beehive huts about six feet in diameter which hung by ropes from large trees. The doors of these huts were round holes in the center of each floor, from which a rope depended so the inhabitants could climb up and draw the rope in after them (T9;8).

hut, Kro-lu The Kro-lus of Caspak build hexagonal huts. A single hut is for a warrior and his mate, but as a warrior picks up more wives and possessions, other hut-cells are added in a cluster (like a honeycomb) to form a larger dwelling (C2;6).

hut, Mezop The Mezops of Pellucidar build spherical huts of sticks and mud atop tree trunks cut off about fifteen feet above the ground. The huts have window slits for light and air and are reached by a ladder jutting up through the trunk of the hollowed-out tree the hut surmounts. Some of these huts are fairly large, having two floors and multiple rooms (P1;8).

hyaenadon The giant prehistoric mastiff-like Oligocene ancestor of the modern hyena (C3;2)(P1;3). See also **jaal; jalok.**

Hyark A large **Athnean** warrior of the **Erythra** who, in 1935, was sent into the arena with armor, sword and spear to kill a naked Tarzan and was easily defeated by him (T21; 24).

hydrophidian A sea serpent (P1;7).

hypophysis gland The gland of the human brain upon which the **Minunian** scientist **Zoanthrohago's** shrinking machine worked (T10;14).

Hyracotherium Proper scientific term for the **Eohippus,** or "Dawn Horse" (P5;4). See also **ecca; orthopi.**

I Am a Barbarian One of Burroughs' few historical novels, a lightly fictionalized biography of **Britannicus Caligulae Servus,** personal slave to the Roman Emperor **Caligula** for 25 years. The book is abbreviated "I" and covers the lives of both slave and Emperor from A.D. 16 to 41.

"I Didn't Raise My Boy to Be a Soldier" Anti-war song originally published during World War I, which experienced a revival as World War II loomed. **Tangor** mentioned it to **Harkas Don,** who replied that if the women of **Unis** had a song, it would be called "I Didn't Raise My Son to Be a Slacker" (B1;4).

I-Gos The 2000-year-old chief embalmer of **Manator** on Barsoom. He was a great artist and had been chief embalmer for at least 1500 years and embalmed many of the people's dead for display, kept the **jeds** in the **Hall of Chiefs** in repair, and shrunk the corpses for the **Gate of Enemies.** He captured **Gahan** in the pits of Manator, but **Tara of Helium** struck him down and escaped, and when Gahan saw him lying prostrate he thought the old man dead. He was only wounded, however, and later recognized Gahan and the harness he had stolen from an embalmed chief and exposed him during the ceremony awarding Gahan victory in the **jetan** games. He alone had the courage to enter the apartments of **O-Mai** after the chiefs had fled the place in terror, and was rewarded by captur-

ing **Tara** there. Later, though, after seeing **O-Tar's** cowardice, he regretted his actions, apologized to **Gahan,** and helped him free Tara (M5;16,18,20–21).

I-Mal The dead and embalmed chief of **Manator** from whom **Gahan of Gathol** took the **harness** and weapons he used to disguise himself as a Manatorian (M5;18).

I.W. (American slang) Itinerant worker (GH;4).

I.W.W. Abbreviation for the Industrial Workers of the World, a radical, socialistic labor organization founded in 1905. Its members were called "Wobblies" and instigated strikes, boycotts and sabotage to achieve their ends. By 1925, the organization had almost completely vanished (C1;4).

I-Zav The **Manatorian** warrior who brought **Ghek** food, only to have the **Kaldane** play a trick on him that nearly frightened him out of his wits (M5;12).

Ibeto The warrior of the tribe of **Mbonga** whose wife was **Momaya** and whose son was **Tibo** (T6;6).

Ibn Aswad, Sheik An Arab slave and ivory raider who abducted **Victoria Custer** from Tarzan's estate in 1912 with the intent of selling her in the north to a black sultan. He was stopped by Tarzan and his **Waziri,** who defeated the Arabs (E1;8–13).

Ibn Dammuk The right-hand man of Sheik **Abu Batn** on his mission to central Africa with the **Zveri** expedition in 1928. It was Ibn Dammuk who engineered the abduction of **La of Opar** from the Zveri camp and later stole her from Abu Batn for himself. When he took her aside from his men to rape her, though, La killed him with his own knife and escaped (T14;8–10).

Ibn Jad Sheik of the el-Harb tribe of Arabs and a member of the clan **Beny Salem Fendy el-Guad.** He brought his tribe into southern Abyssinia to sack the hidden city of **Nimmr** but was hindered several times by the interference of Tarzan, of whom Ibn Jad was rightfully afraid. He eventually did succeed in locating the **Valley of the Sepulcher** and sacking the **City of the Sepulcher** while most of its warriors were away at the annual **Great Tourney** in Nimmr, but got greedy and, encouraged by his easy victory, set forth to sack

Nimmr as well. He was later captured by Tarzan's **Waziri**, and he and his tribe were turned over to the **Galla** people to be sold into slavery (T11;1–2,10,17,23–24).

ice barrier The edge of the land of **Okar** in Barsoom's arctic regions is a mighty ice barrier which rises for hundreds of feet into the air. On land, this barrier can only be passed through by way of the **Carrion Caves** (M3;8).

ichthyosaur A whale-like dinosaur of the **Jurassic** which had a pointed snout full of large, sharp teeth (P1;4). See also **azdyryth**.

Ictl One of the chiefs of the **Coripies** of **Amiocap**, from whose tribe **Mow** came (P3;8).

id (*Pal*) Silver (T8;4).

Id-an "Silver Spear" (*Pal*). A **Waz-don** warrior of **Kor-ul-ja** in **Pal-ul-don**, son of **An-un** and brother of **Pan-at-lee**. He was a swift runner who was sent by **Es-sat** with his father and brother to spy on the **Kor-ul-lul** tribe to get them out of the way, and in the process he was almost killed (T8;4).

Idaho One of the ranch hands of the **Bar-Y Ranch** in 1880s **Arizona** who remained loyal to **Bull** and **Diana Henders** through all of their troubles. Idaho was shot and badly wounded while trying to protect Diana from **Maurice Corson** and his men (HB;8,11–17).

ignition disruptor An electronic device invented in 1939 by **Horace Brown**, which could disrupt the ignition of any internal combustion engine, stopping it cold, at a range of about 3000 feet (T24B;2).

ijan-ale (*Apa*) "Don't let" or "don't allow" (A1;2).

Il-Dur-En An intelligent **hormad** of Barsoom, loyal to **Ras Thavas**, who helped him and John Carter escape **Morbus** and build a boat (M9;15).

Illall The most remote city of **Okar** on Barsoom, which has almost no intercourse with **Kadabra**. John Carter and **Thuvan Dihn**, acting on **Talu**'s advice, claimed to be from this city while in Kadabra (M3;9).

Illana The consort of **Muso**, acting **Jong** of **Korva**, when **Carson Napier** came there in 1930. She was "a quiet, self-effacing woman

of high lineage but no great beauty" whom Muso "usually ignored." He put her out in order to take **Duare** as his woman — a double mistake (V3;5–6,12–13).

Illili One of the smaller Philippine islands (T24;3).

Imba Kali Bwana's traitorous boy on her ill-fated safari of 1931 (T18;3).

Imigeg The old high priest of the **Leopard Men**, who was trapped after their defeat in 1931 in their island temple with no food, no way off the island, and only his **cannibal** followers for company. We must therefore assume that he either starved to death, was eaten by the others, or both (T18;11,14).

immortality pellets The longevity potion of the **Kavuru** tribe appeared in the form of black pellets which kept the imbiber free from all effects of physical aging for as long as they were used (they had to be taken once a month, supposedly on the day of the full moon). Among the pellets' ingredients were the pollen of certain herbs, the spinal fluid of leopards, and the glands of young girls. Tarzan and Jane took the pellets from the Kavuru temple in 1934 and by their power remained young for many years thereafter (T19;28–31).

Imperator (*Lat*) Emperor (T12;9).

In (*Pal*) Dark (T8;4).

In-sad "Dark Forest" (*Pal*). A warrior of the **Kor-ul-ja** tribe of **Waz-don** who went to search for **Pan-at-lee** with **Om-at**, Tarzan, and **Ta-den** (T8;4).

In-tan "Dark Warrior" (*Pal*). The Waz-don warrior of the **Kor-ul-lul** tribe of **Pal-ul-don** who was assigned to guard Tarzan while he was their prisoner, but was killed by the ape-man (T8;5).

incense A strange odor of incense pervaded the entire **Palace of Diamonds**, rendering Tarzan's infiltration of the place more difficult because he was very accustomed to using his nose to search for friends and detect enemies (T9;11,13).

Incitatus Caligula's favorite horse, for whom he had a beautiful house built, gave slave and riches to, and made both a consul of Rome and a priest in Caligula's temple (I;17).

Incubators The incubators of the **green men** of Barsoom are always built at a great distance from the community's normal stomping grounds, though no one is sure why. An incubator is about four feet tall and perhaps 20 or30 feet wide, with thick brick walls and a four inch thick plexiglass roof which acts as a greenhouse to warm the eggs. Some five hundred eggs are selected from the thousands laid in the previous five years by tests for size, weight and specific gravity and kept in a cool cave to prevent incubation, then walled up in the incubator at the end of the five year period — all others are destroyed. It takes five years for them to hatch (during which time more eggs are collected in caves for the next cycle), and the time of return to the incubator by the community can be calculated to within a day or so. This is made possible by the fact that early hatchees die in the heat and late hatchees are left behind to die when the horde leaves the area, so that a tendency toward very exact incubation period has developed over time. When the incubator is opened, children are selected at random by the green women (since it is impossible to determine paternity or maternity) and taught to speak and fight, though beyond this they are really raised by the entire community (M1;7). The incubators of the **red men** (and, we must assume, the other civilized races) hold only a single egg and stand on the roof of the family home, usually under guard (M1;27).

Indiana A large island of Pellucidar which lies across a strait from **Thuria**, where **Hooja the Sly One** collected his followers (called **Hoosiers** by **Abner Perry**, hence the name "Indiana") for his **Mahar**-sponsored invasion of the **Empire of Pellucidar**. **Juag** was made king of the island by **David Innes** after Hooja's power was broken (P2;11–15).

Indians, American Aboriginal people of North America with reddish skins who appear in many places in the works of Burroughs. John Carter compared the appearance of the red Barsoomians to that of American Indians, especially when the former were adorned in their ceremonial feathers (M1;21). See also **Apache**; **Sioux**; **slaves**; biographies of individual Indians.

Indra Sen The officer of **Pnom Dhek** who acted as **Gordon King**'s official host

while he stayed in the palace of **Beng Kher** and led him out of the city later to escape Beng Kher's wrath (HM;12–13).

ink-tah (*Apa*) "Sit down" (A1;19).

Innes, David A blond-haired, blue-eyed native of **Connecticut**, Innes was a trained athlete who inherited his father's prosperous mining business at the age of 19 and invested a large sum of money in the construction of a mechanical mining device invented by one **Abner Perry**. Due to a design flaw, however, the machine could not be turned, so it tunneled with the two down into the hollow interior of the Earth to the land called Pellucidar by its inhabitants. Innes and Perry were captured by the **Mahars**, the dominant race of Pellucidar, but eventually escaped, stealing the **Great Secret** of the Mahars' reproduction in the process. He later took **Dian the Beautiful**, Princess of **Amoz** as his wife and founded the **Empire of Pellucidar**, a confederation of human tribes to whom he and Perry gave sword-and-bow technology and led to overthrow the local Mahars, with "**David I**" as emperor. Eventually, he was forced to return to the outer crust in the **iron mole** for books and information with which to make even more formidable weapons (and other technological innovations) for his people. Due to a mishap, he ended up in **Algeria** instead of America as he had wished, and there met Burroughs, to whom he dictated his story and from whom he received help (P1).

On his return to Pellucidar, he laid out a telegraph line behind the mole, and through this line he later communicated his further adventures within the Earth's core. On this trip he had to rebuild his empire, which had been racked by dissention in his absence thanks to rumors started by his enemy **Hooja the Sly One**. He also had to rescue Dian and destroy the threat posed by Hooja who, with the help of the Mahars, had gathered an army of **Sagoths** and renegade humans with which he planned to crush the now-divided Empire for the Mahars. After some doing Innes managed to save Dian, rebuild his empire and destroy Hooja's power, then set out on a systematic campaign to destroy every Mahar city in the Empire with his new weapons (P1;15) (P2).

Years later, the Empire was threatened by the **Korsars**, descendants of pirates from the Spanish main who had discovered the **polar** opening into Pellucidar and built themselves a nation with their superior weaponry. The invaders were repelled by the Pellucidarians but retreated with hostages, prompting Innes to go after them with Ja of Anoroc as his sole companion. He was captured by the Korsars and imprisoned in a horrible, lightless dungeon beneath the palace of The Cid, ruler of the Korsars. He languished there for almost two years until he was rescued by the O-220 expedition led by Tarzan of the Apes and Jason Gridley of California, who had been summoned to Innes' aid by Abner Perry. Perry had in turn been informed of Innes' imprisonment by Tanar the Fleet One, who had also been imprisoned but escaped (P3) (P4;17).

After his release, Innes led an expedition to find the lost Wilhelm Von Horst of the O-220, finding him at long last in Lo-har (P5;22). On his return from this expedition, however, he was captured by the huge, bearded women of the tribe of Oog and was presumed dead by all but Dian, who set out to search for him herself. After escaping from Oog, he was detained for awhile in the village of the mad Jukans, where he was temporarily reunited with Dian. He was then successively captured by the man-eating Azar, a nest of giant ants, and the black men of the Floating Island of Ruva, where he stayed for a while and achieved considerable fame before escaping to the mainland with a Suvian girl, finding Dian and returning to Sari (P6).

His final recorded adventure took place directly after his return, for he found that Suvi had left the Empire and made war upon Kali in the north. While he went to put an end to this, Dian flew up in a new hot air balloon of Abner Perry's invention which got loose and carried her across the Nameless Strait to the land of the Xexots. Upon his return, Innes followed her in another balloon, saved O-aa of Kali from the Xexots, and was rescued by the men of Ghak the Hairy One in the newly-built EPS John Tyler. They set out in search of Dian, but she had previously escaped the country with the help of Gamba, the go-sha of Lolo-lolo, and returned home, where Innes found her after a long and arduous overland journey (P7).

inns, Barsoomian Barsoomian inns are mostly the same in all places on the planet. Private rooms are usually available only for married couples, singles being given a platform in a public room with others of their sex. One's valuables may be left on the platform, as theft is practically unknown on Barsoom, but guards patrol constantly to protect the occupants against assassination—among the sleepers for the men and outside the room for the women, but female slaves keep watch among the women and call the guards at the least sign of trouble. There are baths supplied, which guests are required to use daily or else leave the premises. Usually, there is also an eating place next door under the same management (see restaurant)(M4). Inns in Manator are marked by a carved thoat's head above the door (M5;16).

insects, giant, Barsoomian Several species inhabit the Forest of Kaol and the Toonolian Marshes, some of them having a wingspread of up to 30 feet (M9;23). See also sith.

Intamo The evil old witch doctor of the Bagalla tribe when the "Tarzan Twins" were their prisoners in 1920. He tried to refute Doc's "big medicine" but failed, and was later killed by Ukundo the pygmy when he came to murder Doc (TT1;1).

intchi (Apa) The wind (A1;4).

intchi-dijin "Black wind" (Apa). The storm wind (A1;4).

International Machine Company Mason Compton's factory in early 20th century Chicago (EE;6).

International Peace Fleet The airborne peacekeeping force organized in 1967, at the close of World War III. It mostly contended with airborne pirates and rebellions of African or Asian peoples until the Lunar invasion of 2050, when that portion of it led by Julian 5th was the sole mode of Earthly defense. Julian 3rd and Julian 4th were also officers in it during their times. Due to the actions of pacifists in Washington, half of the fleet was scrapped in the early 2040s, leaving Earth nearly unprotected when the Kalkars came in 2050 (MM1;1)(MM2;1).

Invak A city-state of Barsoom which lies hidden in the Forest of Invak, out of touch with the other races of Barsoom for millennia. The city is almost entirely roofed, with periodic courtyards to provide ventilation. The roof is covered with vines and the courtyards filled with spreading trees, so that from the air the city is nearly as invisible as its inhabitants are. Those people are invisible in normal daylight due to a special pill they take. The invisibility created by this pill extends about three inches from the skin of the person, thus covering gear, and is negated by special lights with which the entire city (with the exceptions of the courtyards) is lit, so that the Invakians are not always running into each other. John Carter and Llana of Gathol were captured by the Invakians in 1940 while searching for food in their forest, but escaped with the help of Rojas, an Invak noblewoman (M10:4;2–4).

Invak, Forest of A beautiful, forested valley south of Dusar, lying directly on Barsoom's equator. It is a very thick and lush forest comprised of very large versions of normal Barsoomian trees. The forest is home to two city-states, Invak and Onvak, which are inhabited by similar societies of red men who are hereditary enemies of each other (M10:4;2–4).

invisibility Several different methods of invisibility appear in Burroughs' books, four of them in the Mars series alone. Most of the methods involve the use of some substance that can bend light rays, such as the compound of invisibility invented by Phor Tak of Jhama or the sands of invisibility used by the Morgors of Eurobus (M7;10)(M11B;2).

The **invisibility spheres** of Invak are different, as they cause a living body to emit an invisibility aura which extends three inches from the body, thus covering gear or anything else that passes within the area. This invisibility can be negated by means of special lighting (M10:4;4–8).

The most interesting kind of invisibility, however, is certainly that of the Tarids of Ladan, who use a sort of hypnosis by which they will their opponents not to see or hear them, no matter what. This is probably the most effective type of invisibility, as it possesses several advantages: the invisible person can see his own body and those of his fellows (as the hypnosis is only directed toward enemies) and thus can avoid the clumsiness inherent in light-bending forms of invisibility. Sound is negated by this ability as well. The invisibility does have one drawback, however; if a victim knows of the Tarids' power and

repeatedly wills himself to be able to see them, their suggestion can be countered and the victim enabled to see them (M8;18).

invisibility, compound of A pigment invented by Phor Tak of Jhama which would render any object painted with it totally invisible. He planned to use it to render his Flying Death undetectable, but Tan Hadron and Nur An used it to cloak a flier, and Tan Hadron later used it to create a cloak of invisibility (M7;10,12).

invisibility, sands of The ocean beaches of Eurobus are covered with a sand composed of microscopic, magnetic, prismatic crystals which bend light, resulting in invisibility for anything covered with them. The hulls of Morgor ships can be magnetized, then a quantity of these crystals are blown out of vents all over the hull, where they stick, conferring invisibility. When visibility is desired, the magnetic field is turned off and the crystals fall off. Some oceanside villages of Savators are protected by a plaster of the sands of invisibility on the outsides of the buildings. The buildings' positions must then be remembered by secret marks (M11B;2,9).

invisibility spheres Large pills, about the size of marbles, which confer invisibility about an hour after being taken. The invisibility thus created affects a zone extending to about three inches from the skin (thus covering gear) and lasts about 25 hours. The secret of these pills' manufacture is known only to the Invaks and their enemies the Onvaks. The invisibility given by the pills is negated by special lighting within the halls of the cities so that the inhabitants do not keep colliding with each other, but outside, the invisibility is impermeable. Some of the pills were given to John Carter by Rojas, an Invak noblewoman, so that he, Ptor Fak, and Llana of Gathol could escape Invak and take her with them. Carter later used one to sneak aboard the flagship of Hin Abtol and abduct him, thus protecting Gathol until the fleet of Helium arrived (M10:4;8,13).

"Invisible Men of Mars" The title of the fourth book of Llana of Gathol. It originally appeared as a novelette in Amazing Stories magazine in October of 1941, and is abbreviated M10:4.

inzayu (Apa) Die (A1;2).

Io A beautiful girl of Greek mythology who was seduced by Zeus, then transformed into a cow to hide her from the jealousy of Hera, who saw through the deception and placed the tireless watchman **Argus** over the hapless girl (R;5).

Irene (?–1962) A **Hollywood** clothing designer of the 1930s who became the head designer for MGM in 1942 (B1;5).

Iron Cross A medal of high honor of Imperial Germany (C2;1).

iron mole The name given by **Abner Perry** to his 100 foot long, drill-equipped mechanical prospector, which developed more power per cubic inch than any existing engine developed per cubic foot. It was equipped with every precaution imaginable, including specially mounted seats that always remained vertical no matter which way the mole tunneled, but also had one major design flaw: it could not be turned while tunneling through rock. Because of this flaw, Perry and his backer, **David Innes**, ended up drilling through 500 miles of rock and reaching Pellucidar, the world within the Earth (P1;1–2).

Isaac the Jew An honest banker of mid-13th century London who was often used as a go-between in transactions involving large sums of money, particularly when the two parties did not trust one another (OT;5).

Isaza The Waziri "boy" and cook for the English big game hunter **"Lord Passmore"** (alias Tarzan) on his 1929 safari to the **Ghenzi Mountains** region (T15;7).

Iseka, Oda The son of **Oda Yorimoto**, Daimyo of **Yoka** who was captured and interrogated by **Henri Theriere** and **Billy Byrne** when they tried to rescue **Barbara Harding** from Yorimoto's village after the wreck of the *Halfmoon* (K1;11).

Ish-kay-nay "Boy" (*Apa*). A young Apache girl of **Shoz-dijiji**'s own age and tribe with whom he became sweethearts. They planned to marry when Shoz-dijiji reached a warrior's estate, but the girl's father had other ideas — he set a ridiculously high price (50 horses) on her so Shoz-dijiji could not afford her, because he wished her to marry **Juh**, chief of the **Ned-ni** instead. Shoz-dijiji's mission to collect the ponies was protracted, however, and Juh, eager to get the girl, lied and said

that Shoz-dijiji had been found dead. In despair, the girl agreed to marry Juh to make her father happy, since she no longer cared. She was killed by a stray bullet fired at the retreating Apaches after the battle of **Cibicu Creek** in 1881, but lived until the following day, when she was found by Shoz-dijiji just before she died and told him the whole story (A1;2–6,12–16).

Isis An ancient Egyptian fertility goddess, wife of Osiris and mother of **Horus** (T20;21).

Iskandar The chief of a group of **Sumatran** natives who captured **Corrie van der Meer** in the spring of 1944, intending to turn her in to the **Japanese** for a reward. She escaped, however, and Iskandar pursued, only to have most of his men killed by Tarzan and the *Lovely Lady* crew (T22;8).

Island Riker's Island prison in New York (ME;2).

Island of Despair The last and largest of the three large islands off the southern tip of **Unis** on **Poloda**, stretching out toward the continent of **Epris**. It was in past times a Unisan maximum security prison (B1;10).

Island of Trees A large, forested island south of **Indiana** (Hooja's island) in the **Sojar Az** of Pellucidar, where Hooja built a great fleet of canoes with which to invade **Sari** (P2;10).

Isle of Wight An island in the English Channel on which Newport stands (LC;3).

Iss The River of Mystery on Barsoom. Since time immemorial the great majority of those Barsoomians who reached the age of 1000 years (and many before that age) made a voluntary **pilgrimage** down the Iss, one of the two remaining rivers of Barsoom, to the Lost Sea of **Korus** in the **Valley Dor** near Barsoom's south pole, where it was believed a material paradise existed. The **Therns** left boats stocked with provisions at various points along the river (which flows sometimes above ground and sometimes below) to facilitate this journey. Once one embarked upon the pilgrimage, he could never return — indeed, the one man who ever returned in recorded history was immediately put to death by his own people. The source of the Iss is probably within the **Forest of Kaol**, and its one sizeable tributary is the **Syl** (M2;3)(M7; 7-8).

Issus The Barsoomian Goddess of Death and Life Eternal. She was actually an incredibly ancient (approximately 5000 years) black woman, shriveled up and hideous to behold, but as Queen of the **First-Born** she convinced them of her divinity and they in turn convinced the **Therns** and the rest of Barsoom. Issus was also convinced of her own divinity, but not so much so as to stick around when confronted with imminent death. The First-Born actually believed that Issus was wondrously beautiful as well, even though they could plainly see her. Those of the "lower orders" (meaning all non-black Barsoomians), however, could only survive the "blinding glory" of her "divine loveliness" for a single year, mostly because they were thrown to the **white apes** after that time. She had as her slaves only the most beautiful and high-born of women (the First-Born took no male slaves) and they, of course, died within a year of seeing her. Issus was incredibly evil and wicked and encouraged the doctrine of the **Pilgrimage** wholeheartedly in order that the **Therns** might be enriched so the First-Born would have plenty to steal from them. Her career finally ended when the land of the First-Born was invaded by the **Heliumites** and the **green men of Thark** and she was revealed as a fraud by her inability to change matters with her "divine powers." Her incensed followers then tore the old woman apart with their bare hands (M2; 11-13,22).

Issus, Temple of A beautiful golden temple studded with gems situated in the Land of the **First-Born** at the exact south pole of Barsoom. It lies in the midst of indescribably beautiful gardens on the shores of the Lost Sea of **Korus** and is apparently just barely visible from the most remote part of the domain of the **Therns**. A Thern who lived his allotted 1000 years could take a pilgrimage to this temple, where he believed he would meet **Issus** and live forever; what actually happened, of course, was that he was captured by the First-Born, forced to compete in the monthly **Games** of Issus, then eaten when he died. The temple complex is surrounded by a wall 100 feet high and across a huge lawn outside the wall is an amphitheater. In this outer area, **plant men** and **white apes** moved freely

about among the First-Born, of whom they were apparently afraid (M2;9-11).

Italian Somaliland Former name of modern **Somalia**, the country in which Tarzan fought communist agitators in 1928 (T14; 1,16).

Ithaca City in New York state which is home to **Cornell University** (Q;1).

Ithaca The name given by Professor **Arthur Maxon** to the schooner he purchased in **Singapore** to take him to the **Pamarung Islands** (Q;1).

ittindi (*Apa*) The lightning (A1;4).

Ituri Forest A dense, wild jungle area of northeastern **Zaire** in which the **Valley of Diamonds** lies (T17;1-2).

itza-chu (*Apa*) The eagle (A1;3).

Itzamna The Mayan god of the sky, ruler of the gods and son of **Hunab Kuh**, the first god (T24;13).

Itzl Cha A Mayan girl of **Chichen Itza** on **Uxmal** whom Tarzan saved from being sacrificed in their temple and carried off into the forest. She stayed with the castaways of the *Saigon* for six weeks and taught Tarzan Mayan while she learned English and **Penelope Leigh** complained about her nudity and possible morals. Itzl Cha fell in love with Tarzan and betrayed him to the **Ah Kin Mai** out of jealousy over **Patricia Leigh**, whom she thought he loved, but Tarzan survived the trial they put him through and was thus "proved" a god and set free. Tarzan then commanded that Itzl Cha be set free as well (T24; 14,17-18,23-24).

Ivitch, Paul One of the communist conspirators of the **Zveri** expedition when it came to rob the treasure-vaults of **Opar** in 1928. After the failure of the expedition, Tarzan sent him out of Africa under guard (T14;1,17).

Ivory Room One of the private chambers of the royal palace of **Cathne** which was reserved for the exclusive use of the reigning monarch (T16;12).

izze (*Apa*) Medicine (A1;6).

izze-kloth "Medicine cord" (*Apa*). A ceremonial belt made of four strands of twisted buckskin, worn by an **izze-nantan** (A1;3,7).

izze-nantan (*Apa*) Medicine man (A1;3).

J The fictitious conspirator of **Tangor** in his supposed plot to rule **Kapara**, as revealed in the forged diary placed in his desk by **Grunge** (B2;7).

ja (*Pal*) Lion (T8;2).

Ja The chief of one of the **Mezop** tribes of **Anoroc**, an island in the **Lural Az** of **Pellucidar**. **David Innes** saved him from a sea serpent and they were fast friends from then on. It was Ja who first showed Innes a **Mahar** temple and the horrible rites carried out there (P1;8). He later became the **Empire of Pellucidar's** first admiral (P2;17) and accompanied Innes to **Korsar** in search of **Tanar the Fleet One** in 1927 (P3).

Ja-don "Lion Man" (*Pal*). **Ta-den's** father, the chief of **Ja-lur** and a very powerful leader. He protected Princess **O-lo-a** after **Ko-tan's** assassination and also tried to protect the city of **A-lur** from the machinations of **Lu-don**. He failed in this and so withdrew into Ja-lur in order to gather his strength. After Lu-don's defeat, Ja-don was made King of **Pal-ul-don** (T8;2,15–17, 20–21,24–25).

Ja-lur "Lion City" (*Pal*). The largest Hodon settlement of Pal-ul-don outside of A-lur (T8;14).

Ja-ru The country of the **Mammoth-Men** of Pellucidar (P5;7).

jaal (*Cpk*) The **hyaenadon** (C3;2).

jaal-lu "Hyena man" (*Cpk*) A **Caspakian** expression of contempt (C3;2).

jabo (*Ape*) Shield (obviously a Tarzan coinage) (TC).

Jack The name given by **Dr. Van Horn** to **Number Thirteen**, Professor **Arthur Maxon's** only perfect synthetic man, in order to help him fit in with normal humans (Q;5).

Jackie Jack Clayton, Jr.'s nickname (T10;1).

Jackknife Canyon A canyon of the **Rancho del Ganado** (GH;1).

Jackson The chauffeur for the **Scott** family of early 20th century **Scottsville, Virginia** (ME;9).

Jacot, Armand A captain in the French Foreign Legion in **Algeria** who captured the Arab marauder **Achmet ben Houdin** and refused to ransom him to his uncle, Sheik **Amor ben Khatour**. The uncle revenged himself by kidnapping Jacot's daughter, **Jeanne**, and taking her south as a slave. Jacot, by birth the **Prince de Cadranet**, later worked his way up to general and was eventually reunited with his daughter more than nine years after her abduction (T4;5,27).

Jacot, Jeanne The daughter of **Armand Jacot**, abducted at the age of seven from her father's house in **Algeria** by **Amor ben Khatour**, who later told her that he was her real father and renamed her **Meriem**. To escape the French, they fled south across the Sahara to an unexplored part of **Nigeria**, where they lived among the natives by trade and raiding. She was eventually rescued by **Korak**, son of **Tarzan**, passed through many adventures, married him, and was finally reunited with her father more than nine years after her abduction (T4;5,27).

Jacques The servant of the **Count** and **Countess de Coude's** who was bought by **Nikolas Rokoff** to spy for him and help him to carry out his plots (T2;4–5).

jad (*Pal*) The (T8;2).

Jad The jong of the **Samary** of **Houtomai** on Amtor when **Carson Napier** came there to rescue **Duare** in 1930 (V3;3).

Jad-bal-ja "The Golden Lion" (*Pal*). An orphaned lion cub adopted by Tarzan after he found it on his way back from **Pal-ul-don** with his wife and son. He bought from a native village a bitch who had lost her pups and used her to suckle the cub, though the two animals disagreed with the notion at first. Tarzan trained the lion (as only he could) to fetch, follow or kill on command and the lion learned and obeyed the ape-man, growing into a formidable fighting machine in two years. When Tarzan returned to **Opar** for gold in 1917 he left Jad-bal-ja behind, but not for long — the beast escaped and, following far behind on his trail for many weary miles, arrived in the **Palace of Diamonds** just in time to help Tarzan defeat a **Bolgani** attack on him and save **La** of Opar. Tarzan later sent him to "fetch" **Esteban Miranda**, but the lion only succeeded in getting the Spaniard's leopard skin — the one he had drawn a map on to show the location of the stolen gold of Opar

(T9;1–5,14,20). Jad-bal-ja later figured in several of Tarzan's adventures, saving La again in 1928 (T14;12–17) and saving Tarzan himself from the lion Belthar in 1930 (T16;19).

Jad-bal-lul "The Golden Water" (*Pal*). The lake of Pal-ul-don into which the waters of Jad-ben-lul empty. It in turn empties into Jad-in-lul (T8;18).

Jad-ben-lul "The Great Water" (*Pal*). The large central lake of Jad pele ul Jad-ben-otho in Pal-ul-don (T8;14).

Jad-ben-otho "The Great God" (*Pal*). Chief deity of both the Ho-don and Waz-don of Pal-ul-don, whom the Ho-don conceive of as tailless and the Waz-don as tailed. Erich Obergatz believed himself to be Jad-ben-otho and was supported in the contention by Lu-don (T8;2,21–24).

Jad-guru-don "The Terrible Man" (*Pal*). The name given to Tarzan by the Waz-don of Kor-ul-ja after his fight with them upon his first arrival there (T8;3).

Jad-Han The brother of Janai, who fled Amhor when his sister was believed dead, because he feared that Jal Had would have him assassinated as he had their father. He was captured by the Black Pirates and enslaved in Kamtol, where he met John Carter, Pan Dan Chee and Llana of Gathol while they were imprisoned in the pits awaiting their sale as slaves; it was at this time that he explained the nerve-index machine to them. Jad-han and Pan Dan Chee were eventually bought by Nastor and rescued from the valley by John Carter. They then flew to Gathol, where Jad-Han was captured by the Panars and held until after their defeat by the navy of Helium (M10:2;5,11,13)(M10:3;3–4)(M10:4;13).

Jad-in-lul "The Dark Water" (*Pal*). The lake of Pal-ul-don on which the city of Tu-lur was built (T8;16).

Jad pele ul Jad-ben-otho "The Valley of the Great God" (*Pal*). The central valley of Pal-ul-don, heavily forested and well watered, in which the Ho-don live (T8;2).

Jagst, General Count The chief of staff for the old king of an unnamed European country. Upon the king's death, Jagst fled with Prince Michael as per the king's prior orders, but was killed when their ship went down in the Atlantic (LL;1–2).

Jahar An unfriendly and backward country in the southern half of Barsoom's western hemisphere, ruled in the early 20th century by Tul Axtar and almost destroyed by his mad scheme to increase the size of his army by inducing a population explosion. The people of Jahar eventually overthrew Tul Axtar after his fleet's defeat by that of Helium (M7; 5,16).

Jahara Janjong of Korva and daughter of the jong, Kord, when Carson Napier came to Korva in 1930. She was the wife of Taman, the Korvan nobleman whom Napier had befriended (V3;5).

Jake One of the hands on the Rancho del Ganado (GH;16). Another Jake was a cowboy at the Crazy "B" Ranch of 1880s Arizona (A2;18).

jake (American West slang) All right (D;15).

Jal Had The ruling prince of Amhor on Barsoom. When Kor San, Jeddak of Duhor, refused Jal Had's request for his daughter Valla Dia in marriage, Jal Had waited until the Duhorian navy was away at war with Helium, then sacked the city; unfortunately for him, Valla Dia had escaped in the meantime. After her marriage to Ulysses Paxton of Earth, Jal Had gave up on her and eventually decided he wanted Janai as his wife. When she also refused him, he had her father assassinated by Gantun Gur, who was also supposed to kidnap her. She escaped, but was later caught by one of Jal Had's ships and returned to him. At this point he tried to marry her, but was hindered by the plans of his eldest wife, Vanuma, until he had her killed, which touched off a civil war. Jal Had was a cruel, evil man who kept humans locked up as specimens in his menagerie, but his cruelty eventually caught up with him. During the civil war started by his callous disposal of his wife, he was killed with a metal goad by Bal Tab, a green man who had been a prisoner in his zoo (M6;4)(M9;24–27).

jalok (*Pell*) The hyaenadon, a fierce, 500-pound pack hunter and scavenger (P2;7).

Jalu The chief of the Neolithic Zurts tribe of Pellucidar when O-aa of Kali came there in 1932. He was a good man who befriended both her and her man Hodon, who came in search of her shortly thereafter (P7:4; 7–11).

jambe (*Fr*) In a suit of plate armor, the calf protector; also called a greave (OT;15).

James The imaginary butler of the educated vagabond **Bridge** (K2;2).

James, Elizabeth The mate of Julian 8th and mother of Julian 9th, one of the few literate women of her time. She was very attractive and thus stayed home all the time so she would not be seen by the **Kash Guard** and her man murdered by them to get her. **Peter Johansen** especially wanted her and constantly spied on Julian 8th to find some illegal activity he might be arrested for so Johansen could take her for himself. While Julian 9th was away rescuing his father, **General Or-tis** found the hiding place in which her son had left her, and she killed herself rather than be given to a **Kalkar** (MM2; 2–3,6,10).

James, William One of the crew of the captured U-33. He was one of the members of the ill-fated **Bradley** expedition which set out from **Fort Dinosaur** on September 4, 1916; James was killed by a saber-toothed tiger on September 13 and buried there in **Caspak** (C1;6,9).

jan (*Amt*) Daughter (V1;12).

jan (*Ara*) Plural of jin (T14;5).

jan (*Uni*) Seven (B1;3).

Jana, the Red Flower of Zoram A beautiful Pellucidarian girl who fled across the **Mountains of the Thipdars** to escape **Skruk**, Chief of **Pheli**, who wished to mate with her. She was saved by **Jason Gridley** and they fell in love with one another. Alas, the course of true love never did run smooth, and the two had several misunderstandings (not to mention physical separations) before they were finally reunited in the land of the **Horibs** (P4;7–17). Jana then returned to **California** as Gridley's wife (P5;22).

Janai A gorgeous red Barsoomian girl of **Amhor**, coveted by **Jal Had**, who sent assassins to abduct her. While fleeing, she fell into the hands of the **hormads** and was taken to their city, **Morbus**. Three of the **Seven Jeds** claimed her as a slave; during their dispute she was rescued by **Vor Daj** (a.k.a. **Tor-dur-bar**) and hidden away. He later "found" her after **Ay-mad** promised her to him for his help in conquering Morbus.

After escaping the city, she was told by **Sytor** that Vor Daj was dead and Tor-dur-bar intended to keep her for himself, but she did not completely believe him and so he and **Pandar** abducted her, leaving the others stranded. She was soon after recaptured by hormads and rescued again by Vor Daj/Tor-dur-bar, only to fall again into the hands of **Jal Had**, at which time she became the object of an **assassination** plot by the prince's eldest wife **Vanuma**. She was finally saved by Vor Daj/Tor-dur-bar and his friends, revealed that she had long since realized the truth about Vor Daj/Tor-dur-bar, and accepted Vor Daj as her lover when he was restored to his own body (M9;5,10–11,15–16,23–27,31). Later, they were married (M10:2;5).

Jane *see* Clayton, Jane; Porter, Jane

Janhai "Seven-elect" (*Uni*). The ruling body of **Unis** on **Poloda**, which is composed of seven men who hold office for life until age 70, after which they may be re-elected. Elections are otherwise only held to fill vacancies. The Janhai appoints all judges and provincial governors, who in turn appoint other provincial officials and the mayors of cities, who in turn appoint municipal officers. Each member of the Janhai heads a department; these departments are war, foreign/state, commerce, the interior, education, treasury and justice. One member is the **Eljanhai**, or High Commissioner, who is elected for a six-year term and cannot serve two consecutive terms. Each member of the Janhai and each appointee must pass a rigorous intelligence test (B1;3).

Janiculan Hill A hill across the Tiber from the seven hills of Rome (I;19).

janjong "Daughter-King" (*Amt*). Princess (V1;12).

Janos A Mexican town of the **Sierra Madre** in **Sonora** (A1;13).

Jantor The Jong of **Japal** on Amtor in the early 20th century, father of **Carson Napier's** friend **Kandar**. There was a revolution in Japal late in 1930 and Jantor was deposed and fled to the mountains. He returned later to warn his people of a coming attack by the **Myposan** war fleet and was treacherously murdered for his loyalty by **Gangor**, leader of the revolution (V4;8,19–21).

Janviers, Sub-lieutenant An officer of the French cruiser which rescued the Porter party when they were shipwrecked in Angola in February and March of 1909 (T1;24).

Janzara The beautiful princess of Veltopismakus in Minuni whom Komodoflorensal, Prince of Trohanadalmakus wished to take as his wife. She was actually a vicious, spoiled brat who wanted everything her own way and tried to kill Tarzan when he spurned her, but he turned the tables on her and helped Komodoflorensal and Talaskar to abduct her from her city. She finally realized the error of her ways and helped them escape to Trohanadalmakus, where she was received in peace (T10;6,10,19–21).

Japal An Amtorian city of Northern Anlap which lies on the shores of the Great Lake in the northernmost part of that continent (V4;4–5).

Japal, Great Lake of *see* Great Lake of Japal

Japan Island country off the east coast of Asia, probable ancestral home of the Nipon people of post–Kalkar 25th century California (MM3;6).

jar (*Pal*) Strange (T8;12).

Jar-don "Strange Man" (*Pal*). The Pal-ul-don term for a stranger. It was the name given to Korak by Om-at when the former came in search of Tarzan (T8;12).

jarrah (*Eucalyptus marginata*) A hard, weather-resistant timber common in Australia, New Zealand and Caspak, and used by the crew of the U-33 to build Fort Dinosaur (C1;6).

Jarred, Sir Sir Malud's second in his combat with James Hunter Blake in the north ballium of the hidden city of Nimmr in February of 1921 (T11;14).

Jarth The Kalkar who became Jemadar of the United Teivos of America in 2117, after which conditions became much worse. Among other things, he raised taxes and appointed a military governor over each teivos who would have absolute power in that teivos. One of these governors could, for example, establish a closed military court (instead of a fair trial system) or enact any laws he saw fit without consulting with anyone (MM2;2,4).

Jasoom (*Bar*) The Barsoomian name for the planet Earth (M6;3).

Jat Or A padwar in the personal guard of Dejah Thoris who accompanied John Carter on his mission to rescue the princess from the clutches of Ur Jan and the assassin's guild of Zodanga. He was captured by the Tarids on Thuria with John Carter and the others and helped Carter escape. Later, he and Zanda became romantically involved (M8;10, 16,21,24).

jato (*Pal*) The small striped lion hybrid of Pal-ul-don (T8;3).

Jav A man of the lost Barsoomian city of Lothar who took Carthoris and Thuvia of Ptarth prisoner and explained Lothar, its customs, and its history to Carthoris. Jav was a Realist but believed in Komal and was terrified when Tario threw him to the banth-god. After helping Carthoris and Thuvia escape Komal's pit, he took Thuvia for himself by tricking Carthoris with an image of her, but was mauled by Komal in defense of her (M4;10).

A different Jav was the second mate of the EPS *John Tyler* on her maiden voyage (P7:3;4).

javadar (*Van*) Prince. While he was in Laythe, Julian 5th claimed to be a javadar in his own country (MM1;11).

javelins The only Barsoomians who use javelins are the yellow men of Okar (M3;9). The weapon was also used by the U-gas of Va-nah, especially by gentlemen (MM1;11).

Jay A lieutenant on the Barsoom who at first shared a stateroom with Norton but soon moved in with his classmate West and allowed Orthis to move in with Norton, a move which later saved the ship and crew because of the knowledge Norton gained from his friendship with Orthis (MM1;1–2,14).

Jayavarman VIII (Ruled 1243–1295) The last of the great Khmer Kings of Cambodia before the Siamese forced the Khmers out of Angkor (HM;7).

Jeans, Sir James (1877–1946) A British physicist who wrote several popular books on astronomy (V1;1).

jed (*Bar*) A king or chieftain (M1).

jeddak (*Bar*) Emperor (M1).

Jeddak of Jeddaks The title of the ruler of Okar on Barsoom (M3;9). It is also the title held by John Carter as **Warlord of Barsoom** (M3;16).

Jeddak's Award Each year the Jeddak of Helium gives an award to the artwork of greatest beauty produced that year (M5;9).

jeddara (*Bar*) Empress (M6;2).

jedwar The commander of an entire Barsoomian army or navy, corresponding to an Earthly marshal. In Barsoomian military organization, the rank is second only to a jed (M7).

Jeffries, James J. (1875–1953) American boxer from **Ohio** who won the title of World Heavyweight Champion in 1899 by a knockout and also won every challenge for the next five years (except one) by a knockout. He retired undefeated in 1905, but while attempting a comeback in 1910 was himself knocked out by the new World Champion, Jack Johnson (K1;17).

Jeft The **Jong** of **Hangor** when **Carson Napier** and **Ero Shan** were enslaved there late in 1931 (V4;49).

Jehovah The Hebrew name for God (T15;2).

jemadar (*Van*) Emperor. In ancient times, **Va-nah** was divided into ten confederated nations, each with its own jemadar, who competed on a friendly scientific, economic and artistic basis. In later times, though, the only jemadars were those of hidden **U-ga** cities (MM1;6,10). Still later, the Kalkars resurrected the title for use by the Kalkar rulers of conquered Earth (MM2;2), and by the time four centuries had gone by, even humans had adopted the title, and **Julian 20th** was declared "Jemadar of America" after destroying the west coast Kalkars (MM3;9–10).

Jemadar of Jemadars Title given to Orthis by the Kalkars when they made him their absolute ruler (MM1;13–14).

jemadav (*Van*) Empress (MM1;12).

Jensen, Luke A cowboy whom **Shoz-dijiji** saved from death by dehydration in 1881, and who then went to work at the Billings ranch. He was ever afterward a loyal friend of Shoz-dijiji's who defended his reputation whenever necessary (A2;5,15).

Jenssen, Carl A Swedish adventurer who searched for the kidnapped **Jeanne Jacot** with his friend **Sven Malbihn** for several years in order to collect the reward, but eventually gave up and became an ivory raider instead. While attempting to trade with **Amor ben Khatour** for ivory some years later, however, they spotted the child and began to forge plans to capture her and return to **Algeria**, but this plan was foiled by her prior escape from the **Arabs**. Years later, they were trapping animals for a zoo and captured a baboon chief, but **Korak**, son of Tarzan freed the chief and led the baboons to drive the Swedes away. Soon after that, they succeeded in tricking **Kovudoo** into selling **Meriem** (whom he had captured) to them, and Jenssen saved the girl from being raped by his partner — not for any noble reasons, but only to protect his reward. He was soon afterward killed by Malbihn when the latter tried to rape her again (T4;5, 12–14).

Jerome, Jerry The real name of **The Kid**, friend of the **Old Timer**'s and brother of **Jessie Jerome**, a.k.a. **Kali Bwana**. Jerome shot **Sam Berger** in 1930 and fled to Africa, presuming his victim had died. He did not die, though, refused to press charges, and was later killed by someone else, freeing Jerome to go home (T18;23).

Jerome, Jessie "Kali Bwana's" real name. She was the sister of **Jerry Jerome** and came to Africa in 1931 to find him and bring him home (T18;1,5,23).

Jerrold, Captain The captain of the *Lady Alice*, Lord Tennington's yacht (T2;13).

Jerry One of Burroughs' nurses during a hospital stay for an operation early in 1929 (V1;1).

Jervis The white foreman of Tarzan's plantation at the time the Claytons were recivilizing **Meriem**. Jervis was befriended by **Sven Malbihn** so he would have an excuse to hang around and wait for a chance to abduct Meriem (T4;18–19). It was Jervis who was later put in charge of rebuilding the estates after the German **Schneider** had destroyed them and abducted Jane (T9;2).

jetak A Minunian coin (T10;10).

Jetan   Barsoomian chess, played on a square board of 100 alternating orange and black squares with two armies of 20 pieces each. The game is supposed to represent an ancient war between the blacks of the south and the yellow men of the north and is usually played so the black player sits at the south end of the board. The pieces of each player are listed below with their descriptions and moves in order from left to right, back row first.

The Back Row

Warrior: Has two feathers and moves two spaces straight in any direction or combination (such as two forward, or one forward and one right, or one left and one backward). The piece may not cross the same square twice in one move, so forward and back again is not a legal move. The same goes for other pieces with combination moves.

Padwar: Represented by two feathers and can move two spaces diagonally in any direction or combination (as above).

Dwar: Represented by three feathers and can move three spaces straight in any direction or combination.

Flier: A three-bladed propeller. This piece can move three spaces diagonally in any direction or combination and may jump over intervening pieces (as a knight can in Earthly chess). In ancient times this piece was called the **odwar**.

Chief: Represented by a diadem with ten jewels. It can move three spaces straight or diagonal in any combination. If it is taken by any piece other than the opposing chief the game is drawn, but if a chief takes a chief the game is won by the player who does the taking.

Princess: Represented by a diadem with one jewel. She moves as a chief does, but can jump intervening pieces like a flier. The princess cannot move onto a threatened square nor take an opposing piece. She is entitled to one ten-space move (in any direction or combination) during the game, called the Escape. If a princess is taken by any piece, the game is won by the taker.

Flier: As above.
Dwar: As above.
Padwar: As above.
Warrior: As above.

The Front Row

Thoat: A mounted warrior with two feathers. Moves one straight and one diagonal in any direction and can jump intervening pieces.

Panthans: (Eight of them) Represented by a single feather. May move one space forward (straight or diagonal) or one space sideways, but may not move backward at all.

Thoat: As above.

A piece is taken when an opposing piece lands on its square at the end of a move. A game is won when a chief takes a chief or any piece takes a princess. The game is a draw if a chief is taken by other than a chief, or if "both sides are reduced to three pieces or less of equal value and the game is not won in the ensuing ten moves, five apiece."

"The first move may be decided in any way that is agreeable to both players; after the first game the winner of the preceding game moves first if he chooses, or may instruct his opponent to make the first move" (M5).

The people of **Manator** play jetan on a huge board with living pieces. When a piece is moved onto a square occupied by another there is a battle, and the winner keeps the square. In **Manatos** the contests are sometimes decided by first blood or points, but in Manator the game was always to the death. Also, in Manatos only criminals were sentenced to jetan, but in Manator slaves, prisoners and troublemakers were also sentenced to the games, which were often unfair (M5;13).

John Carter owns a tiny portable jetan set whose box folds out to become the board. All of the pieces are exquisitely carved replicas of friends and family, the princesses being **Tara of Helium** and **Llana of Gathol**. Carter carries a magnifying glass with the set so that he may show off the pieces to people, since they are so tiny (M10;1:6).

Jew   The racial stock from which old **Samuels**, a tanner of **Kalkar**-occupied 22nd century **Chicago**, was descended (MM2;4).

Jewel of Nine Colors   The one priceless gem on Barsoom. It scintillates the seven known prismatic colors and the two indescribable colors of the **eighth** and **ninth** rays. The jewel is worn only by the keepers of the **atmosphere plant** (M1;20) and by **Holy Therns** of high eminence (M2;4).

Jewel-room of Opar   A small circular chamber deep beneath the lost city of **Opar** in which the entire gem treasure of the city was kept. It could be reached by a hidden passage or by a second passage leading to the bottom of a well near the city's main treasure room and, like the main room, had been forgotten over the ages (T5;7).

Jezebel   The one beautiful girl in the land of South **Midian** in Africa, who was hated by the others for her beauty. She befriended **Lady Barbara Collis** immediately when the aviatrix landed in Midian after bailing out of her airplane in 1929. Jezebel's high native intelligence made her realize that her fellow Midianites would respect her more if she claimed some special privilege, so she pretended to understand all Lady Barbara said and "interpreted" it to the others. She actually did learn English from Lady Barbara after a while, and taught the Englishwoman her tongue. Jezebel was to be burned on a cross as a heretic after that, but she and Lady Barbara were saved by Dr. **Lafayette Smith** and escaped, only to be captured again by the North Midianites, from whom she escaped alone. Soon afterward she met up with **Danny "Gunner" Patrick**, who had come to the valley with Tarzan in search of Dr. Smith. Jezebel thought that "Gunner" was beautiful (as she thought all male non-Midianites were) and promptly fell in love with him, only to be abducted from him by the **Capietro shiftas**, stolen from them by **Leon Stabutch**, and finally reunited with "Gunner" after the Russian's death. The lovers eventually got married, bought a gas station, and settled down in **California** (T15;2,6,11–14,17–20,23,26).

Jhama   A small fortress far to the west of Jahar on Barsoom which **Phor Tak** discovered and commandeered many years after its inhabitants had all been slaughtered, probably by the **green men**. In it, he planned his revenge against **Tul Axtar**, who had driven him from Jahar after stealing his **disintegration rifle** idea. He thus welcomed the chance arrival of **Tan Hadron** and **Nur An**, who also wished to destroy Tul Axtar (M7;9).

Jhama   The invisible flier built in **Phor Tak's** workshop by **Tan Hadron** and **Nur An**. It was an unusual ship, a totally enclosed four-man flier with a narrow deck on top, two hatchways above and two below. It was pointed at the ends and had portholes with covers which opened out (controlled from within) and a periscope which threw its image to a viewscreen. The ship was equipped with **disintegration rifles** forward and aft and was coated entirely with the blue **protective pigment of Jahar**, and over that a coat of Phor Tak's **compound of invisibility**, so that when the ports and hatches were closed only the tiny lens of the periscope was visible, and that only from the front. *Jhama* came in very handy to Tan Hadron in his rescue of **Tavia**, **Phao** and **Sanoma Tora**, which would scarce have been possible without it (M7;10–14).

jidda   (*Ara*) A large cooking vessel, usually of brass (T11;1).

Jim   A mail carrier of 1917 **Oakdale**, **Illinois** (K3;6). Another Jim was the owner of a stable in 1920s **Ganado** (GH;22). Still another Jim was the chauffeur of **Ogden Secor** (GF;6).

Jimber-jaw   The name given by **Pat Morgan** to **Kolani**, the 50,000-year-old cave man he and Dr. **Marvin Stade** discovered frozen in **Siberia**, after a grizzly bear of the **Yellowstone River** region that Morgan had once seen. Jimber-jaw had been frozen in a blizzard and perfectly preserved until Stade used his new techniques to resurrect him. After several weeks of illness he regained health, learned to speak English, and returned to America with Morgan where, due to his lack of understanding, he became a wrestler, then a boxer, and eventually appeared in movies. He became convinced at that time that the movie star **Lorna Downs** was his lost beloved **Lilami** until he found out what Downs was really like. Disgusted with the modern world, Jimber-jaw decided to refreeze himself in order to find the real Lilami (J).

Jimmy   An electrician on the B.O. Pictures location shoot for *The Lion Man* in 1932 (T17;7).

jin   (*Ara*)(Also *djinn*) An aerial spirit of Arabic mythology which is possessed of great magic powers (T11;21).

Jinja   A town of **Uganda** which lies on Lake Victoria at the beginning of the Victoria Nile; it was the site from which the B.O. Pictures safari set out for the **Ituri Forest** in 1932 (T17;2).

jo   (*Cpk*) Beginning (C2;3).

jo-oo "Beginning bird" (*Cpk*). A pterodactyl (C2;5).

Jobab One of the apostles of the Midianites when Lady Barbara Collis landed in Midian in 1929. She shot him dead when he tried to stop Lafayette Smith from rescuing her (T15;2,14).

jodades "Luck to you" (*Amt*). The Amtorian greeting (V1;8).

Joe A scenarist for B.O. Pictures in the 1930s (T17;1). Another Joe (or possibly the same one) was the host of the 1933 Hollywood party which Reece and Billy Brouke crashed with the unwitting Tarzan in tow (T17;33).

Johansen, Peter A human informer in Kalkar-occupied 22nd century Chicago who wanted Elizabeth James, Julian 8th's woman, as his own and so spent a lot of time spying on him in order to catch him in some illegal activity. In one of these instances he saw Julian 8th's American flag and reported its presence to the new military governor, General Or-tis. Soon afterward, he tried to kill Julian 9th, who responded by breaking his wrist. Later, he spied on Moses Samuels the Jew, and exposed his practice of religion to the Kash Guard, who arrested the old man and tortured him to death for information. After the arrest of Julian 8th, he tried to come and take Elizabeth, and Julian 9th killed him (MM2;2–6,8–9).

John One of the henchmen of Peter of Colfax, who was killed by Norman of Torn in June of 1262 (OT;10). Another John was a faithful servant of Joan de Tany's around the same time (OT;12).

John, King (1167–1216) King of England from 1199 to 1216 who fought a series of wars with his nobles, France and the Pope to keep his throne and eventually died in 1216 after the arrival of the French Dauphin, who had been invited by the nobles to take the throne. On John's death, however, the throne passed to his eight-year-old son, Henry III (OT;1).

"John Carter and the Giant of Mars" The "fictional" John Carter story written for the Whitman Publishing Company for their Big Little Books series of children's books, in which several successful adaptations of Tarzan's stories had already appeared. Burroughs

was uncomfortable with the strict (15,000 words written in a certain way, for children) format required, and recruited his son John Coleman Burroughs to assist him in the writing, which probably accounts for the almost totally different writing style evident in the story. Burroughs later adapted the story "up" for adult readers and published it in a 20,000 word format in *Amazing Stories* magazine in January 1941, where it drew considerable criticism from readers who, of course, recognized the stylistic differences immediately and doubted the story's authorship until research for the book *John Carter of Mars*, in which the offending story was included, revealed the truth.

For purposes of this cyclopædia, "John Carter and the Giant of Mars" will not be regarded as a "true" John Carter story told to his great-nephew by the Warlord himself, but rather a mere fiction created by the author at the request of a publisher. The story was obviously not dictated by Carter, as it contains too many silly plot devices and inconsistencies with known "facts."

It concerns Pew Mogel, one of Ras Thavas' hormads, who creates a synthetic giant called Joog and an army of human-brained white apes with which he hopes to conquer Helium, then all of Barsoom. For some reason antiaircraft fire which can bring down mighty battleships is ineffective against the giant malagors the white apes ride, and the Heliumetic navy (with a flight ceiling of several thousand feet) cannot manage to stay out of the range of a 130-foot-tall giant, so John Carter must save Helium by a silly plan involving crippled ulsios. The book is abbreviated M11A.

John Carter of Mars The eleventh book in the Mars series, which is composed of two novelettes that are of such different character as to merit two separate entries in this cyclopædia. The first is titled **"John Carter and the Giant of Mars"** and the second **"Skeleton Men of Jupiter."** They were published in the same book together in 1964, long after the author's death, in much the same way as **"The Wizard of Venus"** and **"Pirate Blood"** were, because neither is long enough to merit a book of its own.

John Tyler The first clipper ship of Pellucidar, built by the old man whose name was not Dolly Dorcas late in 1931 and named for the president of the United States at the time he left Cape Cod. It was first used to go searching for David Innes and Dian the Beautiful on the other side of the Nameless Strait (P7:3;4).

Johnson   The chief of the Mexicans who ambushed the Apaches with a cannon at the Santa Rita Mine in the late 1700s (A1;11).

Johnson, Porfirio   The second officer of the Pan-American aero-sub *Coldwater* on her fateful voyage "beyond thirty." He was a sullen, dislikable man of about 30 at the time, and was intensely jealous of Lt. Jefferson Turck for his rapid promotion to command. He was jealous enough to sabotage the *Coldwater*'s engines, once it was downed on the ocean surface in a storm, so that prevailing tides and winds would carry the ship beyond the line of 30 degrees longitude, resulting in a mandatory court-martial for Turck. He later seized the ship when Turck was out in a launch, imprisoned the first officer Alvarez, and returned to Pan-America where, after Alvarez's trial and its ensuing results, Johnson went down in history as a villain (LC;1–2,9).

Johnson's Landing   A quay of 1920s Singapore (PB;11).

Johnson's Ranch   A ranch which lay southeast of the Bar-Y in 1880s Hendersville, Arizona (HB;13,17).

Joliet   City of northeast Illinois, site of both the Illinois State Penitentiary (K2;1) and a coal mining industry. In the 22nd century it was the center of the teivos where lay the Kalkar mines to which Julian 8th was sent after being convicted of smuggling (MM2;10).

Jonda   A vookor from Tonglap on Amtor who was a prisoner of the Brokols at the same time Carson Napier was, early in 1931. They eventually escaped together (V4; 25–29).

Jones   One of the crew of the *Kincaid* who remained loyal to Tarzan after the ship exploded, unlike Schmidt, who plotted with Schneider, the first mate (T3;21).

Jones, Doctor   A Los Angeles heart specialist of the 1920s (GH;10).

Jones, Mister   One of Dick Gordon's golf-playing friends (ME;2).

Jones, Robert   A black man from Alabama, private soldier in an American labor battalion of World War I, who was forgotten in Germany when the Americans went home. He made friends, learned German, and joined the German Air Force as a cook, from which position he was drafted by Captain Zuppner to be the cook of the dirigible O-220 on her voyage to Pellucidar (P4;3).

jong   (*Amt*) King (V1;4–5).

Joog   The incredibly large, incredibly stupid 130-foot-tall synthetic title character of "John Carter and the Giant of Mars," an indestructible monster created by the brilliant hormad Pew Mogel to help him conquer Barsoom. The giant was controlled by his creator from an armored howdah atop the thing's head while in battle; it obeyed commands given it through an electronic device implanted in its ear, which apparently forced its obedience. This device allowed John Carter to take over control of Joog from Pew Mogel after slaying the hormad, and he ordered the creature to go away and never come back (M11A;6–14).

Jor   The high chief of the Galus of Caspak in the early 20th century, father of the cos-ata-lo Ajor. Because she was a hope for the future of the Galus in Caspak, he would not let her leave Caspak with Tom Billings (C2;5,7).

joram   (*Amt*) Ocean (V1;9).

Jose   An old, retired Chihuahuan brigand of 1916 Mexico who knew Pesita well, and whom Barbara Harding paid to tell Billy Byrne of Bridge's capture by Pancho Villa's men. He later also told Byrne of Barbara's capture by Esteban and the Siwashes (K2;12,14).

Joseph   The servant of House Van der Tann who helped Barney Custer escape Blentz when he was incarcerated there as Leopold of Lutha in October 1912 (MK1;4).

Joubon   A clerk of the Paris police department in 1910 (T2;4).

ju   (*Cpk*) Stop (C2;2).

Ju-lan-fit   The closest the Laytheans could come to saying "Julian 5th." As a joke, he told them "fit" was a title equivalent to their javadar, and they believed him and thereafter called him either "Ju-lan-fit" or "Ju-lan-javadar" (MM1;11).

Juag The son of the chief of the tribe which originally inhabited **Indiana** before **Hooja the Sly One** took over the island. Juag escaped from Hooja and helped **David Innes** to rescue **Dian the Beautiful** from the Sly One's camp. He was afterward made King of Indiana by David Innes (P2;10,14–15).

Juarez The Mexican city that lies on the southern side of the border across from **El Paso, Texas** (K2;9).

Juba, King Specifically, Juba II (50 B.C.-A.D. 24), the king of Numidia and Mauretania. He was a personal friend of the Emperor Augustus' who was also renowned as a scholar (I;17).

Jubal, the Ugly One A mighty warrior of **Amoz** in Pellucidar who wished to mate with **Dian the Beautiful** and had a right to do so by the customs of their tribe; however she refused him, ran away, and was captured by the **Sagoths**, in whose captivity she met **David Innes**. Jubal, who was seven feet tall and very powerfully built, had earned his sobriquet when half of the flesh of his face was torn off by some wild animal. He was eventually killed by David Innes (with bow, sword and fists) in defense of Dian (P1;4,14).

Jude A warrior of **Hime** in Pellucidar who was captured by the **Coripies** of **Amiocap** and held for their feast along with **Tanar the Fleet One**. They escaped together, but the ungrateful Himean abducted **Stellara**, whom Tanar had just taken as his mate, and fled to Hime with her while Tanar slept. He caught up with them, however, and Jude fled (P3;8–9,12).

judges, Unisan The judges of the country of **Unis** on **Poloda** are appointed for life by the government on the recommendation of what we would call a bar association. They hold office until they are 70 (unless impeached first), after which they may be re-recommended by the association and reappointed. They wear grey uniforms with grey boots (B1;2).

Jugerum (*Lat*) A Roman unit of square measure equal to 28,800 square feet (I;13).

Jugurtha (160–104 B.C.) The King of **Numidia** who was defeated by the Roman general Sulla in 106 B.C. and, after being

displayed in Sulla's triumph, was imprisoned in the **Tullianum**, where he was executed almost two years later (I;4).

Juh Also called "The Butcher," he was the Chief of the **Ned-ni Apache** who wanted to kill the infant **Andy MacDuff** when he was found, and grumbled when **Go-yat-thlay** kept the child. The grumbling later grew to hatred of the boy (now called **Shoz-dijiji**) both because of his hatred of whites and his jealousy-born hatred of Go-yat-thlay. Juh continually opposed Shoz-dijiji in both love and war and brought false evidence forward to "prove" his rival's death when the young brave had been missing for some time. He then took the despondent **Ish-kay-nay** (Shoz-dijiji's betrothed) as his wife (at her father's insistence), but left her for dead after she was shot in the retreat from **Cibicu Creek**. For both the lie that stole his beloved and for Juh's leaving her to die, Shoz-dijiji sought him out and, after a fierce struggle, killed him in Autumn of 1881 (A1;1–2,12–17).

Jukans A race of somewhat erratic humans of Pellucidar who inhabit the valley east of that where **Oog** and **Julok** lie. Jukans' hair grows straight out from the scalp and is usually cut off at about an inch from the scalp. The irises of their eyes are small and their mouths are loose and flabby and often hang open. They range from apparently sane and intelligent folk to raving maniacs or complete idiots, but the majority of Jukans are simply forgetful halfwits. In spite of (or perhaps because of) their mental defects, they are much more advanced than most Pellucidarians — they live in palisaded villages in (mostly) well-constructed houses, practice agriculture, and worship a god called **Ogar** in a temple (P6; 6–10). It is possible that the Jukans may be related (at least in kind) to the maniacs of **Xuja**, whom they resemble both physically and mentally (T7;15–19).

Juke, Daisy The girl of **Glenora** whom both **Johnny Lafitte** and **Frank Adams** loved. She was a descendant of the criminal **Max Juke**, whose family swarmed with thieves, murderers, prostitutes and bums. After the great Glenora oil strike of the 1920s, her family became rich and she became engaged to Frank Adams, whose family had also become rich. Wealth spoiled her, though, and she began to drink too much, which eventually led to the engagement being broken. She then took up with a bootlegger and eventually went from him to an opium smuggler with whom she ran away to Singapore. She quickly tired of him, though, and became an expensive prostitute known as the Queen of Diamonds. She was eventually lured away from this life by the pirate known as the Portuguese, and on his ship she again met up with Johnny Lafitte, who had recently come to the Portuguese from the camp of the Vulture. She bared her soul to him, including the fact that she had always loved him, then went below and shot herself (PB;1,12).

Juke, Max A criminal of the early 1700s who sired a family that produced over 1200 criminals in the next 200 years (PB).

Julia The name of both the mother and sister of Agrippina, both of whom were notorious wantons and adulteresses; the elder Julia was the daughter of Augustus Caesar. Another Julia was the wife of Nero, brother of Caligula, and still another was Caligula's daughter, assassinated along with her father and mother on January 24, A.D. 41 (I;1–2,15,21).

Julia Livilla (A.D. 18–41) The youngest child of Germanicus Caesar, banished with her sister Agrippina for plotting against Caligula and later assassinated by order of Messalina, wife of Claudius (I;6).

Julian, Tribe of The collected descendants of Julian 9th and his allies, who fought the Kalkars for 300 years and eventually drove them into the Pacific Ocean in 2432. Over the centuries of war they lost touch with technology and became nomadic hunters and herders who bought all of their goods from more advanced peoples, such as the Kolrado people. They worshipped The Flag and lived much as the American Indians had, eventually even taking symbolic names like the Indians did. Their feud with the House of Or-tis finally ended when the pure human members of that house joined with the Tribe of Julian and the son of Or-tis 15th voluntarily swore fealty to Julian 20th, who married his sister, Bethelda (MM3).

Julian 1st A career military man who was born in 1896, married in 1916, became a major in 1918, and was killed in the Argonne on Armistice Day of that same year. He thus never saw his son, Julian 2nd (MM1;1).

Julian 2nd A career military man, like his father, who was born in 1917 and killed in Turkey in 1938, early in World War II (MM1;1).

Julian 3rd The reincarnation of Julian 1st, a career military man like his forebears. He was born in 1937 and worked his way to admiral status by the end of World War III in 1967. On Mars Day (June 10, 1967), he met Burroughs and narrated to him the events of *The Moon Maid*, which he remembered from his next incarnation as Julian 5th. They again met in March of 1969, and Julian told the stories of *The Moon Men* and *The Red Hawk*. He belonged to the International Peace Fleet and patrolled the world for the next 25 years, but was killed in the line of duty in 1992. He was thus the first Julian to meet his son, who was born in 1970, but never met his grandson, who was born in 2000 (MM1;1)(MM2;1) (MM3).

Julian 4th The son of Julian 3rd, born in 1970 and eventually killed in the line of duty in the International Peace Fleet, of which he was a commanding officer (MM1;1).

Julian 5th The son of Julian 4th and reincarnation of Julian 3rd, who was born in Chicago in 2000 and, having the same military aptitude as his ancestors, graduated from the Air School at the age of 16. He was an incredibly successful man who made captain by age 24 and was appointed captain of the *Barsoom*, the first Earth-Mars vessel, in 2025. He was appointed to supervise its construction as well as its flight, even though he felt that this duty should have been given to his brilliant, though unpopular, classmate Orthis. Julian tried to make the experience painless for Orthis, but the latter's hatred and jealousy of Julian were too great to permit him to accept Julian's overtures of friendship, and these feelings spurred him to sabotage the *Barsoom*, requiring it to make a forced landing in Va-nah, the world within the moon. There, Orthis and Julian were captured by the Va-gas, who soon afterward also captured Nah-ee-lah, Princess of Laythe, last city of the advanced U-gas. Julian fell in love with her and helped her escape from the Va-gas, but they fell into the hands of the hateful Kalkars; he managed to accomplish her escape from these, but was recaptured himself and confined in a Kalkar prison to await his apportionment as a slave. Here he met **Moh-goh**, a Laythean who helped him escape and took him back to Laythe, where he introduced him to **Ko-tah**, a prince of Laythe who had long planned to usurp the position of the **jemadar**, which plan was accomplished while Julian was in the city (MM1;1–11).

Although he failed to prevent the assassination of the jemadar, Julian was able to kill Ko-tah. His victory was a hollow one, however, because Orthis had joined up in the meantime with the Kalkars and taught them how to make Earthly explosives and artillery in exchange for their making him their ruler, and he and they came to Laythe and sacked it. Julian and Nah-ee-lah escaped the city and eventually succeeded in finding the *Barsoom*, which the crew had repaired after ten years of hard labor directed by Ensign **Norton**, whom Orthis had taught about the ship. They returned to Earth in 2036, at which time Julian and Nah-ee-lah were married (MM1;11–14).

After his return, he became Commander-in-Chief of the **International Peace Fleet** and warned the people of Earth against disarmament, but his warnings were dismissed and so Orthis was able to lead the Kalkars to conquer Earth in 2050, destroying the now-reduced Peace Fleet with a disintegration device he had invented. Julian, however, developed a means of thwarting the weapon, and Orthis, thus cheated of his revenge, blew up his own ship, killing both himself and Julian 5th (MM2;1).

Julian 6th   The son of Julian 5th and **Nah-ee-lah** of Laythe, born in 2036 (MM1; 14).

Julian 7th   The son of Julian 6th and father of Julian 8th. Almost nothing is known of him other than that he lived in Chicago and built with his own hands the house and livestock pen that Julian 8th later inherited (MM2;4–5).

Julian 8th   The son of Julian 7th and father of the hero Julian 9th. He was a small farmer and an intellectual who lived in the **Teivos** of Chicago, a proud man from whom the spirit had been almost completely crushed by the grinding oppression of the Kalkars. It had not been so completely crushed, however, that he would let a Kalkar take either his woman or the illegal flag he had hidden in his mantlepiece. Julian was spied upon constantly by **Peter Johansen**, a Kalkar collaborator who wanted Julian's woman **Elizabeth James** as his own, and this spying eventually led to Julian's arrest and conviction on charges of smuggling. He was sentenced to ten years in the mines, but was rescued by his son and helped him to begin the rebellion that was to finally overthrow the Kalkars 11 generations later. Julian 8th, however, was captured in the first battle and executed (MM2).

Julian 9th   The great-great-grandson of **Julian 5th**, into whom he was reincarnated on Earth on January 1, 2100, being born on that date in what was once **Chicago** as the son of **Julian 8th**, a goat farmer whose ancestors had been heroes and emperors. Julian was a physically powerful young man who killed a pack of vicious dogs with his bare hands and once wrestled a bull to the ground. He killed the dogs to save a girl called **Juana St. John**, whom he fell in love with and secretly married (in defiance of Kalkar law), and who bore him his son, **Julian 10th**. Finally sick of the degradation heaped upon humanity by the Kalkars, he began to perform acts of rebellion, culminating in the revolution that many generations later destroyed the last of the Kalkars. He was captured at the end of the first battle, tried and convicted of rebellion, and executed by **The Butcher** (MM2).

Julian 10th   The son of **Julian 9th** and **Juana St. John**, who grew up in hiding and began to organize in earnest the rebellion his father had given his life to begin (MM2;11).

Julian 15th   A great warrior chief of the line of Julian who lived from 2259 to 2309. He drove the **Kalkars** out of the American West entirely and into the **San Fernando Valley** by the year of his death. They there entrenched themselves and held out against the Julians for another century (MM3;1).

Julian 18th   A great warrior chief of the House of Julian who rode alone to the Pacific Ocean through **Kalkar** territory in 2408 so his people would know how near their goal was. The Kalkars discovered him, however, and although he reached his camp, he died of his wounds later, after telling his people that the sea was no more than a day's ride away and that a beautiful and rich country (the seacoast orchards and vineyards of **California**) lay there (MM3;1).

Julian 19th   The Chief of Chiefs of the tribes of Julian from 2408 to 2429. On August 12th of that year he was killed by an Ortis lance, leaving his son **Julian 20th** as Chief of Chiefs at the age of 20 (MM3;1).

Julian 20th   The reincarnation of Julian 9th. He was Chief of Chiefs of the tribes of Julian from August 12, 2429 (his 20th birthday) until some time after the destruction of the last of the Kalkars. He was called the **Red Hawk** and broke the stalemate that Kalkars and humans had been locked into for over a century by bringing his entire tribe down into the Kalkar valley in 2430 so there would be no inducement to retreat to the desert again. He was thus successful in pushing back the Kalkars, but was caught in their retreat and taken as a prisoner to their **jemadar, Or-tis 16th**. With the help of a pure human member of the Or-tis family who hated the Kalkars he lived among, Julian escaped and found the sea. Heading back east, he encountered the **Nipons** and rescued **Bethelda**, pure human daughter of Or-tis 15th, whom he fell in love with in spite of himself. While he was out hunting, she was captured by the giant **Raban** and Julian pursued, killing many of the bandit's men but eventually being captured himself. He was freed by **Okonnor**, a pure human who was one of Raban's men, when he found that the girl he had helped Raban to abduct was the daughter of Or-tis 15th, to whose family he was still loyal. Julian then crept into Raban's castle and killed the giant before he could take Bethelda as his woman.

After returning to his people, Julian upheld the decision of peace with the House of Or-tis that the **Vulture** had made, and together the humans drove the Kalkars into the sea after two more years of fighting. Julian was then proclaimed **Jemadar of America** and married Bethelda, thus sealing the ancient gap between the two houses (MM3).

Julian 21st   The son of Julian 20th and Bethelda Or-tis, the living symbol of peace between the two houses. He was born around 2432 and had to begin the work of reconstructing America from almost four hundred years of Kalkar domination and war (MM3; 10).

Julok   One of the tribes of the Pellucidarian continent west of **Korsar**, whose women

were large and bearded and men small and weak (P6;2).

Julp   A Bastian warrior of Pellucidar who was set to guard **Wilhelm von Horst** when he was a slave in Basti. Von Horst killed him by knocking him off a high ledge (P5;6).

Jungle Girl   The original title of *The Land of Hidden Men* when it was first published in 1931.

Jungle Island   An island about 50 or 60 miles off the west coast of Africa, due west of the mouth of the Ugambi River, upon which Tarzan was purposefully marooned by **Nikolas Rokoff** for a few weeks in 1912. The island must have been once part of the mainland because lions, panthers, apes and other jungle creatures lived there. It was with the assistance of the **great apes** of the tribe of **Akut** (whom he had befriended) that Tarzan was able to kill a group of black warriors of the **Wagambi** tribe, who had chanced upon the island while fishing, and attacked Tarzan. **Mugambi**, chief of the Wagambi, alone survived the attack and befriended Tarzan, helping him escape to the mainland in his canoe along with Akut, eleven of his apes, and **Sheeta** the panther. Tarzan later returned to the island with the commandeered *Kincaid* in order to return Sheeta and the apes to their homes, and at that time the time bomb that **Alexis Paulvitch** had planted aboard the ship exploded, marooning Tarzan and the crew of the *Kincaid*. Tarzan was soon afterward able to capture the *Cowrie* and returned to England, leaving his beasts behind.

Ten years later, the scientific research ship *Marjorie W.* stopped at the island to make some chemical tests and Akut, still looking for Tarzan, came down to the ship and even let himself be taken aboard and back to England by Paulvitch, whom the ship had just rescued from the Ugambi region, where he had been left ten years before (T3;3–7,19–21) (T4;1).

"A Jungle Joke"   The eleventh short story comprising *Jungle Tales of Tarzan*, abbreviated T6:11. In it Tarzan plays a cruel, but fitting practical joke on the cannibals of the tribe of Mbonga after they set a trap to catch a lion to torture for fun.

Jungle Tales of Tarzan   The sixth book of the Tarzan series, actually a connected series of 12 short stories originally published as a magazine series in 1916 and 1917. The events of the stories concern Tarzan's coming of age among the apes, mostly in the years 1906 to 1910, and were told to Burroughs by Tarzan himself in or around 1914, probably at the same time as he related the events of T5. Each story has its own separate title and will be treated as a separate entity.

junh-gan-hay (*Apa*) Village (A1;16).

Junia Claudilla The daughter of **Junius Silanus** and first wife of the Emperor **Caligula**. She died early in A.D. 38 (I;15–16).

Junius Silanus The Proconsul of Africa and father of **Junia Claudilla**. He was ordered by **Caligula** to commit suicide after a perceived insult in A.D. 39 (I;15,17).

Jupiter Pluvus (*Lat*) Jupiter the Rainmaker (I;7).

Jupiter Tonans (*Lat*) Jupiter the Thunderer (I;6).

Jurassic The second period of the Mesozoic era, which began 181 million years ago and ended 135 million years ago. The plesiosaurs and ichthyosaurs flourished during this period, as did the diplodocus, stegosaurus and rhamphorhyncus (P1).

jury, Barsoomian Barsoomian juries are composed of 31 members of the defendant's own class (M2;17).

jury, Unisan Juries of **Unis** on **Poloda** are composed of five men (B1;3).

K.K.S. Studio The Hollywood motion picture studio for which **Wilson Crumb** worked in the early 1920s (GH;10).

Ka-at The **Brokol yorkokor** (colonel) who first questioned **Carson Napier** when he fell into their hands early in 1931 (V4;25).

ka-chu (*Apa*) The jackrabbit (A1;2).

Ka-e-ten-na A member of **Crawford's Indian Scouts** on their campaign to catch **Geronimo** in March of 1886 (A2;9).

ka-goda (*Ape*) Either "Do you surrender?" or "I surrender" (T1;12).

Ka-yi-tah A Cho-kon-en Apache who was a member of **Crawford's Indian Scouts** and tracked **Geronimo** to his hideout in Sonora in August of 1886 (A2;14).

Kab Kadja Jeddak of the **Warhoons** of Barsoom when John Carter first encountered that horde of **green men** in 1886 (M2;14).

Kabariga The chief of the **Bangalo** people who enlisted Tarzan's aid to rid his people of the depredations of a band of **shiftas** in 1929 (T15;1).

Kadabra The capital of **Okar** on Barsoom. It lies near the north pole and is covered by several domes, the whole being 100 miles in diameter. It has its own **atmosphere plant** (as do all Okarian cities) and is the largest and most important city of Okar. John Carter and **Thuvan Dihn** entered it by a ruse in 1888 in order to find **Matai Shang**, who was a guest of **Salensus Oll**, Jeddak of Jeddaks of Okar, in his palace at Kadabra (M3).

kadar (*Bar*) A guard (M4;8).

Kadour ben Saden The Arab sheik of a tribe who camped to the south of **Djelfa**. He befriended Tarzan after the ape-man bought a horse from him and treated him to dinner in **Sidi Aissa** in 1910. Tarzan then rescued the Arab's daughter, who had been stolen from his **douar** two years earlier and enslaved in a cafe in the town, and returned her to the grateful sheik, who helped Tarzan leave town that very day and rode with him to **Bou Saada**, fighting off the Arabs who pursued him the whole way (T2;7–8).

Kaffa (Also Kefa) A mountainous region of southwestern **Abyssinia** (T16;1).

Kaffir corn A native corn of Africa (T19; 27).

Kaficho An ethnic group which inhabits the **Kaffa** region of Abyssinia (T16;1).

kah (*Apa*) "Arrow" or "foot" (A1).

Kahiya The black headman of the **Zveri** expedition in 1928, whom **Raghunath Jafar** bribed to take his men on a hunt so the Hindu would be left alone with **Zora Drinov**, whom he wished to rape (T14;2).

kahuna (Hawaiian) A priest or sorceror (B1).

Kai Shang One of the leaders of the *Cowrie* mutineers when they stopped on Jungle Island in the autumn of 1912 while Tarzan and the *Kincaid* survivors were marooned there. He was a Chinese criminal and planned with Momulla the Maori to kill Gust, their navigator, after they had recruited Schneider of the *Kincaid* to take his place. Unfortunately for them, Gust saw them coming, guessed their intentions, and escaped to tell Tarzan of the plot. Tarzan then assaulted the *Cowrie* and Kai Shang was killed in the process by Sheeta, the panther (T3;20–21).

Kaibab A plateau and forest of northern Arizona, just north of the Grand Canyon (D;5).

Kaisers A name given to the Kalkars by American nationalists of the 22nd century (MM2;5).

Kaji A fierce tribe of warrior women who dwelt on an isolated plateau at the source of the Mafa River in the Ethiopian Highlands not far from Onthar and Thenar. They were originally black, but wanted to become white, and so used the power of the Gonfal to terrify any blacks who entered their territory, and to lure white men in. Every white man was given as many Kaji wives as the queen allotted (those who paid her the highest bribes, of course). Any baby born black or any male baby at all was destroyed; only light brown or white females were allowed to live. Over time this policy became a part of their religion, so by the early 1900s they ranged from light brown to white in color, but were more savage and vicious in temperament. In 1935 they were freed from the rule of Mafka by Tarzan, who gave them the Gonfal so that they could go out into the world and finance their acceptance into the European civilization so many of their white prisoner-husbands had told them of (T21;1–2,10–11).

Kaji language The language of the Kaji and Zuli was based upon the Galla tongue, but its vocabulary and grammar had been severely affected by the languages of the male prisoners they had taken over the years until it had become a hybrid of Galla and several European languages (T21;4).

kal (*Ape*) Milk (TC).

Kal Tavan A prince of Tjanath, son of the jed of that city and father of Tavia. He ended up as a slave in the house of Tor Hatan of Helium and tried to stop the abduction of Tor Hatan's daughter Sanoma Tora, but was struck down. After being shown a picture of the metal of Jahar, he recognized it as that of the girl's abductors and told Tan Hadron so.

He was later reunited with his daughter after Tan Hadron rescued her (M7;1–2,17).

Kala The young she-ape of the tribe of Kerchak who adopted the infant John Clayton, Jr., to replace her own baby, which had died in a fall when Kala was forced to flee one of Kerchak's periodic rages. She stole the human baby from his cradle in the Clayton cottage while Kerchak killed John Clayton, and she left the corpse of her own dead child in the bassinet. At the time, she was only about ten, but full-grown, and protected the baby she named Tarzan from the other apes until his maturity. They wanted to abandon him because of his slow development — he took years to develop to a point baby apes reach in months. Kala was killed by Kulonga, the first black man ever seen by Kerchak's tribe, with a poisoned arrow, and Tarzan was greatly grieved, searching out and killing Kulonga shortly thereafter. Tarzan always thought of Kala as his mother forever after, even after he knew that he was not her natural child (T1;4–9,25,28).

Kalan (*Ape*) Female (TC).

Kaldane One of the stranger forms of intelligent life on Barsoom. A Kaldane resembles a hideous bluish-grey humanoid head with great, bulging, lidless eyes, a nose that is nothing more than two vertical slits, and a sphincter-like mouth. It is much larger than a normal human head and is soft and boneless, with a huge brain. Kaldanes have six short legs like a spider's and two powerful chelae. When outside, Kaldanes ride about on rykors, headless humanoid creatures whom the Kaldanes control by mental commands through an appendage attached to the rykor's exposed spinal columnar nerves. Underground in their burrows, Kaldanes walk under their own power and leave the rykors aboveground in their silo-like towers.

Kaldanes are hive creatures, hatching from eggs laid by a bisexual king. The rest are all asexual and very similar to each other, even down to likes and dislikes. One egg in a thousand laid by the king of a swarm is another king; several of these special eggs are kept in walled-up enclosures and raised therein because they would attack and kill their "father" if they escaped. When the old king dies a new one is released and takes the name and place of the old. The Kaldanes in these sealed chambers do not suffocate because Kaldanes have no need of air. Ninety percent of a Kaldane is brain and the rest rudimentary support organs. They hate light and open areas and prefer to exist in vast underground tunnel systems where they have stored staggeringly huge quantities of preserved food in preparation for the day Barsoom's atmosphere goes and all other life dies.

To the Kaldanes, brain is everything and uninterrupted thought the purpose of existence. Because of this philosophy, they have developed great mental powers and are able to control a rykor without touching it, from a short distance away, even to the point of having the creature lift up the Kaldane and place it upon its own shoulders. The power can also be used to dominate normal humans, but this requires considerable effort and does not always work. Kaldanes can also recall ancestral memory consciously (instead of in dreams or instincts), giving them a vast store of ancient memories to tap (M5;5–6,12).

Kalfastoban The vental of the mines of Veltopismakus who supervised Tarzan while he was a slave there. He was a bully and a lout who wished to buy the beautiful slave girl Talaskar for himself, and Tarzan eventually had to kill him to save her (T10;11–12,18).

kali (*Swa*) Woman (T8;17).

Kali One of the original member nations of the Empire of Pellucidar; it is the northeasternmost kingdom of the Empire, lying only 40 miles inland from the Lural Az. In 1931 David Innes went there to stop a war between it and Suvi, which had dropped out of the Empire (P2;6)(P7:1;2).

Kali Bwana "Woman Master" (*Swa*). The alias of Jessie Jerome, an attractive young white woman who came to Africa in 1931 to find her brother Jerry, and was captured by the horrible Leopard Men to be their new high priestess after being abandoned by her porters deep in the interior. Chief Bobolo, one of the Leopard Men, then stole her for himself and took her to the village of the Betete pygmies for safekeeping. She was rescued from the pygmies by Tarzan and the Old-Timer, who had fallen in love with her. She realized soon after that she loved him as well, and when she discovered that his partner The Kid was actually her brother, her happiness was complete (T18;1–7,11–15,18–23).

Kaliphe An Arab marauder of the band of Sidi-el-Seghir whom Prince Michael killed in order to save Nakhla (LL;8,10,20).

Kalkar City #337 The Kalkar city into which Julian 5th and Nah-ee-lah accidentally blundered while searching for Laythe. Julian helped Nah-ee-lah to escape but was himself recaptured, escaping later with the help of a Laythean prisoner named Moh-goh, who took him to Laythe thereafter (MM1;9–11).

Kalkars The dominant race of Va-nah and bitter enemies of the Laytheans. They are a mixed race of a slightly darker color than that of the pure U-gas of Laythe (though still not as dark as Earthly Caucasians), with eyes ranging from brown to watery blue and hair ranging from flaxen yellow to dark brown. They have a variety of types of features and are often awkwardly built. A few of them are quite large, ranging up to almost seven feet in height. The word Kalkar originally meant "thinker," and the Kalkar race traces its development back thousands of years to the time when Va-nah was ruled by the pure U-ga race, which had become very technologically advanced. The Kalkars were at this time a secret society of communistic pseudo-intellectuals who sought to abolish the class system and the capitalist system and eventually started a revolution which did so. Civilization was almost completely destroyed thereafter because in a classless communistic society there is no incentive for work, and so no one would (a lesson we on Earth have apparently yet to learn despite many good examples of the process). The Kalkar rulers were too stupid to develop new technology and too lazy to repair the old, nor could they if they had wanted to, because in their fanatical revolutionary zeal they had destroyed all books and records of history, art, literature and technology. To make things worse, the Va-gas followed the Kalkar example, revolted against them, and destroyed what little of civilization was left. The Kalkars have always hated the Laytheans and the other remnants of U-ga nobility in Va-nah, enslaving any they catch and constantly searching for any U-ga cities so they can conquer them (MM1;9–10).

Orthis fell in among the Kalkars sometime in the 2020s and made a deal with them — he gave them the know-how to make explosives and artillery in return for their making him

Jemadar of Jemadars, ruler of all the Kalkars and, with their new weapons, all of Va-nah, including Laythe by 2036 (MM1;13-14). Over the next 14 years he built a fleet of a thousand spaceships for them and in 2050 led an army of 100,000 Kalkars to Earth, which he easily conquered due to its deplorable state of disarmament. After Orthis' self-immolation to destroy Julian 5th, the Kalkars reverted to type and established the same sort of communistic government on Earth as they had in Va-nah, aided and abetted by many ignorant, lazy and foolish Earth people who welcomed a society where the great and intelligent would be dragged down to their level and everyone made "equal" economically. The Kalkars then began to transport more of their kind to Earth for awhile (at the rate of about seven million a year), until all of their ships were lost or broken down. Since none of them knew how to repair or rebuild the ships, their communication with Va-nah then ended, but the Kalkars already on Earth bred like flies, producing millions upon millions of pure Kalkars and millions more half-breeds who hated pure humans even more than the pure Kalkars did. By this time, of course, the world had been reduced to ruins, just as Va-nah had been millennia ago (MM2;1-3).

Under the grinding oppression of the Kalkars, the spirit of humanity was almost totally broken, but there came a point where mankind would fold no more and leaders like Julian 9th arose in the mid-22nd century, starting rebellions that eventually wiped the Kalkars from the face of the Earth entirely after more than 300 years of fighting. Their last stand in the American West was in the San Fernando Valley, where they held off the tribe of Julian for over a century. The particular Kalkars there were of the House of Ortis (the descendants of Orthis), hereditary enemies of the House of Julian for more than 400 years. These Kalkars had bred purely for size and strength since the time of their arrival on Earth, so that by the time of Julian 20th the average Kalkar was over seven feet tall. The last of them were driven from their capital in April of 2430, fleeing out to sea in ships in 2432 (MM2;9-11)(MM3;1-3,9-10).

Kalksus A Barsoomian cruiser-transport ship under command of Vas Kor of Dusar (M4;13).

Kalo (*Ape*) The cow (TC).

kalto (*Amt*) Chemist. This is one of the five ruling classes of Havatoo, who live in a section of the city named for their profession (V2;14).

kalu (*Ape*) Mother (TC).

Kam Han Tor An ancient prince of Horz on Barsoom, brother of the Jeddak of Horz who began his rule in the year 27M382J4 (by the ancient calendar of Horz). He was lured down into the pits by Lum Tar O some 500 years after Hor Kai Lan was, and placed into suspended animation by the old man in the same fashion as he had trapped many others. He awoke when John Carter killed the ancient madman, breaking his spell, but Kam Han Tor and the others were crushed to find Throxeus gone and their world vanished. The millennia postponed by Lum Tar O eventually caught up with his victims, who crumbled into dust less than an hour after awakening (M10:1;9-12).

kamadar (*Van*) A duke (MM1;11).

kamak A Minunian military rank. A kamak commands an amak of 1000 troops (T10;13).

kambo (*Ape*) Jungle (TC).

Kambu The mythological progenitor of the Khmer race, from whose name the word Cambodia was derived (HM;7).

Kamehameha (1758-1819) The king of Hawaii from 1782 to 1819. He united the island chain under his rule and established profitable trade relations with Europe and the United States. Burroughs once dreamed that Kamehameha had come to visit him, but in reality it was John Carter (M10).

kamerad (*Ger*) Comrade (C3;6).

Kamlot An Amtorian of Vepaja who befriended Carson Napier soon after his arrival on Amtor. He was the son of Duran, the man who had first captured Napier and taken him to the palace of Mintep. During an expedition to gather tarel, he and Napier were captured by Klangan agents of the Thorists and taken prisoner aboard the ship *Sofal*, but they there began a mutiny which ended in their possession of the ship. Kamlot was then made second in command after Napier (V1;3-11).

Kamma A she-ape of the tribe of Kerchak when Tarzan was growing up (T6:1).

Kampf, General A fictitious Austrian officer invented by **Barney Custer** to pass an Austrian sentry in September of 1914 (MK2;4).

kampong (Sumatran) Village (T22;1).

Kampong Thum A city of Cambodia which lies on the **Stoeng Sen** River about 100 miles north of **Phnom Penh** (HM;1).

Kamtol The city of the **First-Born** in the Valley of the First-Born in Barsoom's northern hemisphere. It is built of gorgeous white stone with tall, elaborately carved towers and city wall and lies amidst cultivated fields in the fertile, forested valley. The First-Born of Kamtol are independent from those of **Dor**, but sometimes join with them for a very big raid. Kamtol was ruled in recent times by the **Jeddak Doxus**, who was the descendant of a long line that must have either descended from or received its authority from an ancient **Issus** of long ago. Every person in the valley had had his **nerve-index** recorded except Doxus, who thus ruled supreme because he could use his **nerve-index machine** to instantly kill anyone whose nerve-index had been recorded, no matter where on Barsoom he was. He thus prevented escape or insurrection. The population of the city is rigidly controlled at 200,000 because that is the maximum number the valley will support. Of these 65,000 are men, 5000 are slaves, and 130,000 are women and young. 65,000 fighting men is generally considered sufficient for defense (particularly as the valley has never been attacked), but many Kamtolians believe that the number of women should be decreased and the number of warriors increased. Interestingly, most women are of the second belief, because each believes herself to be too beautiful and desirable to destroy and holds that that fate would fall to other women. The population is controlled both by **birth control** and by killing the old, weak and sick (M10:2).

Kamudi A black slave of the **Kaji** who became the headman of the safari organized by the freed Kaji prisoners to leave Kaji country in 1935 (T21;11).

kan (*Apa*) Spirit (A1;4).

Kandar The **Tanjong** of **Japal** on Amtor. He befriended **Carson Napier** when they were both enslaved in **Mypos** in 1930 and they escaped together. Upon his return to Japal, Kandar found that his father had been deposed and killed by the evil **Gangor**, whom Kandar in turn killed with **Napier's** help. He then became **Jong** of Japal himself (V4;4, 18–24).

Kander The King of **Amoz** in Pellucidar after **Dacor the Strong One** either lost or gave up the kingship — we are never told which (P7:1;2,7).

Kando (*Ape*) The ant (TC).

Kandos One of the **Erythra** of 1935 Athne (T21;21).

Kandus A red Barsoomian warrior of **Invak** who acted as John Carter's guide through the forest to the city when he was captured there in 1940. Kandus befriended him and eventually helped him escape, albeit indirectly (M10:4;2–3,6–7).

kane (Hawaiian) Man (B1).

Kaneko, Second Lieutenant Kenzo The officer of a small group of **Japanese** occupation troops who captured Tarzan in Sumatra for a brief while in the spring of 1944. He was a stereotypical Japanese caricature: 5'6" tall, bandy-legged, buck-toothed, and wearing horn-rimmed glasses. He was shot and killed by the **"Foreign Legion"** when they came to rescue Tarzan (T22;28).

Kangaroo People of Barsoom *see* **Gooli**

Kangrey The **Khmer** peasant woman of **Lodidhapura** who found **Gordon King** delirious in the jungle and nursed him back to health with the help of her husband **Che** (HM;3).

Kanje A faithful priest of **Tanga-tanga** whom **David Innes** appointed high priest of **Pu** after banishing **Ope**, the faithless old high priest (P7:3;6).

Kansas A cowhand of the **Crazy "B"** Ranch (A2;15).

Kantchi, Baron The **Karlovan** ambassador to **Margoth** in the early part of the 20th century (R;1).

Kantchi, Ivan The eldest son of **Baron Kantchi**. Ivan was a huge man (standing 6'6"), an officer of the **Black Guard**, and a close personal friend of **Prince Boris**. He was involved in the Prince's hoax against **Margoth**, in which the prince and the outlaw known as The Rider switched places (R;3–6,8,10).

Kantos Kan A padwar of the navy of Helium on Barsoom. He was captured by the green men of Warhoon while searching for the missing Dejah Thoris and met John Carter in the pits of Warhoon. They escaped together, but became separated and did not meet again until a few weeks later in Zodanga. Kantos Kan then got John Carter into the navy of Zodanga with him, and together they found Dejah Thoris. They became best friends, and by the time 20 years had gone by Kantos Kan had worked his way up to jedwar of the navy of Helium (M1)(M2; 16).

kantum (*Amt*) Physicist. This is one of the five ruling classes of **Havatoo**, who live in a section of the city named for their profession (V2;14).

Kantum Lat "Physicist Avenue" (*Amt*). One of the five major "spoke" avenues of the semicircular Amtorian city of **Havatoo**. It leads from the **Tag kum voo Klookantum** in the wall to the **Sera Tartum** on the riverfront (V2;16).

Kanty, "One Eye" A large, scarred bandit of the band of the **Black Wolf** in medieval Derbyshire who was one of the first five men to join **Norman of Torn** after he bested them in 1256. He had formerly been a blacksmith and was made the chief armorer of Torn in the next few years (OT;6,10).

Kao The Vulture's Chinese houseboy (PB;8).

Kaol An empire in one of the few forests left on arid Barsoom. It is a low-lying, wet and swampy area where thrive all manner of strange creatures that are found almost nowhere else on the planet. The forest is thick and tropical and abounds with tall purple grasses with red and yellow fern-like tops. Since the forest is more than moist enough for agriculture, no canals go there, and the surrounding land is high and rough, making surface commerce difficult. The Kaolians have few fliers and no navy because of the thickness of their forest, whose growth they encourage for defense against the navies of other powers. These factors combine to make Kaol very out of touch with other nations, thus the Kaolians tend to be very conservative to the

point of being backward. For instance, they still clung to the discredited **Thern** religion for some time after the reorganization of **Dor**; because of this, **Matai Shang** and **Thurid** fled to Kaol after abducting **Dejah Thoris** and **Thuvia** of Ptarth and hid out in the palace of its jeddak, **Kulan Tith**. The city of Kaol itself has cleverly constructed, practically unscalable, glasslike walls. The source of the River Iss probably lies within the Kaolian forest (M3;5,7).

Kaolian Road The main highway which runs from the outer edge of the Forest of **Kaol** to the city itself (M3;5).

kaor (*Bar*) The universal word of greeting (M1).

Kapara The country of the **Kapars** on **Poloda**. It lies on the continent of **Epris** on the opposite side of the planet from **Unis** and is a horrible place of poverty, oppression and suspicion, where war is worshipped and children turn in their own parents for "treasonous" acts and speech (B1;8)(B2;2–10).

Kaparan The language of the **Kapars** of **Poloda** sounded to **Tangor** "something like the noise that pigs make when they eat" (B1;4).

Kapars On the planet **Poloda**, the deadly enemies of the people of the country of **Unis**, with whom they had been at war for 101 years in 1939. They are a mixed race, with some members who could pass for Unisan but others who were much darker, including some with black hair (B1;2–5).

Kapdor A city-state of **Noobol** which converted to **Thorism** early in the 20th century. It was a backward place, built strongly but with no imagination, and its people were unhappy (at least after the Thorist takeover) (V2;1).

Kapopa The witch-doctor of the village of **Bobolo**, who helped him hide **Kali Bwana** so he could have her whenever he wished without his other wives killing her (T18;13).

kar (*Amt*) Cold (V1;4).

Kar Komak Odwar of the phantom bowmen of **Lothar** on Barsoom. He was commander of the fleets of Lothar in ancient times, but for long millennia his persona was only one of the phantom bowmen materialized by

Tario, Jeddak of Lothar. He was Tario's favorite, however, and every time Tario materialized bowmen, Kar Komak was one of them. Tario believed that by constantly suggesting the reality of Kar Komak several times a day he could eventually make him a permanent suggestion in the minds of all creatures. He eventually succeeded on the day Carthoris and Thuvia of Ptarth reached Lothar in 1889, and Kar Komak became material while pursuing the green men of Torquas. Kar Komak hated Tario, however, because he, as a creature of Tario's mind, knew the evil jeddak only too well, and so decided to accompany Carthoris on his search for Thuvia. Being a creature of Tario's brain, he also had the power to create phantom images, and called forth his utan of bowmen to kill a tribe of white apes who had captured him and Carthoris, and again later to kill a horde of green men. He helped Carthoris free Thuvia, returned with them to Helium, and later helped John Carter learn to project both body and matter from world to world (M4; 10–14)(M5).

Kara Vasa The red Barsoomian girl of Phundahl whom Dar Tarus loved and Sag Or coveted. After Dar Tarus' assassination, she fled Sag Or by going to Helium and seeking the protection of John Carter. She later married the restored Dar Tarus and became the Jeddara of Phundahl (M6;12,14).

karad A Barsoomian degree. By a curious coincidence, the Barsoomians divide a circle into 360 measurements, just as Earth people do. A karad is the basis of all Barsoomian measurement — one degree, or karad, at the equator is the base unit, which is subdivided into 100 haads, or Barsoomian "miles" (M4;6).

Karagan Ocean The Polodan ocean which separates the continents of Epris and Unis by an average of about 3500 miles (B1;8).

Karana (Pell) The Xexot word for heaven (P7:2;4–5).

Karbol "Cold country" (Amt). The outermost zone on Amtor's highly inaccurate circular maps. Karbol is actually the south polar area of Amtor, but is represented as being larger than the temperate zone on the maps. At the time of Carson Napier's arrival

in Vepaja, Karbol was largely unexplored (V1;4).

Karendo A tribe of African traders who were friendly both to whites and blacks (TT1;9).

Kargovitch The last ruling house of the tiny Balkan nation Karlova (R;2).

Karis The northern continent of Poloda (B1;8).

Karlova A tiny Balkan nation, hereditary enemy of its equally tiny neighbor Margoth. In the early part of the 20th century they finally began to negotiate for peace in the face of greater enemies, and were allied by the marriage of Prince Boris of Karlova to Princess Mary of Margoth (R;1,17).

Karnath A great ape of the tribe of Kerchak who grew up with Tarzan and was still with the tribe in 1911 (T2;23).

karoo (Pell) A feast in honor of some noteworthy event (P5;14).

karpo (Ape) Middle (TC).

kas (Ape) Jump (TC).

Kas-ki-yeh Apache name of the Mexican town where Geronimo's wife and three young children were murdered (A1;6).

Kash Flag The Kalkar flag (MM2;3). See also Kash Guard.

Kash Guard A corruption of a Va-nah term, used in Kalkar-occupied 22nd century America to mean either a soldier, a body of soldiers, or the authorities in general (MM2;2).

Kau A Khmer warrior under the command of Vama in 1920s Lodidhapura (HM;5).

Kavandavanda The god-king of the Kavuru, inventor of the immortality pellets which kept him looking like a man in his twenties even though he was hundreds of years old. Kavandavanda believed that there was no God, but that he could learn to become a god over time through the accumulation of wisdom, power and experience. He fell in love with Jane Clayton in 1934 (after capturing her to use in the pellets) and would have broken his vow of chastity with her had not his attempt to do so been cut short by the arrival of Tarzan, who shot Kavandavanda dead with a pistol (T19;27–31).

Kaviri The chief of a tribe who lived along the **Ugambi River** in 1912. He made offers of friendship to **Nikolas Rokoff**'s party and was attacked for his trouble by the evil Russian; because of this, Kaviri immediately assumed Tarzan's force to be hostile as well and so attacked his boat, finding out only too late that it was full of **great apes** of the tribe of **Akut**. After his defeat, Kaviri told Tarzan of Rokoff's passage three days before and promised to help him pursue the Russian's party upriver by providing paddlers for his canoes, since the apes were no good at the job (T3;6–7).

Kavuru A strange tribe of white savages in central Africa who were reputed to be eternally young. No one had ever seen one of them and lived to tell until Tarzan made his way to their country in pursuit of **Buira**, daughter of **Muviro**, whom they had abducted. The Kavuru were dreaded for their ability to spirit off young girls, a trick they accomplished by making a strange, hypnotic sound which drew their victims into the jungle in a trance and allowed the physically powerful Kavuru to carry the pliant victim off through the trees. The trance lasted for several hours, so by the time the girl awakened, it was too late. These women were not abducted for sexual purposes (since the Kavuru were a race of celibate priests who believed that sex with a woman would eventually lead to death), but rather for use in making their **immortality pellets**, the chief ingredient of which was the glands of young women. The pills really did work, and worked well — although all of the Kavuru appeared to be in their twenties, the youngest of the tribe joined it in the early 1800s.

The Kavuru kept madmen as slaves rather than killing them because they believed that killing a madman would release the evil spirit within him to possess another Kavuru. Their village was small, built against the side of a mountain, and surrounded by a stone wall. Within was their temple, which was guarded by pet leopards who ate the dead victims of the Kavuru and also served as a source of leopard spinal fluid, another of the ingredients of the pellets (T19;2,4,10,24,27–31).

kazar An Amtorian animal of **Noobol**, which is about the size and shape of a German police dog, but is feathered and has a head, beak and talons like those of a parrot, but no tail or wings. Klookazar (plural form) screech and make hideous cackling noises and are utterly fearless and ferocious pack fighters, but their predilection for stopping to devour any wounded members of the pack makes their use in war undesirable, though they are sometimes kept for hunting (V2;9).

kazor (*Cpk*) Beware (C2;2).

Kazov, Colonel A **Luthanian** army officer of **World War I** (MK2;11).

Keeling Islands A small chain of islands in the Indian Ocean northwest of Australia (T22;29).

Keeper of the Gate The title given to the knight of **Nimmr** who was on duty for the day as officer in charge of the outer gate of the **Valley of the Sepulcher** (T11;9).

Keewazi The **Waziri** warrior whose duty it was to feed and care for **Jad-bal-ja** in Tarzan and **Korak**'s absence. He carelessly let the lion loose one day while Tarzan was on his trip to **Opar** in the summer of 1917 (T9;5).

keld A Va-nah year, made up of ten **ula** (sidereal months), the only observable standard of time in Va-nah. A keld is thus about 272 Earth days long (MM1;6).

Kelley, James One of **Scott Taylor**'s friends who went with him to Africa to kill **Dick Gordon**. He returned safely from the abortive mission but was killed by **Ben**, King of Beasts while stalking Gordon in the Scott library back in **Scottsville, Virginia** (ME; 2,9).

Kelly One of the members of **Corey Blaine**'s gang, who had a shack in **Sonora** (D;6).

Kelly's Feed Store The honest business establishment of **Chicago** that really had nothing to do with the gang which took its name from the fact that they customarily assembled behind it (K1;1).

Kelly's Gang The turn-of-the-century west side **Chicago** gang that **Billy Byrne** practically grew up in. It took its name from **Kelly's Feed Store**, behind which the gang used to hang out. Like other gangs, it was jealously protective of its territory (K1;1).

Kent One of the southeastern districts of England which lies between the Straits of

Dover and the Thames. **Cingetorix** was its king in the first century B.C. (I;1).

Kenya The present day name of the country Tarzan knew as **British East Africa**, in which his second African estates lay (T7;2). **Peter Zveri** promised to make **Kitembo** King of Kenya for his part in the Russian's plans (T14;16).

Kerchak The "king" (alpha male) of the tribe of **great apes** which eventually adopted Tarzan as one of their own. At the time of the baby human's adoption by the she-ape **Kala**, Kerchak was about 20 years old and weighed about 350 pounds. He had a low, receding forehead, red eyes, and smallish ears for an ape. As is usual among the great apes, he became king by his strength and ferocious temper, which often broke out uncontrollably as that of most of his kind does. In one of these rages he caused the death of Kala's baby, prompting her to adopt the orphaned **John Clayton, Jr.**, as her own. It was also Kerchak who killed **John Clayton** and made the baby an orphan in the first place. Kerchak attacked Tarzan in a fit of jealous rage when the latter was 18 and was killed by him, thus promoting Tarzan to kingship (T1;4,11).

Kesner Building The Chicago office building in which **Maggie Lynch** found her first respectable job (GF;5).

Keta A little **Sumatran** monkey befriended by Tarzan while he was there in the spring of 1944 (T22;22).

Ketchum A small town of Blaine County, Idaho (GF;11).

Khamis The witch doctor of the tribe of **Obebe** the cannibal, who insisted that the captured **Esteban Miranda** was actually a river devil in the guise of Tarzan, and thus kept him from the cooking pots that Obebe (who believed Miranda to actually be Tarzan) wanted to send him to. The real Tarzan later killed Khamis after escaping imprisonment in his village (T9;21)(T10;1,22).

Kheybar Alternate spelling of Khyber, the region of India (today Pakistan) where **Atewy** worked with an archeologist in the late 1920s and learned to speak English (T17;2).

Khmer A people of Southeast Asia (probably of Chinese derivation) who ruled **Cambodia** from the 800s to the early 1400s, at which time they were conquered by the **Siamese** and reduced to vassalage. The Khmers built the giant temple city of **Angkor** and others like it, most of which were abandoned and disappeared into the jungle soon after the conquest (HM;1).

Kho One of the **Sto-lu** of Caspak. He tried to abduct **Lys La Rue** on October 8, 1916, and was killed by **Bowen Tyler** for it (C1; 10).

khusa (*Ara*) A kind of dagger or long knife (T11;1).

Kibbu An African village near the village of **Tumbai** in Utengi (T18;1).

Kibuka A Bantu war god (T23;10).

The Kid The alias of **Jerry Jerome**, a 21-year-old ivory poacher of 1931 Africa who had fled there to escape prosecution for the murder of **Sam Berger**. Unknown to Jerome, the man lived and refused to press charges, so Jerome's sister **Jessie** came to Africa to fetch him home. She finally found him searching for his friend the **Old-Timer**, who had in turn been searching for Jessie, the woman he knew only as **Kali Bwana** (T18;4,18,21,23).

Kidder, Tom The foreman of **Olaf Gunderstrom**'s ranch who first found the old man dead (D;2).

Kiel A German port of Schleswig-Holstein on Kiel Bay off the Baltic Sea. During **World War I** it was the main base of the German Imperial Fleet (C1;2).

Kilimanjaro, Mount Famous volcanic mountain of **German East Africa** (modern Tanzania), from whose southern slopes Tarzan first heard the sounds of **World War I** (T7;2).

Kincaid The steamship upon which **Nikolas Rokoff** and **Alexis Paulvitch** took the kidnapped Tarzan, **Jane** and **Jack Clayton** back to Africa, keeping them separated through the whole trip. When Tarzan later commandeered the ship for his return to England, Paulvitch put a **time bomb** on board. The explosion harmed no one, but did maroon the party on **Jungle Island** (T3;1–2, 18–19).

king The bisexual parent and leader of a swarm of Barsoomian **Kaldanes** (M5;5–6).

King The original leader of the *Arrow* mutineers, who was shot in the back by Snipes (T1;13,17).

King, Gordon A young American physician and adventurer who explored the jungles of Cambodia in the late 1920s in search of herb lore with which he might develop new medicines. He became lost in the jungle and stumbled upon the lost **Khmer** city of Lodidhapura, where he won fame as a great warrior and helped a beautiful slave girl to escape a horrible fate. He returned the girl (named **Fou-tan**) to her own city, **Pnom Dhek**, where he learned that she was actually a princess who was bound by duty to marry the evil Prince **Bharata Rahon**, whom she despised. King was forced to flee the city to escape the wrath of Fou-tan's father **Beng Kher** when he found out that King and Fou-tan loved each other. King was then recaptured by the soldiers of Lodidhapura. He escaped the wrath of its king, **Lodivarman** (which he had earned by stealing Fou-tan from him) by curing him of a loathsome skin condition resembling leprosy, from which he had suffered for many years. He was then made a Prince of Lodidhapura and went to save Fou-tan, whose treacherous fiancée he had seen try to kill her father so he could become king sooner. King killed the traitorous Bharata Rahon, married Fou-tan, and their union was at last blessed by the dying Beng Kher, thus leaving King as King of Pnom Dhek (HM).

King, Lieutenant Samuel Adams A cavalry lieutenant of "B" Troop who was assigned to the **Billings** ranch during the Apache uprising of 1881 and developed a strong attraction to **Wichita Billings**. Because **Shoz-dijiji** thought Wichita loved King, he later spared the soldier during a battle when he easily could have killed him. The story eventually got back to Wichita who, though she did not love King, was glad he was not dead. In 1886, he repaid Shoz-dijiji by helping him escape from the cavalry, and he later found and returned **Nejeunee** to him (A1;15–18)(A2;11–12).

King of Ganado One of the prize bulls of the Rancho del Ganado (GH;1).

King of Glory The legendary Khmer ruler Yacovarman (HM;15).

King's Corridor The main corridor of the four entering the royal dome of the **Minunian** city of Veltopismakus (T10;13).

King's Road A major thoroughfare of Lustadt (MK1;10).

Kinzie Street A street of Chicago's west side, near the railroad yards (K1;1).

Kircher, Fraulein Bertha A German spy of **World War I** who was actually an English agent (named the **Honorable Patricia Canby**) spying on the Germans in **German East Africa**. Lost behind English lines, she was captured by Tarzan after he rescued her from a lion, but succeeded in escaping from him with his **locket**, which had been given to her by **Hauptmann Fritz Schneider** after he took it from Jane. Tarzan later caught up with her and recovered the locket, but spared her life and later even attempted to save her from a group of Germany's native troops who had deserted and taken the girl with them into the interior; he would have succeeded had not the resourceful young lady escaped first. Tarzan then put her under his protection and set up a camp for her near the **great ape tribe** of Go-lat, and she went with the ape **Zu-tag** when he saved Tarzan from the savage **Wamabo** tribe. She there met **Lt. Harold Percy Smith-Oldwick**, also a prisoner of the tribe, who fell in love with her, but the two were recaptured by **Lt. Usanga** and the native troops who had brought Kircher into the interior. Usanga then tried to carry the girl off in Smith-Oldwick's plane but was foiled by Tarzan, and she and Smith-Oldwick flew off together, only to be soon afterward stranded in the deadly **desert** of western **Tanganyika** when the plane was forced down after colliding with a vulture. They were captured by the mad race of **Xuja** and taken to that lost city, where she was abducted by the mad prince **Metak**, saved by Tarzan and the lieutenant, and returned to civilization, at which point Tarzan finally found out her true identity (T7;5–24).

Kiron A well-formed Amtorian soldier of **Thora** who dared to speak out against his government and was to be imprisoned for it. He joined **Carson Napier** in his mutiny aboard the *Sofal* in 1929 (V1;9).

Kitembo A renegade Basembo chief of the 1920s who led the communist **Zveri**

expedition to raid **Opar** for its gold in 1928. He hoped to be revenged against the British (who had made him an outlaw) by this and to get rich and powerful besides. He was later killed by Tarzan when he tried to abduct **Zora Drinov** from the rapidly disintegrating expedition (T14;1–2,17).

kiva A ceremonial building of the Pueblo Indians. A kiva is windowless and can only be entered by climbing to the roof via a ladder, then descending through a trap door in the roof via another ladder inside (T19;24).

kl- (*Amt*) The plural prefix for words beginning with vowels (V1;8).

Kla "New La" (Oparian). The name given by **Gulm** to **Gretchen von Harben** after he abducted her to be the high priestess in exile of the **Flaming God** (TT2;3).

Kla-de-ta-he An Apache warrior who was killed in a trap set by white soldiers in the late 1850s (A1;2).

Klamataamorosal A king of the Minunian city of **Trohanadalmakus** at some time in the distant past who decreed that all noblemen and warriors should mate with slaves to keep new, strong blood coming into the nobility so they would not weaken through inbreeding. The idea caught on in other cities and in modern times is a normal standard of Minunian life (T10;6).

Klangan "Birdmen" (*Amt*). A species of Amtorian humanoid which possesses many of the characteristics of true birds, such as feathers and hollow bones. They had very dark skins and "low, receding foreheads [with] huge, beaklike noses, and undershot jaws; their eyes were small and close set, their ears flat and slightly pointed. Their chests were large and shaped like those of birds, and their arms were very long, ending in long-fingered, heavy-nailed hands. The lower part of the torso was small, the hips narrow, the legs very short and stocky, ending in three-toed feet equipped with long, curved talons. Feathers grew upon their heads instead of hair. Similar feathers grow at the lower extremity of the torso in front, and there is another, quite large bunch just above the buttocks...."
    The feathers on an Angan's head stand erect when the birdman is excited, but usually lie flat; there are no feathers on the creature's

huge, bat-like wings. Klangan can speak but are very stupid and unimaginative. They are perfect slaves as long as they are well-treated, being totally loyal to their master until he dies, sells them, gives them away or whatever; their loyalty is then transferred to the new master. Unless motivated by primitive instincts (hunger, sex, etc.) they will only act under orders. Klangan are very garrulous and love to gossip and sing. Many of them serve the **Thorists** (V1;8,11,14).

Klatz One of the German sailors of the **U-33** on its voyage to **Caspak** in 1916 to 1917 (C3;5).

kle-go-na-ay (*Apa*) The full moon (A1;2).

Kleeto A Suvian slave girl in the palace of **Meeza**, king of a village of **Jukans**, who befriended **David Innes** while he was a "guest" of Meeza's in 1929. When Innes and **Zor** of **Zoram** escaped, they took the girl with them back toward Suvi, planning to do something once there about **Do-gad**, the King of Suvi's nephew, who had pursued her out of Suvi before he had decided he wanted **Dian the Beautiful** instead. Kleeto and Zor were later married and in 1930 had a son (P6;7,12–16,28).

Klein The secretary of King **Alexis III** of **Margoth** who was outwitted by **Princess Mary** so she could escape marrying **Prince Boris** of **Karlova** (R;6).

klij (*Apa*) Snake (A1;2).

klij-Litzogue (*Apa*) The yellow snake; probably either the ringneck snake, the yellow rat snake, or the Western shovel-nosed snake (A1;2).

Kling A dark-skinned people of Southeast Asia related to the Tamils (PB;9).

Klo-sen A Ned-ni Apache runner of the 1870s (A2;1).

kloo (*Amt*) The number two. This is probably pronounced or accented differently than the plural prefix **kloo-**, because both are used as prefixes. In other words, "**klootogan**" means "second high man" and not "high men" (V1;8).

kloo- (*Amt*) The plural prefix for words beginning with consonants (V1;8).

klookor "Two daggers" (*Amt*). An Amtorian military rank roughly equivalent to a major (V4;44).

Kloonobargan "Hairy Men" (*Amt*). A race of ape-like savages of the Amtorian continent of **Noobol** who use slings and bows. They are extremely stupid and unimaginative and smell awful (V1;14) (V2;5).

Klootag Lat "Gates Avenue" (*Amt*). The eight mile long avenue which follows the outer, semicircular wall of the Amtorian city of **Havatoo**, on which many of its shops, businesses and factories are located (V2; 15).

klootogan "Second high man" (*Amt*). The mature eldest son of an Amtorian **togan**, or baron (V5;4).

klootoganja "Second high woman" (*Amt*). The consort of an Amtorian **klootogan** (V5;4).

Klopkoi A famous European portrait painter of the late 19th and early 20th centuries (R;15).

Klovia A small city of **Margoth** that was the site of the king's summer palace (R;6–7).

Klu (*Ape*) The hen (TC).

klu-kal (*Ape*) Egg (TC).

Klufar An Amtorian scientist of about 3000 years ago who propounded the "theory" of relativity of distance (V1;4).

Knibbs, Henry Herbert (1874–1945) The Canadian poet who composed "Out There Somewhere," the poem upon which much of *Return of the Mucker* was based, and which is included (in parts) in that novel (K2;2).

knife, hunting Tarzan's second weapon of proficiency was his dead father's hunting knife, which he found in the deserted **cottage** (after learning how to open it at the age of ten) and promptly cut himself on, thus apprising himself of its use. Only a few hours later it saved his life when he used it to kill **Bolgani**, the gorilla, and he always kept the knife near him or on his person for the rest of his life (T1;6).

knife, Wieroo When a **Wieroo** has advanced to the wearing of a completely red robe (see **colors, Wieroo**), he is given a long, curved knife. Such Wieroos are the only members of their race allowed to carry weapons (C3;3).

Knights of Christ and the Temple of Solomon The full name of the **Knights Templar** (T11;9).

Knights of Columbus A Roman Catholic fraternal organization mentioned by James Hunter Blake to Prince **Gobred** of **Nimmr** when asked what new orders of knighthood had arisen in the outer world since the time of **Richard I** (T11;14).

Knights of Labor The first important labor organization in the United States, founded in 1869, which rapidly declined after the founding of the American Federation of Labor in 1886. It was mentioned by James Hunter Blake to Prince **Gobred** of **Nimmr** when asked what new orders of knighthood had arisen in the outer world since the time of **Richard I** (T11;14).

Knights of Pythias A fraternal organization mentioned by James Hunter Blake to Prince **Gobred** of **Nimmr** when asked what new orders of knighthood had arisen in the outer world since the time of **Richard I** (T11;14).

Knights of the Diamond The name used by James Hunter Blake to explain baseball players to Prince **Gobred** of **Nimmr** (T11;14).

Knights of the Squared Circle The name used by James Hunter Blake to explain boxers to Prince **Gobred** of **Nimmr**. Foremost among them, he said, was **Sir Dempsey** (T11; 14).

Knights Templar Medieval order of knighthood to which James Hunter Blake claimed to belong when he stumbled into **Nimmr** in 1921 (T11;9).

knob stick A short, heavy club used by many African natives as a weapon (T4;12).

knobkerrie see **knob stick** (TT1;7)

ko (*Amt*) Fast (V4;44).

ko (*Pal*) Mighty (T8;2).

Ko A **Mezop** of Pellucidar who was assigned to the EPS *Sari* on her trip to **Kali** in 1931 (P7:2;3).

Ko-tah A powerful **javadar** of **Laythe** in **Va-nah** who wished to marry **Nah-ee-lah** and thus become **jemadar** after **Sagroth's** death. If Nah-ee-lah refused, Ko-tah had planned to kill Sagroth and the girl and take the throne anyway, as he was in line to the throne and very popular in Laythe — a popularity born of fear for Ko-tah's power and money and the things they might accomplish, and not of any love for the man himself. By the request of **Moh-goh**, one of Ko-tah's men whom **Julian 5th** had saved from the **Kalkars**, Julian was made a guest of Ko-tah's, leading Nah-ee-lah to believe that Julian had betrayed her father; she was shown differently when Ko-tah staged his coup and Julian defended Sagroth. Ko-tah did succeed in taking over Laythe, only to have the victory stolen from him by Julian, who put a sword through the over-ambitious noble (MM1;9–10,13).

Ko-tan "Mighty Warrior" (*Pal*). King of the **Ho-don** of **Pal-ul-don**, whose capital was **A-lur**. He hated **Ta-den** and would have put him out of the way to keep him from his daughter **O-lo-a**, but Ta-den fled into the wilds to escape. Ko-tan was not at all pleased with Tarzan's claim to be the **Dor-ul-otho** and was only too happy to collaborate with **Lu-don** against the ape-man, whom he felt was undermining his power. Ko-tan was later assassinated by the drunken **Bu-lot**, whom he had publicly insulted (T8;2,8–11,15).

Ko-va One of the **Floating Islands** of Pellucidar whose black inhabitants are hostile to those of **Ruva** (P6;24).

Ko-vo A kamadar of the Laytheans of **Va-nah** who was a friend of **Moh-goh** the paladar, with whom **Julian 5th** escaped Kalkar City #337. Ko-vo was the honorary guard of the tunnel to Laythe when Moh-goh and Julian arrived (MM1;11).

kob (*Amt*) The basic unit of Amtorian linear measure. One kob is ⅒ of a **hita** (degree) at the equator, roughly 2.5 miles. How this was derived considering the deplorable state of Amtorian cartography is not clear (V2;11).

kob (*Ape*) Hit (TC).

Kobol A city-state of Barsoom's western hemisphere which lies due south of **Bantoom**. It is ruled by a **jed** (M7;1).

Kod The slave-buyer for **Tyros the Bloody**, Jong of Mypos when **Carson Napier** and **Duare** came there in 1930 (V4;7).

Kodj One of the Amtorian crew of the

Thorist ship *Sofal* when **Carson Napier** started a mutiny on it in 1929. He joined the mutineers, but objected to Napier being **vookor** (captain) and immediately started spreading unrest (V1;10).

koho (*Ape*) Hot (TC).

koku A medieval Japanese unit of currency (K1;10).

Kolani The real name of **Jimber-jaw**, a.k.a. **Jim Stone** (J;4).

kolantar "Fast landship" (*Amt*). The equivalent of a fast cruiser among the landships of **Middle Anlap** on Amtor, built to be faster and more navigable than a **tonglantar**, but still very dangerous in battle (V4;44).

Kolchav The name by which **Andresy** first befriended the exiled **Count Lomsk** and got him to write a letter of introduction to **Prince Ferdinand** (LL;9).

Kolk The son of **Goork**, King of **Thuria**. Kolk's sister was **Canda the Graceful One**, who was stolen by **Dacor the Strong One** as a mate. Kolk was the first to bring to **David Innes** news of **Hooja the Sly One's** whereabouts after he had kidnapped **Dian the Beautiful** late in 1913 (P2;6).

Kolrado The name of a tribe of Americans in the post–Kalkar 25th century who apparently had built back up to medieval level of technology because they had excellent steels (they made **long swords, lances** and **knives**), well-established trade routes, and understood the necessity for peaceful co-existence among the tribes once the Kalkars were gone. They traded with all of the peoples of the American West of their time, unmolested because of the excellence of their goods (MM3;1).

Komal The god of **Lothar** on Barsoom. The Lotharians believe that Komal is real and must eat real food in order to radiate the substance of thought that minds form into reality. **Tario** feeds **Realists** to Komal when no **Torquasians** are available, because (as he says) if they believe that they are the only real Lotharians, then they are the only proper food for Komal. Komal is of course a huge **banth**, and so **Thuvia** could control him like any other banth when Tario dropped her, **Carthoris** and **Jav** into his lair, enabling them to escape through the back way (M4;7,9).

Komodoflorensal The Prince of Tro-hanadalmakus in Minuni, son of King Aden-drohahkis. Tarzan saved Komodoflorensal from being devoured by a Zertalacolol woman, for which he was understandably grateful. He taught Tarzan the language and culture of Minuni and was captured by the Veltopismakusians in the same battle as Tarzan and enslaved in their mines. He and Tarzan escaped together and rescued the slave girl Talaskar, who turned out to be a princess of the city of Mandalamakus, whom he married shortly thereafter (T10; 6,12–21).

Kooaad The capital of Vepaja, carved (like other Vepajan cities) from the trunks of living trees more than a thousand feet above the ground (V1;3–5,8).

kor (*Amt*) Dagger (V2;14).

kor (*Ape*) Walk (TC).

kor (*Pal*) Gorge (T8;3).

Kor A Niocene warrior of the tribe of Nu who made the finest spearheads of any warrior in the tribe (E2;2).

Kor-An The leader of the group of Gath-olian herdsmen who captured John Carter near Gathol during the Panar siege in 1940. Carter was still disguised as a Black Pirate after his escape from Kamtol and the herds-men took him for one despite his protesta-tions. They roped him and dragged him be-hind their thoats until he was half dead, but the dragging rubbed off most of his black pig-ment, revealing to the men their mistake. Carter then challenged Kor-An to a duel and made a fool of him, but did not kill him (M10:3;2).

Kor San The Jeddak of Duhor on Bar-soom, whose daughter Valla Dia was a great beauty. He refused to give her in marriage to Jal Had of Amhor because she was his only child and he wished her to marry one of his jeds so that one of his own blood might rule after his death. Because of this refusal, Jal Had sacked Duhor while its navy was away at war with Helium (M6;4).

Kor-ul-gryf "Gorge of Gryfs" (*Pal*). A gorge of Pal-ul-don uninhabited by the Waz-don because of the monstrous gryfs which in-habit it (T8;3).

Kor-ul-ja "Gorge of Lions" (*Pal*). The gorge of Pal-ul-don inhabited by the Waz-don tribe befriended by Tarzan, ruled first by Es-sat, then Om-at (T8;3–4).

Kor-ul-lul "Gorge of Water" (*Pal*). A gorge of Pal-ul-don inhabited by a Waz-don tribe unfriendly to that of Kor-ul-ja (T8;3).

Korad An ancient, ruined city of the Orovars of Barsoom inhabited intermittently by one of the groups of the horde of Thark, as one of their incubators is nearby (M1).

Korak "Killer" (*Ape*). The name given to Jack Clayton by Akut and always used by the young man while in the jungle. He earned the name by his rapid adaptation of the jungle law, kill or be killed, and he always made his kills in silence, just as his father had marked his by a victory scream. A few months after his renaming, and shortly after his rejection by a tribe of great apes, he rescued a little girl named Meriem from her cruel foster father, the Sheik. She became his friend and they ma-tured together thereafter, living in the trees with Akut and communicating in the lan-guage of the great apes. After killing an ape who tried to abduct her, Korak's true feelings for her awakened, but she was abducted shortly thereafter by a black tribe who recog-nized her and wished to return her to the sheik for a reward, thus forcing Korak to pur-sue. He arrived after they had already sold her to Jenssen and Malbihn and, thinking she had been eaten by the savages, he drove them from their village with a baboon army, then went off to live alone in the jungle for another year, not realizing that Meriem was less than one hundred miles away at Tarzan's estate. He eventually wandered into that area and saw her, but would not approach her because he thought she loved the Honorable Morri-son Baynes. He later ran into Baynes and thus learned of the girl's abduction by Malbihn, whom he then pursued. He rescued her, was reunited with his parents, married Meriem, and returned to London (T4;6–27).

Kord The jong of the Amtorian nation of Korva whose power was usurped in the late 1920s by the Zani party and their leader, Mephis. Kord was imprisoned in Amlot after his refusal to rule as a figurehead under Mephis, and his nephew Muso took over as acting jong for the loyalists, who made their stand in the city of Sanara. After repeated refusals to bow to Mephis, Kord was shot dead by the dictator in 1930 (V3;5,10).

kordo (*Ape*) Dance (TC).

kordogan (*Amt*) An officer roughly comparable in rank to a sergeant (V3;7).

korgan "Daggerman" (*Amt*). Warrior or soldier. The only non-scientific ruling class of Havatoo, who live in a large section of the city named for their class (V2;14).

Korgan Lat "Warrior Avenue" (*Amt*). The largest avenue of Havatoo, which leads from the center of the outer wall (at the **Tag kum voo Klookorgan**) to the central hub of the city, bisecting it exactly (V2;15).

Kormor The capital city of **Morov** on Amtor; it was a dirty, drab, grey place, littered and bleak. It had not always been so—once it had been a thriving city filled with living people, but these had been largely replaced by the **zombie** slaves of the mad **jong**, **Skor**, who wished to create a nation of living dead entirely obedient to his will. Very few of the living remained in the city by 1929, and those were very old because they had no way to get **longevity serum** from outside Kormor (V2; 10,12,17–20).

Korsar Az "Korsar Sea" (*Pell*). The ocean which washes the western shores of the Pellucidarian continent on which the **Empire of Pellucidar** lies. It is roughly two thousand miles long from north to south and is connected to the **Sojar Az** by the **Nameless Strait** (P3;3)(P4;16–17)(P7:2;1)(P7:4;1).

Korsars The fierce sea rovers of Pellucidar, descendants of a shipload of pirates ("corsairs") who, lost and trapped by ice in arctic seas, had eventually happened through the north **polar opening** of the Earth and into Pellucidar in the early 1500s. They interbred with Pellucidarian women and so gained many Pellucidarian traits, but not all; for instance, Korsars have facial hair, while true Pellucidarians do not. The Korsars maintain a piratical lifestyle, raiding and conquering rich countries and poor in their huge galleons, high in the poop and forecastle and loaded with sails. The Korsars use **harquebuses** and **cutlasses** and dress in gaudy and colorful clothes with sashes and kerchiefs around waists and heads. They are unbelievably brutal, enjoying killing for the fun of it, and

advancing in social position through assassination and treachery. They first came to the notice of **David Innes** and the **Empire of Pellucidar** in 1924, when they began raiding the northernmost and southernmost portions of the Empire. They were repelled, however, by the Empire's more advanced weaponry (P3;1).

Korth One of the warriors of **Nadara's** tribe. He was a large and ferocious bully who was cordially hated by everyone in the tribe. Korth tried to take Nadara as his own late in 1911, but was killed by **Waldo Emerson Smith-Jones** in protection of the girl (CG1; 4,8–9).

Korus, Lost Sea of The south polar sea of Barsoom, its only remaining above-ground sea, though it is no doubt considerably smaller than in ancient times. Korus is fed only by the river **Iss** and drains into the underground sea of **Omean** (M2).

Korva The Amtorian country occupying Southern **Anlap**, which was ruled by a **jong** until the nationalistic and dictatorial **Zani** party took over there in the late 1920s following a disastrous war. Thanks to **Carson Napier** and the **Toganja Zerka**, the Zanis were overthrown in 1930 and the jong restored to his throne. For this service and that of saving the young **janjong** from abduction, Napier was made a **tanjong** of Korva. The capital of Korva is **Amlot** and its chief seaport is **Sanara** (V3;5–18).

Korvan Don **Tangor's** assumed name when he went into **Kapara** as a spy for **Unis** in 1940 (B2;2).

Korvas A dead city of ancient Barsoom which is mentioned in "**John Carter and the Giant of Mars**" as lying not too far from Helium. It was here that **Pew Mogel** set up his secret base and laboratory, to which he lured John Carter and **Tars Tarkas** in an attempt to kill them. Beneath the city, in a large cavern, was a city of mutated, intelligent **ulsios** (M11A;2–8).

Kota (*Ape*) The tortoise (T7;11).

Kovudoo The chief of the African savages who kidnapped **Meriem** from **Korak** to return her to the **Sheik** for a reward, but were tricked by **Sven Malbihn** and **Carl Jenssen** into selling her to them. His village was later attacked by Korak and his **baboon** allies, who drove the natives away so there were none left from whom Korak could find out what had happened to Meriem (T4;11–15).

kraal (Afrikaans) An enclosed village or stockade (T12;1).

Kramer A shopkeeper of Tafelberg who found the "Mad King" Leopold of Lutha after he escaped from Blentz and brought him to Tafelberg Sanitorium. He also helped Barney Custer after his escape from Blentz, and tracked Coblich and Maenck to their hiding place after they kidnapped the king, then reported the abduction to Custer, thus saving the king (MK1;7,11–12).

Krantzwort, Captain The Luthanian officer of Blentz whom Barney Custer (disguised as Leopold of Lutha) forced to escort him and the Princess Emma von der Tann out of Blentz in September of 1914 (MK2;9).

Kraski, Carl A handsome, well-built Russian dancer of the early 20th century who was one of Flora Hawkes' co-conspirators in her plan to rob Opar of its gold. At Hawkes' suggestion, he got Tarzan to drink a cup of drugged coffee and left him in the jungle for the Oparians to find. Later, after the failure and disintegration of the expedition, Tarzan found the group wandering in the jungle and saved them, but lost his pouch of diamonds while preparing camp. Kraski pocketed the treasure, hoping to take it back to London right under the noses of his benefactor and fellow plotters. He sneaked off into the jungle the next day and encountered Esteban Miranda, who killed him with a spear and took the bag of diamonds (T9;3–7,10,15,18–19).

Krause, Fritz A German wild animal trapper who bought the aphasic Tarzan from Abdullah Abu Nejm late in 1938 to exhibit in a circus as a wild man. After the mutiny aboard the *Saigon*, he was imprisoned by the mutineers, but after the shipwreck, Tarzan kicked him out of camp with the other ones. He came back six weeks later (during Tarzan's absence from camp) and stole guns, supplies, and Janette Laon, but Tarzan caught up with him soon afterward and killed him (T24; 1–8,11,16,19–22).

Krause, Kitty A friend of Jane Porter and Hazel Strong when they were all young ladies in turn-of-the-century Baltimore. She was a social climber who had first married a Mr. Peters (the Cotton King), was widowed, then married Prince Sborov. In 1934, she talked Jane into flying from London to Nairobi with her on her private plane (Jane was headed back to Tarzan's estate and Kitty was embarking on a self-financed expedition to seek out the Kavuru secret of longevity). After her plane crashed she was absolutely useless, carrying on in a hysterical manner until the Prince split her skull open during their first night on the ground (T19; 1–12).

Kraut, General A German (as one might suspect) general stationed in German East Africa just before the outbreak of World War I. He was Hauptmann Fritz Schneider's commander (T7;1).

kree-gor (*Ape*) Scream (TC).

Kreeg-ah! (*Ape*) "Beware" or "Danger" (T6:8).

Kreff, "Smooth" The foreman of Wichita Billings' ranch in 1880s Arizona who tried both to rustle her cattle and make time with her, but fled when he was found out (A2;13,16–19).

kris A wavy-bladed knife favored by Malays (T22;7).

kro (*Cpk*) Bow (C1;9).

Kro-lu "Bow-men" (*Cpk*). The second most advanced human race of Caspak, above the Band-lu but below the Galus. Kro-lu are purely human in appearance and neolithic in development, possessing archery, agriculture, domesticated animals, pottery, organized villages, etc. Given time, a Kro-lu may become a Galu (C1;9).

Kroona An old Amtorian woman of the city of Kormor, one of the few living people of that city. She helped Carson Napier, Duare and Nalte of Andoo hide from Skor after they escaped his palace in 1930. She and the other living Kormorites were old because Skor had banned the production of longevity serum and destroyed existing supplies, since his zombies did not need it (V2;19).

Krovac, Pete A "straw boss" at the International Machine Company of 1910s Chicago. He was a troublemaker who worked for Harold Bince to try to get rid of Jimmy Torrance (EE;18–19).

Kru The Ganak of Pellucidar who became chief of his tribe after **Wilhelm von Horst** killed **Drovan**. Von Horst also helped Kru by killing **Tant**, the only other claimant to the position, but the ungrateful Kru tried to execute von Horst anyway (P5;19–20).

Krutz The butler of the **Smith-Jones** family (CG2;6).

Ku Klux Klan A secret organization of the southern United States formed during the post–Civil War reconstruction to harass, terrify and often eliminate blacks they considered troublesome, i.e., any that showed any spirit or ability to advance beyond the semi-slavery of field work or sharecropping. The organization still exists today, though not as popular or powerful as it once was. Members wear long white robes and tall, hooded masks (T15;13).

Kubla Khan (1215–1294) The Great Khan, the grandson of Genghis Khan. He ruled China from 1279 to 1294 as the first ruler of the Yuan (Mongolian) Dynasty (T22;27).

Kudu (*Ape*) The sun (T6:12).

Kulan Tith The Jeddak of Kaol on Barsoom during the late 19th century. He still believed in the discredited **Thern** religion and allowed **Matai Shang**, **Thurid**, and their hostages to remain as guests of his palace until **Thuvan Dihn** and John Carter exposed them. Since Thuvan Dihn was his great friend, Kulan Tith gave him the benefit of the doubt and ordered Matai Shang to release the red girls with him so that everyone could see if they were really Dejah Thoris and Thuvia of Ptarth, as Thuvan Dihn and John Carter claimed. Matai Shang of course fled with the girls after this, leaving Kulan Tith very much embarrassed. He afterward allied his kingdom to **Helium** and sent men out to help in the invasion of **Okar**. Later, Thuvan Dihn promised Thuvia to him in marriage, but after seeing how much she and **Carthoris** loved each other, he gave up his right to her (M3;7)(M4;14).

Kulonga A black cannibal of west Africa, the son of **Mbonga**, who was the first human (other than himself) Tarzan ever saw. Kulonga killed **Kala**, Tarzan's adoptive mother, and was himself stalked and killed by Tarzan soon afterward, but not until the ape-man had stolen Kulonga's **bow** and **poisoned arrows** and learned the location of his village (T1;9).

kum (*Amt*) Of (V2;11).

kung (*Amt*) The name of the letter which makes the "k" sound (V1;9).

Kung Kung Kung "K K K" (*Amt*). The Amtorian initials of the mutineer group "Soldiers of Liberty" aboard the **Thorist** ship **Sofal** in 1929 (V1;9).

kunh-gan-hay "Fire place" (*Apa*). Camp (A1).

Kurch An Amtorian criminal of **Sanara** who was murdered (in an unrelated crime) the night the **Janjong Nna** was abducted (V3;17).

kut (*Ape*) Hole (TC).

Kut-le A mighty **Apache** warrior of the **Cho-kon-en** who was renowned for his courage (A1;15)(A2;6).

Kwamudi The native headman of B.O. Pictures' safari to the **Ituri Forest** in 1932. He and his men deserted the safari after the **Bansuto** attacked them, but they were caught and killed by the hostiles anyway — all except Kwamudi himself, whom they took back to their village to eat (T17;2,8,10).

Kwantung A province of southeast China (T22;26).

Kyomya A native lad of about 19 who was a slave in **Alemtejo**. He was assigned to the person of **Sandra Pickerall** when she became Goddess of Alemtejo in 1938 and was killed by **Ruiz**, the high priest, while trying to protect Sandra from Ruiz's advances (T23;12,14).

L-42-X The vault beneath building 4-J-21 of Ras Thavas' complex in which lay the bodies of **Hovan Du** and the **white ape** with half of his brain (M6;3).

L-ray *see* Ray L

la In the adolescent Tarzan's letter-naming system, the letter "G" (T6:4).

La-ak A Pellucidarian warrior of the island of **Canda** who captured **O-aa** of **Kali** and tried to take her home as a wife, but was undone when he turned his back on her to fight a **ta-ho-az** and she killed him with his own spear (P7:2;2–3).

La-ja A Pellucidarian slave girl in the village of **Basti** while **Wilhelm von Horst** was enslaved there also in 1927. She was blond and slender and at first very sweet-natured, but she suddenly and inexplicably began to defy, fight against, and even run away from von Horst, who was beginning to fall in love with her. He kept alternately finding and losing her until he finally reached **Lo-har**, her home village, and killed the mighty **Gaz**, a warrior who coveted La-ja and whom she had feared would kill von Horst. It was because she loved von Horst that she had tried to make him hate her, hoping to scare him away so Gaz would not kill him (P5;7,21–22).

La of Opar The high priestess of the Flaming God of **Opar**, last outpost of drowned **Atlantis**. She was a beautiful young woman, descended from a long line of high priestesses, who had (as all Oparian women) long black hair and large black eyes. She usually wore a skin depending from a golden waist belt and a large number of gold ornaments, all studded with diamonds, plus a golden **headdress** such as all the priestesses wore. La would have sacrificed Tarzan to the Flaming God, but he saved her from the murderous rage of the priest **Tha**, and she repaid him by hiding him in the temple, allowing him to escape later through a secret passage that even La did not know about. After seeing the ape-man in action, La fell in love with him and planned to "reveal" him to the Oparians as a messenger from their god whom she would then marry. Tarzan's escape ruined her plans, but she still loved him ever after (T2;20,22,25).

When the amnesic Tarzan returned to Opar in 1913, she again threw herself at his feet, but he (not knowing her in his state) spurned her and stole her sacrificial knife as a weapon for **Albert Werper**, the Belgian whom she had been about to sacrifice when Tarzan intruded. Both for revenge on Tarzan and for recovery of the knife, she and 50 of her priests left Opar (which she had never done before) to track down and destroy Tarzan. They eventually found him (with the help of three **great apes**) and condemned him to death, but La was overcome by love when she saw him again and freed him, escaping with him into the jungle to escape a mad elephant. She eventually returned to Opar with her priests, almost all of whom forgave her—

all, that is, except for the high priest **Cadj**, whom she was later forced to marry by Oparian law (T5;7–8,12–14)(T9;6).

When Tarzan again returned to Opar a few years later and La still did not kill him, Cadj and **Oah**, an ambitious priestess, plotted to overthrow La so Oah could marry Cadj and become high priestess, but La escaped with Tarzan into the neighboring **Valley of the Palace of Diamonds**, where she was captured by the **Bolgani**. Tarzan rescued her and began a revolution among the **Gomangani**, the subhuman Negroes used by the Bolgani as slaves. This revolution resulted in the deaths of most of the Bolgani, and the remainder swore allegiance to La and came with her back to Opar, where they wrested her throne back from Oah and Cadj and killed the latter (T9;7–16).

All went well for La until 1928, when Oah once again succeeded in overthrowing her and forcing her to flee with Tarzan, this time out into the jungle, where she wandered away while he was hunting and became lost. She was captured by the **Arabs of Abu Batn** when they abandoned the **Zveri** expedition, and was taught some English by her fellow captive **Zora Drinov**. She later escaped from the Arabs and met up with **Jad-bal-ja**, Tarzan's lion, who remembered her and protected her until Tarzan was able to find them and return La to her throne, since the Oparians hated Oah and were ready to kill her when La arrived (T14;16–17).

La Rue, Lys The beautiful young fiancée of **Baron Friedrich von Schoenvorts**, a German U-boat commander of **World War I**, who broke off her engagement to him when the war broke out. He later unknowingly sank the ship that she and **Bowen Tyler** were passengers on, and Tyler saved her from the wreck and promptly fell in love with her. After the "allies" captured the U-33, she was accused by the saboteur **Benson** of having had whispered conversations with von Schoenvorts (so as to throw suspicion on her), but it was she who helped the "allies" re-recapture the submarine after the Germans had recaptured it with Benson's help. She and Tyler eventually cleared up the misunderstanding after they had begun to share adventures in **Caspak**, and finally professed their love for one another. On September 11, 1916, she was carried off by **Tsa**, chief of a **Sto-lu** tribe of Caspak, but was rescued a few hours later by

Tyler. They lived for a short while with the Sto-lu, but Tyler became lost on a hunting trip and they were not reunited until October 8, when Lys ran into Tyler while fleeing the advances of Kho, another Sto-lu with amorous intentions. Tyler killed Kho and then he and Lys were married in a simple ceremony of their own devising and set out to await the faint hope of rescue (C1). They eventually moved into the land of the Galus, where they were accepted as friends, and were rescued when Tom Billings and the *Toreador* expedition found them there late in the summer of 1917 (C2;7).

La Salle Street Station   The Chicago train station closest to Billy Byrne's old haunts on the west side (K2;1).

Labor Corps   The Unisan service which replaced trees, repaired broken ground, filled in bomb craters, etc. on the surface of a city after a Kapar attack, wiping out all signs of the bombing to increase Unisan morale and decrease that of the enemy. It was in this Labor Corps that Tangor worked for his first month in Unis (B1;4).

labyrinthodon   A large, carnivorous, salamander-like amphibian of the Triassic period. See also sithic (P1;9).

The Lad and the Lion   A "single" novel first published in 1917, abbreviated LL. It concerns the adventures of Prince Michael who, after fleeing a revolution in his country, becomes amnesiac and winds up wandering north Africa with his only friend, a lion with whom he spent the first few years of his amnesia. There is, of course, a beautiful girl to be won as well.

Ladan   The name given to Thuria (Phobos) by its inhabitants. It is a bizarre world which exists in a peculiar spatial anomaly, such that any object approaching it shrinks to a proportionate size on its surface. Because of this the world is rather large to its inhabitants and possesses forests, lakes and rivers. It is a very rich world where gold, platinum and especially precious gems are to be found in abundance. Indeed, the castle of the Tarids is made of huge blocks carved from the various precious stones. It was to this world that Gar Nal and Ur Jan fled with Dejah Thoris after abducting her, pursued closely by John Carter in the interplanetary flier of Fal Sivas (M8;16).

Ladja   A family and castle of the medieval Amtorian country of Gavo. The Ladjas were friendly to the Pandar and Tolan families until they were conquered and "turned into zaldars" by the wizard Morgas (V5;4,11).

Lady   Lady Greystoke, i.e., Jane Clayton, as she was known to her husband's Waziri followers (T5;9).

Lady Alice   Lord Tennington's yacht, which he took on a cruise around Africa in 1910, bringing along Professor and Jane Porter and William Cecil Clayton and picking up Hazel Strong, her mother and "Mr. Thuran" (a.k.a. Nikolas Rokoff) in Cape Town along the way. On the way up the west coast, the yacht struck a partly-submerged derelict and had her bottom ripped out, forcing the crew and passengers to seek the shore in the lifeboats. One lifeboat (the one with Clayton, Jane and "Thuran" aboard) got separated from the others and drifted for over a week without food, water or oars until it came to shore not five miles south of Tarzan's cottage (unknown to them). The other three boats came to shore quickly a few miles north of the cottage, but their occupants knew nothing of the fate of the lone boat (T2;13, 18,21).

Lady in the Dark   A 1944 movie musical starring Ginger Rogers and Ray Milland (T22;14).

Lafayette Escadrille   A French army flying squadron of World War I which was made up entirely of American volunteers (before the U.S. entered the war). After the U.S. officially entered the war it became the 103rd Pursuit Squadron of the U.S. Army (C1;1).

Lafitte, Jean   (1780–1826) A French-born pirate who preyed upon Spanish and later American shipping in the Gulf of Mexico. From 1806 until the War of 1812 (in which he took part on the American side) he worked the coast of Barataria in Louisiana, and after the War of 1812 he had his base on the site where Galveston, Texas, now stands. In 1820 he fled U.S. reprisals and disappeared from history (PB;1).

Lafitte, John   A small-town boy from 1920s Glenora, California, who after graduating college became a motorcycle cop in order to complete his law studies, then failed the bar exam and was forced to stay in the police for a living. He had never been able to succeed in school or other pursuits to his satisfaction until, as a policeman, he tried to stop his old friend **Billy Perry** from escaping in a homemade dirigible with one million embezzled dollars and was himself hijacked across the Pacific with Perry. He eventually landed on a remote Pacific island where he joined up with a modern-day pirate known as the **Vulture**. He eventually became his second-in-command and stayed with him for two years, until the Vulture caught Lafitte making love to his woman and Lafitte was forced to flee for his life to the island of the **Portuguese**, the Vulture's arch-enemy. He then led the Portuguese and his men to take the Vulture's island, took **La Diablesa** (the Vulture's woman) for himself, and put both the Vulture and the Portuguese out of commission in the process. Lafitte and La Diablesa later married and moved to Paris (PB).

Lafitte, Louis A small-town cobbler of early 20th century **Glenora, California**, a descendant of the pirate **Jean Lafitte** and father of the pirate **John Lafitte** (PB).

Lahore A major city of the Punjab in Pakistan (at that time part of India) from which **Lal Taask** originated (T20;10).

Lajo One of the **Korsar** party who captured **Thoar** of **Zoram** and **Jason Gridley** of **Tarzana** in the **Phelian Swamp** of **Pellucidar** in 1927, thinking Gridley to be a **Sarian** because of his advanced weaponry. Lajo was apparently the most intelligent and capable man of the Korsar party, and was their means of escaping the swamp alive, since their officer had been killed on the way in. Lajo later became the first Pellucidarian to make a parachute jump, over the city of Korsar from the O-220 (P4;14,17).

Lake Dwellers A tribe of people in Niocene Africa who dwelt on a lake in an island in the **Restless Sea**. They were progressing toward a neolithic civilization, as they built houses on pilings and herded **aurochs** (E2;11).

Lake Horus The sacred lake of **Tuen-Baka**, in which **Ashair** and **Thobos** lie. It drains through a small river which passes in a tunnel through the walls of Tuen-Baka, eventually finding the **Zambezi River**. The Ashairians navigate their galleys both upon the river and the lake, which swarms with all

sorts of bizarre fish, many of them predatory (T20;12–17,26–31).

Lake Rudolph A lake of northern **Kenya** (today known as Lake Turkana) which lies right on the **Ethiopian** border (T21;1).

Lake Tana A lake of northwestern **Ethiopia**, source of the Blue Nile. Tarzan was asked to go there in 1935 by **Haile Selassie** to find out what the Italians were up to, but he was sidetracked by running into **Stanley Wood** and being drawn into an adventure in the **Kaji** country (T21;3).

Lakor A Holy **Thern** who accompanied **Matai Shang** on his mission to kidnap **Dejah Thoris** from the **Temple of the Sun** in 1887. He attempted to ambush John Carter, but was killed by **Woola** (M3;2).

Lal Taask A tall, thin Muslim from India, one of the henchmen of **Atan Thome**, who tried to strongarm Tarzan in 1936 after mistaking him for **Brian Gregory**. He was faithful to Atan Thome, and even though he was a coward, he followed Thome all the way to **Ashair**, where they were captured together. He helped Thome in his plans to kill **Queen Atka** and make **Akamen** king, but Thome double-crossed him and Lal Taask swore bloody vengeance thereafter. He was killed by Thome while attempting to make off with the **Father of Diamonds** (T20;1–13,19, 22,29–32).

Lamarck (Full name Jean Baptiste Pierre Antoine de Monet, Chevalier de Lamarck) (1744–1829) A French biologist who proposed a theory of evolution which was later corrected by Darwin and others (T17;25).

Lamech One of the **Midianites** whom **Dr. Lafayette Smith** was forced to shoot dead in order to save **Lady Barbara Collis** from being burned at the stake by the fanatics (T15; 12–14).

Lamour, Dorothy (1914–1996) The stage name of Mary Leta Dorothy Kaumeyer, a film actress best known for her many appearances as a South Seas–type beauty (usually in a sarong), especially in the Bob Hope–Bing Crosby "road" movies (T22;21).

lamp, Barsoomian see **lighting, Barsoomian**

lan (*Ape*) Right (TC).

Lan-O   A Gatholian slave woman in Manator who was given to Tara of Helium to take care of her. It was she who told Tara all about Manator and its customs, and she was the orange princess in the jetan game played for Tara (M5;11,17).

Lan Sohn Wen   The dwar of the first utan of the troops of Horz on Barsoom who captured John Carter when he discovered the Orovars living there. Lan Sohn Wen tried to intercede on Carter's behalf with Ho Ran Kim but failed (M10:1;3–5).

lana   (*Ape*) Sting (TC).

Lana   The sister of Jana, the Red Flower of Zoram in Pellucidar, who was stolen as a mate by a warrior of Pheli (P4;7).

lanai   (Hawaiian) Porch (B1).

lance   One of the weapons of choice of the Julian tribe of post–Kalkar 25th century California. The lance tips were of steel made by the Kolrado people, who traded with the Julians (MM3;1).

The Land of Hidden Men   One of Burroughs' "single" novels, abbreviated HM, which was titled *Jungle Girl* at its first publication in 1931. It concerns the adventures of Gordon King, an American physician on an exploratory trip to 1920s Cambodia who stumbles upon a hidden country deep in the jungle and falls in love with a beautiful princess whom he must rescue from the clutches of the hideous leper king, Lodivarman.

Land of Terror   The sixth book in the Pellucidar series, abbreviated P6. The events within took place in 1929 and 1930, directly after those of *Back to the Stone Age*, and were narrated to Burroughs by David Innes via the Gridley Wave in 1939, but Burroughs did not publish the book until 1944. The events described therein are the adventures of Innes as he fought to get back to Sari after becoming separated from his men on the journey back from Lo-har. He encountered Amazonian warriors, black slave takers, and even giant ants along the way.

Land of the Awful Shadow   The area of Pellucidar over which the Dead World seems to hang, causing permanent darkness at the center and permanent twilight in the penumbra. At the edge of this land lies Thuria, home of one of the more advanced tribes of Pellucidar — the Thurians cultivate land and have domesticated animals, including the enormous lidi (P1;10,15).

The Land That Time Forgot   The first book of the Caspak trilogy, abbreviated C1. The events within took place in 1916 and were found by Burroughs in the summer of 1917 while vacationing in Greenland on his physician's advice. The manuscript was written by Bowen Tyler who, after becoming lost as a captive in a German U-boat, sailed into Caspak and there encountered terrifying adventures while trying to find his way home. He wrote the manuscript, sealed it in his thermos bottle, and hurled it into the sea, from which it was eventually plucked by Burroughs and published in August of 1918.

Lang, Freeman   The B.O. Pictures press agent in charge of covering the 1933 Hollywood homecoming of B.O.'s hottest new starlet, Balza (T17;33).

languages   The following is a list of some of the languages which have appeared in the various works of Burroughs. Not included are the languages Tarzan knew, which are listed below in a separate entry. See individual entries.

Afrikaans	Dialects, 25th Century
Amharic	Kaji
Amtorian	Kaparan
Barsoom, Tongue of	Unisan
Caspak, Language of	Va-nah, Tongue of

languages, Tarzan's   Tarzan was quite a linguist (in addition to his many other accomplishments) and managed to pick up quite a few languages in his life. All of his known languages are listed below, and each has its own entry.

apes, great, tongue of	Minunian
Arabic	Ontharian
Dutch	Pal-ul-don
English	Pellucidarian
French	Swahili
German	Waziri
Latin	West Coast

Lanikai   "A district, a beach, a post office, and a grocery store … on the windward shore of the island of Oahu" in Hawaii, where Burroughs spent some time in the early 1940s and was there visited by John Carter, who told him the story that was later to become *Llana of Gathol* (M10).

Lano (*Ape*) The mosquito (TC).

lantar (Contraction from **lap notar,** "land ship")(*Amt*) The huge, tank-like vehicles used for war in **Middle Anlap** on Amtor. They are built like ships but have multiple rows of huge tank treads, are atomic powered, and bristle with armor and weapons (V4;44).

Laon, Janette The "girlfriend" of **Fritz Krause** when he took Tarzan across the Pacific as a captive "wild man" in 1938. She was a young, black-haired beauty who sided with Tarzan against the cruel treatment afforded him aboard the *Saigon*, and was imprisoned with him after the mutiny. She had been somewhat loose while in the East Indies and her reputation preceded her, making her an "undesirable" to **Penelope Leigh** after the shipwreck. After six weeks on **Uxmal,** she was recaptured by Krause and his men during Tarzan's absence from camp, but was rescued by Tarzan and later married **Hans de Groot,** who did not care about her past (T24;2–4, 7–11,15–24).

lap (*Amt*) Land (V4;44).

Lar The village of the island of **Amiocap** in Pellucidar from which the woman **Allara** was stolen by the **Korsars,** and to which her daughter **Stellara** was taken when she came to Amiocap almost two decades later (P3;3).

Lara A native girl of **Sumatra** who befriended Tarzan and his "**Foreign Legion**" after they killed the **Japanese** detachment posted in her village in the spring of 1944 (T22;14,21–22).

Larok A warrior-artisan of **Dusar** who served **Vas Kor** by duplicating the key to **Carthoris' destination compass** mechanism so Vas Kor could sabotage it (M4;2).

Larsen The captain of the tramp steamer *Saigon* on its ill-fated voyage across the Pacific in 1938 (T24;2).

Lascar (Portuguese) A sailor or soldier of the East Indies (T24;2).

laser, gamma ray A beam of coherent gamma rays is used by the Amtorians for determining the distance of objects and the depth of oceans much as we use radar and sonar (V1;9).

Lasky, Stanley A policeman of Chicago's west side whom **Billy Byrne** saved from some "outside" hoodlums when he was 18, and who later returned the favor by warning Byrne of the false murder rap against him (K1;1).

Lasso Tarzan's first weapon of proficiency, which he learned to make from the grass ropes he had taught himself to braid. He first used the lasso to torment **Tublat,** his hated foster father, and later to kill his enemies (T1;5,9). See also **ga.**

Last Jeddak of Barsoom The title claimed by **Tario, Jeddak** of Lothar (M4;7).

lat (*Amt*) Avenue (V2;13).

Lathrop, June The title character of "**The Girl from Farris's,**" who was for three months a kept woman (under the name **Maggie Lynch**), though she thought herself married to her "benefactor" **John Secor.** She was persuaded by Secor's foster son **Ogden Secor** to "go straight" (he thought her a prostitute), after which she began using her own name again. She worked at ill-paying jobs for a long time while learning stenography at night school, but eventually got a job in Secor's office, though he did not recognize her until she was wrongfully implicated in the robbery of his office some time later. He refused to press charges because he believed in her innocence and she fled west, becoming a waitress in a lunchroom in **Goliath, Idaho,** where the ruined Secor turned up about two years later. They fell in love and she helped him work his way out of alcoholism and poverty, and after she was acquitted of the murder of his foster father, they were married (GF).

latigo A strong leather strip used for tightening the cinch of a saddle around a horse (HB;4).

Latin Although Tarzan had studied written Latin, he could neither speak nor understand the spoken tongue until necessity forced him to learn it while in **Castra Sanguinarius** (T12;7).

Latin, vulgar The inhabitants of **Castra Sanguinarius** and **Castrum Mare,** both Roman and **barbarian,** spoke a vulgar Latin mixed with **Bantu** word elements (T12;6).

lav (*Pal*) "Run" or "running" (T8).

Lavac, Lieutenant Jacques The seaplane pilot who was hired to fly **Paul d'Arnot,** Tarzan, **Mr. Gregory** and their employees from **Loango** to **Bonga** in 1936, but was caught in bad weather and forced down out of gas; he was thereafter a member of the expedition out of necessity. He became infatuated with **Helen Gregory**, and grew moody and brooding after she rejected him. He was imprisoned with Tarzan in **Thobos**, freed with him, and went to rescue d'Arnot and Helen, but was attacked and killed by strange giant sea-horses on the bed of **Lake Horus** (T20;5–14,17–24,29–31).

Lawton, Captain The cavalry officer who replaced **Crawford** as commander of the Indian Scouts after Crawford's death in April of 1886 (A2;10).

Laythe The last city of the civilized U-gas of Va-nah, ruled in the early 21st century by the **Jemadar Sagroth**. It was founded by a group of U-ga nobles who escaped the **Kalkars**, but in their centuries-long flight before finding the perfect hiding place for their city, they lost all records of their technology except for a very few devices. The Laytheans believed there might be other U-ga cities hidden elsewhere in Va-nah, but could not be sure. Laythe was built around the inside of an ancient extinct volcanic caldera, its buildings rising in terraces all around the crater to a prodigious height (the top row was fully a mile above the central plateau of the city). It was of great age, having been built bit by bit over the course of millennia and beautifully landscaped with gardens and artificial streams, pools and waterfalls which could be diverted for fire control.
Julian 5th was brought to Laythe by **Mohgoh**, a Laythean noble whom he had met as a prisoner of the Kalkars. After their escape, Julian became a guest in the house of **Ko-tah**, a powerful noble who aspired to become jemadar by marrying **Nah-ee-lah**, the princess of Laythe. Out of his love for her, Julian accepted Ko-tah's hospitality in order to act as a spy. Ko-tah later staged a coup d'état, killing Sagroth in the process, but was himself killed by Julian soon afterward. The civil war made a surprise Kalkar attack (with Earthly weapons technology given them by **Orthis**) that much easier, though, and the city was sacked and all her people either killed or enslaved except for Nah-ee-lah, who escaped with Julian (MM1;10–14).

Learned Ones The science council of the **Mahars** of Pellucidar. Among their other experiments, they practice vivisection (P1; 10).

leather, Va-ga The leather used by the Va-gas of Va-nah is made from the hides of those killed for food, and is often improperly cured (MM1;7).

lee (*Pal*) Doe (T8;2).

Lee Um Lo The most famous embalmer in Barsoomian history, who lived hundreds of thousands of years ago in Horz. He was supposed to have been such a great embalmer that the dead he embalmed sometimes got up in the middle of their funerals and walked away, failing to realize that they were dead. His end came when the dead wife of a jeddak did not know she was dead after being embalmed by him and walked in on the jeddak and his new bride. Needless to say, that jeddak was none too happy, and Lee Um Lo lost his head the next day (it is not recorded who, if anyone, embalmed him). Prior to his death, he embalmed the corpse of his friend **Lum Tar O**, thus allowing the hideous monster to live on for almost a million years, victimizing the nobility of Horz for ages thereafter (M10: 1;5,9).

Legan A loyalist officer of the army of **Korva** who volunteered to accompany **Carson Napier** on his mission to rescue **Mintep**, **Jong** of **Vepaja**, from the **Zani** capital, **Amlot** (V3;13).

Leicester A British city which was once the seat of **Simon de Montfort, Earl of Leicester** (OT;1).

Leigh, Penelope An English aristocrat, wife of **Colonel William Leigh**, who was with her husband on his yacht when it was taken as a prize by **Wilhelm Schmidt** and his *Saigon* mutineers late in 1938. She was a terrible old nuisance who, after the shipwreck, yammered constantly about Tarzan and **Itzl Cha** being "naked" and nagged her poor husband half to death about how things "should" be done, including kicking the "undesirables" (Tarzan, Itzl Cha, and **Janette Laon**) out of camp. After finding out that Tarzan was actually **Lord Greystoke**, she changed her tune, and they were all rescued by the *Naiad* soon afterward (T24;6–11,15–18,24).

Leigh, Colonel William Cecil Hugh Percival An English aristocrat of the 1930s who owned the *Naiad*, the yacht which was commandeered by **Wilhelm Schmidt** and the *Saigon* mutineers. He was a typical retired army man, but not a bad sort — he took charge of the survivors' camp after the *Saigon* was wrecked on **Uxmal**, establishing order and even following Tarzan's advice most of the time. He and the other survivors were picked up six weeks later by the *Naiad*, which saw their signal fires (T24;6–11,15–18,24).

Leigh-Burden, Patricia The niece of Colonel **William Leigh** who was aboard his yacht when it was captured by **Wilhelm Schmidt** and the *Saigon* mutineers late in 1938. Unlike her aunt, she was not a haughty aristocrat who turned up her nose at Tarzan — as a matter of fact, she started to fall in love with him after the wreck of the *Saigon* and became very angry when he spurned her, reacting by stalking off into the jungle alone to be captured by the warriors of **Chichen Itza** as a sacrifice. Tarzan rescued her soon afterward, and after their rescue from the island told her who he was and that he was already married (T24;6–11,15–24).

Iekay (*Apa*) White (A1).

Leland-Stanford The small but excellent college attended by **Bowen Tyler** in the early 20th century (C1;1).

Lent In the Christian calendar, the 40 days preceding Easter Sunday, a time of fasting and solemn religious observance. The season usually begins in February (T11;12).

Leo The trained lion in **Prominent Pictures**' 1933 film *Tarzan of the Apes*, who went berserk on the set and had to be killed by the real Tarzan (T17;33).

Leopard City The hidden city of **Nimmr**, whose inhabitants wear decorative leopard-skin apparel. Over time, legends among the **Galla** people of the area had come to say that the city was inhabited by a race of **Leopard Men** (T11;12).

Leopard God A huge leopard worshipped by the **Leopard Men** who was supplied with a human voice by the priests via ventriloquism in order to fool its credulous worshippers (T18;9).

Leopard God, Temple of the A huge hut-like structure built on ten foot piles on an island in a small, crocodile-infested river of central Africa. The temple was 200 feet long, 50 feet wide and 50 feet high, with posts to support its roof and a clay-paved altar at one end. Rooms for the priests and priestesses lay behind the altar and a veranda encircled the building, which could not be reached by any landlocked trail, even to get to the banks of the river opposite the island. This precaution proved their undoing, for Tarzan trapped all of the **Leopard Men** who survived the **Utengi** raid of 1931 in their temple, with little food and no way to get to the shore (T18;14).

Leopard Men A cannibalistic African cult of the 1920s and early 1930s who killed their victims with steel claws, wore leopard skins, and filed their teeth down to sharp points in imitation of leopards. They inhabited the **Congo** region and were the followers of **Gato Mgungu**, a once-powerful chief who had slowly lost all of his tribespeople, but had built his power with the Leopard Men in the meantime. They were feared and hated by all other natives, and once Tarzan and the **Utengi** broke their power in 1931, the survivors were either arrested by the European authorities, killed by their own people, or disappeared without a trace (T18).

Leopold II (1835–1909) The King of Belgium from 1865 to 1909, whose barbaric treatment and exploitation of the natives of the **Congo Free State** provoked widespread censure in Europe and forced the black **cannibals** of **Mbonga** to leave that nation and move to the area of **Angola** where Tarzan grew up (T1;21).

Leopold II, King of Lutha Popularly known as the Mad King, Leopold was only a young boy when he was rushed off into imprisonment in **Blentz** castle by his uncle **Peter of Blentz** upon the death of the old king in 1902, leaving Peter as regent until the boy's "mental health" should be restored. He escaped in October of 1912 just as his look-alike cousin **Barney Custer** came to **Lutha** and was taken for Leopold by many people. Leopold lay sick in **Tafelberg Sanitorium** for several weeks before his identity was discovered and he was betrayed to Prince Peter, who had him abducted from the hospital and would have killed him had not Custer rescued him and replaced him on his throne. The ungrateful Leopold, however, realized that the people really loved Custer (who had been impersonating him to thwart Peter's plans) for his courage and nobility, and likewise the Princess Emma von der Tann, Leopold's betrothed, who had fallen in love with Custer. Mad with rage, Leopold ordered his savior executed, and Custer barely escaped with his life (MK1;1–2,7–12).

Leopold turned out to be an even worse ruler than Prince Peter had been, since he had never been groomed for the job and was thus totally unfit for it. His weak nature and worship of those greater than himself allowed Count Zellerndorf, the Austrian ambassador to Lutha, to sway him into allowing Austrian troops into the country at the beginning of World War I and also into pardoning Peter of Blentz and his confederates. Peter promptly lured Leopold back to Blentz and again imprisoned him there, but due to a fortuitous set of circumstances Barney Custer was again able to change places with him and rule the country wisely for a few days while Leopold was forced into Custer's place and almost executed by Prince Peter. The courageous and noble Nebraskan showed up and saved him, but Leopold then tried to trick the Princess Emma into marrying him by convincing her that he was actually Custer impersonating Leopold. The ruse worked too well, however, so that he shot Leopold dead, thus throwing the throne to the nearest and most fit successor — Custer, who assumed Leopold's identity with the blessing of all the nobles (MK2; 2,5–16).

Lepidus, Marcus Aemilius The second husband of Caligula's sister Drusilla, a depraved creature to whom he gave her after dissolving her first marriage. He then took her from Lepidus for himself. Lepidus later became the lover of Caligula's sister Agrippina and she and he plotted with Julia (another sister) to kill Caligula, but they were caught and Lepidus executed in A.D. 39 (I;18).

lepta The plural of lepton, a very small Greek coin which is also used in Cathne (T16;10).

Letari A girl of the village of Lar who fell in love with Tanar the Fleet One when he was captured by the people of Amiocap early in 1925. She later came to the village of Paraht to seek him, but he spurned her and she later

fell in love with Doval, the Adonis of Amiocap, and he with her (P3;4–7).

Lettenhove, Lieutenant Groen de A Dutch guerrilla of Sumatra into whose camp Tarzan came seeking information in the spring of 1944 and joined up with afterward (T22;15–27).

Levy, Nellie A girl of the Teivos of Chicago in Kalkar-occupied 22nd century America who was taken away by one of the Kash Guard to be his woman (MM2;4).

Lewes A British town of East Sussex near which a great battle was fought between the forces of King Henry III and those of the barons on May 13, 1264 (OT;15).

Leybourn One of the sycophantic courtiers of Henry III (OT;1).

Leybourn, Claudia The naive wife of Roger Leybourn, who almost allowed herself to be seduced by de Fulm, Earl of Buckingham in the summer of 1263 but was saved by Norman of Torn (OT;14).

Leybourn, Roger A loyalist baron of medieval England who changed sides after Norman of Torn saved his wife from the advances of de Fulm in the summer of 1263 (OT;14).

liang A Chinese unit of weight equal to approximately 100 grams (CG2;12).

Liba One of the villages of Thuria in the Land of the Awful Shadow in Pellucidar (P7:2;3).

Liberator The series name given to World War II's B-24 bomber (T22;2).

Liberty The magazine in which *Tarzan and the Lion Man* first appeared as a serial.

Lichty A famous Chicago cartoon artist (T22).

lictor (*Lat*) A standard bearer (I).

lidi The Pellucidarian diplodocus, a creature some 80 to 100 feet long which lives only in the Lidi Plains of the Land of the Awful Shadow. Lidis are ridden by the people of Thuria, who live nearby (P1;4,15).

Lidi Plains A large plain frequented by the enormous lidi which lies adjoining (and partially within) the Land of the Awful Shadow (P1;15).

The Life of Our Beloved Mephis A play consisting of 101 episodes, shown in all 100 theaters of **Amlot** every night during the **Zani** period. Attendance of at least one night in ten was obligatory by law (V3;10).

light that devours The Va-ga term for the huge balls of lightning that appear during lunar storms and burn up everything in their paths (MM1;5).

Lightfoot The horse that **Kay White** usually rode while at **Corey Blaine's** dude ranch. It panicked during a lion hunt and nearly killed her (D;5,8).

lighthouse **Tan Hadron** had climbed into an ancient lighthouse of the dead city of **Xanator** to look for signs of **Jahar** when he saw a group of **green men** enter the city with **Tavia** in tow (M7;3).

lighting, Amtorian Artificial lighting is known on most of Amtor, but the scientists of **Havatoo** have developed a soft light which is still brilliant and seems to come from no particular source. This light casts soft shadows, gives off no heat, and can be made to look like sunlight or have any color desirable (V2;15).

lighting, Barsoomian There are several methods by which the Barsoomians light their buildings and streets. The most common is the radium bulb, a glass hemisphere containing the Barsoomian radium powder, which lights dimly but for an immensely long time (M5;4). Barsoomian optical wizardry produces a much brighter light for those able to afford it — rays of light somehow imprisoned between a false glass ceiling and the real ceiling above it (M1;22). The Barsoomian oil lamp generates a gas that burns without a wick, producing a bright and far-reaching light. It is not often used by the **green men** because of the difficulty of obtaining the proper fuel (M1;5). The ancient **Orovars** made torches containing a core of phosphorescent material with a cap on top. The cap can be flipped back to reveal the core, and a thumb button is used to push it up — the more core exposed, the more light emanated. This material gives off no heat and gets no dimmer with age, but even though many of the torches survive as relics from the ancient days, the secret of their manufacture has been lost (M10:1;6). Before the development of this

substance or the discovery of radium, however, the ancients used electric lights not altogether different in principle from our own lighting systems (M7;3).

Barsoomian street lighting is a scientific marvel. The light is completely controlled so that there is no zone of diffused light nor any dense shadows. Reflected light is reabsorbed by the lighting unit and reused (M6;8). Finally, the inhabitants of **Invak** have developed a special light which negates their invisibility, and they use it to light all indoor areas so they can avoid constantly colliding with each other (M10:4;3).

lighting, Minunian Lighting in the dome-cities of **Minuni** is accomplished by the use of windows opening into a central light-and-air shaft, but interior rooms are lit by large (to the Minunians, man-sized) candles 18" tall and 9" wide, which burn very slowly, consuming noxious gases and releasing oxygen in a smokeless fire. The candles were the discovery of an ancient Minunian scientist and were used as much for their gas-burning and oxygen-producing properties as for lighting (T10;12).

lighting, Va-nah The ancient **U-gas** invented a **radium** paint which glows with a phosphorescent light. Rooms which are to be lit are painted with this compound (MM1; 9 10).

Lil The fat old harlot who was the woman of **Pedro**, one of the **Portuguese's** lieutenants (PB;12).

Lilami The beloved of **Kolani**, for whom he had gone bear hunting on the fateful day 50,000 years ago that he had been frozen. **Lorna Downs** bore a striking resemblance to her, enough to convince Kolani until he discovered her true personality (J;3–5).

Limosis Flumen "Muddy River" (*Lat*). The western tributary of the **Tiberis Flumen** in the central **Wiramwazi** valley (T12).

Lincoln The capital of **Nebraska**, which lies about 35 miles north of **Beatrice** as the crow flies (E2;1).

Lincoln Street Chicago street on which **Billy Byrne's** fence operated his business (K1;1).

Lindbergh, Charles (1902–1974) An American aviator who became the first person to fly across the Atlantic solo, nonstop from New York to Paris, in May of 1927 (D;8).

Linee   The closest Sing Lee, Professor Arthur Maxon's Chinese cook, could come to pronouncing "Virginia" (Q;2).

"The Lion"   The eighth short story comprising *Jungle Tales of Tarzan*, in which Tarzan rescued the body of a she-ape from the lion who had killed her because he did not want the lion to eat it and so get the idea that the apes were easy prey. The story took place about 1908 (T6:8).

lion, black   A huge, almost completely black species of lion is native to the valley of Xuja. They are vicious beasts without any fear of man at all, and are as willing to eat humans as any other prey (T7;16–23).

lion, Polodan   Although Tangor never mentioned its Polodan name, he described the beast as lion-like and aggressive, with stripes like those of a zebra (B1;6).

lion, spotted   The normal lion of Pal-ul-don, which is spotted like a lion cub for its whole life (T8;1). See also ja.

lion, striped   A small lion of the forest that rings Pal-ul-don. It is striped like a tiger (T8;1). See also jato.

Lion Man   In the lost city of Cathne, a noble who was born to the position rather than being created so by edict. Each has the responsibility of keeping several war lions for the ruler, and only Lion Men and the ruler may own lions (T16;8,11).

The Lion Man   A B.O. Pictures film shot on location in the Ituri Forest of Africa, starring Stanley Obroski as a wild man raised entirely by lions to manhood as Lord of the Jungle (T17;1–2).

lions, Grabritin   No doubt the descendants of zoo beasts, they were revered by the Grabritin people as the actual rulers of the land, in which they thought of themselves as invaders — "the lions have always been here," they believed. It was necessary to give a human sacrifice to the beasts, especially those inhabiting the Camp of the Lions (ruined London), before a man took a queen as his wife, thereby becoming king (LC;4).

literature, Barsoomian   The ancient Orovars were a very literary race, but most of

their art, literature and records were lost during the untold millennia of war with the green men (M1;11).

Little Boots   *see* Caligula

Little Canyon   A form of execution arena among the Mammoth-Men of Pellucidar; it is literally a little canyon with steep sides. Around the top (some 30 feet above the floor) is a wide ledge where spectators may sit, and in the far end is a barred cave entrance in which **tarags** are kept. In the near end is a corral where several **tandors** are kept. The victims are armed, then both tarags and tandors are released to fight it out with the humans caught in the middle (P5;17).

Little Chamber   A small chamber beneath a small domed temple of Ashair beneath the waters of Lake Horus. It is like a tiny cylindrical closet into which a sacrificial victim is placed. The door is then sealed and water allowed to fill the building above; water then slowly trickles into the Little Chamber, so that after a few hours the victim drowns (T20;24–25).

Little Colorado   A small river near whose headwaters Burroughs camped in the early 1930s and was there visited by John Carter (M8).

Little Eva   A prostitute of late 1910s Chicago who was an habitué of Feinheimer's Cabaret, where she became a friend of Jimmy Torrance's while he was employed there as a waiter. It was her enthusiasm that inspired him to apply for the efficiency expert job at the International Machine Company, where he later got her a job as a stenographer. She fell in love with him, and while his association with her was used as "evidence" of his "bad character" in his trial for murder, observations she had made and evidence she had collected eventually helped to clear him, along with her tireless moral support and speaking out for him to various people. Tragically, she came down with influenza (which developed into pneumonia) after wearing herself down with worry, and died a few hours after Torrance was acquitted, expiring in his arms after telling him that Harriet Holden also loved him (EE;10,15,18–19,22–28).

Little Men   The name given by natives of the Congo region to those people called pygmies by the Europeans (T18;13,15).

Little Mesa   A descriptively named landform of the **Crazy "B" Ranch** in 1880s Arizona (A2;15).

litu   (*Ape*) Sharp (TC).

litzogue   (*Apa*) Yellow (A1;2–3).

Livia   The mother of the Emperor **Tiberius**, whose marriage to Augustus put Tiberius, her child from a previous marriage, in line to the throne (I;6).

Livia Orestella   A Roman girl with whom Caligula became infatuated. He interrupted her wedding ceremony, made love to her in front of everyone, then married her himself, but divorced her a few days later. He banished her in A.D. 40 (I;17).

Livilla   The sister of **Germanicus Caesar** and wife of **Drusus**, son of **Tiberius**. She was seduced by **Sejanus**, who helped her poison her husband, and starved herself to death when she was found out (I;6,15).

Livingston-Browne   An aristocratic family of **Boston** which is friendly to the Smith-Jones family (CG2;4).

The Lizard   A pickpocket and safe cracker of 1910s **Chicago** who tried to rob **Jimmy Torrance** upon the latter's arrival in town, but was sort of befriended by him instead. He was actually a decent sort of fellow who later helped Torrance out when he was badly down on his luck and even got him jobs twice. He was later employed by **Steve Murray** to destroy the accountant's report that would have revealed **Harold Bince** as an embezzler, but did not complete the job after he found Mason Compton's corpse. Thanks to "Little Eva's" belief in Torrance and the friendship he felt for him, The Lizard risked prosecution to reveal in court what he knew, thereby winning Torrance's acquittal (EE;3,8–10,14, 24,28).

lizard, flying, Amtorian   Tiny flying lizards perform the function of pollination for most Amtorian plants, just as bees do on Earth (V4;4).

lizard, white   A great albino lizard, one of the few Barsoomian reptiles, laired in the cavern of the river **Syl** directly beneath **Tjanath** and feasted upon all who came down the river from either upriver or Tjanath until it was killed by **Tan Hadron** and **Nur An** with

weapons left behind by its former victims. It had stinking purple blood and was almost blind (M7;7).

Lizzie   The aging automobile which belonged to the sheriff of early 20th century **Comanche County, New Mexico** (D;2).

Llana of Gathol   The daughter of **Gahan**, **Jed of Gathol** and **Tara of Helium**, and thus **John Carter's** granddaughter; she was as beautiful a woman as her mother and grandmother. While fleeing the bad manners of **Hin Abtol, Jeddak** of the **Panars**, by taking a trip to **Helium**, her ship was attacked by one of Hin Abtol's and she was taken prisoner, but escaped in **Horz** when a group of **green men** attacked the Panars, who had stopped there after Llana sabotaged their ship. She hid in the **pits** of Horz and was found there by John Carter and **Pan Dan Chee**, who promptly threw his sword at her feet in avowal of his dedication. After she brought Carter up to date on events in Gathol, they left Horz by land, Carter's **flier** having been stolen by the now-transportationless Panars. By an error in navigation they ended up at the **Rift of Kamtol**, where they were captured and enslaved by the **First-Born** and Llana was sold to **Van-tija**, the wife of a **dator**. She was eventually rescued by John Carter and they returned to Gathol, where they found the city besieged by the forces of Hin Abtol. Llana was again captured by the Panars and taken directly to **Pankor**, from which her grandfather again rescued her. They headed south toward Helium for aid, but stopped in the **Forest of Invak** for food on the way there and were captured by an invisible Invak patrol. **Ptantus**, Jeddak of Invak, then gave Llana to **Motus**, one of his nobles, but she was again rescued by Carter before the former could do anything dishonorable to her. She was finally returned to her home and accepted Pan Dan Chee as a suitor (M10:1;10–13)(M10:2;1–8,13) (M10:3;4,13)(M10:4;1–2,7–13).

Llana of Gathol   The tenth book in the Mars series, originally published in *Amazing Stories* magazine as a series of four novellas from March to October of 1941. The action of the stories took place around 1939 and were told to Burroughs by John Carter, who visited him in **Hawaii** the next year. The story concerns the title character, Carter's granddaughter, who was captured by and escaped from the **Panars**, a nation of **red men** from the frozen north who planned to conquer **Gathol**. She was discovered hiding by her grandfather and together they adventured among the ancient **Orovars** of **Horz**, the **Black Pirates** of **Barsoom**, the Panars, and the invisible people of the hidden city of **Invak**. The book is abbreviated M10.

lo (*Amt*) Most (V4;24).

lo (*Cpk*) Woman (C2;5).

lo (*Pal*) Star (T8;2).

Lo-har A large village of Pellucidar which lies midway between **Basti** and **Sari** (P5;7).

Lo-har A ship of the line of the Empire of Pellucidar which was taken to the **Korsar Az** by **Hodon the Fleet One** to search for **O-aa** — he found **Dian the Beautiful** instead (P7:3;7).

Loango A seaport of the Congo (about 100 miles north of the Congo River) in which **Paul d'Arnot** first met **Helen Gregory** and her father in 1936 (T20;1–2).

lob (*Ape*) Kick (TC).

Lobongo The chief of the Utengi village of **Tumbai** in the first part of the 20th century (T18;2).

locket The locket of **Lady Alice Greystoke** found by Tarzan in the **cottage** became his greatest treasure, and he wore it about his neck in imitation of the way he had seen the black **cannibals** wear jewelry. He later gave the locket to **Jane Porter** as a token of his love (T1;11,13,20), and it was stolen from her years later by **Hauptmann Fritz Schneider** when he abducted her. Schneider gave it to **Bertha Kircher**, a fact which greatly angered Tarzan when he discovered it (T7;5).

Loco "Crazy" (*Sp*). The name given by the Mexicans to a great **Apache** warrior of the **Chi-hen-ne** tribe in the late 1800s. After the death of **Victorio**, he succeeded to the chiefhood of his tribe (A1;3,20).

Lodas A **Korvan** farmer of Amtor who acted as a spy in **Amlot** for the loyalists during the **Zani** rule. His farm lay five **klookob** (about 12.5 miles) northwest of Amlot (V3;6).

Lodidhapura A lost city of **Cambodia**, hidden in the jungle and forgotten since the time of the **Khmers** almost a thousand years ago. It fought continuously against the nearby

city of **Pnom Dhek**, but had no other contact with the outside world until **Gordon King** stumbled upon it in the early 1920s (HM; 3–5).

Lodivarman The "leper" king of the lost Cambodian city of **Lodidhapura** when **Gordon King** stumbled upon it in the 1920s. Lodivarman was morally as well as physically injured by his condition and wished to spread it to beautiful young women, since he believed a woman had given it to him in the first place. The actual source of the condition was an allergic reaction to the mushrooms he was addicted to eating, and which he would permit no one else to eat. King cured him of the condition (mostly by making him stop eating the mushrooms); Lodivarman was returned to full health after only a few weeks and heaped honors upon King (HM;6–9,13–15).

loincloth, Band-lu The **Band-lu** of **Caspak** usually wear a loincloth made of a snakeskin cured with the head on, and the head depends to the knees in front when worn (C1;9).

Lollia Paulina A very beautiful Roman woman of the 1st century A.D. whom **Caligula** had brought to Rome for his pleasure. He divorced her from her husband **Memmius Regulus**, married her, then divorced her a few days later (I;17,19).

Lolo-lolo A **Xexot** city a few miles south of the **Nameless Strait** in Pellucidar. It was a small, mean city of clay houses and narrow, crooked streets, but was still a walled city an amazing thing in primitive Pellucidar (P7:2;4).

Lomsk, Count Maximilian A sycophantic "friend" of **Prince Ferdinand's** who was already dissolute and lecherous by the age of 17. He was exiled after the incident where he was found with the prince and two common girls in the royal hunting lodge, and while in exile was befriended by the revolutionary **Andresy**. Lomsk gave Andresy a letter of introduction to Prince Ferdinand so Andresy and Ferdinand could hatch a plot to overthrow **King Otto** so Lomsk could go home. After King Otto was overthrown and Ferdinand made king, he called Lomsk home and made him a general and Chief of Staff. It is not known what happened to Lomsk after Ferdinand's assassination (LL;7,9,19,23).

Lonay The pack leader of the sheep and guard dogs of the tribe of Julian in the post-Kalkar 25th century American West. He belonged to the Vulture, Julian 20th's younger brother (MM3;2).

London The capital of Great Britain, one of the dual capitals of the Earth from 1967 to 2050. After the Kalkar conquest, the Eastern Hemisphere was ruled from the city (MM1) (MM2;1). Lord and Lady Greystoke had lived there in the 19th century (TT1;1), and Tarzan maintained a residence there to which he sometimes came to escape the discomfort of the African rainy season (T3;1). London was also the name given by God to the city of gorillas he built in the Valley of Diamonds, which was ruled by Henry VIII (T17;21).

Lone Wolf A professional wrestler of the 1930s whom "Jim Stone" threw from the ring with very little effort (J;4).

longevity Burroughs was apparently obsessed with the topic of longevity, as the theme recurs in many of his books. Most of his races are incredibly long-lived, not to mention individual characters (such as the deathless John Carter, who always looked about 30 and could recall no childhood). Each variation on the theme of longevity is treated below in its own entry.

longevity, Amtorian The scientists of Vepaja on Amtor discovered the Serum of Longevity around A.D. 900. An injection of this serum every two years will keep an individual young forever (at least theoretically). Individuals who have attained a very great age will quickly age and die if the serum is not administered on schedule (V1;5)(V2;19).

longevity, Barsoomian The average Barsoomian lives about 300 years, but this is only because of the incredible violence of life on the planet. About one in fifty lives to the age of 1000 years, and at that age most take the voluntary Pilgrimage down the river Iss. Since at 1000 a Barsoomian looks about 40, one can imagine that old age is indeed a rare phenomenon on Barsoom. Indeed, the few old people to be found there in the past usually lived in countries that did not believe in the Pilgrimage, such as the ancient Ras Thavas (from atheistic Toonol) or the hideous Xaxa (Jeddara of Phundahl), which follows the

religion of Tur rather than that of the Therns) (M1;4)(M6;2).

longevity, genetic The "God" of the intelligent gorillas of London in the Valley of Diamonds had discovered that by implanting the genetic material of young people into his own body he could stay young himself, particularly if he consumed their glands afterward to boost the process by absorbing their young hormones. Unfortunately for him, the only youngsters about at the time were gorillas, so over time he was growing to look like one himself thanks to the genetic instructions implanted in his body by the young cells. He hoped to reverse this process and yet stay young by using the cells and glands of Tarzan and Rhonda Terry when they came to his stronghold as prisoners in 1932 (when he was, incidentally, a very young and virile 99 years old)(T17;24–25).

longevity, Kavuru Kavandavanda, the god-king of the mysterious Kavuru tribe of white savages of Africa, developed an immortality potion sometime in the last thousand years. This potion was derived from the glands and blood of young women and appeared in the form of black, pea-sized pellets which, taken once a month, would keep the user young (20ish) and beautiful indefinitely; some of the Kavuru were hundreds of years old. The pills were taken from the treacherous Kavuru by Tarzan and Jane (who were quite young-looking for their ages anyway) and used by them afterward to stay young for quite some time (T19;31).

longevity, Pellucidarian Although the average Pellucidarian lives only as long as the average Stone Age man did (perhaps a little longer, due to the lack of contagious diseases there), some Pellucidarians (those who do not die a violent death) can live to over 100, particularly persons transplanted from the outer crust to Pellucidar. David Innes at 56 looked no more than 30, and Abner Perry at 101 looked younger than he had at 65, when he first came to Pellucidar. The known record is 134, achieved by the old man from Cape Cod whose name was not Dolly Dorcas, born in 1805 and reported still alive in 1939. The major reason for this must be that, since there is no absolute time in Pellucidar, a person is literally only as old as he feels. Indeed, modern medicine has shown that "thinking young" and staying active can keep a person seeming younger than his chronological age, particularly in clean air without the presence of harmful bacteria (P6;1)(P7: 2;2).

Loo Kotai A Chinese criminal of **Pai-sha** (T3;20).

lor An Amtorian nuclear fuel composed primarily of **element 105** (**yor-san**, or **hahnium**), which undergoes a nuclear chain reaction when exposed to **element 93** (**vik-ro**, or **neptunium**) and releases a tremendous amount of energy (V1;8).

Loras, Mountains of The mountain range which skirts the west coast of the **Polodan** continent **Unis** (B1;6).

Lord An English captive-husband of several **Zuli** warriors who (with 11 others) captured Tarzan while he slept in the **Kaji** country in 1935. Lord saw Tarzan kill **Woora** and take the **Great Emerald**, and though Tarzan had promised to split the treasure with him Lord did not believe him, and so called the Zuli to pursue Tarzan, only to be turned back by the power of the emerald, which also compelled Lord and the other men to follow Tarzan. Lord later stole the emerald from Tarzan (again, while the ape-man slept) but was caught and killed soon after by **Mafka** and the Kaji (T21;4–9).

Lord Forest see **Che** (T24;13)

Lord Greystoke see **Greystoke**

Lord Hills and Valleys see **Huitz-Hok** (T24;13)

Lord with the Large Head, the An Arab epithet for **el Adrea**, the desert lion (T2;10).

Lorquas Ptomel The jed of the **Thark** community which captured John Carter and Dejah Thoris in 1866 (M1).

Lorro A **Zuli** warrior on guard at **Woora's** house when Tarzan was taken there as a prisoner in 1935 (T21;4).

Los Angeles California city used by the **Kalkars** of the 24th and 25th centuries as their capital until they were forced from it after their defeat by the tribe of **Julian** (MM3;4,10).

Los Angeles Athletic Club The gymna-

sium frequented in the early 20th century by **Bowen Tyler, Jr.** (C1;9).

Los Embudos A canyon of **Sonora** in which **Geronimo** met with **General Crook** to parley on March 28, 1886 (A2;8).

The Lost Continent One of Burroughs' "single" novels, abbreviated LC. It was originally titled *Beyond Thirty* and concerns the adventures of one **Jefferson Turck**, the commander of a **Pan-American aero-sub** of the 22nd century, who was accidentally carried across the forbidden line of 30 degrees longitude into the Eastern Hemisphere, where no one had gone in 200 years. The novel describes an alternate future from the "main" or "true" future depicted in *The Moon Maid* and its sequels.

Lost on Venus The second book in the Venus series, abbreviated V2. The events within took place in 1929 to 1930 and were transmitted telepathically to Burroughs by **Carson Napier** soon afterward to be published as a novel in 1933. It begins where *Pirates of Venus* leaves off, with Napier led off into captivity in the city of **Kapdor** in **Noobol**. He escapes and wanders in an attempt to return to **Vepaja**, but instead encounters adventures in the super-scientific city of **Havatoo** and its neighbor, the zombie city of **Kormor**, from which he must rescue his beloved **Duare**.

Lost Tribe of the Wiramwazi Mountains A legendary tribe of white men who live far up in the **Wiramwazi Mountains** of central Africa. They are thought by the neighboring **Bagego** people (whom they both raid and trade with) to be a race of bloodthirsty ghosts, but are actually the descendants of a Roman legion which penetrated into the area in the 1st century A.D. and founded the city of **Castra Sanguinarius** (T12;1). See also **Castrum Mare**.

lot (*Pal*) Face (T8;2).

Lotai The younger daughter of **Gorph**, the Mammoth-Man of Pellucidar. She was a very sweet-natured, pretty girl who liked **Wilhelm von Horst** very much when he was Gorph's prisoner because he was nice to her. She escaped from the chief **Mamth** with **Thorek**, whom she loved, and fled to **Sari** (P5;14–17).

Lotar Canl The servant given to **Tangor** while he was a spy for **Unis** in **Kapara** in 1940. He was a **Zabo** agent, but was a likable fellow nonetheless, and with good reason — he, too was a Unisan secret agent who had been advised of Tangor's coming and protected him while he was there, eventually fleeing back to Unis with him when they both came under suspicion (B2;4–7,11).

Lothar A great seafaring nation of ancient Barsoom whose people fled into the **Highlands of Torquas** in the days when the seas were receding and the **green men** were conquering the planet. Deep within the highlands they found a huge, hidden, fertile, forested valley and built a city they named Lothar after their vanished nation. The walls of the valley are steep cliffs passable only by a single tunnel which goes through them, and the only non-Lotharians who know of the city are the green men of **Torquas**, who periodically attack the city and are repulsed by the **phantom bowmen** (see below). Lothar is still inhabited by the fair-skinned, auburn-haired people who built it, kept alive for over 100,000 years by their amazing mental powers, honed to perfection over the eons. Only a few hundred of the original 20,000 inhabitants had the ability necessary to survive for so long, and of those none were women, so the race is doomed to die eventually. The Lotharians dress in flowing robes and speak a variant of the **Tongue of Barsoom.**

The Lotharians use their mental powers in several ways besides keeping themselves from aging; they also have the power to create amazingly real illusions. The illusion of food they create is so real it can actually provide sustenance, and the phantom bowmen they materialize to protect their city are real enough to kill — the sight of arrows burying themselves in his body is enough to kill a victim in actuality. They use these bowmen to repel the occasional attacks of the Torquasians, but do not bother to venture out of their city because they believe Lothar to be the last city inhabited by humans on Barsoom; they believe the rest of the world to be overrun by green men.

Carthoris and **Thuvia of Ptarth** discovered the city while fleeing the Torquasians and **Tario**, Jeddak of Lothar, tried to keep Thuvia there for himself, but she was rescued by Carthoris and they escaped the decadent city (M4;6–9).

loto (*Amt*) Most high (V4;24).

Loto-el-ho-ganja "Most High More Than Woman" (*Amt*). The title held by **Betty Callwell**, the goddess-queen of the **Brokols** of Amtor's northern hemisphere. She was a pretty Earthwoman with black hair and eyes who had somehow been mysteriously transported across space to Amtor, perhaps as John Carter was to Barsoom. Unlike Carter, she had no memory of Earth until **Carson Napier** reawakened her memory. The Brokols supposed her to come from the fires surrounding Amtor, and her full title was "Loto-el-ho-ganja kum o Raj" (Most High more than Woman of the Fire). After an altercation over Napier's status in Brokol, she was deposed as goddess, regained her memory, and mysteriously disappeared back to Earth as a corpse on September 24, 1931 (V4;24–29).

lotokor "Most high dagger" (*Amt*). A military general (V4;14).

Lotus Millionaire **Anthony Harding**'s yacht, from which his daughter **Barbara** was kidnapped by the *Halfmoon* a few days out of **Honolulu**. The *Lotus* was then disabled and left to drift, but was soon found and repaired by the warship *Alaska* (K1;4,15).

Louis IX (Saint) (1214–1270) King of France from 1226 to 1270, who made a truce and a deal for mercenaries with **Henry III** of England in 1243, after they had warred for some time over the English possessions in France. Henry III planned to use these mercenaries to enforce his will to repeal the Magna Carta (OT;2).

Lovely Lady A B-24 Liberator of World War II sent on a reconnaissance mission to Japanese-held **Sumatra** in the spring of 1944 with RAF Colonel **John Clayton** aboard as an observer. The plane was heavily damaged by anti-aircraft fire and crashed, leaving only Clayton and a few of her crew alive (T22;2).

lu (*Cpk*) Man (C1;9).

lu (*Pal*) Fierce (T8;9).

Lu-bra A Suvian slave girl of the **Floating Island** of Ko-va in Pellucidar whom **David Innes** took as his slave so she could guide him back to the mainland. She eventually recognized him and was very eager to help thereafter (P6;25–28).

Lu-don   "Fierce Man" (*Pal*). The high priest of Jad-ben-otho, god of the Ho-don of Pal-ul-don. He was suspicious of Tarzan's claim to be the Dor-ul-otho from the beginning, particularly after he heard the testimony of a Waz-don slave who had seen Tarzan before. He and Ko-tan both coveted Jane Clayton, who had been brought to Pal-ul-don by Lt. Obergatz several months before Tarzan's arrival. Lu-don supported Mo-sar's claim to the throne after the assassination of Ko-tan because he knew he could rule Pal-ul-don through Mo-sar. Later, when Lt. Obergatz came to A-lur convinced that he was Jad-ben-otho, Lu-don set him up as the god, using him to bring all of A-lur under his control. He would have sacrificed Tarzan to Jad-ben-otho had not Korak arrived in time and shot Lu-don dead (T8;9–11,14–15,21,24).

Lu-tan   The mate of Tha of the tribe of Nu in Niocene Africa. Lu-tan was the mother of Nat-ul (E2;2).

Lu-thans   The tribe of Va-gas which the No-vans defeated while Julian 5th was their captive. They gained from their conquest a new village, an incredible amount of food, ten thousand females and fifty thousand young and lost about half of their own warriors (MM1;6).

lua   (*Cpk*) The sun (C2;3).

Luana   An island and island group off the coast of Phutra in the Lural Az of Pellucidar, inhabited by a Mezop tribe hostile to that of the Anoroc group until 1914, when they joined the Empire of Pellucidar and began competing with the Anoroc on a friendly basis (P1;8)(P2;15).

Luata   The Caspakian god of heat and life, whose name is derived from the words "lua" (the sun) and "ata" (the mystery of life). Luata is worshipped chiefly by the Galus in the forms of fire, the sun, eggs, etc. They use an inverted isosceles triangle as a sign of Luata, putting the figure on their jewelry and making it in the air at sunrise or upon encountering a fire (C2;3). The Wieroos also consider themselves to be Luata's children, but worship him in a different manner than the Galus do—through ritual murders (C3; 2–4).

Luberg   A German army officer stationed in German East Africa during World War I.

Tarzan got information from him which he used to get onto Hauptmann Fritz Schneider's trail (T7;5).

Lucas, Captain Jerry   The pilot of the *Lovely Lady* when it crashed in Japanese-held Sumatra in the spring of 1944. He was a self-proclaimed misogynist since he had been jilted after being away for only two months by his Oklahoma City girlfriend, who had married a 4-F (who was a Republican to boot). He soon got over that in the presence of Corrie van der Meer, who fell in love with him and vice versa. After much hardship they survived to reach Sydney and were married en route by the captain of the British submarine which had saved them (T22;3–30).

Lucius   One of Agrippina's brothers, a sickly child who died young (I;1).

Lucius, the slave of Silvanus   A champion charioteer who was killed in a race in A.D. 23 (I;8).

Lucky   Short for Lucky Strike, a brand of cigarettes (PB).

Ludang   One of the chief lieutenants of the Vulture when John Lafitte joined him in the 1920s. Ludang was half Portuguese and half Polynesian and was a thoroughly dislikable fellow. It was he who gave Lafitte the hardest time after he became second-in-command, and Lafitte had to shoot and kill Ludang in self-defense when he later took over the island from the Vulture (PB;9,13).

lufo   (*Ape*) Side (TC).

Luger   A German 9mm automatic pistol of the mid-20th century, favored for its accuracy and dependability (T12;2).

Lukedi   A black African of the Bagego tribe who was assigned to care for Tarzan while he was their prisoner in 1923 (T12;5).

lul   (*Pal*) Water (T8;3).

Lula   The Samary male of Amtor who led Carson Napier to the village of Houtomai after Duare had been captured by the Samary women (V3;2).

Lulimi   One of the priests of the Leopard Men. It was he who decided that Kali Bwana should be their new high priestess, and in a brilliant political move, assured himself of the succession to high priest once old Imigeg had died. He was trapped in the island temple with no food, no way out and only his **canni-bal** friends for company after Tarzan led the **Utengi** to destroy the power of the Leopard Men (T18;6,11,14).

Lum Kam One of the Chinese servants of the **Van der Meer** family of 1930s **Sumatra** who fled with the family when the **Japanese** came in January of 1942. He and Mr. Van der Meer were caught and killed while providing a distraction for **Corrie** and **Sing Tai** to escape (T22;1).

Lum Kip A Chinese sailor of the *Saigon* in 1938 who could speak the **Lascar** tongue. He overheard the plans of the ship's Lascar crew to mutiny, but the mutiny occurred directly after Lum Kip reported the plan to **de Groot** (T24;3).

Lum Tar O A man of ancient **Horz** with amazing mental powers. He was a weakling and a coward who hated all brave men, and he lured many of the nobility of Horz down to the **pits** of the city, where he dominated their minds and put them into a state of suspended animation that lasted for eons. When he originally died, his body had been embalmed by the great **Lee Um Lo** so well that Lum Tar O did not know he was dead and so continued to exist for almost a million years, trapping and dominating all who dared to enter the pits (and eating many of his victims) until John Carter finished him. This released his victims, dozens of ancient **Orovar** nobles who did not believe that millennia had passed, nor that **Throxeus** was gone, until they saw it with their own eyes. Released from Lum Tar O's influence, they quickly aged and crumbled into dust as the millennia caught up with them (M10:1;8–9).

Luna The Earth's moon, known to the inhabitants of its hollow interior as **Va-nah**. Its surface has only a tenuous atmosphere and supports a rapidly-growing **fungus**-like vegetation and possibly some form of animal life, but no higher forms. Its interior, by contrast, has a breathable atmosphere and a fairly high civilization. Due to sabotage by its jealous inventor, the *Barsoom*, the first Earth-Mars spaceship, made a forced landing on Luna, or rather in it, passing into its hollow interior via a crater. As the ship descended, the crew found that the air pressure and temperature slowly increased until the midpoint of the

journey, after which the pressure slowly decreased while the temperature continued to rise. Va-nah, on the inside of the 250-mile-thick crust, had a low, but tolerable air pressure and an average temperature of about 80 degrees Fahrenheit (MM1;1–2).

Lunar Fallacy The name given by the people of the 22nd century to the communist fallacy, as perpetrated by the **Kalkars**— the belief that each human being is only a part of society and therefore owes everything to society as a whole, and that each individual owns nothing, being only a cog in the greater machine. The result of this, of course, is that with no profit motive or means of individual expression, no one works or even cares (MM2;9).

lupanar (*Lat*) Brothel (I;9).

Lupingu A young Utengi warrior from the village of **Kibbu** who joined the war party against the **Leopard Men** in 1931 because he was a Leopard Man himself and wished to sabotage the expedition and betray it to the Leopard Men. Tarzan found him out, killed him, and threw his corpse into the Leopard Men's village (T18;4–9).

Lupus, Julius The tribune of the **Praetorian Guard** who killed **Caligula's** wife, Ceasonia, and their daughter Julia (I;21).

lur (*Pal*) City (T8;2).

Lural Az The great sea east of **Sari** in Pellucidar, which is actually the same sea as the **Darel Az** of **Amoz** and the **Sojar Az** of **Thuria** (P2;6).

Lure, Gaza de The stage name of a Hollywood film actress (and cocaine addict) of the early 1920s who had originally come from the Midwest. Her real name was **Shannon Burke**, and she had had the misfortune to fall in with the wrong people — specifically, director/actor/dope pusher **Wilson Crumb**, who got her addicted to cocaine and then put her to work selling dope for him, of which she got a percentage. She saved up and bought her mother a small farm near the **Pennington's Rancho del Ganado** in April of 1922 and moved there (as Shannon Burke) after her mother's death in July of that year, beginning a new life and eliminating "Gaza de Lure" (GH;5,10–12).

lus (*Ape*) Tongue (TC).

Lusitania The Roman name for Portugal (I;9).

Lustadt The mountainside capital of Lutha (MK1;1).

Lutha A tiny German-speaking country of eastern Europe on the Serbian-Austrian border in the Dinaric Alps. Its history ran from the late 1500s until World War II, after which it was absorbed into Yugoslavia (MK1;4).

Luud The king Kaldane of Bantoom in whose fields Tara of Helium was captured and to whom she thus belonged by Kaldane tradition. Luud was larger by 50 percent than other Kaldanes and a little bluer in color, with bands of white and scarlet about its eyes and mouth and a band of scarlet and one of white extending from each nostril to the sides of its head. Luud ordered Tara fattened for eating, but when she did not become fat he decided to mate her with a rykor instead. She was saved from this fate by Gahan of Gathol and the Kaldane Ghek, who assassinated Luud with a hurled dagger (M5;5,8).

Luvini The black headman of the Flora Hawkes expedition after Owaza fled with Esteban Miranda to steal the gold of Opar. Luvini was a traitorous type who began a rebellion among the porters that would have resulted in the deaths of all the whites in the party had they not been tipped off by a loyal porter and fled. They met up with Jane Clayton and the Waziri, whose protection they placed themselves under. Luvini followed, mistook Jane for Flora Hawkes in the dark, and abducted her from the camp. The Waziri of course followed and torched his camp after rescuing Jane, burning Luvini alive (T9;15,17,20).

Luzon The largest of the Philippine Islands (K1;15).

Lynch, Maggie The alias of supposed prostitute June Lathrop, who supposedly worked for Abe Farris and was maneuvered into testifying against him by Officer Doarty. It was through the grand jury hearing of this case that she met Ogden Secor, the foreman of the jury, who helped her find respectable employment after the trial. After she got the job, she resumed using her real name again (GF;1–5).

Lysimachus, Alexander A friend of Germanicus Caesar's and the steward of Antonia, whom Caligula had arrested for no particular reason (I;16).

ma (Pal) Child (T8).

ma (Pell) The (P5;13).

Mabel Jerry Lucas' nickname for his mother (T22;24).

Mabido A trading post of British East Africa (ME;2).

Mabunu The toothless old black hag whose job it was to take care of Meriem in the douar of Amor ben Khatour. The sadistic hag delighted in inflicting minor tortures and major cruelties upon the helpless child (T4;5).

MacArthur, General Douglas (1880–1964) American general in command of the U.S. Pacific forces during World War II, who eventually reclaimed most of the territory occupied by Japan at the beginning of the war (T22;25).

McClellan A style of American cavalry saddle of the late 19th century, designed by and named for General George McClellan (1826–1885) (A2;6).

McCulloch A friend of modern-day pirate Johnny Lafitte's who encouraged him to write his autobiography for posterity (PB;1).

McDougal Mrs. Abner J. Bass's Brooklynish chauffeur (R;10).

Macduff, Andrew (1863–?) The only son of Jerry and Annie Macduff, who was taken as an infant by Go-yat-thlay and raised as his own after Go-yat-thlay killed his parents in Arizona a few months after his birth. The Apaches gave him the name Shoz-dijiji (A1;1).

Macduff, Annie The wife of Jerry Macduff, who was killed with him in Arizona in 1863 (A1;1).

Macduff, Jerry (1833–1863) A Georgian of Scottish descent who set out for California along the Santa Fe Trail in 1863 with his wife and young son Andrew and was killed later that year by Apaches under Go-yat-thlay (A1;1).

McGuire, Sergeant A cavalry sergeant

204 MACO • MAFA RIVER

of "K" Troop who went with a detachment into Sonora in the spring of 1886 to search for Geronimo (A2;10).

Maco The grandfather of Go-yat-thlay. Maco was hereditary chief of the Ned-ni Apaches in the early 19th century (A1;2).

McPherson, Aimee Semple (1890–1944) American evangelist of the 1920s who was largely discredited after it was discovered that she had faked her own kidnapping in 1926 to go to a "love nest" with a married man. She later died of a drug overdose (A1;1).

Macro (Died A.D. 38) A Roman prefect who was a friend of Caligula's and assisted him in speeding Tiberius' death along. He committed suicide at Caligula's command after trying to keep the emperor from making a fool of himself one time too many (I;15–17).

Macy, Henri de One of the favorites of Henry III of England, who gave de Macy an old Saxon castle in Derby. De Macy in turn gave it to an old French nobleman as payment for a debt (OT;5).

mad (*Bar*) Man (M9;11).

Mad King *see* Leopold of Lutha (MK1;1)

The Mad King A two-novel set usually published in one volume. The first half, *The Mad King*, took place in October 1912 in the tiny European nation **Lutha** and concerns the American adventurer **Barney Custer**, who traveled to Lutha (his mother's home country) only to find himself involved in court intrigue, war, and rebellion with a beautiful young princess, chiefly because he looked just like King **Leopold of Lutha**, who had been locked away as a madman for ten years. This portion of the story was told to Burroughs by Custer when they were both guests at Tarzan's African estate in 1913 (E1).

In the second half, *Barney Custer of Beatrice*, Custer returned to Lutha on the eve of **World War I** because his Luthanian enemies had tracked him to America and begun to pitch bombs at him. He again had to impersonate the true king, now on the throne at last thanks to Custer, whom the king hated because Custer was so much more noble than he was. The first book is abbreviated MK1 and the second MK2.

The Madison Name by which **Naomi Madison** was popularly known (T17;2).

Madison, Naomi A Hollywood starlet who was chosen to play the female lead in *The Lion Man* in 1932. She was a typical spoiled-rotten Hollywood type, but the hardships of the safari made a new woman of her. She and **Rhonda Terry** were kidnapped by **Ab el-Ghrennem**, who believed the movie's "treasure map" plot to be real and wanted the girls to lead him to the treasure. She was abducted from the **Arabs** by the gorilla **Buckingham** but was soon afterward saved by Tarzan, reunited with the film crew, and returned to Hollywood. She later married the **Prince Mudini**, whoever he was (T17;2–7,9,12,21–23, 32–33).

Madison Square Garden An amphitheater in **New York** used chiefly for boxing matches until 1925, when it was rebuilt as an all-sports arena (T24A).

Madison Street The northern border of **Chicago**'s seedy south side (T15;13).

mado (*Ape*) Lame (TC).

Mae West (WWII slang) A life jacket, named for its fancied resemblance to the buxom American movie actress (T22;2).

Maenck, Captain Ernst One of the henchmen of **Prince Peter of Blentz**. He was the governor of **Blentz** itself and had almost unlimited power within its walls. Maenck was a totally unmitigated scoundrel who would do anything for his own profit, including kidnapping **Leopold of Lutha** from **Tafelberg Sanitorium** and plotting to kill him, which he would have done had he not been shot by **Barney Custer** (MK1;8–11). Maenck was later sent to **Beatrice, Nebraska**, to assassinate Custer, but he failed and was recognized, then fled to **Lutha** with Custer in hot pursuit. He assisted Prince Peter in his villainies through the early days of **World War I**, but eventually and unwittingly served as the agent of good when he shot and killed Leopold in the mistaken belief that he was Custer in disguise. He was himself then shot by **Lt. Otto Butzow** and died, but only after lingering on for long enough to discover his blunder (MK2;1–3, 15–16).

Mafa River A river which comes out the **Ethiopian** plateau where the **Kaji** live, goes over a fall, then down a gorge to join with the Neubari (T21;1).

Mafka The powerful wizard of the Kaji, who with the Gonfal could work incredible feats of magic, such as drawing a person to Kaji in spite of himself once he entered the area, or killing any person he had seen, even from a great distance. He was also an alchemist of great ability, but derived all of his black magic powers from the Gonfal, any possessor of which would have the same powers. When Tarzan came to rescue Stanley Wood in 1935 he was able to defeat and bind Mafka and hand him over to the Kaji, who hated and feared him. They killed him (T21; 2,8–10).

Mafka, Castle of The castle in which Mafka lived was built by the Portuguese in the 1530s when they came to repel Islamic incursions at the request of the emperor, or perhaps earlier by some unknown European group. It had secret passages through the backs of false fireplaces that neither Mafka nor the Kaji knew of, since they had never had enough imagination to look for any such thing (T21;2,8–10).

Magor A bull great ape of the tribe of Kerchak whom Tarzan grew up with. He was still with the tribe in 1911 (T2;23).

Magra A dark Anglo-Indian girl, one of the helpers of Atan Thome, who lured Tarzan into a trap in 1936 when she and Thome mistook him for Brian Gregory. Inexplicably, she stopped Thome from shooting Tarzan when he would not give them the information they wanted. She afterward pretended to turn traitor to Thome, joining the Gregory safari to spy on its activities, but actually felt no loyalty to Thome, who was her guardian. She did, however, fall in love with Tarzan after finding out he was not Brian Gregory. She went into Thobos with Tarzan, Thetan, Gregory and Lavac and was there coveted by King Herat, whom she was forced to flee. She was thereafter captured and briefly held by the minions of Chon, god of Thobos, but escaped with the help of Tarzan, with whom she was still in love, though he tried to discourage her. She afterward returned with the others to the outside world, courtesy of the now-friendly Herat, who had his god and treasure back (T20).

maguey (*Agave shawii*) A plant found in the American Southwest and Mexico and used as a source of fibers and to make the drinks tequila and mescal (A1;4).

maharajah (Hindi) Emperor (T20;10).

Mahars The dominant race of Pellucidar, a highly evolved race of winged reptiles much like the rhamphoryncus of the Cretaceous on the outer crust, but much bigger, averaging some seven or eight feet long with the tail. Mahars have large, powerful wings capable of lifting a man; a narrow, beaked head full of pointed teeth; and webbed feet. They are as much at home in the water as in the air. With the aid of their human slaves (kept in control by their Sagoth guards, with whom the Mahars have a peculiar rapport) they build vast underground cities (lit by refracted sunlight) in which to live. Mahars have no ears and communicate among themselves by a form of telepathy and with their Sagoth slaves by a highly complicated sign language. Mahars are all female — ages ago, they possessed a female-dominated culture and discovered a means of fertilizing their eggs chemically, eradicating the need for males, who thus disappeared over time. The secret of the formula was kept only in a hidden place in the city of Phutra to prevent Mahar scientists from experimenting with it and thereby inducing overpopulation. The Mahars eat human flesh, and in many Mahar cities (though not in their capital, Phutra) humans are kept like cattle, bred and fattened for food value. The Phutran Mahars supposedly did not enjoy eating human flesh, but seemed to relish it enough in their religious rituals, in which some consumed as many as two whole girls at a time. The Mahars were eventually driven out of the Empire of Pellucidar by the forces of David Innes, but fled outside the boundaries of the empire and decided to live in peace with the humans, whom they had finally realized were intelligent. It was these Mahars who told Innes and his people of the coming of the Korsars in 1924 (P1;4–5,8)(P2;15)(P3).

mahout The driver of an elephant, who sits upon the animal's neck and guides it with a baton (HM;15).

Main, Hemmington The "star reporter of a great metropolitan daily" in early 20th century New York, who was in love with Gwendolyn Bass, heir to the Bass millions, and she with him. **Abner Bass**, the girl's father, liked **Main**, but her mother had "higher" ambitions for her. At her father's insistence, Main travelled to Europe in pursuit of mother and daughter and ended up with them in **Demia**, where he and the incognito **Prince Boris** met and developed the plan that eventually brought two countries together as well as Main and Miss Bass, because the plan got botched up. Main was forced to shoot the **Rider** (posing as Prince Boris), who was attempting to marry the girl himself, which showed Mrs. Bass Main's character; she then consented to their marriage, which (after some trouble) took place in Demia a few days later with the real Prince Boris as best man and **Princess Mary** of **Margoth** as maid of honor (R;1,5,7,10–17).

maize, Caspak   A giant variety of corn grows in **Caspak**, with stalks some 50 or 60 feet high, ears as large as a man, and kernels as large as a man's fist (C1;6).

maj   (*Pell*) The mastodon (P4;8).

Makahago   The Chief of Buildings of the **Minunian** city of **Veltopismakus** while Tarzan was imprisoned there (T10;10).

Makonnen, Ras Tafari   The birth name of Emperor **Haile Selassie** of **Ethiopia**, in Tarzan's time the regent (and actual ruler) of Ethiopia in the stead of the Empress Judith, daughter of **Menelek II**, who was Makonnen's cousin. In 1930 she died and he became emperor, taking the name Haile Selassie (T14;13).

makus   (*Min*) City (T10;11).

mal   (*Ape*) Yellow (T17;30).

Mal-gash   "Yellow Tooth" (*Ape*). King of the apes of **Ho-den** in the forest of **Alemtejo**, whom Tarzan defeated in single combat when he came there in 1938 (T23;18).

Mal Un   The living corpse from **Kormor** who attempted to abduct **Carson Napier** from **Havatoo** early in 1930 but was captured, decapitated and cremated (V2;17).

Malacca Strait   A narrow channel of the Indian Ocean which separates **Sumatra** from the Malaysian peninsula. At its narrowest point it is only 20 miles wide (T22;2).

malagors   Huge, extinct Barsoomian birds large enough to be ridden by one man

and a passenger. **Ras Thavas** succeeded in recreating these creatures for his **Hormads** to ride on (M9;3–4). In "**John Carter and the Giant of Mars**," they were also used by **Pew Mogel** to transport his ape-soldiers (M11A; 7–11).

Malbihn, Sven   A Swedish adventurer who, with his friend **Carl Jenssen** searched for the kidnapped **Jeanne Jacot** for several years, hoping to get the huge reward offered for the girl's return. He and Jenssen eventually gave up and became ivory raiders, but while attempting to trade with **Amor ben Khatour** for ivory they caught sight of the child and began to plan a way to get her away from the wily old sheik. Years later, while trapping animals for zoos, he and Jenssen were attacked by a tribe of **baboons** led by **Korak**, whom they had shot at years before when he had tried to join them. Soon afterward, they finally got **Meriem** (née Jeanne Jacot) by a trick and set off to collect their reward, but Malbihn was attracted to her and would have raped her had not Jenssen stopped him. He later shot and killed Jenssen to get the girl, but was stopped this time by Tarzan, who happened upon the camp while on safari from his estate and took the girl back there, setting Malbihn free with a warning. He later shaved off his beard, disguised himself, and came to Tarzan's estate in the guise of a hunter lost in central Africa so he could attempt to abduct Meriem again. After **Morrison Baynes** was asked to leave Tarzan's estate, Malbihn used the girl's attachment to him to trick her away from the estate so he could take her. She escaped from him, and while pursuing her he was shot and wounded by Baynes in revenge, but Malbihn shot Baynes as well. Malbihn was finally killed by **Tantor** when Korak came with him in pursuit of Meriem (T4;5,12–14,17–24).

Malb'yat   "Yellow Head" (*Ape*). The most human-looking of the hybrid creatures driven out of **London** in the **Valley of Diamonds** by the gorillas of that city. He looked just like a handsome, blond human but could not learn English and had the disposition of a gorilla. He tried to take **Rhonda Terry** when she wandered into the hybrids' territory, but Tarzan defeated him and took Terry himself, getting Malb'yat's mate **Balza** in the bargain (T17;29–30).

Malihini (Hawaiian) A non-Hawaiian (B1).

Mallius Lepus The Roman centurion of Castrum Mare who first befriended Erich von Harben upon his arrival in that city. He was a patrician, as it is the custom in Castrum Mare for all officers to be. He was imprisoned with von Harben after Fulvus Fupus convinced Emperor Validus Augustus that the two were spies who sought to overthrow him. He and von Harben later escaped, and Lepus remained in hiding until Tarzan and Cassius Hasta came to liberate Castrum Mare (T12; 6,18,21–23).

Mallory, Billy A clean and athletic young man who was in love with Barbara Harding and was almost killed trying to protect her from Billy Byrne on the deck of the *Lotus* when Byrne came with the crew of the *Halfmoon* to abduct her. Byrne, later a changed man, was glad to find out that Mallory had lived, and saved him from the samurai of Yoka when he and Anthony Harding came looking for Barbara. Upon their return to civilization, Barbara (who thought Byrne dead) became engaged to Mallory, but broke it off upon finding out that Byrne was alive (K1;4,15–18).

Malmsey A sweet, strong Madeira wine (OT;3).

Maltor A bandit city-state which lies near Falsa in Middle Anlap. During Falsa's war with Panga, the Maltorians made a habit of stealing Falsa's herds (V4;45).

maltu (*Amt*) Hail (V3;8).

Maltu Mephis "Hail Mephis" (*Amt*). The prescribed verbal salute for all occasions during the Zani period of Korva (V3;8).

Malud, Sir One of the knights of Nimmr when James Hunter Blake came there in 1921. He was a very arrogant and intolerant man who immediately took to ridiculing Blake, particularly after he saw how the Princess Guinalda (whom Malud wished to marry) looked at Blake. When Blake returned his insults, Malud challenged him to a duel, which Blake won by the use of some pretty unorthodox methods. Malud later spread vicious rumors about Blake's feelings for the princess, but these were eventually disproved (T11;9–14,20).

Maluma The hairdresser to Nemone,

Queen of Cathne. She leaked important information to Phobeg, and he to Tarzan (T16;16–17).

Mamka A she-ape of the tribe of Kerchak who was killed by a lion when Tarzan was a teenager. Tarzan took great pains to recover her body before the lion could eat it, lest the lions learn that the great apes were easy prey (T6:8).

mammal, Barsoomian "There is only one mammal on Mars, and that one [is] very rare indeed...." It would seem likely, however, that what John Carter means in this case is that there is but one animal that still gives milk, as it seems obvious that Barsoomian humanoids were once mammalian, as they have breasts and hair, and the same goes for other known Barsoomian animals (M1;5,8).

Mammoth Men (Translation of the Pellucidarian "Tandor Gilak") A tribe of Pellucidar which inhabits the land of Ja-ru near Basti, north of the Forest of Death. They are called Mammoth Men because they both hunt and domesticate the mighty tandor of Pellucidar (P5;6–7,12–13).

Mamth The chief of the Mammoth Men of Ja-ru when they captured Wilhelm von Horst early in 1928 (P5;13).

Man-apes Pellucidarian creatures who resemble Negroes, but with more pronounced features and very sloping foreheads. They have longer arms than do humans, opposable toes, and a prehensile tail. Except for their hairlessness, they are very much like a more primitive cousin of the Waz-don of Pal-ul-don, who are both more intelligent and more culturally sophisticated. A tribe of these creatures captured David Innes and Abner Perry shortly after their arrival in Pellucidar (P1;2–3).

"The Man-Eater" A novella of African adventure last published in 1957 in a combined volume with *Beyond Thirty*. Its abbreviation is ME. The story is comprised of a long series of unusual coincidences involving a lost will and marriage certificate, a beautiful heiress, her evil and greedy cousin, a noble and brave young man who was the son of her father's best friend, and a man-eating lion.

Man-eaters Cannibalistic savages who inhabit the wilds of the Toonolian Marshes on Barsoom (M9;21).

man-eating genius One of the creatures imagined by **Esmerelda** to be lurking in the African jungle (T1;22).

man-flower A Barsoomian plant of the **Kaolian Forest** which has hands and eyes and eats insects (M3;5).

Man-Lat The guard officer who was assigned to guard John Carter in the palace of **Doxus, Jeddak of Kamtol** (M10:2;10).

man-tree A carnivorous plant of **Eurobus** which has eyes and constricting tentacles which it uses to ensnare prey even as large as a human (M11B;8).

The Man Without a Soul The original title of ***The Monster Men*** at its first publication in 1929.

Manai The wife of **Hamlar**, Chief of the **Tandarites**, when they captured **Dian the Beautiful** upon her landing on their island in 1931. As slave-drivers go, she was really not so bad (P7:3;3).

Manat A Pellucidarian tribe of the far side of the island of **Tandar** in the **Korsar Az** who are hostile to the **Tandars** of the near side. They raise **ta-hos** from cubhood for war and hunting, just as the Tandars raise **tarags** (P7:3;5).

Manataj The most distant city of **Manator**, from which **Gahan of Gathol** pretended to come in order to enter the **jetan** game and win **Tara of Helium** (M5;16).

Manator A country and city to the northeast of **Bantoom** and the west of **Gathol** on Barsoom. It is inhabited by **red men**, but their country is so isolated by the horrible terrain surrounding it (hundreds of miles of rough, dry country incapable of supporting any plant or animal life, and many chasms that create treacherous updrafts which make aviation difficult) that the people are unacquainted with the higher technology of Barsoom, such as firearms or **fliers**. They are a sword-and-bow technology people who have been out of touch with the rest of Barsoom for many thousands of years. One example of their backwardness is the practice of adorning themselves with many feathers (usually only done for ceremonial purposes on modern Barsoom) and body paint of ocher, blue and white (M5;9).

The architecture of Manator is of a style

younger than that of the dead cities of the **Orovars** but older than that of even the most ancient of modern Barsoomian cities, dating back to a time when the oceans were still receding and huge marshes covered the planet. The city was built to be defended "against ... spear and arrow with spear and arrow," a sort of medieval Barsoomian style. The streets of the city are walled with tall buildings and the city's outer walls are about 50 feet thick and are pierced by both large and small gates. Large Manatorian buildings have halls and runways large enough to comfortably admit saddle **thoats**, and these animals are frequently ridden in the buildings.

Probably the most interesting aspect of Manatorian culture is the ancient custom (dating back to Orovar times) of perfectly embalming the dead and placing them in lifelike postures on the roof or balcony of the house in which the family lives. In the palace of the **Jeddak** of Manator is the **Hall of Chiefs**, where embalmed jeddaks sit upon their embalmed thoats in full battle regalia (M5;11).

The Manatorians are great lovers of **jetan** and play the game as a martial sport with living men. The games are also used as a method of punishment or execution, for a person can be sentenced to a piece in the game, and possession of a square is determined by mortal combat. The sentences range from one game for a mild offense to ten for a serious one — no one has ever survived a series of ten.

The Manatorians get most of their slaves from Gathol (which lies 22 degrees east of Manator itself and is thus the closest city) by making secret raids on Gathol's outlying provinces every few years. Since they leave no witnesses, no word of Manator's existence is carried back to Gathol itself (M5;13).

The city was conquered in 1915 by the combined forces of **Helium** and Gathol (with the help of **Manatos**) to rescue **Tara of Helium**, Gahan of Gathol, and all the Gatholian citizens enslaved in Manator. After this, Manator was reorganized with **A-Kor** as jeddak and joined the Heliumetic Alliance (M5;22).

Manatos The second city of **Manator**, which was in modern times ruled by the "**Great Jed**" **U-Thor**. Manatos is a powerful city, and was more justly ruled than Manator as a whole. In Manatos only criminals were sentenced to **jetan**, and games between others were sometimes decided by first blood or by points rather than fought to the death (M5;13).

Manchuria   A region of northeastern China which was conquered by the Japanese in 1937 and reorganized as the puppet state of Manchuko (T22;26).

Mandalamakus   A city of Minuni which lies at a great distance from Veltopismakus. From this city came the mother of Talaskar, the slave-girl Tarzan befriended in the quarries of Veltopismakus (T10;11).

Mandan Ocean   One of the four oceans of Poloda, which lies between Auris and Epris. It is roughly 2000 miles across (B2;2).

Mandecote, Sir John   An English knight of the mid–13th century who after being declared an outlaw by Henry III, joined the band of Norman of Torn and became one of his captains (OT;12).

Mangani   (*Ape*) The great apes (T4;10). See also Gomangani; Tarmangani.

Mangas   The son of the great Mangas Colorado, who was 18 when his father was killed in 1863 (A1;1).

Mangas Colorado   The chief of the Bedon-ko-he Apache who was treacherously murdered by the U.S. Cavalry at Fort McKane, Arizona in 1863 (A1;1).

Manhattan Island   The name given by Barbara Harding to the little, rocky island in a river on Yoka where she and Billy Byrne camped and recovered their strength for two months after he rescued her from the samurai of Yoka (K1;14–15).

Manila   The capital of the Philippines (T24;3).

Manilius   A didactic poet of Augustan Rome, author of the *Astronomica* (I;9).

Manill, John   Elias Henders' best friend and partner in his Bar-Y Ranch and gold mine of 19th century Arizona; he was also the brother of Henders' wife. Manill managed the New York interests of the partnership, and so lived there. Only a few days after Henders' death, Manill died as well, leaving Diana Henders sole owner of the business, because Manill felt that, since Lillian Manill was only his step-daughter, she should not inherit (HB;2,8,16).

Manill, Lillian   The daughter of John Manill's wife, who was not related by blood in any way to Diana Henders. Elias Henders and John Manill had signed an agreement that only blood children would partake in the division of their joint property when they died, and that meant Diana alone, but only Lillian Manill and her partners Maurice Corson and Jefferson Wainright knew this, and so they conceived of a plan to swindle Diana out of half of the ranch and gold mine. Lillian was a good-looking, well-educated girl from New York who was very flirtatious with the ranch hands, to Diana's chagrin. Even though her plan would have worked (Diana in her ignorance was willing to give Lillian half of the operations' profits every month), Lillian got greedy and wanted cash, and so went along in the plan to rob Diana, even stooping to seducing Hal Colby to get him on her side. She was found out, however, by Bull, and after a final bid for cash she and her cronies were kicked out of town at gunpoint (HB;9–19).

manioc   (*Manihot esculenta*) A tropical African shrub (also known as cassava) which is cultivated for its edible roots, from which tapioca is made (T18;9).

maniple   (*Lat*) A unit of the Roman military, consisting of two centuries of 100 men each. Three maniples make a cohort of 600 men (T12;6).

Manius   A charioteer of early 1st century Rome (I;8).

Mankar Pol   "Mankar Park" (*Amt*). The beautiful park at the hub of the Amtorian city of Havatoo. The Sera Tartum is located within it (V2;15).

Mankar the Bloody   Sobriquet given to Mankar, Jong of Havatoo, during his life because of his ruthless policies. See also Mankar the Savior (V2;14).

Mankar the Savior   Sobriquet given to Mankar, Jong of Havatoo, after his death owing to the positive effects of his reforms on later generations of Havatooites. He destroyed all politicians and appointed learned men to their positions, then forbade breeding by any whom the scientists declared unfit and had those individuals sterilized to enforce the decree. All defective infants were destroyed, and fit people encouraged to raise children. He then formed the Sanjong, abdicated his own throne to them, and ended his reign by abolishing all laws and allowing individuals to make their own moral judgments henceforth (V2;15).

mantalia A large (eight to twelve feet tall) Barsoomian plant which grows almost entirely without fresh water and is prized for the delicious, though slightly acidic milk it produces. The milk is either drunk as is or used to produce a cheese-like food. The plant produces eight to ten quarts of milk per day, the milk being obtained by tapping the trunk as maple trees are tapped to obtain syrup on Earth. The plants grow in small groves or clusters in the arid regions of the planet (M1;5)(M7;4).

Mantar A friend of the **Toganja Zerka's** in **Amlot** to whom she entrusted **Carson Napier's** safety while he was spying in that Amtorian city in 1930 (V3;8).

Manu (*Ape*) The monkey. These small relatives of the apes speak a very limited form of the **Tongue of the Great Apes** and are fond of teasing their huge cousins. **Meriem** was friendly with them and they often got food for her or warned her of the presence of carnivora (T1;9)(T4;10).

Manuel The guard of a Mexican wagon train who was killed in an **Apache** raid by **Shoz-dijiji** in the summer of 1877 (A1;5).

Manyuema A cannibalistic tribe of Negroes of central Africa who acted as temporary slaves for the **Arabs** when they came to the jungles seeking ivory and slaves. The Manyuema would betray other black tribes to the Arabs, who would leave the Manyuema behind when they went back to the desert with the betrayed blacks, whom they would sell as slaves in the north (T2;15).

Maori The native people of New Zealand (T3;20).

Maral The wife of **Avan**, chief of the **Clovi** tribe of Pellucidar. She was a woman of **Zoram** who had been stolen as a wife in her youth, and immediately accepted Tarzan's friendly intentions as such (T13;11).

Marcus, Gordon Z. An aging Hollywood actor who was chosen to play the white trader, father of the love interest, in B.O. Pictures' 1932 film *The Lion Man* (T17;1).

Marcus Bibuli A tribune of the **Praetorian Guard** who brought **Caligula's** sentence of death to **Tiberius Gemellus** (I;16).

Marcus Vinicius The husband of the Emperor **Caligula's** youngest sister, **Julia** (I;21).

mare (*Lat*) Sea (T12;6).

Mare Orientis "Eastern Sea" (*Lat*). The shallow lake at the east end of the central **Wiramwazi** valley, whose shores blend into papyrus marshes and at whose center is the island on which lies **Castrum Mare**, the lost Roman city. The reed marshes are inhabited by "barbarians" of **Bagego** descent, who live in raised huts just above the water (T12;6).

Marentina A city of **Okar** on Barsoom. It is nestled in a small valley with a tiny entrance pass in the middle of some of the most rugged country in Okar, about 30 miles from **Kadabra**. Since Okar is "a country with neither **thoats** nor **fliers**," Marentina is almost impervious to attack because of these topographical defenses. Like other Okarian cities, Marentina is heated by a huge greenhouse dome in the summer, and excess heat is stored for the long arctic winter. The city has its own **atmosphere plant** and its streets are made of ocher moss-covered sod. The people of 19th century Marentina hated **Salensus Oll** and his religion and helped their prince **Talu** to the throne of Okar (M3;9).

Margaret A young lady friend of Victoria **Custer's** who was fond of bridge (MK2;1).

Margaretha Street The street at whose foot lies the main gate of **Lustadt** (MK1;10).

Margoth A tiny eastern European country, hereditary enemy of **Karlova**, which was allied with that country on the eve of **World War I** by the marriage of Margoth's **Princess Mary** to Karlova's **Prince Boris**. Margoth lay west of Romania in what was until recently Yugoslavia (R;1,10).

Maria, Princess The princess of an unnamed European country of the early 20th century whom King **Otto** wanted his son Prince **Ferdinand** to marry because her country was very rich, but not strong in arms, while Otto's was the opposite. The prince eventually married the ugly, bucktoothed girl because it was a good political move, but when Ferdinand became king and moved his mistress into the palace, Maria went home to daddy (LL;10,12,19).

Marie Mrs. Louisa Smith-Jones' maid (CG2;7).

Mariel, Luis The son of Pedro Mariel, who was born in 1866. He was spared by Shoz-dijiji with his father in 1885, and again the next year, and repaid him by intentionally misleading the troops that were on his trail. Luis later went back to San Carlos with the troops as a camp follower and fell into the employ of "Dirty" Cheetim, luckily for Wichita Billings, because Luis was a good man and helped to bring her rescue about when Cheetim abducted her soon afterward. He then went to work on Wichita's Crazy "B" Ranch (A2;7,11,16–19).

Mariel, Pedro A Mexican woodchopper of Casa Grande whom Shoz-dijiji freed from a felled tree in 1880 and who repaid the Black Bear's kindness by helping him escape a Mexican ambush the next day (A1;6–7). Years later, in 1885, he was again spared by Shoz-dijiji, this time from an Apache attack (A2;7).

Marjorie W. The ship which, on a scientific mission to the Ugambi region, rescued Alexis Paulvitch from the jungle. It later stopped on Jungle Island in search of some mineral deposits, and the ape Akut, still pining for Tarzan after ten years, came in a friendly manner to the landing party to see if Tarzan was there. He was very civil to Paulvitch, who took him aboard and back to England (T4;1).

Marks, Joey "One-Punch" Mullargan's manager, who accompanied the champion to Africa on vacation in 1939 and almost got both of them killed because of his constant hay fever sneezing (T24A).

Marlborough A fashionable California prep school (T13;8).

marriage Marriage was made illegal after the Kalkars conquered Earth because they wanted no legal boundaries to their stealing of human's wives and daughters. The only thing like marriage was the custom that if a man chose a woman as his and she did not wish to be, she had 30 days to choose another (whom the Kalkars would usually kill if the original man who chose her had been one of them)(MM2;5).

marriage, Barsoomian The rules governing Barsoomian marriage are much as on Earth, but much more rigid — once a woman has given her consent, the couple is married, and the ensuing ceremony is only a formality. In the ceremony, padlocked golden collars connected by a chain are locked onto the couple, and the symbolic locking together is nevertheless very real. One would gather that divorce is unheard of, as even taking a lover would be the height of disgrace for a red woman. Even expressing love without physical contact to someone other than one's betrothed or husband is strongly frowned upon. A Barsoomian woman may not marry the man who kills her husband or betrothed, even if he did so in self-defense (M1;22,25).

In backward Manator, the wedding ceremony is different than in other countries; the bride enters the room alone, followed by the guests, and the bridegroom (wearing a ceremonial mask) enters last, after a short consultation with his dead ancestors. Golden manacles are used rather than collars (M5;22).

Mars The Red Planet, called Barsoom by its inhabitants. It was the planet to which John Carter found himself drawn after his apparent death in Arizona, and upon which he had many amazing adventures. It is of course the setting for all 11 books in the Mars series.

Mars Day June 10, 1967 — the day on which the first broadcast message from Mars to Earth was released to the public (MM1).

marsupial, Barsoomian Besides the Goolians, the only pouched creature on Barsoom is a reptile (M9;20).

Marsupial, Pellucidarian The only pouched creature in Pellucidar is the hideous trodon (P5;1).

Mart One of the members of Cory Blaine's gang, who was shot dead by Buck Mason when he came to rescue Kay White from Mart and Eddie (D;6,19).

Marteen A Ned-ni Apache, member of Crawford's Indian Scouts, who arranged for a parley between Geronimo and Lt. Gatewood in 1886 (A2;14).

Martha A woman of the land of Midian who was censured by Abraham, son of

Abraham for her fear of the sound of **Lady Barbara Collis'** plane (T15;2).

Martin A ranch hand of the **Rancho del Ganado** (GH;1).

Marvel, Bruce Ostensibly, a very inexperienced guest at **Cory Blaine's dude ranch,** but actually **Buck Mason** in disguise, investigating those he suspected of the murder of **"Ole" Gunderstrom.** In several instances circumstances forced him to drop his pretense of inexperience, but he still maintained it sufficiently to avoid blowing his cover long enough to complete his investigation and save **Kay White** from Blaine's gang, after which his true identity was revealed (D;3–23).

Mary The younger sister of **Victory, Queen of Grabritin.** She tried to release **Lt. Jefferson Turck** from captivity so he could rescue Victory from **Buckingham** and avenge the death of their mother at his hands (LC;4).

Mary, Princess (Full name Mary Constantia Deodora Theresa Eugenie Sylvia) The American-educated crown princess of the tiny eastern European nation **Margoth,** who was betrothed by diplomats to **Prince Boris** of **Karlova,** Margoth's hereditary enemy, to seal a centuries-old breach. As one might imagine, the young lady was none too happy about the idea, especially after seeing the ugly brute with whom Prince Boris had switched places to avoid the marriage, to which he was equally adverse. She therefore fled and was mistaken for her school friend, **Gwendolyn Bass** (because of a sketchy description) by the real Prince Boris, masquerading as **The Rider,** with whom he had switched places. Boris wished to capture Miss Bass so his new friend **Hemmington Main** could marry her in spite of Mrs. Bass. During the events which followed, the prince and princess fell in love with one another and so were matched by fate in the marriage the diplomats had tried to force. Because they did not know each other's true identities, love could blossom, and it remained even after they knew the truth. Thus, the two feuding countries were joined (R).

Masenas The cat-men of **Ladan;** savage, basically humanoid creatures of proportionate size and shape to humans, but with some strange features. The following is taken from John Carter's description of one of the creatures: "The shape of his skull was similar to that of a human being but his features were most inhuman. In the center of his forehead was a single, large eye about three inches in diameter; the pupil being a vertical slit, like the pupils of a cat's eyes ... the fingers of his hands and four of the toes of each of his feet were much longer than in the human race, while his thumbs and large toes were considerably shorter than his other digits and extended laterally at right angles to his hands and feet. This fact and the vertical pupil of his eye suggested that he might be wholly arboreal or at least accustomed to finding his food or his prey in trees.

"But perhaps the most outstanding features of his hideous countenance were his mouths. He had two of them, one directly above the other. The lower mouth, which was the larger, was lipless, the skin of the face forming the gums in which the teeth were set, with the result that his powerful white teeth were always exposed in a hideous, death-like grin. The upper mouth was round, with slightly protruding lips controlled by a sphincter-like muscle. This mouth was toothless.

"His nose was wide and flat, with upturned nostrils ... two small orifices near the top of the head and at opposite sides served [as ears] ... starting slightly above his eye, a stiff yellowish main about two inches wide ran back along the center of his cranium."

The Masenas have the ability to match the color of any background to a much higher degree than an Earthly chameleon can. They are primitive and mostly savage and display a few very cat-like behaviors, such as playing with their prey before killing it. They eat by biting off the head of the prey, sucking its blood out with the upper mouth, then eating the flesh with the lower. They speak their own mewing, purring language and can also speak the tongue of the humans of Ladan. They wear leather kilts with belts and fight with their natural weapons. Masenas are arboreal and live in houses built high in the trees in the forests of less populated areas. They are not a very numerous people. Masenas eat humans as they would any other prey, but let John Carter go for helping **Umka** escape the **Tarids** (M8;17–18,24).

Masoerai A Sumatran mountain near which Tarzan was captured by the **Japanese** in the spring of 1944 (T22;28).

Mason The name of the cousin of Price and Westcott Clark on whose Mexican border ranch Billy Byrne, Bridge and the Hardings made a stand against Pesita's men in March of 1916 (K2;17). Another Mason was one of the best friends of Wichita Billings' father, supposedly killed by an Apache warrior in 1884 but actually killed by one of "Dirty" Cheetim's men (A2;3,12).

Mason, Buck A young cowboy who was a deputy sheriff in early 20th century Comanche County, Arizona. He was 24 at the time of the events of *The Deputy Sheriff of Comanche County*, where he was accused of the murder of "Ole" Gunderstrom because of a long-running dispute with the old man. He disappeared and went undercover to investigate the murder by posing as a "dude" from back East named Bruce Marvel in order to stay at Cory Blaine's dude ranch, because he suspected (and later proved) that Blaine was the leader of a notorious outlaw band that had killed Gunderstrom. While there, he fell in love with Kay White, whom Blaine later had kidnapped in an elaborate plot to win her by pretending to rescue her. Mason tracked down and rescued Kay and returned her to camp, rounding up the rest of the gang in the process (though he had to kill all but one of them). He was exonerated from blame for the murder and won the heart of the lovely Kay White as well (D).

The Master Mind of Mars The sixth book in the Mars series, abbreviated M6, which was first published in the *Amazing Stories* annual for 1927. The events in it took place from 1918 to 1920 and the story sent to Earth in manuscript form by John Carter in 1925. The novel concerns Ulysses Paxton, an Earthman who was drawn to Barsoom much as John Carter had been in 1866. He falls into the hands of Ras Thavas, a great surgeon who has perfected brain transplantation and uses it to switch the brains of the lovely Valla Dia and the hideous Xaxa, Jeddara of Phundahl. Paxton falls in love with Valla Dia and must capture Xaxa from her own palace in order to switch the brains back.

Master of Life and Death Upon Barsoom One of the titles held by Matai Shang, leader of the Therns of Barsoom (M2;7).

Matai Shang The Holy Hekkador of the Holy Therns, Father of Therns, Master of Life and Death Upon Barsoom, Brother to Issus, Princess of Life Eternal. The leader and chief priest of the Therns, probably the least misguided and most evil of the whole race. He reacted quickly to the destruction of the Therns' supremacy by kidnapping Dejah Thoris and Thuvia of Ptarth and fleeing northward to Kaol and then Okar, superstitious and out-of-touch countries which he knew would still believe in his discredited religion. He was of course eventually foiled by John Carter, and in trying to keep Thurid from stealing Dejah Thoris for himself, Matai Shang was killed by the black (M2)(M3).

matchlock An obsolete form of firearm in which powder and ball are muzzle-loaded and set off by a trigger which activates an S-shaped arm with a burning wick on the end that touches the powder and sets it off (T11;1).

Matin The Paris newspaper that Nikolas Rokoff intended to inform of the Countess de Coude's "affair" with Tarzan before the latter "persuaded" him to do otherwise (T2;5).

mating, Amtorian On Amtor there is no marriage as we know it, but couples live together by choice and these bonds (like Earthly cohabitation) are often more firm than those of modern Earthly marriage. Infidelity is practically unknown on Amtor. A girl is not allowed to mate until she is 20, and the daughter of a jong may not even talk to or see a man outside her own family until then (V1;5,12).

mating, Barsoomian Mating among the green men is directed by the chieftains for improvement of the breed. The green men apparently have very little sex drive (except for a few like Tal Hajus) and are uninterested in marriage. Each green warrior is responsible for several women, but these are in no sense his wives and he often does not mate with any of them (M1;12). Among the red men, mating is handled in a more Earthly fashion (see marriage, Barsoomian).

mating, Pellucidarian If a man of Pellucidar fights another man for a woman, he must afterward either take her hand and hold it, signifying that he wants her as a mate, or else hold it up over her head and release it, signifying that he does not. To do neither is to claim the woman as a slave, meaning no one else can mate with her (P1;4). On the island of **Amiocap**, love is considered important for mating, and if one of the partners in a marriage ceases to love, the marriage is dissolved (P3;6). Among the **Mammoth Men of Ja-ru**, if a woman wants a man who does not want her, and a champion (her father, brother, or friend) can defeat her chosen in combat, he can be forced to accept her as a mate (P5;14).

Matsuo, Captain Tokujo The **Japanese** officer of **World War II Sumatra** to whom Chief **Hoesin** betrayed **Corrie van der Meer** in the spring of 1944 (T22;1).

Matt A loyal cowhand of the **Crazy "B" Ranch** (A2;16).

Matteawan A New York state mental hospital for the criminally insane, in Duchess County (D;9).

Maud, Lady One of the ladies-in-waiting to **Eleanor of Provence** who was a frequent playmate of young **Prince Richard's** and was assassinated by **Sir Jules de Vac** when she caught him kidnapping the young prince in July of 1243 (OT;2–3).

Maus, Lieutenant An officer who was assigned to help **Captain Crawford** find **Geronimo** when the war chief went to **Sonora** in 1885 (A2;8).

Maximus Praeclarus The officer of **Castra Sanguinarius** who brought **Tarzan** before the Emperor **Sublatus**. He befriended **Tarzan** after the ape-man saved his sweetheart **Dilecta** from being forced by **Fastus**, the emperor's son, and helped **Tarzan** escape the clutches of Sublatus by hiding him in his own house. He was found out, arrested, and sentenced to die in the arena, but escaped with **Tarzan** and helped to start the revolution that deposed Sublatus (T12;9–20).

Maxon, Professor Arthur An old biological genius, wealthy by inheritance and a **Cornell University** professor by choice, who discovered the secret of creating artificial life in the 1920s and fled to the East Indies to pursue his experiments uninterrupted. There he created a dozen horrible monsters and slowly slipped into madness, intending to marry his daughter **Virginia** to **Number Thirteen**, who had emerged as a perfect human specimen. The traumatic events of the next few months, during which his camp was attacked and his

daughter stolen by **Dyak** head-hunters under command of the **Rajah Muda Saffir**, succeeded in restoring his sanity and producing in him a hatred of his creatures. He set off in pursuit of **Virginia** to **Borneo**, where he found her with **Number Thirteen** (now called **Bulan**) and was told the truth about the man — that he was not a monster at all, but an amnesiac castaway found by **Sing Lee** and substituted for the real **Number Thirteen** so **Virginia** would not be forced to marry a monster. He then approved of their marriage (Q).

Maxon, Virginia The beautiful young daughter of **Professor Arthur Maxon** who accompanied him to **Borneo** in the 1920s when he went there to complete his experiments in secret. She was kidnapped by **Dyak** head-hunters a few months later and taken into the interior, pursued by **Bulan**, the man-monster who loved her, and by her father's assistant **Dr. Van Horn**, who wished to marry her to inherit Maxon's fortune. After several escapes, adventures and recaptures, **Bulan** finally saved her, at which time she fell in love with him. Eventually, his true identity as a real human was revealed, and the two were married in **Singapore** (Q).

May, Lieutenant The commander of the shore party from the U.S.S. *New Mexico* who rescued **Professor Arthur Maxon** and his party from **Borneo** (Q;17).

Maya The girl who introduced **Tarzan** to the film producer **Abe Potkin** at a Hollywood party in 1933 (T17;33).

Maya An aboriginal American culture of **Mexico** which flourished in the first millennium A.D. but collapsed around A.D. 900 and was replaced by the **Toltec** culture, which occupied many of its cities and borrowed much of its culture. The **Maya** had a high degree of art, science and architecture and built huge stepped pyramids and elaborate monuments (T24;1).

Mayapan The capital of the **Cocom** family of tyrants in ancient Mexico. It was destroyed in 1451 by **Chab Xib Chac**, the Red Man (T24;1).

Mbeeda A black of the following of **Amor ben Khatour** whom **Carl Jenssen** and **Sven Malbihn** paid to bring **Meriem** to them. **Mbeeda** was unfortunately discovered by the **Arabs** and killed (T4;5).

Mbonga The chief of the tribe of west African cannibals who moved into the area frequented by the great apes of Kerchak in the first decade of the 20th century and were the first humans (other than himself) that Tarzan ever saw. Mbonga's son **Kulonga** killed **Kala** and was in turn killed by Tarzan, who haunted the tribe for a long time afterward, playing tricks upon them that unnerved their superstitious minds and filled them with fear of the white devil-god who came and went at will and spoke with the beasts of the jungle. Mbonga and all of his savages were exterminated in March of 1909 by Lt. Charpentier and a force of French soldiers in retribution for the capture, torture and (so the sailors believed) killing of Lt. d'Arnot, who had actually been rescued by Tarzan the night before (T1;9–11,21–22).

Mbuli The headman of the **Atan Thome** safari to **Ashair** in 1936 — the safari he had stolen from **Mr. Gregory** by deceit before the man got to **Bonga** to leave with it (T20;8).

M'duze A hideous old black hag of Cathne, a slave who had strong control over Queen Nemone. It was rumored that M'duze was Nemone's mother, which would explain her control over the haughty queen. Eventually, though, she pushed Nemone too far, and the queen killed the old woman in a fit of rage (T16;10–11,17).

meat, Va-ga Since most of the creatures of Va-nah are poisonous, Va-gas are the primary source of meat both for themselves and for the higher races of Va-nah. There is apparently a lack of bacteria in Va-nah's soil, because Va-ga meat that is wrapped up and buried will keep almost indefinitely (MM1;6).

mechanical brain The greatest achievement of Fal Sivas of Zodanga on Barsoom was a mechanical brain, a metal sphere the size of a large grapefruit that was similar to Earthly computers in that it functioned quickly and without making mistakes, but could not originate thought. Unlike Earthly computers, it could receive and respond to thoughts from a person who knew its secret, even across the distance between worlds. Fal Sivas installed the brain in his **interplanetary flier** in order to control it at his direction (M8;5–6).

med (*Amt*) Million (V4;31).

Medain Salih A ruined town of northwestern Arabia near which lies the legendary rock el-Howwara, site of a tower full of cursed treasure which is guarded by an afrit (T11;1).

Medek One of the fat, soft black men kept as slaves by **Kavandavanda**, god-king of the **Kavuru**. He was killed by Ogdli to help Jane Clayton escape the Kavuru in 1934 (T19;24,28).

Medicine Hat A city of Alberta, Canada, with no particular significance to Tarzan (T21;19).

Meeta (*Ape*) The rain (T11;6).

Meeza The Jukan king of Pellucidar by whose men David Innes was captured while passing through their valley in 1929 (P6;6).

megatherium A species of giant ground sloth of the Pleistocene period. See also **dyryth** (P1;3).

Mekong The largest river of Indochina, which roughly bisects **Cambodia** from north to south (HM;2).

melilotus Specifically, *Melilotus alba*, or white sweet clover, used as a cover crop in the American West because it enriches the soil with nitrogen. It smells like new-mown hay when crushed (GH;9).

melodeon A small reed-organ which derives its air flow from a bellows (ME;1).

Melrose The tail gunner of the *Lovely Lady*, killed when the bomber's tail was shot off over Japanese-held **Sumatra** in the spring of 1944 (T22;24).

Melton The guide hired by "One-Punch" Mullargan for his African safari in 1939 (T24A).

Memet A famous warrior of Thobos who was killed fighting a huge Ashairian prisoner as punishment for a crime (T20;19).

Memphis The capital of Egypt during the Old Kingdom of the third millennium B.C., and an important city for many centuries afterward (T15).

memsahib (*Swa*) Ma'am (T14;10).

"Men of the Bronze Age" The second book comprising *Savage Pellucidar*, originally published in *Amazing Stories* magazine in 1942 (P7:2).

menagerie, Barsoomian Jal Had, Prince of Amhor kept a menagerie with specimens of just about every kind of creature on Barsoom, including the various human races and a Kaldane from Bantoom. Vor Daj/Tordur-bar was put into this zoo when he was captured by the Amhorians and later succeeded in escaping from it, releasing everything else as well to create confusion (M9; 24–26).

Menelek II (1844–1913) Emperor of Abyssinia from 1889 to 1913, a powerful king who created the united nation of Abyssinia from a collection of feudal kingdoms. In 1913 he sent Abdul Mourak and a detachment of soldiers in pursuit of Achmet Zek, who had had the effrontery to make a raid in Abyssinia a few months before (T5;15).

Menelek XIV The Emperor of Abyssinia who began the conquest of Europe in the 2080s and ended up completely dominating the main bulk of the now savage continent by the 2130s; this dominion was threatened only by China. Menelek was a man made fat and disgusting by dissipation, but still managed to carry himself with some dignity (LC;8).

Menofra The shrewish wife of Phoros, revolutionary dictator of 1935 Athne. She was a remarkably ugly, manlike woman with red hands and a noticeable moustache. After Phoros tried to kill her she seized power herself and so the former prostitute became Queen of Athne. When the Cathnean army came to overthrow her a few days later, she was killed by some of their war lions, and good riddance (T21;20–25).

Mentheb The Queen of Thobos, wife of King Herat, when Tarzan came there in November of 1936. She conceived of a liking for the ape-man and summoned him to her apartment, where he was discovered by Herat and was barely able to vindicate himself (T20;19–21).

menzil (Ara) Camp (T11;1).

Mephis A common soldier of Korva who, after a disastrous war in that country, arose to leadership at the head of the Zani party and usurped all Korvan government functions for himself, then demanded that the jong, Kord, resign those powers to Mephis and rule as a figurehead. After Kord refused for a while,

Mephis killed him. After authoring many tragedies and acts of hatred, Mephis himself was poisoned by the Toganja Zerka late in 1930 in revenge for his having killed her ooljagan during the last war for some imagined insult against himself and the Zanis (V3; 5–15).

mephitis (Lat) A noxious or poisonous vapor from the ground (ME;7)(I;4).

Merchant Man-of-War The bulk of the Pan-American navy of the 22nd century was made up of these craft, which carried cargo and mail to earn their keep as warships rather than simply patrolling aimlessly or waiting in reserve (LC;1).

Merchants and Farmers Bank A financial institution of early 20th century Oakdale, Illinois (K3;2).

Meriem The name given to Jeanne Jacot by Amor ben Khatour after abducting her from her true parents in revenge for the capture of his nephew, a raider, by her father, a French army officer. She was most ill-treated by the Arabs and their black allies, and after three years of flight from Algeria and much cruelty at the hands of her captors, she only dimly remembered her former life. Her only playmate during this time was Geeka, the hideous doll that had been made for her by a kindly slave, which she carried everywhere. She was eventually rescued by Korak, who saw the Sheik mistreat the girl and punched him out, then took the girl away to the jungle to live with him and Akut. She grew into early womanhood, learning on the way the language of the great apes and the secrets of woodcraft, and they lived together for a few years until she was eventually abducted by a great ape while Akut and Korak were away. After Korak rescued her from the ape, his true feelings for her were awakened, but she was again abducted that very day by a black tribe who recognized her and planned to return her to ben Khatour for a reward. They instead sold her to Sven Malbihn and Carl Jenssen (who wanted the reward from her real father) and taken northward. She was rescued from being raped by Malbihn a few days later by Tarzan, on safari from his African estates, and taken there to live until Korak should come for her, though neither Tarzan nor Meriem realized that Korak was Tarzan's son until they later met. Over the next year, she gave

Korak up for lost and was re-civilized by the Claytons, eventually developing a fascination (which she mistook for love) for the honorable Morrison Baynes, a young English guest of the Claytons who had anything but honorable intentions for her — he planned to take her back to Europe as his mistress. Instead, Malbihn (disguised as "Mr. Hanson") tricked her to his camp in the west and abducted her. She escaped from him, only to fall again into the hands of ben Khatour, from whom she was rescued by Korak soon afterward. He took her back to Tarzan's estate and was thus reunited with his parents. Meriem and Korak married, and she was later reunited with her real father (T4;5–14,17–27).

merk   A small gold coin of the Middle Ages (OT;3).

Mesnek   One of the slave women of Mentheb who was sent by the queen to fetch Tarzan to her boudoir after he defeated a warrior in the arena of Thobos in November of 1936 (T20;21).

mesquite   Any of several species of small trees of the genus *Prosopis*, indigenous to the American Southwest. Its pods are sweet and can be eaten by humans or livestock and its wood is dense and makes an excellent fuel (A1;2).

Messalina   The wife of the Emperor Claudius, who almost ruled the Roman Empire herself for the first few years of his reign, until he had her executed in A.D. 48 for publicly staging a mock marriage with her lover to show her disdain for Claudius (I;6).

Messerschmitt   The largest manufacturer of German fighter planes in World War II, whose models included the excellent Me 109 (B1;1).

metae   (*Lat*) The columns which mark the ends of the laps in a Roman circus (I;8).

Metak   The son of Herog XVI of Xuja. Upon seeing Bertha Kircher for the first time, he abducted her, attacking anyone who came to intervene. He escaped with her to the house of Veza, where Tarzan met and killed him (T7;19,23).

metate   (*Apa*) Mortar (A1;11).

metempsychosis   Transmigration of souls (B1;2).

Metnal   The Mayan underworld, conceived of as a dank, gloomy place far beneath the ground, ruled by Hun Ahau, god of the dead (T24;13).

Meyer   An unkempt, sneaky little communist revolutionary of the early 20th century who plotted the assassination of the old king with Prince Otto and was double-crossed and killed by Otto's men afterward. He had been abused by his father as a child and had a lust for power as a result (LL;1–3,7).

Mezops   The red men of Pellucidar, a tall (males average about 6'5"), handsome race which inhabits the islands of Pellucidar's seas. They were the only race the Mahars were never able to dominate, because they lived in secret places on their islands and were very vicious warriors who never gave up fighting until killed. The Mahars wisely decided that attempting to enslave such a people was not worthwhile, and so made a pact with them, giving them peace and certain goods in exchange for the Mezops' supplying them with fish and allowing them to build their hidden temples on Mezop islands (P1;8). The Mezops later became the seafaring people of the Empire of Pellucidar, much of the navy being manned by (and all of it built by) Mezops (P2;14–15).

M'ganwazam   The chief of a cannibal tribe of the upper Ugambi region of west Africa through whose village Nikolas Rokoff passed with the captive Jane late in the summer of 1912. Rokoff warned M'ganwazam against Tarzan and his "evil powers," with the result that M'ganwazam lied to Tarzan when he later interrogated the tribe, saying that there had been no white woman with Rokoff's party and that he did not know where his safari was, when it was in fact close by. M'ganwazam was a crafty, ugly, short, ape-like fellow with absolutely no redeeming characteristics. Rokoff had originally planned to give Tarzan's son Jack to him to be raised as a cannibal, but after the death of the baby he thought to be Jack, he decided to give Jane to M'ganwazam as a wife. Fortunately, she escaped (T3;11–13).

mias pappan   (Dyak) Orang-utan (Q;12).

Michael, Prince   The 14-year-old heir to the throne of an unnamed European country who was forced to flee when his father was overthrown and killed in a revolution that ended with Michael's uncle **Otto** on the throne. His steamship went down in the Atlantic and Michael was hit by floating debris, resulting in permanent amnesia of an extreme type. He was rescued by an evil old deaf-mute epileptic who inhabited a derelict ship and raised the youth as his slave, made to fish and do everything else for the old man. The boy befriended the ship's only other inhabitant, a young caged lion who had been part of the derelict's cargo. This lion eventually killed the old man in defense of Michael after escaping his cage. The ship soon afterward ran aground in north Africa and Michael and the lion went ashore, learning to hunt together. They soon afterward saved the beautiful **Nakhla**, daughter of an **Arab** sheik, from being raped by bandits, and Michael and the girl fell in love at first sight, though he could not speak to her because his amnesia had robbed him of all memory of language and the deaf-mute had taught him only sign language. Nakhla taught him Arabic and they grew closer until the treacherous **Ben Saada** found him alone and told him she had married another (LL;1–14).

He went away from there and befriended **Marie Vivier**, the daughter of a French army officer whom he rescued from bandits. She taught him French, and in a roundabout way and completely unintentionally she helped him find out that Nakhla had not been married. He returned to her father's **douar**, saved her from Ben Saada and from more bandits, and was severely injured in the head in the process, causing his original memory to return. Even then, he preferred to stay and marry his desert beauty rather than return to the political turmoil of his homeland (LL; 15–25).

Michel   The squire of **Sir Richard Montmorency** (T11;9).

Midian   The name given by its roughly 1000 inhabitants to the volcanic caldera in which they live. It is five miles in diameter, surrounded by steep cliffs and lies in the **Ghenzi Mountains** of Africa. The Midianites are the descendants of the fanatical Pauline Christian **Angustus the Ephesian**, who went there with his slave girl around A.D. 63 out of fear that he would be martyred, and founded an unhappy race of epileptic fanatics. Inbreeding has made the Midianites ugly and

twisted: They have exceptionally large noses (large enough to be called deformed) and almost no chins. They do not wash or keep their black hair combed, and the men all have beards. Their religion is the only thing important to them, dominating their lives entirely, and is like a fanatical Pentecostal biblical fundamentalist belief, embracing such concepts as speaking in tongues and the idea that all fun is sinful. In addition, these fanatics believe that **Paul of Tarsus** was the son of God, and they practice human sacrifice of "sinners." Occasionally, one is born among them with the recessive genes of Angustus' slave girl, and such are generally hated and reviled and eventually killed unless captured by the north Midianites, who kill blond men and keep blond women as slaves. North Midianites separated from the south Midianites long ago and are different in appearance and temperament, though not in religion, except that they believe that Paul was blond, while the south Midianites believe he was dark-haired. The north Midianites kill all deformed, black-haired or epileptic children and have thus purified their blood to some degree and are more advanced, cleaner and slightly less twisted than their cousins in south Midian, though no less fanatical (T15; 2,19).

Mighty Ones   A Mayan epithet for the gods (T24;13).

Miguel   A Mexican from whom **Billy Byrne** and **Bridge** purchased some food upon first arriving in Mexico in 1916, and in whose home got in trouble with the bandito **Pesita** (K2;6).

Mik-do   The semi-legendary ancestor of the **Nipons**, whom they conceived of as living on an island in the middle of the sea (probably **Japan**), where they go when they die. The name probably derives from the Japanese word "mikado," meaning emperor (MM3;6).

Mike   A former Russian nobleman who was the doorman at a restaurant frequented by **Dr. Lafayette Smith** in the late 1920s (T15;14).

Miles, General Nelson A.   (1839–1925) American cavalry general who replaced **General Crook** after **Geronimo** and his band slipped away from the former after surrendering to him in March of 1886. Miles put prices on the renegades' heads and harried them with **Apache** troops until they finally surrendered on September 4, 1886 (A2;14).

milk, Amtorian Amtorian milk has a strong, almost pungent, but not unpleasant taste (V1;3).

Mill Creek A landmark of the TF **Ranch** in early 20th century **Porico County, Arizona** (D;3).

Miller One of the crew of the *Halfmoon* who joined the **Theriere/Byrne** faction after the ship was wrecked on an uncharted Pacific island. He was killed by the followers of **Oda Yorimoto** when they came to abduct **Barbara Harding** (K1;9–10).

Millsville A small **Illinois** town west of **Oakdale** (K3;7).

Milwaukee A city of Wisconsin which, after the **Kalkar** conquest was the center of a **teivos** in which the taxes were so high that the people had nothing left for themselves 10,000 of them starved to death one month in 2120 (MM2;2).

Mimbres A river of southwestern **New Mexico** which begins in the Mimbres Mountains and terminates in the deep desert of Luna County (A1;1).

Mine of the Rising Sun One of the gold mines of **Cathne** (T16;16).

minkala (Also mankala) A game favored by many African peoples, including the **Gallas of Ethiopia**. It is a counting and capture game played with stones or counters and a board containing 14 pits or cups; it can be played in a series of little pits dug in the ground (T14;1).

Minsky Sidekick of **Tom Crump** when he came to Africa looking for the bounty on Tarzan's head in 1938. After Tarzan was cleared the two decided to find **Sandra Pickerall** and hold her for ransom instead, so they made their way into the **Ruturi** region, where they were captured by the **Gallas of Sultan Ali** and enslaved. They escaped during a battle with the **Alemtejos** soon afterward and met up with the false Tarzan for a while, during which time they stumbled upon the Alemtejo gold mine and took far too much gold to carry. Soon afterward, a hunger and thirst-crazed Crump killed Minsky with a large gold nugget for his share of the gold neither could carry (T23;7–13,17,20,23,29).

Mintep The 700-year-old Jong of **Vepaja** on Amtor at the time of **Carson Napier**'s arrival there in 1929. He was, like most Vepajans, fanatically duty-bound and followed his country's traditions and rules exactly, even when they caused him great pain, as in the case of his daughter **Duare**. He was imprisoned in the **Zani**-controlled city of **Amlot** in 1930 while searching for her and was later saved by Napier, but after finding out that Duare had mated with Napier, he was duty-bound to bring her back to **Kooaad** for trial, even though it would mean her death. He did so (half heartedly) but was saved from the anguish of seeing his beloved daughter executed when Napier rescued her from the royal palace itself (V1;4–5)(V3;7,11,14–16,19–20).

Minuni The land of the Ant Men, a pleasant country of ancient volcanic basins surrounded by wooded hills, and beyond that the **Great Thorn Forest**. In the rocky, precipitous hill country dwell the **Zertalacolols**, massive, muscular creatures with a gender-reversed paleolithic culture. The Minunians themselves, who live in the rest of the country, are only 18 inches tall and ride on **diadets**, a small species of antelope. They are a very efficient people, working quickly and with no lost movement. Their large, conical city buildings are quickly and efficiently constructed and can house thousands of Minunians each. They possess a slave society, but the slaves of the second and third generations are well treated, and if any noble takes a slave as a spouse (a practice encouraged by Minunian governments for strengthening noble bloodlines) the slave is raised to the rank of the spouse (T10;6).

Minunian Race name of the Ant Men. See **Minuni** (T10;6).

Miocene The fourth (and second to last) epoch of the Tertiary Period, which lasted from 25 million to 13 million years ago. Dinotheria and the earliest mastodons appeared then, and also many of the giant mammals which gained precedence later.

Miranda, Esteban A Spanish-born silent film actor who bore a striking resemblance to Tarzan and was recruited by **Flora Hawkes** (whom Miranda quickly fell in love with) for her 1917 expedition to steal the gold of **Opar.** He went about in the jungle disguised as Tarzan in order to destroy his reputation, then led the Hawkes expedition to Opar while Tarzan was elsewhere and stole its gold. He later took Tarzan's place among the **Waziri,** pretending to have had a relapse of his amnesia from the last trip to Opar, and led them to steal the gold from the Hawkes expedition, conspiring with **Ozawa** (the Hawkes headman) to hide the gold and return for it later. He soon afterward came upon the embattled safari (who had been betrayed by **Luvini,** Ozawa's successor) and captured Flora Hawkes, taking her away with him in full view of **Jane Clayton,** who mistook Miranda for Tarzan and was thus understandably hurt and confused by his "saving" another woman instead of her. By this time Miranda had fallen victim to the delusion (spurred on by fear and privation) that he was indeed Tarzan, and Flora his mate, and in this delusion he remained for some time. When he stole the diamonds from **Kraski** that the Russian had taken from the real Tarzan, Miranda became greedy enough to abandon Flora, but still believed himself Tarzan. When the true Tarzan caught up with him, though, he fled down the Ugogo River into the hands of the tribe of **Obebe,** who imprisoned him, planning to keep him until he died in order to find out whether "Tarzan" was a mortal or not (T9; 3–6,10,15–21).

About a year later, he succeeded in escaping by tricking **Uhha,** the daughter of the witch doctor **Khamis,** into helping him, and took her with him in his search for a trail west. She eventually realized that he was neither Tarzan nor river-devil, and struck him unconscious one night while he slept, taking his diamond pouch when she left. This left Miranda truly amnesic, but he was soon found by the Waziri and taken to Tarzan's bungalow as him — unfortunately for Miranda, the truth was soon discovered when the real Tarzan returned (T10;1,4,9–10,22).

Mirando A black savage of the tribe of **Mbonga** whom Tarzan strangled, stripped, and threw into the village square, causing all of the natives to flee in superstitious terror (T1;13).

Misenum The Roman city where the Emperor **Tiberius** died in A.D. 37 (I;15).

Mississippi The largest river of North America and the third longest on Earth. The **Gerlat kum Rov** of the Amtorian continent of **Noobol** is comparable in size to the Mississippi (V2;11).

Missouri Pacific The railroad which built the first lines west of the **Mississippi** River and eventually expanded all over the West and South (K2;5).

mistal An Amtorian animal, rat-like and about the size of an Earthly house cat (V2;8).

Mix, Tom (1880–1940) A hero of silent (and early sound) movies best known for his overstated cowboy costumes (enormous white hat, hand-carved leather, etc.) (D;3).

mo In the adolescent Tarzan's letter-pronunciation scheme, the letter "D" (T6:4).

mo (*Pal*) Short (T8;2).

Mo-sar "Short Nose" (*Pal*). A powerful chief of the **Ho-don** of **Pal-ul-don** who was a pretender to the throne on the basis that his great-grandfather had been a king. After his son assassinated **Ko-tan,** he started a civil war to get the throne and was supported in his claim by the priest **Lu-don,** who supported Mo-sar because he knew that he could manipulate him and thereby rule Pal-ul-don himself. While trying to kidnap **O-lo-a** for his son, Mo-sar saw **Jane Clayton** (who was being held in O-lo-a's quarters) and stole her for his own, but she escaped him, and when Tarzan came looking for her in **Tu-lur,** Mo-sar tricked him into a trap. Later, while helping Lu-don gain control of Pal-ul-don, he was shot and killed by **Korak** (T8;2,15–18,24).

Moak A king Kaldane of **Bantoom** on Barsoom. **Tara of Helium** was first sighted by the Kaldanes at the edge of his fields and one of Moak's men claimed her, but was killed by **Ghek,** who claimed her for **Luud** since she was actually caught in Luud's fields (M5;4).

Moekemoeko A town on the west coast of **Sumatra** (T22;29).

moghreby (*Ara*) A wizard (T11;1).

Moh-goh One of the huntsmen of **Ko-tah,** the noble who aspired to the throne of **Laythe** in **Va-nah.** Like many Laytheans, Moh-goh was only loyal to Ko-tah because of fear. He had been captured by the **Kalkars** and was imprisoned with **Julian 5th,** who helped him escape. Moh-goh then led Julian back to Laythe. He was a **paladar** (count) and was able to get Julian a place in the palace of **Ko-tah** so he could live in **Laythe** (MM1; 10–11).

Mohammed One of the men of the 1920s Arab bandit **Sidi-el-Seghir** (LL;20).

Mohammed Beyd The second-in-command to **Achmet Zek**. He was left in command of Zek's village while the sheik went south to steal Tarzan's gold from where the **Waziri** had buried it during Tarzan's amnesia in 1913. He made a deal with **Albert Werper** for **Jane Clayton** and the jewels of **Opar** that Werper had stolen from Tarzan, and rode with him northward until greed and lust induced him to double-cross Werper to get Jane and all of the jewels for himself. While trying to rape Jane during the night, he was shot and killed by Werper (T5;20–21).

Mohammed Dubn An imaginary **Arab** sheik whom young **Jack Clayton** (alias **Waja, Chief of the Waji**) pretended Mr. **Harold Moore** was when he bound and gagged the tutor, who was trying to stop the over-muscled lad from sneaking out to see **Ajax** (T4;2).

Mohar A **korgan kantum** (warrior-physicist) of the Amtorian city of **Havatoo** who authorized **Carson Napier** and **Nalte of Andoo** to be tested for their fitness to live (V2;14).

Mohave A small sandy desert of southern **California** (C2;2).

Mohawk A peculiar form of haircut named for the Mohawk Indians who originated it. It consists of shaving the head entirely except for a ridge of hair about two inches wide running down the center from forehead to neck. Members of the **Zani** party of early 20th century **Korva** on Amtor distinguished themselves by such a haircut (V3;6).

Moko The son of **Meeza**, the **Jukan** king of Pellucidar, whose men captured **David Innes** in 1929. Innes tried to kill Moko to save **Dian** from him, but he was only wounded— luckily for Innes, because his reappearance caused the distraction Innes needed to escape (P6;7,10,14).

mola salsa (*Lat*) Coarsely ground spelt flour mixed with salt, which was strewn on the victim of a sacrifice (I;6).

Molak The king ape of the tribe of **Jungle Island** who attacked Tarzan soon after his arrival on the island and was killed by him (T3;3).

molop (*Pell*) Fire (P1;10).

Molop Az "Fire Sea" (*Pell*). In the cosmology of the **Gilaks** of Pellucidar, the flaming sea upon which the flat Pellucidar floats. Dead people who are buried in the ground are believed to be taken bit by bit to Molop Az by tiny demons, thus accounting for decomposition. Because of this belief, only the bodies of enemies are buried in Pellucidar (P1;10). See also **Dead World**.

Momaya A black woman of the tribe of **Mbonga** whose child **Tibo** was stolen by Tarzan to be his "son." She tried to get both her tribal witch doctor and **Bukawai** (another, more fearsome witch doctor) to make magic to get the child back, but of course it did not work. Tarzan later returned the reluctant child to his mother when he realized that the child would pine away for her and die if he were not returned (T6;5). A few months later, Bukawai returned and demanded payment from her for the spell he had never cast, and when she did not pay Bukawai stole Tibo, intending to hold him for ransom. Tarzan soon rescued the child, however, and returned him to Momaya (T6;6).

Mombasa The most important port of Kenya, which lies on an island slightly off the coast (T7;1).

Momulla the Maori One of the leaders of the *Cowrie* mutineers when they landed on **Jungle Island** in the latter half of 1912 at the same time as Tarzan and the *Kincaid* survivors were marooned there. He ran into **Schneider** of the *Kincaid* (after overhearing his plan to kidnap **Jane Clayton**) and recruited him as navigator for the *Cowrie* so Schneider could get off Jungle Island safely and Momulla could dispose of his rival, **Gust**. Unfortunately for the **Maori**, Gust escaped and led Tarzan to the *Cowrie* just in time for him to raid it with his beasts. Momulla was one of the few survivors (T3;21).

Monarch of the Morning A somewhat inflammatory newspaper of early 20th century **Chicago** (GF;2).

Monchensy, William de One of the barons who rebelled against **Henry III** of

England. He was present at the Battle of Lewes on May 13, 1264 (OT;16).

money   At first, Tarzan did not understand money or its usage, but learned quickly and came to appreciate the necessity of having it. His first money was a sum of 10,000 francs won in a bet with a big game hunter that "Monsieur Tarzan" could not kill a lion armed only with a lasso and a knife (T1;26). Tarzan quickly learned to enjoy money, and felt greed for gold when he saw the many pieces of gold jewelry possessed by the Waziri, resolving to have them lead him to the place from which their supply of it had come. They did so, and the gold that Tarzan later stole from Opar made him a very rich man (T2;15,22,26). He later returned for more several times (T5)(T9)(T14).

money, Barsoomian   Barsoomian money is decimal and similar to that of Earth. The coins are oval and come in three denominations: Pi, worth about one cent (1941 money), which are bronze; teepi, worth about ten cents, which are silver; and the gold tanpi, worth about one dollar. Paper money is issued by individuals as needed and redeemed in gold or gems twice yearly. If a man issues more than he can redeem, the government redeems the money for him and the man must work off the debt as other debtors do (M1; 20)(M10:2;11).

money, Kalkar   In Kalkar-occupied 22nd century America, paper money was printed and issued to the Kalkar officials, who would then use it to buy wares from the humans, who were not allowed to refuse it. The government, however, would not take paper money to pay taxes (accepting only goods or specie) and so the paper money was totally worthless (MM2;2).

money, Korvan   The money of the Amtorian country of Korva is all coin, each coin being made of the same metal and of the same diameter but different thicknesses, and the centers have shapes punched out of them — different-sized circles, squares, ovals and crosses. The value of each coin is determined by the weight of the metal it contains, and the coins stack easily. Thicker pieces of course stack higher, and so the expression "a tall stack" means "a lot of money" (V3;17). See also Pandar.

monkey-men   A typical World War II propaganda image of the Japanese used by Burroughs in *Tarzan and the Foreign Legion*. They are also called "sub-men" therein and their speech described as monkey-like chatter. In his book *Edgar Rice Burroughs: Master of Adventure*, Richard Lupoff poked fun at this usage: "presumably," he wrote, "ape-men are of a far higher order" (T22;1).

monochord   A one-stringed musical instrument which produces one note. Such an instrument is strapped to the left forearm of a dancer participating in the Dance of Barsoom, and is bowed by a ring wound with gut and worn between the first and second joints of the right index finger. The dancers thus provide their own music, which never changes over the years (M5;1).

The Monster Men   A single novel, abbreviated Q for lack of a better one (since both M and MM are already taken). It is the story of Number Thirteen, a synthetic man from the vats of Professor Arthur Maxon, who rose above both his fellow monsters and mere humans in courage, appearance and intelligence and aspired to the hand of Virginia Maxon, the professor's daughter, who loved him in return. It is also the story of Number Thirteen's quest to rescue the girl from peril and the search for his own soul. The events took place in the late 1920s and were published as a novel in 1929.

Monstery, Colonel   Barney Custer's fencing master, who had made him a master of the sabre (MK1;9).

Mont Blanc   The highest point in Europe, 15,771 feet above sea level at its summit (MK1;2).

Montana goats   What Angora goats were erroneously called in Kalkar-occupied 22nd century America (MM2;2).

Montfort, Bertrade de   Daughter of Simon de Montfort, Earl of Leicester and thus first cousin to Norman of Torn, who first met her when he rescued her from abduction by the men of Henry III in May of 1262. He later saved her again from the castle of Peter of Colfax, but dared not reveal his true identity to her, wooing her instead as "Roger de Conde." She was betrothed by her father to Prince Philip of France and went with her mother to visit him there for two years, but upon returning to England in 1264 she realized that she loved Norman too much to give him up and openly avowed it, marrying him after he was revealed as the lost Prince Richard, though she would still have otherwise (OT;7–12,16–19).

Montfort, Guy de The third son of Simon de Montfort, who was present at the Battle of Lewes on May 13, 1264 (OT;16).

Montfort, Henry de The eldest son of Simon de Montfort and brother of Bertrade, who was sent out by their father when she was overdue from the Castle de Stuteville in June of 1262. He also went to Castle Torn in search of her and made overtures of friendship to Norman of Torn when the latter rescued Bertrade from Peter of Colfax. Henry was later one of the generals at the Battle of Lewes on May 13, 1264 (OT;9–10,16).

Montfort, Simon de, Earl of Leicester (1200–1265) The brother-in-law of Henry III of England, who was unjustly accused of treason by the king in 1243 and afterward led a series of rebellions and civil wars against the very unpopular Henry. He was very fond of the young Prince Richard and was crushed when the boy was kidnapped in July of 1243, but the boy unknowingly helped his uncle's cause when he grew up (and became Norman of Torn), because the chaos created by his raids in the late 1250s helped make his uncle the virtual ruler of England. After Henry's defeat in 1264, de Montfort practically became ruler in fact, then became Richard's father-in-law as well. De Montfort died in battle the next year after many of his own allies turned against him and sided with the king (OT;1–6,17–19).

Montfort, Simon de, Jr. The second son of Simon de Montfort, Earl of Leicester (OT;10).

month, Barsoomian A Barsoomian month is about 70 Earth days long (M10:3;3). See Teean.

month, Sidereal The only natural and observable measurement of time available to the U-gas of Va-nah. See ula (MM1;6).

Montmorency, Sir Richard One of the knights of Nimmr who was the officer of the gate to the Valley of the Sepulcher when James Hunter Blake stumbled across it in 1921. The two quickly became friends and Sir

Richard helped Blake adjust to the ways of Nimmr, teaching him how to fight and joust (T11;9–12).

moon *see* Luna

moon fish A small fish of both the Atlantic and Pacific coasts of North America (V4;4).

The Moon Maid The first book in Burroughs' moon trilogy, abbreviated MM1, which was first published in 1923. The events in it took place in 2024 to 2036 and were told to Burroughs aboard a transoceanic airship on June 10–11, 1967, and sent back to the 1920s by some strange telepathic means of which we know nothing. The story concerns Julian 5th, the reincarnation of Julian 3rd, from whom Burroughs received the story. Julian 3rd had the peculiar ability to "remember" his future lives as well as his past, and so could relate the adventures of Julian 5th. The latter was the commander of the Barsoom, the first Earth-Mars vessel, which was sabotaged by one of its inventors out of jealousy of Julian and crash-landed inside the hollow moon. Julian was soon separated from his men and had to travel about the world within the moon, seeking to rescue the moon maid Nah-ee-lah from her captors.

The Moon Men The second novel in the moon trilogy, originally published in *Argosy All-Story Weekly* in the February and March issues for 1925. The action of the story takes place in 2120 and was related to Burroughs in March of 1969 by Julian 3rd, who was reincarnated as his descendant Julian 9th, hero of the story. Julian 3rd had the peculiar ability to "remember" his future lives and so knew of the events before they happened. Julian 9th lived in Chicago under the rule of the Kalkars, who (led by the human traitor Orthis) had conquered the Earth in 2050. The story concerns the events leading up to Julian 9th's beginning a revolution against the Kalkars. It is abbreviated MM2.

moons, Barsoomian Mars has two moons. The nearer, Phobos (called Thuria by the Barsoomians), is inhabited and has some bizarre physical properties. The farther, Deimos (called Cluros by the Barsoomians), is unexplored (M1)(M8).

Moore, Harold Ten-year-old Jack Clayton's tutor in London, "a bilious-countenanced, studious young man," who took everything too seriously. When he tried to stop the boy from going to see the trained ape **Ajax**, the muscular lad bound and gagged him, then went anyway. After this incident, the hapless tutor resigned (T4;2).

Moosko An ongyan of **Thora** who was aboard the ship **Yan** when it was taken by **Carson Napier**'s privateer **Sofal** in 1929. Moosko was taken aboard the **Sofal** as a hostage and later helped abduct **Duare** from the ship, caused Napier to be imprisoned in the newly **Thorist** city of **Kapdor**, and would have used Duare for his sadistic sexual pleasure had not Napier saved her and killed Moosko (V1;12–14)(V2;1–3).

Mor The Cloud Man of Amtor who guided **Carson Napier**, **Duare** and **Ero Shan** through the **Mountains of the Clouds** to **Southern Anlap** after they saved him from a tharban at the end of 1931 (V4;55).

Morbus An ancient lost city in the **Toonolian Marshes** 700 miles south of **Amhor**. It was a substantial city which had been efficiently and logically laid out and executed, but the buildings were totally without ornamentation. Nothing else was known about the inhabitants, who left few records. The city was discovered and occupied in the early part of the 20th century by **Ras Thavas**, who created and worked to perfect his **hormads** there. The **Council of the Seven Jeds** took over the city from Ras Thavas, and later **Ay-mad** took over from the other six jeds and proclaimed himself **jeddak**. The city was later bombed by the **Heliumetic** fleet to destroy the growth from **Vat Room #4** (M9;4,15,31).

Morga Sagra An attractive young **Unisan** woman, a secretary in the office of the Commissioner of War, who wished to defect to the **Kapars** because she was a warmonger who believed that the Kapars would eventually conquer Unis anyway. She was in contact with Kapar spies in Unis and tried to get **Tangor** to defect with her. He consulted with the **Eljanhai** about it, and they decided he should go with her in order to steal the secret of the Kapar **power amplifier** which might allow a plane to travel to other worlds. Morga Sagra was happy upon first arriving in Kapara but soon found that it was not what she had hoped it would be, and was a nervous wreck in two months. She was eventually turned in to the **Zabo** by the horrible **Horthal Gyl** and died under torture after saying that Tangor was a spy, though she did not actually know that to be true (B2;1–7,11).

Morgan, Patrick (Wild Pat) An Irish-American pilot, inventor, and amateur boxer of the 1930s who decided to defect to the Soviet Union when the U.S. government refused to let him patent or manufacture his experimental aircraft engine and fuel, probably because of interference from the oil companies. While en route, however, the plane developed engine trouble over **Siberia**, necessitating an emergency landing for repairs. It was at this time that he and his passenger **Dr. Marvin Slade** discovered "Jimber-Jaw" and thawed and reawakened him with a process Slade had developed. The Russians would not believe their story, however, and forced them to return to America, where Morgan introduced "Jim" to modern society and was his friend and agent until his "suicide" (J).

Morgas A self-proclaimed wizard of the medieval Amtorian country **Gavo** in the early 20th century who was supposed to be able to turn people into **zaldars**, a feat he accomplished through hypnosis, chicanery and propaganda in order to control his little corner of Amtor. He was also a **togan** and had a powerful force of warriors. Morgas was quite insane and was himself unable to tell the difference between humans and zaldars any more. **Carson Napier** defeated him by the use of the telepathic powers he had learned from **Chand Kabi**—he made Morgas think that he was being pursued by **tharbans**, and the wizard leaped to his death from the top of his castle (V5;4–11).

Morgors The dominant race of **Eurobus**. Morgors look like human skeletons, as their skin is thin, translucent, parchment-like, and pulled tightly over their bones, leaving them visible in full detail. Under good lighting conditions, even their internal organs are visible through the skin. They are totally hairless and have deep-set, completely black eyes with no whites or irises. Morgors wear only a g-string and a very simple **harness** with which to support their weapons—sword, dagger and a pocket pouch. Morgors are totally warlike, living only for war and the love of war as other races live to reproduce. They are thoroughly brutal and completely without honor, having no respect for anything but war — even their technology was stolen from the Savators. The only education received by Morgor youth is military education, and their graduation exercises are combat games fought against slaves and criminals, two Morgors to each opponent. Those Morgors who survive are inducted into their highest caste, the warrior caste (obviously). Morgors have absolutely no art or decoration of any kind — on their buildings, weapons, harness, or anything else — nor any concessions to comfort. Even Bandolian, their Emperor, was only differentiated from the others by having a different insignia on his harness.

The cities of the Morgors are all made entirely of a brown volcanic stone unbroken by decoration of any kind, and are walled and perfectly rectangular. The cities are divided into exactly square blocks by precisely laid out streets and are very large, 16 miles wide by 25 miles long being average. All their buildings are rectangular and only the fact that they are different sizes breaks the monotony. The cities are totally free of vegetation and are located at respectful distances from the immense volcanoes which dot the planet (M11B;3).

Having conquered all of Eurobus, they next turned their attentions to warlike Barsoom as an excellent new conquest. To this end they observed Barsoom for years, learning all they could of its military strength, defenses, etc., then abducted John Carter to verify all of that information. They had decided to attack Helium first because, being the most powerful Barsoomian nation, it would give them the most interesting fight (M11B;2–4).

Mori, Antonio A Filipino communist lackey who came to Africa in 1928 with Wayne Colt, the American "communist." He eventually saw the error of his ways and renounced communism (T14;1,15–17).

Morley, Sir One of the knights of the City of the Sepulcher when it was invaded by the Arabs of Ibn-Jad in 1921 (T11;17).

Morov A semi-civilized part of the Amtorian continent of Noobol which was ruled by the mad jong, Skor (V2;9).

Mors Kajak The Jed of Lesser Helium on Barsoom, son of Tardos Mors, Jeddak of Helium, and father of Dejah Thoris. He and Tardos Mors were shipwrecked in Okar in

1887 by the Guardian of the North and imprisoned, but later fought their way out with John Carter's help. Other than this incident, Mors Kajak is a rather shadowy figure in John Carter's manuscripts (M1)(M3).

Morton, Mary The wife of Reverend Sangamon Morton, who was killed in the Wakanda uprising shortly after he was (ME).

Morton, Ruth The daughter of Reverend Sangamon Morton, who married the American big-game hunter Jefferson Scott, Jr. After the Wakanda uprising and the ensuing deaths of Scott and her parents, she went with her young daughter to live in Virginia with her father-in-law (ME).

Morton, Reverend Sangamon An American Methodist missionary of turn-of-the-century Belgian Congo who was killed when the Wakanda tribe revolted against European rule (ME).

Mosby The name taken by an Apache spy in "D" Troop of the U.S. Cavalry in 1881 (A1;14).

moss, Barsoomian The most prevalent vegetation of Barsoom is a sort of spongy, ocher-colored moss that covers most of the dead sea bottoms which make up the greater part of Barsoom's land area. The moss is so spongy that tracks do not last for long on it, and its softness muffles the sound of feet or wheels. Most of the Barsoomian herbivores (see thoat) find all the moisture they need by eating this moss (M1).

Most High The Kaparan mode of address for anyone in a high position (B2;5).

Mosula A black west African tribe whose members often acted as porters for white Europeans on safari (T3;6).

Mother Hubbard A loose, flowing gown for women, unconfined at the waist, chiefly remembered as the garment which missionaries forced upon native women they had converted (T24;18).

Mother Kruger's A roadhouse of 1910s Chicago (EE;26).

Motlog An Arab raider of the el-Harb tribe who helped Fahd to capture Tarzan in 1921 (T11;1).

Motus A nobleman of Invak who kicked John Carter in the groin while the Warlord was a prisoner of the Invaks. Although he was invisible at the time, Carter managed to get a grip on him and punch his lights out, thus making a great enemy of Motus. Llana of Gathol was given to Motus at the request of the jealous Rojas, who thought Carter loved her. Later, Carter arranged a duel with Motus to give the invisibility spheres time to take effect. Motus was greatly hated (as were Pnoxus and Ptantus) by the people of Invak, but they also feared him because he was the greatest swordsman in the city. Everyone was thus pleased, albeit very surprised, when it became obvious that Carter was the better swordsman. After toying with him for a while, Carter easily dispatched Motus (M10:4; 3,7–10).

mountain ranges The following is a list of the many mountain ranges which have appeared in the works of Edgar Rice Burroughs. See individual entries.

Artolian Hills	Mountains of Thip-
Barren Hills	dars
Black Mountains	Otz, Mountains of
Dinaric Alps	Pare Mountains
Ethiopian Highlands	Ruturi Mountains
Ghenzi Mountains	Santa Monica
Golden Cliffs	Mountains
Grampian Hills	Terrible Mountains
Highlands of Torquas	White Mountains
Mountains of the	Wiramwazi Moun-
Clouds	tains

mountains The following is a list of mountains that appear in the works of Burroughs. See individual entries.

Borson	Midian
Gartolas	Mont Blanc
Gojam	Pastar-ul-ved
Hohr	Stein's Peak
Kilimanjaro	Tuen-baka
Masoerai	Xarator

mountains, African Several African mountain ranges are home to lost civilizations, most notably the Wiramwazi, the Ghenzi, the Ruwenzori, and the Ethiopian Highlands.

mountains, Barsoomian There are many mountains on Barsoom, particularly along the shores of the former oceans, but few are over 4000 feet in height, leading one to the conclusion that the seas of Barsoom must have been shallow by Earthly standards, perhaps no more than one or two thousand feet deep (M1;10).

mountains, Euroban The mountains of Eurobus are often tremendous, reaching heights of 20 miles or more. The volcanoes of the planet, however, are even more awe-inspiring, as they have craters up to 100 miles in diameter (M11B;3–4).

mountains, Va-nah The mountains of Va-nah are enormous, jagged, and numerous and tower to great heights (MM1;2).

Mountains of the Clouds A large, steep, high mountain chain of the continent on which the Empire of Pellucidar lies. Men say that they are visible from half of Pellucidar (P1;10).

Another range with this name is the Amtorian mountain range which separates Middle Anlap from Southern Anlap. It is passable only to the Cloud People, who live in it and know it well, because even the very lowest passes of the range are far up in the thick, eternal inner cloud envelope of Amtor and could not be seen to be explored even if they could be discovered in the first place (V4;54).

Mountains of the Thipdars A mountain range of Pellucidar which lies on the Pellucidarian continent west of the Korsar Az (P4;6).

Mountford, Lord and Lady A British couple who disappeared in 1915, captured by the fierce women warriors of Kaji after being abandoned by the superstitious blacks of their safari when they entered the forbidden Kaji territory. Lady Mountford was killed after bearing a daughter because the Kaji wanted white males to marry — for this reason, they did not kill Lord Mountford. He sent a letter out by a native bearer, but the man died of thirst en route and the letter went undiscovered until Tarzan stumbled upon the skeleton of the messenger in 1935. Mountford himself escaped earlier in that year, but was killed by the black magic of Mafka before he could reach civilization. He did, however, meet Stanley Wood before he died and warned him off, to no avail (T21;1–2).

Mow A young Coripi from the grotto of Ictl deep below the island of Amiocap in Pellucidar. He was captured by the Coripies from the grotto of Xax to be saved for a great feast, and befriended Tanar the Fleet One when he was captured also. They helped each other escape, but Mow was killed in a fall (P3;8).

Mpingu   The trusted **Bagego** slave of **Dilecta**, the sweetheart of **Maximus Praeclarus** in **Castra Sanguinarius**. He was a very trusted slave who served as interpreter for **Tarzan** when he first arrived in the city, but was later forced by threat of torture to betray both Maximus Praeclarus and Tarzan to the agents of **Sublatus**. He was imprisoned with them and also escaped with them (T12;9–20).

Another Mpingu was the chief of the cannibalistic **Buiroo** tribe of **Northern Rhodesia**, who captured **Helen Gregory** for a feast in 1936 (T20;7) and who also captured Tarzan for a brief while in 1939 (T24B;4).

Mpugu   A native chief of the **Belgian Congo** who was friendly to white men and owed Tarzan a debt. The Lord of the Jungle left **Stanley Obroski** with him when he was stricken with fever in 1932 (T17;20).

mtu mla watu   Cannibals (T23;9).

mu   (*Ape*) "She" or "female" (T6:4).

mu   (*Pal*) Strong (T8).

Mu Tel   The Prince of **Toonol** on Barsoom, nephew and heir to the **Jeddak** of Toonol, **Vobis Kan**. He was more popular than his uncle, but the people's loyalty to their jeddak and the idea that Mu Tel might prove even worse than his uncle, were he to become jeddak, kept him from the throne for a long time. He became friends with **Gor Hajus** so the assassin might help him to get the Toonolian army on his side, and helped **Ulysses Paxton** and his party on their mission to kidnap **Xaxa** of **Phundahl** (M6;9).

mucker   (American slang) A vulgar roughneck or hoodlum (K1).

The Mucker   The story of **Billy Byrne**, a "mucker" from **Chicago** who finds himself shipwrecked in a jungle of the Far East and must use all of the wisdom and ability the streets taught him to win freedom for himself and the woman he has fallen in love with, the rich girl **Barbara Harding**, who is separated from him by such a wide social gulf that even if he wins her, he loses her. The story was published in 1914 and abbreviated K1.

Muda Saffir, Rajah   A Malay prince and pirate of the 1920s who, upon discovering the beauty of **Virginia Maxon**, immediately began to plot to possess her for his own. He abducted her from her father's island and fled

into the **Bornean** interior with her, then lost, recaptured and lost her again before fleeing into the interior before the white man's law in the person of the U.S.S. *New Mexico* (Q;1–2,6–16).

Mudini, Prince   Some obscure royal person whom **Naomi Madison** married in 1933 (T17;33).

mugalla   In the terminology of the **Bagalla** tribe of east Africa, a subchief (TT1;3).

Mugambi   The chief of the **Wagambi** tribe of west Africa who led an expedition to **Jungle Island** in 1912 and attempted to attack Tarzan while there, but was attacked himself by **Sheeta** and the apes of **Akut** in response to Tarzan's call. He alone of all his warriors escaped the carnage and fled, but was apprehended by Tarzan, who made Mugambi a deal to take him and his apes to the mainland in return for Mugambi's life. He traveled with Tarzan and the apes up the **Ugambi** River in search of **Nikolas Rokoff**, and Tarzan left him to lead the apes and Sheeta while he went ahead to scout. He was with the apes when they rescued Tarzan from the cannibals' dance of death, and later led the pack in pursuit of Rokoff's canoe when they thought Tarzan killed by a crocodile. He became Tarzan's devoted follower, following him to Jungle Island, thence to England, and later to Tarzan's estate in **Uziri** as his lieutenant (T3;5–10,15–21).

It was Mugambi whom Tarzan left in charge of his bungalow when he went to **Opar** in 1914 so that Jane would have a trustworthy and fearless protector, and Mugambi who was the sole survivor of the attack of the band of **Achmet Zek** to abduct Jane. Mugambi tracked the **Arabs** back to their camp, but Jane had already escaped when he arrived. He followed her trail east, but was captured by the same **Abyssinian** patrol which had previously captured **Albert Werper**. A few days later Mugambi escaped, after having seen Werper carrying the pouch Mugambi recognized as Tarzan's. He stole the pouch of jewels from Werper, but they were in turn stolen from him by the **great ape Chulk** while he slept and not rediscovered until much later. He was eventually reunited with Tarzan and his adopted **Waziri** tribe (T5;6,10,15,19,24).

mukaad   (*Ara*) The men's quarters of an Arab domicile (T11;1).

Mukarram, Abul A young Arab of the band of Sheik Ibn Aswad who coveted Victoria Custer after the band abducted her from near the Greystoke estate in 1913. He abducted her from the band and was killed by the pursuing Nu, son of Nu, when he tried to have his way with her (E1;11–12).

Mullargan, "One-Punch" The new world heavyweight champion in 1939, who went to Africa on vacation after defending his title six times and there encountered Tarzan, who planned to kill the "champeen" for his brutal hunting with a machine gun. After their capture by the **Babango cannibals**, Mullargan showed real penitence for his misdeeds and also showed self-sacrificing courage to save **Joey Marks**. As a result, Tarzan relented and saved him, only sending him out of Africa instead of killing him (T24A).

Multis Par The Prince of **Zor** on Barsoom, son of the **Jeddak Zu Tith**. Multis Par was a cruel and hated tyrant who was always urging acts of rebellion against **Helium**, acts the people of Zor had no stomach for. He disappeared in the late 1930s, and after that Zor gave Helium no further trouble. Actually, Multis Par had been captured by the **Morgors** from **Sasoom**, to whom he gave information and help because they wished to conquer Barsoom. It was he who developed the plan to abduct John Carter, using **U Dan** as bait (M11B;1–2).

Mulungu (*Swa*) God (T12;1).

Mumal The wife of **Gorph**, one of the Mammoth Men of Pellucidar, when **Wilhelm von Horst** was their prisoner in 1928 (P5;14).

Mumga An old, toothless she-ape of the tribe of **Kerchak** in Tarzan's youth (T6:1). Another Mumga was the old high priestess of the **Leopard Men**, replaced by **Kali Bwana** in 1931 (T18;7).

munango-keewati (*WA*) A devil-god of the jungle, such as the people of **Mbonga** thought Tarzan to be (T1;13).

Mungo A bull great ape of the tribe of Kerchak (T1;12).

Munsey, Frank A. *see* Frank A. Munsey Company

Munsey's Magazine The magazine in which *The Girl from Hollywood* first appeared as a six-part serial, beginning in June of 1922.

murder, Wieroo Murder has an important ritual significance to the **Wieroos** of Caspak—a person who gets away with a certain number of undiscovered murders is promoted, and rooms where many murders have been committed are feared and shunned. See also **colors, Wieroo** (C3;3).

Murphy The personal servant of **Dick Gordon**. Murphy resembled "a Methodist minister crossed in love" (ME;2).

Murray, Steve A labor leader of early 20th century **Chicago**. He was a disreputable sort who tried to make a pass at **Elizabeth Compton** in **Feinheimer's Cabaret** one Christmas Eve, only to have the hell beat out of him by **Jimmy Torrance** on behalf of the young lady. He later went to work for **Harold Bince** to attempt to cover up the latter's embezzlement of Miss Compton's father's business. It is not known what legal repercussions befell him after his misdeeds were revealed in court (EE;10–11,22,28).

Museum of Natural History The pride and joy of the Amtorian city of **Voo-ad**. The **Vooyorgan** paralyze (from the neck down) all visitors to their city after taking them by surprise with pretended friendliness, then hang them on the walls as living exhibits forever (V4;31–32).

Muso The acting **Jong** of **Korva** in the loyalist city of **Sanara** on Amtor after **Kord**'s imprisonment by the **Zanis** in 1930. Muso was unpopular with the people, who preferred the noble **Taman**, and he planned to betray Sanara to **Mephis** in order to become Jong of Korva. After he was caught in the act and deposed in favor of Taman, he abducted the **Janjong Nna** in order to extort himself back to the throne, but was caught and killed by **Carson Napier** instead (V3;5–8,12–13,16–17).

Mussolini, Benito (1883–1945) The premier of Italy from 1922 until his death, and the founder and leader of the Fascist movement. He was allowed by King Victor Emmanuel III to reform the Italian government in October of 1922 after threatening to attack Rome and, by 1926, was really dictator of Italy (LL;15).

mutants, Londonian As part of the natural tendency of the human genetic material in their gametes to express itself, children with a mixture of human and gorilla traits were often born to the intelligent gorillas of London in the Valley of Diamonds; a rare few of these were fully human. These mutants were usually destroyed at birth by the superstitious parents, and those who were not were usually driven out of London as soon as they became adults. The outcasts then settled at the south end of the valley along with others like themselves. Most of these that survived, however, were mentally gorillas, even some of those that looked almost human; it was for this reason that they were driven out. The most successful of these hybrids was the fully human Balza, who later became a Hollywood star (T17;28–33).

Mutimbwa The chief of the Waruturi cannibals when Rand (the false Tarzan) started to steal his women and children (T23;2).

Muviri *see* Muviro (T7;1)

Muviro Tarzan's lieutenant, one of the mightiest of the Waziri warriors. It was he who rallied the Waziri after the destruction of Tarzan's farms by the German Schneider and led them to rebuild the estates while his master was away searching for Jane, whom the Germans had abducted. He also accompanied Tarzan on his expedition to Pellucidar to rescue David Innes, and took nine Waziri warriors with him (T4;14)(T9;2)(T13;2). In 1934, his daughter Buira was captured by the mysterious Kavuru and Muviro set out to find her, meeting Tarzan on the way and following him thereafter on a mission to raid the Kavuru stronghold and rescue Buira. The mission was eventually successful, though not in the way Muviro would have envisioned it (T19;2,13–16,20,25,29–31).

muzimo A protecting spirit of east African myth, the spirit of the ancestor for whom one was named. After Tarzan was hit by a tree in 1931 he was convinced by a young warrior named Orando that he was the youth's muzimo, and believed it afterward until he recovered his memory (T18;1–4,12).

m'wa (*Ape*) Blue (TC).

M'wa-lot The king of the Sagoth tribe which captured Tarzan on his expedition to Pellucidar in 1927. Perhaps because his tribe was not dominated by the Mahars, they were more primitive than most Sagoths, going naked and using only clubs as weapons (P4;4).

M'walat A great ape of the tribe of Toyat who released Tarzan from his bonds after Tantor rescued him from the tribe el-Harb in 1921 (T11;3).

Mweeza A black cannibal of the tribe of Mbonga who was killed by a lion when he attacked it, thinking it to be Tarzan in disguise (T6;11).

My Dear Jane Clayton, as she was known to Meriem, because it was what "Bwana" (Tarzan) always called her (T4;14).

Myos-Hormos An ancient Egyptian port on the Gulf of Suez (T12;10).

Mypos The city of the fish-men of Amtor, a walled city of no great size built on the shores of the Lake of Japal in the northern part of Noobol. It was apparently built without benefit of any sort of surveying or plumbline, completely by eyesight. Since the Myposan sense of straightness and balance is very poor, all of the streets of Mypos are crooked and winding, as are the wood or limestone buildings, which look hastily and shoddily thrown together. Doors and windows are all of different sizes (V4;4).

Myposans The fish-men of Amtor, who inhabit the city-state of Mypos. They have webbed hands and feet, gills on their necks, protruding lips, and bug eyes. They have heavy black beards and hair and their bodies are absolutely perfect, with well-developed muscles and practically no fat. Myposans have a peculiar life cycle — after mating (once a year, and always with a member of one's own family) the females go into pools in their homes and produce tens of thousands of tiny, fish-like babies who go out through channels into the Great Lake of Japal, thence to the open sea as salmon do. Like salmon, the few who survive a year find their way unerringly to the pool in which they were spawned and there develop into amphibians, then full humanoid adults. Their parents can recognize their own offspring by instinct and will kill all alien babies who wander into their pool, though this is a rare occurrence because of their homing instinct. Usually only one or two babies out of a spawning survive, and sometimes none at all (V4;3,10).

Myr-Lo The operator of the nerve-index machine of **Kamtol** on Barsoom, successor to the device's inventor. He could operate the machine perfectly but could not possibly have repaired or rebuilt it, since the secret of its construction died with the inventor. John Carter killed him and took his harness to help disguise himself, then smashed the hellish machine (M10:2;5,13).

Na-chi-ta (1858–?) The son of **Cochise** who led his people into battle (during his father's illness) against the Mexican cavalry in May of 1874, then became the chief of the **Cho-kon-en** after his father's death in June of that year. He accompanied **Geronimo** in his 1884 rebellion and surrendered with him at **Skeleton Canyon** on September 4, 1886, and was imprisoned at **Fort Marion, Florida**, until his death (A1;3–4)(A2;6,14).

Na-tanh An Apache warrior of the **Be-don-ko-he** in the late 19th century (A2;1).

Nacori A Mexican army outpost town of late 19th century **Sonora** (A2;8).

Nacozari A Mexican town of **Sonora** which lies near the headwaters of the **Rio Yaqui** (A1;8).

Nadara The beautiful young "cave girl" of the story of that name who fell in love with **Waldo Emerson Smith-Jones** after he involuntarily saved her from the "**Bad Men**" who had captured her in 1911. In her naiveté, she believed him to be an immensely brave fellow, and after she taught him the beginnings of jungle craft she wanted him to come to her village and kill two mighty brutes who wanted her. He fled in fear and did not return until six months later, after he had built up his musculature, his courage and his skill to the point where he actually could kill them and take Nadara for himself. She forgave him for running away and led him to her tribe, where he became king (CG1;2–11).

He ruled for some time, until a great earthquake killed most of the tribe except for Smith-Jones (now called **Thandar**), who lucked out, and Nadara, who had just been reabducted by the Bad Man **Thurg**. She was rescued from him by the crew of the *Priscilla*, who had come in search of Smith-Jones, and when she found out that her rescuer was her mate's father, she told him about the earthquake in which she thought him dead. Mr. Smith-Jones took her aboard the yacht (much to his wife's chagrin) and would have taken her back to **Boston** as his daughter-in-law, but she was abducted by the yacht's villainous first mate **Stark** and taken to another island, which was inhabited by head hunters who made Nadara their goddess. Smith-Jones rescued her from the temple after following her with great difficulty (because of the poor healing of his earthquake-inflicted wounds) and returned with her to his parent's yacht, where her true origin as the daughter of the **Count** and **Countess of Crecy** was discovered and she and Smith-Jones were officially married in Honolulu on the way home to Boston (CG2).

Nadara's Island A very large tropical island inhabited only by white Stone Age and pre–Stone Age savages. It lies at 10 degrees south, 150 degrees west and was discovered by **Captain Cook** in 1773 but was of little interest commercially and so was not often visited by mariners. It is not known where the ancestors of the islanders came from, but it might be assumed that they were originally shipwrecked mariners of ancient times (CG1;6)(CG2;6).

nagaina Feminine of **naga** (HM;4).

nagas In Hindu mythology, the Cobra People, who have seven heads, are great workers of magic, and are able to change their shape at will. Great kings or warriors often claimed to have a **nagaina** as a wife or ancestress, as these female nagas sometimes married human warriors or kings (HM;4).

nagoola In the language of the white savages of **Nadara's Island**, the black panther (CG1;3).

Nah-ee-lah The Moon Maid, princess of the city of **Laythe** and daughter of its jemadar, **Sagroth**. She fell into the hands of the **No-vans** after being swept away from Laythe by a sudden windstorm while she was flying above the city. **Julian 5th** promptly fell in love with her and rescued her soon afterward from the No-vans and from **Orthis**, to whom the No-van chieftain had given her while they waited for the ransom they planned to demand for her return. After wandering for a while, she and Julian mistakenly entered a **Kalkar** city, and even though he succeeded in getting her to safety, he himself was captured by the Kalkars. She made her way home, where Julian found her after his escape from the Kalkars, but she pretended to not even know him because she believed (because he was staying in Ko-tah's palace) that he had betrayed her trust. When Julian defended her father against the assassins sent by Ko-tah, Nah-ee-lah realized the truth and apologized to him. Together they escaped the doomed city with flying wings and lived for a few months on a deserted island until they saw the *Barsoom* in the distance and flew over to it, then returned to Earth and married. Nah-ee-lah became the mother of **Julian 6th** in 2036, the year they returned to Earth (MM1;6–8,12–14).

Naiad The British yacht owned by Colonel **William Leigh**, which (while on an expedition to explore deep sea life in the Pacific late in 1938) was captured by **Wilhelm Schmidt** and the *Saigon* mutineers and put under a prize crew. Apparently, the crew did not hold to Schmidt's ideas and instead cruised around for six weeks, and eventually rescued the *Saigon* castaways, including the Leighs (T24; 6–7,24).

Naika The daughter of **Gupingu**, witch doctor of the **Bukena**. Naika was abducted by **Ydeni** the **Kavuru** and rescued from him by Tarzan (T19;10,13).

Nairobi The capital and chief city of Kenya, to which Tarzan often traveled for supplies and news from his African estates, which lay south of Nairobi (T7;1).

Nakay-do-klunni (?–1881) An Apache *izze-nantan* (medicine man) of the **Be-don-ko-he** tribe who tried to save **Cochise** from death by sickness in May of 1874, but could not. He began to foment an uprising in September of 1878 by establishing a dance which he claimed would raise the great dead warriors, but which could only work if the white men were driven from the land, because their presence was holding the dead down. He was killed at the Battle of **Cibicu Creek** in 1881 (A1;3,15).

Nakhla The beautiful daughter of Sheik Ali-es-Hadji in early 20th century northwest Africa. She was saved from being raped at the hands of bandits by the amnesiac **Prince Michael** and his lion and immediately fell in

love with the handsome youth. A week later, she began to teach him her language so they might communicate, since his amnesia had also robbed him of any knowledge of spoken language. After considerable opposition from her father and interference from the treacherous **Ben Saada** was overcome, they married and Prince Michael (now called **Aziz**) joined her father's tribe (LL;10–25).

nala (*Ape*) Up (T21;24).

Naliny A Galla of Abyssinia who was the father of Ulala, better known as **Fejjuan** (T11; 10).

Naliza A great Apache warrior of the late 1800s, friend to **Cochise**. He was, like most of his race, very taciturn (A1;2).

Nallah One of the young sisters of **Julian 20th** (MM3;1).

Nalte, voo jan kum Baltoo "Nalte, the daughter of Baltoo" (*Amt*). The beautiful daughter of the **Jong of Andoo** who was taken prisoner by **Skor**, Jong of Morov after she escaped from those who had abducted her from her own country during a war. She escaped from Skor with **Carson Napier** in 1930 and fled with him to **Havatoo**, where she was declared fit to work as a **yorgan** and lived as such until she was recaptured by the creatures of Skor, who had come from **Kormor** (which lay directly across the **Gerlat kum Rov** from Havatoo) in search of human subjects for Skor's experiments. She was again rescued by Napier and later mated with **Ero Shan** of Havatoo (V2;10–21).

Nameless Strait A 1000 mile long, 200 mile wide strait joining the **Sojar Az** to the **Korsar Az** in Pellucidar, south of the great continent on which both the **Empire of Pellucidar** and **Korsar** lie (P7:2;1).

names, Invak The names of nobles of **Invak** indicate that status, since the names of male nobles (such as **Motus**) end in -us and the names of female nobles (such as **Rojas**) end in -as. Royal names follow the same pattern but also begin with two consonants (like **Pnoxus** or **Ptantus**)(M10;4;4).

Nan-ta-do-tash An Apache *izze-nantan* (medicine man) of the **Cho-kon-en** tribe who could not save **Cochise** from his death by illness in May of 1874 (A1;3).

Nan-tan-des-la-par-en "Captain with the brown clothes" (*Apa*). Apache name for Major-General George Crook, U.S. Army (A2;1).

Nanay An Apache chieftain of the Chihen-ne tribe in the late 1800s (A1;3).

Nao A young priestess of Opar who became infatuated with Wayne Colt when he was captured there for sacrifice in 1928. She helped him escape the city, killing the priest Firg in the process (T14;9–10).

Napier, Carson The young blond-haired, blue-eyed Anglo-American pioneer of spaceflight. He was born in 1902, the son of a British army officer and an American girl from Virginia, and was raised in India, where he learned the powers of telepathy and the projection of psychic images, which he later used to send the narrative of his travels to Edgar Rice Burroughs. After inheriting a huge sum of money from his uncle, Judge John Carson, he designed and built a huge rocket torpedo with which he intended to journey to Mars, but a miscalculation in his flight plan (he neglected to account for the gravity of the moon) caused him to end up on Venus instead. He fell in with the people of Vepaja, a beautiful country in which the people live in cities carved out of the upper branches of living trees. He was adopted by the Vepajans and even given their serum of longevity, but fell in love with Duare, the forbidden daughter of the Jong of Vepaja, who eventually returned his love — a worse sin than his daring to love her. On an expedition with Kamlot (his best friend there) he was captured by the Klangan and taken aboard a Thorist ship, where he eventually started a successful mutiny, took the ship, and rescued Duare, who had been imprisoned on another Thorist ship. After he later saved her from being abducted by a spy among the crew, she avowed her love to him, but in the rescue he was captured by the recent Thorist converts of Noobol, a mostly-savage country near Vepaja (V1).

After escaping the Noobolians, they wandered in the wilderness for a time before being captured by Skor, the mad Jong of Morov, who had created a whole nation of zombies to serve him. Duare soon escaped them, and Napier later, rescuing in the process Nalte, Janjong of Andoo. They ended up in Havatoo, a super-scientific city built on the shores of the Gerlat kum Rov directly across from the zombie city of Kormor in the Strabolian part of Noobol. Napier was there almost executed by the Havatooites for his inherited genetic imperfections, but proved his worth by his knowledge of astronomy and aeronautics, sciences unknown on Amtor. Nalte was soon afterward abducted to Kormor, and when Napier went there to save her, he found that Duare had since been recaptured and imprisoned in the city. He rescued both of them and returned to Havatoo, only to have the Havatooites conclude that Duare was one of Skor's creatures and sentence her to death, which sentence would have been carried out had not Napier escaped with her in the airplane the Havatooites had helped him build (V2).

After their escape they flew to the continent of Anlap, where they landed in the friendly city of Sanara, under siege by the forces of the Zani party, which had taken over the government of Korva (the country in which Sanara lies) after a disastrous war with nearby Ator. Napier accepted a commission from Muso, the acting Jong of Korva, to act as a secret agent in Amlot (the capital of Korva) by posing as a Zani himself. He there discovered that Duare's father Mintep was a prisoner in the Gap kum Rov of Amlot. After saving Duare from Muso (who in Napier's absence had tried to take her as his woman) Napier returned to Amlot and rescued Mintep, helping to defeat the Zanis at the same time and also exposing Muso as a traitor. In the confusion, he became separated from Duare and returned to Sanara to find that she had returned to Vepaja in the anotar with her father to stand trial for the crime of mating with Napier. Before pursuing them Napier had to rescue Nna, Janjong of Korva, from Muso, who had had her abducted in a bid to recapture the throne. He did so, killing Muso in the process, and was declared Tanjong of Korva for his service. He then returned to Vepaja in the nick of time to save Duare, and together the two escaped toward Korva in the anotar (V3).

They were caught en route in a deadly Amtorian hurricane, however, and although they did not crash, they were driven thousands of miles off course into Amtor's unexplored northern hemisphere, where they were captured and enslaved by the fishmen of Mypos.

They escaped, but Napier, upon returning a fellow slave to his home in nearby Japal, became embroiled in a civil war there. Luckily, Duare was for once out of harm's way at the time. Napier was then captured by the hideous plant men of Brokol and taken to their country as a sacrifice, but was rescued by Duare in the anotar. They then flew over to Anlap, but because of a poorly-made repair on the anotar were forced to land in Voo-ad, the country of the Vooyorgan, who tricked them, drugged them into paralysis, and hung them up as museum exhibits. Here they again met Ero Shan of Havatoo and were given the happy news that Duare's death sentence in Havatoo had been reversed and they were again welcome there. Once again Duare had to save Napier from this predicament — a Vooyorgan mutant fell in love with her and brought her the paralysis antidote, then abducted her, but she eventually got free from him and returned to Napier and Ero Shan. They then flew south into Middle Anlap, where (because of Napier's excessive curiosity and an unprotected propeller) they were shot down in a war between two fleets of huge, land-going ships. Duare was again separated from him and he and Ero Shan were impressed into military service, eventually ending up after the war was over as slaves in a barbaric outlaw city, where by chance Duare had also ended up. They eventually escaped and made their way across the Mountains of the Clouds in a scout lantar, and back to Korva (V4).

Napier and Ero Shan then built another anotar to replace the lost one so Ero Shan could return to Havatoo, but while they were testing it they became lost in a freak weather condition (coupled with instrument failure) and were forced down in the country of Gavo on the continent Donuk, where a medieval technology prevailed. While there, they helped the inhabitants of the country defeat Morgas, a self-proclaimed wizard who had the ability to convince people that he could turn them into zaldars through a combination of hypnosis and propaganda. To defeat him, Napier used the power to project psychic images he had learned in his youth, both to escape Morgas' guards and to kill Morgas by convincing him that he was being pursued by tharbans, whereupon he leaped to his death from the top of his castle (V5).

Napolapart Bruma, the Jukan high priest of Ogar, mispronounced "Napoleon Bonaparte" this way when David Innes used the French Emperor's name as an alias to enter the palace of Meeza (P6;13).

Napoleon Bonaparte Name taken by David Innes when he returned to the Jukan village of Meeza to rescue his friend Zor late in 1929 (P6;13).

Naratu A huge black woman, the jealous and shrewish wife of Sgt. Usanga, whose fear of Naratu kept Fraulein Bertha Kircher safe from Usanga's amorous attentions for a while (T7;8).

nargily (Ara) A tobacco pipe (T17;12).

Narrow Canyon The descriptively named site of the Samary village of Houtomai in the hill country of Noobol on Amtor (V3;2).

Narvon An Atorian scholar living in Amlot during the Zani period whom Carson Napier was ordered to arrest while posing as a Zani officer. Narvon had contacts with the Toganja Zerka, who was almost discovered at his house when Napier came to arrest him. He was killed by torture, half-betraying Zerka in the process (V3;11).

nasara (Ara) Plural of Nasrany (T17;2).

nasrany (Ara) An infidel (T11;1).

nasrawia (Ara) Feminine form of Nasrany (T11;21).

Nastor A Dator of the First-Born of Kamtol on Barsoom who was the enemy of Xaxak and gave him two-to-one odds against John Carter, a wager which Nastor of course lost, for which he was none too happy. His wife bought Llana of Gathol as a slave and he tried to buy Llana from her, but the woman refused because she feared Llana's beauty. He then tried to rape Llana, for which he was killed by John Carter (M10:2;7–9,13).

Nat-ul A beautiful cave girl of Niocene Africa 100,000 years ago. She was the daughter of Tha and the beloved of Nu, son of Nu. She asked him to bring her the head of Oo, the saber-toothed tiger, as proof of his courage, and during an earthquake soon afterward he was trapped in Oo's cave, where mysterious gases kept him in suspended animation until 1913. Nat-ul meanwhile died and was reincarnated as Victoria Custer, to be reunited with her lover at last when another earthquake freed him. After Nu saved her from the Arabs, Victoria was "possessed" by the psyche of Nat-ul and returned with Nu to the past by some mysterious means. She there relived her last few weeks of life, during which she was abducted by the covetous Hud, escaped from him, then was captured by the Boat-Builders. She followed Nu to an island to which he had gone himself to escape the Boat-Builders, and after he rescued her they returned to their home in the village of Nu. She was killed soon afterward when a stupendous earthquake destroyed the village by hurling the cliff in which it was built into the Restless Sea, and Nat-ul with it (E1;5–7,12–13)(E2).

Natando The black head man of Dr. Karl von Harben's 1920 safari to find his kidnapped daughter Gretchen (TT2;10).

Natch-in-ilk-kisn An Apache warrior of the Be-don-ko-he tribe who helped Shoz-dijiji bring back the bear he killed in the spring of 1873 (A1;2).

Navajo An Indian tribe related to the Apaches, with whom they were not friendly because their territories were too closely contiguous (the Navajo lived in Utah and Arizona). They were raiders, but surrendered to "Kit" Carson in 1865 and were given a large reservation which they inhabit to the present day (A1;3).

Ndalo An African chief who was an ally of Abdullah Abu Nejm's and told the Arab of Tarzan's affliction with aphasia in 1938 (T24;1).

Ned-ni An Apache tribe of Arizona, ruled in the 1860s and 1870s by Juh (A1;1).

Neeta (Ape) Bird (TC).

Neeta One of the young sisters of Julian 20th (MM3;1). Also, a female ape-child of the tribe of Kerchak who drowned when Tarzan was about ten (T1;5).

negative gesture, Caspak Hands raised, palms away from the body. This conveys the same meaning as our shaking of the head (C1;9).

Nejeunee "Friend" (Apa). Shoz-dijiji's favorite pinto, which he rode from the time he first began warrior-testing in the mid–1870s until many years later, with rare exception.

When the Apaches were starving while under siege early in 1886 and were eating their horses, Shoz-dijiji drove Nejeunee away so no one could eat him. The pony was later found by Lt. King, recognized, and sent to the Billings ranch, where Shoz-dijiji later found and reclaimed him (A1;8,12–18)(A2;10–12).

Nemone The Queen of Cathne when Tarzan came there early in October of 1930. She was an exceptionally beautiful but exceptionally cruel woman who had women more beautiful than her disfigured or even killed. She became completely infatuated with Tarzan after seeing him in the arena and wanted to marry him, but was stopped from attempting it by the old hag M'duze, who exerted a strange hold over the otherwise uncontrollable Nemone. She continually threw herself at Tarzan's feet but he, repulsed by her evil and happily married to a better woman anyway, spurned her until she could bear it no more and ordered him executed in a Grand Hunt. This was to prove her undoing, however, since her hunting lion Belthar was killed by Jad-bal-ja as a result of the hunt and she, believing herself somehow linked to Belthar, committed suicide as a result (T16; 9–19).

Nene (Ape) The beetle (TC).

neo (Amt) Small (V4;44).

neolantar "Small landship" (Amt). The equivalent of a destroyer in Middle Anlap on Amtor, measuring some 300 feet long and 40 feet wide (V4;44).

neozaldar "Small zaldar" (Amt). The small, pig-sized zaldar of Donuk and other regions of Amtor (V5;3).

nephrite A more common form of jade (E2;11).

neptunium A heavy radioactive element (atomic number 93) used on Amtor to trigger the release of T-rays from element 97 (berkelium) and to cause the substance lor to undergo a nuclear chain reaction. Its Amtorian name is vik-ro (V1;8).

Nero Caesar The older brother of Caligula—not the emperor of the same name, who was Caligula's nephew. He was arrested in A.D. 29 for plotting against Tiberius and was exiled to Ponza, where he committed suicide by starving himself in A.D. 31 (I;3,15).

Nerva (A.D. 35–98) The Emperor of Rome from A.D. 96 to 98. He accused **Marcus Crispus Sanguinarius** of treason (probably rightfully), which prompted the prefect to flee Egypt with the third cohort of his tenth legion and found **Castra Sanguinarius** deep in the African interior (T12;10).

nerve-index machine A machine invented by an ingenious inventor of **Kamtol** on Barsoom. It could record the unique "nerve index" (a sort of "print" of a person's nervous system, possibly like an electro-encephalogram) of any person and keep it on file, then send out a burst of short waves attuned to that person's nervous system, causing instantaneous death no matter where the victim happened to be. The nerve-index reading was taken by a subsidiary machine while the person was exposed to a broad spectrum of stimuli so that all of his reflexes and mental states could be recorded. The machine's inventor was executed long ago by **Doxus**, **Jeddak** of Kamtol so he could have absolute power over everyone in the city, slave and free. The machine was so delicate that it could be easily damaged, and as the secret of its construction had died with its inventor, it could not be repaired and so was carefully guarded from harm. John Carter killed its guards and smashed the machine before escaping Kamtol, or else the machine could have been used to kill him even after his escape (M10:2; 4–5,13).

Nesen (*Ape*) The grasshopper (TC).

Nestor, Cogden An English adventurer of the early 20th century who discovered David Innes' hidden telegraph line in the Sahara desert in May of 1914 and wrote Burroughs about it so the author was able to again communicate with Innes and receive news of Pellucidar (P2).

Netherland East India The name by which Indonesia was called until it was occupied by the Japanese in January of 1942 (T22;1).

nets The hormads of Barsoom used nets to capture their prey so they might be returned to Ras Thavas unharmed (M9;3).

Neubari River An Ethiopian river which is possibly a tributary of or identical with the Wabi Shebelle or the Ganale Dorya (T21;1).

New Gondar The Abyssinian border city of the early 22nd century which stood on the spot occupied by ancient **Berlin**. It was built largely of materials taken from the ruins of that city (LC;8).

New Mexico, U.S.S. The flagship of the U.S. Pacific fleet in the 1920s. It rescued **Professor Arthur Maxon** and his party from Borneo at the end of their adventure there (Q;17).

New Story magazine The magazine in which *The Return of Tarzan* first appeared as a serial from June to December of 1913.

The New York Evening World The newspaper in which "The Man-Eater" first appeared as the serial "Ben, King of Beasts" from November 15th to November 20th of 1915.

Newport An English city on the **Isle of Wight** of which Lt. Jefferson Turck found no trace when he landed there in 2137 (LC;3).

NGC 7006 A globular cluster 220,000 light years from Earth, known to the **Polodans** as **Canapa** (B1;2).

Ni-yo-ka-he An Apache warrior who was killed in a trap set by white soldiers in the late 1850s (A1;2).

Niaka The brother of **Hafim**, the **Galla** whom Tarzan rescued from a **Grand Hunt** in **Cathne** in October of 1930. Niaka was the head slave of the gold mines of Cathne, south of the city, and in thanks for Tarzan's rescue of his brother, he hid the girl **Doria**, whom Tarzan had rescued from the Temple of Thoos and Nemone's plan for her execution (T16;15,19).

Niaux A cave at Ariège, France, in which may be found Cro-Magnon cave paintings (C2;3).

nielsbohrium *see* hahnium

Niger A large river of west Africa, on an unexplored Nigerian tributary of which the tribe of **Amor ben Khatour** camped whenever they were raiding the area. Twice a year they traveled north to **Timbuktu** to trade (T4;5).

Niger A famous racehorse of the Blue Stables of early 1st century Rome (I;8).

Nigger Joe The huge Negro second mate to the **Portuguese**. He tried to kill the first mate **Pedro** one night and **Johnny Lafitte** shot him, thus winning Pedro's loyalty (PB;13).

"The Nightmare" The ninth short story in the collection *Jungle Tales of Tarzan,* in which the young Tarzan ate some stewed elephant meat he had stolen from the natives of Mbonga's tribe and developed food poisoning from the meat, that of an elephant which had died of sickness several days before the feast. The story describes not only the sickness but also the horrible delirium which came with it. The story took place in 1908 and is abbreviated T6:9.

nihilism Name applied by its opponents to a radical political philosophy of late 19th century Russia. Alexis Paulvitch was a nihilist in **Petrograd** for some time and learned to make **time bombs** there, but eventually betrayed his fellows for gold and immunity from legal prosecution (T3;18).

Nimmr A fabled treasure city of **Abyssinia** which lies somewhere in the area called **el-Habash** by the Arabs. Specifically, it lies in the hidden **Valley of the Sepulcher** and is inhabited by the descendants of a lost group of English knights from the **Third Crusade.** The inhabitants of Nimmr are always ruled by a prince called **Gobred** and have never given up on the crusade, which they consider unfinished, even though the inhabitants of the rival **City of the Sepulcher** do consider it finished. Because of this the two cities have been technically at war since the time of the crusades, though the only expression of that war is the highly formalized annual **Great Tourney** (T11;1,9–12).

Ninaka A panglima (chieftain) of the **Signana Dyaks** of **Borneo** who betrayed his Rajah, **Muda Saffir,** by leaving him behind when he fell out of his **prahu** after a struggle with the captive **Virginia Maxon** (Q;10).

999 Priscilla Avenue The American address of **Townsend J. Harper, Jr.,** better known in **Borneo** as **Bulan** (Q;17).

ninth ray The ninth solar ray, unknown on Earth, can be separated by the Barsoomians from sunlight and used to produce atmosphere. See **atmosphere plant** (M1;20).

Niocene A biological epoch which ended about 100,000 years ago. At that time primitive man and the **great apes** spoke very sim-

ilar languages and could to some degree understand one another (E1;1).

Niocene Tongue The primitive human tongue of the **Niocene** period in Africa 100,000 years ago. It was similar to the language of the **great apes,** and **Victoria Custer** could speak it fluently after **Nu, son of Nu,** reappeared (E1;7,12).

Nip (WWII slang) A **Japanese** person or soldier. Short for Nippon, the Japanese name for their nation (T22;29).

Nipons A race of pygmies who inhabit the hills around the **San Fernando Valley** in the heart of 25th century **Kalkar California.** They average about three feet tall for a full grown male and are of Oriental stock, probably descended from one of the large communities of **Japanese** people in modern California, as evidenced by their name for their race. They believe themselves to be descended from a "giant" (normal human) named **Mik-do** who came from "an island far, far out in the middle of the sea," probably Japan. They believe that Mik-do still lives there and that they go to be with him when they die. The Nipons are a happy, peaceful and hospitable people who are very affectionate to one another, but they hated the Kalkars and would ambush them every time they came into the hills, so the Kalkars eventually left them alone. **Julian 20th** encountered the Nipons while trying to get back to his people after escaping from the Kalkar capital, and they gave him food, water and information. The Nipons also knew **Bethelda** and gave her food, but were unable to stop **Raban** from kidnapping her while Julian was away hunting (MM3;6–7).

Nisho, Hawa One of the warriors of **Oda Yorimoto** whom **Barbara Harding** killed by surprise when he discovered the corpse of his **daimyo,** whom she had also surprised and killed (K1;11).

Nkima A little **Manu** (monkey) who was adopted by Tarzan as a sidekick in the early 1920s and figured in several of his adventures thereafter, even helping to rescue him on several occasions. Like most of his kind he was terrified of everything and believed that everyone he met was coming specifically for the purpose of killing him. Tarzan sent him to get the **Waziri** when he was trapped in the

Colosseum dungeons of Castra Sanguinarius in the summer of 1923, and by the middle of August, Nkima successfully returned with the Waziri in tow. He performed a similar function when Tarzan went to Opar to stop the Zveri expedition in 1928 (T14;1–6,10–17) and was with Tarzan for the entire duration of his 1931 adventure among the Leopard Men, constantly upbraiding the amnesiac ape-man to try to make him remember his identity, which finally succeeded. He later saved Tarzan from the Betete pygmies by summoning Zu-tho and Ga-yat to Tarzan's aid (T18). In 1934, he accompanied Tarzan on his quest to rescue Buira from the dreaded Kavuru tribe, and his "monkey-see-monkey-do" antics actually alerted Tarzan to Jane's danger by getting a note to him from her. He was rewarded for his faithful service by being given a share of the Kavuru immortality pellets, making him the world's first immortal monkey (T19).

Nna The Janjong of Korva on Amtor, daughter of Taman, who became jong in 1930. She was abducted by the former jong, Muso in a bid to return himself to power, but was rescued and returned home by Carson Napier (V3;17).

no (*Amt*) A prefix derived from not (with); it fills the same purpose as the English suffix "-y," as in bar (hair) and nobar (hairy) (V1;14).

no (*Pal*) Brook (T8).

No-doyohn Canyon A canyon of southeastern Arizona which was home to the Ned-ni Apaches in 1827 (A1;1).

No-po-so The Apache of the Ned-ni tribe who was the father of Alope, and was thus Geronimo's father-in-law (A1;6).

No-vans The tribe of Va-gas of Va-nah who captured Julian 5th and Orthis, and from whom they learned the language of Va-nah. The No-vans were ruled by a large and intelligent chief named Ga-va-go, and they did not eat Julian 5th and Orthis right away because they feared the strange Earth people might have poisonous flesh like many other animals of Va-nah. Julian of course encouraged this idea. He eventually escaped from the No-vans with Nah-ee-lah, leaving Orthis for dead after he tried to rape the girl (MM1; 5–8).

Noada In the religion of the Xexots of Pellucidar, a female messenger from their god Pu, sent as a sort of Christ-figure to save the souls of the believers. Both Dian the Beautiful and O-aa of Kali were taken to be the Noada by the Xexots, Dian in Lololo and O-aa in nearby Tanga-tanga (P7:2; 4–5).

Noak The assistant to Goofo, major-domo of the palace of Meeza in the land of the Jukans in Pellucidar while David Innes was their "guest" in 1929. Noak was a dangerous maniac, a man to be avoided at all costs. One day he decided to kill Goofo, which made things worse for Innes because Noak then replaced Goofo and was neither as forgetful nor as harmless as his predecessor. He was killed by Innes soon afterward (P6;7–8).

nobar (*Amt*) Hairy (V1;14).

nobargan "Hairy man" (*Amt*). A savage; see Kloonobargan (V1;14).

nobility, titles of Many strange titles of nobility appear in the works of Burroughs on the various planets, worlds, and countries. Below is a list of those titles. See also individual entries.

Chief of Chiefs	Jeddak of	ongvoo
chieftain	Jeddaks	paladar
dator	jeddara	prince
go-sha	jemadar	princess
imperator	jemadav	rajah
janjong	jong	tanjong
javadar	kamadar	togan
jed	maharajah	toganja
jeddak	nonovar	vadjong

nobility, Wieroo The Wieroos of Caspak progress in rank by literally getting away with murder. See colors, Wieroo (C3;3).

Nobs Bowen Tyler's nickname for his dog, Crown Prince Nobbler (C1;1).

noellat (*Amt*) Mighty (V4;9).

Noellat-Gerloo "Mighty Water" (*Amt*). The Amtorian ocean into which the Lake of Japal empties, between Noobol and Anlap in the northern hemisphere (V4;9).

Noice, Clarence The sound director for B.O. Pictures on *The Lion Man* location shoot in 1932. He was killed in a Bansuto ambush just as the company was leaving the Bansuto country (T17;1,7).

Nojo Ganja "Lucky Woman" (*Amt*). The name of the pirate vessel which picked up Carson Napier en route from **Anlap** to **Vepaja** to rescue **Duare** (V3;19).

Nolach One of the king **Kaldanes** of **Bantoom** on Barsoom. One of his men acted as arbiter in deciding whether **Moak** or **Luud** should get **Tara of Helium** when the Kaldanes captured her (M5;4).

Nolat A dator among the **First-Born** of **Kamtol** on Barsoom who owed a great deal of money to **Nastor**, a debt which Nastor promised to cancel if Nolat won a fight against John Carter. This persuaded the prince to fight a slave, an almost unheard-of idea which caused great excitement, especially when Carter won. As he had no quarrel against Nolat, Carter spared his life even though the crowd cheered for his death (M10:2;7–9).

nonovar (*Van*) Princess (MM1;12).

Noobol An Amtorian continent which stretches from the south temperate zone (**Trabol**) far into the equatorial zone (**Strabol**). It was only partially civilized and was largely converted to **Thorism** in the 1920s (V1;13–14)(V2;1). The countries of **Havatoo, Morov,** and **Andoo** lie in the Strabolian portion of this continent, and the countries of **Mypos,** **Japal** and **Brokol** in that portion of it which reaches into the northern hemisphere (V2)(V4;2).

Noola The **Vootoganja** of **Pandar** in **Gavo** on Amtor, consort to **Tovar**. She was "a wild-eyed looking dame with dishevelled hair and a haunted expression" when **Carson Napier** landed in their country while lost over **Donuk** in 1932. She was of the **Ladja** family and distrusted Napier and **Ero Shan**, whom she thought confederates of **Morgas**. Later, when her daughter **Vanaja** was restored to her, she regained her sanity (V5;4,10).

Norge expedition An Arctic expedition arranged by the Norwegian explorer **Roald Amundsen**, which succeeded in crossing the North Pole in the dirigible *Norge* in May of 1926, just a few months before **Jason Gridley** began to plan his expedition to Pellucidar (P4;1).

Norman of Torn The name given to Prince Richard Plantagenet by his old foster

father, **Sir Jules de Vac,** to cover his true identity, of which the young man knew nothing because he had been only three at the time of his abduction in 1243. He was known as Norman of Torn for many years afterward, when as a bandit leader of a thousand men he conducted raids on the king and barons throughout the 1250s and 1260s. The evil influence of old de Vac was tempered in him through the years, however, by the influence of the kindly Father Claude, who taught him the knightly virtues. As a result, Norman preyed only upon the rich, never the poor, and never mistreated a woman or allowed one to be mistreated. In 1262 he met (and later fell in love with) **Bertrade de Montfort,** his first cousin (she was the daughter of the great **Simon de Montfort**), after rescuing her twice from abduction by the awful **Peter of Colfax,** who lusted after her. Norman wooed her not as Norman of Torn, but as "**Roger de Conde,**" and in this alias she fell in love with him and they vowed their love to each other. After this he raided only the barons who were loyal to the king, and made several friends among the nobles who followed de Montfort by his acts of courage and chivalry, especially in defense of women like **Joan de Tany.** When the axe finally fell (so to speak) between king and barons, Norman threw his bandit force behind the barons, turning the tide of battle at Lewes (May 13,1264) in their favor. He then revealed himself to Bertrade de Montfort, only to find that she loved him in spite of who he was and stood by him when de Vac betrayed him to the king (this was done to finish his revenge by having the father order the son hanged). The old man's plot failed, however, because he had made such a good swordsman of Norman that no one could take him but de Vac himself. In the fight they both went down, and de Vac sputtered out the truth as he died — unwittingly, soon enough to save Norman from death. Norman was then reaccepted into the royal family after the truth was proved by his close resemblance to his brother and a distinctive birthmark. He married Bertrade and lived for some time afterward, but his story was later mysteriously stricken from history, probably by his brother (later Edward I), who was jealous of Norman's popularity (OT).

Norman the Devil Appellation applied to **Norman of Torn** by Henry III, who did not know that the famous bandit was his own lost son **Richard** (OT;6).

Norris, Captain   The captain of Anthony Harding's steam yacht, *Lotus* (K1;4).

North Pass Trail   The main road into Hendersville, Arizona, in the 1880s, along which lay **Hell's Bend Pass** (HB;2).

Northern Rhodesia   The British territory which is today called **Zambia**. Tarzan's first African estates were in the westernmost part of the territory (T5).

Norton   The 17-year-old ensign of the *Barsoom*, the first Earth-Mars vessel. Orthis became friendly with him and the young man cultivated that friendship because of the knowledge it gave him, knowledge which allowed him to eventually refill the lunar **eighth** ray tank and get the ship safely back to Earth (MM1;1–2,14). Another Norton was the president of a bank of early 20th century **Chicago** who had been a friend of **Ogden Secor's**, but deserted him when he lost his fortune (GF; 10).

Norwich, Bishop of   A great clergyman who was robbed and made a spectacle of by **Norman of Torn** in May of 1262 (OT;8).

not   (*Amt*) With (V1;14).

Notae Tironianae   (*Lat*) A system of shorthand developed by Marcus Tullius Tiro, private secretary to **Cicero** (I;5).

Notan   The royal **psychologist** of **Zodanga**, a man skilled in reading minds, including those of the recently dead (M1;22).

notar   (*Amt*) Ship (V1;12).

novand   A Minunian military unit comprised of 250 men divided into five **entex** of 50 men each. Four novands make up an **amak** of 1000 men. Novand is also the title of the officer who commands this unit (T10;13).

nsenene   (*Swa*) The grasshopper (T12;4).

Nsenene   "Grasshopper" (*Swa*). The native girl of the village of **Bobolo** who had a crush on "**The Kid**" and so warned him of Bobolo's planned treachery. She also told him about **Kali Bwana**, whom he was anxious to find (T18;21).

Ntale   The native who took over as chief of the **Capietro** band of **shiftas** after the Ital-

ian's death. He was killed the very next day by "**Gunner**" **Patrick** (T15;24–25).

Nu, son of Nu   A powerful caveman of the **Niocene** period 100,000 years ago who was the son of the **Chief of Chiefs** of his people. After killing a saber-toothed tiger, he became trapped in a cave where strange gases kept him in suspended animation until 1913, when an earthquake released him and reunited him with his true love **Nat-ul**, who had been reincarnated as **Victoria Custer**. After saving her from **Arabs**, he and she returned to the cave in which he had slept and again were hit by an earthquake which somehow returned them to the Niocene to relive their lives there. Nu had been forced to pursue and rescue Nat-ul, who had been captured by the **Boat-Builder** people living to the south of his tribe. After various adventures, he succeeded in winning Nat-ul but insisted on hunting out **Oo**, the saber-toothed tiger, whose head he wanted as a trophy for Nat-ul. He succeeded in killing it but was trapped in its cave when a mighty earthquake hit, killing him and imprisoning him within the cave, where he was found in 1913 by Victoria and **Barney Custer**. All the incidents in 1913 with Nu had been only a vision of Victoria's, but all of the other events were real, though they happened 100,000 years ago (E1)(E2).

Nu of the Niocene   The original title of *The Eternal Savage* when it first appeared in *All-Story Weekly* on March 7, 1914.

nudity   Barsoomians go almost completely naked most of the time, wearing only a **harness** (often jeweled) with which to carry weapons, pouches, etc., and many ornaments also. Women tend to wear even less than men (M1).

Numa   (*Ape*) The lion, distinguished from **Sabor**, the lioness, by his mane (T1;9). The **Bolgani** emperor of the **Valley of the Palace of Diamonds** was named Numa and was a huge, man-eating lion that Tarzan eventually killed (T9;9–14).

Numabo   The chief of the **Wamabo** tribe whose warriors captured **Lt. Harold Percy Smith-Oldwick** in the winter of 1915 when he was forced to land his plane in western **Tanganyika** (T7;9).

Number One   The first and most hideous of **Professor Maxon's** synthetic men. It was very tall and hugely built, "a great mountain of deformed flesh ... its face was of the ashen hue of a fresh corpse, [with] ... white hair and pink eyes ... one eye was fully twice the diameter of the other, and an inch above the horizontal plane of its tiny mate. The nose was but a gaping orifice above a deformed and twisted mouth. The thing was chinless, and its small foreheadless head surmounted its colossal body like a cannon ball on a hill top. One arm was at least twelve inches longer than its mate, which was itself long in proportion to the torso, while the legs, similarly mismated and terminating in huge, flat feet that protruded laterally, caused the thing to lurch fearfully from side to side as it lumbered ...." The thing was the first to escape the compound into the jungle, carrying **Virginia Maxon** with it. It was killed by **Number Thirteen**, who heard her screams and came to save her (Q;3–4).

Number Ten One of the toughest of **Professor Arthur Maxon's** synthetic men, one of the only two to resist the leadership of **Number Thirteen** in the beginning. He was one of the last three left alive after repeated encounters with the **Dyak** head hunters who had abducted **Virginia Maxon**, but was later shot dead when he attacked **Sing Lee** in a rage (Q;8,11–12).

Number Thirteen The last of **Professor Maxon's** synthetically created humans, well formed and very intelligent, a handsome young man by any objective standard. To help him feel more human, he alone was given a name by **Dr. Van Horn**—**Jack**. After his escape from the compound, he became known to the natives of **Borneo** as **Bulan** (Q;5).

Number Three One of **Professor Maxon's** synthetic men, a mindless brute who seemed to parrot the actions of the brighter **Number Ten**. With Number Ten, he resisted **Number Thirteen's** leadership at first, but then followed him to rescue **Virginia Maxon** and was one of the last three left alive after repeated encounters with the Dyaks who had abducted her. He was killed by one of the headhunters when he and Numbers Twelve and Thirteen finally rescued Virginia from them. Number Three was covered with black hair and looked something like an orang-utan (Q;8,11–14).

Number Twelve The most advanced, most intelligent and least hideous of **Professor Arthur Maxon's** synthetic men, discounting **Number Thirteen**. He was the last of the monsters to be killed after continued encounters with the **Dyak** head hunters on **Number Thirteen's** quest to save **Virginia Maxon** (Q;7,11,14).

Number Two One of **Professor Maxon's** synthetic men, who was (at least in some ways) much better formed than **Number One** (Q;3).

numbers, Minunian The **Minunians** use a peculiar system of squares, cubes and multipliers to form their numbers in the same way that we use multipliers alone. For instance, a Minunian expresses the number **aopontando** (512,000,021) as $800^3 + 21$, or rather $(23 \times 100)^3 + (10 \times 2) + 1$, but thinks of it as a single number, just as we express 37 as $(3 \times 10) + 7$ but think of it as a single number (T10;13).

numbers, Vooyorgan The **Vooyorgan** of Amtor each have a number rather than a name, with the system working thus: **Kloomeds** (two millions) and above are servants; **voo-meds** (one millions) with no **du** (letter) are artisans; voo-meds with a du are middle class; nobles run from **voo-yor-yorko** (100,000) to voo-med, and the **jong** is always **vik-vik-vik** (999) (V4;31).

Numerius A Roman charioteer of the early 1st century A.D., the slave of **Helvidius Pius**. He was a Spaniard and extremely good-natured — he became **Britannicus'** best friend and eternal rival for the beautiful **Attica**, whom Britannicus eventually won. He was the namesake of Britannicus' only son (I;8–18).

Numerius Tiber Britannicus The only son of **Britannicus Caligulae Servus**, born late in A.D. 40 of Attica, the slave of **Milonia Caesonia**. He was named for **Numerius**, his father's best friend, and for the Emperor Tiberius, whom his father greatly respected (I;20–21).

Numgo A bull ape of the tribe of **Kerchak** while Tarzan was growing up (T6;1).

Numidia An ancient kingdom of northern Africa which is today known as **Algeria** (I;4).

nur (*Ape*) Lie (untruth) (TC).

Nur An A Jaharian noble and enemy of Tul Axtar, from whom he fled to Tjanath, where he was imprisoned as a spy by Haj Osis. He and Tan Hadron were sentenced to die The Death and went down the river Syl to Ghasta. They escaped that frightful city and ended up at Jhama, the fortress of Phor Tak, where Nur An was forced to wait while Tan Hadron went to rescue Tavia, Phao and Sanoma Tora. He was eventually rescued and reunited with his beloved Phao (M7;5–10,17).

Nurn A large, one-eyed pirate aboard the faltar *Nojo Ganja* when it picked up Carson Napier in 1930 (V3;19).

Nutus The Jeddak of Dusar, father of Astok. He did not disapprove of his son's abduction of Thuvia of Ptarth, but when he saw the anger of Helium, Ptarth and Kaol over the matter, he commanded Astok to find her and kill her secretly, thus removing any possibility of Dusar being implicated in her death. What he did not know was that Astok already had her as a secret prisoner in the palace (M4;12).

Nuuana Pali *see* Nuuana Valley (M10)

Nuuana Valley A scenic valley on the Hawaiian island of Oahu (K1;3).

Nyalwa The Betete chosen as chief by his people after Tarzan killed the old chief Rebega in 1931 (T18;19).

Nyamwegi A black warrior of the village of Tumbai who went to the nearby village of Kibbu to court a young lady one night in 1931 and was murdered by the horrible Leopard Men on the way back. His best friend Orando later came to believe that Nkima was the spirit of Nyamwegi because he helped Tarzan, whom Orando believed to be his muzimo (T18;1,3).

nyanza (*Swa*) Lake (ME;2).

Nyuto The chief of the Bagego tribe of the outer Wiramwazi Mountains when they captured Tarzan in 1923 (T12;5).

o (*Amt*) North Amtorian word for "the" (V4;26). See also **voo**.

o (*Pal*) "Like" or "similar" (T8;2).

O-aa The beautiful young chatterbox and compulsive liar who was the daughter of

Oose, King of Kali in Pellucidar. When Fash, King of Suvi, conquered her village in 1931, he took her for himself, but she escaped and took up with Hodon the Fleet One as he escaped Kali also. They were together captured by and escaped from the Sabertooth Men and cornered in a cave, at which time they fell in love with each other (P7:1;3–7). When Hodon fought the warrior Blug for her, O-aa ran away because she thought Blug would kill him; she was captured soon after by a warrior from the island of Canda, whom she killed by a trick, then drifted in her canoe until she was picked up by the derelict EPS *Sari*. When the sailors abandoned the derelict ship she refused to go with them, remaining on board until the ship washed up on the shore of the Xexot country, where she was proclaimed Noada by the people of the city of Tangatanga and got into trouble with the priest and the king for her habit of giving the temple revenues back to the people (P7:2;1–4,7). When David Innes came to Tanga-tanga in search of Dian, he and O-aa conspired, eventually escaping the Xexots aboard the EPS *John Tyler*, which had come to rescue Innes (P7:3;1–7). She later leaped off the ship to get away from Ah-gilak, who considered a woman aboard ship to be bad luck, and ended up in the friendly Zurts country, from which she was later rescued by Hodon and taken home (P7:4).

O Ala The wife of Han Du, the Savator of Eurobus who befriended John Carter while he was there (M11B;9).

O-dan "Like Rock" (*Pal*). A Waz-don warrior of the Kor-ul-ja tribe of Pal-ul-don who went with Om-at, Tarzan and Ta-den to search for Pan-at-lee (T8;4).

OGPU The acronym of the Obyedinyonnoye Gosudarstvennoye Upravlenie (Unified State Political Administration), the Soviet Secret Police from 1923 to 1934, after which the organization passed through five successive name changes to become the KGB in 1955. Both Peter Zveri and Leon Stabutch were OGPU agents sent to Africa to cause trouble in Tarzan's country (T15;1).

O-lo-a "Like Star Light" (*Pal*). The daughter of Ko-tan, King of Pal-ul-don. She loved and was loved by Ta-den, but her father hated him and tried to put him out of the way, so he fled. Tarzan later met her and gave her news of Ta-den, in return for which she helped him escape the searching priests who wanted him dead. She was eventually carried to safety by **Ja-don** during the civil war and married Ta-den after his father became King of Pal-ul-don (T8;2,13,22–25).

O Mad (*Bar*) The green Barsoomian term for a man with one name. The only way to gain a second is to kill a chieftain in fair combat, taking his metal and his surname (M1;14).

O-Mai the Cruel The Jeddak of Manator on Barsoom about 5000 years before O-Tar. He died in his bedchamber one night, and when he was found, the hideous expression of fear on his face (together with the fact that there was not a mark on him to explain death) drove all who looked upon him mad. His corpse was left to rot where it lay and his suite was closed up and forbidden by tradition, which held the chamber to be haunted by O-Mai and a horde of **corphals**. In superstitious Manator, his room was the perfect hiding place for **Gahan** of **Gathol** and **Tara of Helium**, who were brought there by **Tasor** of Gathol (M5;18).

O-ra The gold-digging sweetheart of U-val of Ruva in Pellucidar, who would only marry U-val if he got himself a slave (P6;25).

O-Tar The Jeddak of Manator on Barsoom for 433 years (from 1482 to 1915) — a cruel and sadistic man who reveled in his deadly games of jetan. Like most bullies, he was also a coward, and after **Ghek's** display of power was afraid to kill him, and sentenced him to jetan instead. He was accused of cowardice by his **jeds** and chiefs for not seeking **Gahan** of **Gathol** in the chamber of **O-Mai** and eventually acquiesced, but fainted at the sound of Gahan's chilling scream in the dark bedroom. O-Tar wanted to marry **Tara of Helium** after her capture by **I-Gos**, but was foiled by Gahan and I-Gos when the latter showed proof of O-Tar's cowardice. After the overthrow of his power by **U-Thor** (with the help of **Helium** and **Gathol**), he honorably committed suicide to make way for **A-Kor**, thus redeeming himself in the eyes of the honor-loving Manatorians (M5;14–22).

O-220 The great dirigible built in **Friedrichshafen** in 1927 for **Jason Gridley's** expedition to Pellucidar to rescue **David Innes**

from the dungeons of the **Korsars**. It was built entirely of **harbenite**, a metal as light as cork but stronger than steel, and obtained its lifting power from six axial vacuum tanks rather than from hydrogen or helium; this design was only possible because of harbenite's enormous strength-to-weight ratio — any other material would have either collapsed under air pressure or not left the ground. To keep the dirigible's weight low, all of its engines, tanks and fittings were also constructed of harbenite (wherever possible), and to maintain its aerodynamic qualities all crew quarters, engine rooms and supply tanks were internal. It had six landing tires and eight propellers and set out for Pellucidar in June of 1927. Here are its specifications:

Length: 997 feet
Diameter: 150 feet
Mass (empty): 75 tons
Maximum Airspeed: 105 mph
Total Lift: 225 tons
Lifting Tanks: 6
Motors/Propellers: 8
Motor Type: Air cooled
Motor Power: 700 hp each
Total Power: 5600 hp

O-Zar A great warrior of **Manataj** whom Gahan of Gathol pretended to know in order to win the favor of the new keeper of the Towers of Jetan (M5;16).

Oah A priestess of **Opar** who plotted with the high priest **Cadj** to do away with **La** and make Oah high priestess, Queen of Opar and Cadj's mate. She was overthrown when La returned with Tarzan and a small army of **Bolgani** and was replaced on her throne (T9; 7,16). Oah again succeeded in overthrowing La in 1928 with the help of **Dooth**, the new high priest, but was herself overthrown and killed by the loyal followers of La within a few months, and Dooth and Oah's followers were killed as well (T14;4,17).

Oahu The second largest island in the Hawaiian chain, site of the capital, Honolulu. Burroughs spent some time there in the early 1940s (M10)(B1).

Oak Park The **teivos** just west of that of **Chicago** in **Kalkar**-occupied 22nd century America, extending along the Desplaines River and encompassing a considerable area. **Juana St. John** lived there until the **Kash Guard** impounded her father's house and killed both her parents. She escaped to Chicago and met Julian 9th (MM2;4).

Oakdale The Illinois town in which the events of *The Oakdale Affair* took place (K3;2).

The Oakdale Affair A novel which concerns the further adventures of Billy Byrne's friend Bridge, the educated hobo. It is thus considered a sequel to *The Mucker* and as such is abbreviated K3. The events within took place in 1917, after Bridge's release from the Texas army hospital where a bullet from one of "General" Pesita's men landed him in March of 1916. He returned to Illinois, where he met and befriended a naive, cowardly boy who claimed to be a hardened criminal, and had pockets full of loot to prove it. Together they had to flee both the law and a group of murderous hobos who would stop at nothing to get at the loot they knew the boy to have.

Oakdale Tribune The only newspaper of 1917 Oakdale (K3;2).

The Oaks The ancestral home of the Scott family in Scottsville, Virginia (ME;2).

Obambi Lafayette Smith's "boy" on his adventurous 1929 expedition to the Ghenzi Mountains of Africa (T15;7).

Obebe A cannibal chief of Africa who captured Esteban Miranda and (mistaking him for Tarzan) kept him a prisoner for quite some time (T9;21).

Obergatz, Lieutenant Erich A German army officer who was attached to the command of Hauptmann Fritz Schneider in German East Africa during World War I. He abducted Jane and fled with her after the destruction of Tarzan's bungalow, taking her into the Belgian Congo for a time. After the German rout in Africa, he fled his own troops with her in tow, intending to head for South Africa but ending up in Pal-ul-don instead. Once there, they were attacked by the Ho-don and Jane was captured, but Obergatz escaped and fell into the hands of the Waz-ho-don while trying to get out of Pal-ul-don. He later escaped and again encountered Jane, who had also escaped her captors, and tried to reabduct her; she was able to threaten him into leaving her alone, and he wandered lost for a time. Obergatz eventually went completely mad and went to A-lur, where he

proclaimed himself **Jad-ben-otho** and demanded worship, which **Lu-don** ordered that he be given (since it suited the evil priest's purposes). Obergatz was eventually shot dead by **Korak** while trying to sacrifice Tarzan to himself (T7;1,7)(T8;17,19,21,24).

obol A small Greek coin, worth 1/6 of a drachma, which is also used in **Cathne** (T21; 18).

Obregon, Alvaro (1880–1928) Mexican soldier and president. As a soldier he fought against the popular revolutionaries **Pancho Villa** and **Emiliano Zapata**. He was assassinated shortly after being elected to his second term as president (T14;1).

Obroski, Stanley A champion marathon runner who was cast to play the title role in B.O. Pictures' *The Lion Man*, filmed on location in the **Ituri Forest** of Africa in 1932. He was a great coward who looked very much like Tarzan, but he was forced to be brave when he was captured by the fierce **Bansuto** tribe. He was later rescued by Tarzan and, racked with fever, placed in the care of friendly natives. Tarzan, amused by his resemblance to the man, took his place for a while, but when he went to get the real Obroski he found that he had died of his fever. Tarzan let all of Obroski's friends believe that his acts of courage had actually been performed by Obroski, and so the coward went to his grave a hero (T17;1–2,7–8,14,16, 20–33).

obstruction evader A device invented by **Carthoris** for a self-explanatory purpose. It is a radar device attached to an automatic pilot, which moves a flier automatically out of the path of any obstacle within about 100 yards (M4;1).

oceans, Pellucidarian The oceans of Pellucidar occupy approximately the area of the continents on the outer crust and vice versa, so Pellucidar is about 70 percent land and 30 percent water (P1;6).

oceans, Va-nah Va-nah has three oceans (MM1;10).

ochre The yellowish-red color of the soft, moss-like vegetation which carpets most of the dead sea bottoms of Barsoom (M1).

Octavia (?–11 B.C.) The sister of Octavian (later known as Augustus Caesar), who was married to Mark Antony before he ran out on her to be with Cleopatra (I;5).

od (*Amt*) The pronoun "it" (V4;32).

od (*Pal*) The number 90 (T8).

O'Donnell, Officer Patrick The Chicago policeman to whom Jimmy Torrance did not turn in "The Lizard" after the latter picked his pocket. O'Donnell had it in for Little Eva and decided he didn't like Torrance either, because of his associations with her and The Lizard. His testimony of circumstantial details helped to implicate Torrance in Mason Compton's murder (EE;3,17,25–28).

odwar (*Bar*) A general or admiral (M4; 10). Also, the ancient name of the jetan piece presently called a flier (M5;16).

og (*Pal*) The number 60 (T8).

Ogabi An African tribesman who lived in Tarzan's country and was personally known to him. He was sent out by Paul d'Arnot and Mr. Gregory in October of 1936 to get Tarzan to bring him to Loango to speak with them about the missing Brian Gregory. He then accompanied the Gregory safari into the interior, even though he was terrified of approaching the forbidden Ashair, and rightfully so; he was dragged overboard by an Ashairian warrior when Tarzan and the party commandeered an Ashairian galley, and was presumably drowned (T20;1,4–17).

Ogar The beast-god worshipped by the Jukans of Pellucidar through very strenuous forms of devotion, like cartwheeling. They also offer him human sacrifices (P6;6,12–13).

Ogdli The Kavuru warrior who captured Jane Clayton while she was attempting to leave the jungle after surviving the crash of the Sborov plane in central Africa in 1934. He fell in love with her and tried to help her escape, but failed; he himself escaped, however, and told Tarzan where she was (T19;24, 27–30).

Ogonyo A Bagego warrior who was posted to guard Tarzan while he was their prisoner in 1923, and whom Tarzan used to scare the villagers by letting Ogonyo overhear him talking to Nkima. He was later one of the prisoners of Castra Sanguinarius who escaped with Tarzan (T12;5,18).

A different Ogonyo was the head man

of the Lafayette Smith expedition of 1929 (T15;5).

O'Grady, Patrick The assistant director for B.O. Pictures' 1932 *The Lion Man*; he was a happy-go-lucky sort, unlike Tom Orman. O'Grady managed to get the safari through to Omwamwi Falls while the director searched for the kidnapped Naomi Madison and Rhonda Terry (T17;2,9,31).

"Oh, Frenchy" A popular comedy tune of World War I (words by Sam Ehrlich, music by Con Conrad; copyright 1918) which was often hummed by Ulysses Paxton, to Ras Thavas' great annoyance (M6;5).

"Oh, Gaberelle!" The favorite exclamation uttered in fear by Esmerelda, Jane Porter's maid, the exact meaning of which is unclear (T1;14).

Oju A brutal young orang-utan of 1944 Sumatra who refused to accept his tribe's friendship for Tarzan until the latter defeated Oju in combat. He later tried to abduct Corrie van der Meer and was killed by Tarzan for his pains (T22;11,19).

okapi (*Okapia johnstoni*) An African ruminant related to the giraffe, but with a smaller body and a much shorter neck (T18;3).

Okar The racial name of the yellow men of Barsoom as well as the name of their country, which lies in the icy north polar regions of the planet. Several semi-independent cities comprise Okar, but its chief city and capital is Kadabra. Each city of Okar is covered by a glass-like dome which acts as a greenhouse to heat the city, and each has its own atmosphere plant. There are no thoats in Okar nor any fliers, except for the strange automobile-like ground fliers. The Okarians were very reclusive but observed the outer world secretly and knew its geography, political setup and major events. The religion of the Therns was still accepted there even after its discredit upon most of Barsoom, so Matai Shang and Thurid fled there after escaping John Carter in Kaol. They there enlisted the aid of Salensus Oll, Jeddak of Jeddaks of the north, but were eventually defeated when the combined forces of John Carter's allies invaded Kadabra. After the invasion Talu, the rebel prince of Marentina, was made Jeddak of Jeddaks and the country of Okar was opened to its new allies (M3).

Okar The flagship of **Phor San, odwar** of the **Panar** fleet at the siege of **Gathol.** It was over 100 years old and, while not in as bad a condition as most of the ships, it was still pretty bad (M10:3;5,8).

Oklahoma City The Oklahoma hometown of AAF Captain **Jerry Lucas,** pilot of the B-24 *Lovely Lady* (T22;1).

Okonnor A pure Yank who was loyal to the pure human **Or-tis** family in **Kalkar**-controlled 25th century **California** and joined **Raban** the giant's gang after the assassination of **Or-tis 15th** and the subsequent purging of pure humans by **Or-tis 16th.** He joined Raban merely so he could kill Kalkars and was happy to free **Julian 20th** and help him rescue **Bethelda** (daughter of Or-tis 15th) from Raban by gathering up all the pure humans of the **House of Or-tis** into an army and leading the **Julian** tribe to the house of Raban (MM3;8–9).

ola The U-ga day or hour, lasting roughly six hours and thirty-two minutes Earth time. One hundred ola make **ula,** or **sidereal month,** the only observable basis of time measurement in **Va-nah** (MM1;6).

Olathe A small **Kansas** town of Johnson County, 20 miles southwest of Kansas City (K2;5).

Old Forest The forest of **Lutha,** which lies below **Lustadt** (MK1;1).

Old Ones A Mayan title for the gods, a strange and unpredictable lot in Mayan thought (T24;13).

Old Timer A 30-year-old ivory poacher of 1931 Africa whose only known given name was Hiram. He found **Kali Bwana** lost in the jungle and would have taken her back to his camp, but she was abducted from him by the **Leopard Men.** He set out after her and was captured by them himself, but escaped with Tarzan's help and was reunited with her after they saved her from the **Betete** pygmies, to whom she had been given for safekeeping by Chief **Bobolo,** a Leopard Man who wanted her as a wife. By this time the Old Timer was totally in love with her, a feeling she eventually reciprocated. He returned to America with her and her brother, his friend "The Kid," soon afterward (T18;4–5, 9–23).

Ole Bill A Cape Cod sailor of the wrecked *Dolly Dorcas* who was "a mite tough and rank" to eat (P7:1;7).

O'Leary A bookmaker of turn-of-the-century Chicago (K1;7).

Oligocene The third and middle epoch in the **Tertiary** period, which ran from about 36 million to about 25 million years ago, when many of the mammal forms began to become more recognizable as ancestors of the modern types. Mesohippus, baluchitherium, and hyaenadon first appeared in the Oligocene.

olo (*Ape*) Wrestle (TC).

Olson The engineer of the British tug which rescued **Lys La Rue** and **Bowen Tyler** from the English Channel after their liner was sunk by a U-boat on June 4, 1916. He was of course also with the crew when they captured that U-boat later in the day and accompanied it to **Caspak,** where he was left in charge of **Fort Dinosaur** in the absence of Tyler and **Bradley** (C1;2,6)(C3;1).

Olson, Sergeant A U.S. cavalryman of "D" Troop who shot at **Shoz-dijiji** in the summer of 1881 (A1;14).

Olthar An Amtorian warrior of the city of **Kooaad;** he was a son of **Duran**'s (V1;4).

Olivia Marthis The princess of **Hastor** on Barsoom who married **Djor Kantos** while **Tara of Helium** was thought dead, thus freeing Tara to marry **Gahan,** Jed of Gathol (M5;1,22).

om (*Pal*) Long (T8;2).

Om-at "Long Tail" (*Pal*). A Waz-don of **Pal-ul-don** who fought with Tarzan when he first arrived there but called a truce with him when their fight was interrupted by a striped lion; they afterward became friends, and Om-at helped **Ta-den** to teach Tarzan the tongue of Pal-ul-don. They returned with him to his tribe, that of the **Kor-ul-ja,** where he killed and replaced **Es-sat,** the chief who had driven him away, then set out after his sweetheart, **Pan-at-lee,** who had fled the advances of Es-sat. Om-at aided **Ja-don** and Ta-den to invade **A-lur,** became an ally of the **Ho-don,** and married Pan-at-lee (T8;2–5,24–25).

Omat One of the nephews of **Jeft, Jong** of **Hangor,** when **Carson Napier** was a slave there in 1931. His mother had been a **Pangan** slave, and Omat took after her — sensible and decent, rather than awful like the other Hangors. He was the guard to whom Napier was assigned to work, and helped him to see **Duare** (V4;50).

Ombra A city-state of **Ladan** in which **Gar Nal** and **Dejah Thoris** were rumored to have been seen, but John Carter never got to visit because **Fal Sivas** called his ship back to **Zodanga** (M8;24).

Omean The buried south polar sea of Barsoom. It lies in a tremendous domed cavern two miles below the surface of Barsoom that glows with a phosphorescent light which is nearly as bright as daylight. The sea is dotted with small islands replete with colorless, fungus-like vegetation. Omean is the home of the **First-Born**, who keep their enormous navy on its waters (the ships are equipped with both air and water propellers). The sea is reached by a volcanic shaft a thousand feet wide from the apex of the dome up to a basaltic caldera on the surface, in the middle of an ice field north of the **Mountains of Otz**. Omean is fed by the **Lost Sea of Korus**, which is smaller than it is and lies a bit to the south of it. Four enormous pumps keep the water in the sea at a normal level by pumping it north through huge conduits to the reservoirs of the red men, who have apparently forgotten the ancient arrangement, since the source of their water is mysterious to them (M2;8).

Omos The sun of **Poloda**, a very small star in comparison with our own (probably a white dwarf). It has 11 planets which all share a single orbit about it, connected by an atmosphere belt. The arrangement is probably artificial (created by some super race for unknown purposes), as all of the planets are of equal size and similar composition, and such weird orbital mechanics obviously do not occur in nature. Omos lies about 450,000 light years from Earth in the direction of NGC 7006. Each planet lies about a million miles from the center of Omos, and less than 600,000 miles from each neighbor — a little more than twice the distance from the Earth to the moon. The atmosphere belt of Omos is roughly 7200 miles wide (B1;2–3,8).

Ompt The island in the **Toonolian Marshes** of Barsoom on which **Gooli** is located, and of which **Anatok** was jed (M9;20).

Omtag (*Ape*) The giraffe (TC).

Omwamwi Falls A great waterfall of the Belgian Congo, just south of the **Valley of Diamonds** (T17;9).

on (*Apa*) Are (A2;6).

on (*Pal*) The number ten (T8;4).

onager A light catapult (T12;19).

Onar The large capital city of **Falsa**, an Amtorian nation of **Middle Anlap** (V4;44).

One Mile Creek A landmark of early 20th century **Arizona** (D;6).

Onesiphorus A noble house of ancient Ephesus to which **Angustus the Ephesian** belonged (T15).

ong (*Amt*) "Great" or "exalted" (V1;12).

ongvoo "Great one" (*Amt*). A hereditary Amtorian title of nobility occasionally conferred on noblemen for meritorious service to the **jong** (V3;6).

ongyan "Great friend" (*Amt*). The title held by the one hundred members of the ruling committee of **Thora** (V1;12).

Onthar The valley in the **Ethiopian Highlands** in which **Cathne** (the City of Gold) lies, due south of the volcano **Xarator**. Onthar is known as the Land of Lions (T16;3).

Onvak A city of the **Forest of Invak** whose people are an offshoot of **Invak** and also possess the secret of **invisibility**, but are hostile to Invak and raid it whenever possible (M10:4;4).

"Onward, Christian Soldiers" The only hymn known to the members of the secret church near **Chicago** to which **Julian 8th** and his family belonged. It was **Julian 9th's** favorite song (MM2;7).

oo (*Cpk*) Bird (C2;5).

Oo (Niocene) The saber-toothed tiger (E1;1).

Oo-oh "Bird Place" (?) (*Cpk*). The island of the **Wieroos** of **Caspak**, the more northerly of the two islands in Caspak's warm central sea. On it is a very large and inconceivably ancient city with piles of houses built one atop the other like stacked blocks made from stone, wood and brick, not to mention millions of human skulls used for decoration, support and even pavement. Everything about the city is incredibly old because the Wieroos keep using the same buildings, with the result that every stone in every floor or street is worn smooth with age and even rutted pathways are visible in well-traveled areas. The city is undeniably that of an aerial species, as many doorways are on top of buildings and there are no streets per se — only short, narrow, winding blind alleys that connect at most a few buildings that could not otherwise be reached from the air. Most of the city is built and painted in a seemingly chaotic manner, giving a bizarre (but not unpleasant) appearance. There are three such cities on Oo-oh (C3;2–4).

Oog A primitive tribe of the Pellucidarian continent west of the **Korsar Az**, where women are large, fierce and hairy and men are small, frail and retiring (P6;2–3).

oolja (*Amt*) Love (V3;5).

ooljagan "Love man" (*Amt*). The word used in **Korva** to mean a woman's mate (V3;9).

ooljaganja "Love woman" (*Amt*). The word used in **Korva** to mean a man's mate (V3;5).

Oose The King of **Kali** in Pellucidar when it was at war with **Suvi** in 1931. He was caught in a Suvian ambush and imprisoned in his own village, much to **David Innes'** chagrin when he got there too late to stop the war. He and Kali were later liberated by an expeditionary force under **Ghak the Hairy One** (P7;1,2,7)(P7;2;1).

Opar The fabulous lost city of central Africa, located in the mountains above the source of the **Zambezi** River in the very southernmost part of what is today the Republic of Zaire. It was founded about 12,000 years ago by the Atlanteans as a mighty fortress in a high mountain valley from which they might mine the plentiful gold of the region. Opar was at that time a seasonal city, inhabited by great throngs of Atlanteans during the dry season but by only a few hundred troops, merchants and priestesses during the rainy season. It was during such a rainy season that **Atlantis** sank, so that the few Atlanteans there were eventually overcome and almost destroyed by a combination of their own great anguish at the loss of their civi-

lization and the rebellion of the black tribes they had used as slaves for so long. Over time, the location of the city was forgotten by the blacks and its name passed into their legends. The Oparians then began to degenerate, associating with the **great apes** (whom they call the "**First Men**") and even mating with them, even though this was a crime punishable by banishment if it were discovered. By modern times the male Oparians had become very ape-like, being short-legged, long-armed, very muscular, and extremely hairy, but the females were very human and often very beautiful, probably because each sex was indirectly selected for those traits. Oparian men are even ape-like in behavior, and sometimes fall into inexplicable murderous rages just as the apes do. Modern Oparians even speak the **tongue of the great apes** as their everyday language, retaining their Atlantean tongue only for religious purposes.

The Oparians have long since lost the ability to repair their gorgeous city, except for routine maintenance like removing plants and trees from the more often used buildings; the rest of the city is in ruin. The riches of Opar are tremendous, as the gold of many years of mining is stored there, as well as countless pieces of gold jewelry worn by the inhabitants, gold temple trappings, and gold decorations, like a room with seven golden pillars and another with a golden floor. It was for this gold that Tarzan first came to Opar after finding out about it from the **Waziri**, who had encountered the city in their old chief's childhood and captured many pieces of gold jewelry from the Oparians they had killed. Tarzan was led to the city by the Waziri, but they would not go in with him because of their superstitious terror; as a result, he was captured by the beast-men as a sacrifice to the **Flaming God**. After breaking his bonds and saving the high priestess **La** from the murderous rage of the priest **Tha**, Tarzan was helped to escape by La. Soon after a patrol was sent to look for him, Tarzan stole 100 huge ingots of gold from the forgotten treasure vault of Opar. The patrol captured **Jane Porter** from her castaway camp on the coast and took her back to Opar as a sacrifice, so that Tarzan was forced to return to the city to save her (T2;19–25).

He returned to Opar in 1913 to steal more gold in order to renew the fortune he had lost in a bad business deal, but on the way he was rendered amnesic by a concussion from falling debris in the treasure vault. On this trip he discovered the hidden jewel room of the city and so stole both gold and jewels. He also found out that La still loved him and awaited his return (T5;2–8,12–14). He returned four years later after his fortune was again used up (this time in fighting World War I), but this time was replaced en route by his look-alike Esteban Miranda, who had been given Opar's location by Flora Hawkes, Tarzan's former maid, who planned to rob Opar herself. Once again, Tarzan got gold and became involved with La, this time saving her from a coup d'état (T9); he was forced to return again in 1928 to stop the Zveri expedition from robbing Opar, and once again had to save La from her treacherous followers (T14).

Opatah   An Indian tribe of Sonora, enemies of the Apaches. The Opatah enthusiastically accepted Christianity and Spanish customs and language and disappeared as a separate population by the late 19th century (A1;8).

Ope   A high priest of Pu at Tanga-tanga when O-aa was proclaimed Noada there in 1931. Unlike Hor of Lolo-lolo, Ope was faithful and truly believed in the divinity of his Noada, since he was not in the religion business purely for profit. He was, however, afraid of the go-sha, Furp, and so did not take sides in his war against David Innes (whom they thought was Pu), for which Innes banished him after winning the war (P7:2;7)(P7:3;1–6).

Or-tis   The Va-nah way of pronouncing Orthis, the name of the first Jemadar of Jemadars of Va-nah (MM1;13). Or-tis was also the name of Orthis' son by a Kalkar woman (MM2;1).

Or-tis, Brother General   The military governor of the teivos of Chicago, a descendant of Orthis' who was appointed to his post by Jarth, who became Jemadar of America in 2117. General Or-tis was cruel and hated "Yanks" (as American nationalists were called), and suspected Julian 8th of being one. He spied on him mercilessly to prove it, and eventually arrested and imprisoned him on a trumped-up charge of smuggling. When he first saw Juana St. John, he tried to force her to work for him as a maid, but she refused; then he later tried to claim her as his woman,

but Julian 9th did so instead, an act which earned him Or-tis' undying hatred. When Julian 9th went later to rescue his father from the mines, Or-tis and the Kash Guard found Juana where Julian had secreted her and carried her off, but when Or-tis later tried to rape her, Julian caught up with him and killed him with his bare hands (MM2;4,7–8,11).

Or-tis, House of   The descendants of Orthis, who eventually became the ruling clan of Earthly Kalkars. The feud between the Houses of Or-tis and Julian continued as the humans slowly wiped out the Kalkars over the next 300 years. Indeed, the last Kalkar Jemadar of the Valley of the Kalkars was an Or-tis, Or-tis 16th, who proposed peace to Julian 20th, but was refused. Over the centuries, the Or-tis line became completely human, as none but Orthis himself had ever taken a Kalkar woman to wife, preferring humans instead. Eventually, this human Or-tis family began to feel a kinship for their fellow humans and grew to despise the horrible Kalkars they ruled, eventually planning to separate from them. One of these human Or-tises, condemned to death by his half-caste cousin Or-tis 16th, helped Julian 20th escape from the Kalkar capital and went to the Tribe of Julian, making peace with them and leading them by a secret way into the Kalkar capital. The ancient feud between the houses was finally healed when the son of Or-tis 15th voluntarily swore fealty to Julian 20th, who married Bethelda, the daughter of Or-tis 15th (MM3).

Or-tis 15th   A wise and good Jemadar of the Valley of the Kalkars, a pure human descendant of Orthis' who had come to despise his ancestor and the ruin he had brought upon the Earth by bringing the Kalkars to it. Feeling a kinship for his fellow humans, he had planned to renounce his post as jemadar and go with the few hundred pure human nobles who felt as he did to join the Tribe of Julian in the desert and help Julian 19th undo the crime his ancestor had committed. Unfortunately, the Kalkar nobles got wind of the plan and Or-tis 15th was assassinated by a half-breed nephew of his, who proclaimed himself Or-tis 16th. Or-tis 15th's son, the true Or-tis 16th, was meanwhile condemned to death by the usurper, but he and Julian 20th escaped (MM3;4–5).

Or-tis 16th The Jemadar of the Valley of the Kalkars, last foothold of the Kalkars in America. Like all of the Or-tis line, he was very human looking, and proposed peace to Julian 20th in 2430 out of fear, but was refused. He was not the rightful heir to the throne but a half-breed nephew of Or-tis 15th, whom he assassinated and whose throne he usurped. He was a Kalkar to the heart and actively sought to destroy all pure human Ortises (MM3;4).

Oran A port of northern Algeria (210 miles WSW of Algiers) which Tarzan passed through on his way to Sidi-bel-Abbes as a French agent in 1910 (T2;7).

Orando A young warrior of Utengi in the early 1930s; he was the son of Lobongo, Chief of Tumbai. Orando freed Tarzan from beneath a tree which had fallen on him (producing amnesia) and, after seeing him in action, became convinced that Tarzan was his **muzimo**, a benevolent spirit who would help him wipe out the **Leopard Men** who had killed Orando's best friend Nyamwegi the night before. Orando and his men were then led by Tarzan to destroy the Leopard Men and killed most of them, burned their village, and trapped the remainder on an island from which there was no escape (T18;1–14).

orang-utan "Forest man" (Malay). A large, man-like, orange-haired anthropoid ape (*Pongo pygmaeus*) of the Malay Archipelago. It is chiefly herbivorous but, like other anthropoid apes, is a very powerful creature owing to a lifetime of swinging through trees (T22;4).

Oratharc A Minunian warrior of Veltopismakus who helped Zoanthrohago and the Princess Janzara to escape that city along with Tarzan and his friends (T10;20–21).

ord (*Bar*) The Barsoomian year, 670 padans long (687 Earth days). An ord is subdivided into ten teeans, or Barsoomian months. The Barsoomians make adjustments for leap years in much the same way we do.

Oregon, University of The American university attended by Lt. Kumajiro Tada before World War II. It was there that he picked up his excellent idiomatic English (T22;11).

orluk An elephantine predator of the Barsoomian arctic which is hunted for its meat and its gorgeous black and yellow striped fur (M3;9).

Orm-O A young red Barsoomian slave of Jal Had, Prince of Amhor, who brought food to Vor Daj/Tor-dur-bar while he was a prisoner in Jal Had's menagerie. Vor Daj befriended the boy, who then brought him news of Janai's status in the palace (M9;25).

Orman, Tom A director for B.O. Pictures who traveled to the Ituri Forest in 1932 to make *The Lion Man*. He drank far too much Scotch and had far too short a temper where the porters were concerned, which eventually led them to desert the safari. After this he shaped up a lot, stopped drinking, and did what he should have done in the first place — became a good leader. He did not succeed in finding Naomi Madison and Rhonda Terry after they were kidnapped by Arabs, but did get to Omwamwi Falls, made his movie, and returned to Hollywood to marry Rhonda, whom Tarzan had rescued (T17; 1–2,6–9,13,16,22–23,32–33).

El Orobo Ranch A large American ranch in Mexico, not far from El Paso, to which Billy Byrne and Bridge were headed when they were captured by the men of Pesita. It was owned by Anthony Harding, who took a vacation there with his daughter Barbara in March of 1916, but they were forced to flee when Pesita raided the place soon afterward (K2;6–9,15–17).

Orovars The ancient white-skinned, blond or auburn haired race of Barsoom from which the Therns and Lotharians sprang. They lived from about one million to about 500,000 years ago and were a powerful seafaring race in whose now dead and deserted cities the green men live. As the seas receded, the Orovars built their cities to follow the seas down the slopes of the continents until they were eventually left high and dry and conquered by the green men. As the seas dried up, most of the Orovars entered into a cooperation with the black and yellow races, and their interbreeding over ages produced the modern red race. Besides the aforementioned white splinter groups, a small fragment of the race survived into modern times in the city of Horz, keeping their presence secret by killing every visitor to the city who discovered them (M1)(M7;3)(M10;1;4).

Orthis The man who almost single-handedly destroyed human civilization. He was a brilliant military man and scientist, excelling at both sports and studies, and would have been the pride of his class in **Air School** had he not happened to have been in the same class as the "boy wonder" **Julian 5th**, who edged him out in sports, studies and cadet honors. Orthis developed a great jealousy of Julian which later turned to hatred when the latter was appointed to supervise construction of the **Barsoom**, the Earth-Mars ship that Orthis' discoveries had made possible. In 2024, he succeeded in isolating the **eighth rays** of the sun, Mercury, Venus, the moon, and Jupiter, which would allow a ship to negate the gravitational pull of those bodies and so make interplanetary travel possible. He also designed an engine capable of generating sufficient power from light to propel the craft at half speed if the main engine should break down.

To make matters worse, Orthis (by this time a lieutenant commander) was chosen as a crew member of the *Barsoom*, but Julian 5th was placed in command. To be fair, the latter's progression was based partly on the fact of his excellent personality, while Orthis, despite his genius, had an unsavory character, as exemplified by some of his deeds after leaving the academy (such as abandoning his wife and joining a subversive group). The choice of Julian over him seems to have been the last straw for Orthis, who gained his revenge by sabotaging the *Barsoom* by opening up the lunar eighth ray tank and destroying the auxiliary engine, with which sufficient power could have been generated to escape the moon's gravity and go on to Mars. After the crew was able to make a soft landing in Va-nah, the world within the moon, Orthis begged for forgiveness, saying it was only his drunkenness that had made him act irrationally, and Julian and the crew foolishly forgave him. Soon afterward, he and Julian were captured by Va-gas and taken away, but were not eaten by the creatures, who thought them poisonous. Orthis promised their chief that he would lead them to a land filled with food, and the Va-gas believed him and even gave him the captive Princess **Nah-ee-lah** as a present, but when Julian caught him attempting to rape her, he beat him senseless and, leaving him for dead, fled with the girl into a storm (MM1;1–7).

Orthis later managed to escape the Va-gas himself and fell in with the **Kalkars**, to whom he gave the secrets of making explosives and artillery in return for their making him **Jemadar of Jemadars**, ruler of all Va-nah. His first act in his new position was the destruction of **Laythe** so the Kalkars could overrun it (MM1;13–14). Over the next 14 years he built up a fleet of ships, and in 2050 led the Kalkars to Earth, where he conquered the disarmed planet in no time, destroying the remnants of the **International Peace Fleet** with the **electronic rifle** he had invented. When Julian 5th defeated the rifle's power, however, Orthis blew up both himself and Julian with a self-destruct device in his ship, leaving Earth at the mercy of the stupid Kalkars, who quickly reverted to type and destroyed Earth as they had the U-ga civilization of Va-nah (MM2;1).

orthopi The tiny four-toed **Eohippus** of Pellucidar, which is favored by the **Gilaks** as a food animal (P1;14).

ortij (*Amt*) The possessive pronoun "my" (V3;19).

Orvis The capital city of **Unis** on the planet **Poloda**; it was the city where **Tangor** first appeared when he was mysteriously transported to the planet. Like all Unisan cities, it consists of buildings which can be raised or lowered like elevators, with underground highways, streets and immobile buildings (B1;1–3).

Oskaloosa A city of Mahaska County, Iowa (K3;1).

Oskaloosa Kid A criminal of 1910s Illinois, an ex-boxer with a bullet head. The name was mistakenly applied by the hobo band of the **Sky Pilot** to the disguised **Abigail Prim** when she encountered them after robbing her own safe in 1917. It was the real Oskaloosa Kid who tried to kill **Hettie Penning** (whom **Bridge** took to be Miss Prim) after his murder of **Reginald Paynter**, and the false "Kid" who, with Bridge's help, saved Miss Penning. Abigail continued to use the male alias of "the Oskaloosa Kid" until she was finally revealed as she was about to get lynched. The real "Kid" meanwhile wrecked in his car and made a deathbed confession of the murder of Paynter, thus clearing Bridge, Abigail and Hettie (K3;3–10).

Ostend The chief fishing port of Belgium, which was used as a submarine base by the Germans in **World War I**. It was the site of **Lt. Jefferson Turck's** first landing on the European continent in July of 2137. He found it as devastated as he had found England (LC;6).

Ostia A Roman port city at the mouth of the Tiber (I;6).

Otho (*Pal*) God (T8;2).

Otobu A black **Wamabo** tribesman who was a slave in the lost city of **Xuja**. Tarzan promised to help him escape to his people in return for his help, which proved invaluable in the escape because he could lead the party by back ways and communicate with the Xujans (T7;22–24).

Otto, Prince The younger brother of the old king of an unnamed European country of the early 20th century. He cooperated with communist revolutionaries to assassinate his brother, leaving Otto as king when **Count Jagst** fled the country with the young **Prince Michael**. Otto double-crossed the revolutionary **Meyer** by denying him a new constitution after he came to power, thus earning himself almost universal hatred, especially since he was a bad ruler as well. About four years later he was assassinated by **Carlyn**, leaving his son **Ferdinand** as king (LL;1–17).

Otz, Mountains of The mountains surrounding the **Valley Dor** at the south pole of Barsoom, in which the palaces, galleries and habitations of the **Therns** are built. The plateau at the summit of the mountain range is at least five miles wide and is covered with gardens, farms, courtyards and galleries. The outer ramparts extend completely around the pole for the whole length of the mountain range and are impregnable to ground-based attack. The outer slopes of the mountains are the sites of the palaces of the greatest Therns, and the cliffs themselves are honeycombed with dark, labyrinthine passages inhabited by the Therns' slaves and prisoners, including numerous **banths** which are allowed to roam free at night. The inner cliffs of the mountains are called the **Golden Cliffs** because of the great wealth of that metal in them, which gives them a golden color. They are also full of every kind of gem imaginable and are for all intents and purposes unscalable, unless

you know the secret passage up through a huge hollow tree near the cliff (M2;2–5).

Oubanovitch The engineer of the tramp steamer *Saigon* when it carried Tarzan as a captive "wild man" across the Pacific in 1938. He mutinied along with **Schmidt** and the **Lascars**, even though (being a Red Russian) he hated Germans. He swore revenge on Tarzan when, after the wreck of the *Saigon*, he cast him out with the other mutineers to fend for themselves. They returned six weeks later to raid **Camp Saigon** and he was shot dead by **Tibbet** soon afterward (T24;3–11,19–22).

ouled-nail (*Ara*) A dancing girl who performs in coffee houses, usually as a slave of the cafe owner or another. Tarzan was helped to escape **Nikolas Rokoff's** ambush in a cafe in **Sidi Aissa** in 1910 by an ouled-nail, whom he then rescued from slavery and returned to her father, Sheik **Khadour ben Saden**. She later rescued Tarzan from the **douar** of the **Arabs** who captured him for Rokoff (T2;7–10).

Our Beloved Mephis One of the titles taken by **Mephis**, **Zani** dictator of the Amtorian nation of **Korva** in the 1920s (V3;9).

Ouse A river of southern England which empties into the Channel not far from **Lewes** (OT;16).

Out of Time's Abyss The third and final book of the **Caspak** trilogy (abbreviated C3), in which **Bradley**, lost from **Fort Dinosaur** on an exploration in *The Land That Time Forgot*, encountered weird adventures of his own after being abducted by a **Wieroo** and carried off to their hideous city in September of 1916. From there he had to escape with a beautiful **Galu** girl. The story was told to Burroughs by Bradley himself after his return to the *Toreador*, upon which Burroughs was a passenger, and published in *Blue Book* magazine in December of 1918.

The Outlaw of Torn A story which Burroughs dug up among some extremely old manuscripts in an equally old European monastery, the Father Superior of which was related to his wife's cousin. It was first published in 1914 and is abbreviated OT. The action concerns **Richard**, the lost prince of England, and his adventurous life as the outlaw **Norman of Torn**, raised as a bandit (ignorant of his true heritage) by a wily old man to get revenge on the prince's father, **Henry III** of England. The story runs from 1243 to 1264 and chronicles Norman's development from pure bandit to protector of the weak and raider of crooked royalist strongholds, then to the mightiest noble in England.

ov (*Bar*) The number seven (M9;4).

Ovan A ten-or-eleven-year-old boy of the tribe of **Clovi** in **Pellucidar** whom **Tarzan** saved from a **ryth** in 1927. The youth then brought Tarzan back to Clovi and urged his father, Chief **Avan**, to accept the ape-man as a friend. Ovan later helped Tarzan and **Jana** escape the death sentence his tribal council had imposed on Tarzan (T13;11–13).

"Over There" A popular **World War I** tune (copyright 1917 by George M. Cohen) often hummed by **Ulysses Paxton**, to **Ras Thavas**' great annoyance (M6;5).

Owaza The black head man of the **Flora Hawkes** expedition to rob **Opar** in the summer of 1917. He was a greedy man who talked **Kraski** into attacking a tribe of **Arab** raiders for their ivory once the gold of Opar was stolen from them by **Esteban Miranda**. Later, Miranda talked Owaza into acting as guide for a share of the stolen gold. Owaza then double-crossed Miranda and stole the gold himself, but was tricked by a native chief into delivering it directly to Tarzan's bungalow (T9;10–12,21).

Oxford A well-respected English university, alma mater of every male of the **Henders** family of **Kentucky** since old **Sir John Henders** had established the American branch of the family (HB;2). It was also the university from which **God** graduated in 1855 (T17; 24–30).

Oxford Statutes A series of agreements between **Henry III** of England and his barons, signed in 1258, which threw all legislative and judicial power into the hands of a council of 24 barons, assisted by a body of knights (four from each county). Henry was forced to sign the document after a successful series of rebellions by the barons, but slowly regained his full power over the next few years with the help of his son **Edward** (OT;12).

Ozara The jeddara of the **Tarids** of **Ladan**, a very young, beautiful, intelligent and perceptive woman who took a liking to John Carter's looks immediately. She realized

that Carter could both see and hear the Tarids, but **Ul Vas** would not believe her. Ozara was actually a **Domnian** prisoner among the Tarids and helped Carter and his companions to escape both for the reason of empathy with their plight and also to get rid of **Dejah Thoris**, whom her husband proposed to replace her with. She also fell in love with John Carter herself and planned to keep him, but of course this could not be so. She was later restored to her father, the **Jeddak** of Domnia (M8;18–24).

Paabu A **Bagalla** youth who tried to brain **"Doc"** with a stick and received a good punch from **Dick** instead when the **"Tarzan Twins"** were captured by the Bagalla in 1920. When "Doc" later made their knives disappear by sleight-of-hand, he told the Bagalla that the knives had gone into Paabu's head, with unfortunate consequences for Paabu. After "Doc" saved him by reversing the "magic," Paabu in gratitude helped the twins escape (TT1;4,7–9).

Pacco (*Ape*) The zebra (T6:8).

padan (*Bar*) The Barsoomian day (24 hours, 37 minutes Earth time), which is divided into ten **zodes**, or Barsoomian hours. Sixty-seven padans make one **teean**, or Barsoomian month.

padang (*Pell*) "Friend" or "friends" (P7: 4;6).

Padang A coastal city of **Sumatra** which lies about one degree south of the equator on the island's west coast (T22;2).

padwar A Barsoomian military rank corresponding to an Earthly lieutenant. It is also the name of a **jetan** piece with a move of two spaces diagonally in any direction or combination (M5).

Pagth The ape-king whose tribe witnessed the slaying of **Gobu** by **Esteban Miranda** while he was disguised as Tarzan. They of course believed that the real Tarzan had done it and so began to fear him (T9;4).

pah (Niocene) Man (E2;2).

Pai-sha A Chinese port with a bad reputation (T3;20).

paint, body The ancient Britons painted their bodies with a bright blue pigment called woad before going into battle (I;1).

pak (*Cpk*) Land (C2;4).

pal (*Pal*) "Place" or "land" (T8;2).

pal-e-don-so "Place where men eat" (*Pal*). A banquet hall (T8;15).

Pal-ul-don "Land of Man" (*Pal*). A hidden valley in what is today the Republic of Zaire, somewhere to the north of Opar. It is surrounded by huge, rough mountains with few passes and is beautifully forested, as is the area outside the mountains. Surrounding the whole is a wide, almost impassable morass, and around that a vast, dry steppe covered almost completely with thorn bushes; the valley thus presents several natural barriers to penetration from the outside. The central valley of Pal-ul-don, Jad Pele ul Jad-ben-otho (the Valley of the Great God) is dominated by three large lakes which flow one into the other, then empty via a gorge into the outer morass. Branching off from the central valley are several steep gorges, which terminate in the mountains. These gorges are inhabited by the Waz-don, a group of hairy, black, tailed humans, while the valley floor is inhabited by the slightly more advanced (though no more intelligent) Ho-don, a species of almost hairless, white, tailed humans. Besides these intelligent species, the area is home to several other unusual species of flora and fauna, most notably the spotted lion (ja), the smaller striped lion (jato), and the enormous gryf, a descendant of the triceratops.

Into this hidden land came Lt. Erich Obergatz (with Jane Clayton in tow), who had tried to reach South Africa and become hopelessly lost on the way. Tarzan, following an almost nonexistent trail, came after them, and found in Pal-ul-don one of the strangest adventures of his career. After eventually liberating Jane they escaped Pal-ul-don, leaving its political structure somewhat changed in the bargain (T8).

Pal-ul-ja "Place of lions" (*Pal*). The lion pit of the city of Tu-lur in Pal-ul-don, a large dungeon room with barred windows into which prisoners are placed to be eaten by lions. Tarzan was trapped within the room by a trick of Mo-sar's in order to hold him hostage, but the ape-man of course escaped (T8;18).

Palace Dining Room A lunch counter of early 20th century Goliath, Idaho, where June Lathrop worked after fleeing Chicago (GF;11).

Palace of Diamonds The great citadel of the Bolgani in the Valley of the Palace of Diamonds to the east of Opar. It covered about 15 acres of ground and was actually an accumulation of weird and unearthly buildings built in different periods, though all of great antiquity. A large proportion of the exterior of the buildings was covered with inlaid gold and thousands (perhaps millions) of diamonds. Unlike the Oparians, the Bolgani race was not in decline, and Tarzan even noticed the construction of a new building going on while he was there in 1917 (T9;9–11).

Palace of Peace In Ptarth, the building which houses the various embassies of foreign powers. The ambassadors themselves inhabit palaces in the district where nobles live (M4;2).

paladar (*Van*) A count (MM1;11).

Palastokar The name of a Minunian warrior invented by Komodoflorensal so as to have an excuse to pass through Hamadalban's quarters to find those of Kalfastoban and rescue Talaskar (T10;17).

Palatine One of Rome's seven hills (I;5).

Palensk, Alexander The son of the Prime Minister of Karlova before World War I. He was an officer in the Black Guard and a close friend of Prince Boris', and so was involved in the Prince's hoax involving The Rider (R;3–10).

Paleocene The earliest epoch of the Tertiary Period, which lasted from 63 million to 58 million years ago.

palla (*Lat*) A type of cloak or mantle (I;3).

palthon A rare and beautiful Barsoomian stone, blood-red in color with gorgeous white markings, which can be polished to a high luster (M6;11).

palus (*Lat*) Marsh (T12;6).

Palus Meridien "Southern Marsh" (*Lat*). The papyrus marsh along the south shores of Mare Orientis in the central Wiramwazi valley (T12;6).

Palus Septentrionum "Northern Marsh" (*Lat*). The papyrus marsh along the northern shores of Mare Orientis (T12).

Pamarung Islands A small chain of islands which lies in the western part of the Straits of Macassar near **Borneo**. Professor **Arthur Maxon** travelled to the islands in the late 1920s in order to continue his artificial life experiments undisturbed (Q;1).

Pamba (*Ape*) The rat (T1;13).

pan (*Pal*) Soft (T8;2).

Pan-American Federation In *The Lost Continent*, all the nations of North and South America formed a confederation after **World War I** and eventually became one country by the 1970s. This country ruled the seas and forbade all contact with the Eastern Hemisphere (bounded by the lines of 30 degrees and 175 degrees west longitude) in 1931, and kept the ban up for 206 years—until involuntary explorations by Lt. **Jefferson Turck** convinced the government to lift it in 2137 (LC;1).

Pan-at-lee "Soft-tail-doe" (*Pal*). A **Wazdon** woman of the **Kor-ul-ja** tribe of **Pal-ul-don**, **Om-at**'s sweetheart. She fled the advances of **Es-sat** and made her way to the **Kor-ul-gryf**, where she hid for a while and was rescued by Tarzan, only to be captured and sent as a slave to **A-lur**, where she was given to **O-lo-a**. The two women became friends, and Pan-at-lee was eventually freed to marry Om-at (T8;2–7,10,25).

Pan Dan Chee A warrior of the **Orovars** of **Horz** who was set upon by **green men** in his city and rescued by John Carter, whom he then tried to warn away because he knew of his city's policies regarding strangers. As a result of his actions he was condemned to death along with Carter. Pan Dan Chee was a rather extreme person who fell in love with **Llana of Gathol** after seeing her likeness, into which the princess of John Carter's miniature **jetan** set was carved. Upon meeting the real thing, he was absolutely awe-struck and immediately threw his sword at her feet. He left Horz with Carter and Llana and journeyed with them overland toward **Gathol** (M10:1;2–13), ending up instead at **Kamtol**, where they were captured and enslaved by the **First-Born**. He was eventually rescued by John Carter, who disguised himself as a **Black Pirate** for the escape (M10:2;1–6,13). They then flew to Gathol, which they found under siege, and Pan Dan Chee was captured by **Panars** while Carter was gone for a short while (M10:3;3–4,13). He

was rescued when the fleet of **Helium** defeated that of **Hin Abtol**, and Llana of Gathol finally accepted him as a suitor (M10:4;13).

Pan-sat "Soft Skin" (*Pal*). A priest of the temple of **Jad-ben-otho** in **A-lur**, one of **Ludon**'s most trusted aides. It was he who Ludon sent to parley with **Mo-sar**, and to kidnap Jane from **Ja-lur**, where Tarzan had left her while he went with **Ja-don** to attack Ludon's army. He was shot dead by **Korak** while trying to sacrifice Tarzan (T8;15,20,23–24).

Panars A race of **red men** who live in a distant portion of the frozen north of Barsoom, far from **Okar** and unknown to everyone (including the Okarians) until they tried to conquer the planet. They are a race of technological pirates who innovate nothing, but instead steal all the technology they need, which is usually obsolete because of the scarcity of opportunity to steal it. Their ships are usually several hundred years old and their instruments obsolete; what instruments they do have they are usually too ignorant to use. Even the domes of their cities are of a design stolen from the Okarians, but shoddily built—John Carter's **flier** was able to break right through one of the domes, something one would imagine would not happen with a dome of true Okarian manufacture. The Panars are cowards and dirty fighters, but like many cowards believe themselves to be brave and fierce. They are more brutal than even the **green men** and ignore any kind of ethics of civilized warfare, preferring, for instance, to gang up on their foes four-to-one. The Panars are also lazy, lax in discipline, and dirty, and cannot keep their stolen ships in repair. There are, however, some decent Panars, like **Gor-don** and his family. Almost all of the Panars hated **Hin Abtol** and his dreams of conquest, mostly because the lazy Panars felt that conquest required too much effort and required them to leave **Pankor**, where life was easy (M10:1;10–11)(M10:3;6–7,11–13).

Pand (*Ape*) The thunder (T11;6).

pand-balu-den "Thunder stick" (*Ape*). Gun (obviously a Tarzan coinage) (TC).

panda (*Ape*) Noise (TC).

pandar (*Amt*) A **Korvan** coin worth about one dollar (1930 U.S. currency) (V3; 17).

Pandar   A Phundahlian warrior of Barsoom who was captured by the **hormads** and taken to **Morbus**, where he helped acquaint John Carter and **Vor Daj** with the situation at hand. He later became one of the lieutenants of Vor Daj/**Tor-dur-bar** and helped **Sytor** to double-cross him and escape with **Janai**, only to be recaptured by the hormads (M9;4,16,19).

Pandar   A noble house and castle of the Amtorian nation of **Gavo** (V5;4).

Panga   A nation of **Middle Anlap** on Amtor. The people of Panga have a powerful military force but are not really a military people, and inefficiency and thoughtlessness mark their military endeavors. They managed to defeat and capture the **Falsan** navy by trickery in 1931, then began a punitive campaign against the city-state of **Hangor** which would have easily succeeded had the Pangans planned it just a little, but failed because of their carelessness (V4;48).

Pangani   A river of **Tanganyika** which flows from **Mount Kilimanjaro** into the Indian Ocean opposite **Zanzibar** (T7;5).

panglima   (Dyak) Chieftain (Q;10).

pangos   A palm-like tree of tropical Pellucidar (P6;22).

Panizo Circle   A street of Hollywood (GH;10).

Pankor   The capital city of the **Panars** of Barsoom's frozen north. It is like **Kadabra**, the capital of **Okar**, but much, much smaller, and its dome is not as well built. Outside the city hung a million fighting men who had been kidnapped over the past hundred years from all over northern Barsoom and frozen in ice in suspended animation until **Hin Abtol**, Jeddak of the Panars, should need them for his plan of conquest (M10:3;11–12).

panthan   (*Bar*) A mercenary; a fairly common occupation on warlike Barsoom. Panthans are well-paid, but usually find that the money burns a hole in their pocket pouches. In times of war, any panthan within a country's territory may be impressed into service for that country (M4;11)(M6;9). Panthan is also the name of a **jetan** piece which moves one space forward (straight or diagonal) or one space sideways, but never backward (M5).

Papago   A small Indian tribe which inhabited the area south of the **Gila** River in Arizona (A1;3).

paper chase   A game in which one player, the "hare," runs about in a wilderness area, occasionally dropping bits of paper so as to provide a trail for the pursuers to follow (D;11–14).

papyrus   (*Cyperus papyrus*) A tall reed which grows profusely in shallow African lakes; it was used in ancient times to make paper. The shallow areas of **Mare Orientis** are choked with the reed (T12;4).

Parachute   An aviation safety device not used on Barsoom except in "**John Carter and the Giant of Mars**" (M11A;10,12).

Paraht   The village of **Amiocap** in Pellucidar where **Fedol**, father of **Stellara**, ruled as chief, and where she and **Tanar the Fleet One** were accepted as guests (P3;6).

parang   A Malay machete, often used as a weapon (T22;7).

Pare Mountains   The mountain chain of Tanzania of which **Kilimanjaro** is a peak (T7;2).

parking lots, Barsoomian   Barsoomian parking lots are found inside buildings at about 60 feet above the street (M9;24).

Parr, Catherine   The sixth wife of the gorilla king **Henry VIII** who, unlike his historical namesake, was married to him concurrently with the other five. She was the only one who was friendly to **Rhonda Terry** when she was imprisoned in Henry's women's quarters in 1932, and told her all about the bizarre gorilla civilization (T17;20).

parrot   A large species of parrot is worshipped by the people of **Xuja**, who greatly fear and respect the exceptionally intelligent birds. These creatures can repeat almost word-for-word information given them by the monkeys of the Xujan forest and carry it verbatim to the inhabitants of the city (T7; 17–19).

Parsons, Louella   A Hollywood gossip columnist of the 1930s (T17;33).

Parthak   A **Zodangan** youth who brought food to John Carter while he was imprisoned in the **pits** of **Zat Arrras**. John Carter tricked

Parthak into bringing a note to **Carthoris**, and Carthoris tricked him into revealing Carter's location (M2;19).

Parthia The successor to the Persian Empire, contemporary to the Roman Empire (I;17).

Pasadena A city in **California**, the ruins of which were inhabited by **Kalkars** in the 24th and early 25th centuries. The captured Julian 20th was taken there to meet **Or-tis** 16th, last of the Kalkar **jemadars**, who wished to propose peace to him (MM3;4).

Pass of the Ancients The main pass down into the **Valley of the Kalkars**, probably Cajon Pass (MM3;2).

Pass of the Warriors The single, river-carved pass through the cliffs that separate the valleys of **Onthar** and **Thenar** in the Ethiopian Highlands. The road from **Athne** to **Cathne** runs through the pass alongside the river (T16;4).

Passmore, Lord An alias taken by Tarzan to flush out a band of **shiftas** in the Ghenzi region in 1929 while the **Stabutch** and **Smith** expeditions were also in the area. He was supposedly a big game hunter, but all of his porters and **askaris** were actually armed **Waziri** warriors (T15;5–7,24–26).

pastar (*Pal*) Father (T8;2).

Pastar-ul-ved "Father of Mountains" (*Pal*). The largest, steepest and most treacherous mountain of **Pal-ul-don**, where the warriors of the **Waz-don** go to prove their courage by climbing around it (T8;2).

Pastor A Roman noble whom **Caligula** invited to a banquet directly after executing one of his sons (I;20).

patricians The noble class of ancient Rome (T12;6).

Patrick, Danny "Gunner" A hoodlum of 1920s **Chicago** who was the right-hand man of a powerful mobster whom he double-crossed for $20,000 in 1929. "Gunner" was found out and fled the country, joining **Dr. Lafayette Smith**'s expedition to Africa on the off chance that it might be fun. He grew to really like the shy professor, despite their great differences, and also had great respect for Tarzan, whom he classified as "a real big shot." He managed to wreak great havoc on

the **Capietro shiftas** with his "typewriter" on two separate occasions, and for a while he and Tarzan were in the habit of saving each other. They entered the land of **Midian** together in search of Dr. Smith, but "Gunner" became separated from Tarzan and met and fell in love with the beautiful **Jezebel**, who was stolen from him by the aforementioned shiftas. He managed to catch up with them just in time to see **Leon Stabutch** fleeing the camp with her, followed them, and arrived soon after Tarzan killed Stabutch. The smitten "Gunner" married Jezebel, bought a gas station in **California** and settled down to be "legit" for a change (T15;3,5,10,16–20,24–26).

Patton The shop foreman at the **International Machine Company** of 1910s **Chicago** (EE;18).

Paul of Merely One of three English knights, the first such that **Norman of Torn** ever saw, who came to his castle in 1255. He was killed by Norman in a duel after attempting to touch his person (in a search for birthmarks) against his wishes (OT;5).

Paul of Tarsus, Saint (A.D. 3–62) A probable paranoid schizophrenic of the 1st century A.D. who, converted to Christianity late in the 4th decade A.D., changed it to fit his own particular views and beliefs and spread it throughout the Mediterranean world. Perhaps it was his own madness that attracted other unstable individuals to him, such as **Angustus the Ephesian**. Paul is worshipped as the Son of God by the **Midianite** descendants of Angustus (T15;2).

Paulvitch, Alexis **Nikolas Rokoff**'s valet, a scoundrel as bad as Rokoff himself who helped the latter pursue his plans against the **Count** and **Countess de Coude** and Tarzan, but was protected from legal prosecution with Rokoff by the Countess, who could not bring herself to turn in Rokoff, her brother. It was Paulvitch who, in disguise, accused the Count of cheating at cards and who attempted to strangle the Countess, but was foiled in both pursuits by Tarzan, earning him the enmity of the Russians. Some time later, Paulvitch managed to steal back the secret papers Tarzan had stolen from Rokoff, thus opening the way for them to throw Tarzan overboard from the ship onto which they had followed him from **Algiers** (T2; 1–2,12).

No more was heard of Paulvitch until he helped Rokoff escape from prison in 1912, at which time the two hatched a plot of revenge against Tarzan, kidnapping his infant son and luring him into a trap aboard their chartered steamship, the *Kincaid*, with the idea of taking them to Africa and there disposing of them separately. After the death of Rokoff, Paulvitch planned revenge on Tarzan by planting a time bomb on the *Kincaid*, which Tarzan had commandeered. It blew up, setting the ship on fire, but the occupants fled to Jungle Island in lifeboats before the boiler exploded. Paulvitch meanwhile returned to the mainland and was lost to white men for quite some time. It was later found that he had double-crossed Rokoff by leaving the Clayton baby in London with a confederate and substituting another to fool Rokoff, hoping to get a huge ransom for the child behind Rokoff's back. He was in turn betrayed by his confederate, who ransomed the child to Tarzan's lawyers soon after Paulvitch left England (T3;1,18–21).

Soon after his flight inland, he was captured by one of the tribes he and Rokoff had terrorized, and was brutalized by them for ten years, being beaten, tortured, and used as a slave to the point where, although less than 40 years old, he looked at least 60 — he was incredibly emaciated, toothless, and grey-haired, and his mind was almost completely gone. He took the name Michael Sabrov when he was rescued by the *Marjorie W.* ten years later and was taken back to England. On the way back the ship stopped at Jungle Island, and Tarzan's friend Akut came to the landing party to look for Tarzan, whom he still missed. He was disappointed at not finding him, but allowed Paulvitch to take him aboard the ship and back to England, where Paulvitch exhibited him as a performing animal named Ajax. This went on until Tarzan and his son showed up at a performance one night and the ape recognized both Tarzan and the father's features in the son. After speaking to Tarzan Akut refused to perform any longer, and so Paulvitch (whom Tarzan could not recognize, so much had he changed) eventually sold the ape to him, giving Tarzan the promise that he would be returned to Jungle Island as soon as possible. In the meantime, Jack and Akut had become great friends, so when Paulvitch tried to kill the boy (and frame Akut for the murder) in

revenge against Tarzan, the ape became enraged, broke his bonds, and killed the evil Russian, finally ending his career of hate (T4; 1–3).

Pausanius   The assassin who killed Philip of Macedon for Philip's wife, Olympias (I;21).

Paxton, Ulysses   A captain in the United States Infantry during World War I who, after having his legs blown off by a shell in France, found the same ability within himself as the great John Carter had, to throw off his physical bonds and transport himself to Mars, having read about Barsoom in the works of Burroughs at an earlier time. He alighted within the manor of Ras Thavas, a brilliant Barsoomian surgeon whom he saved from assassination. Thavas taught him the Barsoomian language and made him his apprentice, since he could trust no Barsoomian with his secrets. While there, Paxton fell in love with the beautiful Valla Dia, into whose body Ras Thavas had transplanted the brain of the hideous Xaxa, Jeddara of Phundahl. Paxton escaped from Thavas, abducted Xaxa, and eventually succeeded in returning Valla Dia to her own body, then married her and became a Duhorian noble and a friend of John Carter's (M6).

Paynter, Reginald   The most eligible bachelor in 1917 Oakdale, Illinois, who was robbed, killed and thrown from a car on the same night as Abigail Prim disappeared. He was with the (real) Oskaloosa Kid and Hettie Penning at the time, and was killed by the Kid for fighting with him over the girl, whom witnesses thought was Abigail Prim (K3;2,10).

Payson   A small Illinois town which was connected with Oakdale by a well-paved road (K3;7).

pecunia numerate   (*Lat*) Cash money (I;8).

Pedestal of Truth *see* Throne of Righteousness

Pedro   The chief lieutenant to the Portuguese; he was almost killed one night by Nigger Joe, but was saved by Johnny Lafitte, who thus won Pedro's respect and admiration. Pedro later returned the favor by shooting the Portuguese to save Lafitte from him. In return for that favor, Lafitte left Pedro with leadership of the pirate band (and both the Vulture's and Portuguese's ships) when he quit the pirate business and went to Paris with his bride (PB;12–13).

Peebles, John One of Flora Hawkes' co-conspirators in her 1917 plan to rob **Opar** of its gold. He was a former pugilist and was part of the expedition's muscle. With **Bluber** and **Throck**, he succeeded in evading the traitorous bearers of their safari when the men revolted, and Tarzan eventually arranged for their transportation to the coast (T9;3,17–19).

Peebles, Miss The secretary of the "Society for the Uplift of Erring Women"; she was the **Reverend Theodore Pursen's** cousin (GF;6).

pele (*Pal*) Valley (T8;2).

Pellucidar The name given by its inhabitants to the Earth's inner world, which exists on the inside of the 500-mile-thick crust of the Earth and is lit by its own tremendous inner sun, which never moves and never sets, sitting always at noon and thereby confounding any computation of passing time. In Pellucidar, the areas of land and water are roughly reversed from their places on the surface world, so that seas lie in the positions where continents do outside and vice versa, giving Pellucidar a much greater land area than that of the outer Earth — some 124 million square miles, more than twice the outer Earth's land area. The flora and fauna of Pellucidar are for the most part like those of the outer Earth from the **Mesozoic** on up, with many Ice Age–type animals and even a few dinosaurs, but also with some variant evolutionary lines, such as the **Mahars**. These creatures probably originated on the outer Earth at various times during the planet's history, and there may have even been periodic "waves" of migration from the outside to the inside through the **polar opening** (P1;3–6).

Pellucidar The second book in the Pellucidar series, abbreviated P2. The events of the book took place from 1913 to 1915 and were communicated to the outer Earth through the telegraph line laid out by **David Innes** upon his return to the inner Earth in 1913. Burroughs finally found the long-lost line and copied the story down, publishing it later that year. The events of the story concern Innes' return to the inner Earth; his search for the

town of **Sari** and **Dian the Beautiful**, his wife; his capture by and escape from the hideous **Mahars**, rulers of Pellucidar; and the final overthrow of the latter.

Pellucidar, Empire of The confederation of human tribes founded by and first ruled by **David Innes of Connecticut**, originally begun to establish human dominance over Pellucidar and overthrow the **Mahars**, the previous ruling race. The continent on which it lies is like a huge peninsula, bounded on the east by the **Lural Az/Sojar Az**, on the west by the **Korsar Az**, on the south by the **Nameless Strait**, and on the north by the Arctic Ocean. It is 700 miles wide at its narrowest point (west of **Sari**) and more than a thousand miles wide at its widest point. The narrowest point of the continent mentioned above is some 1400 miles north of the Nameless Strait, 5000 miles from Sari by sea (P1;15) (P7;4;1).

Penelope A character in **Henry Knibbs'** poem "Out There Somewhere," an allusion to the faithful wife of Odysseus in Greek myth. **Bridge** used Penelope as a symbol for each man's "right" woman, waiting somewhere out in the world for him (K2;2,6).

Penning, Hettie A young woman of Payson, Illinois, who was mistaken for **Abigail Prim** while on a drive with **Reginald Paynter** and the **Oskaloosa Kid** on the day in 1917 when the latter murdered the former. To shut her up, the Kid shot her and threw her from the car, but she did not die — she was saved instead by **Bridge** and the false Oskaloosa Kid — the real Abigail Prim! Bridge assumed that Miss Penning was Abigail Prim, and she did not deny it. She accompanied them in their flight because she did not want to bring shame on her father by being involved with murderers, however indirectly. After being caught by **Detective Burton**, though, she spilled everything just in time to save the real Abigail Prim and Bridge from a lynch mob who thought them guilty of the murder of Abigail Prim! (K3;3–10).

Pennington, Colonel Custer The good-natured patriarch of the Pennington family of the **Rancho del Ganado, California**, a veteran of the Spanish-American War who had gone to California in 1900 to die and found instead rejuvenation. The war was as nothing, however, compared with the heartaches of 1922 to 1923, which his family bravely bore and finally came through — a little disheveled, but none the worse for wear (GH).

Pennington, Custer, Jr. The younger Mr. Pennington, son of Colonel Pennington of Rancho del Ganado, California— a noble and upright young man who found himself thrust into various tragedies in 1922 and 1923. The first was the decision of his childhood sweetheart Grace Evans to go away to Hollywood in search of stardom, separating her from her loved ones forever after a sleazy Hollywood director and drug pusher got hold of her. In September of 1922 Pennington was framed for bootlegging by Slick Allen, a real bootlegger who had forced Pennington's best friend Guy Evans (Grace's brother) into the business as well. Pennington took the rap for Evans, refusing to let him confess lest Eva Pennington (Custer's sister and Evans' fiancée) be crushed by the knowledge; after all, she knew Custer was innocent, so she could not be hurt as much by his being falsely convicted as by Evans' being justly convicted. He served his six-month sentence, and after Grace's death in Hollywood began to realize that he loved Shannon Burke, who had been in love with him for some time. Thus, when Wilson Crumb (the man who had ruined and killed Grace) annoyed Shannon outside the Pennington house in August of 1923, Custer wanted to kill him, but got drunk and passed out. He was arrested the next day, however, because Guy Evans really had killed Crumb, but had since gone insane (after finding Eva apparently dead from a suicide attempt) and so could not confess. Custer was once again convicted for a crime committed by Guy— this time murder. He would have been hanged had not Shannon doggedly worked to restore Guy to sanity in time for him to confess, thus saving Custer. Despite the facts of Shannon's sordid past (which came out in the course of the trial), Custer yet loved and married her (GH;1–10,21–23, 27–37).

Pennington, Eva The sister of Custer Pennington; she was a bit of a scamp and more than a bit of a flapper, and was engaged to Guy Evans. As could be expected, she was greatly affected by the tragedies which befell her family and friends in 1922 and 1923, but still continued to plan her wedding to Evans until the arrival of Wilson Crumb, his attempted seduction of her, and his reve-

lation to her that Guy was a bootlegger who had let her brother Custer take the rap for his crime and do time in jail for it. In her sadness and confusion, she attempted suicide the next day, but was rescued by excellent surgeons and lived to regret the attempt, especially after Custer explained that he had forced Guy to keep quiet for her sake (GH; 1–30,33–37).

Pennington, Julia The wife of Colonel Custer Pennington, who had married him in 1895. They lived with their children (Custer, Jr., and Eva) on the Rancho del Ganado in southern California of the 1920s (GH;4).

Pennington, William A New York cousin of the Penningtons of Rancho del Ganado, California (GH;17).

The People That Time Forgot The second book in the Caspak trilogy, abbreviated C2. It is the story of Tom Billings (Bowen Tyler's secretary) and his attempted rescue expedition to Caspak in 1917, soon after Burroughs' finding of Tyler's manuscript sealed in a thermos bottle in the summer of that year. Burroughs went on the trip with Billings and thus observed a few of the events firsthand, hearing the others from Billings after he returned to the ship. He then published the story in *Blue Book* magazine in October of 1918.

Percival, Sir Not the Arthurian knight, but a Knight of the Sepulcher that James Hunter Blake was mistaken for when he sneaked into the ranks of those knights to rescue the Princess Guinalda of Nimmr (T11; 19).

Percy-Standish A aristocratic family of early 20th century Boston, acquaintances of the Smith-Joneses (CG2;4).

Perez, Captain Santa Anna A Mexican infantry officer who ordered an attack made on Crawford's Indian Scouts on January 11, 1886, in the mistaken belief that the men were hostile Apaches (A2;8).

periosaurus An anomodont reptile of the Triassic, to which the gorobor of Pellucidar is analogous (P4;13).

peristyle (Greek) An area enclosed by a system of columns around the outside of a building; a porch (I;2).

peritoneum A membrane that lines the abdominal cavity and completely covers the viscera. The peritonea of Pellucidarian dinosaurs were used by **Abner Perry** for such needs as the sails of ships and the gas bag of his prototype balloon (P7:1;3)(P7:2;2).

Perry, Abner A brilliant, though erratic inventor of the turn of the century who, with the backing of the **Innes** Mining Company, built a huge mechanical prospector which was designed to burrow through solid rock, and which developed so much power it was able to do so at an average speed of seven miles per hour. Unfortunately for Perry (and his backer David Innes), the device's turning mechanism did not work, and so once started it drilled through into Pellucidar, the world within the hollow Earth. Perry and Innes were soon captured by the **Mahars**, Pellucidar's dominant race, but eventually escaped, taking with them the secret of the Mahars' reproduction. Perry and Innes gave the humans of Pellucidar sword-and-bow technology, and later gunpowder and guns, allowing them to overthrow the Mahars and form the **Empire of Pellucidar** (P1;1–6,11–15). Later, with the books and tools brought back from the outer Earth by Innes, Perry was able to design and have built ships, weapons of war, telephones, wireless and steam locomotives (P2;14–15).

As might be expected from such an erratic inventor, he accidentally discovered the **Gridley Wave** while attempting to build a radio receiver, and so entered into communication with **Jason Gridley** of **Tarzana**, alerting him and Burroughs to the plight of David Innes in 1926 (P3).

Perry later developed a hot-gas balloon, the *Dinosaur I*, which carried **Dian the Beautiful** off after she demanded to be allowed to ride aloft in it and it slipped its moorings. He was then forced to create the *Dinosaur II* so Innes could fly off after her in the hopes that the prevailing winds would carry him to the same place as they had carried her (P7:1)(P7:2).

Perry, Billy A college chum of **Johnny Lafitte's** in 1920s Glenora, California, whose father owned a small bank. After his father's death, the bank passed into other hands, and Perry became a teller. One day he stole over a million dollars in gold, currency and securities and took off in a small dirigible of his own design, but was boarded by Lafitte, who had become a police officer. Perry refused to give up and set the ship adrift, refusing to land the hard-to-control craft even after Lafitte had thrown out the loot, and as a result the two men were propelled aimlessly out over the Pacific. He turned the craft toward the East Indies and eventually showed Lafitte how to fly it, but Lafitte dared not turn back because he knew that Perry would only head toward the Indies again during his watch, resulting in them going in circles. After six days the engine quit and, faced with imminent death, Perry went mad, tried to kill Lafitte, then hurled himself overboard to his death (PB; 1–4).

pesh (*Apa*) Iron (A1;10).

pesh-litzogue "Yellow iron" (*Apa*). Gold (A1;10).

Pesita, "General" A pillaging Mexican bandito of 1916 who unsuccessfully tried to cloak his activities under the guise of political revolution à la **Pancho Villa** or **Emiliano Zapata**. Pesita hated Americans but hired **Billy Byrne** as one of his captains after being convinced by **Bridge** that Byrne was actually a German colonist. Byrne served him for awhile, but eventually realized his true motivations, and when he invaded the **El Orobo Rancho**, Byrne of course defended its occupants, including its owner, **Anthony Harding**. Because of this they were forced to flee, and Byrne shot Pesita dead when the bandito caught up with them (K2;7–10,17).

Peter One of the mutineers of the *Arrow*, who made a map of the location of the treasure they stole from **Professor Porter** (T1;17).

Peter of Blentz, Prince *see* **Blentz, Prince Peter of**

Peter of Colfax An English nobleman of the mid-13th century who wanted the hand of **Bertrade de Montfort** and, failing to win it, tried to abduct her in May of 1262, only to be foiled by the intervention of **Norman of Torn**. He tried again a few weeks later, and was successful because of the help of **Jules de Vac**, who wanted to make Norman look bad in order to hasten his end. Norman soon rescued her, but Peter escaped in the confusion and returned to England two years later to fight with **Henry III** against his barons at the Battle of **Lewes**. After the battle he was caught and killed by Norman of Torn, who had promised Bertrade his head (OT;7,9–10,17).

Peter the Hermit One of the bandits of the band of the Black Wolf in medieval Derbyshire; he became one of the first of five followers of Norman of Torn after he bested them in combat in 1256. He later became major-domo of Torn (OT;6,10).

Peters The cotton king of early 20th century Baltimore, who married Jane Porter's friend Kitty Krause. When he died, he left her "so many millions she didn't have enough fingers to count 'em on; so the poor woman will never know how rich she is" (T19;1).

Peter's Inn A disreputable hotel on a dirt road in a gloomy wood not far north of the old Roman road in early 20th century Karlova, just east of Sovgrad. It was haunted both by ruffians and by Prince Boris' little band of friends (R;3).

Peterson The alias taken by Zubanev in 1939 when he and Joseph Campbell joined the Ramsgate safari in Northern Rhodesia after being shot down by Lt. Cecil Giles-Burton while pursuing him for the secret Horace Brown plans. As "Peterson," he was killed by Campbell the night after Giles-Burton's murder so Campbell would not have to share the proceeds from the sale of the plans with him (T24B;6–7).

Petit Sahara That portion of the Sahara Desert which lies north of the Atlas Mountains in Algeria (T2).

Petko, General The Serbian ambassador to Lutha in the years preceding World War I. Leopold of Lutha was invariably nasty to him, so he was very much surprised when Barney Custer, posing as Leopold, asked him for help in September of 1914 (MK2;10).

Petrograd A Russian city which was first called St. Petersburg, then Petrograd, then Leningrad, then St. Petersburg again. Alexis Paulvitch belonged to the nihilist movement there and betrayed his fellows when it became expedient to do so (T3;18).

Pew Mogel A hormad of Barsoom with a microcephalic head and genius brain who appeared in "John Carter and the Giant of Mars." He claimed that Ras Thavas had taught him all of his secrets, but this is very doubtful in view of the master mind's known character traits. In any case, he somehow knew those secrets and used them to create an

"invincible" army of white apes with the brains of red men, and a 130-foot-tall synthetic giant named Joog who, like all hormads, was practically indestructible (in addition, Joog instantly repaired all damage to his body). With these, he hoped to conquer all of Barsoom (starting with Helium) after disposing of John Carter and Tars Tarkas. Like most hormads, he was deformed, though not as badly as most. On his tiny head he had no eyelids, and his left eye tended to pop out of its socket and hang on his face; he was also entirely hairless. Aside from that, he looked fairly normal. Eventually, he was killed by John Carter (M11A;5–8,13).

Pew Mogel, His Life and Wonderful Works The title of Pew Mogel's autobiography, the sole copy of which lay in his own library in Korvas (M11A;5).

Pfennig (*Ger*) Penny (P5;20).

Phaidor The daughter of Matai Shang, Holy Hekkador of the Holy Therns of Barsoom. Phaidor was a beautiful white girl with blond hair, every inch a goddess. Like the others of her kind she totally believed in the divinity of the Thern race and of Issus until she was slapped in the face by reality. She fell in love with John Carter and vowed revenge when he spurned her for his wife, the beautiful Dejah Thoris. She was captured by the First-Born and enslaved, then later imprisoned within the Temple of the Sun with Dejah Thoris and Thuvia of Ptarth, during which time she tried to murder Dejah Thoris but was stopped by Thuvia. She was freed by her father before the year of imprisonment was up and fled north with him to Kaol and then Okar. After Thurid killed her father she killed him, then committed suicide to repent for her wickedness (M3;15).

phantom bowmen of Lothar Creatures which are materialized by the mental powers of the men of Lothar on Barsoom, and kill by the power of suggestion (M4;7). See also Kar Komak.

Phao A Jaharian slave girl in the palace of Haj Osis, Jed of Tjanath on Barsoom, the beloved of Nur An. She helped Tan Hadron to rescue Tavia, but they were recaptured and the men were sentenced to die The Death. She and Tavia were again rescued by the men after they returned from Jhama, but this time they were betrayed by **Sanoma Tora**, who helped **Tul Axtar** of Jahar kidnap **Phao** and strand **Tan Hadron** and **Tavia** in the land of **U-gor**. She was re-rescued by Tan Hadron and reunited with **Nur An** (M7;6,12–17).

Pheli A Pellucidarian village which lies at the southern foot of the **Mountains of the Thipdars**, north of **Korsar**. The men of Pheli often steal wives from the mountain people of **Zoram**, a fate the Zoramite women deplore because they hate the lowland Phelians. Pheli lies in the horrible **Phelian Swamp** and is a little village of log longhouses with sharpened stakes set all about to keep away the giant reptiles that infest the swamp (P4;7,12).

Phelian Swamp A dismal swamp at the southern foot of the **Mountains of the Thipdars** in Pellucidar. It is heavily infested with reptiles, including snakes so huge that they can swallow a **trachodon** whole (P4;12).

Phil Sheridan Military Academy The western military academy at which **Dr. Lafayette Smith** taught for about a year before setting out for Africa in 1929 (T15;1).

Philander, Samuel T. The fussy and silly assistant, secretary, and long-time friend of **Professor Archimedes Q. Porter**, who always had to keep his employer out of the trouble the senile old professor was constantly wandering into. He was stranded after the *Arrow* mutiny with Porter and his party on the same spot of coast where Tarzan's parents had been two decades before as evidenced by the presence of the abandoned cottage built by the latter. Soon after their landing, Porter wandered off into the jungle and had to be pursued by Philander and **William Clayton**. He was later rescued by Tarzan and returned to the cottage with Professor Porter, then was saved and returned to civilization on a French cruiser a few months later (T1;13,16,24). As usual, he accompanied the Porters on their cruise around Africa on the *Lady Alice*, which wrecked and left them on shore not five miles north of where they had been marooned before (T2;21).

Philip, Prince The nephew of **Louis IX** of France to whom **Simon de Montfort** betrothed his daughter **Bertrade** in 1262. He came to England for a betrothal party with her and her mother in May of 1264, and there met **Norman of Torn**, but despite Norman's

good reason to dislike him, they liked and respected each other from the first — enough for Philip to draw sword in Norman's defense when he was caught in the Castle of **Battel** with Bertrade by the King, de Montfort and their men (OT;11,18–19).

Philip, Sir An English statesman of the 1930s (LC;5).

Philip Augustus (1165–1223) The King of France from 1180 to 1223; **Richard I** was supposed to meet him for the **Third Crusade** at the port of **Acre**, but was delayed by his stopping to conquer **Cyprus** (T11;12).

Philip of Macedon (382–336 B.C.) The conqueror of Greece and father of Alexander the Great (I;21).

Pho Lar A bully among the **Savator** prisoners in the capital of the **Morgors on Eurobus** who tried to pick a fight with John Carter and was flattened by him within a minute, earning the Warlord great respect among the other prisoners. As it turned out, Pho Lar was really a decent man whose impending death sentence had frazzled him considerably. He was an excellent swordsman and helped the prisoners destroy the Morgor graduating class under Carter's leadership, then escaped with him (M11B;7–8).

Phobeg A temple guard of **Cathne** who was imprisoned (for stepping on "God's" tail) in the same dungeon as was Tarzan in October of 1930. He befriended Tarzan and told him all about Cathne and its queen, **Nemone**, but he was a stupid lout who was fond of bragging about himself and his prowess, so Tarzan did not really like him very much. They were later compelled to fight each other in the arena, but Tarzan refused to kill Phobeg after defeating him. Later, Phobeg warned Tarzan of a planned attempt on his life by **Erot**, and of the plots against **Gemnon** and **Thudos** as well (T16;6,9,13,17).

Phobos Mars' nearer moon. See also **Thuria**; **Ladan**.

Phor San The **odwar** commanding **Hin Abtol's** fleet at the siege of **Gathol**, a drunken slob whom John Carter tricked into making him the dwar of a ship, the *Dusar*, while Phor San was drunk. He later came aboard the ship to arrest Carter, but "fell" overboard soon after the ship took off (M10:3;5,8–9).

Phor Tak An aged Barsoomian scientist of Jahar who invented the disintegration rifle and its corresponding protective pigment, then was driven from Jahar by the jealousy of the other scientists of that city. He discovered and occupied Jhama, a small fortress far to the west of Jahar, and there planned his revenge against Tul Axtar, assisted by Tan Hadron and Nur An. He designed and built the Flying Death (a kind of guided missile) and the compound of invisibility to render it invisible. Finally, he also developed replaceable cartridges for the disintegration weapon which enabled it to disintegrate wood or flesh instead of metal. He was killed by Tan Hadron in self-defense a short time later (M7;5,9–11,16–17).

Phordos The father of Gemnon, Tarzan's Cathnean friend. Phordos was the hereditary Captain of the Hunt for the ruler of Cathne (T16;19).

phororhacos An extinct, flightless, carnivorous bird of the Miocene which stood about five feet tall. See also dyal (P4;6).

Phoros The dictator who usurped the throne of Zygo, King of Athne after their revolution in the mid-1930s; he was a coarse, brutal man who was a typical communist-type dictator. He tried to kill his shrewish wife, Menofra, but she survived, seized power, and had Phoros imprisoned with Gonfala in order to torture him. When he tried to force the beautiful Amazon, she killed him with a dagger (T21;20–25).

photography, Barsoomian Like all other branches of optics (see telescope; atmosphere plant; lighting) photography is a high art on Barsoom. For instance, photographs taken for registration of palace guards are reproduced instantly in five government offices at once, two of them in other cities (M3;10).

photostatic machine The Barsoomians have photostatic copying machines just as we do on Earth, which are capable of reproducing pictures in books, etc. (M7;2).

Phundahl An ancient, backward and superstitious city-state on the western end of the great Toonolian Marshes on Barsoom. Ras Thavas called the Phundahlians "egregious sentimentalists, filled with crass stupidities and superstitions, slaves to every

brain-withering conceit." Phundahlians believe that their jeddak rules by divine right and so will fight and die for him no matter how awful he is; the jeddak is also the high priest of their god Tur. Because of the fundamentalist religion of Tur and its anti-scientific teachings, Phundahl has only a very small navy (M6;2,10).

Phutra The Mahar city of Pellucidar to which David Innes and Abner Perry were taken after being captured by the Sagoths in 1903. Given its favored status, it was probably the Mahar capital. Like other Mahar cities, it consisted of a vast network of underground passages and buildings lit by reflected sunlight. It was destroyed by the army of the Empire of Pellucidar late in 1914 (P1;4–5, 8–11)(P2;15).

Phystal The procurer and keeper of slaves for Fal Sivas of Zodanga (M8;3).

pi The smallest of the oval coins of Barsoom, made of copper and worth about one cent (1941 American money). There are ten pi in a teepi and a hundred in a tanpi. The word is pronounced "pie" (M10:2;11).

Pickerall, Sandra The daughter of Timothy Pickerall, who came to Africa with her father in 1938 and was abducted by Colin Randolph, the false Tarzan. He then lost her to the Waruturi, from whom she was rescued by the real Tarzan and returned to her father's safari. The false Tarzan then kidnapped her again and took her to Alemtejo, but left with her soon afterward when he realized King da Gama's intentions for her. By this point she realized that he was an innocent pawn of da Gama's, a mystery man suffering from amnesia and convinced that he really was Tarzan. As she helped him over his delusion, she grew more fond of him, and when they were reunited after several misadventures, she realized that she loved him. When he finally regained his memory, they flew back to civilization in his plane, which had miraculously landed itself after he had bailed out two years before (T23;2–5,8–16,20–33).

Pickerall, Timothy A Scottish millionaire, manufacturer of Pickerall's Ale, who came to Africa with Pelham Dutton on safari in 1938 and almost suffered a heart attack when his daughter Sandra was abducted by Rand, the false Tarzan (T23;2).

Pickerall's Ale   The alcoholic beverage which made Timothy Pickerall of Edinburgh his fortune (T23;2).

Pickford, Mary (1893–1979)   The professional name of Gladys Marie Smith, one of the most popular actresses in film history. She was especially popular in the silent films of the 1910s and 1920s, and in 1919 founded United Artists along with Douglas Fairbanks, Charlie Chaplin and D.W. Griffith (GH;32).

pieces of bronze   The coins of the Xexots of Pellucidar, octagonal bronze coins of government-designated value (P7:2;5).

Pierre   The valet to Romanoff, whose safari joined the Ramsgates' in Northern Rhodesia in 1939. Pierre was in love with Violet, Lady Ramsgate's maid (T24B;5).

pigment   John Carter always carried with him a vial of the same type of pigment as was first given to him by the Ptor brothers, so that he could stain his skin red to disguise himself among the red men of Barsoom (M1;20). In the Valley of the First-Born, he used the same sort of pigment to disguise himself as a Black Pirate (M10:2;13).

pigment, protective   The substance which can dissipate the rays of a Barsoomian disintegration rifle is a hideous blue, so that all Jaharian fliers, painted with the substance to protect them against the rays, were this same blue color (M7;5). Julian 5th developed a similar protective pigment to protect his ships from Orthis' electronic rifle, but that pigment was grey (MM2;1).

pike, Roman   The javelin-like spear used both by Roman soldiers of ancient times and the barbarian subjects of the Romans in the central Wiramwazi Mountains (T12;6).

Pilgrimage   The Barsoomian term for the great journey (usually taken at the age of 1000 [Earth] years, but sometimes earlier) down the River Iss to the Valley Dor, which was supposed to be the Barsoomian paradise (M2).

Pima   A tribe of American Indians of the Gila and Salt River valleys of southern Arizona who were related to the Papago, who lived to the south of them (K2;14).

pimalia   A large Barsoomian flowering bush cultivated for its gigantic and beautiful blooms (M4;1).

Pimo see **Pima** (A1;3)

Pimos Canyon   The canyon pass southeast of San Carlos, Arizona (A2;4).

pindah-lickoyee   "White eye" (*Apa*). Deprecatory Apache term for the white man (A1;1).

Pindes   An officer of the guard of Cathne in the late 1920s. He was a friend of Xerstle's and helped him in his plan to kill Tarzan in a Grand Hunt. The plan of course failed, much to Pindes' amazement and Xerstle's chagrin (T16;14–15).

Pinkerton   A famous and well-respected American private detective agency, founded in 1850 (K3;8).

Pinkham, Lydia E. (1819–1883)   The manufacturer of "Pinkham's Vegetable Compound," one of the most widely used and advertised patent medicines of late 19th century America (GH;2).

Pinsar   A small cargo flier owned by Ras Thavas which Ulysses Paxton sent out under remote control as a decoy to trick Ras Thavas into sending the *Vosar* in search of it (M6;7).

pintle   A hinge pin or bolt (Q;11).

Pirate Blood   One of Burroughs' single novels, abbreviated PB. Whether it is a "real" autobiography or a "mere" work of fiction there is no way of knowing, since it was written in 1932 and then put away, to be published posthumously in 1970. It tells the story of Johnny Lafitte, former football player and cop, who got lost over the Pacific in a damaged dirigible after trying to foil a bank robbery getaway. He got adopted into a pirate band and eventually became their leader, a career his ancestor (the pirate Jean Lafitte) would have approved of.

Pirates of Venus   The first book in the Venus series, abbreviated V1. The events of the story took place in 1929 and were communicated to Burroughs by Carson Napier, the hero of the story, through the medium of mental telepathy in that year and the next and were published as a book by Burroughs in 1932. The story concerns Napier's attempt to reach Mars by rocket torpedo, only to be thrown off course to land on Venus instead, there to be plunged into a series of adventures among the inhabitants of that world and to fall in love with the gorgeous but forbidden **Duare**, Princess of **Vepaja** on **Amtor**, the name given Venus by its inhabitants.

Pisah (*Ape*) The fish (T1;9).

pisang The Malay name for the banana, or a similar fruit of Africa (T7;13).

Piso, Gaius A Roman patrician with whose bride, **Livia Orestella**, the Emperor **Caligula** became infatuated at their wedding, and with whom he openly made love in front of the whole wedding party, then took for himself (I;17).

Piso, Gnaeus The Roman governor of Syria from A.D. 17 to 19. **Germanicus Caesar** quarreled with him and dismissed him from his post in A.D. 19, then died in Syria shortly afterward; because of this **Agrippina** blamed Germanicus' death on Piso, who committed suicide in A.D. 23 during his trial for poisoning Germanicus. **Britannicus** characterized him as a "bull-headed, egotistical ass" (I;6,12).

Piso, Lucius The Roman magistrate who presided over the trial of **Agrippina** and her son **Nero** (I;15).

pistol, Barsoomian The Barsoomian pistol is a revolver that fires the usual **radium bullets** (M1). Both pistols and rifles were unknown in **Lothar** and **Manator** (M4)(M5).

pistol, Polodan Polodan pistols of the 1940s were small machine guns, perhaps like our modern Uzis, though a bit slower (B1;4).

pistol, R-ray A simple but ingenious Amtorian weapon consisting of a lead-lined chamber and barrel. The chamber is divided into two compartments by a lead shutter that is raised by pulling the trigger, allowing the radiation of one heavy element to act upon another, which results in the release of the very deadly R-rays (possibly hard gamma rays). The weapon emits a staccato hum when activated (V1;6,10).

Pit of Plenty A method of slow torture and execution in **Kadabra** on Barsoom. The pit is 100 feet deep, with smooth and perfectly transparent glass sides. The victim is placed in the pit with no food, and once a day a light is turned on, allowing the prisoner to see food and drink beyond the walls, thus increasing

his hunger by the power of suggestion. The victim eventually goes mad, dehydrates, or starves. John Carter was placed in the pit by **Salensus Oll**, but escaped with the help of one of the spies of **Talu** (M3;11–12).

Pithecanthropus The ancient hominid stock from which the **Ho-don** and **Waz-don** of **Pal-ul-don** were probably descended (T8;1).

pits Under every Barsoomian city are an interconnected series of dungeons and catacombs called the pits. Only the top levels of these are usually connected, and those are guarded, but the lower levels are often unconnected and completely forgotten over time. The pits of **Tjanath** are not as dark as most, as they are lit by gratings and **radium bulbs** (M7;5).

Placina The wife of Gnaeus Piso, whom Britannicus characterized as a "spiteful, jealous troublemaker" (I;6).

plane, Polodan *see* **aircraft, Polodan**

Plant Men of Amtor *see* **Brokol** (V4;24)

Plant Men of Barsoom Burroughs' description is classic: "A race inhabiting the **Valley Dor**. They are ten or twelve feet in height when standing erect; their arms are very short and fashioned after the manner of an elephant's trunk, being sinuous; the body is hairless and ghoulish blue except for a broad band of white which encircles the protruding, single eye, the pupil, iris and ball of which are dead white. The nose is a ragged, inflamed, circular hole in the center of the blank face, resembling a fresh bullet wound which has not yet commenced to bleed. There is no mouth in the head. With the exception of the face, the head is covered by a tangled mass of jet-black hair some eight or ten inches in length. Each hair is about the thickness of a large angleworm. The body, legs and feet are of human shape but of monstrous proportions, the feet being fully three feet long and very flat and broad. The method of feeding consists in running their odd hands over the surface of the turf, cropping off the tender vegetation with razor-like talons and sucking it up from two mouths, which lie one in the palm of each hand. They are equipped with a massive tail about six feet long, quite round where it joins the body, but tapering to a flat, thin blade toward the end, which trails at right angles to the ground" (M4).

I might add a few notes: The "hairs" are actually ears, and move independently of each other, writhing constantly; the plant men can suck blood with their mouth-hands as easily as they suck up vegetation; baby plant men grow from the armpits of adults by a stalk in the head until they get too big and fall off. The plant men hop about like kangaroos, and one of their favorite battle tactics is to leap over opponents in order to crush their skulls with a blow of the tail. The plant men attack pilgrims to the Valley Dor, killing them and sucking their blood. They are held sacred by the **Therns**, who consider them to be one of the four primordial creatures of Barsoom, and who believe that the souls of Therns who die before the age of 1000 pass into the bodies of plant men to finish the 1000 years. If the plant man dies, the soul passes to a **white ape**, and if the ape dies one minute before the 1000 years (timed from the moment of the original Thern's birth) are up, the soul is lost and passes into the body of a slimy **silian** in the **Lost Sea of Korus** (M2;4).

Plantagenet The family name of the Kings of England from Henry II to Richard II, derived from the surname taken by Geoffrey of Anjou, Henry's step-father (OT;1).

Planter's Punch A tropical concoction of shaved ice, rum, sugar and lime juice which was popular in the African colonies (T20;1).

plebeians The peasant class of ancient Rome (I;3).

pleisiosaur A large aquatic dinosaur of the **Jurassic** with a large body, fins for legs, a long tail, and a long neck supporting a tiny head full of sharp teeth. See also **Tandoraz** (P1;4).

Pleisiosaurus olsoni The pleisiosaur species of **Caspak**, named by **Bradley** of the U-33's prize crew for **Olson**, the engineer, who struck the death blow to one of the creatures which stuck its head into the U-boat's conning tower to get him (C1;4).

Pleistocene The first epoch of the **Quaternary** Period, which began about one million years ago and ended about 8000 B.C. During this epoch the ice-ages came, so animals from the period (such as woolly mammoths) grew massive coats of hair for warmth.

Plesser One of the German crew of the captured U-33, on whose behalf **Bowen Tyler** reprimanded **Captain von Schoenvorts** for hitting the man with his swagger stick (C1;6). Much later, he revenged himself for that blow (and many others like it) by killing von Schoenvorts with a bayonet after he broke his word and double-crossed the English (C3;5).

Plin A **Myposan** warrior who had been sold into slavery to the **jong, Tyros**, for making love to one of his master's concubines. He alone of the Myposans did not believe that **Carson Napier**'s R-ray pistol could kill by touch, and so he eventually stole it from him, but was forced by Tyros to throw it into his pool, so terrified of it was he (V4;13–15).

Pliocene The fifth and last epoch of the **Tertiary** Period, which lasted from 13 million to 1 million years ago. **Mammoths** and other large herbivores appeared on the scene around this time.

plurals, Amtorian Plurals in the Amtorian language are formed by adding the prefix **kl-** to words beginning with a vowel and the prefix **kloo-** to words beginning with a consonant (V1;8).

plurals, Pal-ul-don Plurals in the tongue of **Pal-ul-don** are formed by doubling and voicing the initial letter, thus: **Kor** (gorge), **k'kor** (gorges); **don** (man), **d'don** (men). Apparently, they are spelled the same, perhaps with a diacritical mark of some sort to mark the plural (T8;5).

Plymouth A major port and harbor of southwest England. The city proper lies some miles inland, up the River **Tamar** (LC;2).

pneumatic subway A method of transport on Barsoom, used between Greater and Lesser Helium. The rider lies down in the car (which looks like an eight-foot bullet), sets a pointer to his destination on a mechanism, and is automatically routed to the correct tube and shot pneumatically to his proper destination in seconds (M4;2).

Pnom Dhek A lost **Khmer** city of Cambodia; the enemy of **Lodidhapura**. It was ruled in the early 20th century by **Beng Kher**, then after his death by his daughter **Fou-tan** and her husband **Gordon King** (HM;5,17).

Pnoxus The Prince of **Invak**, son of the **jeddak, Ptantus**. He and his **invisible men**

captured John Carter and **Llana of Gathol** when the two stopped to gather food in the **Forest of Invak**, and took them back to the city. **Ptor Fak** sized Pnoxus up as "a calot and the son of a calot and the grandson of a calot." Pnoxus hated his father, who returned the favor (M10:4;2–5).

po (*Ape*) Hungry (TC).

pocket-pouch A small pouch attached to a Barsoomian **harness**, used to carry small items.

Point Conception A cape on the California coastline (in Santa Barbara County) where the coast changes direction from due south to almost due east (PB;2).

pol (*Amt*) A park (V2;15).

Polan The westernmost surviving city of **Unis** on **Poloda**, which lay some thousand miles inland from the ruins of **Hagar** (B1;6).

polar bear (*Ursus maritimus*) An enormous carnivore of the Arctic regions that Burroughs went to hunt in March of 1969, leading to his second meeting with **Julian 3rd** when the latter's airship picked him out of the Arctic Ocean after he had fallen into it during the hunt (MM2;1).

polar opening The north polar opening into Pellucidar is probably about six hundred miles in diameter and lies in the vicinity of 85 degrees north latitude all around the world, though the O-220 encountered it north of **Siberia** and **Alaska** in the vicinity of 170 degrees east longitude. It is possible to sail a ship directly through the opening and into the **Korsar Az** of Pellucidar, but one must imagine that it is a pretty rough trip (P3;14)(P4;2).

Polnik, Captain The captain of the guard at the **Margothian** palace of **Klovia** prior to World War I (R;9).

Poloda One of the 11 planets of the star Omos, a world of roughly the same technological development as Earth when **Tangor** was mysteriously transported there after dying in an aerial battle over Germany in 1939. Poloda lies 230,000 light years beyond NGC 7006, 450,000 light years from Earth. Its atmosphere is very thick and maintains high pressure for a long way up (because it blends with the **atmosphere belt** which connects Poloda with the other planets of Omos) and

is breathable to an altitude of 15 miles. Poloda has five continents (**Unis, Karis, Heris, Auris** and **Epris**) and four oceans (including the **Karagan**, the **Voldan** and the **Mandan**) (B1; 1–2,6,9).

Polodan The human beings of **Unis** on **Poloda** are well-formed and of a very pale white skin color (from living underground). Males have blond hair and females have hair of a very unusual copper color. Only very old Polodan men have beards, and even those are quite sparse. The **Kapars** are a darker, mixed race with varying hair colors (B1;2).

polodona (*Bar*) Equator (M5;1).

pom (Kapar) Great (B2;4).

Pom Da "Great I" (Kapar). The title given to each supreme leader of the **Kapars** of **Poloda**, who then sheds his own name for the title (B2;4).

Pompedius A Roman senator who was arrested after speaking to others about a plot against **Caligula**'s life (I;21).

Pompeius Pennus A Roman senator who was pardoned by **Caligula** after the old man agreed to kiss the mad Emperor's feet (I;20).

Pomponius One of the consuls of Rome at the time of **Caligula**'s death (I;21).

Ponza A small island off the west coast of Italy. It was the site of the Roman prison to which **Nero** was sentenced in A.D. 30; he later committed suicide (I;15).

popo (*Ape*) Eat (TC).

por (*Ape*) Mate (TC).

por-atan "Male mate" (*Ape*). Husband (TC).

por-kalan "Female mate" (*Ape*). Wife (TC).

Porico County The Arizona county in which the TF Dude Ranch lay (D;3).

Porta Decumana "Tenth Gate" (*Lat*). One of the waterbound gates of the lost Roman city of **Castrum Mare** (T12;10). Also, one of the gates of **Castra Sanguinarius** (T12;19).

Porta Praetoria "Praetorian Gate" (*Lat*). One of the gates of the lost Roman city of

Castra Sanguinarius, to which Appius Applosus was transferred out of suspicion that he might help his friend Maximus Praeclarus escape the Colosseum when the latter was imprisoned there in August of 1923 (T12;17).

Porta Principalis Dexter "Right Main Gate" (*Lat*). The right main gate of Castra Sanguinarius (T12;19).

Le Portel   A French cave which contains Cro-Magnon cave paintings (C2;3).

Porter, Professor Archimedes Q. An American professor from Baltimore, father of Jane Porter. He had at one time been brilliant, but his former absent-mindedness had blossomed into full-grown senility by the time the crew of his ship, the *Arrow*, mutinied off the coast of Africa and landed the professor and his party at the same point on the coast as Tarzan's parents had been left 20 years before (they chose the spot because of the presence of Tarzan's cottage). Shortly after their landing, Professor Porter wandered off into the jungle, necessitating his pursuit by William Cecil Clayton and Mr. Philander; he was rescued and brought back to the cottage by Tarzan.

The reason for the trip to Africa in the first place was that the professor had purchased a treasure map from the owner of a bookstore in Baltimore and had actually found the treasure — it was for this treasure that the crew had mutinied, but Tarzan stole it from them. The party was eventually rescued by the crew of a French cruiser which had captured the *Arrow* and interrogated its crew. They were taken back to civilization, but without the treasure, which Tarzan later returned when he realized to whom it belonged. The return of the treasure allowed Professor Porter to pay back Robert Canler, from whom he had borrowed $10,000 for the expedition; the treasure came to about $241,000 (T1;13–19,24–28).

He was later with the *Lady Alice* on its cruise around Africa which resulted in shipwreck not far north of where he had been marooned after the *Arrow* mutiny two years before. A few months later, they were rescued by the same French cruiser that rescued them before (T2;21,26).

Porter, Jane   The daughter of the American professor Archimedes Q. Porter who later fell in love with Tarzan and vice versa. She was stranded on the African coast along with her father, his secretary, their maid, and Tarzan's cousin William Clayton when she was nineteen (in 1909) and became acquainted with Tarzan through the written notes he left in camp for her, but did not know that he was the same "forest god" who twice saved her life, and with whom she had fallen in love. Jane was a beautiful young girl with snowy white skin and waist-length blond hair. She defended Tarzan against the attacks of the others, who believed him to be the adopted member of some cannibal tribe, and even kept the French rescue ship from leaving without Tarzan for over a week; unfortunately, Tarzan was too busy nursing Paul d'Arnot to return, and the cruiser left without them, returning Jane to Baltimore against her will (T1;13–24).

She was forced upon her return to America to accept the proposal of Robert Canler in order to cancel the huge debt her father owed him, but took a trip to her mother's family's farm in Wisconsin to escape for awhile. She was caught in a forest fire, from which she was rescued by the now-almost-civilized Tarzan, who arrived in the nick of time to save her from both the fire and the forced marriage; he brought back Porter's treasure, allowing him to pay Canler back. Furthermore, he throttled Canler until the man released Jane from her promise. At this point she was completely overcome with confusion, unsure whether her love for Tarzan was merely physical and equally unsure that he could ever be fully civilized. During this confusion, William Clayton again asked for her hand and she impulsively accepted, regretting the decision an hour later when Tarzan also proposed, because she then realized the depth of his devotion to her. It was for her sake that Tarzan decided to hide the truth about his birth, because if he had claimed his rightful title and estate from William Clayton, he would also be taking them from Jane, who would have still kept her promise to marry Clayton (T1;27–28).

She continued to put off her marriage to Clayton for some time, insisting that it wait until their return from a cruise around Africa on Lord Tennington's yacht, *Lady Alice*. She ran into her friend Hazel Strong while the yacht was stopped in Cape Town for a few days, and Lord Tennington invited Hazel, her mother and "Mr. Thuran" (the disguised Nikolas Rokoff) aboard. It was at this time that Jane found out about Tarzan's apparent death from Hazel, who had known him on a ship as "John Caldwell" and had a photo of him. A few days up the African coast the yacht struck floating debris and was wrecked, and the whole party landed near where Tarzan had come ashore after Rokoff had thrown him from the liner. It was also near the site of Tarzan's cottage, where she had met him two years before. Jane was with William Clayton and "Mr. Thuran" in a lifeboat, lost and without food or water, and came to shore less than ten miles south of the other party (and less than five miles south of the cottage). They lived there in a crude shelter for about two months before they were menaced by an old, sick lion before which Clayton quailed. After Tarzan (who had happened upon the party in the nick of time) saved them with a well-aimed spear thrown from concealment, Jane berated Clayton for his cowardice and told him she could never marry him, nor any lesser man than Tarzan (T2;12–14,21).

Soon afterward, while Clayton was out hunting and "Mr. Thuran" lay in a fever, Jane was captured by a patrol of Oparians that had come looking for Tarzan, and they took her back to Opar to be sacrificed. She was saved from them by Tarzan, who had followed at great speed after being told of her plight by a great ape who had witnessed the abduction. She and Tarzan were married early in 1911 by Professor Porter (who was also a minister) in the cottage of Tarzan's father and returned to Europe on Lt. d'Arnot's ship, which (on its customary patrol) saved them as it had two years before (T2;23–26). For more of Jane's adventures, see Jane Clayton.

The Portuguese   A pirate of the 1920s South Seas, enemy of the Vulture for ten years before the arrival of Johnny Lafitte on the former's island. Unlike the Vulture, the Portuguese was a hoarder rather than a spender, and he was more aggressive in his persecution of the Vulture than vice versa. After escaping from the Vulture (who wanted to kill him for making love to La Diablesa), Johnny Lafitte joined up with the Portuguese and led him to conquer the Vulture's island. He would have killed Lafitte afterward, but was shot down by his own lieutenant, Pedro, whose life Lafitte had previously saved (PB;8,12–13).

Portuguese West Africa *see* Angola

Potkin, Abe   A Hollywood film producer who wanted Tarzan to play the role of Tarzan in his upcoming movie when the ape-man came incognito to Hollywood in 1933 (T17;33).

Poughkeepsie   A city on the Hudson River in Dutchess County, New York (D;9).

Povak   The second Zodangan assassin sent out to kill John Carter while he was undercover as "Vandor." As with Uldak, Carter easily killed him (M8;8).

Powell, Captain James K.   John Carter's companion during his prospecting in Arizona from 1865 to 1866. He was "a mining engineer by education" and a former Confederate officer who, with Carter, discovered a fortune in gold, but was killed by Apaches on March 3, 1866 (M1;1).

power, Unisan   The power of Unis on Poloda is all derived from their sun, Omos, and is broadcast by long band radio waves to all parts of a city from its central power station; even cars and airplanes run on this broadcast power (B1;4).

power amplifier   A device developed by the Kapar scientist Horthal Wend of Poloda around 1940 for use on the engines of airplanes. It served to amplify the broadcast power emissions received by the plane from its power plant, and therefore allowed the plane to attain far greater speed and altitude, and possibly to travel to the other planets of Omos. It was eventually perfected and stolen from the Kapars by Tangor (B2).

Powers   A ranch hand of Shannon Burke's farm in 1922 Ganado, California (GH;24).

Praetorian Guard   The elite guard of the emperors of ancient Rome. The former gladiator Tibur became a member after Germanicus' German campaign of A.D. 17 (I;2).

prahu *see* proa

Prang   A huge brute who lived alone in the Cambodian jungle near Pnom Dhek. He was a runaway slave from that city and stole the girl Fou-tan from Gordon King (after the latter had rescued her from Lodidhapura), only to lose her in turn to soldiers from Lodidhapura. He was himself later rescued from a fallen tree by King and promised to help him find the girl; he did so, then disappeared into the jungle (HM;10–12).

Prentice, Susan Anne A childhood friend of **Gordon King**'s, a "peach of a girl" with whom he had grown up over the years. She had always lived next door, and the two were like sister and brother (HM;2).

Preswick, Major A British army officer of the Second **Rhodesian** Infantry in **World War I**, whom Tarzan had met in London (T7;3).

Prim, Abigail The 19-year-old daughter of **Jonas Prim** who disappeared en route to meet **Sam Benham**, an old man her mother wished her to marry. She cut off her hair and adopted a male alias (the **Oskaloosa Kid**), then robbed her own room and set out on the road, falling in with a group of murderous hobos soon afterward. Forced to flee, she met up with (and eventually fell in love with) **Bridge, Billy Byrne**'s educated hobo friend, who protected her first from the hobos, then from the law that she claimed to have broken. They ran into various adventures along the way, but were eventually cornered and almost killed by the hobo band of the **Sky Pilot**, who caught up with them at **Payson**. They were saved from death by the timely arrival of **Detective Burton** and his men, who arrested them, but were then dragged from custody by a lynch mob who wished to hang them for the "murder" and "robbery" of Abigail Prim. She was only able to save them by revealing her true identity, surprising both the mob and Bridge, who had not previously understood his unaccountable attraction to the "boy." They were married after Bridge was revealed as the prodigal son of a wealthy **Virginian** (K3;3–10).

Prim, Jonas The president of the First National Bank of **Oakdale, Illinois** in 1917 (K3;1).

prince, Barsoomian On Barsoom, a prince (the Barsoomian term is unknown) ranks below a **jed** but above a **chieftain**. John Carter was made a prince of the House of **Tardos Mors** of Helium until he was made Warlord of Barsoom. See also **dator**.

Prince de Cadrenet The title borne by **Armand Jacot**, **Meriem**'s father and **Jack Clayton**'s father-in-law (T4;27).

Prince of Wales The title held by the Crown Prince, both in England and in the **Valley of Diamonds** (T17;18).

Princeps A famous racehorse of early 1st century Rome, sire of **Certus** (I;8).

princess Besides having the usual meaning, if a Barsoomian man addresses a woman as "my princess," he is calling her his lover. It is considered bold effrontery to use the term to a woman without her consent. See also **chieftain**. Princess is also the name of a **jetan** piece with a three space move, the capture of which by any opposing piece ends the game (M5).

A Princess of Mars The first book of the Mars series, abbreviated M1. The events of the book took place from 1866 to 1876 and were written down by Captain John Carter of Virginia, the book's hero, in 1885, to be published by Captain Carter's great-nephew, Burroughs, in 1912. The action follows Captain Carter's adventures on Mars (called Barsoom by its inhabitants) after he was mysteriously transported there following his apparent death in **Arizona**, and his attempts to win the hand of the radiant **Dejah Thoris**, the title character.

Princess Theater The moving-picture house where **Adolph Bluber** saw the African safari movies that had given him his conception of the dark continent (T9;5).

Pringe, Heber An Arizona rancher who was killed by **Apaches** in April of 1882 (A1;19).

Pringe, Molly The wife of an **Arizona** rancher, friend to **Wichita Billings**, who was killed by the **Apache Tats-ah-das-ay-go** in April of 1882 (A1;19).

Priscilla John Alden Smith-Jones' steam yacht, which he sent out to find his son **Waldo** in 1911, then returned on himself in 1912 (CG2;1,6).

proa A type of large, oceangoing, lateen-sailed canoe used by the natives of Indonesia (T22;29).

Prohibition Like the United States, the Minunian city of **Veltopismakus** once tried to prohibit the use of alcohol, only to find that it was an impossible and needlessly costly law to enforce (T10;11).

Prominent Pictures A Hollywood film studio which unknowingly rejected the incognito Tarzan to play himself in their 1933 movie *Tarzan of the Apes*, saying that he was not the type. They cast Cyril Wayne, an adagio dancer, in the part instead (T17;33).

Prophet of Paul The title held by the leader of the Midianites in the Ghenzi Mountains of Africa (T15;2).

Pruell, Abbie The spinster aunt of Kay White; she was a guest at Cory Blaine's dude ranch (D;3).

Prunt An Amtorian criminal of Sanara who took part in the abduction of the Janjong Nna for Muso in 1930 (V3;17).

psychologist, Barsoomian The psychologists of Barsoom have, through their training, considerable telepathic powers, including the ability to read the minds of even the recent dead (M1;22).

Ptang One of the warriors of Xaxak of Kamtol on Barsoom. When John Carter, whom Xaxak had purchased as a slave, easily defeated Ptang (who was an excellent swordsman), Xaxak knew he could fight Carter in the lesser games and win a great deal on him. Ptang, unlike Dator Thurid of the First-Born of Dor, held no enmity against Carter for his defeat, but rather befriended him, helped him train, and bragged of his skill to the other warriors of the First-Born (M10:2;6–7).

Ptantus The Jeddak of Invak in the early 20th century, father of Pnoxus, whom he hated and vice versa. Like many jeddaks of Barsoom's lost peoples, he was a cruel tyrant who was feared by his people. He gave Llana of Gathol to Motus at the jealous request of Rojas (because she thought John Carter loved Llana), and later arranged a duel between Carter and Motus which allowed the former to escape (M10:4;4–13).

Ptarth A great city-state of Barsoom's northern hemisphere, staunch ally of Kaol and the only Barsoomian nation which had intercourse with that forest country. Unlike Kaol, Ptarth is a modern and advanced country. It became an ally of Helium after the rescue of Thuvia of Ptarth from Okar (M3;6, 16). It is especially known for its navy (M6;8) and its wine (M7;16).

pteranodon A huge flying reptile of the Cretaceous, to which the thipdar of Pellucidar is closely related (P4;3).

Pthav The Kalkar who operated the coal concession for the teivos of Chicago in the early 22nd century. His woman was a human who had gone to him willingly (albeit out of fear) and so was shunned by the local Yanks. Julian 9th saved their child from a mad bull in the marketplace, and Pthav was grateful but could not express it because General Ortis, who hated Julian, was nearby. He was later just as bad as he had ever been, and at the beginning of the revolution his woman killed him and carried his head out on a pole (MM2; 2,5,8,11).

Ptolemy The son of King Juba. He was a cousin of the Emperor Caligula's who was put to death out of jealousy for applause Ptolemy once received in Caligula's presence (I;17).

ptome In the language of Ashair, a lesser priest who is assigned to go out into Lake Horus with a special suit to spear fish, tend garden, and keep the underwater temple (T20;20,25).

Ptor The family name of three Zodangan brothers of Barsoom who were farming officers near the atmosphere plant in the late 19th century. They assisted John Carter in getting to Zodanga with food, money, instructions, and a red skin dye so he could blend in with the inhabitants (M1;20).

Ptor Fak One of the three Ptor brothers who helped John Carter enter Zodanga a few months after his arrival on Barsoom (M1;20). Over 70 years later, John Carter was able to repay the debt by helping Ptor Fak escape from Invak, where he had been imprisoned when his flier's experimental engine had given out over the city during an equatorial circumnavigation of Barsoom (M10:4; 4–12).

Pu The god of the Xexots of Pellucidar, who is said to live in Karana. When David Innes arrived in Tanga-tanga by balloon in 1931 he was thought to be Pu, and ruled the city as the god for some time, winning many followers and defeating the go-sha, Furp, who was disloyal to "Pu" (P7:2;5)(P7:3;1–2,4–7).

Puant, Dan The Hollywood film writer who wrote the script for a Tarzan movie for Prominent Pictures in 1933 (T17;33).

Publius Scorpus A Roman freedman of the early 1st century A.D. He was the superintendent of the White Stables and was a former charioteer (I;13).

Pud A city on the Polodan continent of Auris which was held by the Kapars when Tangor came there as a spy in the spring of 1940 (B2;2).

Pudding Foot A horse of Cory Blaine's dude ranch which was noted for its exceptionally large and round hooves (D;18).

Pudgy Jonas Prim's nickname for his second wife (K3;1).

Pulchra "Beautiful" (*Lat*). A famous mare of early 1st century Rome, dam of Spatium (I;8).

Punos A country of Poloda which lies on the continent of Epris southeast of Kapara; it was one of the first countries to be conquered by the Kapars in the early 19th century. Its inhabitants have since been reduced to a state of near-savagery by the Kapar oppression and practice cannibalism, but only on captured Kapars. They were formerly allies of Unis, and still befriend downed Unisan fliers (B1;8–9).

Pursen, Reverend Theodore A politically outspoken clergyman of early 20th century Chicago who tried to "help" Maggie Lynch for his own purposes. He was the founder of the "Society for the Uplift of Erring Women" and eventually married Sophia Welles (GF;2,6,10).

Puteoli A Roman town across the Baian Gulf from Bauli (I;17).

Pwonja An African chief of the 1930s whose village lay on the Upindi River (T23;6).

pygmies A tribe of African natives of the Congo region known for their small stature (adult males average just over four feet in height). A group of them attacked the remnants of the Hawkes expedition in 1917, but the whites were saved by Tarzan (T9;18).

pygmies, Noobolian A kind of small, very hairy little savages who inhabit the Amtorian continent of Noobol. They are probably related to the kloonobargan, but are of a lower scale of development, and use no weapons or clothing (V2;11).

python Any of several species of powerful constrictor snakes of Africa, Asia, Australia and the Pacific which kill by forcing the breath from their prey, asphyxiating it (T22; 11).

Q-138 The huge European submarine which tried to sink a Brazilian tanker off Bermuda in the fall of 1972; it was the last vessel from the Eastern Hemisphere ever sighted by Pan-American eyes (LC;1).

Q.P. Saloon The bar which Ogden Secor frequented during his first few weeks in Goliath, Idaho (GF;11).

quaestor Any ancient Roman official in charge of public funds; a treasurer (T12; 10).

quagmire Bogs and quagmires, fueled by hidden springs, are fairly common in Caspak. Some of them are almost invisible until one steps into them (C2;7).

quail A game bird whose call is the signal between Tarzan and his Waziri warriors (T19;29).

Quakers Popular name for the Society of Friends, the religion which Juana St. John and her parents secretly practiced in Kalkar-occupied 22nd century America (MM2;4).

queen, Grabritin The Grabritin people of the 22nd century England of *The Lost Continent* were ruled by a king, but the king was the man who had taken for his woman the queen, through whom the bloodline is traced. This was done because there was never any doubt as to the identity of a child's mother, though the paternity might be in doubt. They believed this bloodline to be carried back to the 20th century rulers of England. Aside from granting the authority to rule to her man, the queen had no real power, and she had no real choice of her man, either, if no one opposed his taking her (LC;4).

Queen of Diamonds Daisy Juke's alias as a famous and expensive prostitute of Singapore (PB;12).

Quesada A priest of 1930s Alemtejo who wished to become the high priest, and was made so by da Serra after da Gama and Ruiz fled a revolution brought about by their refusal to accept Tarzan as the true god when he came to Alemtejo in 1938, even though the people believed he was (T23;12,21).

THE QUEST OF TARZAN • RACES, BARSOOMIAN 273

The Quest of Tarzan The title under which *Tarzan and the Castaways* (T24) was first serialized in *Argosy* magazine in 1941, not to be confused with *Tarzan's Quest* (T20). For some reason, the title which appeared in *Argosy* was not Burroughs' working title, which was *Tarzan and the Castaways*.

Question Box The torture chamber of the **Zabo** in the **Polodan** country of **Kapara** (B2;7).

quid (American Western slang) A plug of chewing tobacco (D;2).

Quincy Adams-Coots An aristocratic family of **Boston**, acquaintances of the **Smith-Joneses** (CG2;4).

Quintilia A beautiful Roman actress of the 1st century A.D. who was tortured by **Caligula** for information about a plot against him that he supposed her to possess. She did not talk, and was eventually released (I;21).

Quintus Horatius Flaccus (65–8 B.C.) Full name of Horace, the great lyric poet and satirist of ancient Rome (I;6).

quirt A small riding whip with a short handle and a lash of braided leather (HB;2).

quisling (WW II slang) A traitor; one who betrays his country to a conqueror in exchange for political power. The word is derived from the name of Vidkun Quisling (1887–1945), leader of the Norwegian Nazi party and Norway's Minister of Defense, who betrayed Norway to Germany in **World War II** (T22;10).

R-ray A ray of extremely short wavelength (possibly gamma rays) emitted when two certain radioactive materials are placed in close proximity. See **Pistol, R-ray** (V1;6).

ra (*Amt*) Also (V1;8).

Ra-el A Niocene girl of the tribe of **Nu**; she was the daughter of **Kor** the spear-maker (E2;2).

Rab-Zov A warrior of the bodyguard of **Hin Abtol**, **Jeddak** of the **Panars**, who was claimed to be the strongest man on Barsoom. When Hin Abtol ordered John Carter to wrestle with Rab-Zov, he picked up the warrior and threw him at Hin Abtol's feet (M10:3;13).

Raban A giant **Kalkar** bandit of the early 25th century. He was nine feet tall and very

powerfully built, with bestial features, a low forehead, and shaggy black whiskers and hair that he never combed. He was a cruel and vicious monster who had been born of normal Kalkar parents in the Kalkar capital somewhere around A.D. 2400, a time when the average Kalkar was over seven feet tall and some were as tall as eight feet. Raban preyed only upon Kalkars until the assassination of **Or-tis 15th**, after which he commandeered the dead **jemadar**'s palace and began to prey upon the pure human Or-tis clan as well.

While **Julian 20th** was away hunting, Raban came to the village of the **Nipons** and kidnapped **Bethelda**, daughter of Or-tis 15th, with whom Julian had fallen in love. Julian of course pursued, and after a running fight in which he killed many of Raban's men he was himself captured, but escaped with the help of **Okonnor**, a pure human Or-tis who had joined Raban. The giant was killed by Julian shortly thereafter when he tried to take Bethelda as his woman (MM3;7–9).

Rabba Kega The witch doctor of the tribe of **Mbonga** in **Angola** when Tarzan was growing up. Due to Tarzan's intervention in the kidnapping of **Tibo** by **Bukawai**, Rabba Kega's magic was shown up, and he was very embarrassed and angered (T6:6). He was killed late in 1908 by a lion after Tarzan tied him in his own tribe's lion trap as bait in place of the kid they had originally placed there, which Tarzan had stolen and eaten. It goes without saying that the warriors of Mbonga were shocked and afraid when they went to the trap the next day (T6:11).

races, Amtorian The following is a list of the semi-human races of Amtor, discounting the dominant human race. See also individual entries.

Brokols	pygmies,
Cloud People	Noobolian
Klangan	Samary
Kloonobargan	Timal
Myposan	Vooyorgan

races, Barsoomian The following is a list of all of the races mentioned in the Mars books, including human variations. See also individual entries.

First-Born	Man-Eaters	rykors
Goolians	Orovars	Therns
green men	Panars	yellow men
hormads	Plant Men	
Kaldanes	red men	

races, Lost The following is a list of Earthly lost races, including most of the major groups. See also individual entries.

Ashairians	Mayans	Wieroos
Bolgani	Midianites	Xujans
Galus	Minunians	Yokans
Ho-don	Ontharians	Zertalacolols
Kavuru	Oparians	
Khmers	Waz-don	

races, Pellucidarian The following is a list of known races of Pellucidar, including human, humanoid, and non-human. See also individual entries.

Black Men	Gorbuses	Mezops
Brute-Men	Horibs	Oog
Coripies	Korsars	Sabertooth Men
Ganaks	Mahars	Sagoths
Gilaks	Man-apes	Xexots

radio The Barsoomians monitor Earthly radio communications, and some savants have succeeded in learning Earthly languages, most notably English, Urdu, Russian and Chinese (M6;9).

radio, Amtorian The only Amtorian nations known to have radio are the countries of **Middle Anlap** (V4;45) and **Havatoo** (V2;16). Neither the **Thorists, Korvans**, nor **Vepajans** have it (V1;10).

radio-aerogram Upon Barsoom, a wireless radio message. They are seldom, if ever, used for dispatches of importance (and never during wartime) because of the power and versatility of Barsoomian code-breaking devices (M2;16,20). In **"John Carter and the Giant of Mars"** this policy is ignored, with predictable results (M11A;4–8).

radium Burroughs believed that radium was the base of the powder used to make Barsoomian **bullets** explode, and also the fuel of almost all Barsoomian motors (M1;13).

radium paint A paint invented by the ancient U-gas of Va-nah which was painted on interior walls to provide nearly eternal illumination (MM1;9).

Raffles The name given to a large lion who was in the habit of killing Tarzan's sheep while Burroughs and **Barney Custer** were guests at his estate in 1913. He was killed by **Nu** of the Niocene to save **Victoria Custer** (E1;5–6).

Raghunath Jafar A swarthy East Indian communist who came to Africa with the Zveri expedition in 1928 to cause war between France and Italy. He conceived of a passion for **Zora Drinov** and tried to rape her, but was stopped by the timely arrival of **Wayne Colt**. He later tried to murder Colt, but was himself killed by Tarzan (T14; 1–3).

rah (*Pell*) Kill (P7:4;9).

rahla (*Ara*) A march (T11;1).

rahna (*Pell*) Killer (P5;13).

Rahna "Killer" (*Pell*). The name given by O-aa to the trained **jalok** she found early in 1932 after its master had met with some unknown fate (P7:4;5).

Railway Exchange Building The Chicago building in which **Ogden Secor** had his offices (GF;7).

Rain Cloud The youngest brother of Julian 20th. In 2430 he was 16 years old and noted for his handsomeness, intelligence and (for the time) advanced ideas, which everyone else thought strange. He was a thinker rather than a warrior and was doubtless a major force in prodding Julian's tribe back toward civilization after the **Kalkars'** defeat (MM3;1).

rainy season, African The rainy season of Africa lasts from June to September (T4;2)(T16;1).

raj (*Amt*) Fire (V4;26).

Raj A chief of the **Mezops** of Pellucidar who was the captain of the EPS *Sari* in the 1920s and 1930s (P7:2;3).

Raja David Innes' collie when he was a teenager, after whom he named the **jalok** whose broken leg he set and nursed back to health, then kept as a pet (P2;7).

rajah (Hindi) King (Q;1).

rak (*Ape*) Yes (TC).

rala (*Ape*) Snare (no doubt a Tarzan coinage) (TC).

Ram Head A great promontory which marks the edge of **Plymouth Bay** in southwest England (LC;2).

ramba (*Ape*) Lie down (TC).

ramp Ramps are used in all Barsoomian buildings instead of stairs, which are almost totally unknown there (M1).

Ramsgate, Lady Barbara A British noblewoman and a friend of Lt. Cecil Giles-Burton's, whose 1939 safari Burton met up with after being shot down over Northern Rhodesia and wandering for a time, lost and starving (T24B;5).

Ramsgate, Lord John A British nobleman, brother of Lady Barbara Ramsgate, whose 1939 safari to Northern Rhodesia was joined by their friend Lt. Cecil Giles-Burton after he was shot down over the area and became lost (T24B;5).

Rana The sweetheart of Zor, David Innes' fellow captive in Oog. Rana had been abducted from Zoram, and it was during his pursuit of her that Zor was captured by the Amazons of Oog (P6;4).

Rancho del Ganado "Cattle Ranch" (*Sp*). A ranch of southern California in the early 20th century, which lay 100 miles south of Los Angeles. It belonged to the Pennington family (GH;1).

rand (*Ape*) Back (TC).

Rand Nickname of Colin T. Randolph, Jr. (T23;32).

Randolph, Colin T., Jr. A West Virginian adventurer, pilot and compulsive gambler who emulated Tarzan and made a bet that he could live like Tarzan for a month in Africa. On the way to Africa in his plane, however, it developed engine trouble and he was forced to bail out, parachuting into the lost city of Alemtejo and striking his head upon landing, causing severe amnesia and resulting in the delusion that he actually was Tarzan. Since he had fallen from the sky, he was proclaimed God by King da Gama in order to control the populace, and da Gama further urged him to go out and find a goddess so his power could be doubled. Unfortunately, most of the women Randolph found were black and thus suitable only as slaves to da Gama, who believed that gods should be white. Tarzan's reputation was thus tarnished by this amnesiac who, although he looked nothing like Tarzan, fit his description in behavior and dress and could thus be taken for him by people who did not know him by sight. Randolph finally

succeeded in abducting a white woman, Sandra Pickerall, whose father offered a reward for Tarzan's death or capture that drew bounty hunters after him, prompting him to seek Randolph with murderous intent. After a short while, Miss Pickerall realized what condition the man was in and began to feel sympathy, then love for the noble, brave pseudo-Tarzan who had done evil only under orders from da Gama, but had treated her as a gentleman would. He rescued her from Alemtejo after seeing da Gama's plans for her, then again from the Galla village of Sultan Ali. After he regained his memory, they returned to civilization together aboard his plane, which had glided to an unharmed landing nearby after he had bailed out (T23;1–16, 20–33).

Ranee The mate of Raja, David Innes' pet jalok; she later became as much Innes' pet as her mate (P2;12).

Rapas, the Ulsio An assassin of Zodanga who took a liking to John Carter while he was in that city on a secret mission, and who got Carter work as an assassin with his best client, Fal Sivas. Angered by Carter's besting him at swordplay in front of Fal Sivas, Rapas then went to the assassin's guild and told them that Carter (whom he knew by the alias "Vandor") was Fal Sivas' assassin; as a non-member of the guild, this made "Vandor" subject to punitive assassination for practicing his trade in Zodanga. Rapas was very useful to Carter on several occasions afterward, because he had a very loose tongue (M8;1–4,7–9,24).

ras An Ethiopian title of nobility, equivalent to a prince (T15;7).

Ras Tafari *see* Makonnen, Ras Tafari

Ras Thavas The most brilliant medical mind upon Barsoom; by his own estimation, the most brilliant mind, period. When he met Ulysses Paxton he was a small man (about 5'5"), very old and stooped, with an enormous balding head and a skinny, emaciated body. He had at that time been alive for about two thousand years, and had been involved in new and undiscovered fields of medical knowledge for over half of that time. He is from Toonol, and carries the Toonolian tendency for detached, unemotional, scientific thought to an extreme; emotions are beyond his comprehension, as are ordinary concepts of good and evil. Ras Thavas has invented many amazing medical devices, including a bone saw, a blood pump, and special surgical tape. He has developed a fluid that can keep a body fresh in suspended animation almost indefinitely, and has perfected transplantation to such an art as to be able to effect a complete brain transplant in only four hours. His skill is so great, he can even raise the dead if the body is fresh enough.

Ras Thavas made Ulysses Paxton his bodyguard and assistant, positions to which he could trust no Barsoomian, because Paxton had no reason to betray him and every reason to stay with his only friend on a hostile world. In the process, he taught Paxton to transplant brains so he might transplant Thavas' brain into a fresh young body of his choosing, which Paxton did. He later used this skill to replace the brains of Xaxa and Valla Dia, whose brains Thavas had switched earlier so the hideous Xaxa might have a beautiful body. For this service and all others Thavas charged enormous fees — to pay for his many expensive experiments rather than to get rich, as he cares very little for money (M6;1–4).

His tower was later taken from him by Vobis Kan, Jeddak of Toonol, and Thavas was forced to agree to a code of experimental ethics in return for aid to get it back (M6;14). This expedition was defeated, however, and Thavas was missing and presumed dead for many years, until John Carter and Vor Daj discovered him in the dead city of Morbus, deep in the Toonolian Marshes, working on the perfection of his synthetic men, the hormads, who had grown numerous enough to take over the island and force Ras Thavas to work for them, turning out enough synthetic men to conquer Barsoom. When John Carter was captured by the hormads and made one of their officers, Ras Thavas immediately recognized him through the red pigment he was disguised with, and took him into his confidence. He and John Carter discovered a secret passage out of Morbus and escaped, then built a boat to get back to Carter's hidden flier, then to Helium, where Dejah Thoris lay dying and in need of Ras Thavas' medical genius. He of course healed her, then returned with John Carter to Morbus, where he restored Vor Daj's brain (which had been placed in a hormad so he could spy) to its rightful body. They then left again so the city

could be destroyed (and the hormads with it); it is unknown what Ras Thavas did next (M9; 1–6,15,29–30).

Rasoom The Barsoomian name for the planet Mercury (M6;2).

rat, Pellucidarian Some of the larger rats of Pellucidar (such as those found in the dungeons of the Korsars) can grow to be up to three feet long and a foot high. They are incredibly vicious (P3;13).

ratel (*Mellivora capensis*) A burrowing animal of Africa, also called the honey badger. Ratel burrows are often used as campsites by Minunians when in the field (T10;20).

Rateng A Galla hunter of the village of Sultan Ali who abducted Sandra Pickerall for himself after she escaped his village in 1938. She grabbed an arrow from his quiver, however, and killed him with it (T23;27–28).

rations Barsoomian food rations are in the form of small, concentrated lozenges, and are common everywhere on the planet (M3; 11).

rattan Any of several species of palm of the genus *Calamus*; they have extremely long, thin stems, jointed like bamboo, which are used for wickerwork (CG2;11).

Rattlesnake One of the warrior chiefs under Julian 20th in the post–Kalkar 25th century American West (MM3;1).

Ravenna A provincial city of the Roman Empire, located in northern Italy. It was the chief port of Rome's northern Adriatic fleet (I;1).

Ravine of the Kings A ravine in the valley of the Jukans in Pellucidar which is filled with caves which are used by the mad Jukans of Meeza's village for no purpose, except for the one cave which hides the exit to Meeza's secret passage (P6;14).

Raxar A Barsoomian city-state which lies far to the north, but not within the polar lands. It lies between Pankor and Gathol and is ruled by a jed (M10:3;7).

ray gun, Amtorian *see* pistol, R-ray

ray gun, Barsoomian An imaginary weapon of unknown effect which appears only in "John Carter and the Giant of Mars" (M11A;1).

Ray L The Barsoomian term for cosmic rays, which are collected from space by **Morgor** ships and used as a method of propulsion in interplantary space (M11B;3).

rea (*Ape*) Word (no doubt a Tarzan coinage) (TC).

Realists One of the two philosophical schools of **Lothar** on Barsoom; the other is the **Etherealist** school. Realists believe that mind can control matter, but that matter does exist. They also believe that all Etherealists have no material existence and are only pure mind, because if they had bodies, they would have to eat to stay alive; however, they do not eat, and yet live, therefore they are unreal. **Jav** was the leader of the Realists (M4;7).

Rebega The chief of the **Betete** cannibals in 1931, friend to **Kapopa**, the witch doctor of **Bobolo**. At Kapopa's request, Rebega kept **Kali Bwana** in his village so Bobolo could secretly have her whenever he wished, as his village was near Bobolo's. Rebega was killed by Tarzan a few days later when he and his people tried to eat the girl (T18;15,18).

reclamation laboratory The facility in **Morbus** in which dismembered **hormad** parts were dumped into **culture vats** to grow new bodies, heads or limbs (M9;4).

Red Book Magazine The magazine in which the first part of *Tarzan the Untamed* was first published as a serial from March to August of 1919.

Red Butte An Arizona prominence not far from the **Bar-Y Ranch** of the late 19th century (HB;6).

Red Flower of Zoram The appellation given to the Pellucidarian girl **Jana** of the village of **Zoram** (P4;7).

Red Hawk The tribal name of **Julian 20th** (MM3;1).

The Red Hawk The third novel in the moon trilogy, originally published in *Argosy All-Story Weekly* in September of 1925. The action of the story took place in 2430 and was told to Burroughs in 1969 by **Julian 3rd**, who had the uncanny ability to "remember" his future lives as well as his past ones. By some unknown method the story was sent backward to 1925 and novelized. It concerns the efforts of **Julian 20th** to destroy the very last

group of the **Kalkars** who had conquered his world almost 400 years before and left humanity in a primitive state. Since the novel is a short one, it is usually published in the same volume as *The Moon Men*. Its abbreviation is MM3.

Red Lightning An outlaw five-year-old bay stallion owned by **Hoffmeyer**, a human agent of the Kalkars in the **Teivos** of **Chicago** in the 22nd century. The animal was so vicious that no one could tame it, so Hoffmeyer was happy to sell it to **Julian 9th** for one goat, but Julian succeeded in breaking it and it became a very good-natured and tractable (though spirited) animal (MM2;8). The horse of every Julian thereafter was always called Red Lightning (MM3;1).

Red Man Sobriquet of the ancient **Mayan** rebel **Chab Xib Chac** (T24;1).

red men of Barsoom The dominant race of Barsoom is a hybrid one, resulting from the mixture of the ancient white, black and yellow races during the period of their cooperation to fight the **green men** and build the **canals** and **atmosphere plant**. They are a very beautiful people with copper-colored skin, dark eyes, and jet-black hair. The red race has long since reached and surpassed the long-lost achievements of the ancient cultures and are the inventors of practically every modern technological device on Barsoom, including **fliers**. They are a warlike race except as compared to the green men, relative to whom they are positively pacifistic (M1).

red men of Pellucidar *see* Mezops

red robe A symbol of high office among the **Wieroos** of **Caspak**. Anyone, no matter how high ranking, who kills a red-robed Wieroo is put to death by torture (C3;3). See also **colors, Wieroo**.

Red Stables One of the four officially sanctioned racehorse syndicates of 1st century Rome (I;8).

Redcoat Dick Gordon's horse (ME;2).

Reece A young man who acted as Tarzan's guide on his first (and only) visit to Hollywood in 1933 (T17;33).

reefer (American slang) A marijuana cigarette. The drug was made illegal in 1937, but the laws were not really enforced until the 1960s (T22; 24).

Regulus, Memmius   A commander of the Roman army in Macedonia, whose wife, **Lollia Paulina, Caligula** had him send to Rome for his own use (I;17).

reincarnation   Julian 1st, an American officer of **World War I**, was reincarnated several times that he could remember, coming back as his own descendants **Julian 3rd, 5th, 9th and 20th.** The beings of **Va-nah** believe in reincarnation, and the **Kalkars** further believe that anyone who falls into a crater is never reincarnated again (MM1;1,10–11)(MM2;1) (MM3).

Rela   "Darkness" (*Pell*). The daughter of **Avan**, Chief of the **Clovi** tribe of Pellucidar. She was the sister of **Ovan**, who befriended Tarzan (P4;11).

Rela Am   "River of Darkness" (*Pell*). A river of Pellucidar which flows from the **Gyor Cors** into the **Korsar Az** (P4;14–15).

relativity of distance   A peculiar bit of Amtorian nonsense first propounded 3000 years ago by a "scientist" called **Klufar**; it insists that since all circles have 1000 hita (Amtorian degrees), each is equal, and only appear different to flawed human perception. The "true" distances may be reconciled by multiplication of the "apparent" results by i (the square root of -1). This "theory" is used to reconcile the facts with the religious notion that the "inner" border (toward the pole) of Amtor's south temperate zone is actually the "outer" border (toward the equator) (V1;4).

religion   As under most communist regimes, religion was outlawed by the **Kalkar** government of America on the grounds that the priests and ministers were attempting to foment rebellion. Sometime in the 2060s, the **Twentyfour** had all clergymen executed, but **Julian 8th's** family and a few others (16 in all) still practiced a simple and nondenominational religion in an underground church hidden in the woods near **Chicago** (MM2; 3,6–7).

rem   (*Ape*) Catch (TC).

rep   (*Ape*) Truth (TC).

reptiles, Barsoomian   Reptiles are practically extinct on Barsoom, except for the darseen, but there are still a few fearsome examples floating about in hidden places. See Chamber of Reptiles; lizard.

reptiles, Pellucidarian   Giant reptiles rule the seas of Pellucidar, but few are to be found in the drier land areas — land reptiles are mostly limited to damp areas like the Phelian Swamp.

reptiles, Va-nah   Besides the U-gas and Va-gas, the highest life forms in **Va-nah** are reptilian (MM1;3–4).

restaurants, Barsoomian   In Barsoomian restaurants the food is prepared and served mechanically in response to push-button ordering at the tables. No human hand other than that of the diner ever touches it (M1;21).

restaurants, Wieroo   The Wieroos of Caspak have restaurants in which are several large, birdbath-shaped stone fonts, each with four seats (wooden with a metal support) projecting from it. A mess of food (a sort of Wieroo chop suey) is deposited in the bowl, from which all of the Wieroos seated at the font eat in common, usually too quickly (they have terrible table manners). Strict Wieroo laws prohibit any sort of argument or fighting in such an eating place (C3;2).

Restless Sea   A great shallow lake or sea of central Africa in the **Niocene** period 100,000 years ago. It may have been this same sea whose shores **Opar** was built upon (E1;9).

"The Resurrection of Jimber-Jaw"   A short story which to this date has only appeared in *Tales of Three Planets* (with "The Wizard of Venus" and *Beyond the Farthest Star*). It is abbreviated J and concerns the thawing out of a cave man found frozen in the wilds of **Siberia**, and his attempt to adjust to the modern world.

The Return of Tarzan   The second novel in the Tarzan series, abbreviated T2, which was published in 1913. The events of the book took place in 1910 to 1911 and came to Burroughs from the same source as did the first Tarzan story. It concerns Tarzan's adventures on an ocean liner traveling from America (where he had left **Jane Porter**, who had impulsively promised to marry **William Clayton**) to France; the enemies he made on the liner, who would follow him for several years;

his adventures in France and north Africa; and his eventual return to the jungle, where he became chief of the noble **Waziri** tribe and first journeyed to the lost city of **Opar**, where he found both great treasure and great peril.

Return of the Mucker The sequel to *The Mucker*, abbreviated K2, in which **Billy Byrne** must stand trial for a murder committed by an old enemy — the same false murder charge that had forced him to flee **Chicago** over a year before. He is convicted, but escapes to Mexico, where he takes part in a revolution and meets up again with **Barbara Harding**, the woman who loves him, but he will not allow himself to have.

"The Return to Pellucidar" The first book of *Savage Pellucidar*, published in *Amazing Stories* magazine in 1941.

Reyd, Doctor The Dutch doctor of **Sumatra** who was a member of the guerrilla band with whom Tarzan and his "Foreign Legion" joined up while in **Japanese** territory in the spring of 1944 (T22;24).

rhamphorhynchus A small flying reptile of the **Jurassic**, the probable ancestor of the **Mahars** of Pellucidar (P1;5).

Rhine One of the great rivers of Europe; it rises in southeast Switzerland, flows through Austria, Germany and the Netherlands, and empties into the North Sea. Lt. **Jefferson Turck** and his men explored it in their motor launch and found no inhabitation anywhere along it (LC;6).

Rhodes A Greek island off the coast of Turkey, where **Angustus the Ephesian** acquired the fair-haired slave girl who was to bear his descendants (T15).

Rhodesia, Northern *see* **Northern Rhodesia**

Rhump One of the women warriors of **Oog** who captured **David Innes** while he was passing through their country in 1929 (P6;2).

riata (*Sp*) Lasso; it is from this word that the English "lariat" (from "la riata") was derived (K2;12).

Rice, Deacon Edmund (1594–1663) An ancestor of **Carson Napier**'s (and Burroughs') who came to Sudbury, **Massachusetts**, about 1639 and was a descendant of **Cole Codoveg**, a Briton king (V4;6).

Richard, Earl of Cornwall, King of the Romans (1209–1272) The younger son of King John of England, who was chosen Holy Roman Emperor by one faction of the electors in 1256 while Alfonso X was chosen by the other faction. He returned to England in May of 1264 to help his brother, **Henry III**, and was captured by his nephew, **Norman of Torn**, for the barons at the Battle of Lewes on May 13th. He was a good ruler and one of the richest men of the 13th century (OT;16).

Richard, Prince The younger son of **Henry III** of England, forgotten by history after his kidnapping by **Sir Jules de Vac**, the King's swordmaster, in revenge for an insult the cowardly king had given him. The boy was only three at the time of his abduction, and by the age of six had forgotten his former royal life and knew himself only as **Norman of Torn**. He thought that de Vac was his father, and as he developed he grew to hate the old man, but did not find out the truth about himself until 1264, when de Vac, thinking his revenge complete, sputtered out the story in his last moments of life (OT;2–8,19).

Richard I (the Lion-hearted) (1157–1199) The King of England from 1189 to 1199; he went on the **Third Crusade** in 1191, but stopped to conquer **Cyprus** along the way, so the ships of **Sir Bohun** and **Sir Gobred** were lost in a storm and shipwrecked in Africa (T11;12).

Richmond The city of **Virginia** which was the Earthly home of John Carter, and in which his original body was buried in a strange mausoleum of his own design (M1).

The Rider A notorious bandit of early 20th century **Karlova** who terrorized the southern part of that tiny kingdom for some four years before moving to the vicinity of its capital around 1913. He was captured at that time by **Prince Boris** of Karlova, who sort of befriended him, and the two (who looked nothing alike) switched identities for a time, during which The Rider made a fool of himself as a prince. He eventually showed his true colors by trying to fool a rich American heiress named **Gwendolyn Bass** into marriage with his "royal" self, but was shot in the attempt, escaped, and blabbed the story to **Bakla**, the serving-girl at **Peter's Inn**, who told the authorities and thus saved both **Hemmington Main** and the real Prince Boris from execution. What happened to The Rider afterward is unknown (R;1–6,10–11,14–17).

The Rider   A "single" novel, published in *All-Story Weekly* in 1918 as *H.R.H. the Rider.* It was written in 1915 and the events within took place in the last days before World War I. The story concerns **The Rider**, a most successful highwayman, who interferes in the marriage plans of two royal families whose intermarriage will seal a centuries-old rift between their countries. The story is abbreviated R.

rifle, Barsoomian   The Barsoomian rifle is made of a white metal (an alloy of aluminum and steel) and is stocked with wood. It weighs very little, has a very long, narrow barrel which fires the same small, explosive **bullets** as other Barsoomian firearms do, and its magazine holds 100 rounds. Barsoomian rifles are equipped with wireless finders and sighters which render them extremely accurate and deadly; their theoretical range is 300 miles, but even with the wireless equipment the range is "but a trifle over 200 miles." The **green men** are particularly deadly with these weapons (M1;3). Firearms were unknown to both the **Lotharians** (M4) and the **Manatorians** (M5).

rifle, disintegration, Amtorian *see* T-rays

rifle, disintegration, Barsoomian *see* disintegration rifle

rifle, electronic   A weapon similar to the disintegration rifle invented by **Phor Tak** of Barsoom. It was invented by **Orthis** and could entirely disintegrate any substance to which it was attuned, usually aluminum. He only built one and used it to destroy almost the entire **International Peace Fleet** before **Julian 5th** discovered its secret and destroyed it (MM2;1).

rifle, Express   A heavy hunting rifle favored by Europeans and Americans on safari in Africa (T3;15).

Rift of Kamtol   A deep canyon northwest of Gathol on Barsoom. It is about two miles deep, ten miles wide and almost a hundred miles long. Since it has a denser atmosphere and is protected from the parching winds, it is very fertile, forested and well-watered, with several rivers leading into a large central lake. It is known to its inhabitants, the **Black**

Pirates of Barsoom, as the **Valley of the First-Born**, and their colony of **Kamtol** lies within it (M10:2).

Rift Valley, Great   The largest rift valley on Earth, formed by the splitting of the African and Asian plates by tectonic forces in the Earth's mantle. The valley runs from Mozambique through the eastern portion of Africa (Lake Malawi and Lake Tanganyika lie in it), then through **Ethiopia** to the Red Sea, which was formed when the rift widened sufficiently (in prehistoric times) to admit ocean water. The Dead Sea of Palestine marks its northernmost portion, and Madagascar was split off from the African continent by it as well. It was to study the Great Rift Valley that **Lafayette Smith** came to Africa (T15;1). The tortuous terrain in and along it hid the lost lands of **Xuja** (T7), **Minuni** (T10), the **Valley of the Sepulcher** (T11), **Midian** (T15), **Onthar** and **Thenar** (T16), **Tuen-baka** (T20) and possibly **Opar** (T2), the **Valley of the Palace of Diamonds** (T9), and the **Lost Empire** (T12) as well.

ring of warning   One of the few priceless gems of Barsoom looks like a lump of bituminous coal, but fragments cut from the same mother stone react electrically to each other's presence, causing a pricking sensation in the finger if a ring is made with this gem in its setting and the wearer approaches another such ring within 50 feet. Rings such as these were worn by the spies of **Talu** in **Kadabra** so they might know one another (M3;9).

ripotamus   Another Esmerelda malapropism (T1;22). See also **hipponocerous.**

River of Death   The buried river which flows beneath the largest **Wieroo** city of **Oo-oh** in **Caspak**, into which the headless corpses of the dead are dropped and float down to the warm central sea of Caspak to be devoured by the reptiles there. Garbage is disposed of in the same way (C3;3). See also **Gerlat kum Rov** (V2;17).

rivers, Barsoomian   The only major river on Barsoom is the River Iss, the river of the **Pilgrimage**, but there are others, most notably the River **Syl**, which runs beneath **Tjanath** and through the **Valley Hohr**, and is probably a world-spanning tributary of the Iss (M7;7–8). The great underground river that runs beneath **Manator** (M5;12) is probably identical with the Syl, and the stream of the Valley of **Bantoom** (M5;3) is probably a tributary of it. There are small rivers which flow into the Iss through the **Valley of Lost Souls** (M2;8), and an underground river with several tributaries that enters the Iss beneath the **Mountains of Otz** (M3;1–2); these rivers derive from the melting of Barsoom's south polar ice cap. Small rivers can be found in the Valley of **Kamtol**, but these all empty into the valley's central lake (M10:2;3).

rivers, Va-nah The world within the moon is replete with rivers, all of which empty into its three oceans (MM1;5).

Riverside Drive The name given by Billy Byrne to the part of "Manhattan Island" where he built **Barbara Harding's** hut while they hid from the samurai of **Yoka** (K1;14).

ro In the adolescent Tarzan's letter-naming system, the letter "Y" (T6:4).

Ro One of the henchmen of **Noak**, majordomo of the palace of **Meeza**, King of the Jukans of Pellucidar. Ro was a mean man with a good memory, for a Jukan (P6;8).

ro (*Amt*) The number three (V1;8).

ro (*Pal*) Flower (T8).

Ro-tai The Chief of the **Ruvans** when David Innes was captured by them near the end of 1929. Ro-tai was very friendly to Innes once he had shown the Ruvans several new ideas, but would not permit him to leave Ruva, making him a full warrior instead and insisting that he stay (P6;23–28).

Ro Tan Bim An ancient Orovar of Horz on Barsoom who was hypnotized and put into suspended animation in ancient times by **Lum Tar O**, the hideous old man of the pits. He was the last man that Lum Tar O ate before being destroyed by John Carter (M10:1;8).

Ro-ton The Brokol high priest of **Loto-el-ho-ganja** when **Carson Napier** came to Brokol in 1931 (V4;25).

roan A horse of bay, chestnut, or sorrel color mixed with grey or white (D;1).

Robey Street One of the borders of Chicago's rough west side (K1;1).

Robot pilot A Unisan invention with which all ships designed to fly very great distances were equipped so the pilot might sleep, eat and rest (B2;10).

Rochere, General The chief of the bureau of the French War Department with which Tarzan held his first and only salaried position, having received the job through the intercession of the **Count de Coude** (T2;6).

Rochester A British town in Kent where the forces of **Henry III** suffered a crushing defeat at the hands of the baronial army in 1262 (OT;12).

Rock One of the warrior chiefs under Julian 20th in the post–**Kalkar** 25th century American West (MM3;1).

Rogers, Ginger (1911–1995) American dancer and actress, partner of Fred Astaire; she was especially popular in the 1930s and 1940s (T22;14).

Rojas A noblewoman of **Invak** who helped John Carter to escape the city by bringing him some of the Invakian invisibility spheres. She also pretended to be in love with him so he would take her with him when he left, because she wanted to get out of Invak (M10:4;3–13).

Rokoff, Nikolas The brother of **Olga, Countess de Coude**; a villainous Russian who tried to use his sister to blackmail French military secrets from her husband in order to sell them to Russia. For this purpose he tried to frame the Count for cheating at cards, and the Countess for having a tryst with another man, both for the purpose of getting blackmail material with which to extort the secrets from the Count. Tarzan foiled both of these attempts, earning him Rokoff's undying wrath. Although Rokoff was a villain, his sister would not give him up to the police because he had some blackmail material on her (a girlhood romance with a man who turned out to be a criminal) which might ruin her marriage, but was not strong enough for his primary blackmail scheme. He later manipulated Tarzan and the de Coudes so that the Count would find Tarzan in an apparently compromising position with the Countess, but Tarzan sought him out afterward and forced him to sign a confession of his manipulation of the circumstances. The incident did, however, induce the Count to challenge Tarzan to a duel, and made Rokoff hate Tarzan more than ever (T2;1–6).

Olga later paid Rokoff 20,000 francs to leave France and never return, but he took the money to Algeria and used it to hire Arabs to kill Tarzan for him, a plot that failed. Tarzan later found him again in Bou Saada, discovering that it was Rokoff to whom Lt. Gernois was giving military secrets, forced to do so by more blackmail. Tarzan took the secrets and warned Rokoff that if he ever crossed his path again or showed up in any French territory, Tarzan would kill him. Rokoff did not heed the warning; he signed onto the same ship taken by Tarzan to Cape Town (under the alias "Mr. Thuran") and attempted to woo Jane Porter's best friend, Hazel Strong, who was also on the ship. When Tarzan again confronted him on the ship, Rokoff and his valet Alexis Paulvitch sneaked up behind the apeman and heaved him overboard into the Atlantic, thus returning him to the jungle, and successfully stealing back the papers Tarzan had taken from him in Bou Saada (T2;7–12).

He then continued to woo Hazel Strong, and accompanied her and her mother aboard the *Lady Alice* for the cruise back to England. He was thus aboard when the ship wrecked near the spot where he had pitched Tarzan overboard, which was also the spot where Tarzan's cottage lay. He was with William Clayton and Jane Porter in the lost lifeboat, and showed his true colors in the week of starvation and thirst which followed, as well as in the two months of primitive living which ensued after they reached the coast. After Jane's abduction by the Oparians, Clayton contracted a fever and Rokoff left him to die, heading north on foot toward civilization and running into the camp of the main body of the castaways soon afterward. He was arrested by the French naval personnel who came to rescue the castaways after Tarzan showed up and told them of his actions; at this time the ape-man was again able to take the secret papers from him and return them to France (T2;13–14,18,21–26).

Rokoff was tried, convicted and interred in a French military prison for about a year and a half, after which he escaped with the help of Paulvitch. They succeeded in kidnapping Tarzan's infant son, Jack, from Tarzan's London residence by planting a confederate therein, and also kidnapped Tarzan and Jane, leaving Tarzan marooned naked on Jungle Is-

land and taking Jane to the mainland, where she escaped with the help of Sven Anderssen, the Swedish cook of Rokoff's ship, the *Kincaid*. Rokoff pursued them upriver, leaving a clear trail of villainy for Tarzan to follow after he escaped the island, until the latter was captured by a group of cannibals Rokoff had paid off. Tarzan of course escaped and Rokoff fled his wrath, eventually catching up with Jane and Anderssen, then taking the girl and leaving the wounded Swede to die. He was furious when he discovered that the baby he had abducted (and mistakenly believed to be Jack) had died of a fever, as he had planned to give the child to the cannibal chief M'ganwazam to raise as his own. In replacement he decided to give Jane to the chief as a wife, but she escaped and fled downriver in a native canoe. Rokoff, deserted by his men, had no choice but to pursue her in another canoe, and was himself pursued by Mugambi and the apes of Akut the whole way. He finally landed on the opposite riverbank after discovering that Jane had commandeered the *Kincaid* and would shoot him if he attempted to board, but was soon rescued by his shore party and regained the ship — just in time to be attacked by Tarzan, Mugambi, Akut and his apes, and Sheeta the panther, who leaped upon Rokoff and tore him to shreds, ending his career of evil forever (T3;1–3,6–17).

rokor "Three daggers" (*Amt*). An Amtorian military rank corresponding to a sub-lieutenant (V4;44).

Romanoff An expatriate Russian noble whose safari met and joined with the Ramsgate safari in Northern Rhodesia in 1939, since they were both going the same way (T24B;5).

Rome The greatest city on Earth for a thousand years, center of an empire that ruled most of Europe, part of Asia, and some of Africa. After the collapse of the empire, two of its outposts, Castra Sanguinarius and Castrum Mare, continued to exist as though Rome had never fallen, cut off as they were deep within the Wiramwazi Mountains of Africa (T12;10).

Romero, Miguel A Mexican communist who went to Africa with the Zveri expedition in 1928. He eventually renounced communism after seeing the true colors of the Russian communists as typified by Zveri (T14;15–17).

rondel   The midriff protector of a suit of plate armor (OT;15).

Roof   The "Bad Man" of Nadara's Island with whom Thandar made friends after the earthquake that killed almost everyone on the island. Roof had witnessed Nadara's rescue from Thurg by the *Priscilla* party and told Thandar about it, then helped him to build the hide-covered canoe with which he set out to search for her (CG2;9).

Room of Seven Doors   An Amtorian torture chamber of the city of Kapdor that consists of a circular room with seven identical doors, only one of which leads to freedom (the one through which the prisoner is admitted, which is lost to him by extinguishing the lights and spinning the floor around quickly). In the center of the room is a table with seven foodstuffs and seven drinks, and hanging above the table is a noose placed so the victim may commit suicide, but only by slow strangulation, since there is no room to drop and break one's neck. All but one of the foods and all but one of the drinks is poisoned. The deaths beyond each door (which are spring-loaded and cannot be held open) are activated by stepping on a hidden trigger in the floor of the hall beyond, and are as follows:

1) Long, sharp spikes impale the victim
2) A spark ignites a flammable gas in the room, and the victim is burned to death
3) R-rays kill the victim immediately
4) A tharban which has been starved for days is released and devours the victim
5) Hidden jets spray acid on the victim; the acid destroys his eyes and slowly corrodes his flesh — this is a very slow and painful death
6) The walls close in very slowly (almost imperceptibly) and eventually crush the victim between them
7) The exit

The chair and cot in the room are covered with sharp needles so as to give no rest to the victim, and if he attempts to sleep on the floor, scores of poisonous serpents are released into the room to either kill him or force him through a door (V2;1–2).

Room of the Three Snakes   A room in the Temple of Kavandavanda, god-king of the Kavuru. It was labeled by the device of three preserved snake heads affixed above the door, and was the room in which Jane Clayton and Annette were held as prisoners of the Kavuru in 1934 (T19;28).

Room of the Two Snakes   A room in the Temple of Kavandavanda labeled by the expedient of two preserved snake heads affixed above the door. It was next to the Room of the Three Snakes and was the room where Prince Sborov was kept as a captive of the Kavuru in 1934 (T19;29).

The Roosevelt   A luxury hotel of Hollywood (T17;33).

Roosevelt, Eleanor   (1884–1962)   The First Lady of the United States during the Great Depression and most of World War II, wife of President Franklin D. Roosevelt; she was important in her own right as a social activist and lecturer (T22;23).

rope, grass   By playing with the long African grasses and braiding them as children so often do, the young Tarzan learned how to make ropes. He later discovered how to make knots in the ropes, including slip-knots, and later lassos. Such a grass rope was always part of the ape-man's equipment thereafter (T1;5).

Rosetti, Staff Sergeant Tony "Shrimp"   The ball turret gunner of the B-24 Liberator *Lovely Lady* on her ill-fated observation mission over Japanese-held Sumatra in the spring of 1944. He had a strong dislike for the British that was eventually overcome by Tarzan's likability, and a strong dislike of women (engendered in him by his mother, the widowed gun moll of a Chicago gangster) that was eventually overcome by the likability of Corrie van der Meer. He later fell in love with Sarina, a Dutch-Indonesian "dragon lady" who was a friend of Corrie's. Like many woman-haters, when he fell in love he fell hard, and after surviving months of privation they made it to the coast, set out to sea, were rescued by a British submarine, and were married by the submarine's commander on the way to Sydney (T22;3–7,23–30).

rota   (*Ape*) Laugh (TC).

Rothmund, Ralph   Burroughs' secretary at his Tarzana office (V1;1).

Rotik   "Three-eye" (*Amt*). A huge sea monster of Amtor which can attain lengths of up to a thousand feet; it has a huge maw and bulbous, protruding eyes. The creature has a third eye on an erectile shaft about 15 feet long, which it uses as a periscope to cruise just below the water's surface. Rotiks often lie resting on the ocean's surface (V3;19).

rov (*Amt*) Death (V2;17).

Rovos One of the 11 planets orbiting the star **Omos**. It lies between **Antos** and **Vanada** (B1).

Royal Geological Society The British scientific club from which Burroughs was almost bodily thrown for narrating the story of Pellucidar there (P1).

Royal Horse Guards of Lutha The elite cavalry of **Lutha** (MK1;1).

Royal Observatory A large, flat boulder at **Greenwich**, Pellucidar, from which **David Innes** made the first determination of magnetic north in the inner Earth (P2;1).

Rozales, Captain Guillermo One of the "captains" under "**General**" **Pesita**. He hated "**gringos**," including **Billy Byrne**, and it was his group of banditos that chased Byrne, **Bridge** and the **Hardings** almost to the border. Byrne killed Rozales during the subsequent battle with a mighty blow to the face (K2;7–8,17).

Ru A river of **Lutha** which runs between **Blentz** and **Lustadt**, forming a natural barrier between the two by the steep ravine through which it flows (MK2;15).

Rubinroth The ruling house of **Lutha** for 300 years (MK1;11).

Rubinroth, Princess Victoria Barney and Victoria Custer's mother, who was literally stolen from **Lutha** (though willingly) by Barney's father, an American adventurer (MK1;1,9–12).

Rudolph A young Luthanian boy who was a servant to the brigand band of **Yellow Franz** because his father owed the robber a great deal of money, and Franz was keeping the boy as a hostage pending payment. He rescued **Barney Custer** (believing him to be **Leopold of Lutha**, as did practically everybody) when Custer was being held for ransom by Yellow Franz, but in the escape was killed by a brigand's fire (MK1;6).

Rudolph, Lake *see* Lake Rudolph

Rue Maule A dark, narrow street of Paris, known for its criminals and danger at night, down which Tarzan was fond of walking while in Paris. Nikolas Rokoff set a trap for him there by hiring a woman to pretend to be in trouble so Tarzan could come to her rescue; she would then turn him into the police (whom Rokoff had previously summoned) as her actual attacker. It was left to **Paul d'Arnot** to untangle the matter with the police, whom Tarzan easily escaped (T2;3–4).

Rufinus The half-breed officer of the watch when **Erich von Harben** was brought as a prisoner to **Castrum Mare** in 1923 (T12;6).

Ruiz The high priest of **Alemtejo** in the 1930s who refused to believe that the false Tarzan was a god, even if he did fall from the sky. He did not let his knowledge on to his followers, however, as it was not politically expedient to do so. Ruiz was overthrown at the same time as was **da Gama**, due to his failure to recognize the true Tarzan as the true god (T23;4,11–12,21).

Rumla One of the husbands of **Gluck**, chief of the gender-reversed Pellucidarian **Oog** tribe (P6;3).

Rungula The chief of the fierce **Bansuto** tribe of the **Belgian Congo** when the film crew of *The Lion Man* passed through their territory in 1932. He was an inveterate savage to whom Tarzan showed the error of his ways after he attacked the safari of the film crew (T17;10,14).

Rupes Flumen "Rock River" (*Lat*). The southern river which flows through the **Palus Meridien** into **Mare Orientis** in the central **Wiramwazi** Valley (T12;6).

Rush Street A **Chicago** street which crosses a bridge over the Chicago River (C3;1).

Rutherford, Alice The British noblewoman who married **John Clayton, Lord Greystoke**, and accompanied him on his ill-fated trip to west Africa in 1888, during which she was put ashore with him after the crew of their ship mutinied. Clayton built a cabin for them, and a few months later he was attacked by a **great ape**, which Lady Alice shot; before it died, however, it leapt to attack her, and she fainted. Though the creature did not even touch her, the shock proved too much to her already shattered nerves, and she entered a hysterical state in which she believed herself to be home in London. She bore Clayton's son **John, Jr.** (later to be called Tarzan), that very night and lived for a year afterward, passing away quietly from no obvious cause in her sleep, never again having realized where she and her husband actually were. Her remains were discovered and buried by **William Clayton** and the **Porter** party about 20 years later (T1;1–3,17).

Ruturi Mountains A mountain chain of Africa near which the **Waruturi** cannibals live, and from which they get their name. Their foothills are surrounded by a difficult-to-pass thorn forest, and deep within the range lies **Alemtejo** (T23;2,7).

Ruva The largest of the **Floating Islands** of Pellucidar (P6;23).

Ruzaar The Barsoomian battleship on which John Carter and Ras Thavas returned to **Morbus** after the latter had healed **Dejah Thoris** (M9;28).

ry (*Ape*) Crooked (TC).

ry-balu-den "Crooked branch" (*Ape*). Bow (obviously another Tarzan coinage) (TC).

rykor A strange breed of Barsoomian humanoid which resembles a gorgeous human body of either sex with no head, just a hole where the neck should be. In this cavity is its mouth and an exposed spinal nerve clump. The creatures exist only in **Bantoom** and are the property of the **Kaldanes**, who look like bodiless heads with six legs and a pair of chelae. A Kaldane can climb up a rykor and sit upon its neck orifice, grasping the spinal cord with a special set of nerves in its back, then control the rykor — the Kaldane can not only work the rykor's muscles, but can also feel through its sensory nerves. Rykors are the descendants of exceedingly stupid humanoid creatures selectively bred by the Kaldanes over eons for strength, health, beauty and microcephaly. The physical attributes of the stock have also been improved over time by mating them with captured **red men**, whom they physically resemble.

Each rykor wears a leather belt and shoulder strap from which depend a pocket pouch and a long sword; males and females wear the same thing, and are used equally by the Kaldanes. Each rykor also wears a thick leather collar to make the Kaldane's seating arrangements more comfortable. All in all, rykors are lower than cattle, since they can do nothing for themselves other than feed from a trough (if guided to it) by blindly throwing food into their mouth-orifices. They cannot even mate without Kaldane direction. The Kaldanes also eat rykor flesh, and fatten female rykors for the purpose. Old rykors (ten years or more) who are no longer capable of satisfactory labor are left out at night for the **banths** to devour, because they are too tough for eating by that point (M5;5–6).

rympth A creature of **Va-nah** which looks like a five foot long snake with four toe-like legs and a flat head with a single large eye. Rympths move by a combination of slithering and scuttling and are amphibious, very retiring and afraid of humans. Their flesh is poisonous and cannot be eaten (MM1;3–4,6).

ryth The gigantic cave bear of Pellucidar, eight feet tall by twelve feet long while on all fours (P1;13).

Sab Than The Prince of **Zodanga** on Barsoom who kidnapped **Dejah Thoris** to attempt to force her into marriage, but was foiled by John Carter and **Kantos Kan** and killed by **Tars Tarkas** (M1).

Sabertooth Men A strange humanoid race of Pellucidar, closely related to the **Man-apes**, whom they strongly resemble. The Sabertooth Men also look like black people with low foreheads and long, prehensile tails; unlike the Man-apes, however, they have a pair of saber-teeth that curve down from the upper jaw like those of a **tarag**. They are not arboreal, but rather cliff-dwelling, and live in the mountainous volcanic country north of **Kali**. They are man-eaters, and captured **Hodon the Fleet One** and **O-aa** to eat after the two escaped the capture of Kali in 1931 (P7;1;7).

Sabinus, Cornelius A member of the **Praetorian Guard** who helped to kill the Emperor **Caligula** (I;21).

Sabor (*Ape*) The lioness; lions are the only lower animal whose male and female are distinguished by the **great apes**, on the basis of the mane possessed by **Numa**, the male lion (T1;5).

sabre A slightly curved sword with one edge. Sabres were made and used by the inhabitants of the lost city of Xuja, a fact which surprised both Tarzan and Lt. Smith-Oldwick (T7;16–18).

Sabrov, Michael Alexis Paulvitch's alias after he was rescued by the *Marjorie W.* after ten years in the Ugambi region of Africa. He also went by the name after his return to London, and so physically changed was he by all of his years of torture that no one ever recognized him, even after he was killed (T4;1–4).

sad (*Pal*) Forest (T8;4).

sadok The Pellucidarian rhinoceros, an enormous double-horned animal much like a **brontotherium** (P1;4,15).

Saffarrans, Colonel An officer who taught a jungle survival course to American GI's in the Pacific during World War II (T22;3).

Sag, the Killer A savage warrior of Nadara's Island who tried to kill Waldo Emerson Smith-Jones (a.k.a. Thandar) after he had developed his body, and was killed by the American with a primitive spear (CG1;5).

Sag Or A favorite noble of Xaxa, Jeddara of Phundahl, who had Dar Tarus killed so his brain could be transferred to Dar Tarus' body by Ras Thavas. Sag Or's own body was ugly, but Dar Tarus was handsome, and in the young warrior's body the noble hoped to win the love of Dar Tarus' girlfriend, Kara Vasa. He was eventually returned to his own body and swore fealty to Dar Tarus (M6;11–14).

Sago-zhu-ni "Pretty Mouth" (*Apa*). The wife of the Apache chief Mangas; she was a great brewer of tizwin (A2;6).

Sagoths The gorilla-men of Pellucidar, who are built much more lightly than a gorilla, but much more heavily than a human. They are of human proportion in the limbs, but have shaggy brown hair all over and very gorilla-like faces. Those Sagoths who serve the Mahars wear tunic-like garments and carry spears and hatchets supplied them by their masters. The Sagoths speak a variant of the tongue of the great apes, to whom they are probably closely related, and those Sagoths who serve the Mahars also speak a pidgin language with which to communicate with the Gilaks. After the defeat of the Mahars within the Empire of Pellucidar, many Sagoths swore fealty to David Innes and served as imperial troops (P1;3–4)(P3) (P4;4).

Sagroth The Jemadar of Laythe, last city of the advanced U-gas of Va-nah; the father of Nah-ee-lah. He was regal and noble, every particle an emperor, and was a man of great learning besides, being acquainted with even the prehistoric legends of his world. He was also very intelligent and accepted the truth of Julian 5th's narrative of how he had come to Va-nah. Sagroth was killed by assassins sent by the usurper Ko-tah, even though both he and Julian fought bravely to protect him (MM1;6,12–13).

sahar (*Ara*) A magician, sage or mystic (T11;1).

sahib (*Swa*) Sir (T14;10).

Saigon The tramp steamer which carried the trapped Tarzan and a good number of African animals from Mombasa across the Pacific late in 1938. Its crew mutinied and it was later wrecked on the uncharted island of Uxmal in the South Pacific (T24;1–10).

Sailor Byrne Billy Byrne's prizefighting name (K1;18).

St. Helena The remote south Atlantic island on which the wreckage of the *Fuwalda* was found in July of 1888 (T1;1).

St. John, Charles Edward (1857–1935) An astronomer of the early 20th century who measured the amount of oxygen and water vapor in the Venusian atmosphere (V1;1).

St. John, Juana A farm girl from the Teivos of Oak Park in Kalkar-occupied 22nd century America. Her parents were killed by the Kalkars, forcing her to flee to Chicago, where she was rescued from the hellhounds by Julian 9th and moved in with Jim Thompson and Mollie Sheehan, who had a spare room. She and Julian fell in love with one another and were married in the secret church the Julian family belonged to, but not until after Brother General Or-tis tried to claim her as his woman. After the arrest of Julian 8th, her husband hid her in the ruins of the secret church while he went to rescue his father, but Or-tis and the Kash Guard discovered her and took her away. Julian 9th rescued her before Or-tis could wrong her, and she escaped on **Red Lightning** with **Julian's American flag** and later bore **Julian 10th,** whom she raised as a great rebel leader (MM2;3–7,10–11).

St. Luke's A major hospital of downtown Chicago where **Ogden Secor** was treated following his injury at the hands of criminals who were robbing his office (GF;9).

Saj One of the priests of **Pu** in the city of Lolo-lolo in Pellucidar. He apparently hanged himself after failing in his mission (ordered by **Hor**) to kill the "Noada," **Dian the Beautiful,** in 1931 (P7:2;6).

sak *(Bar)* Jump (M1;4).

Sakkan The Rajah Muda Saffir's principality in the interior of **Borneo** (Q;10).

Saku The chief of the Nipon tribe that **Julian 20th** encountered while escaping from the **Kalkar** capital. He was a kind and wise little man who aided Julian and gave him information (MM3;6).

Salee's Flats A salt flat of northern Mexico near the **Arizona** border which turns into an impassable barrier in heavy rain (HB;19).

Salensus Oll The Jeddak of Jeddaks of Okar on Barsoom, a coarse and evil man who was unpopular with most of his people because of his cruelty and his religion. He gave asylum to **Matai Shang** and **Thurid,** but coveted **Dejah Thoris** as his queen and took her from Matai Shang. He ordered John Carter executed in the **Pit of Plenty** so he could legally marry Dejah Thoris, but Carter escaped and killed Salensus Oll in the middle of his premature wedding ceremony (M3;14).

Sally Corwith The sailing ship which **Waldo Emerson Smith-Jones** met at **Nadara's Island** in 1911, and upon which he sent a letter to his mother in **Boston** (CG1;6) (CG2;6).

Salt Creek The site of the **Kash Guard** station for the teivos of Oak Park in Kalkar-occupied 22nd century America until the Kalkars seized the home of **Juana St. John's** parents in 2122 (MM2;4).

salutation, Barsoomian Consists of placing one's right hand on the other person's left shoulder and or saying "kaor" (M1).

salute, Barsoomian The Barsoomian military salute consists of raising both hands, palms forward, over the head (M2;8).

salute, Korvan The salute given royalty in the Amtorian nation of **Korva** consists of raising the arms at a 45 degree angle from the horizontal with the palms crossed (V3;5).

salute, Wieroo The **Wieroo** salute consists of placing the back of one's hand against one's face (C3;2).

Sam One of the cowboys of the **Crazy "B" Ranch** (A2;18).

Samaritan Hospital A charity hospital of early 20th century **Oakdale, Illinois** (K3;2).

Samary A large tribe of Amtorian Amazons who inhabit the hill country of **Noobol** parallel to the **Gerlat kum Rov** in **Trabol** (V3;2).

Sammy The lanky office-boy of **John Secor and Company, Chicago,** at the time that **June Lathrop** worked there. He wanted to be a detective, and practiced "shadowing" people; it paid off when he tracked **Stickler** and proved him to be the criminal behind the Secor robbery. He later became a real detective (GF;7–9,14).

sampot A simple garment of Indochina which is worn like a diaper about the loins by members of both sexes (HM;3).

Samuel A Negro beggar of early 20th century Scottsville, Virginia (ME;3).

Samuels, Moses A Jewish tanner of the teivos of Chicago in Kalkar-occupied 22nd century America. He was an excellent tanner and would have been rich, but almost all of his clients were Kalkars who paid him in worthless **paper money.** He was one of the worshippers at the **secret church** and was discovered returning from it one day by **Peter Johansen,** who then reported him to the **Kash Guard.** They tortured him to death in an effort to get him to reveal the names of the other worshippers (MM2;4,7–8).

samurai A type of aristocratic warrior-knight of feudal Japan. Samurais were masters of the sword and were sworn to an extremely rigid code of honor (T22;3).

san *(Amt)* The number five (V1;8).

san (*Pal*) The number 100 (T8).

San Carlos A fort in late 1880s Arizona to which **Geronimo** was transferred from **Hot Springs** after his capture in 1877. It was here that **Shoz-dijiji** came to be with him and learned English until Geronimo was freed three months later (A1;7).

San Carlos Indian Agency, the A branch of the Bureau of Indian Affairs located at Fort **San Carlos, Arizona** (A1;19).

San Clemente A Pacific island which lies about 30 miles south of **Santa Catalina** island, about 70 miles west of San Diego in the Gulf of Santa Catalina (PB;2).

San Fernando Valley A California fault valley which lies primarily within Los Angeles County (PB;2). See also **Valley of the Kalkars.**

San Quentin The California state penitentiary, near San Francisco (GH;36).

San Simon A river which runs across Cochise County in southeastern **Arizona**; it empties into the **Gila** River at the north end of the county (A1;10).

San Tothis The commander of the **Gatholian** cruiser *Vanator*, who held his ship steady in the great hurricane of 1915 (M5;3).

San-za An **Apache** warrior who was killed by American soldiers through trickery in the late 1850s (A1;2).

Sanada One of the 11 co-orbital planets of the star **Omos**. It lies between **Vanada** and **Uvala**, almost opposite **Poloda** (B1).

Sanara The largest seaport of the Amtorian nation of **Korva**; it was the last stronghold of the royalists after the **Zani** takeover in the 1920s. It repulsed Zani forces for years until 1930, when it was finally liberated after the fall of Zani power thanks to **Carson Napier, Duare,** the **Toganja Zerka,** and her counter-revolutionary forces (V3; 4–6,15–17).

Sanchez, Admiral An elderly officer of the **Pan-American** navy of the early 22nd century who claimed that he could smell the forbidden line of 30 degrees longitude (LC;1).

Sancho One of the **great ape** servants of **Alemtejo,** who helped **Colin Randolph,** the false Tarzan, abduct **Sandra Pickerall** in 1938.

He later abducted her for himself, but lost her in a fight with the apes of **Ungo** (T23; 8,24).

Sanders, "Red" One of the sailors of the *Halfmoon* with Billy Byrne; he was in on the plan Byrne and **Henri Theriere** had hatched for double-crossing the skipper and **Larry Divine** (K1;4).

Sanguinarius, Marcus Crispus A Roman general who fought the Germans in the 839th year of Rome (A.D. 86). Fourteen years later he took his legion (the Tenth) to Africa to escape the wrath of the Emperor Nerva, penetrated deep into the interior, and founded the city of **Castra Sanguinarius** with the third cohort of that legion, the only one to survive the whole trip. He then declared all of his officers **patricians,** thus founding a ruling class (T12;6,9).

Sanjong "Five-king" (*Amt*). The five-man ruling body of the Amtorian city of **Havatoo.** It is made up of one member from each ruling class: A **sentar** (biologist), an **ambad** (psychologist), a **kalto** (chemist), a **kantum** (physicist), and a **korgan** (warrior). Achievement of the post is based on merit and a test which must be passed every two years to retain the post. The sanjong does not technically rule Havatoo, which has no laws; it merely guides and judges (V2;14).

Sanoma Tora The beautiful but shallow daughter of **Tor Hatan, Odwar** of the 91st **Utan** of the troops of **Helium** on Barsoom. **Tan Hadron** loved her, but she wished to marry **Tul Axtar, Jeddak** of Jahar, because of the riches and position she believed he would give her. Tul Axtar had her kidnapped, however, instead of marrying her honorably, and Tan Hadron came in pursuit and rescued her from slavery in Tul Axtar's harem, only to be betrayed by the faithless girl after Tul Axtar promised to make her his **jeddara.** After Jahar's defeat, Sanoma Tora was taken back to Helium and spurned by Tan Hadron in favor of **Tavia** (M7;1,13–17).

Santa Ana A small **California** town of Orange County which lies between Los Angeles and **Ganado** (GH;30).

Santa Anna An ornery horse of the **El Orobo Ranch** which no one could ride (K2;11).

Santa Catalina A Pacific island which lies about 20 miles due south of Los Angeles (PB;2).

Santa Cruz A large Pacific island which lies about 15 miles south of Santa Barbara, California (PB;2).

Santa Fe The popular name of the Atchison, Topeka and Santa Fe Railway Company, one of the largest American railroad systems, which covers most of the Southwest and, though today limited to freight hauling, was at one time famous for its luxurious and speedy passenger trains (K2;2).

Santa Fe Trail The main path of westward migration in 19th century America. It stretched from Independence, Missouri, in the East to Santa Fe, New Mexico, in the West, but fell into disuse after the Santa Fe railroad went through in 1873 (A1;1).

Santa Monica A city of Los Angeles County, California, which was a major shipbuilding site in the early 20th century (C1;1).

Santa Monica Mountains A small coastal mountain range of California which lies primarily within Los Angeles County (PB;2).

Santa Rita A copper mine near the headwaters of the Rio Mimbres where the Mexicans ambushed a large number of Apaches after luring them there for a fiesta in the late 1700s (A1;11).

sar (*Pal*) Nose (T8;2).

Saracen Medieval term for a Muslim Arab (T11;7).

Saran Tal The major-domo of Carthoris (M4;3).

Sari One of the more highly developed cultures of Pellucidar lives at Sari on the southern shores of the Darel Az. The country was ruled in David Innes' time by Ghak the Hairy One, and it was one of the first two kingdoms to form the Empire of Pellucidar (the other was Amoz, which was ruled by Ghak's nephew Dacor the Strong One) (P1;4,15). Later, Innes made Sari the capital of the Empire (P2;6).

Sari The name of a Pellucidarian naval ship, named for the first, ill-favored *Sari* that David Innes and Abner Perry built in 1913. It

was wrecked in a hurricane and abandoned by its crew when it came abreast of Anoroc, then eventually washed up on the shore of the Xexot country (P7:2;3–4).

Sarina A female member of the Sumatran outlaw band who captured, then lost Tarzan in the spring of 1944; she was the only person who could tell Hooft, the outlaw leader, what to do. Sarina was a mixed Eurasian and knew Corrie van der Meer because she had worked for her family a few years back. They had been kind to her when she got in trouble with the law, and even hired her an attorney. Because of this, Sarina helped Corrie escape when she was captured by the outlaws. She later left them and joined up with Captain van Prin's guerrillas, as had been her intent from the start. She and "Shrimp" Rosetti fell in love with each other, partly because he was so impressed with her ability to take care of herself. After months of hardship, they reached the coast and were married by the captain of the British submarine which rescued them (T22;14–17,23–30).

Sarkoja The eldest among the green women of Tars Tarkas' retinue (about 900 years old at the time of John Carter's arrival on Barsoom); coarse, brutal and hideous, she was among the worst of her kind. Insane with jealousy, she tried to cause Carter's death and that of Dejah Thoris on more than one occasion. It was Sarkoja who had exposed Gozava to Tal Hajus while Tars Tarkas was away, resulting in the former's execution by torture; she would have exposed Tars Tarkas as well if she could have proven his crime. When Tars Tarkas discovered her treachery, she fled his wrath by taking the Pilgrimage (M1;10–24).

Sarnya, Count Paul A captain of the palace guard of the old king of an unnamed European country of the early 20th century, who was made general and chief of staff in place of General Jagst after the death of the old king and Jagst's flight with Prince Michael. He grew into a powerful general, head of the army and secret police, and practically ruled the country for King Otto, whom he had grown to hate; it was Sarnya that the revolutionaries were worried about, rather than King Otto. After the latter's assassination the new king, Ferdinand, made Sarnya commander of the frontier forces instead, thus removing his power from the capital, but

Sarnya soon returned and led a coup that left Ferdinand dead and Sarnya in control. He later became dictator of the country (LL; 1–15,19,23,25).

sarong A skirt-like garment of cotton or silk cloth which is worn by both genders of Indonesian islanders (T22;29).

sarong, Vepajan A woman of Vepaja wears a long scarf of colored silk as a sort of sarong. It is wound around the body under the arms to confine the breasts, then around the hips, between the legs and up through the waist, the end then falling to the knees. A girdle is usually worn with it (V1;3).

Sarus One of the slaves of the family of **Dilecta** in **Castra Sanguinarius** of 1923 (T12;9).

Sasoom (*Bar*) The planet Jupiter (M11B;1).

sat (*Pal*) Skin (T8;2).

sato (*Ape*) Kind (TC).

Sato One of the principal lieutenants of the **Vulture**; Sato was a very bright and crafty Japanese (PB;9).

Sator Throg A Holy Thern of the Tenth Cycle on Barsoom. He was the Thern on watch when **Thuvia** came down the River Iss, and claimed her as his own pleasure-slave. Fifteen years later, she killed him with the help of John Carter, and Carter, who resembled him, donned his blond wig and accoutrements and posed as Throg (M2;4).

Savage Pellucidar The seventh and final book of the Pellucidar series, abbreviated P7. The events of the book took place around 1931, not long after **David Innes** had returned to **Sari** after the events of *Land of Terror*, and were narrated to Burroughs in the same series of **Gridley Wave** transmissions (in 1939) as was the aforementioned book. They were published by Burroughs in four novelettes, one in 1941, two in 1942, and one (posthumously) in 1963. It is the story of David Innes' search for **Dian the Beautiful** after she floated off in **Abner Perry**'s newly invented hot air balloon. It is also the story of **Hodon the Fleet One**, who pursued the little compulsive liar called **O-aa**, whom he had fallen in love with, to save her from all sorts of trouble.

"Savage Pellucidar" The title of the fourth part of the novel of the same name,

first published as part of the novel edition in 1963, 13 years after Burroughs' death.

Savators The human race of **Eurobus**, who have light blue skin which looks purple under Eurobus' reddish volcanic light. They have no hair except for eyebrows, eyelashes and a thick head growth. Savators are the slaves of the **Morgors** because they are an artistic, scientific and peace-loving people who were therefore easily conquered by the vicious Morgors. Savators usually wear only a g-string with no **harness** (M11B;3–4).

Savoy A luxurious London hotel (T19;1).

sawbones (American Western slang) A physician (HB;3).

Sawbuck, Tiny A 237-pound professional wrestler whom **Jim Stone** threw from the ring with almost no effort (J;4).

Sawtelle A part of **Santa Monica**, California; site of an old soldiers' home in the 1920s (PB;2).

Sawyer, "Bony" One of the sailors of the *Halfmoon* with **Billy Byrne**; he was in on the plan that Byrne and **Henri Theriere** had for double-crossing the skipper and **Larry Divine** (K1;2,4).

Sborov, Prince Alexis The second husband of **Kitty Krause** of **Baltimore**, who was old enough to be his mother. He was a typical effete aristocrat, useless and snobbish, and was completely impatient with Kitty, whom he had only married for her seventy million dollars. He tried to kill two birds with one stone by murdering Kitty and framing **Neal Brown** (whom he hated) for the murder, but the scheme backfired and the others suspected, then became sure, that Sborov was the murderer. He at that point tried to kill Brown, but was discovered in the attempt and fled into the jungle. Tarzan later found him, but Sborov refused to go with him and eventually went mad from guilt and fear. He was then abducted by **Ydeni**, the **Kavuru**, because that tribe kept madmen as slaves. He later tried to escape the **Temple of Kavandavanda**, but was torn apart by the leopards kept in its courtyard (T19;1–12,15–23,26–29).

Sborov, Princess *see* **Krause, Kitty** (T19;1)

Scar Foot Jefferson Billings' favorite horse (A2;13).

Scarb The chief of the Boat Builder tribe of Niocene Africa who captured Nu, son of Nu and would have burned him at the stake had Gron not interfered (E2;10).

Schenectady A city of New York state, northwest of Albany, from which Jim Stone supposedly came (J;4).

Schmidt A sailor of the *Kincaid* who was recruited by Schneider for his plot to kidnap Jane and leave Jungle Island. After the beasts of Tarzan had done their work, he was one of the few surviving plotters (T3; 20–21).

Schmidt, Wilhelm The second mate of the *Saigon* when it took Tarzan across the Pacific as a captive "wild man" late in 1938. When he found out that World War II had begun, he used it as an excuse to take over the ship "for the Führer" and use it for piracy. When they wrecked on Uxmal, he and the other mutineers were kicked out of camp by Tarzan, only to return six weeks later to raid the camp in his absence. The ape-man caught up with him soon afterward and killed him (T24;2–3,11,16,19–22).

Schneider The first mate of the *Kincaid*, the ship on which Nikolas Rokoff had the kidnapped Tarzan and Jane brought to Africa. After the ship exploded and marooned the crew on Jungle Island, Schneider grew tired of waiting for the completion of the ship his men were building to reach the mainland, so he proposed making a dugout, taking three men loyal to him, and kidnapping Jane to the mainland, then demanding money from her to take her back to civilization. His conversation with Schmidt was overheard by Momulla the Maori of the *Cowrie* mutineers, who then recruited Schneider to navigate the *Cowrie* so Gust could be disposed of; he of course agreed so he could kidnap Jane more easily. The plan succeeded, but Tarzan and his beasts caught up before the plotters could escape, and Tarzan killed Schneider with his own hands (T3;20–21).

Another Schneider was an often-robbed saloon keeper of turn-of-the-century Chicago's west side. He was murdered by "Coke" Sheehan, who framed Billy Byrne for the murder (K1;1).

Schneider, Hauptmann Fritz A German army officer stationed in German East

Africa who treacherously invaded and pillaged Tarzan's estate while the ape-man was away, before he even knew that Germany and England were at war. After several months of tracking, searching and fighting, Tarzan caught up with Schneider and cut out his putrid heart before the German could tell him that Jane was still alive (T7;1,6).

Schneider, Major A German army officer whom Tarzan exacted revenge upon for the "murder" of Jane, mistaking him for his brother, Hauptmann Fritz Schneider, by their same last names. He threw Major Schneider into a pit with a trapped lion after abducting him from a staff meeting in plain sight of several other officers (T7;2,5).

Schonau, Lieutenant Karl A Luthanian officer of the guards at Blentz castle when Barney Custer was taken there as Leopold of Lutha in October of 1912. He insulted the Princess Emma von der Tann and would have killed Custer if not for the intervention of Lt. Butzow (MK1;3).

Schwartz A German non-commissioned officer of the U-33; he was a brute who found great pleasure in striking prisoners with a stick. He was killed by an arrow from Co-tan while he was attempting to kill her beloved John Bradley (C3;5).

Schweinhund "Pig-dog" (*Ger*). A deprecatory term (C3;5).

Schwerke A German sailor of the U-33 who was driven mad by Captain von Schoenvorts' incredible cruelty and committed suicide (C3;5).

Scilly Islands A group of islands off the southwest coast of England which mark the beginning of the English Channel (LC;2).

scimatines Some sort of food the great apes enjoy (T7;13).

scimitar, Wieroo Only Wieroos with blue in their robes, and then only those who guard the Temple of Luata in Oo-oh, carry such weapons —He Who Speaks for Luata uses two (C3;4).

Scott, Jefferson, Jr. An American big game hunter who came to the Morton Mission in central Africa for a few months, and there met and married Ruth Morton, with whom he decided to stay. He was killed in the Wakanda uprising, but his wife and daughter escaped to America (ME).

Scott, Jefferson, Sr. A well-to-do Virginian, father of Jefferson Scott, Jr., who supported his son's widow and daughter from the time of their arrival after the Wakanda uprising until his own death 19 years later (ME).

Scott, Virginia The daughter of Jefferson Scott, Jr., and Ruth Morton Scott; she was one year old at the time of the Wakanda revolt and went afterward with her mother to live with her grandfather in Virginia until she was 20. After the old man's death Scott Taylor of New York (Virginia's cousin) cast doubts on her legitimacy in order to inherit the Scott fortune himself. He even went so far as to pursue Richard Gordon (who had gone to Africa to find the marriage certificate) in order to kill him. When Virginia found out, she pursued Gordon as well in order to warn him, but fell victim to Taylor, who captured her. She escaped and found Gordon, warning him; together, they then returned to America, and after the real will and marriage certificate were found, the two were married (ME).

Scott, Washington The Negro butler of The Oaks, ancestral home of the Scott family in Scottsville, Virginia (ME;9).

Scottsville The Virginia home town of General Jefferson Scott, Sr.; it must be assumed that his family founded the place (ME;1).

scrofula Obsolete term for tuberculosis of the bones or lymphatic system, especially in children (I;6).

Scurv The chief of the village of Garb on the island of Hime in the Korsar Az of Pellucidar. He was the father of Balal, whom Tanar the Fleet One saved from a codon (P3;10).

sea horse, giant A species of giant, horned sea horse as large as a man prowls the bottom of Lake Horus in Tuen-baka, attacking any quickly-moving prey with its sharp horns. How the animal then eats its prey is unknown, considering the mouth-parts of a normal sea horse (T20;31).

seas, Barsoomian Barsoom once had five oceans, now dried up except for Korus, which is nonetheless severely reduced in size. The mightiest of these was Throxeus, which

covered much of the northern hemisphere. The bottoms of these former seas are the stamping grounds of the green men (M1) (M2;1–2)(M4;9).

Secor, John A rich Chicago businessman, foster father of Ogden Secor, who dropped dead of a heart attack in Farris's brothel after "visiting" Maggie Lynch there. It was he who was to blame for the "ruin" of June Lathrop, whom he married under the pretense that he himself was not married, changed her name to Maggie Lynch, and kept her in a brothel until his heart attack, after which she found out the truth (GF;1,12–14).

Secor, Ogden The foreman of the grand jury which heard Maggie Lynch's evidence against Abe Farris and voted no bill. He himself, however, made up his mind to help the girl, and spoke to her after the hearing to help her find more respectable employment. She was eventually hired as his secretary and served well in that position until Stickler fired her. On that same day Secor was severely beaten while attempting to stop a robbery of his office; afterward, due to Stickler's mismanagement and embezzlement, Secor's company went bankrupt, leaving him completely broke except for a farm in Idaho. He became an alcoholic, and was swindled out of what little money he had on the way West, so he had to work as a clerk for several months in Ketchum, Idaho, in order to save enough money to get him to his farm and start working it. The farm turned out to be useless, but he prospected in its river for gold, and eventually the government bought the land for a new city project, making him comfortably well-off again. It is not known whether the conviction of Stickler resulted in the renumeration of any of the $25,000 stolen from him directly or the countless thousands embezzled later, but Secor did marry June Lathrop (a.k.a. Maggie Lynch) afterward (GF; 3–4,7–14).

Secretary of Peace The cabinet minister in the Earth government of the 21st century who was responsible for diplomacy and the administration of the International Peace Fleet (MM1;2).

Segrave, Nicholas de One of the rebel barons of England, who was the general in charge of the London troops at the Battle of Lewes on May 13, 1264 (OT;16).

Sei-yo-jin (Japanese) Occidentals (K1;11).

Sejanus, Lucius Aelius (A.D.?- 31) A sycophantic **patrician**, "friend" of **Drusus Caesar** (Tiberius' son). He was the author of many of the evils that beset the royal family of Rome, which he caused to further a plan to gain the throne for himself. Part of it involved seducing **Livilla**, Drusus' wife. He eventually made himself Tiberius' favorite and succeeded in warping the old man's mind in the seclusion of his retreat on **Capri**, hoping to get rid of **Germanicus'** entire family so he could be declared heir by Tiberius. The plan backfired when the news came out of how he had poisoned Drusus with Livilla's help, and Sejanus was dragged through the streets to his death (I;6-7,14-15).

Semeler, Madame Helen The wife of a French army officer of 1920s **Algeria**. Her husband was attached to the command of **Colonel Vivier**, and Madame Semeler considered herself a mother figure to **Marie Vivier**; because of this she stuck her nose in to break up the "unseemly" relationship between Marie and **Aziz** (LL;16,18).

Senator A bay stallion which belonged to **Grace Evans** (GH;1).

Senorita The schooner yacht captured by **Johnny Lafitte** to prove to the **Vulture** that he would make a worthy second-in-command. It was a good ship, a worthy replacement for the Vulture's old ship, which the **Portuguese** had sunk a month or so before (PB;9-10).

sentar (*Amt*) Biologist. This is one of the five ruling classes of **Havatoo**, who live in a portion of the city named for their profession (V2;14).

Sept A Kaldane of **Bantoom** who was high in the estimation of **Luud**. He brought **Ghek** and **Tara of Helium** into Luud's presence (M5;5).

Septimus Favonius A patrician of **Castrum Mare**, descendant of a long line of patricians from the centurion ancestor who had been made a patrician by **Marcus Crispus Sanguinarius** when **Castra Sanguinarius** was founded. Favonius was the uncle of **Mallius Lepus**, the centurion who befriended **Erich von Harben** upon his arrival in Castrum Mare. Favonius was very rich, and famous for the strange guests he always had for dinner.

He was the father of the beautiful **Favonia**, whom **Erich von Harben** fell in love with (T12;6,8).

sequins The clothing of the people of **Unis** on **Poloda** is skin-tight, elastic, and looks as though it were made entirely of shiny sequins, except for the knee-boots that go with the costume (B1;1).

sera (*Amt*) Central (V2;15).

Sera Tartum "Central Laboratories" (*Amt*). Both the research facilities and government buildings of the scientifically advanced technocratic state of **Havatoo** lie in the same building complex, located in the hub of the city on the **Gerlat kum Rov** (V2;15).

Serbia A European country which in World War I bordered Austria-Hungary on the south. **Lutha** lay between it and Austria and was hence caught up between the two warring powers when **World War I** started in July of 1914 (MK2;1).

Serenus The fat major-domo of the house of **Germanicus Caesar** during **Caligula's** childhood (I;2).

Serra, Osorio da A noble of 1930s **Alemtejo** who had designs on the kingship of that lost city. He was the captain-general of the warriors of Alemtejo and befriended **Tarzan** when he came there in 1938. With Tarzan's help, he became king of Alemtejo because he claimed that Tarzan was a true god, the people believed him, and **da Gama** denied it, precipitating the old king's fall from grace (T23;12,19-21).

serum of longevity A drug which was perfected around A.D. 900 in **Vepaja** on Amtor; administered every two years, it arrests aging and repairs damaged tissue, thus prolonging life indefinitely. Because of it, strict **birth control** became necessary, so that only sufficient numbers of children to replace those killed by accident would be born. The secret of the proper manufacture of the serum of longevity was eventually lost in **Thora** because of the incompetence of their economic system, and so old age began to reappear there (V1;5).

Servilia An ambitious noblewoman of 1st century B.C. Rome, stepsister of Cato Uticensis and mother of Brutus. She was at one time a mistress of Julius Caesar's (I;7).

Servius Tullius One of the legendary seven kings of Rome, who ruled from 578 to 534 B.C. and was famous for his building projects and expansion of Rome's boundaries (I;4).

sestertium A Roman coin of some small value, equal to about five cents in U.S. currency of 1948 (I;5,17).

Seven Jeds, Council of *see* **Council of the Seven Jeds**

Seven Mile Hill An Arizona landmark east of **Fort Apache** (A1;15).

Seven Worlds to Conquer The original title of ***Back to the Stone Age*** when it was first published in 1936.

Seymour, Jane The third wife of the gorilla king **Henry VIII**, who unlike her namesake was married to him concurrently with the other five (T17;20).

Shador A prison islet near the north shore of **Omean** (M2;9).

Shandy, Red A bandit of the band of the **Black Wolf** in medieval **Derbyshire**, who was wounded by **Norman of Torn** in 1256 and was afterward one of the first five to join his band of outlaws. He was a huge, red-haired fellow who became Norman's principal lieutenant (OT;6–8).

Shane, Maggie The girlfriend of "Coke" Sheehan (K2;1).

shanghai (American slang) To force an unwilling man into service on a ship, usually by drugging him (K1;2).

Sharu The slave woman of **Ghasta** on Barsoom who brought **Tan Hadron** the dagger and needle he needed to make his plan of escape work (M7;9).

shaving Because the black savages he saw were beardless, **Tarzan** learned to shave because he feared he might turn into an ape if he let his facial hair grow (T1;13).

Shawnee A small **Kansas** town of Johnson County (near Kansas City along the **Missouri** border) where **Detective Flannagan** of **Chicago** almost caught **Billy Byrne** (K2;4–5).

Shea, John Burroughs' secretary at Tarzana from 1919 to 1922. Together they were always "in the saddle before sunrise." Shea often played chess with Burroughs (M5).

shee-dah (*Apa*) Myself (A1;2).

Sheehan, "Coke" A boy who was nearly killed by **Billy Byrne** with a brickbat when he was 12; he later falsely implicated Byrne in the murder of old Mr. **Schneider**. He later came clean and confessed, letting Byrne off the hook (K1;1)(K2;1,17).

Sheehan, Mollie **Jim Thompson's** woman, the female half of the only couple whom the **Julian 8th** family could trust. She had killed two female babies she had had rather than let them grow up to be raped (both figuratively and literally) by the **Kalkar** soldiers. She adopted **Juana St. John** as her own after **Julian 9th** saved the girl from the **hellhounds**. She was widowed in the first battle of the revolution, then vanished from history (MM2;3,11).

Sheeta (*Ape*) The leopard, a persistent foe of ape-children (T1;9). While marooned by **Nikolas Rokoff** on **Jungle Island**, Tarzan rescued a leopard trapped beneath a fallen tree, and when the animal followed him, he fed it and purred to it, eventually gaining its respect and friendship. He took it on his search for Rokoff into the African interior, where it served him well several times and was the final agent of Rokoff's destruction. Tarzan then returned it to its home on Jungle Island (T3;4–21).

sheik (*Ara*) A chieftain or leader of an **Arab** tribe (T2;7).

Sheik, the **Amor ben Khatour**, as he was known to his "daughter" **Meriem**, whom he had actually stolen from her true father, **Armand Jacot**, in revenge for the death of the Sheik's nephew, **Achmet ben Houdin**. Meriem feared and despised him because he constantly beat and kicked her whenever he had the chance, and never gave her any love or kindness whatsoever. **Korak** saved the girl when she was 11, beating the Sheik mercilessly before taking her into the jungle with him. Five years later, he encountered and recaptured her, but Korak again freed her and the Sheik was trampled to death by **Tantor**, who had come along (T4;5,9,23–25).

Sheol The ancient Hebrew underworld; Hell (P1;10).

Shepherd's Star A poetic term for the planet Venus (V1;13).

Sherman Hotel A luxurious hotel of early 20th century Chicago (T15;7).

sheyk *see* sheik

Sheytan (*Ara*) The Devil (T11;1).

shield, Amtorian Amtorian troops carry shields made of a metal that is resistant to T-rays and impervious to R-rays (V3;4).

shield, Barsoomian Shields are practically unused upon Barsoom, except in a few isolated cases. The yellow men of the north use a small, cup-shaped buckler to protect themselves from hooked swords (M3;9), and the Phantom Bowmen of Lothar use a long, oval shield (M4;5).

shield, Kro-lu The shield of a Kro-lu of Caspak is very large and oval, made of rhino hide, and has a small hole in the center. A warrior who is attacked by a large carnivore will fall upon his back, pulling the shield over himself like a turtle's shell, and strike with his long dagger through the hole when the creature gets on the shield to try to break through (C2;5).

shiftas (Amharic) Organized, mounted native bandits of Abyssinia who prey upon other natives for food, goods and slaves (T15;1).

ship, Amtorian Amtorian ships are made of metal and have no stacks, because they are driven by a nuclear-powered engine in which element 93 (vik-ro, or neptunium) is exposed to a substance called lor, which contains mostly element 105 (yor-san, or hahnium); the resulting chain reaction annihilates the lor, releasing considerable energy. Fuel for the life of the ship could be carried in a pint jar (V1;8).

Shis-inday "Men of the Woods" (*Apa*). The Apache's name for themselves (A1; 2–3).

Shoa A mountainous area of central Abyssinia (T16;1).

Shogan A kantum (physicist) of the Amtorian city of Havatoo; he was the chief of the Sanjong at the time of Carson Napier's arrival in the city in 1930 (V2;15).

shogun The Japanese term for a warlord who establishes himself as ruler of a country by force and politics (K1;9).

***Shorewater,* H.M.S.** A British sloop-of-war that met the *Cowrie* while Tarzan was in command of it and headed toward England. Through its wireless he discovered that his son was safe in London, and on it they returned home (T3;21).

Short, Colin One of the members of Tom Billings' expedition to rescue Bowen Tyler, Jr., from Caspak in the summer of 1917 (C2;1).

short line Any small railroad; in the late 19th and early 20th centuries there were thousands of these spread out across the country; most connected at one end to a major rail line (GF;10).

Short Line Hotel "The most pretentious hostelry of Goliath [Idaho]" in the 1920s (GF;13).

Shorter, Eddie The son of Billy Byrne's Kansas benefactor, Mrs. Shorter. He had run away from home years before and was not heard from until Byrne ended up in Mexico in 1916, where he found Eddie as a ranch hand at the El Orobo Ranch in Chihuahua. Eddie "looked the other way" while Byrne escaped from Pancho Villa's men. Later, he went with Byrne to save Barbara Harding from the Indians, and was killed by their gunfire (K2;5, 12–16).

Shorter, Mrs. The 1910s Kansas farm woman whom Billy Byrne saved from being robbed and killed by the hobos Dink and Crumb. In gratitude, she gave him some money and hid him when the Kansas City police came looking for him on the false murder charge he was fleeing (K2;5).

Shorty One of the crew members of B.O. Pictures' *The Lion Man* safari in 1932 (T17;7). Another Shorty was a 6'3" cowpoke at the Bar-Y Ranch in 1880s Arizona who was totally loyal to Bull and Diana Henders through all of their troubles (HB;4,9,13–19).

Shoshone The county seat of Lincoln County, Idaho (GF;11).

shoz (*Apa*) Bear (A1;2).

Shoz-dijiji "Black Bear" (*Apa*). The name earned by Andy MacDuff, the adopted son of

Go-yat-thlay, by killing a black bear by himself at the age of ten in the spring of 1873. He had been raised as an Apache and knew nothing of his true origins. He became a great warrior over the years, but was known among the Apaches for not torturing his victims after a battle, and also for not killing women and children; because of this he was accused of cowardice by some, most notably his enemy Juh, Chief of the Ned-ni. He eventually won many over, however, and at 16 was already a war chief in his tribe, an honor presented to him because of his great feats of cunning and warriorship. He loved the maiden Ish-kay-nay, but her father wished her to marry a chief and so set the exorbitant price of 50 horses on her. Shoz-dijiji went to get them, but the mission took longer than he had expected, and in the meantime Juh succeeded in finding enough false "proof" to declare Shoz-dijiji dead and claim the despondent and apathetic Ish-kay-nay for himself, at her father's insistence (Al;1–14).

By the time Shoz-dijiji returned from his failed mission, he found that his tribe had meanwhile gone to war, and with the help of Wichita Billings, a white girl he had previously saved from rape, he was able to get back on his people's trail, arriving just in time to find Ish-kay-nay, who had been wounded by a soldier's bullet, abandoned by Juh and dying. He then sought out and killed Juh before returning to his tribe. It was during this period that, as a lone raider in northern Mexico, he became known as the Apache Devil. After coming home to his tribe, he went on a raid and again saved Wichita Billings' life, this time from another Apache warrior. He carried her off to his tribe, where they lived until the hostile Apaches and pursuing cavalry had left the area, at which time he brought her home; in the meantime, however, the two had fallen in love, though Wichita did not realize it until Shoz-dijiji had gone (Al; 15–20).

They did not meet again until three years later, when Geronimo (Go-yat-thlay) was going out of the reservation to raid again. About that time, Shoz-dijiji again saved her from "Dirty" Cheetim (the man who had tried to rape her before), then went out with Geronimo on the warpath over confiscated Apache cattle in May of 1885. They harried Arizona, Sonora, Chihuahua and New Mexico for over a year before they were finally forced to a stand by General Miles. During this period Shoz-dijiji became a notorious raider and always spoke for more war against the white men he hated. When Geronimo and the others surrendered to Miles at Skeleton Canyon on September 4, 1886, Shoz-dijiji would not go, preferring to remain renegade; it was at this time that Geronimo told him the truth about his birth (A2;1–14).

Friendless and without even a people to belong to, Shoz-dijiji returned to Arizona, where he had a final reckoning with "Dirty" Cheetim, who had framed him for several murders. He was then finally reunited with Wichita Billings, who broke through the boundaries of her own prejudice against Indians to love him. He settled down with her to run the Crazy "B" Ranch, with a chance for happiness at last (A2;15–19).

shoz-lekay (*Apa*) The white bear (A1).

Shrud A Pellucidarian woman of Tandar who took Gamba as a slave when he and Dian the Beautiful landed on the island after escaping the Xexot country in 1931. Shrud maltreated him, though, so he eventually killed her (P7:3;5).

si-chi-zi (*Apa*) Twilight (A1;2).

siamang (*Symphalangus syndactylus*) The black gibbon of Sumatra, largest of all the gibbons (T22;3).

Sidi Aissa A city of Algeria (about 120 miles SSE of Algiers) in which Tarzan stopped for a day in 1910 on his way from Sidi-bel-Abbes to Bou Saada. He was there attacked with murderous intent by a group of Arabs whom Nikolas Rokoff had hired to kill him (T2;7).

Sidi-bel-Abbes A city of French Algeria (about 50 miles south of Oran) to which Tarzan was sent by the French War Department to spy on Lt. Gernois, who had been accused of treason (T2;7).

Sidi-el-Seghir An Arab bandit of 1920s Algeria who abducted Nakhla with intent to sell her into slavery. He was killed by Aziz, who came to save the girl (LL;20–22).

Sierra de Antunez A small mountain range of Sonora (A2;13).

Sierra de Quarequa A mountain range along the Pacific coast of Panama (CG1;1).

Sierra de Sahuaripa A small mountain range of **Sonora** (A2;2).

Signana A Dyak tribe of **Borneo**, who were ruled in the 1920s by the **Rajah Muda Saffir** (Q;10).

Sikorsky Amphibian A helicopter of the 1920s which had pontoons for water landings (V1;1).

Sil Vagis Senior **teedwar** of the 91st **Umak** of the troops of **Helium** on **Barsoom**, who performed all of the regular duties for his lazy **odwar, Tor Hatan**. Sil Vagis was a coward who had bought his position, and he ran away from the men who abducted **Sanoma Tora** (M7;1).

Silanus The Roman governor of Syria under the Emperor **Tiberius**, who was recalled in A.D. 17 and replaced with **Gnaeus Piso** (I;6).

silians Slimy sea serpents of the **Lost Sea of Korus** on **Barsoom**; they are believed by the **Therns** to be the repositories of damned Thern souls. See also **Plant Men** (M2;4).

silks and furs The Barsoomian bed, even among the advanced human races, consists entirely of silks and furs, placed on an elevated platform when indoors, and stowed away during the day (M1).

silo The buildings of the **Kaldanes** of **Bantoom** are like grain silos, tall and domed, about 40 feet wide and 60 feet tall, but embrasured for defense and equipped with prism-faceted crystal domes at the top. The center of each tower is a cylindrical well faced with highly reflective white tile which is designed to reflect light into the rooms of the tower and into the underground passages below the tower, the first few hundred feet of which are faced with the white reflective tile. Unlike most Barsoomian buildings, these towers are equipped with stairs rather than ramps (M5;4).

simba (*Swa*) The lion (T5;3).

simm (*Ara*) Poison (T11;21).

Simms, Skipper The captain of the *Halfmoon*, aboard which **Billy Byrne** was shanghaied to Asia in 1914 (K1;2).

simnel bread A fine bread made in England until the late 18th century. It was made of finely-ground flour and cooked partially or completely by boiling (OT;3).

Simpson The sailor of the *Marjorie W.* who stuck the friendly ape **Akut** with a pin when the ship was stopped to make tests at **Jungle Island**. In response, the enraged ape nearly bit Simpson's shoulder in half, leaving him very sore for a while (T4;1).

Sinclair One of the crew of the captured **U-33** on its voyage to **Caspak** in July of 1916. He was one of the men who accompanied the ill-fated **Bradley** expedition from **Fort Dinosaur** on September 4, 1916, and did not return until the 11th, having lost three men, including Bradley (C1;6)(C3;1).

Sing The Chinese cook of the **El Orobo Ranch** in 1916 Mexico. He remained loyal to **Anthony Harding** when "General" **Pesita's** men attacked the ranch (K2;17).

Sing Lee The faithful old Chinese cook of the *Ithaca*, Professor **Arthur Maxon's** schooner. It was he who substituted the amnesiac **Townsend J. Harper, Jr.**, for Professor Maxon's **Number Thirteen** (after destroying the malformed creature) so **Virginia** would not have to marry a monster (Q;1,17).

Sing Tai One of the loyal Chinese servants of the **van der Meer** family of 1930s **Sumatra**; he fled into the hills with them when the **Japanese** invaded the island in January of 1942. He was bayonetted in the spring of 1944 (when the Japanese found their hiding place) but did not die; he ran into **Tarzan** and the crew of the *Lovely Lady* two days later and told them his story. After his wounds healed he rejoined **Corrie van der Meer** and Tarzan's crew and went with them on their break for the coast, but he was killed when a Japanese ship sunk the **proa** in which the party hoped to reach **Australia** (T22;1,4, 26–30).

Singh, Jabu A Lascar sailor of the tramp steamer *Saigon*; he joined the mutineers who took over the ship in 1938 (T24;3–4).

Singing Frog Nickname of Koiso Kuniaka (1880–1950), the premier of **Japan** from 1944 to 1945 (T22;26).

Sinkhole Canyon The next canyon west of **Cottonwood Canyon** in 1880s **Arizona** (HB;2).

sinus (*Lat*) Sea (T12;10).

Sinus Arabius (*Lat*) The Arabian Sea (T12;10).

Sioux Indian tribe of the mid- and northwestern plains states of the United States, eventually driven through Iowa and Missouri up into the Dakotas and Canada. Like the Apaches, they resisted white intrusion with warfare (A1;2). John Carter fought among them for several years (M1;1).

Sir Galahad The great black charger ridden by James Hunter Blake in the Great Tourney of the Valley of the Sepulcher in 1921 (T11;19).

Sir Mortimer Norman of Torn's great black stallion, which he broke and trained himself (OT;5–6).

sirrah Archaic term used to address men and boys in a contemptuous manner; often used by nobility when addressing servants or peasants (OT;3).

sith A huge, hornet-like monster of the Kaolian Forest on Barsoom. "Bald-faced and about the size of a Hereford bull. Has frightful jaws in front and mighty poisoned sting behind. The eyes, of myriad facets, cover three-fourths of the head, permitting the creature to see in all directions at one and the same time." The creature has been hunted nearly to extinction in Kaol both for its venom (which has "certain commercial uses," and of which each creature has about two gallons in its poison sacs) and for protective reasons, as the creatures are very aggressive, totally unafraid of humans, and formerly very numerous (M3;5).

sithic The giant labyrinthodont of Pellucidar, which weighs several tons and is fully 20 feet long. The sithic is carnivorous and is perfectly content to dine upon any sort of warm meat, including that of humans (P1;9).

Sitting Bull (1831–1890) English name of Tatanka Iyotake, a great Sioux Indian leader who led his people in war against the white invaders (including the destruction of Custer's force at Little Big Horn in 1876) until his death at the hands of the army in 1890 (A1;2).

Siva The third person of the Hindu trinity of Godhead, Siva the Destroyer, causes all created things to come to an end in their time (T20;1).

siwash (American Western slang) Deprecatory term for an Indian (K2;15).

Six Tribes, the The six free Apache tribes of the late 19th century: The Cho-kon-en (Chihuicahui), Be-don-ko-he, Ned-ni, Chihen-ne, Sierra Blanco (White Mountain), and Chi-e-a-hen (A1;3).

Ska (*Ape*) The vulture (T7;6).

Skabra The Vadjong of Mypos, woman of Tyros the Bloody, when Carson Napier and Duare came to Mypos in 1930. She was incredibly jealous, which kept Duare out of the hands of Tyros (V4;7).

skeel A Barsoomian hardwood which is used for doors, floors, ship decks, or what have you. The skeel tree is tall and straight and produces large, edible nuts which are delicious (M4;2)(M10:4;2).

Skeleton Canyon The Arizona site where Geronimo and Na-chi-ta surrendered to General Miles on September 4, 1886 (A2;14).

Skeleton Men of Jupiter *see* Morgors

"Skeleton Men of Jupiter" The name of the second novelette which comprises *John Carter of Mars*. It was originally published in *Amazing Stories* in February of 1943 and was intended to be the first of four novelettes describing John Carter's adventures after being kidnapped to Jupiter by the Morgors, the skeleton men of the title. He must then not only escape the Morgors, but also return to Barsoom to prepare them for the coming Morgor invasion. The events in it must have happened around 1940, just after Carter's return from Hawaii (M10), but when or how they were dictated to Burroughs will forever remain a mystery. Since it is the second half of *John Carter of Mars*, it is abbreviated M11B.

skinner (American slang) A mule-driver (A1;5).

Skinny Philander Samuel Philander's nickname as a boy in the 1850s, when he and Professor Porter first became friends (T1;16).

Sko-la-ta (*Apa*) A camp of the Be-don-ko-he Apache in 1878, south of Casas Grandes (A1;11).

Skopf, Herr   The proprietor of the hotel in which Jack Clayton and Akut stayed upon their arrival in Africa. They fled the hotel after Akut killed Condon, the American criminal who tried to rob Jack. Herr Skopf was a portly man who was very mystified at the disappearance of "Mrs. Billings" and her "grandson," to whom he had rented the room, and who had actually exited through the window—something no old lady could have done. Burroughs knew him as an acquaintance, but had not seen him for several years by the time of these events (T4;4).

Skor   The mad Jong of Morov on Amtor when Carson Napier came to that country in 1930. He had discovered a process by which he could imbue the dead with a sort of pseudo-life, and these creatures were entirely subject to his will. He continued to experiment on living victims, however, in an attempt to imbue his creatures with actual life. Napier and Duare became his prisoners late in 1930 but escaped, and Napier also freed the Janjong Nalte kum Andoo in the process. The creatures of Skor later recaptured both of the girls, but they were re-rescued by Napier, who fled with them to Havatoo (V2;9–12,17–20).

Skrag   An Amtorian criminal of Sanara who took part in Muso's abduction of the Janjong Nna in 1930 (V3;17).

Skree   (*Ape*) The African wildcat (T10;20).

Skruf   A Pellucidarian warrior of Basti whom Wilhelm von Horst met and befriended by saving him from a jalok in 1927. Skruf, however, felt no such kinship, and soon betrayed von Horst and Dangar to the Bastians as slaves. He and Frug (the Chief of Basti) were later captured by the Gorbuses and escaped with von Horst and La-ja. Skruf then abducted La-ja and was pursued by von Horst and shot, but did not die. This was fortunate for von Horst, because Skruf later gave David Innes information on his location (P5;4–5,10–11,18,22).

Skruk   The chief of the lowland village of Pheli in Pellucidar who pursued Jana, the Red Flower of Zoram, across the Mountains of the Thipdars to get her for a mate despite the protests of his followers (P4;7).

skulls   The Wieroos of Caspak decorate their city, Oo-oh, with the skulls of their victims, placing them on posts above their homes and inserting them in plaster around the eaves of houses, both inside and out. There are many millions of skulls in the city, and one tower is built entirely out of them. Indeed, there are some places where alleys are even paved with them (C3;2).

Sky Pilot   The leader of the band of hobos who pursued the false "Oskaloosa Kid" after "he" supposedly robbed Abigail Prim's safe in 1917. He was old, fat and grizzled, but extremely wise and crafty; his name derived from the fact that he had formerly been an ordained minister. He was later arrested with his gang by Detective Burton when they again tried to kill the "Kid," Bridge, "Abigail Prim" and Giova south of Payson the next night (K3;1–4,10).

Slankamen   A town on the Danube at which the power of the Ottoman Turks was broken in 1691. Its name was the password through the Austrian lines around Blentz when Barney Custer was taken prisoner there in September of 1914 (MK2;9).

Slats   A lion trained by Charlie Gay; he was used by B.O. Pictures for their jungle movies (T17;13).

slavery, Barsoomian   Slavery is common on Barsoom. These slaves are almost always prisoners of war, and most are well-treated. Barsoomian gentlemen are permitted female slaves, but John Carter (perhaps unable to shake off all Earthly conventions of his time) chose to have only male body-slaves (M2;14).

slaves   The name given to the American Indians by the Kalkars, who used them as such. The white nomads of the post–Kalkar 24th and 25th centuries used them thus as well, but were kinder to them, and upon moving on left them to their own land. These Indian slaves had a more established oral tradition than the whites and so actually remembered the ancient times better than the Tribe of Julian did (MM3;1–6).

slaves, Minunian   The Ant Men of Minuni have a society in which the slaves greatly outnumber the masters, but they have very little trouble with revolts because of the system of treatment used. Most slaves are captured in raids on other Minunian cities; each of these is given a green tunic with the insignia of his home city stamped on the back and that of his master's house on the front. They are used in the work of quarrying and building, and worked very hard at that. The children of these slaves also wear green tunics, but with the master's insignia stamped on the front and back, and are given more privileges than their parents. The slaves of the third generation are given white tunics, taught a skill, and move about with even more freedom; the highest-ranked, most loyal slaves actually form a skilled and prosperous middle class among the Minunians. In addition, it is the Minunian custom for nobles to marry slaves in order to keep their bloodlines free from inbreeding, because the slaves must obviously be of foreign stock. Any slave thus espoused is raised to the caste of his or her spouse and freed from slavery (T10;6).

Slaves' Corridor One of the four major corridors leading into the royal dome of the Minunian city of Veltopismakus, on the north side of that dome (T10;16–17).

Sleeping Sickness The nickname given Stanley Obrowski by Gordon Marcus during the 1932 location filming of *The Lion Man*, because of Obrowski's slothful habits (T17;2).

sling, Zertalacolol The "sling" used by the Zertalacolol women of the Minunian hills is a walnut-sized stone attached to a rawhide thong. This weapon is used as a sling would be, except that the thong goes with the pebble. Each Zertalacolol woman wears a "skirt" of these thongs for ready use in hunting or man-catching (T10;2–3).

Sloo The wife of Scurv, chief of the Himean village of Garb. Like all Himean women, she was a great shrew, but had been pretty and loving in her youth on Amiocap, from which she had been abducted by Scurv; years of Himean life, however, had made her just as bad as the natives (P3;11).

smilodon The saber-toothed tiger of the Pleistocene (P1;6). See also **tarag; jato.**

Smith The alias of Joseph Campbell when he and Zubanev joined the Ramsgate safari while lost in Northern Rhodesia in 1939 after being shot down by Lt. Cecil Giles-Burton, whom they also had shot down. After joining the safari he recognized Giles-Burton in the party and murdered both him and Zubanev for the Brown plans (T24B;5–7).

Another Smith was the butler of the Harding family in 1910s New York (K1;18), and another a juryman of the grand jury which voted no bill on the case of Abe Farris's holding Maggie Lynch prisoner (GF;4). Yet another was a cowhand at the El Orobo Rancho in 1916 (K2;9).

Smith, Gum The somewhat ineffectual sheriff of 1880s Hendersville, Arizona, who also owned the town's most profitable saloon. He was totally crooked and could be paid off by anyone, including Maurice Corson and his friends, and even Hal Colby, the notorious Black Coyote, from whom he was getting a percentage of the loot. He was run out of town when the truth was discovered (HB; 1–3,13–19).

Smith, Joseph (1805–1844) The founder of the Mormon church, who was murdered by his enemies before his 39th birthday (A1;1).

Smith, Lafayette, A.M., Ph.D., Sc.D. A young wunderkind geologist who graduated from college at 17 and had his doctorates by 21, only to find that college boards laugh at 21-year-old professors. He taught for a year at Phil Sheridan Military Academy, then set out for Africa in 1929 to study the Great Rift Valley; he met Danny "Gunner" Patrick on the ship en route and took him along. While examining the Ghenzi Mountains, he became separated from his safari and stumbled into the land of Midian just in time to save Lady Barbara Collis and Jezebel from being crucified and burned. The group was soon captured by the only slightly less fanatical North Midianites, and Smith would have been buried alive as a trial by ordeal had not Tarzan rescued them. Smith later found that he had fallen for Lady Barbara, and although she did not "fall" for him, it was plain to see that there was some affection there, because she invited him to stay at her home for a while, ostensibly to teach him to shoot straight (T15;1–3,7–9,12,19,26).

Smith, Lem The first farmer of Oakdale, Illinois, to get a threshing machine (K3;6).

Smith, Milton The vice-president in charge of production for B.O. Pictures in the 1930s; it was he who conceived of the idea of shooting *The Lion Man* on location in Africa (T17;1).

Smith, Miss The stenographer that **June Lathrop** replaced in **Ogden Secor**'s office (GF;7).

Smith, Sergeant An American cavalryman of "D" Troop who killed the **Apache** medicine man **Nakay-do-klunni** after the Battle of **Cibicu Creek** in 1881 (A1;14).

Smith-Jones, John Alden The father of **Waldo Emerson Smith-Jones**, who sent a well-equipped expedition out to find his son after the young man was lost at sea in 1911 (CG1;11). He returned with a second expedition in 1912 and rescued **Nadara**, who told him of Waldo and was accepted by him as a daughter-in-law. He later gave his blessing to their marriage when Waldo was found (CG2; 6–7,12–13).

Smith-Jones, Louisa Mrs. John Alden Smith-Jones, the mother of **Waldo Emerson Smith-Jones**, whom she had spoiled too much for his own good, but educated admirably. She went on the *Priscilla* expedition to rescue Waldo in 1912 and there met **Nadara**, of whom she instantly disapproved on principle. When she found out that the girl was actually the orphaned child of a lost French count and countess, however, she accepted her (CG1; 1–2)(CG2;6–7,12).

Smith-Jones, Waldo Emerson The false name given by Burroughs to the Bostonian aristocrat hero of *The Cave Girl* who, of course, wished to remain incognito when his story was told. He was 6'2", blond-haired and blue-eyed, and at 21 was skinny, pale and sickly until he went on a South Pacific cruise in 1911 (on doctor's orders, to improve a chronic cough) and was washed overboard and onto an island inhabited by stone-age people, where he was forced to develop his neglected body in order to survive at all. When he first arrived on the island he spent 22 days on the beach in a state of terror, but eventually encountered the savages, two of whom he managed to kill with a heavy stick when they cornered him. This act of "courage" so impressed the beautiful cave girl **Nadara** that she named him **Thandar** (the brave one) and fell in love with him. She tried to get him to come to her tribe with her, but he fled and remained distant for six months, during which time he exercised and practiced with weapons (CG1;5–8). At the end of this time he searched her tribe out and killed the

horrible **Korth**, then saved Nadara from the equally awful **Flatfoot** and mated with her. Soon afterward, his father's yacht came looking for him after his position was reported by another ship, but he avoided the yacht until he could convince Nadara to return to Boston with him; unfortunately, they were held up by an encounter with the "**Bad Men**" and the *Priscilla* sailed without seeing them (CG1; 9–11)(CG2;1–2).

Nadara then brought him back to her people, of which he became king. He had great plans for the island, but they were disrupted by an earthquake which killed everyone except himself (who escaped by luck) and Nadara, who had been abducted earlier that evening by the "Bad Man" **Thurg**. She was rescued by Waldo's father and the *Priscilla* (who had returned for another search), but told them that Waldo had died in the earthquake, so they sailed away. He was of course not dead and so made a boat with which to pursue Nadara after speaking to the island's only other survivor, who had witnessed everything. He landed on an island north of theirs, where he found out from a pirate chief whose life he saved that a tribe of head hunters on the island had a white girl prisoner. He rescued her, and after a harrowing run-in with the pirates (from which they were saved by the grateful chief) they were reunited with Waldo's parents on the *Priscilla* and married in **Honolulu**, moving afterward to Boston (CG2;3–13).

Smith-Oldwick, Lieutenant Harold Percy The British air scout stationed in **British East Africa** during **World War I** whose plane stalled above northwest **Tanganyika** in the winter of 1915 during a solo scouting mission. While attempting to repair his engine, he was abducted by a party of warriors of the savage **Wamabo** tribe and would have been eaten if not for the intervention of the great ape **Zu-tag**, who led eight great apes to the rescue of **Tarzan**, who had also been captured by the Wamabo and was to have been eaten along with Smith-Oldwick. Later, Smith-Oldwick and **Bertha Kircher** (with whom he had fallen in love) were captured by the brutal **Sergeant Usanga**, who forced Smith-Oldwick to teach him to fly. They were again rescued by Tarzan and flew off towards civilization, only to hit a vulture and be forced down into the deadly **desert** of western Tanganyika and captured by the mad race of **Xuja**. Tarzan once again came to their rescue, and they finally returned to civilization (T7;9–24).

Smuts, General Jan (1870–1950) The commander of the British forces from **South Africa** in the East African Campaign of **World War I**; he later went on to become the prime minister of South Africa (T7;5).

snakes, Amtorian There are many varieties of snakes on Amtor; some are large, some small; some have horns, external ears, or saber-teeth. They can be of almost any conceivable color, but blue, red, green, white and purple are the most common (V2;2).

snakes, Pellucidarian Some of the predatory snakes of Pellucidar (found primarily in the **Phelian Swamp**) are so huge they can swallow a **trachodon** whole. These tremendous monsters are so stupid, however, that they seldom perceive tiny humans as food (P4;12).

Snider One of the three sailors of the aero-sub *Coldwater* who was in the power boat with **Lt. Jefferson Turck** when he was abandoned by his ship around 20 degrees west longitude in 2137. He was an unpleasant sort of person who became lustful of **Victory**, to whom he lied about Lt. Turck's motives toward her. He later abducted her and stole the launch, but she killed him when he tried to have his way with her (LC;2,6–7).

Snipes A little rat-faced man, chief among the *Arrow* mutineers, whom Tarzan stopped from shooting **William Clayton** in the back by throwing a spear through his shoulder before he could fire. This let the castaways know that he was indeed watching them, as the note he had left them had informed them he would. Snipes was later killed by **Tarrant** with a pickaxe (T1;13,17).

snow (American slang) Cocaine. The coca plant–derived white powder was made illegal in 1914, but was until the early 1970s considered a "safe" drug, though one whose high price tag restricted it to use by the "in" crowd (T22;24).

so (*Amt*) A prefix which means the same as the suffix "-er" in English; thus, **fal** (kill), **sofal** (killer) (V1;12).

so (*Ape*) Eat (T22;22). See also next entry — this may be an instance of confusion on Burroughs' part.

so (*Pal*) Eat (T8;15).

So-al The **Band-lu** woman of **Caspak** who was the mate of **To-mar**. They had always come up together, and their rise to **Kro-lu** status was no exception — it took place on the day **Tom Billings** and **Ajor** passed through their country, and they accompanied the two as far as the Kro-lu country (C2;4).

So-ta The wife of **To-jo** the **Band-lu** in **Caspak**; she aided **Bowen Tyler** to escape her people in late September of 1916. She was very advanced, about to become a **Kro-lu**, and so ran off with him to join that tribe (C1;9).

Sobito The old witch doctor of the **Utengi** village of **Tumbai**, who hated Tarzan from the first because he stole the old man's thunder. Sobito spoke out against war with the **Leopard Men**, chiefly because he was one of them. He tried to call Tarzan down, but Tarzan (who now believed himself a **muzimo** because of amnesia) defied the old man and his magic, making a fool of him and breaking his hold on the tribe. When Tarzan found out that Sobito was a Leopard Man, he abducted him from the **Temple of the Leopard God** itself and gave him to the Utenga for justice. Sobito escaped from them and conspired with **Bobolo** for a while, but Tarzan eventually recaptured him and returned him to the Utenga, this time making sure that he did not escape (T18;4,11,14,16,21,23).

The Society for the Uplift of Erring Women Reverend **Theodore Pursen**'s charity, which sought to reform prostitutes by having them attend prayer meetings and lectures instead of finding them decent employment which made them at least as much money as prostitution (GF;6).

sod (*Pal*) Eaten (T8).

sof (*Bar*) A Barsoomian "inch," equivalent to 1.1694 English inches. There are ten sofs in a **sofad** (M8;12).

sofad (*Bar*) A Barsoomian "foot," which equals about 11.694 English inches. There are ten sofads in an **ad**, or Barsoomian "yard," and one sofad is made up of ten sofs, or Barsoomian "inches" (M4;6)(M8;12).

Sofal "Killer" (*Amt*). The **Thorist** ship which took **Carson Napier** prisoner a few months after his arrival on Amtor in 1929. He started a mutiny that left him in command

and turned the *Sofal* into a pirate ship preying on Thorist shipping (V1;8–11).

Soft Shoulders The B.O. Pictures movie (starring Balza) that premiered the night Tarzan arrived in Hollywood on his first (and only) visit to California in 1933 (T17; 33).

sog (*Pal*) Eating (T8).

sojar (*Pell*) Great (P2;6).

Sojar Az "Great Sea" (*Pell*). The Pellucidarian sea east of Thuria, which is actually a part of the same ocean as the Lural Az is (P2;6).

Sokabe, Lieutenant Hideo The lieutenant to Captain Matsuo. Sokabe was the Japanese officer who captured Corrie van der Meer in Sumatra in the spring of 1944 (T22;1).

Sol-to-to The Mahar who interviewed David Innes when he returned to Phutra after escaping it in 1903 (P1;10).

Sola A green Barsoomian woman, the secret daughter of Tars Tarkas. Unlike most of her kind, she was compassionate and merciful, and was often mocked and scorned on this account until Tars Tarkas acknowledged his paternity. She was John Carter's nurse and teacher among the green men, and saved his life by helping Dejah Thoris to prevent Sarkoja from blinding him during his fight with Zad (M1).

Solan An aged yellow man of Barsoom who controlled the various utilities of Kadabra from a secret room in the palace of the Jeddak of Jeddaks. The atmosphere plant, heating system and Guardian of the North were all controlled and maintained by him. Thurid bribed him to let him escape with Dejah Thoris by turning off the magnet, but the old man would have double-crossed him had John Carter not killed him first so he could throw the magnet switch to save the approaching fleet of Helium. Solan was probably the best swordsman John Carter ever fought (M3;11–13).

solar power The Polodans derive all power from their sun, Omos. See **power, Polodan** (B1;4). The Barsoomians also use solar power for lighting and heating, and to run their atmosphere plant.

solar rays The Barsoomians have discovered two solar rays unknown on Earth. See **eighth ray; ninth ray.**

Soldiers of Liberty The secret organization of mutineers Carson Napier founded aboard the Thorist ship *Sofal* while he was imprisoned on it in 1929 (V1;9).

Solent The channel between the Isle of Wight and Great Britain (LC;3).

solution, ray-repelling A chemical solution known only in Havatoo is used to render any substance impervious to both the T-rays and R-rays of Amtorian guns; to what degree is unknown (V3;4). A similar solution protects the lantars of Middle Anlap, and special shells containing an acid to dissolve the coating are fired from enemy lantars (V4;45).

Somalia An east African nation which borders on the Red Sea and the Gulf of Aden. It was known in Tarzan's time as Italian Somaliland (T14;1).

somp The pulp of the fruit of the sompus tree (M10;4;2).

sompus A Barsoomian tree which produces a very sweet, grapefruit-like fruit with a thin red rind, which is considered a great delicacy on Barsoom (M4)(M10;4;2).

son (*Pal*) Ate (T8).

The Son of Tarzan The fourth book in the Tarzan series, abbreviated T4, which was published in 1915. When the events of the book took place (if at all), to whom, and how they reached Burroughs, are all mysteries. To explain: The events of the story are supposed to take place roughly ten years after those of *The Beasts of Tarzan*, which took place in 1912, so at the earliest *The Son of Tarzan* should start in 1921. To make matters worse, the story covers some six years, and so should end in 1926, eleven years after the book was written. To complicate things further, Korak (ostensibly Tarzan's son Jack) appears as an adult in *Tarzan the Untamed* and *Tarzan the Terrible*, which took place in 1914 and 1915. It is possible, of course, that in Burroughs' original manuscript he changed the dates (as he did the names), but he would have had to add some twelve years to the dates for the numbers to work out, so that Tarzan would have had to have been born around 1876 instead of

1888, and thus would be over 60 years old at the time of his last adventures, rather than pushing 50. Possible, to be sure, but... The story, in any case, concerns **Alexis Paulvitch**'s escape from Africa and his subsequent plans to gain revenge on Tarzan by luring his son away, plans which failed because of the intervention of **Akut**, who had come back to England with Paulvitch in a search for Tarzan. Together Akut and Jack fled to the jungle, after which the boy came to feel that he could never go back, and instead learned to live the wild life as his father had and grew into a man in the jungle.

Sondergros An American cavalryman who was killed at the Battle of **Cibicu Creek** in 1881 (A1;14).

"The Song of Love" Barsoom's most beautiful melody, which was sung by **Tara of Helium** to inspire **Ghek** and distract **Luud** (M5;8).

Sonora A northern Mexican state which lies west of **Chihuahua** and south of **Arizona** (A1;3).

Sons-ee-ah-ray "Morning Star" (*Apa*). The youngest wife of **Go-yat-thlay** and adoptive mother of **Shoz-dijiji** (A1;1).

Soor The **Kalkar** tax collector for the teivos of **Chicago** in Kalkar-occupied 22nd century America; he was a small man with red hair and beady eyes who charged **Julian 8th** a ridiculously high tax and then demanded a present from him as well. He gave Julian's pen in the marketplace to **Vonbulen**, another farmer, but **Julian 9th** kicked him out and then threw the bribe Soor had demanded (a cheese) directly into the tax collector's face. Julian was tried for this crime, but let go with a warning. Soor was killed at the beginning of the rebellion by Julian 8th, who bayonetted him (MM2;2,5–6,11).

Sophronia The black maid of the **Scott** house in early 20th century **Scottsville**, Virginia (ME;2).

sopu (*Ape*) Fruit (TC).

sorak A little, six-legged animal that red Barsoomian women keep to play with; a Barsoomian "cat" (M1;14)(M9;7).

Soran The Prince of **Ptarth** on Barsoom, son of **Thuvan Dihn** and brother of **Thuvia**.

He was the **jedwar** of the navy of Ptarth (M4;1).

sorapus A Barsoomian hardwood, not as sturdy as **skeel** (though still very strong) but more fine and beautiful, which is used for attractive constructions like furniture, doors, etc. The sorapus is a spreading tree which produces a large, succulent fruit with a hard, nut-like shell. It also produces large, beautiful flowers and is used for ornamental purposes (M3;2)(M7;1).

Sorav Commander of the palace guards of **Salensus Oll**, Jeddak of Jeddaks of Okar on Barsoom, at the time John Carter and **Thuvan Dihn** joined the palace guards in search of **Matai Shang** (M3;10).

sord (*Ape*) Bad (T22;11).

sorrel A horse color; reddish or yellowish brown (D;9).

sound-detectors The country of **Unis** on **Poloda** uses incredibly sensitive microphones to pick up the sound of plane engines from a great distance, but Unisan planes contain a special device that emits an ultrasonic vibration which enables the detectors to recognize them. The exact frequency of this vibration is changed every day for security (B1;7).

Soup Face One of the murderous hobos who tried to rob the **"Oskaloosa Kid"** after the "robbery" of the **Prim** house. He was red-haired, pudgy and "battered." He was arrested by **Detective Burton** with the rest of the gang when they caught up with the "Kid" and "his" companions south of **Payson** the next night and again tried to rob and kill them (K3;1,10).

South Africa The Dutch-colonized nation at the southern tip of the African continent. Lt. **Erich Obergatz** was headed there with **Jane Clayton** when he stumbled upon **Pal-ul-don** (T8;17).

South Clark Street A street in **Chicago** which **Brady** said Caspak reminded him of, because it is "no place for an Irishman" (C3;1).

South Island The southernmost of the three main islands of the **Anoroc** group in the **Lural Az** of Pellucidar, home to the only tribe of Anoroc Mezops who were not loyal to **Ja**, until they joined the **Empire of Pellucidar** in 1914 (P2;15).

Southern Pacific A U.S. railroad which began as a branch of the Central Pacific into southern **California** and eventually grew to extend from the Pacific to **Illinois** (GH;13).

Sov A captain of guards in the Amtorian city of **Kapdor** when **Carson Napier** was imprisoned there in 1929 (V2;1).

Sovan *see* **Soran**

Sovgrad The capital city of **Karlova**, which lay in a fertile valley surrounded by low hills (R;3).

Sovong "Defender" (*Amt*). The sister ship of the *Sofal*; **Duare** was taken prisoner aboard it, but was rescued when the *Sovong* was taken by the *Sofal*, which had come under **Carson Napier's** command through a mutiny (V1;10).

spahis The French-officered **Arab** troops of **Algeria** during the period when it was a French colony (T2;7).

spalpeen An Irish epithet meaning "rascal" or "rogue" (HB;2).

Spartacus (?–71 B.C.) A slave and gladiator who led a slave revolt against Rome from 73 to 71 B.C., ranging up and down the Italian peninsula creating havoc and defeating several Roman legions until he was defeated by Crassus in 71 B.C. and killed in battle (I;4).

Spatium "Race-Track" (*Lat*). A champion racehorse of the **Green Stables** of early 1st century Rome; his sire was **Fortis** and his dam **Pulchra** (I;8).

spear, Amtorian The Amtorian spear is actually a short, heavy javelin with a cavity for a **tarel** cord in its rear. When it is thrown, the cord (which is tied to the wrist of the thrower) is trailed behind, and the thrower can use it to pull the spear back. This is a necessary precaution for hunting in the giant trees of **Vepaja** (V1;6).

spear, Barsoomian The spear, or rather lance of the **green men** of Barsoom is almost forty feet long (M1;3).

spear, Va-ga A well-balanced, six foot long weapon with a narrow, sharp head with a backward-pointing hook beneath it and a short, sharp point above it. The spear can be used to kill or subdue, since it can be thrown backward to strike shaft first, and the hook will catch on limbs or clothing. The **Kalkars**

use a smaller version of the same weapon (MM1;4,11).

spectacles So poor was the sight of the ancient **Ras Thavas**, he could only see with the aid of incredibly thick and powerful spectacles he had designed himself (M6;4).

Spehon A powerful member of the **Zani** party of the Amtorian nation of **Korva**, head of the Zani guard and secret police, whom **Muso** planned to conspire with to betray **Sanara** and so become **Jong** of Korva. After the death of **Mephis** in 1930, Spehon was the ruler of Korva for a very short time (V3;8–9,15).

Spencer A .52 caliber carbine used by the U.S. Cavalry in the Indian Campaigns of the late 19th century (A1;2).

Sperry, Judge A notable of early 20th century Scottsville, Virginia (ME;1).

Spider One of the sailors of the *Lady Alice*, who ended up in a foodless lifeboat with **Jane Porter**, **William Clayton**, "**Mr. Thuran**" and two other sailors after the ship was wrecked. When he lost the lottery "Thuran" had proposed to see who would be eaten, he committed suicide by jumping from the boat (T2;18).

spiders, Barsoomian The spiders of Barsoom are 12-legged and venomous. In the **Valley Hohr** lives a species of giant spider which spins an incredibly tough web to which the spider is confined because it lacks the ability to crawl on the ground. This is because its legs grow upward from its back, which allows very fast movement along the web but none on the ground. The webs of these giant spiders are made into a fabric by the slaves of **Ghasta**; this fabric is tougher than leather but infinitely lighter and more beautiful, and is woven so tightly it can hold water (M7;7). See also **tarel**.

Spike One of the white hunters attached to the 1935 **Wood** safari to the **Sudan** and **Ethiopia**. After he was rescued by Tarzan from six months of captivity among the **Kaji**, he and **Troll** stole the **Gonfal** and the **Great Emerald of the Zuli** and fled with them, only to find they could not cause them to function; they then abducted **Gonfala** because they figured she could. They fled into the **Ethiopian Highlands** and were captured there by the revolutionary government of **Athne** and enslaved until Tarzan rescued them a few weeks later. He then had them escorted out of Africa for good (T21;2,9–11,14,17,20,25).

spina (*Lat*) The wall which divided a Roman circus lengthwise, around which the race track ran (I;8).

Spitzbergen A Norwegian island in the Arctic Ocean from which Arctic expeditions traditionally set out (T13;2).

Spizo the Spaniard The sole traitor in the ranks of **Norman of Torn**; he was paid by de Vac to spy upon Norman (OT;9).

Splay One of the **Ganaks** of Pellucidar when **Wilhelm von Horst** was captured by them early in 1928 (P5;19).

spoon, Wieroo The eating utensil used by the **Wieroo** of **Caspak** is a sharpened wooden skewer used to spear large chunks of food, with a small clamshell fastened to the other side for use as a spoon, to get small, soft or mushy food (C3;2).

sports, Havatoo The sports of the Amtorian city of **Havatoo** are meant to balance the otherwise structured lives of its people, and as such are extremely dangerous and often result in injury or death, especially in the case of the **Great** War Game (V2;16).

Spring Creek Site of "Ole" Gunderstrom's cabin in early 20th century New Mexico (D;1–2).

Springfield Any rifle produced or adapted at the U.S. Armory in Springfield, **Massachusetts**; they were standard infantry issue from 1873 to 1938. The Springfield .30/06, used from 1906 to 1938, was so accurate that many were modified into hunting rifles after they were retired (A1;3)(D;17).

squaw (American slang) An American Indian woman (C2;6).

Squibbs A family of the outskirts of 1890s **Oakdale, Illinois**. They were all found murdered mysteriously around 1895 (K3;3).

Squint Eye The nickname of **Bender Ward**, first mate of the *Halfmoon* on its last voyage in 1914 (K1;9).

SS-96 The obsolete class of **Pan-American aero-sub** to which the *Coldwater* belonged (LC;1).

Stabutch, Leon An agent of the OGPU of Stalinist Russia, sent to Africa in 1929 to kill Tarzan in retribution for the death of Peter Zveri and also to remove him as a stumbling block to further subversive activities in Africa. For a while, he hitched up with a band of **shiftas** led by the Italian communist **Dominic Capietro**, but killed the latter in a drunken quarrel over **Jezebel**, the beautiful Midianite girl they had captured after **Danny** "Gunner" **Patrick** had led her out of Midian. Stabutch fled with the girl, chanced upon Tarzan, and attempted to assassinate him, but failed and was himself killed by Tarzan (T15; 1,7,20–22).

Stade, Professor Marvin An American biochemist of the 1930s who tried to defect to the Soviet Union when the SPCA and Department of Health banned his experiments in cryogenics. He flew there with **Pat Morgan** and was responsible for the resurrection of Jimber-Jaw. When Stade and Morgan showed up in Moscow with the cave man, however, the Russians threw a fit and basically kicked them out (J;2–4).

stairs, Barsoomian The towers of the **Kaldanes** contain stairs, an architectural element unknown elsewhere upon Barsoom (M5;4). John Carter tried to introduce stairs into his palace in **Helium**, but the difficulty the Barsoomians had with such things eventually caused him to replace them with the **ramps** which normally serve the function on Barsoom. The Barsoomians had great trouble navigating the stairs in the Castle of the **Tarids** on **Ladan** as well (M8;17).

stairs, Laythean In **Laythe**, broad stairways served as avenues to connect various levels of the conical city (MM1;11).

Stalar A slave overseer in the city-state of **Hangor** when **Carson Napier** was enslaved there late in 1931. He was a typical bully (V4; 50).

Stalin, Joseph (1879–1953) Born Iosif Vissarionovich Dzhugashvili; the dictator of the Soviet Union from 1929 to 1953. He was a despot who solidified Soviet power in Asia and Europe and raised the USSR from a backward agricultural nation to an industrial power while simultaneously turning it into a police state. In 1929 he dispatched **Leon** Stabutch of the OGPU to kill Tarzan for his interference in Stalin-ordered subversive activities in Africa (T15;1).

Stanford The California university from which Jason Gridley graduated (P3).

Stanley, Henry Morton (1841–1909) An Anglo-American explorer of the late 19th century who explored and mapped much of the African interior. It was with his 1878 expedition that the old white man Tarzan found in the Palace of Diamonds in 1917 had come to Africa, as a boy. He had been captured by unfriendly natives and taken away from the expedition, escaped from them later, become totally lost, then stumbled into the Valley of the Palace of Diamonds (T9;13).

Stark, William The first officer of the *Priscilla* on its second journey to find Waldo Emerson Smith-Jones in 1912. He was an intelligent and experienced man, but was too arrogant in front of the crew, which led them to cordially hate him. After Nadara was brought aboard the *Priscilla* by Waldo's father, Stark tried to rape her and, when he failed, he abducted her to a nearby island, where he was killed by head hunters (CG2;6–8).

Statilius Taurus A Roman amphitheater of the Tiberian period. Caligula held games there in A.D. 41 in which he had members of the audience driven into the arena (I;3,20).

steel, Barsoomian Most Barsoomian steels are alloyed with aluminum (M1).

Stefan Princess Mary of Margoth's chauffeur (R;6).

stegosaurus An ungainly, awkward armored dinosaur of the Jurassic, about 20 feet long and possessed of a very tiny brain. The dyrodor of Pellucidar would seem to have evolved from this creature (P4;12).

Stein, Doctor The new physician brought for the "Mad King" Leopold of Lutha in 1912 by Prince Peter of Blentz; he was to have removed Leopold permanently. Dr. Stein was later killed by Lt. Butzow while attempting to kidnap Leopold from Tafelberg Sanitorium along with Maenck and Coblich (MK1;1,9).

Stein's Peak A mountain of southern Arizona, namesake of the Stein's Peak Range (A1;1,19).

Stellara The "daughter" of The Cid, chief of the Korsars of Pellucidar; she was a beautiful blond girl of exactly the opposite nature of her "father"—sweet, brave and fair-ness-loving—since she followed her mother's bloodline. She was not afraid to stand up to The Cid and tell him what she thought, which impressed Tanar the Fleet One as much as her looks when he was captured by the Korsars in 1925. Stellara was the daughter of Allara, a woman of the island of Amiocap who was already pregnant when she was captured by The Cid, who ever afterward thought the child was his because he did not know that she had the birthmark of her Amiocapan father. She and Tanar felt a strong attraction for each other, and that feeling only increased when they were left alone together on a foundering derelict vessel abandoned by the other Korsars in a storm. They eventually drifted to Amiocap, where she was reunited with her true father, kidnapped by a Korsar party, rescued by Tanar, then abducted by a warrior from Hime. She was then retaken by the Korsars and eventually re-rescued by Tanar, and the two escaped to Sari (P3;1–2, 5–9,12–17).

Sterling The chief of Indian scouts at Fort San Carlos, Arizona, who was killed by Apaches in the spring of 1882 (A1;20).

Stetson A famous manufacturer of felt cowboy hats (D;1).

Stickler Ogden Secor's office manager, who hired June Lathrop (a.k.a. Maggie Lynch) as a stenographer in Secor's absence. He watched her constantly, and when he found out about her past from Officer Doarty, he tried to use it to have his way with her, and fired her when she refused him. It was he who planned the robbery in which his employer was injured and ruined, and he who destroyed what was left of the business afterward by constant embezzlement. He was eventually caught and convicted, but it is not known whether he had to repay any of the money (GF;7–10,14).

Stimbol, Wilbur A pushy American stockbroker friend of James Hunter Blake's who went on safari in east Africa with him in 1921. Because of Stimbol's brutishness and temper, the two eventually split up the safari and went their separate ways. Soon afterward, Stimbol chased a gorilla down with his rifle and would have killed him had not Tarzan

308 STIMBOL AND COMPANY, BROKERS • STUTEVILLE, MARY DE

heard and intervened. He then arranged for Stimbol to be escorted to the coast, in spite of the American's protestations. Soon afterward, the men of his safari abandoned him after he disobeyed Tarzan's injunction to him against hunting, and he wandered alone through the jungle for days until he encountered the **Arab** tribe **el-Harb**, into which he was taken after promising them great rewards. He was later tricked by **Ibn-jad** into attempting to kill Tarzan, but Tarzan tricked Stimbol by substituting the **Sheik**'s unconscious brother, **Tollog**, in his own place. Stimbol was again left to wander in the jungle, but found by **Blake** and escorted back to civilization, much chastened by his experiences (T11;4–8,13–15, 22–24).

Stimbol and Company, Brokers, New York The company owned by **Wilbur Stimbol**, big game hunter and nuisance to Tarzan (T11;4).

sto (*Cpk*) Hatchet; actually, a stone hand-axe (C1;8–9).

Sto-lu "Hatchet-man" (*Cpk*). The race of Caspakian humanity next in development above the **Bo-lus**. The Sto-lus live in natural caves, make simple stone weapons, use fire, and have some social order. They are hairy, have coarse features and prognathous jaws, and wear no clothing. After a time, a Sto-lu may develop into a **Band-lu** (C1;8–9).

Stone, Jim The name by which **Jimber-Jaw** became known in Beverly Hills after **Pat Morgan** brought him there. He became a wrestler, then a boxer, then a movie actor before he finally "committed suicide" a few months later (J;4–5).

Stone, Jimmie The second assistant production manager for **B.O. Pictures**, who was in charge of producing **Balza**'s 1933 movie, *Soft Shoulders* (T17;33).

stra (*Amt*) Hot (V1;4).

Strabol "Hot Country" (*Amt*). The innermost region or circle on Amtor's highly inaccurate pole-equator reversed maps. It is of course really the equatorial region and is extremely hot, though not intolerably so as the inhabitants of the southern hemisphere believe. The countries of **Morov** and **Havatoo** lie in Strabol (V1;4).

Stripes Tarzan's nickname for a tiger, be-

cause he did not know the local ape-word for such a creature (T22;3).

Stroebel, Prince The kindly Prime Minister of the tiny eastern European kingdom of **Margoth** who conceived of the plan to marry **Princess Mary** to **Prince Boris** of **Karlova**, thus sealing the two countries' centuries-old breach (R;1).

Strong, Hazel **Jane Porter**'s best friend in **Baltimore**, to whom she wrote the letter that Tarzan appropriated; through this medium he discovered why the Porter party was in Africa, as well as the fact that they did not know that the savage white man who had helped them was the same Tarzan of the Apes who had written them notes (T1;18).

He later met her in person (while acting as a French agent under the alias **John Caldwell**) aboard an ocean liner headed from **Algiers** to **Cape Town** on a pleasure trip with her mother. She liked him very much, and was the first person to notice his absence after he was thrown overboard by **Nikolas Rokoff** (whom she knew as "**Mr. Thuran**"), who was engaged in wooing the naive girl with his smooth talk. After she arrived in Cape Town and stayed there for a few months, she ran into Jane Porter in a jeweler's; Jane was in Cape Town on a stop during her cruise on **Lord Tennington**'s yacht, the *Lady Alice*, with her father and **William Clayton**. Hazel, her mother, and "Mr. Thuran" were invited aboard the yacht for the return trip to England and accepted, so they were aboard the yacht when it was wrecked off the coast of **Angola** a few days later. It was during this cruise that Hazel acquainted Jane with the "death" of Tarzan, whom she had known as John Caldwell. Hazel was with the main group of lifeboats after the wreck, the group which came ashore a few miles north of **Tarzan's cottage** and had all the food and firearms. She was married to Lord Tennington early in 1911, right after they were rescued by the same French cruiser which had rescued the Porter party from the same spot two years before (T2;12–13,21,26).

Stuteville, Sir John de An English knight whose estate lay in **Derbyshire** not far from **Torn**. In March of 1262 his castle was captured by **Norman of Torn** (OT;5,7).

Stuteville, Mary de The daughter of **Sir John de Stuteville**; a friend of **Bertrade de**

Montfort's in mid–13th century England. She introduced "Roger de Conde" (a.k.a. Norman of Torn) to Joan de Tany, much to the later sorrow of many people, including the two (OT;7,12).

sub-men A typical World War II stereotype of the Japanese. See also Monkey-men (T22;1).

subhumans The slaves of the Bolgani in the Valley of the Palace of Diamonds could only be called subhuman, though the Bolgani called them Gomangani. They were Negroid but of a very low type, having short legs, long arms, sloping foreheads, and prognathous jaws, and almost no hair except a reddish-brown head growth. They were very stupid, spoke only the tongue of the great apes, lived in houses and used implements fashioned for them by Bolgani craftsmen. With Tarzan's help, they overthrew the Bolgani by sheer force of numbers in 1917 (T9; 8–9,16).

Sublatus The Emperor of the West in Castra Sanguinarius when Tarzan was taken there as a prisoner in 1923. He was a cruel tyrant who was universally hated by his subjects, and was killed in the rebellion begun by Tarzan that August (T12;9,13–20).

submarine, Barsoomian The only submarine used on Barsoom lies in an artificial pool in a building in the center of one of the few islands of any considerable size in Omean. The pool is actually the top of a long column of water connected not to Omean, but rather to a water-filled tunnel far beneath the bottom of the sea that connects with the bottom of a similar submarine pool in a cavern beneath the southern end of the Valley Dor, a good bit inland from the Sea of Korus and presumably at the same elevation as the island in Omean at the other end of the tunnel. This submarine is used to travel from Omean to the tunnel complex beneath the Temple and gardens of Issus, the only part of the land of the First-Born in open air. The ground level there is reached from the submarine cave by an electromagnetic elevator cage. One must assume that there are other means of travel between Omean and the temple, for many more First-Born go back and forth than one submarine could carry; it is likely that the submarine is merely the fastest route (M2;9).

Subura A commercial quarter of Rome which was inhabited by many prostitutes. It lay between the Esquiline, Viminal and Quirinal hills (I;7).

Sudan, An African country to the south of Egypt and northwest of Abyssinia, which is today a republic but in Tarzan's day was ruled jointly by the British and Egyptians (T11;1).

Sudbury A Massachusetts town, just west of Boston, in which Deacon Edmund Rice settled about 1639 (V4;6).

Suffolk A gorilla lord of London in the Valley of Diamonds; he was in charge of Henry VIII's guards (T17;18).

Sullivan One of the crew of the Kincaid who remained loyal to Tarzan after the ship's explosion, and so had to be gotten out of the way for Schneider's plan to succeed (T3;21). Another Sullivan was an American cavalryman killed at the Battle of Cibicu Creek in 1881 (A1;14).

Sulphur Springs A valley of southeastern Arizona which runs from north to south across Cochise County (A1;10).

Sultan of Swat One of the nicknames given to "Babe" Ruth, the great baseball player. Apparently, John Carter must have heard it on one of his visits to Earth, because he gave it as his own title to an Invakian who overheard him telling Ptor Fak that Dotar Sojat was not his real name. He further went on to explain that a sultan is "a Jeddak of Jeddaks" and that Swat is in India (M10;4; 4,9).

sumpitan A blowgun used by the Dyaks of Borneo to shoot poisoned darts (Q;14).

sumpter beast Archaic term for a pack horse (OT;7).

sun, Pellucidarian The eternal noonday sun of Pellucidar is three times the apparent diameter of the real sun and, sitting as it does at the Earth's center, it never sets. It is the dominating force of all life within Pellucidar, and its lack of change is what gives Pellucidar its feeling of timelessness. The inner sun's actual diameter is roughly 100 miles, but what causes it to burn or remain in place are mysteries so far unexplained (P1;2).

Superlative Pictures The chief rival to B.O. Pictures in the 1930s (T17;1).

Suvi One of the original member nations of the Empire of Pellucidar (P2;6). In 1931, it dropped out of the Empire to make war upon Kali, and was punished by David Innes for it (P7:1;2).

sva (*Cpk*) The (C2;3).

Swahili A Bantu language which serves as the common tongue of east and east central Africa. It is the preferred method of communication between Ancient Egyptian-speaking Ashairians and their primarily local black slaves. Tarzan was also fluent in it (T20;13).

Sweetheart Primeval The original title of the second part of *The Eternal Savage* when it first appeared as a separate story. It is abbreviated E2.

swell (American Western slang) Someone who is extremely fashionable; a fop; a fashion-plate (D;1).

Swenson One of the sailors of the *Half-moon*, who joined the Theriere/Byrne faction after the shipwreck. He was killed by the men of Oda Yorimoto when they came to abduct Barbara Harding (K1;9–10).

swimming, great ape The great apes can swim, but do not like to. Tarzan, however, after entering the water to escape a lioness, decided he enjoyed swimming and became quite good at it (T1;5).

swimming, Laythean *see* bathing, Laythean

sword, hooked A strange weapon of the Okarians of Barsoom — it is a broad-sword with a hooked end which is used to ensnare opponents and pull them to oneself (M3;9).

sword, long, Amtorian The Amtorian long sword is a two-edged affair, slightly wider at the point than the hilt (V1;6).

sword, long, Barsoomian A very strong, light, narrow, straight weapon with a needle-like point; the weapon of preference for most fighting men on Barsoom. It can be thrown accurately for up to 30 feet (M1;19). The Okarian version is a bit shorter and broader (M3;9).

sword, long, Julian The long sword was one of the weapons of choice of the Tribe of Julian in post–Kalkar 25th century California but, since they lacked the technology to make them, they bought them from the medieval Kolrado people, with whom they traded periodically (MM3;1).

sword, Mayan The ancient Mayan colonists of Uxmal in the Pacific use a peculiar sword made of heavy, strong wood with two blade edges of obsidian, a volcanic glass which can hold a razor-sharp edge (T24;11).

sword, short, Barsoomian A strong, double-edged sword which is useful for close combat. Like the **long sword**, it can be thrown (M1)(M3;4). The First-Born use a curved version of it, perhaps more like an Earthly broadsword (M2;6–7).

Swords of Mars The eighth book of the Mars series, abbreviated M8, which was originally published as a six-part serial in *Blue Book* magazine from November of 1934 to April of 1935. The events of the story took place around 1930 and were told to Burroughs by John Carter a few years later. In the story, John Carter has decided to end the power of the assassins of Barsoom once and for all, singlehandedly if need be, but finds that it is more difficult than he had imagined. In the meantime, he discovers the secret of two feuding scientists of Zodanga who are racing to the nearer moon, to which Dejah Thoris is abducted so John Carter will surrender his war against the assassins.

Sycamore Canyon A canyon of southern California not far from the Rancho del Ganado (GH;1).

sycee Pure silver in lumps of different sizes, stamped with an assayers' seal to fix value. It was at one time a form of money in China (CG2;12).

Sydney A major port city of Australia's east coast (T22;30).

Syl One of the few remaining Barsoomian rivers; it runs underground for its entire length except where it passes through the Valley Hohr. It is actually larger than the Iss and is probably a tributary of that river; it may also be identical with the river that passes beneath Manator. For much of its length, its cavern is very large and is lit by phosphorescent rock, inhabited by monsters and dotted with weird, colorless fungus-plants. The Syl waters a gorgeous forest of prehistoric plants in the Valley Hohr, then continues on underground (M7;7–8).

Synthetic Men of Mars The ninth book in the Mars series, abbreviated M9, which was originally published as a six-part serial in *Argosy* magazine from January 7 through February 11, 1939. The events took place around 1935 and 1936 and were sent to Earth via **Gridley Wave** by Ulysses Paxton in 1937. The story is that of **Vor Daj**, a padwar in the guard of John Carter, who goes on a mission with the Warlord to locate **Ras Thavas**, who was lost after attempting to retake the **Tower of Thavas** from **Toonol**. They discover that Ras Thavas has succeeded in creating life—the malformed synthetic men, who plan to conquer Barsoom. Vor Daj must stop the synthetic men, save the woman he loves, and destroy the horrible creature from **Vat Room #4**, which threatens to grow uncontrollably until it covers the entire surface of Barsoom.

Syracuse A rich Greek city-state of pre-Roman Sicily (I;5).

Sytor Dwar of the hormad scouting party that captured John Carter and Vor Daj near **Phundahl** and brought them back to **Morbus**. He was a red man and was very courteous and kind to the prisoners. His actual rank was dwar of the 10th Utan of the 1st Dar of the jed's guard of Morbus, but he was originally from **Dusar**, and he became one of Vor Daj's lieutenants when the latter's brain was in **Tor-dur-bar's** body. He later betrayed Vor Daj by telling **Janai** that Vor Daj was dead and Tor-dur-bar was hoping to keep her for himself. He then abducted her and wrecked the other boat so he could not be pursued. He, Janai and **Pandar** (who was helping him) were later recaptured by hormads and returned to Morbus (M9;4,16,19).

T-ray A destructive Amtorian disintegration ray which is fired only by heavy cannons. The ray will disintegrate holes in anything (including the gun itself, which is eventually ruined by T-ray seepage) and is created when **element 93** (**vik-ro**, or **neptunium**) is exposed to **element 97** (**berkelium**) inside the gun barrel when a shutter within the barrel is opened by a crank behind the gun (V1;8).

Ta (Niocene) The woolly rhinoceros (E1;1).

Ta (*Pal*) Tall (T8).

Ta-den "Tall Tree" (*Pal*). A Ho-don warrior of Pal-ul-don whom Tarzan saved from a lion soon after entering the hidden valley; he then befriended Tarzan and began to teach him the tongue of Pal-ul-don. Ta-den was in exile from his people after fleeing the jealousy of his king, **Ko-tan**, with whose daughter **O-lo-a**, Ta-den was in love. Ta-den also befriended **Om-at**, the **Waz-don** chief of the tribe of **Kor-ul-ja**, and later led an army of both Ho-don and Waz-don to invade the city of **A-lur**, where he helped rescue Tarzan and place his own father, **Ja-don**, on the throne. He then married O-lo-a, whose father had earlier been killed by an angry noble (T8;1–3,24–25).

ta-ho The enormous cave lion of Pellucidar; not as large or dangerous a beast as a **tarag**, but close (P7:1;6).

ta-ho-az "Sea lion" (*Pell*). Not the playful pinniped of the Pacific, but a type of ravenous, surface-hunting Pellucidarian elasmosaur (P7:2;3).

Tabernarius A fabric merchant of the lost Roman city of **Castrum Mare** in the 1920s. He was accustomed to sending his son to the house of **Septimus Favonius** for deliveries, a habit the criminal youth later used in a plan to abduct **Favonia**, the daughter of Favonius (T12;22).

tablinum (*Lat*) A balcony or terrace (I;2).

Tabo A Galla warrior of **Abyssinia**, brother to **Fejjuan** (T11;10).

tabu (Also taboo) A magical ban, violation of which means suffering or death (T18;1).

The Tacoma Tribune The newspaper in which **The Girl from Farris's** first appeared as a 26-part serial beginning on February 24, 1920.

Tada, Lieutenant Kumajiro A Japanese officer in occupied **Sumatra** to whom the presence of Tarzan and his "**Foreign Legion**" was reported by **Amat**, a native collaborator, in the spring of 1944. He was killed by **Jerry Lucas** when he tried to behead "Shrimp" Rosetti and "Datbum" Bubanovitch (T22;11–13).

Tafelberg A tiny mountain hamlet of Lutha, home to a famous sanatorium which was one of Lutha's few "claims to the attention of the outside world" (MK1;1,7).

tag (*Amt*) Gate (V2;13).

tag (*Ape*) Neck (T7;10).

Tag kum voo Klambad "Gate of the Psychologists" (*Amt*). One of the five main gates of the Amtorian city of Havatoo; it leads onto Ambad Lat. It was the gate through which Carson Napier first entered the city in 1930 (V2;13).

Tag kum voo Klookantum "Gate of the Physicists" (*Amt*). One of the five gates of the Amtorian city of Havatoo, near which Carson Napier's airplane-building facility lay (V2;16).

Taglat A great ape whose tribe Tarzan joined while amnesiac in 1913. Taglat accompanied him on his search for Jane, whom he felt a vague recollection of when he saw her in the clutches of Achmet Zek and his raiders. Taglat, however, had also conceived of a passion for Jane, and abducted her while Tarzan was otherwise occupied. He was surprised by a lion while trying to gnaw off Jane's fetters and was killed (T5;16–19).

Tagulus A Roman general of the 1st century A.D. who was the commander of the Roman forces in Kent (I;1).

Tagwara An African city in which Sheik Ibn Aswad planned to sell Victoria Custer after he abducted her from Tarzan's estate in 1913 (E1;8).

Tah-clish-un The father of Go-yat-thlay (A2;1).

Tajiri, Colonel Kanji The Japanese officer commanding the sector of occupied Sumatra in which Tarzan and his "Foreign Legion" had set up base in the spring of 1944. He led his men into battle against the Americans and Dutch, but they were wiped out in an ambush planned by Tarzan. He himself was killed by "Shrimp" Rosetti (T22;22).

Taka-mi-musu-bi-no-kami The legendary ancestor of the Japanese people (K1; 12).

Taku Muda A native Sumatran chief who gave asylum to the van der Meer family

in February of 1942 and was killed by the Japanese and his village destroyed for his kindness (T22;1).

tal The Barsoomian "second," which is equal to about .886 second. There are 200 tals in a xat, or Barsoomian "minute" (M2;16).

Tal Hajus The jeddak of the green men of Thark on Barsoom in the 19th century. He was one of the worst of his race — cruel, vicious and depraved. He was the only one of his race known to have experienced what we would term sexual desire, and woe betide the woman of any race who fell into his hands. Sarkoja delivered Dejah Thoris and Sola into his clutches, but they were released by John Carter, and Tal Hajus was later slain in combat by Tars Tarkas, who became the new jeddak (M1).

Talaskar A slave girl of the mines in the Minunian city of Veltopismakus who befriended Tarzan as soon as he arrived there as a quarry slave. She had been born far underground in the quarry and never left the cave in which she was born because she did not wish to mate with a Veltopismakusian. She was very beautiful, but had the unusual ability to alter her facial appearance at will to look ugly. She fell in love with Komodoflorensal, prince of Trohanadalmakus, who was also a prisoner in the mines, and when he and Tarzan escaped from the mines they took Talaskar with them. She married Komodoflorensal when they reached his city, after having told him that she was actually the Princess of Mandalamakus (T10;11–12,15–21).

Talaskhago The king of the Minunian city of Mandalamakus; father of the Princess Talaskar (T10;21).

Talbot, Benson A guest at Cory Blaine's dude ranch (D;3).

Talbot, "Birdie" The fat, bridge-loving wife of Benson Talbot (D;3).

talent A Roman measure of precious metals, equal to 6000 denarii (T12;21)(I;5).

Talu The Prince of Marentina, a city of Okar on Barsoom. Talu was at war with his uncle, Salensus Oll, Jeddak of Jeddaks of Okar, whose government and religion most Okarians (especially those of Marentina) despised. If not for fear of Salensus Oll, Talu would have been made ruler of Okar long before, but with the help of John Carter and his invasion force of red and green men, that situation was changed. Talu helped John Carter and Thuvan Dihn to enter Kadabra by disguising them as yellow men, and gave them a way to recognize one of his agents in that city. After Salensus Oll's death, he became Jeddak of Jeddaks (M3;9–17).

Taman   The Korvan nobleman whom Carson Napier befriended and brought into Sanara across the Zani lines in his anotar in 1930. Taman was of royal blood, married to the Janjong Janhara, and was next in line to the throne after Muso, nephew of Kord, but he was far more popular than Muso, which Muso hated him for. Taman became Jong of Korva after Muso was proven a traitor, and he later made Napier his tanjong for valorous service above all expectation (V3;5–6,16–18).

Tamar   A river of southwest England which pours into Plymouth Bay at Devonport (LC;2).

Tambudza   The oldest wife of M'Ganwazam, Chief of the Waganwazam. While Tarzan was in their village late in the summer of 1912, he was kind to Tambudza, and she repaid this kindness by telling him that there had been a white woman (Jane) with Rokoff's safari (which M'Ganwazam had repeatedly denied to Tarzan), then leading him to their camp (T3;11,14).

Tamil   A dark-skinned Dravidian people of southern India and Ceylon (PB;9).

tan   (*Amt*) Son (V3;5).

tan   (*Pal*) Warrior (T8;2).

Tan   A Galu warrior of Caspak, father of the cos-ata-lo, Co-tan, whom John Bradley married late in 1917. He would not permit her to leave Caspak because of her value as a cos-ata-lo, but was foiled when Bradley simply abducted the girl (with her consent) (C3;5).

Tan Gama   A warrior of the horde of Warhoon on Barsoom at the time they captured Tars Tarkas (M2;14).

Tan Hadron   A nobleman and warrior of Hastor, a city of the Heliumetic Empire on Barsoom. He was the son of the Odwar Had Urtur and a princess of Gathol, and was thus welcomed in the courts of Barsoom even though he was not wealthy. At the time of his greatest adventure he was a padwar in the 5th Utan of the 11th Dar of the 91st Umak, commanded by Tor Hatan. Tan Hadron fell in love with Tor Hatan's daughter Sanoma Tora and vowed to rescue her when she was abducted from her father's palace. Acting on information given by an eyewitness, he headed for Jahar, but detoured to Tjanath on the advice of Tavia, a slave girl he rescued on the way. He was there imprisoned and sentenced to die The Death, which involved being dumped into the cavern of the River Syl; with Nur An, another prisoner, he traveled down the buried river to the hideous city of Ghasta, ruled by the mad Jed Ghron. He and Nur An escaped that place of madness and torture by making a makeshift hot-air balloon out of the amazing silk of Ghasta (see spiders) and filling it with hot air from the palace's great chimney. They eventually ended up in Jhama, where he met Phor Tak, who enabled him to build the invisible flier (called *Jhama* after the castle) in which he rescued Tavia and Sanoma Tora, only to be betrayed by the latter and stranded in U-gor by Tul Axtar, Jeddak of Jahar. After a few days, Tan Hadron and Tavia found the *Jhama*, which had been abandoned by Tul Axtar, and in it they escaped back to Jahar in time to save the attacking fleet of Helium from utter destruction at the hands of the Jaharian fleet and its disintegration rifles. Tul Axtar then stole both Tavia and the *Jhama*, but Tan Hadron was able to regain them both at Phor Tak's laboratory and dispense with both Tul Axtar and the mad Phor Tak. He then married the sweet and faithful Tavia instead of the shallow and faithless Sanoma Tora (M7).

Years later, while searching for John Carter and Llana of Gathol, Tan Hadron was shot down by the Panars and impressed into their navy. He was later found by John Carter, who was disguised as a Panar officer and had swung command of a ship, aboard which he made Tan Hadron second padwar. When the crew mutinied, Tan Hadron was kept as navigator; he was finally rescued after Hin Abtol's defeat (M10:3;7–10)(M10:4;13).

Tan-klu   (*Ape*) Rooster (TC).

Tana   A female ape of the tribe of Kerchak whose husband was in the habit of abusing her (T1;12).

Tanar, the Fleet One The son of **Ghak the Hairy One**, King of **Sari**; Tanar was thus the Prince of Sari and **Dian the Beautiful's** first cousin. He was a special favorite of hers and of **David Innes'** which made the shock even worse when he was abducted by the **Korsars** during their retreat from **Thuria** in 1925, prompting Innes to launch an expedition in pursuit. He escaped from the Korsars with **Stellara**, the daughter of their ruler, and after several adventures ended up imprisoned in a Korsar dungeon in their capital. He eventually escaped again with Stellara and made his way back to Sari, where he told **Abner Perry** about David Innes' incarceration under the palace of Korsar, thus enabling Perry to radio Burroughs to send help for Innes (P3).

Tanar of Pellucidar The third book in the Pellucidar series, abbreviated P3. The incidents of the book took place from 1924 or 1925 to 1926, when they were communicated to Burroughs by **Abner Perry** via **Gridley Wave** transmission in an urgent desire to summon him to help his friend **David Innes**, who had been captured and imprisoned by the fierce **Korsar** sea rovers, descendants of a shipload of pirates who had become trapped in the Arctic Ocean and eventually escaped northward into Pellucidar. The book is the story of **Tanar the Fleet One**, son of **Ghak the Hairy One**, who was dispatched as a messenger to the Korsars by Innes and was imprisoned by them. He escaped and was forced to find his way home across a savage world accompanied only by the Korsar girl **Stellara**.

tand (*Ape*) "No" or "not"; also used to form the reverse of some other words, as in the case of "nala" (up) and "tand nala" (down) (T17;14)(T22;9).

tand-ho "Not many" (*Ape*). Few (TC).

tand-litu "Not sharp" (*Ape*). Dull (TC).

tand-lul "Not wet" (*Ape*). Dry (TC).

tand-nala "Not up" (*Ape*). Down (T22;9).

tand-panda "No noise" (*Ape*). Silent or silence (TC).

tand-popo "Not eat" (*Ape*). Starve (TC).

tand-ramba "Not lie down" (*Ape*). Get up (TC).

tand-unk "No go" (*Ape*). Stay (TC).

tand-vulp "Not full" (*Ape*). Empty (TC).

tanda (*Ape*) Dark (TC).

tandak (*Ape*) Thin (TC).

Tandar An island in the **Korsar Az** of Pellucidar to which a storm carried **Dian the Beautiful** after she escaped from the Land of the **Xexots** in 1931. She was enslaved among the Tandar people, who keep **tarags** trained from cubhood as pets, war beasts, guards, and sources of fur. The **Menats**, who were an enemy people of the far side of the island, kept **ta-hos** in the same way (P7:3;3–5).

tandlan (*Ape*) Left (TC).

tandor The Imperial mammoth of Pellucidar (P1;4).

tandoraz "Sea mammoth" (*Pell*). The Pellucidarian word for a **pleisiosaur**, one of the many terrors of a Pellucidarian ocean (P1;4).

Tanga A port on the coast of **Tanganyika**, northwest of **Zanzibar** (T7;2).

Tanga-tanga The northernmost city of the Land of the **Xexots** in Pellucidar; it lies right on the **Nameless Strait**. Like **Lolo-lolo**, it is a small walled city of clay houses, but a true city nonetheless (P7:2;4).

Tanganyika The name given to **German East Africa** after it was taken over by the British following **World War I** (T7;1).

Tangor "From Nothing" (*Uni*). The name given to the American fighter pilot hero of *Beyond the Farthest Star* by Harkas Yen, the psychiatrist who examined and cared for him when he first appeared on **Poloda**. Tangor did not give his real name in the book because of the publicity-shyness of his Earthly family — suffice to say that he went to Europe to fight for the British against **Hitler** in **World War II**, was shot down in September of 1939, and was somehow mysteriously transported to the city of **Orvis** in the country of **Unis** on the planet Poloda. He was adopted by the Unisans and became loyal to that country, eventually becoming a flier in their air force and fighting the 101-year-old war with the conquering **Kapars** of the planet's far side. He was shot down twice, once behind enemy lines, but managed to escape and return to Orvis both times (B1).

He later went to **Kapara** on a secret mission

when a defector approached him to join her; he went for the purpose of stealing, if possible, the plans for a secret **power amplifier** supposedly developed by the Kapars. He told the Kapars of his non–Polodan origin and said he had been working on an interplanetary ship on his own world, but did not let them know that he knew about the amplifier. During this period he was closely observed and managed to convince the authorities that he was a good Kapar, so that after the inventor of the amplifier was executed for treason (on the evidence of his own son), Tangor was recruited to finish the prototype. He did so, then fled back to Unis with the only working model after committing the plans to memory and destroying all other records of the device. Soon afterward, he and **Handon Gar** took a prototype ship to **Tonos,** but whether they ever returned from that trip, and how Tangor was able to activate Burroughs' typewriter in **Hawaii** without being physically present, are mysteries that may never be explained (B2).

"Tangor Returns" The second novella comprising *Beyond the Farthest Star,* which recounts the further adventures of Tangor on **Poloda** as a spy for his adopted country of **Unis.** It is abbreviated B2 and took place in 1940.

tanjong "Son-king" (*Amt*). Prince (V3;5).

Tann A small river of **Lutha,** for which the noble **von der Tann** family was named. Their castle, also called Tann, lies in the **Old Forest** on the banks of the River Tann (MK1; 1–2).

tanpi An oval gold Barsoomian coin worth roughly one U.S. dollar, 1941 standard. One tanpi is made up of ten **teepi** or 100 **pi** (M10:2;7,11).

Tant The Ganak of Pellucidar who tried to challenge **Kru's** claim to the chieftainship of his tribe after **Drovan** was killed by **Wilhelm von Horst** early in 1928. Von Horst later killed Tant as well (P5;19).

Tantor (*Ape*) The elephant; the only animal able to strike fear into the hearts of the mighty bull apes. Tarzan made friends with the elephants, gaining some measure of influence over the mighty beasts, and often rode on their backs; he was also rescued on more than one occasion by Tantor (T1;4,9). **Korak**

also befriended Tantor and could influence him (T4;23–27).

Tanus A Barsoomian warrior of **Gathol** who accompanied **Gahan** in his search for **Tara of Helium** during the great hurricane of 1915 (M5;3).

Tany, Joan de A friend of **Mary de Stuteville's** who enabled **Norman of Torn** to meet with Mary for word of **Bertrade de Montfort** in the summer of 1263. While visiting at Castle de Tany, Norman became very friendly with Joan and was also very drawn to her, but did nothing about it because he loved Bertrade. Joan fell in love with him, but could not have married him even had he loved her because she would never be allowed to marry a man who was low-born (as Norman was thought to be). After he rescued her from **de Fulm** and returned her home, he revealed his true identity as the great bandit to her, and with a broken heart she committed suicide (OT;12–14).

Tany, Sir Richard de An English knight of Essex who **Norman of Torn** met and let pass on his way to London in the summer of 1263 (OT;12).

Tanzania The modern name of the country **Tarzan** knew first as **German East Africa** and later as **Tanganyika** (T7;1).

tape, surgical One of the many medical inventions of **Ras Thavas;** this tape is used to close wounds. It is antiseptic, locally anaesthetic, promotes healing, and is much quicker to apply than stitches (M6;1).

tapestries, Barsoomian The Zodangans produce a tapestry that, while quite opaque from one side, is as transparent as gauze from the other. It was the custom to hang such tapestries a few feet from the walls when decorating royal chambers, thus providing a corridor in which guards or spies could stand (M1;22).

tapida (*Apa*) Dawn (A1).

Taprobane The ancient name for Ceylon, from which a great merchant fleet carrying Oriental treasure and slaves came every year to **Myos-Hormos** in Egypt, from there to be carried overland to the **Nile,** downriver to Alexandria, then to Rome. In A.D. 98 **Marcus Crispus Sanguinarius** captured the caravan as it reached the Nile, providing all of his men with wives, treasure and slaves (T12;10).

tar (*Ape*) White (T1;5).

tar-bur "White cold" (*Ape*). Snow (possibly a Tarzan coinage) (TC).

Tar-gash "White Tooth" (*Ape*). A Sagoth of the tribe who captured Tarzan on his expedition to Pellucidar in 1927. Tar-gash quickly came to respect the ape-man after he saved the Sagoth's life by alerting him to an assassination attempt on him by M'wa-lot, Tar-gash's king. They became friends and travelled together as Tarzan searched for his companions and the O-220. He returned to his people after Tarzan was carried off by a thipdar (T13;4–9).

Tara of Helium The daughter of John Carter and Dejah Thoris. She is every bit as beautiful as her mother, but more spoiled by her father, and is accustomed to having her own way. She was insulted by Gahan of Gathol's forwardness at a court function in 1915 and went out alone in her personal flier, but was carried off by a rare Barsoomian hurricane and blown halfway around the planet to Bantoom, the city of the Kaldanes, who captured her and would have eaten her or worse had not Gahan and Ghek (a Kaldane whose latent emotions Tara had released through her words and singing) rescued her. They were later captured and imprisoned while seeking food and water near Manator, but she was again rescued by Ghek's cleverness and Gahan's skill and courage. She was then recaptured by the Manatorians and made a stake in their jetan game, won by Gahan in disguise, again recaptured, and finally freed from a forced marriage to O-Tar, Jeddak of Manator, by the armies of Manatos, Gathol and Helium, which invaded Manator and overthrew O-Tar. She later married Gahan and they had a daughter, Llana of Gathol, who also became embroiled in adventures (M5)(M10).

tarag The huge saber-toothed tiger of Pellucidar, an enormous carnivore which is colored much like a Bengal tiger, but with greater contrast in its colors. The things are incredibly vicious and eat almost any meat (P1;6). At least some of them have progressed to a higher plane of intelligence and are capable of joint action to herd huge groups of animals together for a mass kill (P4;5).

Tarawa A city on an atoll of the Gilbert Islands (modern Kiribati) in the Pacific Ocean. It is the capital of those islands and the site of the mission where Sarina learned to speak English (T22;23).

Tardos Mors The Jeddak of Helium and its empire on Barsoom; the grandfather of Dejah Thoris. Tardos Mors is the greatest of the red jeddaks of Barsoom, and his empire is the largest, most powerful, most technologically advanced, and richest. John Carter became a prince of his house by marrying Dejah Thoris (M1). While searching for Carthoris, he and Mors Kajak became marooned and imprisoned in Okar, thanks to the Guardian of the North, but they were later discovered and helped to escape by John Carter (M3).

tarel A light, extremely strong Amtorian fiber which is used in cordage and clothesmaking. It is taken from the web of the targo; a piece as thick as wrapping twine can support the weight of ten men (V1;6).

targo A huge, hairy black tree spider of Amtor from whose web tarel is collected. The targo's only markings are yellow spots the size of saucers, one over each eye. It emits horrible shrieking screams when attacking or threatened, and its venom paralyzes man-sized creatures in a deathlike state for about a day (V1;6–7).

Tarids One of the humanoid races of Ladan; the Tarids have milk-white skin and blue hair. They were once a powerful nation, but were destroyed in a war and retreated to a distant corner of their world; there are only about a thousand of them left, and they live in a gorgeous castle built of precious gems. One of their wisest men developed the ability to implant a hypnotic suggestion in the minds of others, thus rendering him invisible and inaudible, and he taught this power to the other Tarids. It is only this power, their seclusion, and their policy of killing all strangers that has kept them safe since their retreat. The power can be nullified by a person if he uses self-hypnosis to defeat their suggestion of invisibility with one of his own that they are visible. The Tarids wear armor of gold and use medieval weapons, being fairly low in technological development. They believe in astrology and worship the Sun, Barsoom and the stars. Both Gar Nal's and John Carter's interplanetary flier landed at the castle of the Tarids when they came to Ladan, and both parties were captured and imprisoned by their invisible foes, who planned to sacrifice them to the sun god at the most astrologically propitious moment (M8;16–18).

Tario The Jeddak of Lothar on Barsoom and leader of the **Etherealist** school of philosophy of that city; he had been jeddak for more than 100,000 years, at least since the founding of Lothar after the collapse of the Orovars' empires around that time. Because of the lack of real women in Lothar, Tario had long ago issued an edict prohibiting the materialization of women, because he believed it would be easy for the citizens to control himself and others through these phantom women's charms. He at first believed **Thuvia of Ptarth** to be such a phantom, but after he discovered her to be real he decided to make love to her, for which attempt Thuvia put a knife in him. He recovered quickly enough to dump her, **Carthoris**, and **Jav** into the pit of **Komal**, the banth-god of Lothar, to whom Tario was wont to feed **Realists** when no **Torquasian** prisoners were available (M4;8).

Tarmangani "White Great Ape" (Ape). The white man (T4;10).

Tarrant The sailor of the *Arrow* mutineers who killed the bossy **Snipes** with a pick while the group was burying the treasure they had mutinied to steal from **Professor Porter** (T1;17).

Tars Tarkas Originally a chieftain of a small community of green Barsoomians of the horde of **Thark**, he later became jeddak of that entire horde (by killing **Tal Hajus**) and several smaller ones. He was a great warrior and statesman and the first Barsoomian to have any contact with the Earthman John Carter; Tars Tarkas attacked Carter at the Thark **incubator**, which he thought him to be breaking into. They later became great friends and comrades-in-arms, for this savage green man had many of the finer emotions which were entirely lacking in his fellows, including the capacity for love. Tars Tarkas fought alongside John Carter in the sack of **Zodanga**, during which he demonstrated his amazing leadership abilities by temporarily uniting 150,000 green men, comprising at least seven hordes (M1;3–17,24–27).

Tars Tarkas later made the **Pilgrimage** (for reasons which are never adequately explained) and helped John Carter fight his way out of the **Valley Dor**. He later again led his combined hordes to invade the Land of the **First-Born** (M2) and **Kadabra**, the capital of **Okar**. It was he who announced to John Carter his appointment as **Warlord of Barsoom**, and they ever after remained good friends as Tars Tarkas strove to bring civilization to his long-benighted people (M3).

tartum (*Amt*) Laboratory (V2;15).

Tarzan The famous ape-man, born **John Clayton, Jr.**, the son of the castaway British Lord Greystoke, who was set ashore in west Africa when the crew of his ship mutinied. Lord Greystoke was later killed by the king great ape **Kerchak**, and his infant son was taken away by **Kala**, a she-ape whose own baby had been killed earlier that day. She named the baby Tarzan, which in the **tongue of the great apes** means "Whiteskin," and adopted him, nursing him at her breasts and raising him as an ape. He grew slowly compared to the ape-children, but was of course much brighter than they, and even much brighter than most humans — he taught himself to do things that almost no one else could do, such as learning to make ropes out of grass (though he had never seen a rope) and teaching himself to read (though he initially had no idea what a book was for). The young Tarzan developed physically more quickly than most humans, and by age 10 was stronger and more physically developed than most adult men. In youth, he developed clever tricks to play upon the older apes which made him their equal, such as his game of lassoing the neck of **Tublat** and choking him senseless. His speed and cunning kept him alive as a child, and these and his immense strength brought him to ascendancy over the other apes by the time he reached manhood (T1;3–7).

Tarzan's first great adventure happened on the day he discovered the secret of opening the door of his late father's **cottage** and discovered the books with which he would later teach himself to read. He also discovered his late father's **hunting knife**, which saved his life soon afterward because upon leaving the cottage he was attacked by **Bolgani**, the gorilla, and killed the huge adversary with the knife. He was maimed and left at death's door by the battle, but Kala nursed him back to health; he bore the scars of this encounter for life. Soon after he reached manhood, at about age 18, Kala was killed by a black cannibal called Kulonga, who was the first human other than himself Tarzan had ever seen. He killed the man, but not before taking his bow and arrows (which he had seen him use) and learning the location of his village, which he afterward frequented to steal supplies and food, and also to have fun by playing tricks on the superstitious natives. A few months after the death of Kala, he was challenged by Kerchak and killed him, thus promoting himself to the kingship. He was soon afterward challenged by Terkoz, son of Tublat, and defeated the great bull but did not kill him, leaving him instead to the kingship so Tarzan could go off on his own. In the fight, a great piece of his scalp was torn loose, leaving a scar on his forehead that ever after turned red when Tarzan became angry (T1;6–13).

Tarzan then moved to his father's cottage by the sea and there encountered white men for the first time — the party of Professor Archimedes Q. Porter, who had been put ashore by mutineers who wished to steal the treasure that Porter had come to Africa to recover. He fell in love with Jane, the professor's beautiful daughter, and saved her from a lioness. He also saved the professor, his secretary, and his own cousin William Clayton from being lost in the jungle. Furthermore, he dug up the treasure from where the mutineers had buried it and moved it to the natural clearing used by the apes for meetings — not because he knew what was in the chest, but rather because he knew it must be something valuable and, like an ape, wished to imitate the act of burying the chest (T1;13–17).

Tarzan provided food for the Porter party for a month and even wrote Jane a love letter, but he was never able to give it to her because she was abducted by Terkoz. Tarzan killed Terkoz, then took Jane for himself and brought her to a hiding place in the jungle where he fed and protected her, then returned her to her father the next day; it was at this time that she fell in love with him. Directly after he returned her Tarzan rescued Lt. Paul d'Arnot, a French naval officer from the cruiser that had arrived shortly after Jane's abduction, from the tribe of Mbonga, who had captured him when he led a search party

into the jungle to look for Jane. The lieutenant was weak and dying; Tarzan nursed him back to health, afraid to move him or leave him alone for long. By the time he could travel (a week later), the cruiser had left with the Porter party aboard, having given up Tarzan and d'Arnot for dead. Tarzan, however, determined to follow Jane to America, where d'Arnot (who had taught him a little French) had said she was going. Tarzan and d'Arnot journeyed north to a European outpost (while d'Arnot taught Tarzan human language, manners and customs along the way) and they chartered a boat, fetched Professor Porter's treasure, then returned to France, where Tarzan's fingerprints were taken and compared with those of the infant Lord Greystoke recorded in his father's diary, thus proving that Tarzan was indeed that child and the rightful Lord Greystoke (T1;19–28).

Even after saving Jane from having to marry Robert Canler by returning her father's treasure, Tarzan did not acquaint her with the facts of his birth because the girl, confused by her inner conflict over her passion for Tarzan, had already given her promise of marriage to William Clayton; if Tarzan revealed himself, Clayton's title and estates would pass to him (their rightful owner), thus depriving Jane of them as well. He then went back to Paris, but on the ship saved the Count and Countess de Coude from the trumped-up accusations of dishonor placed upon them by the countess' evil brother, Nikolas Rokoff, who hoped to blackmail the count into giving him French military secrets to sell to the Russians. In this way Tarzan gained the friendship of the de Coudes and the hatred of Rokoff and his valet, Alexis Paulvitch, who tried to have Tarzan killed and then falsely arrested soon after his arrival in Paris; they failed on both counts. Tarzan became a close friend of the countess', but Rokoff was able to use the friendship to form a new blackmail plot against her to replace his old one, thus keeping her from turning him into the authorities and manipulating the count into challenging Tarzan to a duel. Tarzan let the count shoot him, but the wounds were not fatal and Tarzan afterward showed him the signed confession he had forced out of Rokoff which, in conjunction with his impression of Tarzan's incredible courage and nobility, caused the nobleman to become Tarzan's friend. He got Tarzan a job as an agent for the French War Office, in pursuit of which he travelled to **Algeria** to spy on **Lt. Gernois**, a suspected traitor whom he discovered had dealings with Rokoff (T1;28) (T2;1–7).

On several occasions, Rokoff paid men to kill Tarzan, but Tarzan escaped him every time, making several friends along the way and completing his mission successfully by stealing back the papers Rokoff had blackmailed Gernois for, causing the hapless officer to kill himself and freeing Tarzan for his next mission in **Cape Town**. On the ship to Cape Town, he met Jane's friend **Hazel Strong** and befriended her, then learned that Rokoff was on board in disguise. That night, Rokoff and Paulvitch surprised Tarzan and threw him into the Atlantic after stealing back the Gernois papers. Tarzan managed to make it to shore, finding to his astonishment that he had been thrown overboard almost exactly opposite his cottage. He soon travelled inland to explore and befriended the warlike but noble **Waziri** tribe after saving one of their warriors from a lion, for which service he was adopted into the tribe. After leading them to victory over a group of **Arabs** a few months later, Tarzan was made chief of the Waziri, because the old chief had died in the fight (T2;8–17).

The Waziri soon led Tarzan to the lost city of **Opar**, whence their fathers had gotten a large amount of gold in a skirmish many years before. The Waziri would not go far into the frightening ruin with Tarzan, and he was captured by the ape-like men of Opar as a sacrifice to the sun, but escaped with the help of the high priestess **La**, whom he saved from the berserk rage of the priest **Tha**. She hid him in a subterranean room connected to a long-forgotten secret passage which led to the secret treasure vault of Opar, then out of the city through barred doors to an exit atop a huge granite boulder about a mile west of the city wall; this boulder was impossible to climb for anyone besides Tarzan. He then returned with his Waziri, robbed the treasure vault, and secretly buried the gold in the amphitheater of the apes, as he had the professor's treasure two years before. He then returned to check on his cabin and saved the shipwrecked William Clayton and Jane from a lion (unknown to them), but did not stay long enough to watch Clayton kiss Jane, and so did not hear her repudiation of him (T2;19–22).

He rejoined the tribe of Kerchak for a short

while, then heard of the capture of Jane by the Oparians and rushed to her rescue, arriving just in time to save her from being sacrificed. They were soon afterward married in Tarzan's cottage by Professor Porter and rescued by d'Arnot's ship, cruising in its habitual patrol of the African coast. Tarzan at that time captured Rokoff and took back the secret papers, then turned Rokoff in to the French navy and returned to England a rich man with his titles, lands and Oparian gold after William Clayton died of a fever and Tarzan was revealed as the true Lord Greystoke (T2;23–26).

Tarzan lived in peace for awhile until Rokoff escaped from prison and kidnapped his infant son **Jack** in the latter part of 1912, then lured Tarzan into a trap and kidnapped him and Jane as well. Rokoff left him on an uninhabited island off the African coast after telling him what he planned for young Jack, but no sooner had the ship gone out of sight than Tarzan was attacked by a group of great apes of a slightly different species than those among whom he had grown up. He killed their king and defeated **Akut**, their strongest bull, thereby immediately gaining their respect and loyalty, especially that of the highly intelligent Akut, whom he later saved from a stalking panther. He later saved another panther from a fallen tree which had pinned it to the ground and taught it to follow him by giving it half of his kills, eventually training it to obey his summons and kill on command. Soon afterward, he was attacked by the **Wagambi** tribe (who had come to the island by chance) and killed them all (with the help of the apes and the panther **Sheeta**) except for their chief, **Mugambi**, whom he impressed into service to take him, Sheeta, Akut, and 11 other apes to the mainland in his canoe. He pursued Rokoff up the **Ugambi** River for several days and was eventually captured by a cannibal tribe that Rokoff had promised presents to, but was saved by Akut's tribe and Sheeta (T3;1–10).

He then continued in pursuit of Rokoff, guided by the Swede **Anderssen**, who had helped Jane to escape and been shot and left to die by Rokoff for his good deed. Tarzan chased Rokoff back down the Ugambi to the **Kincaid**, which he and his beasts boarded, defeating Rokoff's crew and rescuing Jane. Tarzan would have killed Rokoff, but he was beat to the punch by Sheeta, who tore the Russian to shreds. Tarzan then took the

Kincaid to Jungle Island to return Sheeta and the apes of Akut home, but a bomb secretly planted aboard by Paulvitch exploded, marooning the party on the island until Tarzan and his apes defeated the crew of the *Cowrie*, a mutiny ship that had landed and abducted Jane. Tarzan took that ship back to England, leaving the panther and apes behind, and found when he got there that his son was actually safe at home, because Paulvitch had double-crossed Rokoff and ransomed the real baby to Tarzan's lawyer, giving Rokoff a foundling instead (T3;11–21).

The next portion of Tarzan's life is a bit confusing; according to *The Son of Tarzan* he spent the next ten years living in London, raising Jack in ignorance of his life story until the night father and son were reunited with Akut in a music hall where the ape had been brought to perform by a much-changed Paulvitch. Since Jane would not allow Akut to live with them, Jack ran away to Africa with the ape and was kept there by a chain of bad circumstances; the Claytons then returned to their African estates and Tarzan established a sort of frontier order over the area. He would permit no white hunter to use poisoned bait, kill too many animals, or maltreat his porters, and thus came to be loved and respected by all virtuous Africans (black and white) and feared and hated by evil ones. He eventually found his son and brought him back to civilization (T4;1–4,14–18,27). While the bit about Tarzan's establishing order is certainly true, there are some nagging questions about the rest, not the least of which are Jane's rather bizarre and uncharacteristic behavior and the problem of Jack's jumping age, plus the fact that the events of the next ten years are clearly recorded, and do not include any long periods spent in England; see **Clayton, Jack** for a more complete discussion.

In 1913, Tarzan lost his entire fortune in a bad investment and was forced to return to Opar for more gold, only to be felled by falling debris in an earthquake and rendered amnesiac, a condition that would later recur whenever he experienced head injury. After this accident, he discovered the lost jewel room of Opar and took a pouch full of gems with him, only to have them stolen from him by the Belgian **Werper**, who had followed him to Opar and whom he had saved from sacrifice there, precipitating the anger of La, whom he unknowingly spurned again. After escaping La

and her priests, Tarzan set out on Werper's trail, but lost it through a strange combination of circumstances. On the way, however, he saw Jane attempting to escape **Achmet Zek** (who had abducted her after destroying Tarzan's farm) and vaguely recognized her, so he captured her from the Arab with the help of two Great Apes, one of whom abducted her from him. He eventually regained his memory with the help of Werper, but was then captured by a detachment of Belgian troops who had come to arrest Werper and thought Tarzan was his accomplice. With the help of the apes he escaped, rescued Jane, tracked down the Waziri (whom he had lost after his accident), and rebuilt his farm with the gold from Opar and the jewels, which he later recovered from Werper's corpse (T5).

In the autumn of 1914 his new estate (in **Kenya**) was destroyed by a German detachment after the beginning of **World War I**, and Jane was abducted and made to look dead. Tarzan exacted revenge on the Germans responsible for the deed, fought the German army as a guerrilla for a few months, then headed for the interior to try to forget about Jane, only to be forced by conscience to rescue **Lt. Smith-Oldwick**, a downed British flier, and **Bertha Kircher** (whom Tarzan thought a German spy) from savages, then from the lost city of **Xuja**, which lay deep in a hidden, forested valley in the middle of a desert wasteland in western **Tanganyika**. At the end of the adventure, he discovered that Jane was alive, and set out on the months-old trail to rescue her (T7). It eventually led into the hidden land of **Pal-ul-don**, where Tarzan met and befriended members of the strange **Ho-don** and **Waz-don** races and found Jane a prisoner in **A-lur**, capital of the Ho-don, where Tarzan came pretending to be a god. After several setbacks Tarzan rescued Jane, helped overturn the millennia-old priesthood which controlled Pal-ul-don, installed a good and noble king on the throne, and left for home, leaving the stuff of legends and myths to grow behind him (T8).

On the way home, he adopted a lion cub whom he named **Jad-bal-ja** and trained, and who (two years later) tracked him all the way to the **Valley of the Palace of Diamonds**, into which Tarzan had escaped from Opar with La after having been drugged by the members of the **Hawkes** expedition (who wanted to rob Opar) and left to be captured by the

Oparians. In this valley, he and Jad-bal-ja succeeded in overthrowing the rule of the Bolgani, the mighty gorilla-men who had ruled the valley for ages, and with the help of the surviving Bolgani he returned La to Opar and her throne. He then set out to locate the Hawkes expedition, but was forced by circumstances into helping them instead. He was then reunited with his family, but lost the trail of Esteban Miranda, a member of the expedition who looked just like Tarzan and had been impersonating him. Through the treachery of Kraski, another expedition member, Tarzan lost the bag of diamonds he had brought from the valley, but he did get back the gold the expedition had stolen from Opar, albeit in a roundabout way (T9).

Even the diamonds were later recovered by the Waziri warrior Usula while Tarzan was missing in the land of the Minunians, where he had crashed his airplane on his first solo flight. He was well-received at the city of Trohanadalmakus after rescuing their prince from a zertalacolol, but was captured in battle by the inhabitants of the city of Veltopismakus, reduced to their stature (about 18") by scientific wizardry, and set to work as a quarry slave. He finally escaped, fled Minuni, and eventually regained his size and his home (T10).

A few years later he fell victim to a charging elephant shot at by an Arab raider, and was thus thrust into an adventure; he had to stop the Arabs from raiding the lost city of Nimmr, inhabited by the descendants of lost crusaders, and also rescue James Hunter Blake, a young American whom Tarzan had met and taken a liking to. Eventually, thanks more to the efforts of the Nimmrites and Tarzan's Waziri than to Tarzan himself (for a change) the raiders were driven from the Valley of the Sepulcher, captured, and given to the Gallas as slaves. Meanwhile, Tarzan had also located Blake, who as it turned out was in Nimmr and needed no help. The treasure the Arabs had taken from the City of the Sepulcher (rivals of Nimmr) Tarzan took and added to his already great wealth (T11).

In 1923 Tarzan journeyed to the Wiramwazi Mountains in search of Erich von Harben, son of his missionary friend Dr. Karl von Harben, and there discovered a pair of lost outposts of ancient Rome which had been founded by the rogue general Marcus Crispus Sanguinarius in A.D. 86. After almost

being executed several times, Tarzan managed to start a slave revolt in Castra Sanguinarius, overthrow its corrupt emperor, place a good one on the throne, and locate von Harben, then returned home with his faithful Waziri (T12).

In 1926, he was asked by Burroughs and Jason Gridley of Tarzana to lead an expedition to Pellucidar to free David Innes from the dungeons of the Korsars. Tarzan accepted, taking along Muviro and nine other Waziri warriors, only to find that much of his woodcraft was hampered (if not rendered completely useless) by the alien conditions of Pellucidar. He fought his way through, though, making friends along the way, until he finally reunited with the Waziri, then Gridley, and finally the rest of the force. After freeing Innes from the Korsars, the expedition headed home and Tarzan returned to his own familiar jungle late in 1927 (T13). Directly upon his return, however, before he even reached home, he was interrupted by the necessity of foiling the Zveri expedition, led by a Russian communist who hoped to conquer Africa. In his own inimitable style, he caused terror and dissent among the Russian's native troops until they finally deserted and Zveri's plans were foiled. During the same period he had to find La of Opar, whom he had rescued from imprisonment in Opar's dungeons and then become separated from. Eventually, he led his Waziri to return La to her throne once again, only to find that the usurpers Dooth and Oah, with their traitorous followers, had already been executed by the loyal Oparians (T14).

About a year later, one Leon Stabutch was sent by Moscow to kill Tarzan for his part in the Zveri fiasco; Stabutch caught up with Tarzan while he was in the Ghenzi region fighting a marauding band of shiftas, whom Stabutch promptly allied himself with. During the same period, Tarzan also tracked Lafayette Smith, a lost American geologist, into the hidden land of Midian, where a race of hideous religious fanatics practiced their twisted religion; he rescued Smith and Lady Barbara Collis, a downed British aviatrix. With the help of his Waziri and Danny "Gunner" Patrick (a tommy gun–toting, displaced Chicago mobster) the shiftas were defeated, but Tarzan needed no help to kill Stabutch and thus restore peace to the jungle for awhile (T15).

In September and October of 1930, Tarzan travelled to Cathne, the City of Gold in the Ethiopian Highlands, and there became the object of infatuation of the mad Queen Nemone. Because of the queen's favor, Tarzan became the target of several plots which he defeated, but his repeated spurning of the queen eventually turned her against him as well and she tried to have him killed, but died by her own hand after Jad-bal-ja killed her lion, Belthar, with whom she had a strange rapport (T16).

In 1931, Tarzan went on a mission to destroy the evil cult of the Leopard Men, and in the process was hit on the head by a falling tree and suffered a relapse of his amnesia. During this period he was convinced by Orando, a young Utenga warrior, that he was his muzimo (the spirit of Orando's ancestral namesake), and went with the Utenga warriors to destroy the Leopard Men. After regaining his memory he helped even more effectively, rescuing a white ivory poacher from the Leopard Men and trapping the few surviving cult members on an island from which they could not escape. He then saved a white woman called Kali Bwana from a pygmy tribe, was himself saved from them by his old friends Zu-tho and Ga-yat, and informed the European authorities of the whereabouts of the remaining Leopard Men (T18).

In 1932, Tarzan was ranging in the Belgian Congo when he encountered a film crew making a movie called The Lion Man on location in the Ituri Forest. The safari had encountered considerable trouble from the hostile Bansuto natives, and matters were made worse when the Arabs who had accompanied the film crew decided to abduct the female lead and her double. Tarzan had to save the safari from the Bansuto, collect its wandering members, and save both of the girls from the intelligent, English-speaking gorillas of the Valley of Diamonds, who were the end results of genetic engineering experiments by a 100-year-old English biologist who called himself God and wished to use Tarzan and the actresses' genetic material to rejuvenate his aging body. Tarzan of course escaped, rescued the girls, brought the safari back together, and helped them finish their movie. A year later, he travelled incognito to Hollywood, where he was rejected for the part of Tarzan in an upcoming movie. After visiting

Burroughs at Tarzana (the town named in his honor, which lies only a few miles from Hollywood) Tarzan quickly fled back to Africa (T17).

In 1934, Tarzan set out to rescue Buira, the daughter of Muviro, who had been abducted by the Kavuru, a race of white savages of central Africa who made a habit of abducting young women in order to use their glands in an immortality potion. Unknown to Tarzan, Jane was on a plane which crashed nearby and she, too, had become a prisoner of the Kavuru. Tarzan saved both Jane and Buira, put a stop to the Kavuru's abductions, and stole their supply of immortality pellets so he and Jane could thereafter be eternally young. Thus, the oldest Tarzan ever looked was a very youthful 46, and Jane a few years younger, because the immortality pellets kept them looking as though they were in their 20s thereafter (T19).

In 1935, Tarzan was asked by Haile Selassie to spy on the Italians (who were attempting to invade Ethiopia), and on his way to do so he found a lost American travel writer, Stanley Wood, who had escaped from the fierce Amazons of Kaji, only to be drawn back to their country by the power of the Gonfal, a huge diamond with mystic powers owned by Mafka, an evil old wizard. Tarzan entered the country, killed Mafka, and freed Wood, his companions, and Gonfala, Queen of the Kaji, who was actually the daughter of the long-lost British nobleman, Lord Mountford. Gonfala was soon abducted and the Gonfal stolen by Spike and Troll (two hunters who had been with Wood) and taken by them to Thenar, where they were all enslaved. Tarzan followed them by way of Cathne, where he got into a little trouble with his old enemy Tomos, but came out all right; he then went to Athne, where he found that the old king and government had been overthrown and a dictatorship established. Tarzan escaped with his old friend Valthor, and the nobles of Cathne came to restore the old government in Athne so they would have an enemy worth fighting. Tarzan then brought the prisoners back to civilization and returned home (T21).

In 1936, Tarzan was reunited with his old friend Paul d'Arnot (now a captain), who asked him to help an acquaintance find his son, Brian Gregory, who had been imprisoned in the Forbidden City of Ashair while searching for the legendary Father of

Diamonds. In typical style, Tarzan led a small safari to Ashair, saved everyone from danger several times, and finally managed to escape both Ashair and its enemy Thobos after recovering the Father of Diamonds for the Thobotians from where it had lain since the Ashairians attempted to steal it years before (T20).

In 1938 an American adventurer crashed his plane and was rendered amnesiac in the accident, thereby becoming convinced that he was his boyhood hero, Tarzan, and falling into the hands of the inhabitants of the lost city of Alemtejo. The king of that city proclaimed him a god and sent him out to get a goddess, which he did by abducting a large number of tribeswomen and a Scottish millionaire's daughter, thus ruining Tarzan's name and forcing him to pursue the man with murderous intent. Tarzan passed through Alemtejo, encountering difficulties along the way, and rescued from a Galla village a man who later turned out to be the best friend of Rand, the false Tarzan; he had bailed out just before Rand had and landed among the Gallas. They eventually met up with Rand and Sandra Pickerall (the millionaire's daughter) and everything was explained to Tarzan, who then forgave Rand after his friend succeeded in restoring his memory (T23).

Later that year Tarzan suffered another head injury and this time became a victim of aphasia (which left him fully aware of his identity and memory but rendered him unable to speak or understand language for a few months), during which time he was captured by his enemy Abdullah Abu Nejm, who sold him to an animal trapper as a "wild man." He regained his linguistic abilities a few weeks later, and after a mutiny aboard the steamer, escaped his cage and pulled a counter-mutiny during a typhoon in which the ship was wrecked on Uxmal, an uncharted Pacific island which was home to a lost colony of Mayans. After a series of adventures involving the mutineers and the Mayans (who were looking for human sacrifices), Tarzan was eventually "proven" to be a god through a trial by ordeal and was released. Six weeks later they were rescued by another ship the mutineers had captured, now under friendly control, and taken back to civilization (T24).

In 1939, Tarzan acted for a time as a formal detective, using his keen observational powers and sharp mind to solve the murder of the

son of his friend (Colonel Gerald Giles-Burton), who was carrying secret plans to his father in Bangali when his plane was shot down. The son had been murdered in the jungle on the way to his father's bungalow by the criminal who was following him for the plans and who had shot him down (T24B).

The final recorded adventure of Tarzan took place during World War II, when Tarzan again joined the war effort for Britain, this time as a uniformed regular (an RAF colonel). He was assigned to observe a reconnaissance mission early in 1944 on the American B-24 bomber Lovely Lady, but the plane was shot down and Tarzan, by now world-famous, led the crew through miles of beast- and enemy-infested jungle to the Sumatran coast, then into a boat from which they were rescued en route to Australia by a British submarine and returned to civilization (T22).

It is probable that Tarzan had more adventures after these, particularly considering the unrest, tribal warfare, communist revolutions, evil governments, poachers, environmental damage and other troubles which beset Africa in the 1950s, 1960s, 1970s, and beyond, but we know nothing of these adventures; perhaps Tarzan has decided that he would be more effective fighting these various perils from a position of secrecy. It is certainly impossible to believe that he could be anything but alive today.

Tarzan, Jean C. The name used by Tarzan while in France (T2;1).

Tarzan and the Ant Men The tenth book in the Tarzan series, abbreviated T10, which took place in 1918 and was narrated to Burroughs by Tarzan a few years later, to be published in 1924. In the book, Tarzan was taught to fly an airplane by his son Jack and crash-landed beyond the Great Thorn Forest in the land of the tiny Ant Men, where he was well-treated until he was captured by a rival city who shrunk him to their size and enslaved him, necessitating his escape.

"Tarzan and the Black Boy" The fifth of the short stories comprising *Jungle Tales of Tarzan*; it is abbreviated T6:5. It concerns Tarzan's abduction of a child from Mbonga's village so he could have a "balu" of his own, with predictable results. The events took place around 1907 or 1908.

Tarzan and the Castaways The twenty-fourth (and last) book in the Tarzan series, abbreviated T24. The events of the story took place in 1938 and were published by Burroughs as a serial in *Argosy* magazine in 1941. In the story Tarzan, suffering from aphasia due to unexplained injuries, is captured by wild animal trappers who plan to exhibit him as a "wild man" in a circus, but they are marooned on an uncharted Pacific island, where Tarzan finds a lost **Mayan** colony which still practices human sacrifice. The story was for some reason originally serialized as *The Quest of Tarzan* (Burroughs did not choose the title), leading to some confusion with T19, ***Tarzan's Quest***. Also contained in the modern novel format are two short stories, "Tarzan and the Champion" and "Tarzan and the Jungle Murders," which are described under their separate titles.

"Tarzan and the Champion" A short story appearing in the same volume as *Tarzan and the Castaways* and hence abbreviated T24A. In it, there is a confrontation (probably imaginary) between Tarzan and "One-Punch" Mullargan, the world heavyweight champion. The story first appeared in *Blue Book* magazine in 1940.

Tarzan and the City of Gold The sixteenth novel in the Tarzan series, abbreviated T16, which was first published as a serial in *Argosy* magazine from March 12 to April 16, 1932. The events themselves began in September of 1930 and were related to Burroughs sometime in 1931. In the story, Tarzan finds the lost cities of **Athne** (the City of Ivory) and **Cathne** (the City of Gold) and falls into the hands of the beautiful but mad Queen **Nemone** of Cathne, who orders Tarzan to marry her or die in the jaws of her trained lions.

"Tarzan and the Elephant Men" The second novella comprising *Tarzan the Magnificent*, which deals with Tarzan's return to Cathne. This time, however, he went on to Athne, the City of Ivory, where a revolution was taking place, and where **Stanley Wood** and **Gonfala** were being held prisoner by the revolutionaries.

Tarzan and the Forbidden City The twentieth book of the Tarzan series, abbreviated T20. The events described within followed the rainy season of 1936 and were published by Burroughs as a serial in *Argosy* magazine from March 19 to April 30, 1938. The story concerns Tarzan's expedition to the lost underwater city of **Ashair** in search of the adventurer **Brian Gregory**, whom **Paul d'Arnot** had asked Tarzan to rescue. At the same time he also had to stop **Atan Thome**, who also wished to reach Ashair in order to steal the legendary **Father of Diamonds**.

Tarzan and the Foreign Legion The twenty-second book of the Tarzan series, abbreviated T22. It is a "fictional" Tarzan story (according to Burroughs' foreword) and not a "true" Tarzan story, but for the sake of continuity it will be treated normally herein since (unlike the "fictional" Barsoom story, M11A) it does not contain anything which contradicts the rest of the canon; it also may be at least loosely based on "actual" events. It is set early in 1944, written later in 1944, and is the story of Tarzan's leading of the internationally mixed crew of a downed bomber (his **"Foreign Legion"**) across **Japanese**-occupied **Sumatra** to rendezvous with a rescue ship.

Tarzan and the Golden Lion The ninth book in the Tarzan series, abbreviated T9, which was published in 1922. The action began in 1915 (on Tarzan's trip back from **Pal-ul-don**), but the main action did not take place until 1917. The book concerns the plot of a group of European treasure hunters who replaced Tarzan with a double in order to steal the treasure of **Opar**, and also with Tarzan's efforts to save **La**, high priestess of Opar, from the rebellion caused by her saving Tarzan from sacrifice once again. Together they fled into the **Valley of Diamonds** near Opar; Tarzan then had to restore La to her throne, foil the treasure seekers, and expose his evil double.

Tarzan and the Jewels of Opar The fifth book in the Tarzan series, abbreviated T5, which was published in 1916. The events of the story took place in 1913 or early 1914 and came to Burroughs through Tarzan himself in 1914. The story concerns Tarzan's return to **Opar** to renew the fortune he lost in a bad investment in London. While within the treasure vaults, he was hit by falling debris and contracted amnesia, causing him to forget all civilized life and become as an ape again, unable to assist Jane, who had been captured by **Arab** slave raiders.

"Tarzan and the Jungle Murders" A novelette, set in 1939, in which Tarzan acted as a formal detective to solve several murders in a safari. The story first appeared in *Thrilling Adventures* magazine in 1940, but today is usually printed in the same volume as *Tarzan and the Castaways* and is hence abbreviated T24B.

Tarzan and the Leopard Men The eighteenth book of the Tarzan series, abbreviated T18, which probably took place in 1931, but was not published by Burroughs until 1933, after *Tarzan and the Lion Man*, perhaps because Burroughs was not as happy with his adaptation of T18. In any case, the story involves Tarzan's becoming amnesiac again and becoming convinced that he is a muzimo, a spirit who must fight the savage Leopard Men, whose secret cult practices human sacrifice. Even after the recovery of his memory, Tarzan continues to fight the Leopard Men, finding in addition that he must save a white man and a beautiful white girl who have fallen into their evil clutches.

Tarzan and the Lion Man The seventeenth book in the Tarzan series, abbreviated T17. The events within happened in 1932 and were told to Burroughs in 1933, to be published by him as a serial in *Liberty* magazine from November 11, 1933, to January 6, 1934. In the story, Tarzan had to save an American movie company safari which came to Africa to make a movie and encountered both hostile natives and intelligent gorillas.

Tarzan and the Lost Empire The twelfth book of the Tarzan series, abbreviated T12, which took place in 1923 and was told to Burroughs some time later, to be published as a magazine serial in 1928 and 1929. The story involves Tarzan's search for Erich von Harben, son of a missionary friend of his, who had become lost in the supposedly haunted Wiramwazi Mountains. There Tarzan found two outposts of ancient Rome, locked in a struggle with one another for almost two thousand years, and had to free both himself and von Harben, who had been sentenced to die in the arena.

Tarzan and the Madman The twenty-third book in the Tarzan series, abbreviated T23. The action of the story took place in 1938 and was written into a novel in 1940, but was not published in any form until 1964, 14 years

after the author's death. The story involves another Tarzan impersonator (the madman of the title) ruining Tarzan's reputation by stealing and enslaving women of various tribes, including the daughter of a British millionaire who retaliates by putting a price on Tarzan's head. The trail of the impostor takes Tarzan to the lost city of Alemtejo, where he finds the usual perils that must be overcome to reach his goal — the death of the impostor.

"Tarzan and the Magic Men" The first of the two novellas comprising *Tarzan the Magnificent*; it deals with Tarzan's mission to rescue Stanley Wood, an American travel writer, from the Kaji (a tribe of warrior women) and the strange magician who ruled them by the power of the Gonfal, a huge diamond with hypnotic powers.

Tarzan and the Tarzan Twins The first book of the two-volume Tarzan Twins series, abbreviated TT1 which, unlike Burroughs' other children's books (such as "John Carter and the Giant of Mars"), was based on "real" events in the life of Tarzan, or rather the "Tarzan Twins," English schoolboys who he was distantly related. We must assume the events (which took place in 1920) came to Burroughs through Tarzan himself.

Tarzan and the Tarzan Twins with Jad-bal-ja the Golden Lion The rather lengthy title of the second Tarzan Twin book, the events of which took place soon after those of the first in the summer of 1920. In it the "Twins" again become lost in the jungle while on a foray with Tarzan and save young Gretchen von Harben from captivity in the hands of a group of renegade Oparians. It is abbreviated TT2.

Tarzan at the Earth's Core Both the fourth book in the Pellucidar series and the thirteenth in the Tarzan series. In entries regarding things Pellucidarian, it is abbreviated P4; in matters more Tarzanian, T13. The events of the story took place in the years 1926 and 1927 and were told to Burroughs by Jason Gridley on his return to Tarzana late in 1927, to be put into story form as a serial in *Blue Book* magazine from September of 1929 to March of 1930. It concerns the efforts of Jason Gridley to organize an expedition into Pellucidar to rescue David Innes from the Korsars. Tarzan heads the expedition owing to his ability to survive and lead in savage jungles, of which Pellucidar has its fair share. Mishaps occur, however, and the party is split up, so its mission becomes twofold: Save David Innes, and find the lost party members.

Tarzan-go   "Whiteskin-black" (Ape). The nickname given by his schoolmates to the black-haired English "Tarzan Twin," Dick (TT1).

Tarzan, Guard of the Jungle   The original title of Tarzan the Invincible when it appeared as a serial in Blue Book magazine from October of 1930 to April of 1931.

Tarzan-jad-guru   "Tarzan the Terrible" (Pal). The name given Tarzan by the Waz-don of Pal-ul-don when they experienced his terrifying fighting style (T8;3).

Tarzan, Lord of the Jungle   The eleventh book in the Tarzan series, abbreviated T11. The events within took place in the winter of 1921 and were narrated to Burroughs by Tarzan some time later, to be published as a magazine serial in 1927 and 1928. The story concerns the lost Valley of the Sepulcher, inhabited by the descendants of British crusaders who became very lost, and its invasion by a band of Arab slave traders. Tarzan's task is to stop the Arabs and rescue James Hunter Blake while simultaneously protecting himself from his own displaced countrymen.

Tarzan of the Apes   The original book of the Tarzan series, abbreviated T1, which was first published in 1912. The events of the book took place between 1888 and 1910 and the story was given to Burroughs by a man "who had no business to tell it to me, or to any other," but who this person was and how he came to know the story in such exact detail are unknown. He was probably one of Tarzan's friends and possibly even appears in some of the books, because he was eventually able to get Burroughs an introduction to Tarzan himself (E1), from whom Burroughs got the later adventures. The story concerns (as practically every civilized human on Earth knows by now) a castaway British lord and lady, who died in Africa, and their baby son, who was adopted by a she-ape (who had lost her own baby) and raised as an ape in the jungle. The book concerns the ape-man's early adult life, his steps toward humanity, his first

meeting with white men, and his finding a mate in the beautiful Jane Porter. It is a little recognized fact that the names of the characters in the book are not the real names of the participants, since Burroughs changed the names to protect their privacy.

"Tarzan Rescues the Moon"   The twelfth and last short story comprising Jungle Tales of Tarzan, in which Tarzan "rescues" the moon from being "devoured" during a lunar eclipse by shooting arrows at the beast that is "devouring" it. The story is abbreviated T6:12.

Tarzan-tar   "Whiteskin-white" (Ape). The nickname given by his schoolmates to the blond-haired American "Tarzan Twin," "Doc" (TT1).

Tarzan the Invincible   The fourteenth book in the Tarzan series, abbreviated T14, which was originally published as a serial in Blue Book magazine from October of 1930 to April of 1931 under the title Tarzan, Guard of the Jungle. The events within took place early in 1928, just after Tarzan's return from Pellucidar (as a matter of fact, before he even reached home) and the story was communicated to Burroughs by Tarzan late in 1928 or early in 1929. In it, Tarzan had to again save La of Opar from the treachery of her own people, fight off a group of Arab slave raiders, and defeat communist agents who were attempting to start a war between France and Italy by spreading lies and inciting trouble in Italian Somaliland.

Tarzan the Magnificent   The twenty-first book of the Tarzan series, abbreviated T21. The events of the story happened in 1935 (before those of T20; some of the later Tarzan books are chronologically out of sequence) and actually fall into two more or less distinct sequences: "Tarzan and the Magic Men" (published in 1936) and "Tarzan and the Elephant Men" (published in 1937). The general storylines of the two appear under their individual entries.

Tarzan the Terrible   The eighth book in the Tarzan series, abbreviated T8, which was first published in 1921. The events of the story took place in 1915 and were delivered to Burroughs as a manuscript around 1917. The story is a direct sequel to Tarzan the Untamed, in which the German Lt. Obergatz abducted Jane and fled into the interior after making it seem that she was dead. Tarzan found out the truth and tracked Obergatz and Jane to **Pal-ul-don**, a hidden valley in a cluster of mountains surrounded by a vast morass and inhabited by tailed humans who possess a very ancient and complex, though primitive, culture. Somewhere in the valley, Tarzan had to find Jane, battling weird humanoids and even dinosaurs as he went.

Tarzan the Untamed The seventh book of the Tarzan series, abbreviated T7, which was originally published in two parts in *Red Book* magazine in 1919 and 1920. The story took place in the autumn of 1914 and winter of 1915 and was given to Burroughs as a manuscript (probably together with the text of *Tarzan the Terrible*) by Tarzan himself in 1916 or 1917. The story concerns Tarzan's part in the African campaigns at the beginning of World War I, and how Tarzan's home was again destroyed by invaders. As in the other incident (T5), Jane was abducted, but this time a ruse made Tarzan believe her dead by German hands. The story then follows Tarzan's fight against the German army, his seeking revenge for the "killing" of his wife, and his trek across a hidden desert to a city of madmen to find the man responsible for the deeds.

Tarzan Triumphant The fifteenth book of the Tarzan series, abbreviated T15, which took place in 1929 and was communicated to Burroughs in 1930, to be published as a serial in *Blue Book* magazine from October of 1931 to March of 1932 under the title *The Triumph of Tarzan*. In it, a Russian assassin named **Leon Stabutch** came to kill Tarzan for his part in the death of **Peter Zveri**, and hitched up with a band of **shiftas** whom Tarzan had set out to defeat. Complicating the matter, though, was the presence of the safari of an American geologist **Lafayette Smith**, who got himself lost in a hidden land ruled by maniacs while his safari was captured by the shiftas. Tarzan's mission, then, was threefold: Defeat the shiftas, rescue Smith, and stop Stabutch, of whose presence he was completely unaware.

Tarzan Twins Two young boys (born around 1906) whose mothers had been identical American twins, one of whom had married an American and one an Englishman who

was a distant cousin of Tarzan's. The boys were sent to an English public school together and, as each resembled his mother, they looked very much alike; although they were not true twins, they were called such by their schoolmates, who called them the "Tarzan Twins" because of Dick's (the English "twin") relationship to the famous ape-man. The boys decided to live up to the nickname by becoming great athletes and tree-climbers and were called "**Tarzan-tar**" (Tarzan white) for the blond American "**Doc**" and "**Tarzan-go**" (Tarzan black) for the dark-haired English Dick. In 1920 they were invited to Tarzan's estate for a vacation, but their train derailed on the way. They left the train, became lost in the jungle, and were captured by the fierce **Bagalla** cannibals, but escaped with the help of two other prisoners and were saved from the pursuing tribesmen by Tarzan and his **Waziri**, who had been tracking the lost boys for weeks (TT1). They later went on an excursion with Tarzan, again became lost, and saved young **Gretchen von Harben** from a group of renegade **Oparians** who wished to make her their high priestess in exile (TT2).

Tarzana The town founded by Burroughs around his ranch in the 1910s, just west of Los Angeles; it is today a suburb of that city. It was named, of course, for Tarzan of the Apes. In the early 1920s, **Jason Gridley** moved there and met Burroughs, whom he was able to acquaint with his discovery of the Gridley Wave (P3).

"Tarzan's First Love" The first short story in the collection **Jungle Tales of Tarzan**. It concerns Tarzan's first experience with unrequited love in the person of **Teeka**, a beautiful young she-ape who would not mate with the (to her) ugly Tarzan. The story took place about 1906; it is abbreviated T6:1.

Tarzan's Quest The nineteenth book in the Tarzan series, abbreviated T19. The events within took place in 1934 and were published by Burroughs as a serial from 1935 to 1936. In the story, the daughter of **Muviro** (acting chief of the **Waziri**) was abducted by the mysterious **Kavuru** and Tarzan had to rescue her; meanwhile, Jane crashed in an airplane and was exposed to terrible dangers before becoming a prisoner of the Kavuru herself.

Tas-ad (*Cpk*) The Wieroo way, or philosophy; it is a very difficult concept to explain.

Basically, Tas-ad means the traditions and laws (both written and unwritten) of the Wieroo, and the practice of always doing things in a certain way; it also encompasses the science and mental abilities of the Wieroos. Tas-ad dominates the Wieroos to the point where few even think outside its lines; because of this, all Wieroos think very much alike and are generally unhappy, especially because part of Tas-ad is to commit undiscovered murders in order to gain social promotion (C3;4).

Tasor The young Gatholian nobleman of Barsoom whose father died in vain trying to save **Gahan** of Gathol's father from assassins. He was later taken as a slave to **Manataj** where a rich woman bought him, fell in love with him, married him (after having her husband assassinated), then moved secretly to **Manator** with him after spreading the rumor that she had died. She later really died in Manator after buying him a post in the **jeddak's** guard. In Manator, Tasor went by the name of **A-Sor**. He recognized Gahan as his jed and helped him and **Tara of Helium** to escape the searchers while they were fleeing in the palace of **O-Tar** (M5;18).

Tats-ah-dahs-ay-go "Quick Killer" (*Apa*). An Apache war chief of the Chi-e-a-hen tribe who led a raid in **Arizona** in April of 1882 in which **Shoz-dijiji** joined. He was killed by Shoz-dijiji when he tried to harm **Wichita Billings** during that raid (A1;19).

tats-an (*Apa*) Dead (A1;4).

Taug A great ape of the tribe of **Kerchak** who was one of Tarzan's childhood playmates. He fought with Tarzan for possession of **Teeka** when Tarzan was about 18, but the fight was interrupted and Teeka chose the handsome Taug as her mate; Tarzan later saved him from a trap set by the tribe of **Mbonga** and sent him back to Teeka, whom Tarzan no longer desired (T6:1). He attacked Tarzan again when he thought Tarzan would be a threat to his baby by Teeka, but Tarzan defeated him and later proved his good intentions by saving the baby from a leopard (T6:3). After that, Taug was always Tarzan's friend and admirer (T6:10).

taun besar (Dyak) White man (Q;11).

Tav One of the **Kalkar** followers of **Raban**, the giant Kalkar bandit of Kalkar-dominated 25th century **California** (MM3;8).

Taveta The border town of German East Africa (about 25 miles southeast of Mount Kilimanjaro) near which was the German camp from which Tarzan abducted Major Schneider of the beginning of World War I (T7;2,11).

Tavia The daughter of **Kal Tavan**, Prince of Tjanath, who was abducted as a child and enslaved in **Jahar**. She escaped from the palace of **Tul Axtar** by disguising herself as a man and was captured by **green men** near **Xanator**, but was rescued from them by **Tan Hadron**. They escaped to Tjanath in the flier she had stolen from Tul Axtar, but were there imprisoned by her grandfather as Jaharian spies. Tan Hadron later escaped and rescued her and she helped him in his mission to rescue **Sanoma Tora**, even though she had fallen in love with him and did not think he loved her. She was stranded with him in U-gor, from which they only barely escaped, and later was again abducted by the invisible Tal Axtar while Tan Hadron was looking the other way. He again managed to rescue her and at last realized that he had fallen in love with her. He then married her, and found out some time later that the slave girl was actually a princess (M7;4–5,12–17).

Taylor One of the three sailors of the aero-sub *Coldwater* who were in the power boat with **Lt. Jefferson Turck** when their ship abandoned them in mid-ocean in 2137 (LC; 1–2).

Taylor, Dorothy Scott The younger sister of **General Jefferson Scott, Sr.**; mother of **Scott Taylor** (ME;1–2).

Taylor, Scott Jefferson Scott, Sr.'s nephew, **Virginia Scott's** first cousin once removed, who was two years her senior. He was an awful person and a troublemaker who came looking for a fortune when Scott died, even though the old man had banned him from the house several years earlier. He intended to defraud Virginia of her rightful inheritance by throwing doubt on the legitimacy of **Ruth Scott's** marriage to **Jefferson Scott, Jr.** (Virginia's parents). When **Dick Gordon** went to Africa to find the documents to prove the marriage, Taylor followed to kill him, but failed to do so because of the arrival of Virginia, who had come to warn Gordon. He then followed Gordon to America, where he would have killed him at the Scott house if not for a jammed automatic and the arrival of **Ben, King of Beasts** from a derailed circus train. Ben took revenge for Taylor's killing of his mate a month before by promptly killing Taylor (ME).

Tchek A **Khmer** warrior of the command of **Vama** in 1920s **Lodidhapura** (HM;5).

te (*Amt*) An Amtorian hour, of which there are 20 in the Amtorian day. Each is about 80.895 minutes long and the first te begins at mean sunrise (V1;10).

Tebuk A city of northwestern Arabia, north of which lies the fabled ruined city of **Geryeh** (T11;1).

ted (*Amt*) An Amtorian unit of linear measure, equal to about 13.2 feet. There are 1000 ted in a **kob** (V4;22).

tee (*Bar*) The number ten (M9;4).

teean (*Bar*) The Barsoomian month, an arbitrary unit (in other words, not directly calculated from the motions of any heavenly bodies) made up of 67 **padans**, or Barsoomian days. Ten teeans make one **ord**, or Barsoomian year. Note that since the Barsoomian day is longer than that of Earth, a teean is equal to about 69 Earth days (M10:3;3).

teeay "Ten-one" (*Bar*). The number 11 (M9;4).

Teeaytan-ov "Eleven hundred seven" (*Bar*). A **hormad** of **Morbus** who ridiculed **Tor-dur-bar** when his head was cut off. He tried to make friends with **Vor Daj**, and after Vor Daj's brain had been transferred to the skull of Tor-dur-bar (whom he then took the place of) he made friends with Teeaytan-ov, who had since been made a member of the bodyguard of the third **jed** of Morbus and could get Vor Daj/Tor-dur-bar a position in the guard by virtue of the latter's enormous strength. He later became Vor Daj/Tor-dur-bar's spy within the palace of **Ay-mad**, but was killed in a fight with hormads; it is unknown whether he was ever regrown (M9;4,9, 16,18).

teedwar A Barsoomian military rank corresponding to an Earthly colonel (M7;1).

Teeka Tarzan's first love, a beautiful young she-ape whom he fought his former playmate **Taug** for. Although the battle was interrupted by the advent of a panther, Teeka eventually chose the handsome Taug over the ugly Tarzan, causing Tarzan great emotional anguish until he realized that she was not of his own kind and therefore not a proper mate (T6:1). She later had a baby by Taug, and Tarzan saved it from a leopard when it was very young; this made Teeka so thankful she would then let Tarzan play with the baby (T6:3). Another time, she was abducted by an ape called **Toog**, necessitating her rescue by Taug and Tarzan. As it went, Teeka actually saved her rescuers from an ambush by Toog and his tribe when she found a handful of bullets in Tarzan's pouch and threw them at Toog. One exploded by chance and scared all the hostile apes away (T6:10).

teepi An oval silver Barsoomian coin worth roughly ten U.S. cents (1941 standard). There are ten teepi in a **tanpi**, and ten pi in a teepi (M10:2;11).

teivos A **Va-nah** word used in **Kalkar**-occupied America to mean either a district or "the administrative body that misadministers its affairs" (MM2;1).

telepathy All Barsoomians are telepathic. Much of their language, the **tongue of Barsoom**, is telepathic rather than spoken, and is intelligible even to lower animals, though to a lesser degree. John Carter discovered that, while he could often read the minds of Barsoomians (as they sometimes can each others'), no Barsoomian could read his (M1;7). The same held true for Ulysses Paxton (M6;4).

telephone, Havatoo The telephone-like device of the Amtorian city of **Havatoo** is wireless, like our cellular phones (V2;16).

telescopes The telescopic equipment on Barsoom is so advanced that it can pick out individual objects on Earth no larger than a blade of grass. Thus, Earth history is known on Barsoom practically as well as Barsoomian history is. They can pick out objects in this way on all the planets (except for cloud-covered Venus and Jupiter) and on many stars (M1;11). In **Phundahl**, telescopes are forbidden because the **Turgan** says that there are no worlds other than Barsoom (M6;10).

temple, Mahar Mahar temples are large, oval stone buildings with only one ground-level entrance for slaves; the Mahar entrance is a large hole in the roof through which they can fly into the building. These temples have no floor, consisting entirely of a large, deep tank of water containing artificial granite islands on which the human slaves who are to be ceremonially eaten are placed. Mahars sport and play in the water of their temples, and also sleep in them; they do not do these things elsewhere very much, and although the Mahars of **Phutra** claimed they did not eat humans, they did so in their temples. The actual ceremony involves a Mahar using a mind-control power on a human woman or child, drawing the victim into the water from the island she occupies to the shore, underwater all the way, then reversing direction several times. After several of these underwater passes (during which the Mahar's mind control protects the victim from drowning), the victim is in such a deep trance that she does not notice when the Mahar eats one of her arms, then (on the next pass) the other arm, then breasts, then face; on the final pass the victim is completely devoured. After the queen Mahar goes first, all of the others go together, leaving the men of the group for the **thipdars** to eat (P1;8).

Temple of Beauty   The official art museum of **Helium** on Barsoom (M5;9).

Temple of Issus *see* **Issus, Temple of**

Temple of Knowledge   The huge state library and museum of **Helium**, which is much like our own Smithsonian Institution and Library of Congress combined (M7;2).

Temple of Reward   The court building of **Helium** on Barsoom where people are awarded their "just deserts"—it is in this building that heroes are decorated and criminals punished. It lies at the terminus of the **Avenue of Ancestors** (M2;16).

Temple of the Flaming God   The best-preserved building of ancient **Opar**—a vast structure of **concrete** and granite which is decorated in many places with huge amounts of gold and possesses a maze of passages beneath, including one (forgotten by the Oparians) that leads to their secret treasure vault, then out of the city altogether (T2;20–22).

Temple of the Gryf   A small temple in the temple complex of **A-lur** in **Pal-ul-don**. Its front is carved in the likeness of a gryf, and there are numerous trap doors within for the purpose of dropping victims into the tem-

ple's cellar, where a great gryf is kept. It was here that **Jane Clayton** was kept by **Lu-don**, and here that Tarzan first caught wind of her presence (T8;14).

Temple of the Sun   A prison in the center of the **Temple of Issus** in the Land of the **First-Born** of Barsoom. It is very tall and thin, enclosed for its total length (except for a minaret at the top) in solid rock. The temple consists of 687 (actually, the number is probably 670; see **padan**) circular chambers, one below the other. Each has but a single door and a single passage to the temple through the rock, and the whole turns in place once in a year, so that the door of each chamber is exposed for only one day a year. A person may be placed within with insufficient food to last a year, or any of several other means of torment. **Dejah Thoris** was placed in the temple with **Thuvia of Ptarth** and **Phaidor** when John Carter's armies invaded the Land of the First-Born. Thuvia saved Dejah Thoris when Phaidor would have killed her, but they all were later kidnapped by **Matai Shang** and **Thurid** through the use of a little-known secret door (M2;20–22)(M3;3). See also **Temple of the Flaming God**.

Temple of the Virgins   The temple at the apex of the pyramid of **Chichen Itza** on the island of **Uxmal**, so called because it was kept by virgin priestesses. These priestesses could at any time resign and marry if they so desired, and when they did so they were much sought after by nobles and warriors (T24;22).

tenderfoot   (American Wesern slang) An inexperienced cowboy (D;3).

teniente   (*Sp*) Lieutenant (A2;16).

Tennington, Lord   William Clayton's friend, who insisted on inviting him, **Jane Porter**, her father and some others on a cruise around Africa on his yacht, *Lady Alice*. After Jane ran into **Hazel Strong** in Cape Town, Hazel, her mother, and **"Mr. Thuran"** joined the company just in time for the shipwreck off the coast of **Angola** a few days later. Lord Tennington married Hazel shortly after their rescue by the same French cruiser that had rescued the Porter party two years before (T2;9,12–13,26).

Terkoz   The son of **Tublat**; thus, the foster brother of Tarzan. After Tarzan killed **Kerchak** and became king, Terkoz continually looked for an opportunity to slay Tarzan and thus become king. Tarzan defeated him in combat but let him live, and left the tribe after Terkoz acknowledged Tarzan's supremacy; thus, Tarzan left Terkoz as king without losing face himself. It was Terkoz who gave Tarzan the great scar across his forehead that turned red when the ape-man was angry. Terkoz proved to be a cruel and vicious king, and he was eventually driven away by the other bulls of the tribe in combination, as Tarzan had admonished them to do if they ever had a bad king. He thus became a renegade, and took Jane Porter away to be his new mate; for this he was killed by Tarzan, who tracked him down before he could injure Jane (T1;12–13,19).

Terkoz A great wolfhound Tarzan owned in the 1910s and named for his foster brother. It befriended **Victoria Custer**, and in her vision she tracked down **Nu of the Niocene** with it. It was then very protective of both her and Nu, and killed **Curtiss** when he would have killed Nu. In real life, the dog was fiercely protective of her, but did not kill anyone (E1;7–13)(E2;15).

Terrible Mountains A nearly impassible mountain range of Pellucidar which lies between the **Zurts** country on the west coast and the rest of the continent of the **Empire of Pellucidar**. It is as high and rough as the Himalayas and runs for quite a long way north (P7:4;7,11).

Terror A famous racehorse of the **Blue Stables** of early 1st century Rome (I;8).

Terrorists The name given to the inner circle of the revolutionary party of an unnamed European country of the 1920s (LL;9).

Terry The companion of the Oskaloosa Kid on the night he killed **Reginald Paynter** in 1917 **Oakdale, Illinois** (K3;4,10).

Terry, Rhonda The stand-in for **Naomi Madison** in B.O. Pictures' 1932 film *The Lion Man*, filmed on location in the **Ituri Forest**. Terry had more talent than "The Madison," which Madison resented until she realized how well Terry treated her. Because of her strong resemblance to Madison, **Sheik Ab el-Ghrennem** abducted them both for his treasure hunt, since he could not easily tell them apart. She escaped, only to be captured by the English-speaking gorillas of the **Valley of**

Diamonds and taken to God. She was eventually rescued by Tarzan, went back to Hollywood, married **Tom Orman**, and became a star herself (T17;1–9,12,15–20,26–33).

tertia cena (*Lat*) Third course (I;6).

testudone (*Lat*) An ancient Roman siege engine (T12;22).

Texas Pete A cowboy of the **Bar-Y Ranch** in 1880s **Arizona**; he was a self-proclaimed balladeer who constantly sang a long ballad of his own improvisation, much to the chagrin of the other cowboys. He was always decked out in silver-inlaid spurs and hand-carved leather, with saddle and harness to match, and thus presented a vivid spectacle even when broke. He was a good and honest man and a loyal friend of Bull's, who would not believe the gossip spoken against him. He also stood by **Diana Henders** through all her troubles (HB;1–3,14–19).

TF Ranch A ranch of **Porico County, Arizona**, which had been foreclosed on and leased to **Cory Blaine**, who had opened up one of the first **dude ranches** there (D;3).

Tha One of the half-human priests of **Opar**. After being judged against by **La** in a dispute with another priest, Tha went into a murderous rage and would have killed La had not Tarzan broken his bonds and killed Tha with his bare hands, for which service La saved Tarzan's life by hiding him in the temple so he would not be sacrificed (T2;20). Another Tha was a hunter of the tribe of Nu in Niocene Africa; he was the father of the beautiful **Nat-ul** (E1;1).

Thabis The last butcher and cook for **Issus**, Goddess of Death on Barsoom (M2; 11).

thag The Pellucidarian **aurochs** (P1;6).

thagosoto (*Min*) King (T10;11).

Thak Chan A Mayan warrior of **Uxmal** whom Tarzan saved from one of the lions he had released onto the island from the wreck of the *Saigon* late in 1938 (T24;12).

Thaka A bull ape of the tribe of **Kerchak** (T1;12)(T6:1).

Thames The river which runs through **London**, both in England and in the **Valley of Diamonds** (T17;21).

than (*Bar*) Warrior (M10:3;6).

Than Kosis The last Jeddak of Zodanga on Barsoom. He was the father of **Sab Than** and made war on **Helium** so his son could have **Dejah Thoris**, but he was foiled and killed by John Carter (M1).

Thandar "Brave One" The name given by **Nadara** to **Waldo Emerson Smith-Jones** because his own name was far too long and difficult. Thandar was the name he went by exclusively while on **Nadara's Island** (CG1;5,11)(CG2;1).

Thar Ban A jed of the **green men** of **Torquas** on Barsoom. He killed the agents of **Astok** and abducted **Thuvia of Ptarth** from them while in **Aanthor**, but was pursued by **Carthoris** (M4;4).

tharban A cat-like Amtorian predator; the Amtorian tiger. It has stiff, bristly hair all over its body, with red and white stripes running lengthwise and a bluish belly; it also has a mane like a horse's and very pointed ears. Tharbans are very ferocious but have the habit of roaring and growling for no good reason, thus warning the wary of their approach (V2;1,6)(V4;39).

Thark The horde of green Barsoomians who captured John Carter soon after his advent on Mars. It is one of the largest hordes, numbering about 30,000 members, and rules an area which stretches between 40 and 80 degrees south latitude. Their capital is the ancient ruined city of Thark, located in the southwest portion of their territory near the crossing of two **canals**. There are 25 communities of Tharks, five within the city and 20 nomadic. Through the work of John Carter and **Tars Tarkas**, the Tharks became the first **green men** ever to ally themselves with the **red men** (specifically, those of **Helium**) (M1; 3–7,16,26).

Thavas, Tower of The ancestral home of **Ras Thavas'** family, built within sight of **Toonol** on a rocky island southeast of the city in the **Toonolian Marshes** by an expatriate Toonolian noble by the name of Thavas 23,000 years ago. The family was later allowed back into the city, but kept the tower and its support buildings as their home. In Ras Thavas' time, the tower became a vast collection of buildings forming a great medical institution which was presided over by Ras

Thavas himself and served the purpose of a huge hospital and research laboratory. It was occupied by **Vobis Kan**, Jeddak of **Toonol**, (for fear of Ras Thavas' power) around 1920, but Ras Thavas escaped and organized a small army under **Gor Hajus** to retake the tower. It failed and Ras Thavas was again forced to flee (M6;2,6,13–14) (M9;1).

theater, Korvan The theaters of the Amtorian nation of **Korva** are arranged with the seats facing the back wall, away from the stage, where a huge mirror is placed to reflect the action taking place on stage; special lighting and other mirrors allow for special effects to be created. The practice dates from a past time when acting was considered dishonorable, so actors could not be looked at directly; like many customs, however, it has continued long past its reason for existence (V3;10).

Thebae The Latin spelling of "Thebes," the Greek name for the Egyptian city of Luxor. There **Marcus Crispus Sanguinarius** was stationed with his legion until he fled south to escape the wrath of **Nerva** (T12;10).

Thenar A valley in the **Ethiopian Highlands** where lies **Athne**, the City of Ivory. Thenar is the country of elephants and lies due east of the volcano **Xarator** (T16;3).

Theriere, Henri, Count de Cadenet The second mate of the *Halfmoon* on its 1913 cruise to kidnap **Barbara Harding**. He had been cashiered from the French navy (where he had been an officer) and was a polished gentleman with a cruel heart. He had his own plans regarding Barbara Harding, and after her abduction managed to convince her that he had been tricked into his present situation and was really her friend, an assertion he proved through his constant intercession on her behalf and his manly courage in the face of all sorts of danger. He eventually really did fall in love with her, and his true nobility was reborn along with a feeling of respect and friendship for **Billy Byrne**, who was himself awakening to honor, courage and nobility. The two risked their lives to save Barbara from the **samurai** of the island of **Yoka** after the *Halfmoon* wrecked there, and he and Byrne were just beginning to realize the friendship they felt for one another when Theriere died of his wounds (K1;3–13).

Theriere, Jacques The brother of Henri Theriere; he was a French deputy of the early 1900s (K1;13).

Therns The last remnant of the ancient white race of Barsoom. The Therns ruled the Mountains of Otz and the Valley Dor and, through disguised agents all over Barsoom, spread the doctrine of the Pilgrimage for eons. Though the Therns represented the Valley Dor as a place of eternal happiness and rest, in reality the pilgrims were set upon by Plant Men and killed. The Therns then ate the human flesh "from which the defiling blood of life" had been sucked by the plant men. The Therns often took pilgrims as slaves and bred them for service or meat. Although the race from which they sprang was gifted with golden-blond hair, all male Therns are now bald, but wear blond wigs at all times because they are ashamed of their baldness. They are excellent but unscrupulous swordsmen, and were for the most part totally convinced of their own divinity and truly believed themselves the blessed of Issus, as a higher form of life who were perfectly justified in treating the "lower orders" as cattle. There are two kinds of Therns: Lesser Therns, who comprise most of the race, and Holy Therns, the leaders. There are at least ten cycles, or levels of nobility, among the Therns, with Holy Therns occupying the tenth cycle; their leader was always called the Holy Hekkador and Father of Therns. The Therns conceived of the Temple of Issus much as the outer world conceived of Dor; unknown to the Therns, the parallel was exact (see First-Born). John Carter put an end to the Therns' long deception after appearing in the Valley Dor upon his return to Barsoom in 1886, and the Thern society was reorganized so they could begin to cooperate with the other peoples of Barsoom instead of exploiting them (M2;3–4,8)(M3).

Thetan A warrior of Thobos whom Tarzan saved from a small Tyrannosaurus of the region. He was the nephew of King Herat of Thobos and was on a secret mission outside Tuen-baka when Tarzan saved and befriended him. He brought Tarzan, Mr. Gregory, Lavac and Magra to Thobos on a captured Ashairian galley, thinking they would be well-received by the king, but he was mistaken; Herat threw the men in prison and set about wooing Magra, so Thetan helped them

escape to make up for his mistake. He later helped convince his uncle to befriend the outsiders and let them leave Tuen-baka with honors (T20;14,17–23,31–32).

thievery "Thievery is practically unknown upon Barsoom. Assassination is the ever-present fear of all Barsoomians" (M1;21).

thipdar The huge, man-eating, tailed Pellucidarian pteranodon, which is capable of carrying a full-grown man. The Mahars keep them as pets and guard animals, and feed them humans (P1;4,8).

13th Cavalry The U.S. Cavalry unit which pursued "Pancho" Villa's men across the border into Mexico on March 9, 1916, after Villa's attack on Columbus, New Mexico. It did not catch Villa, but it did defeat "General" Pesita's forces at the Clark ranch and rescue Billy Byrne, Bridge and the Hardings (K2; 17).

Thirty-six A barbarian warrior of the Elephant Country of early 22nd century Grabritin who accompanied Lt. Jefferson Turck and his men to the continent. He could not count, and did not know the meaning of his peculiar name. He was shot dead by Snider when the latter proposed to abduct Victory (LC;6).

thirty-thirty Term for a rifle firing a .30 caliber cartridge with a 30 grain charge (T13;8).

tho (Ape) Mouth (TC).

Thoar A warrior of Zoram in Pellucidar who was rescued from a dyal by Tarzan and the Sagoth Tar-gash in the summer of 1927 and befriended them, essaying afterward to teach Tarzan the common tongue of Pellucidar. He was the brother of Jana, the Red Flower of Zoram, and later helped Jason Gridley find her (P4;6,8,12–17).

thoat "A green Martian horse. Ten feet high at the shoulder, with four legs on either side; a broad, flat tail, larger at the tip than at the root which it holds straight out behind while running; a mouth splitting its head from snout to the long, massive neck. It is entirely devoid of hair and is of a dark slate colour and exceedingly smooth and glossy. It has a white belly and the legs are shaded from slate at the shoulders and hips to a vivid yellow at the feet. The feet are heavily padded and nailless" (M4).

Thoats are ridden without bit or bridle and are guided entirely by telepathic means. They are ill-tempered and inclined to stampede, and are generally treated poorly by their green masters. They can live entirely without fresh water, gleaning all of the moisture they need from the ochre moss which forms most of their diet (M1).

The red Barsoomians breed and keep a smaller, more docile species of saddle thoat, and there is also another species which is kept exclusively for meat (M10:2;3).

The name also applies to a jetan piece with a move of one space straight and one diagonal, in any direction (M5).

Thobos The second city of Tuen-baka, which lies at the far end of the lake and is eternally at war with Ashair. It lies close to the shore, and a path leads from it out of Tuen-baka, but this path is known only to Thobotians. Thobos was the original home of the Father of Diamonds before it was stolen by Ashair, and after the stone was returned to Thobos by the priest Herkuf in November of 1936, Thobos set out with its navy and conquered Ashair, reducing it to vassalage (T20;13–14,23,29–32).

Thome, Atan An evil east Indian — plump, greasy and treacherous — who wished to buy Brian Gregory's map to Ashair from Tarzan, whom he thought was Gregory. He eventually reached the forbidden city with the map after getting Wolff to steal it for him, but became a prisoner of the Ashairians, whom he then told about the Gregory safari in an effort to ingratiate himself to his captors. He later became involved in an intrigue with the noble Akamen, then betrayed him to Queen Atka in hopes of currying favor with her; instead, she had him imprisoned in the temple with Akamen and Lal Taask in full view of the stone he coveted. He escaped with Tarzan's help, but then stole the stone and fled, since by this time he had gone quite mad. He killed Lal Taask for the treasure, but himself died of heart failure after he saw what he had killed several people for (T20;1–14,17–22,29–32).

Thompson The British air scout who discovered Lt. Smith-Oldwick's abandoned plane and, while searching for him by air, the lost city of Xuja as well (T7;20).

Another Thompson was an honest man of Hendersville, Arizona, into whose keeping Bull gave Hal Colby after unmasking him as the Black Coyote. Thompson was shot and killed when Gum Smith's men rescued Colby later that evening (HB;17–18).

Yet another Thompson was a card cheater whom Ogden Secor accidentally killed in self-defense a few weeks after his arrival in Goliath, Idaho (GF;11).

Thompson, "Big Bill" Nickname of William Hale Thompson who, while running for mayor of Chicago in 1927, promised to "biff King George on the snoot" if he dared to come to Chicago. Thompson's comment reflected the Anglophobia of his times (T15;3) (T22;2).

Thompson, Jim The best friend of Julian 8th, who lived in the next farm upriver from Julian's in the teivos of Chicago in the early 22nd century. His woman was Mollie Sheehan, and they were Julian and his family's only confidantes. After Julian 9th saved Juana St. John from the hellhounds, they adopted her and took her to their house to live. Thompson joined the rebellion begun by Julian 9th and was killed in the first battle (MM2;3,11).

Thompson submachine gun The famous "tommy gun" favored by Chicago mobsters of the 1920s for quick, complete "rubouts." It was .45 caliber and could hold 50 rounds in its characteristic circular magazine (T15;5).

Thoos The god of the Cathneans; an old, mangy lion who was fed human sacrifices during temple ceremonies (T16;6–7,16).

Thor A laborer and criminal of Old Vepaja (about A.D. 1400) who founded the communistic Thorist movement which preached class hatred and eventually overthrew the old system to establish a tyrannical and totalitarian new order over most of what used to be Vepaja (V1;5).

Thora, Free Land of Those portions of what used to be the Amtorian nation of Vepaja now ruled by the Thorists. It is an unhappy totalitarian state under the guise of a democracy (as many communist countries were on Earth) and is ruled by a committee of 100 people called the Klongyan (the "exalted friends") (V1;8,12).

Thorek A Mammoth Man of Pellucidar who escaped from slavery in Basti along with Wilhelm von Horst in 1927 (P5;6).

Thorian The chief of all the lesser Therns of Barsoom (M4).

Thorists The Amtorian communists, who were founded about A.D. 1400 by a criminal leader named **Thor**. The Thorists spread vicious propaganda against the upper classes and eventually fomented a rebellion which resulted in the overthrow of the government of Vepaja and the establishment of a new totalitarian order (V1;5).

thorrib (*Ara*) A head garment used to cover and protect the head and face from sand (T11;1).

Thrilling Adventures The magazine in which "Tarzan and the Jungle Murders" first appeared in 1941.

Throck, Dick One of Flora Hawkes' co-conspirators in her 1917 plan to rob the treasure vaults of Opar. He was a former pugilist, part of the muscle of the expedition. After the safari's betrayal by Luvini, Throck escaped with Peebles and Bluber and was eventually escorted to the coast by Tarzan's command (T9;3,15–19).

Throk One of the Lake-Dwellers of Niocene Africa; he captured Nat-ul after she escaped from Tur of the Boat-Builders. Nu, son of Nu took Throk's place as sentry when he came to rescue Nat-ul (E2;14).

Throne of Righteousness The central witness platform in the Temple of Reward in Helium on Barsoom around which the defendants sit, facing the jury and audience (M2;17).

Throwaldo The chief of agriculture of the Minunian city of Veltopismakus while Tarzan was imprisoned there (T10;10).

throwing one's sword Barsoomian swords can be thrown in combat, but the act of throwing one's sword at a man's feet means, "my sword, my body, my life, my soul are yours to do with as you wish. Until death and after death I look to you alone for authority for my every act. Be you right or wrong, your word shall be my only truth. Whoso raises his hand against you must answer to my sword." This oath is generally only paid to "a jeddak

whose high character and chivalrous acts have inspired the enthusiastic love of his followers," but sometimes is paid to a woman with whom one is deeply in love. The proper response of acceptance is to pick up the sword, kiss its hilt, and buckle the weapon back onto its owner with one's own hands. Many men threw their swords at John Carter's feet during his career, but the first was Hor Vastus of Helium (M2;16).

Throxeus The largest of the five ancient oceans of Barsoom which covered a large portion of the northern hemisphere, including the area now occupied by several red nations. It is sometimes referred to as Throxus (M4;9).

thub (*Ape*) Heart (TC).

Thudos A powerful noble of Cathne when Tarzan came there in October of 1930. He was head of the faction which wanted to place Alextar, Nemone's supposedly mad older brother, on the throne in her place; he eventually fell into disfavor and was imprisoned, but was released after the queen's suicide (T16;13,17–19). Five years later, when Tarzan returned to Cathne, Alextar (who was now under the influence of Tomos, who hated Tarzan) tried to have the ape-man executed, but the people rebelled at this injustice, causing Alextar to kill himself, and putting Thudos on the throne (T21;19).

Thuran, Monsieur The alias adopted by Nikolas Rokoff when he signed aboard the same liner from Algiers to Cape Town as Tarzan had. Tarzan recognized him and threatened to throw him overboard, but "Mr. Thuran" managed to turn the tables, as he and Alexis Paulvitch heaved Tarzan into the Atlantic by surprise that very night. Afterward, "Mr. Thuran" wooed Hazel Strong for her money, almost convincing her to marry him, and accompanying her and her mother aboard Lord Tennington's yacht, *Lady Alice*, on its ill-fated cruise up the African coast. Tarzan later exposed him as Rokoff and he was arrested by the French navy (T2;12–13,26).

Thurds A horde of green Barsoomians who were bitter enemies of the horde of Torquas (M4;11).

Thurg The chief of the "Bad Men," whose arm Waldo Emerson Smith-Jones broke in rescuing Nadara from him early in 1911. Smith-Jones again met and defeated him almost a year later, and soon after that Thurg brought his whole tribe to attack Nadara's; they were defeated, but he stole into their settlement later that night and abducted Nadara. She escaped from him and holed up in a cliff for a while as Thurg watched, and he caught her coming down for food and would have had her, but was shot dead by Captain Burlinghame and First Officer Stark of the *Priscilla*, who were there in search of Smith-Jones (CG1;3)(CG2;1–8).

Thuria The larger, nearer moon of Mars, called Phobos by Earth men. It lies about 5800 miles from Mars and circles the planet in about seven and a half hours. It is usually conceived of poetically as female and as married to Cluros, the farther moon. A peculiar relationship exists between Thuria and Barsoom; any spaceship traveling from Barsoom to Thuria will somehow shrink until that moon seems a whole world — which, incidentally, is inhabited (see Ladan). The mineral wealth of the satellite is tremendous: gold, platinum and gems occur there in abundance (M8;16). The Black Pirates of Barsoom were once popularly supposed to come from Thuria, until John Carter exploded that myth (M2;8).

Thuria An advanced settlement of Pellucidar within the Land of the Awful Shadow. The Thurians practiced some agriculture and domestication of animals, and joined the Empire of Pellucidar in 1913. They are somewhat shorter and stockier than most Gilaks, and have very white skin from lack of sunshine (P1;15)(P2;6–8).

Thuria Astok, Prince of Dusar's personal flier, aboard which he went south to collect Vas Kor to kill Thuvia of Ptarth for him. It was the swiftest, best armed and best armored flier in Dusar (M4;14).

Thurian Tower One of the Towers of Jetan in Manator on Barsoom; Tara of Helium was imprisoned there while in the city in 1915 (M5;11).

Thurid A dator among the First-Born of Barsoom whom John Carter knocked out and bound in his own harness to prove that he could do so to any dator, and that the blacks were thus unjustified in reviling Xodar, whom Carter had previously bested (M2;10). Thurid later attempted revenge by helping Matai Shang to abduct Dejah Thoris from

the Temple of the Sun and flee with her. He later became infatuated with the beautiful princess, however, and killed Matai Shang so he could have her for himself. He was in turn killed by Phaidor, Matai Shang's daughter (M3;1–15).

Thuvan Dihn The Jeddak of Ptarth on Barsoom; he was the friend and ally of Kulan Tith, Jeddak of Kaol, and the father of Thuvia of Ptarth. He stepped forward in John Carter's behalf when the Kaolians would have killed him for heresy at the urging of Matai Shang and Thurid. The reason for this was that he had heard rumors of the truth about the Valley Dor and also about how John Carter had treated his daughter. When Matai Shang and Thurid fled Kaol with their prisoners (including Thuvia) because they feared Thuvan Dihn would sway Kulan Tith, the former accompanied John Carter in pursuit, adventuring with him into frozen Okar in the north (M3). He later promised his rescued daughter to Kulan Tith, much to her chagrin and that of Carthoris, but granted his permission for her to marry Carthoris after Kulan Tith gave up his claim (M4;1,14).

Thuvia, Maid of Mars The fourth book in the Mars series, abbreviated M4, which contains a glossary of Barsoomian names and terms as an appendix. The events within took place in 1889 and 1890 and were written down by John Carter when he was on Earth for three months in 1898. They were then published as a novel by Burroughs in 1916. In the novel Carthoris, son of John Carter and Dejah Thoris, had to rescue his beloved Thuvia of Ptarth from the clutches of Astok, Prince of Dusar. Along the way they discovered Lothar, a lost city of Orovars with mysterious mental powers. Worst of all, Carthoris was only saving Thuvia for another — Kulan Tith, Jeddak of Kaol, to whom her father had promised her.

Thuvia of Ptarth A princess of the city-state of Ptarth on Barsoom, daughter of the Jeddak, Thuvan Dihn. For some inexplicable reason she took the Pilgrimage while still quite young, and ended up enslaved by the Holy Thern, Sator Throg. She helped John Carter to escape the Chamber of Mystery and the Mountains of Otz, but fell into the clutches of the Black Pirates of Barsoom and was later imprisoned in the Temple of the

Sun along with **Phaidor** and **Dejah Thoris**, whose life **Thuvia** saved when **Phaidor** tried to stab her. They were abducted by **Matai Shang** and **Thurid** before their year of imprisonment was up and taken north to **Kaol**, then **Okar**. Several times during these adventures she was able to use her strange ability to control **banths** to save herself or her friends (M2)(M3).

She and **Carthoris** later fell in love, but she had been promised to **Kulan Tith**, Jeddak of **Kaol**. **Astok**, Prince of **Dusar** also coveted her and had her abducted and taken to the dead city of **Aanthor**, where he lost her to a **green man**. After escaping the green men, she and Carthoris found the lost city of **Lothar**, but after escaping it (again, thanks to her ability to control banths) they were attacked again by green men. She was then again abducted by Astok and rescued by Carthoris, and in the end Kulan Tith gave up his claim to her after seeing how much she and Carthoris loved each other (M4).

Tiang Umar A native **Sumatran** chief in whose village **Corrie van der Meer** and **Sing Tai** found asylum from the **Japanese** from 1942 to 1944 (T22;1).

Tibbet The second mate of the English yacht *Naiad* when it was captured by **Wilhelm Schmidt** and the *Saigon* mutineers late in 1938 (T24;6).

Tibbs Prince **Sborov**'s unflappable English valet, who accompanied him on his ill-fated flight to Africa in 1934. He really served very little help either in the jungle or in the later rescue of **Jane Clayton** and **Annette**, though he did happen to wake up in time to save **Neal Brown** from the Prince's treachery. Tibbs received one-sixth of the **immortality pellets** that Jane took from the **Kavuru**, but probably sold his share because he claimed that he would "rather dislike pressing trousers for so many years" (T19;3,19,21,31).

Tibdos The father of **Erot**, a young **Cathnean** who was elevated to the nobility; Tibdos was a cleaner of lion's cages (T16;8).

Tiberis Flumen "Tiber River" (*Lat*). The river which flows into the west end of **Mare Orientis** in the **Wiramwazi Mountains** (T12).

Tiberius Claudius Nero Caesar (42 B.C.–A.D. 37) The second emperor of Rome

(A.D. 14–37) and stepson of Augustus Caesar, who adopted Tiberius as his heir after Augustus' daughter Julia was banished for adultery and both Lucius and Gaius (her sons and Agrippina's brothers) had died young. Tiberius was a fair but unpopular ruler whose memory was soiled by the vindictive Agrippina, who had always hated him and spread rumors of debauchery at Tiberius' palace on Capri after he retired there in A.D. 26. Tiberius sickened while there, but before he died he disposed of Agrippina and the schemers Nero and Drusus. Near death, he travelled back toward Rome but took sick and died in Misenum, aided to his demise by Caligula and Macro (I;1,14–15).

Tiberius Gemellus The grandson of the Emperor **Tiberius**, son of **Drusus** and **Livilla**, who was born when **Caligula** was seven. He was adopted by Caligula as his son upon Tiberius' death, but was later forced by Caligula to take his own life (I;1,16).

Tibo A ten-year-old black boy whom Tarzan stole from **Mbonga**'s village around the beginning of 1908 out of an urge to have a human child of his own to care for. As might be expected, the child was terrified and cried constantly for his mother. Homesick, fearful of the jungle, and unable to appreciate the available food, Tibo quickly lost health even as he gained respect and trust for Tarzan and a working knowledge of the **tongue of the great apes**. Tarzan eventually let him return to the village with his mother when he realized that it was wrong to keep him (T6:5). A few months later he was again abducted, this time by the witch doctor **Bukawai**, who claimed credit for his safe return and wanted payment. Tarzan rescued him from Bukawai and brought him home (T6:6).

Tibur A legionary of **Germanicus**' legion who had been a Greek gladiator before being conscripted for the German campaign. He became a good friend of the boy **Britannicus** and was transferred to the **Praetorian Guard** at the end of the campaign. Tibur was later assigned to protect the person of **Caligula** and was elevated to the status of Tribune of the Guard upon Caligula's accession to the throne. He remained Britannicus' lifelong friend and tried to take the blame when he killed a Roman citizen in defense of **Attica**, for which Tibur was nearly executed.

Britannicus characterized Tibur in his memoirs as big, dumb and loyal (I;1–2,6–10,15–16).

Tige The dog of the Shorter family of 1915 Kansas, who was killed by **Dink** and **Crumb** while they were trying to rob Mrs. Shorter (K2;5,13).

"Tiger Girl" The third book of *Savage Pellucidar*, originally published in *Amazing Stories* magazine in 1942.

Tigerland The name given by Lt. Jefferson Turck and his men to ancient **Devon** for the enormous numbers of savage tigers they found there roaming free, apparently descended from ancient zoo specimens (LC;3).

Tigre The region of Abyssinia inhabited by the Semitic Tigrean minority; it is the northern part of **Eritrea** (T16;1).

tik (*Amt*) Eye (V3;19).

Til, Old An ancient lower-class crone of 13th century London whose hovel **Sir Jules de Vac** rented to keep **Prince Richard** in after abducting him in July of 1243. He later had to kill her to keep her from reporting him to the authorities (OT;3–4).

Tillie The toothless, ugly old wife of Peter, owner of **Peter's Inn** in early 20th century Karlova. Despite her appearance she was a tremendously good cook, a true culinary artist (R;4).

Timal An aboriginal tribe of Amtor's northern hemisphere. They inhabit the mountain country and are very human except for their horns and short tails. Although the Timal are primitive, they are intelligent, well-mannered and honorable. They never break their word, and their friendship (once earned) is never lost unless one betrays that friendship (V4;19).

timba In the **Bagego** language, the black cow (T12;5).

Timbuktu An ancient city of west Africa (today in the country of Mali) which was in ancient times a center of trade and learning, later only a center of trade, and today only a tourist attraction. It lies in the northern bend of the Niger River and was thus a trading point from the desert of the north to the grassland and jungle of the south. It was to Timbuktu that the **Arabs** of the tribe of **Amor**

ben Khatour travelled twice yearly to trade their goods and theft profits (T4;5).

time, Amtorian measure of How the Amtorians decided upon their year is unknown because there are no observable astronomical phenomena upon which to base its calculation. It is most probable that the year is either a biological or arbitrary unit which is derived by merely assigning a number of days to the unit. See also **te; day, Amtorian**.

time, Barsoomian measure of The Barsoomian day is roughly 24 hours, 37 minutes long. This is divided into ten periods called **zodes**, the first of which begins at winter dawn. Thus, each zode is equivalent to 2 hours, 27 minutes, 42 seconds Earth time. Each zode is further divided into 50 **xats**, each of which is equal to 2 minutes, 57 seconds. Each xat is further divided into 200 **tals**, each of which is .886 second long. Barsoomian clocks have three hands and three rings of markings (M2;16).

time, Pellucidarian Time does not seem to exist in Pellucidar because its sun never moves. **David Innes** tried to establish timekeeping by observing the rotation of the Dead World (Pellucidar's "moon"), but the Pellucidarians hated it so much he decided to abolish it (P3;1).

time, Va-nah measure of The advanced U-gas of Va-nah measure time by observing the difference in sunlight coming up through the **hoos** (craters) from the moon's exterior. One sidereal month they called an **ula**, and divided it by mechanical means into 100 **ola**, each of which was roughly equal to 6 hours, 32 minutes Earth time. Ten ula made up a **keld** (their version of a year), which was 272 days long (MM1;6).

Timothy One of the Midianite **apostles** when **Lady Barbara Collis** fell into **Midian** in 1929 (T15;2).

Tippet, John One of the crew of the captured U-33 when it became stranded in Caspak in July of 1916. Tippet was one of the members of the ill-fated **Bradley** expedition which set out from **Fort Dinosaur** on September 4, 1916; he was killed by a **Tyrannosaurus** in north Caspak on September 10th and was buried there (C1;6,8).

Tippoo Tib (1837–1905) A partially-black Arab slave and ivory trader of the late 19th century who built a commercial empire in the upper Congo region until it was forced into collapse by Leopold II of Belgium. His grandfather was an immortal medicine man who was supposed to have granted Tarzan eternal youth some time in the 1910s (T22;25).

Tiro, Marcus Tullius (103–4 B.C.) The private secretary of Cicero, who wrote his notes in the Notae Tironianae, a form of shorthand he devised himself (I;5).

Titius Sabinus One of the friends of Agrippina; his open bribery of one of Tiberius' retinue to assassinate the Emperor resulted in Sabinus' immediate arrest and execution (I;14).

Titus Livius (59 B.C.–A.D. 17) The full name of Livy, a Roman historian revered not so much for the historical accuracy of his work as for the style and skill with which it was written (I;4).

tizwin (*Apa*) A potent alcoholic beverage brewed from maize and mescal (A1;2–3).

Tjanath A city-state southwest of Jahar in the distant southern half of Barsoom's western hemisphere. Tjanath is a backward city with archaic architecture and obsolete technology. The people are superstitious and ignorant (though not so much as those of Phundahl) and greatly feared the power of Jahar after Tul Axtar began his plans for the conquest of Barsoom; the jed, Haj Osis, imprisoned everyone he suspected of being Jaharian (M7;5).

to (*Amt*) A prefix meaning "high" or "over" (V3;9).

to (*Pal*) Purple (T8).

To-jo The chief of the Band-lu tribe of Caspak who captured Bowen Tyler late in September of 1916 (C1;9).

To-mar The Band-lu warrior of Caspak who became a Kro-lu the morning Tom Billings and Ajor passed through the Band-lu country. After Billings saved To-mar's mate, To-mar became his friend and travelled north with him as far as the Kro-lu country. He later hid Ajor from the renegade Galu, Du-seen, while Billings was busy elsewhere (C2;4,6).

To-yad One of the Sagoths who captured Tarzan on his trip to Pellucidar in 1927 (T13;4).

toad, flying One of the common creatures of Va-nah is a toad-like, leathery-winged creature that flutters around in the trees, eating insects and uttering "plaintive cries." Its flesh is poisonous and cannot be eaten (MM1;3–4).

tob (*Amt*) The basic Amtorian unit of weight, which equals about one-third of a pound; whether Carson Napier meant this to mean a pound on Earth or a pound under Venus' lighter gravity is unknown. All Amtorian weights and measures are decimal and are derived from the tob (V1;7).

Tobey Professor Archimedes Q. Porter's manservant in Baltimore (T1;27).

Tobin, Father A gorilla priest of the Valley of Diamonds who was faithful to God against the forces of Henry VIII (T17;28).

Tofar The captain of the guard at the palace of Mintep, Jong of Vepaja, when Carson Napier first arrived on Amtor in 1929 (V1;4).

toga virilis (*Lat*) The toga of manhood, a garment which bore the same place in Roman society as the business suit does in ours (I;6).

togan "High man" (*Amt*). An Amtorian title of nobility roughly equal to a baron. When a togan has a son old enough to assume the duties himself, he becomes known as a vootogan (first high man) and his son a klootogan (second high man) (V5;4).

toganja "High woman" (*Amt*). An Amtorian title of nobility roughly equal to a baroness (V3;7)(V5;4).

Tojo, General Hideki (1884–1948) An important Japanese general of World War II, prime minister of Imperial Japan, who was responsible for all Japanese military operations during the War; he resigned in disgrace in the spring of 1944 because of the reverses suffered by the Japanese in the Pacific. He was arrested as a war criminal in 1945, tried, convicted, and executed on December 23, 1948. He was the uncle of Lt. Hideo Sokabe (T22;3,26).

tokordogan "Over-sergeant" (*Amt*). The Amtorian military rank which corresponds to our lieutenant (V3;9).

tola A Pellucidarian shellfish with a spherical shell (P1;10).

Tolan A family and manor of Gavo on Amtor who were friendly to the Ladja and Pandar families. They were defeated by Morgas and "turned into zaldars" until Carson Napier came along and broke Morgas' hold on the area in 1932 (V5;4).

Toledo A large town of Illinois, south of Payson (K3;10).

Tollog The brother of Sheik Ibn-Jad of the el-Harb tribe. Tollog wished to become sheik and so plotted against his brother with Fahd, one of Ibn-Jad's men who wanted to marry the sheik's daughter, but was refused. Tollog tried to kill Tarzan, for which Tarzan rendered him unconscious and placed him in the tent Ibn-Jad thought Tarzan was in. Thus, when Ibn-Jad sent Wilbur Stimbol to kill Tarzan, it was Tollog who got the knife (T11;2,15).

Tom One of the mutineers of the *Arrow* (T1;17).

Tomar One of the warriors of Clovi in Pellucidar when Tarzan came there in 1927 (T13;8).

Tomlin Lord John Ramsgate's valet on his photographic safari to Northern Rhodesia in 1939. He was in love with Violet, Lady Barbara Ramsgate's maid (T24B;5).

Tommy (WWI slang) The slang name for a typical British soldier, short for "Tommy Atkins," the sample name which appeared on army enlistment forms. Compare the American "G.I. Joe" (T7;24).

Tomos The Cathnean noble (Nemone's councillor) who interviewed Tarzan when he arrived in Cathne by accident early in October of 1930. He wished to marry Nemone, but the mysterious M'duze would not permit it, possibly because he was rumored to be Nemone's father (T16;5,11). Tomos was a powerful noble, and when Tarzan returned to Cathne in 1935, he found that Tomos had been able to bring the spineless King Alextar (Nemone's brother) under his control to a much higher degree than he had ever been

able to control Nemone, making Tomos the virtual ruler of the city. He made one fatal mistake, though — he threw Tarzan into prison and tried to have him executed. The people would not have this done to their hero (whom they had not forgotten in five years) and rose up in rebellion. When they took the palace, the mad Alextar killed Tomos, then committed suicide (T21;18–19).

Tompkins One of the sailors of the *Lady Alice* who was in the same lifeboat as William Clayton, Jane Porter and "Mr. Thuran" after the ship was wrecked. He died of starvation and thirst a week after the wreck, and would have been eaten by Wilson had the others not objected (T2;18).

ton (*Pal*) The number 20 (T8).

Tonda A town of German East Africa (T7;5).

tong (*Amt*) Big (V4;25).

Tongani (*Ape*) The baboon (T15;8).

tonglantar "Big landship" (*Amt*). The largest type of lantar used in Middle Anlap; it corresponds to a dreadnought in Earthly navies. Klootonglantar are roughly 700 to 800 feet long and 100 feet wide, with the upper deck about 30 feet above the ground; a superstructure rises some 30 feet above that. They are incredibly well-armored and bristling with weaponry (V4;44).

Tonglap "Big Land" (*Amt*). A large continent and nation of Amtor's northern hemisphere. It lies north of Anlap (V4;25).

tongue of Barsoom The semi-telepathic universal language of Barsoom, which dates back to the days of the last great alliance between the black, white and yellow races and is intelligible on some level even to lower animals. The language is so cleverly crafted that when a new word is needed for a new discovery, there is only one word that could possibly fit that concept, so even widely separated groups have the same technical terminology, though they arrived at it independently. Although the spoken language is universal, the written language of each country is different, though it is sometimes decipherable to foreigners (M3;11). The Lotharians speak an early form of the language, but even that was still intelligible to Carthoris and Thuvia of Ptarth (M4;6). The only remnant of any other language was the ancestral tongue of the First-Born, from which we must assume certain words in use among them (such as **dator**) were derived (M2;6).

tongue of Va-nah The language of Va-nah is musical; the meaning of a syllable depends on which of five notes it is sung in. Most words are only one or two syllables long, the longest words being three. The language is very beautiful to hear, and has been compared to "living constantly in grand opera" (MM1;5).

tongzan "Big beast" (*Amt*). A ferocious arboreal predator which inhabits the forests of giant trees in **Vepaja** and **Anlap** on Amtor. The tongzan is as large as a Bengal tiger and has clawed, hand-like paws with which it can climb trees. Projecting from its shoulders in front of its forelegs are two heavy chelae, and it has a single eye growing on a stalk from its forehead. Its forelegs are longer than its hind, and it is furry and striped lengthwise in bands of red and yellow. Klootongzan are very vicious and will attack anything, even a **tharban** (V1;3)(V4;39).

Tonle Sap A large lake of western Cambodia; during the rainy season the **Mekong** backs up into it and it grows to about 4000 square miles, 65 miles wide and up to 45 feet deep, and becomes navigable. In the dry season, however, the Tonle Sap flows into the Mekong and shrinks into a reedy swamp of about 1050 square miles, 22 miles wide and 3 to 10 feet deep, at which time it is navigable only by small boats in certain areas (HM;2).

tonneau The rear part of an old-fashioned touring car, which had a seat enclosed by low sides (R;7).

Tonos One of the two planets of **Omos** nearest **Poloda** in its weird shared orbit. **Tangor** was dispatched there in a plane equipped with the **power amplifier** to find out if conditions there were suitable for a mass migration of all **Unisans** to that world (B2;1,10).

Tony One of the vaqueros of the El Orobo Ranch in 1916 Mexico; he went with **Bridge** to collect the payroll from **Cuivaca** (K2;9).

Toog A renegade bull ape who one day came upon Tarzan's friend **Teeka** and her baby **Gazan** as they foraged at an unhealthy

distance from the rest of the tribe. Toog almost killed Gazan by causing him to fall from a tree, then overpowered Teeka and took her away with him, necessitating pursuit by Tarzan and Teeka's mate, **Taug**. After a few days they caught up with Toog, who had by then recruited two of his own tribe for help; they would have killed Tarzan and Taug had not one of a handful of bullets thrown by Teeka (she found them in Tarzan's pouch, and he in his father's **cottage**) exploded and scared the enemy away (T6;10).

Toonol An advanced, scientific city-state of Barsoom which lies at the east end of the great **Toonolian Marshes**. The Toonolians are atheistic and cultivate detachment, logic and unemotionality, but this is more true among the upper classes than the lower. Toonolians are objectivistic and success-oriented, and never break their given word. Owing to its presence in the marshes, Toonol is not really a flying nation; although there are many **fliers** there, the numbers are not nearly as high as in **Helium** or **Ptarth** (M6;2, 8–9).

Toonolian Marshes The largest wetlands on Barsoom, which are practically impassable on the ground and impossible to land in from the air. The swamp extends for some 1800 miles from east to west and nearly 300 from north to south, and is dominated by **Toonol** in the east and **Phundahl** in the west. Because of their inaccessibility, the fierce beasts which roam there, and the presence of two hostile nations, the marshes are a mystery to most Barsoomians. Outside of the cities, the marsh is only populated by **giant insects** and **reptiles** and fierce tribes of primitive humans. It is also the site of **Morbus**, an ancient city to the west of Toonol, which **Ras Thavas** reclaimed to perform his synthetic man experiments in. The city was later conquered by the **hormads** and had to be destroyed due to the failure of the experiments (M6;6)(M9; 2–6,20–23).

tor (*Bar*) The number four (M9;4).

tor (*Pal*) Beast (T8;6).

Tor-dur-bar "Four million eight" (*Bar*). A hormad of Morbus who befriended **Vor Daj** when he was captured by the hormads. Tor-dur-bar was decapitated in the fight against Vor Daj and John Carter and was sent to the culture vats to grow a new body; this new body was huge and powerful, and Tor-dur-bar still remembered Vor Daj after the regrowth process, which proved to Ras Thavas that he was an unusually intelligent hormad. In exchange for an oath of loyalty to Ras Thavas, Tor-dur-bar's brain was transferred to the body of Gantun Gur, an assassin from Amhor; thereafter, the hormad used the name Tun-gan. Tor-dur-bar's huge and powerful body then became the seat for Vor Daj's brain so the Heliumite could spy on the Seven Jeds and find his beloved Janai. Vor Daj was then known as Tor-dur-bar until he was restored to his own body. After Vor Daj/Tor-dur-bar rescued Janai, Sytor told her that Tor-dur-bar wished to possess her for his own and not for Vor Daj, and that he would have his (supposedly) hormad brain transferred to Vor Daj's body to woo her. Vor Daj knew of this lie, but did not wish to tell Janai the truth for fear that she would forever associate him with the hideous hormad body even after he was in his own body again, and thus be repulsed from him. What he did not foresee was that the wise girl had already seen the truth and loved his brain in spite of its hideous body, which was destroyed after Vor Daj was restored (M9;4,8–9,19,31).

Tor Hatan The odwar of the 91st Umak of the troops of Helium on Barsoom; he was a lesser noble of Helium and the father of Sanoma Tora. He was very rich because he had invested the spoils he had gained in war very wisely, multiplying the sum over time. He was notoriously lax in his duties and was a great social climber, for which purpose he cultivated the acquaintance of Tan Hadron who, though poor, was of noble blood and thus welcome in the great palaces of Helium (M7;1).

tor-ho The only large carnivorous beast of Va-nah, discounting the Va-gas. It is about the size of an Earthly mountain lion, but is reptilian and is quite a bit fiercer and tougher than a mountain lion. It is hairless and has long, sharp fangs and claws which are poisonous (as is its meat), owing to the fact that its diet consists primarily of rympths and flying toads, to which it is not at all averse to adding human meat. Tor-hos are fairly rare, but are found in all parts of Va-nah (MM1;8).

Tor-o-don "Beast-like man" (Pal). A primitive cousin of the Ho-don and Waz-don of Pal-ul-don; it is a large, hairy, tailed creature of a slightly higher level of development than the great apes (T8;6).

Toreador Bowen Tyler, Sr.'s yacht. After his death late in the summer of 1917, the ship was used for the expedition to rescue Bowen Tyler, Jr., from Caspak (C2;1).

Torith The dator of the island of the submarine pool in Omean on Barsoom (M2;12).

Tork A poker-like Amtorian game played with tiles like those used in Mah Jongg (V1;6).

Torkar Bar The Dwar of the Kaolian Road on Barsoom; a lesser noble of Kaol. He saved John Carter from a sith, then sent him on his way to Kaol (M3;5).

Torko The Zani governor of the Gap kum Rov in Amlot, under whom Carson Napier was detailed while spying in that Amtorian city in 1930 (V3;10).

Torlac A city of Northern Anlap on Amtor. It lies about 700 klookob (1750 miles) from Japal by water and is one of that nation's chief trade partners (V4;9).

Torlini, Lieutenant The pilot of the Italian pursuit plane sent out by Mussolini with Joseph Campbell and Zubanev aboard to bring down Lt. Cecil Giles-Burton and retrieve the secret plans Giles-Burton had recovered from the two. Torlini was killed by Burton during the dogfight that occurred over Northern Rhodesia when the pursuit plane caught up with Burton's plane (T24B;1–2).

Torn The name given by Sir Jules de Vac to the ancient Saxon castle in which he raised the young Prince Richard as his own son in the mid–13th century. It was later enlarged and repaired by Richard (now known as Norman of Torn) with the gains from his robberies and raids (OT;5–6).

Torndali The Chief of Quarries of the Minunian city of Veltopismakus while Tarzan was imprisoned there (T10;10).

Torp The chief of the Gorbuses of Pellucidar; he refused to release Wilhelm von Horst and La-ja, ordering instead that they be fattened to be eaten later. In his previous life, he had killed seven women (P5;10).

torpedo, rocket The huge rocket ship by which **Carson Napier** planned to reach Mars, but ended up instead on Venus. It was a 60-ton torpedo-shaped craft with engines capable of propelling it at ten miles per second and a year's supply of food, oxygen and electricity for a 45-day trip. Like the United States' early spaceships it was disposable, and after slowing sufficiently upon descent into an atmosphere, its pilot would bail out and parachute to the ground (V1;2).

torpedo, wheeled Wheeled torpedoes (mounted on three-wheeled undercarriages) are used in **lantar** engagements in **Middle Anlap** on **Amtor** with the intention of disabling the treads of enemy lantars. The torpedoes are effective only at short range because uneven terrain will deflect them (V4; 45).

Torquas A large, fierce **horde** of the **green men** of Barsoom who completely rule the **Highlands of Torquas**, which was once a continent in or bordering one of the five ancient seas. The Torquasians take their name (as is the custom) from the name of the ancient city from which they operate; Torquas, which lies north of **Aanthor** on the northeast corner of the Highlands. The Torquasians are the only green men who have developed artillery, which is why the **red men** seldom pass through their country. It was into their hands that **Thuvia of Ptarth** fell while she was a prisoner of **Astok**, Prince of **Dusar** in Aanthor. They took her to their camp outside **Lothar**, which they planned to besiege, but they were defeated by the Lotharians (as usual) and **Carthoris** rescued her from there (M4;5).

Torrance, James, Jr. Full name of Jimmy Torrance, a star football player, first baseman and boxer at "one of America's oldest and most famous universities" in the late 1910s. He was not, however, a good student and graduated last in his class, barely squeaking by at all. He was from **Beatrice, Nebraska**, and his father was the President of **Beatrice Corn Mills, Inc.** Torrance moved to **Chicago** soon after his graduation to look for a job, but soon found that this would not be easy because everyone wanted prior experience and few wanted a college graduate. He worked as a ladies' hosiery clerk, but quit after he met up with **Elizabeth Compton**, a beautiful and rich girl whom he had once changed a tire for and had a sort of crush on. He then got a job as a waiter at **Feinheimer's Cabaret** thanks to **The Lizard** (a pickpocket he had befriended), but lost it after defending Miss Compton from **Steve Murray**, one of the restaurant's best customers. He then worked as a sparring partner for a crooked boxer named **Brophy**, whose manager had seen him beat up Murray, but he lost this job by ruining Brophy's scheme to take a dive by beating him up in front of reporters — and Miss Compton again. His next job (as a milkman) was again acquired for him by The Lizard; in its pursuit he again met up with Miss Compton at the home of her friend **Harriet Holden**, who offered Torrance a better job which he turned down because he felt she was only doing it out of charity. He lost this job due to a strike (EE; 1–14).

He later (through falsified credentials) got a job as an efficiency expert at the **International Machine Company**, which unknown to him was owned by Miss Compton's father. He quickly discovered **Harold Bince's** embezzlement of the company and hired accountants to check the books and catch him, but Bince hired Steve Murray to get rid of Torrance, which Murray did by arranging for Torrance to be framed for the murder of **Mason Compton**, which Bince had actually committed. Thanks to the tireless efforts of Harriet Holden and **Little Eva**, and the eleventh-hour testimony of The Lizard, Torrance was acquitted. Tragically, Little Eva died of pneumonia directly afterward, but Torrance eventually married Miss Holden and became the General Manager of the International Machine Company (EE;15–28).

Torrance, James, Sr. The president and general manager of **Beatrice Corn Mills, Inc.**, in early 20th century Beatrice, Nebraska; the father of James Torrance, Jr. (EE;2).

Torres The Mexican governor of **Sonora** whose troops joined with the U.S. Cavalry to fight **Geronimo** in the spring of 1886 (A2;10).

Tousley, Reverend The preacher recruited by **Robert Canler** to perform the wedding ceremony for him and **Jane Porter** (T1;28).

Tovar The **vootogan** of **Pandar** in the Amtorian country of **Gavo** when **Carson**

Napier and Ero Shan came there in 1932 (V5;4).

Tower of Diamonds One of the many towers of the castle of the Tarids on Ladan; it was made of solid diamond. In it, Dejah Thoris and Zanda were imprisoned to await Ul Vas' pleasure (M8;19).

Another Tower of Diamonds was the easternmost tower of the Palace of Diamonds in the land of the Bolgani, in which were stored all of the millions of diamonds mined by the Bolgani since the days of Atlantis. They mined far more than they could possibly use because they believed that one day the Atlanteans would return and buy them (T9;16).

Tower of London A prison of London in the Valley of Diamonds, modeled after the original in England (T17;18).

Tower of the Emperors The tower of the Palace of Diamonds in which the throne room of Numa lay (T9;14).

Towers of Jetan A prison in Manator on Barsoom composed of a set of towers confining the prisoners who will be forced to play at jetan in the next set of games. Tara of Helium was kept there while in Manator (M5;11).

Toyat A king ape who hated Tarzan because the ape-man had once kept him from becoming king of a tribe; he wanted to kill Tarzan when his tribe encountered him in 1921 (T11;3). Tarzan had many other encounters with Toyat and his tribe over the next few years (T14;13–14).

tra (*Amt*) Warm (V1;4).

Trabol "Warm country" (*Amt*). The "middle belt," or temperate zone, of Amtor's southern hemisphere, where most of its known nations are located. Trabol is the only part of Amtor drawn to more or less accurate proportions on the highly inaccurate Amtorian maps (V1;4).

trachodon A herbivorous, bipedal, duck-billed dinosaur of the Cretaceous which measured some 40 feet from nose to tail. Relatives of the creature still live in Pellucidar (P4;12).

traffic, Amtorian The only automotive traffic on Amtor is found in the scientifically advanced city of Havatoo, where it is handled in a startlingly efficient fashion. All the cars function on broadcast power, on different frequencies for different directions. When a vehicle comes within 100 feet of an intersection, it automatically switches (via a photoelectric beam which "tells" the car where it is) into a special power frequency that is intermittently turned on and off for cars moving from wall to hub of the city or for cars moving parallel to the walls. When the power is interrupted, automatic brakes immediately stop the car; thus, only cars moving in one direction at a time are allowed through the intersections, eliminating both the need for traffic signals and the results of ignoring them, because when the "red light" goes on at an intersection (so to speak), the cars moving in that direction automatically stop and those moving perpendicular to it automatically resume travel all at once. Because only cars within 100 feet of an intersection are affected, cars between intersections continue to move. Pedestrians travel along a series of viaducts which connect all buildings in the city at the second-story level (V2;13).

traffic, Barsoomian Barsoomian traffic regulations are simple. The normal medium of transport in a city is a small flier with a ceiling of about 100 feet and a top speed of about 60 miles per hour. All streets are one way to traffic, and east-west traffic is forced to rise above north-south at intersections by means of a ramp placed directly before the intersection. Turning is accomplished by rising above both lanes and settling back in when there is an opening. Parking is inside buildings at about 60 feet above the street. Pedestrian traffic follows sidewalks on both sides of the street and continues through intersections on north-south streets, and through underpasses on east-west streets (M9;24). Police and emergency vehicles have a higher-altitude zone all to themselves, and transports between cities move in a higher zone still (M4;2).

trag (*Pell*) To launch a deadly missile; to fire (P2;13).

trail, Mezop The trails made by the Mezops of Pellucidar from the shores of their islands to their villages are very tortuous and are broken in many places by points where the trail user must go through trees, over bushes, or along logs to another nearby leg of the trail. This ingenious method keeps enemies from finding Mezop villages easily, since it is hard enough for the natives of an island to learn all the twists and tricks, and nearly impossible for enemies (P1;8).

Trajan (53–A.D. 117) The Roman emperor who ruled after **Nerva** (T12;10).

Trans-Siberian Railroad Originally completed in 1916, it crossed Siberia from Moscow to Vladivostok. Its ruined portions were restored by the **Chinese** Empire as far as Moscow by 2137 (LC;9).

Tree of Life The mythological source of all life on Barsoom. According to legend, the tree flourished in the center of the **Valley Dor** 23 million years ago. It was apparently of prodigious size, as the nut-like fruit it bore were each a foot in diameter. For ages the fruit evolved, changing from plant to half plant and half animal, and finally to animal. The fruit evolved brains, and after many eons began to drop off the tree, shattering into quarters. Each quarter was a sealed chamber in which a creature lived. In the first (which shattered open) was a tiny **Plant Man**, who remained attached to the tree. In the second was a sixteen-legged worm, in the third a **white ape**, and in the fourth a black man — all in miniature, of course. The latter three creatures remained encased in their shells and hopped about blindly, trying to free themselves, and in the process many fell into lakes and rivers and were washed up all over Barsoom. Many generations lived out their lives in the shells and died, struggling to get out, before a black man burst his shell and then began to break open others, at first out of curiosity and then, presumably, out of a need for companionship. It is from this myth that the blacks call themselves the **First-Born** of Barsoom.

The plant men eventually learned to detach themselves and grew huge; the Tree of Life died soon afterward. The 16-legged worm gave rise to all of the multi-legged lower life forms of Barsoom and the white ape to the present white apes and **green men**; the other human forms resulted from the mating of renegade blacks with the white apes. Most of the other inhabitants of Barsoom have their own version of this myth, though of course the first human is not usually conceived of as being of any particular color (M2;7).

trees, Amtorian The foliage of Amtorian trees is pale and of purplish colors

(especially orchid, heliotrope and violet), but the boles are of brilliant colors and shine as though they were lacquered (V2;5).

trees, Barsoomian While the trees along the canals of Barsoom are large, those of the Valley Dor are simply monstrous, some being fully 100 feet in diameter and 1000 feet tall, with trunks and leaves of all manner of colors. The trees of the **Gardens of Issus** are smaller, but just as dazzlingly beautiful; they have white trunks and purple flowers (M2;1,9). See also **calot tree; skeel; sompus; sorapus; usa**.

trees, Euroban The trees and plants of **Eurobus**, deprived as they are of true sunlight, do not have very good photosynthetic ability, and are all of a pallid, deathly color. They are almost all carnivorous and can eat even fairly large animals. Their nervous systems, however, are of a very low order and their reactions are consequently very slow, especially to pain and the like. The blossoms are the brains and nerve centers and are equipped with eyes and vicious, toothy jaws. They close up in the presence of smoke, so travelers in Euroban jungles must keep a smoky fire burning for protection while camped. Most of the trees have very pliable limbs that may be cooked and eaten; they taste much like veal when so prepared (M11B;8).

trees, Va-nah The trees of Va-nah are distinctly flesh-toned, and many bear huge, beautiful flowers and succulent fruit of various types (MM1;3).

trees, Vepajan The trees of the Amtorian continent of **Vepaja** are absolutely immense; many of them reach all the way up to the inner cloud envelop of Amtor and attain a diameter of fully 1000 feet at the base. Like other Amtorian trees, their leaves are of varying shades of lavender, heliotrope and violet (V1; 3–4,7).

Trent A fairly large river of central England which empties into the Humber in Yorkshire (OT;7).

Trent, Duncan One of the members of the **Ramsgate** safari to **Northern Rhodesia** in 1939; he was attempting to woo **Lady Barbara Ramsgate** (T24B;5).

triangle An inverted isosceles triangle is a symbol used by the Galus of **Caspak** for their god **Luata**. It is placed upon jewelry and other items and is drawn in the air at sunrise or upon first encountering or making a fire (C2;3).

Triassic The first period of the Mesozoic Era, which began about 230 million years ago and ended about 181 million years ago. The forests of the Triassic were dominated by cycads, primitive conifers, and tree-ferns, and the earliest dinosaurs appeared in this period.

Tribbolet An American rancher and moonshiner of **Sonora** who sold strong whiskey to soldiers and **Apaches** for ten dollars a gallon in the 1880s (A2;9).

tribes, African The following is a list of at least most of the many African tribes mentioned in the Tarzan books and several others. See individual entries.

Babango	Galla	Pygmies
Bagego	Ho-den	Urambi
Bagesu	Kaji	Utenga
Bangalo	Kaviri	Wagambi
Bansuto	Kavuru	Waganwazam
Bantango	Kor-ul-ja	Wakanda
Bantu	Kor-ul-lul	Wamabo
Basembo	Kovudoo	Wamboli
Batoro	Manyuema	Waruturi
Betete	Mbonga	Waziri
Buiroo	Mosula	Zertalacolol
Bukena	Mpugu	Zuli
Buliso	Obebe	

tribes, Indonesian Several tribes of Indonesia and the Malay archipelago were mentioned in various of Burroughs' books; see **Battak; Dyak; Maori**.

tribes, Pellucidarian The following is a list of most of the known tribes of Pellucidar. See individual entries.

Amiocap	Hime	Oog
Amoz	Ja-ru	Ruva
Azar	Juka	Sari
Basti	Julok	Suvi
Canda	Kali	Tandar
Clovi	Ko-va	Thuria
Daroz	Mammoth Men	Zoram
Gef	Manat	Zurts
Go-hal	Mezops	

trident The chief weapon used by the **Myposans** of Amtor (V4;3).

trident, wooden The only weapon given to the slave-guards among the **Myposans** of Amtor (V4;8).

trireme A galley with three banks of oars (I;5).

The Triumph of Tarzan The original title of *Tarzan Triumphant* when it appeared as a serial in *Blue Book* magazine from October of 1931 to March of 1932.

tro (*Ape*) Straight (TC).

Trocadero A Hollywood social club of the 1930s (J;5).

trodon An awful monster of Pellucidar which looks sort of like a 15-foot-tall winged reptilian kangaroo with the head of a pteranodon. It has a long tail for balance, a pouch large enough for a human to fit in, and both wings and foreclaws, making it a six-limbed creature. It also has a needle-like poisoned tongue with which it spears its victims through the spine at the base of the neck, paralyzing them below the neck for quite a long time; while paralyzed, the victim needs neither food nor water. The trodon then makes a great circle of its many victims in its pit-like lair, laying them with the heads turned outward after having laid a great circle of eggs first, so that each egg is just beyond one victim's head. In the next few weeks each baby hatches in turn, eats its own shell, then eats its still-living victim whole. It then sleeps for a few days to digest its meal, then flies away. The poison never wears off during this several-weeks-long period, but if a victim is removed from the lair, the paralyzation wears off a few days after the time which would have been sufficient for the baby to hatch and eat (P5;1–3).

Trog The subchief of the **Mammoth Men** of Pellucidar who tried to drive **Ah Ara, Ma Rahna**, the rogue **tandor**, with fatal results for one of his fellow tribesmen (P5;13).

troglodyte (Greek) Cave dweller (E1;1).

Trohanadalmakus The **Minunian** city ruled in 1918 by King **Adendrohahkis**, which consisted of 11 domes and was inhabited by 500,000 people, with another 500,000 slaves living underground in the well-lit and ventilated mine galleries. Because Tarzan had rescued their prince, **Komodoflorensal**, from being eaten by a **zertalacolol**, Tarzan was received in Trohanadalmakus as an honored guest (T10;6).

Troll One of the white hunters of the 1935 **Wood** safari to the **Sudan** and **Ethiopia**. After he was rescued by Tarzan from the Kaji, he and Spike became angry that they were not to get a share of the proceeds from the sale of the Gonfal and the Great Emerald of the Zuli and so decided to steal the gems and flee. They later abducted Gonfala from Stanley Wood (thinking that she was the key to making the Gonfal function) and headed north for a hidden valley Spike knew of. In a fight over the girl, however, Troll suffered a serious concussion and became amnesiac, as a result of which he became convinced that Gonfala was his sister, whom he had to protect from Spike. On the way to the valley, they passed through Thenar and were enslaved by its revolutionary government; they were eventually rescued by Tarzan, and Spike and Troll were booted out of Africa under guard (T21;14–19,25).

Trun The Ganak of Pellucidar who captured La-ja, Wilhelm von Horst's beloved, early in 1928 (P5;19).

Truth One of the Mammoth Men of Pellucidar, who was assigned to guard Frug of Basti while he was their prisoner early in 1928 (P5;13).

Tsa A mighty Sto-lu of Caspak who captured Lys La Rue from Fort Dinosaur on September 15, 1916, and took her back to his tribe with the intent of mating with her; Bowen Tyler caught up with him, however, and shot him dead (C1;8).

Tsao Ming A Chinese pirate of the South Seas whom Thandar saved from a headhunter when they were both shipwrecked on the same island in 1912. He was extremely grateful and did everything possible to help Thandar in his search for Nadara. His crew later captured both Thandar and the *Priscilla* crew and would have killed them all had not Tsao Ming come upon the scene and saved them (CG2;10,12).

tsoch (*Apa*) A papoose carrier or cradle (A1;1).

tu In the adolescent Tarzan's letter-naming system, the letter "O" (T6:4).

tu (*Ape*) Broken (T1;4).

tu (*Pal*) Bright (T8;16).

Tu-al-sa The Mahar whom Hooja the Sly One substituted for Dian the Beautiful when David Innes returned from Pellucidar to the

outer Earth, and whose life he spared when he could easily have taken it. She later repaid his kindness by begging the Mahar queen to spare his life when he was captured by the Mahars of Phutra and sentenced to die in the arena. Her prayer was heeded because she was of royal blood, having been descended from the last male Mahar ruler in the distant past (P1;15)(P2;1,5).

Tu-lur "Bright City" (*Pal*). The city of Pal-ul-don which was ruled by Mo-sar, pretender to the throne of Pal-ul-don (T8;18).

tuano (*Min*) Good night (T10;12).

Tublat "Broken Nose" (*Ape*). The male ape of the tribe of Kerchak who was Kala's mate, and thus Tarzan's foster father. He hated Tarzan and was in turn hated by him, and so became the butt of innumerable practical jokes launched by the young ape-man, such as his game of lassoing Tublat's neck by surprise and choking him for a while. The other apes of the tribe thought this incredibly funny, since no one liked Tublat anyway. During a berserk rage that began after a Dum-dum ritual when Tarzan was 13, Tublat tried to kill Kala and was killed by Tarzan (T1;4–7).

Tubuto The young warrior of the tribe of Mbonga who replaced Rabba Kega as witch doctor after Tarzan caused the old man's death (T6:11).

Tuen-baka An extinct volcano in Northern Rhodesia. Its caldera is filled with water, thus forming the sacred Lake Horus upon and beneath whose waters Ashair and Thobos lie. The volcano and the cities are both tabu to the natives of the area, and Ashair is called the Forbidden City (T20;10).

Tul Axtar The Jeddak of Jahar on Barsoom; he was a very evil and dishonorable man who dreamed of conquering Barsoom with an enormous, recently-bred army equipped with the disintegration rifles of Phor Tak, but was too much of a coward to carry out the actual invasion after making all of his preparations. He made marriage illegal among the middle and lower classes of Jahar because he felt that indiscriminate mating would increase the birth rate; the plan succeeded too well, giving Jahar a disastrous population explosion (see U-gor). For this and his other excesses and perversions (like a palace full of 1500 personal slave women) he was hated by most Jaharians.

Tul Axtar was informed of the beauty of Sanoma Tora and abducted her from Helium, which resulted in his being pursued by Tan Hadron and eventually captured in his own palace. He bribed Sanoma Tora to release him while Tan Hadron slept by promising to make her his jeddara. After his fleet's defeat, his people stormed the palace seeking his destruction, but he stole aboard the *Jhama* (in which Tan Hadron had come to re-abduct him) under the cloak of invisibility he had stolen from Tan Hadron, and took both the ship and Tavia; unfortunately for him, he then made the mistake of going back to Phor Tak's laboratory to regain his help and was there caught and killed by Tan Hadron (M7;1,5,13–17).

Tullianum A maximum security prison of ancient Rome which was built by the semilegendary Servius Tullius (I;4).

tumal (*Pell*) A native beer brewed by the Mammoth Men of Pellucidar from wild maize, herbs and honey — it is a potent brew with "the kick of an army mule" (P5;15). The same name was applied to a beverage brewed by the people of the Floating Islands, probably made from their own native plants (P6;24).

Tumbai An African village of Utengi (T18;1).

Tun-gan The new name of Tor-dur-bar after his brain was transplanted to the body of Gantun Gur, the assassin of Amhor. The name was a transposition of the first two syllables of the assassin's name. As Tun-gan, Tor-dur-bar served Vor Daj (whose brain was in Tor-dur-bar's old body) until Vor Daj wished to return to Morbus, at which point Tun-gan deserted him. He was later picked up by an Amhorian cruiser whose crew thought he was really Gantun Gur, so he began to use that name and took the assassin's place completely (M9;9,19,23).

tunb el-beyt (*Ara*) The main support rope of a tent (T11;13).

Tunbridge Wells An English town of southwest Kent, roughly 30 miles SSE of London (LC;5).

tunic The garment worn by both the Laytheans and Kalkars of Va-nah was a short tunic which hung to about mid-thigh and was made of rich (often diaphanous) fabric for the Laytheans and leather or cheap fabric for the Kalkars (MM1;6,9).

Tunis The capital of Tunisia (formerly a French possession), which lies near the ancient site of Carthage (T24B;3).

Tunk, Mag An old woman of medieval London, a friend of Old Til's (OT;4).

Tunzo Bor A Unisan prisoner in a Kaparan labor camp when Tangor was imprisoned there after "defecting" to Kapara in the spring of 1940. Tangor met and befriended the man, thinking he might lead him to the missing Handon Gar. He did, and they later planned to escape the prison together until Gar became convinced that Tangor was a traitor (B2;3–4).

Tur The god of Phundahl on Barsoom. The Phundahlians are like Earthly biblical fundamentalists in that they deny any scientific evidence that conflicts with Turgan, the book of Tur's religion. Tur is supposed to be the only god, but the Phundahlians worship many different idols of him with meaningless rituals that they (of course) take on faith. At each idol, a different ritual is performed and money is deposited. Because of their slavish devotion to this idiotic religion, the people of Phundahl are the most backward on Barsoom. The priests of Tur mostly realize that their religion is a scam, but many of them are never completely sure about Tur's divinity — except for the high priest (the Jeddak of Phundahl), who knows all the secrets. See also The Great Tur (M6;10–11).

Tur A warrior of the Boat-Builder tribe of Niocene Africa who tried to capture Nat-ul and was forced to follow her out to a small group of islands in the Restless Sea after she was carried there by a supposedly extinct giant pterodactyl. He abducted her and would have mated with her had not Nu, son of Nu, come to the rescue. Tur later recaptured her and fled to another island, where he would have killed both her and Nu had not Gron, his jealous wife, killed him first (E2; 4–9,12–14).

Turan The alias adopted by Gahan, Jed of Gathol, to hide his identity from Tara of Helium after rescuing her from Bantoom. He posed as a panthan in order to win her respect more easily than if she had known who he truly was (M5;8).

Turck A naval family of the 20th to 22nd centuries, from which Jefferson Turck sprang (LC;1).

Turck, Jefferson The hero of *The Lost Continent*. Born in Arizona in 2116 of the famous naval Turck family, he took his first command on the aero-sub *Coldwater* in 2137, which led him to penetrate the forbidden line of 30 degrees longitude when his ship malfunctioned; he eventually brought back a story which led to the lifting of the ban against contact with the eastern hemisphere. After the failure of the gravitation screen generators of the *Coldwater*, her engines were sabotaged by Porfirio Johnson, the second officer, who out of jealousy for Turck wanted the ship swept beyond 30, which would result in a mandatory court-martial for its commander. When Turck refused to submit to arrest after being blown across the line by the wind, Johnson succeeded in seizing control of the now-repaired ship while Turck was out in a boat, then abandoned him in mid-ocean. Turck and his small launch crew effected a landing on the island of Great Britain, finding it reduced to barbarism, and while he was there he rescued and fell in love with Victory, the Queen of Grabritin, as they called their country (LC;1–6).

The party then continued on to mainland Europe, finding it as devastated as Britain, and there Turck was betrayed by Snider so that he was eventually captured and enslaved by the soldiers of the Abyssinian Empire. He eventually found Victory (who had also been enslaved) and rescued her from the Abyssinian emperor, who wished her for himself. Turck in turn was then rescued by the forces of the Chinese Empire, who had been attacking the Abyssinian-held area for some time. In the beneficent hands of the Chinese, Turck and Victory were married and soon returned to Pan-America, which (thanks to the work of Lt. John Alvarez of the *Coldwater*) had decided to re-establish relations with China. Not long afterward, Turck headed Pan-American forces on their mission to reclaim Britain (LC;7–9).

Turck, Admiral Porter The first famous Turck, who was a naval commander of the late 20th century. He had quite a store of books on the history and geography of Eu-

rope, even though such things were generally frowned upon (LC;1–2).

Turgan The holy book of the religion of Tur on Barsoom, supposedly written by Tur himself. Like Earthly biblical fundamentalists, devotees of Tur deny all scientific knowledge that conflicts with Turgan. For instance, they believe that Tur lives in the sun, where he created a flat Barsoom 100,000 years ago and flung it into space. Because of this, the teaching of history prior to 100,000 years ago is forbidden as a lie (even though this history is authenticated), and aviation is not permitted far beyond the city lest a flier circumnavigate Barsoom, thus disproving its flatness. Telescopes are forbidden because Barsoom is the only world, and even biological reproduction is denied, because all life is created directly by Tur. In Phundahl, Turgan is the only textbook (M6;10).

Turjun The alias used by Carthoris while posing as a panthan in order to infiltrate Dusar, which (with two other nations) was planning to war on Helium over the abduction of Thuvia of Ptarth (M4;13).

Turquoise Tower One of the many towers of the castle of the Tarids on Ladan; as its name suggests, it was made of solid turquoise. John Carter, Gar Nal, Ur Jan, Jat Or and Umka were incarcerated there to await their sacrifice to the sun (M8;19).

Tusculum A town of ancient Latium, about 12 miles southeast of Rome; it was the site of one of the villas of Antonia, Germanicus Caesar's mother (I;15).

Twentyfour The ruling committee of a Kalkar city of Va-nah, analogous to an Earthly politburo or central committee, and composed (obviously) of 24 members (MM1; 10). Later, the term came to be applied to the Kalkar government of Earth in general. There was an actual Twentyfour, a council composed of that many members, but as they were all appointed by the jemadar and could be removed by him at will, they had little real power (MM2;2,6).

Twenty-fourth Street A Chicago street of the south side on which Farris's bar and brothel lay in the 1910s (GF;1).

267M9436 Tangor's number while he was a prisoner in a Kaparan labor camp in the spring of 1940 (B2;3).

Two Spot   One of the horses of the Billings ranch in 1886 Arizona (A2;13).

Tyler, Bowen J., Jr.   The son of Santa Monica shipbuilder Bowen Tyler, Sr., who on his way to France to join the American Ambulance Corps in World War I was on a liner torpedoed in the English Channel by a U-boat on June 3, 1916. He and Lys La Rue, a young woman with whom he subsequently fell in love, were rescued by a tugboat which soon afterward encountered and captured the U-33, which had sunk the liner. After several weeks of cruising with some instruments gone and others sabotaged thanks to a German spy among the crew, the U-boat became completely lost and ended up in the South Pacific, where it landed in the "lost continent" of **Caprona** without enough fuel to escape it. They later found a source of crude oil in Caprona (called **Caspak** by its inhabitants) and, with a little luck, were able to refine it sufficiently to refuel the U-boat; at this point the Germans stole back the ship, leaving Tyler and the Englishmen stranded (C1;1–7).

Tyler and Lys finally admitted their love to each other on September 10, but she was abducted the next day by Tsa, chief of the Sto-lu of Caspak. Tyler rescued her, killing Tsa in the process, and they lived with the Sto-lu for a while until he became lost while hunting one day. He was captured by a Band-lu tribe, escaped, then set up housekeeping in a cave atop the barrier cliffs of Caspak, which he had finally managed to scale. A short time later he again met Lys and killed another Sto-lu who was chasing her; they then married each other and set out to await rescue after Tyler threw his journal of the adventure out to sea from the top of the cliffs in his tightly-capped thermos bottle on October 8th (C1;8–10). They later befriended the **Galus** of northern Caspak and moved into one of their cities, from which they were finally rescued by **Tom Billings** and the crew of the *Toreador* late in the summer of 1917 (C2;7).

Tyler, Bowen J., Sr.   A famous ship and submarine builder of **Santa Monica, California**, in the early 20th century. He died en route from **Honolulu** to Santa Monica to meet Burroughs for news of his son, Bowen Tyler, Jr., late in the summer of 1917 (C2;1).

tylosaurus   A 26-foot marine dinosaur of the Cretaceous; its Pellucidarian cousin is 40 feet long (P7:4;2).

typewriter   Chicago gangland slang of the 1920s for a **Thompson submachine gun** (T15;5).

Tyrannosaurus rex   A fearsome, bipedal, predatory therapod dinosaur of the Cretaceous which had an oversized head, under-sized forepaws, and a limitless appetite; it measured some 50 feet long from nose to tail and stood about 20 feet tall. See also **zarith** (P5;8–9). A miniature species of the creature which stands about eight feet tall and weighs almost 1000 pounds prowls the area about the sacred volcano **Tuen-baka**, but it is very rare, almost extinct (T20;14).

Tyros the Bloody   The Jong of Mypos when **Carson Napier** came there late in 1930. After spending some time as a slave in Mypos, Napier was finally able to get near Tyros, and killed him with his pistol after he tried to rape **Duare** (V4;3–16).

Tze-go-juni   The ancient medicine woman of the **Cho-kon-en** Apache in the late 19th century (A1;9).

tzi-daltai   (*Apa*) An amulet made by an Apache warrior from the wood of a lightning-struck tree (A1;3).

tzi-ditinde   (*Apa*) A ceremonial noise-maker, whirled about the head to produce a whistling noise; a bullroarer (A1;3).

U-boat   (Abbreviation of *Unterseeboot* [undersea boat]) (*Ger*) A submarine, particularly a military one; U-boats were the backbone of Germany's navy in both World Wars (C1;1).

U Dan   A padwar in the guard of Zu Tith, Jed of Zor on Barsoom, who gladly swore allegiance to Helium when his tyrannical ruler was overthrown and Zor added to the Heliumetic Empire. U Dan was forced by **Multis Par** to lead John Carter into a Morgor trap by abducting U Dan's beloved, **Vaja**, and threatening her with rape and un-ending torture without death. As almost any man would, he acquiesced, but later helped John Carter and **Dejah Thoris** escape the Morgors, rescuing Vaja in the process (M11B; 1–2,6).

U-Dor   The dwar of the 8th Utan of O-Tar, Jeddak of Manator on Barsoom. U-Dor and his men captured **Tara of Helium** and **Ghek** the **Kaldane** outside the walls of Manator, and he was the orange chief in the jetan game played for Tara against the black chief, **Gahan of Gathol**, who killed U-Dor in the game (M5;10,17).

U-gas   The more human-like of the two humanoid races of **Va-nah**; the term was generally only applied to the pure U-ga race, discounting the mixed **Kalkars**. U-gas had marble-white skin and totally black hair, with totally black eyes. They were a very beautiful race of great scientific achievement, and at one time had an advanced civilization with telecommunications, aircraft and trains; all of this was destroyed, however, by the revolution inspired by the communistic Kalkars, who overthrew the ruling class and proclaimed everyone equal (resulting, of course, in no one wanting to work). Like Earthly fanatics, the Kalkars burned and destroyed what they did not understand, including books, and even the remnant of true U-gas who built the hidden city of **Laythe** lost almost all of their learning while on the run from the Kalkars. The last pure U-gas were all either destroyed or enslaved by the Kalkars after the sack of Laythe in 2036. The U-gas ate Va-gas, both those killed in the wild and those kept and fattened for slaughter, because Va-gas were the only available meat in Va-nah, where every other animal is too poisonous to eat (MM1;6–7,10,13–14).

U-Gor   Once a rich agricultural province of **Jahar** on Barsoom, it was destroyed by a hundred years of **Tul Axtar**'s mad plan to increase his manpower. The population explosion created by the plan resulted in the depletion of U-Gor's crops, then reduced it to a wasteland. By the time Tul Axtar dropped **Tan Hadron** and **Tavia** there, it was inhabited only by roving bands of savage cannibals (M7;14).

U-Kal   The alias adopted by Gahan of Gathol while posing as a Manatorian (M5; 16).

U-33   The German U-boat that sank the ocean liner upon which **Bowen Tyler** and **Lys La Rue** were bound for France, and which was later captured by the crew of the British tug that rescued them. Due to sabotage by the spy Benson, the vessel was thrown far off course, and due to a counter-mutiny by the Germans, a return to the British, and a final bit of sabotage by Benson, it eventually ended up lost far in the South Pacific and reached the island of **Caprona**, where the hidden land of **Caspak** lies. They were stuck there without fuel for a time, but after the discovery and refinement of a source of crude oil in Caspak the Germans fueled up the U-boat, stole it back, and set out for home without the British (C1;1–7). They themselves could not use the damaged instruments, however, and after wandering lost for some time and narrowly escaping destruction in allied waters, they headed back to Caspak to refuel, at which time the sub was recaptured by **Bradley** and the other British and used to return to **California** by following the yacht **Toreador** (C3;5).

U-Thor   The Jed of **Manatos**, second city of Manator on Barsoom. He is a good, noble man and much loved by the people of Manator, for which he was hated by the Jeddak O-Tar, whom the people respected but did not love. In his city, jetan was a martial sport instead of butchery as in Manator. He married Princess **Haja of Gathol** (who had been a slave in Manator) and thus made her again a princess; he also became very incensed at the mistreatment of her son **A-Kor**. In 1915 U-Thor declared open hostilities against O-Tar and camped his forces at the **Gate of Enemies**, where he was joined by many Manatorians and aided from within the city by Gahan of Gathol and his friends. After the fleets of Helium and Gathol also showed up, O-Tar committed suicide and A-Kor was placed on the throne (M5;13–14,20–22).

U-Val   A warrior of **Ruva** who was a prisoner of the giant ants of Pellucidar along with **David Innes** late in 1929. After their escape he treacherously bound Innes as he slept and carried him off to Ruva as a slave. He later picked a fight with Innes and was killed by him almost immediately (P6;20–25).

U-Van   A warrior of Manator on Barsoom who saw Ghek's headless rykor while Ghek was exploring some ulsio burrows and was scared half to death (M5;12).

Ubooga   The eldest and chief wife of **Bobolo**, whom he placed **Kali Bwana** in the care of after stealing her from the **Leopard Men** in 1931 (T18;13).

ubor (Ape) Thirsty (TC).

ud (Ape) Drink (TC).

Uda The little son of Che and Kangrey, the Khmer peasants of Lodidhapura who nursed Gordon King back to health after he stumbled into their country in a delirium (HM;3).

Udalo The chief of the Bukena who was so deathly afraid of his mysterious neighbors, the Kavuru, that he would give Tarzan no information regarding them; he instead decided that Tarzan was a Kavuru spy and took him prisoner (T19;4).

ug (Ape) Bottom (TC).

Ugalla The east African homeland of the Bagalla tribe (TT1;3).

Ugambi The land of the Wagambi tribe in west Africa, and the name of the main river which flows through the area (T3;5).

ugla (Ape) Hate (TC).

Uglo The king of the orang-utan tribe of Sumatra whom Tarzan encountered and befriended in the spring of 1944 after saving one of their balus from a python. Uglo was old, however, and did not dare to interfere when the young and brutal Oju challenged Tarzan (T22;11).

Ugogo An African river down which Esteban Miranda fled Tarzan, and upon which he became a prisoner of the cannibal tribe of Obebe (T9;21).

Uhha The daughter of Khamis, witch-doctor of the tribe of Obebe. Esteban Miranda succeeded in befriending her while he was a prisoner of the cannibals and thus accomplished his escape, with her in tow. She later realized that he was neither Tarzan nor river-devil and so struck him unconscious while he slept, stole the diamonds that he had stolen from Kraski (and Kraski from Tarzan) and escaped, only to be eaten soon afterward by a lion, which allowed Usula the Waziri to find the diamonds among her remains on the trail some time later (T10;1,4,8,10,22).

uhlans A lancer in a cavalry unit, especially of the German Empire (T12;21).

Ukena The central African homeland of the Bukena tribe (T19;4).

Ukundo A pygmy who was a captive of the Bagalla tribe at the same time as the "Tarzan Twins" in 1920; he taught them the rudiments of his language and helped them escape (TT1;5-10).

ul (Pal) Of (T8;2).

Ul The leader of the tribe of Noobolian pygmies who threatened Carson Napier and Nalte when they came to the savages' country while escaping from Skor of Morov (V2;11).

Ul-To A Panar of Barsoom who picked a fight with John Carter while the latter was in Pankor, and was thrown across the room by him. He later volunteered to sword-fight with Carter, with predictable results (M10:3;13).

Ul-Van The brightest of the Ruvans of Pellucidar when David Innes was there in 1930. He proposed treating Innes as a friend since he came in peace and was willing to teach them new things (P6;23).

Ul Vas The jeddak of the Tarids of Ladan; he was a fat, oldish man who was very suspicious and superstitious, and he wanted to sacrifice the Barsoomian visitors to the "Fire God" (the sun), who was supposed to be his father. Ul Vas was a Bluebeard (no pun intended) who killed off his jeddara whenever he found a more beautiful one to replace her (M8;18-20).

ula (Van) The name given by the U-gas to a sidereal month, observable by them because of the difference in sunlight coming in through the hoos into Va-nah. The ula was mechanically divided into 100 parts called ola, and ten ula made a keld, or Va-nah year (MM1;6).

Ulah A slave girl to Ozara, Jeddara of the Tarids of Ladan, who helped John Carter rescue Ozara (M8;19,23).

Ulala The Galla birth-name of Fejjuan (T11;10).

Ulan One of the warriors of the village of Clovi in Pellucidar who urged Chief Avan to accept his son's word as to Tarzan's friendliness when he came there in 1927; he himself befriended Tarzan soon afterward (T13;11-13).

Another Ulan was a loyalist officer in the army of Korva on Amtor during the Zani period. He volunteered to accompany Carson Napier on his mission to rescue Mintep of Vepaja from Amlot, the Zani capital (V3;14).

Uldak The first assassin of Zodanga dispatched by Ur Jan to kill "Vandor"; the latter, who was actually John Carter in disguise, made short work of Uldak (M8;4).

Ulirus A Myposan officer of the group of Myposan troops who captured Carson Napier and Duare in 1930. He was not fond of Tyros or his policies and would have let his prisoners go had he not been in fear for his life from Tyros. As it was, he treated them as well as was possible under the circumstances (V4;3).

Ullah *see* Allah

Ulp An unpopular member of the Oparian renegades who was especially disliked by Gulm, their high priest. He unwittingly helped the "Tarzan Twins" rescue Gretchen von Harben from his band while trying to get rid of her himself so he could not be sacrificed by her. He was later killed by an arrow fired by "Doc" (TT2;3,7).

ulsio The Barsoomian rat. "The Martian rat is a fierce and unlovely thing. It is many-legged [six-legged] and hairless, its hide resembling a newborn mouse's in its repulsiveness. In size and weight it is comparable to a large Airedale terrier. Its eyes are small and close-set, and almost hidden in deep, fleshy apertures. But its most ferocious and repulsive feature is its jaws, the entire bony structure of which protrudes several inches beyond the flesh, revealing five sharp, spadelike teeth in the upper jaw and the same number of similar teeth in the lower, the whole suggesting the appearance of a rotting face from which most of the flesh has sloughed away." The creature has broad feet which it uses to push away the dirt it excavates from its burrows with its teeth. These feet are useless for combat, but the teeth are excellent weapons. The creature is fierce but cowardly, and is the ever-present scourge of Barsoomian dungeons, which it honeycombs with its burrows, then lies in wait to attack sleeping, weak or dead prisoners. Kaldanes love the taste of ulsios and find their burrows fascinating places to explore (M5;12)(M10:1;5). In "John Carter and the Giant of Mars," ulsios were mistak-

enly said to be three-legged; the tribe living under Korvas in that book were intelligent and built dome-shaped huts of human bones coated with mud; they got these bones from the dumping pit of Pew Mogel's lab. They captured John Carter by sheer weight of numbers and were going to sacrifice him in a strange ritual, but he escaped and later used them to save Helium by scaring away the invading army's malagors (M11A;3–5,13–14).

Uluki A small river of the Belgian Congo, site of the nearest Belgian command post to the Morton mission (ME).

Ulzanna An Apache warrior of the late 1800s who was respected for his intelligence (A2;6).

umak A Barsoomian military unit which consists of 10,000 men commanded by an odwar (M7).

Umanga The chief of the first African village Tarzan, Jane and Korak encountered after leaving Pal-ul-don. He gave Tarzan a bitch whose puppies had died so Tarzan could let his newly-adopted orphan lion cub, Jad-bal-ja, nurse on her (T9;1).

Umka The Masena who was locked up in the castle of the Tarids of Ladan with John Carter and taught him the language of the humans of that world, as well as a little of its history and politics. He also taught Carter how to see the "invisible" Tarids, and helped him escape (M8;18,21).

umpalla A plant of Euroban beaches; it is a single, leafless stalk one or two feet tall with a single fuzzy blossom on top. They are used by the people of Han Du, the Savator, to mark the location of their invisible houses (M11B;9).

un (*Pal*) Eye (T8;4).

Una The sister of Nu, son of Nu (E2;2).

Uncle Ben Burroughs' Negro body-servant during his life in Virginia; he mixed a mean mint julep (M2).

Uncle Jack John Carter, as he was known to his family in Virginia (M1).

Under the Moons of Mars The original title of *A Princess of Mars* when it was published in *All-Story* magazine as a six-part serial from February through July of 1912.

Unfriendly Isles A group of islands in the Sojar Az of Pellucidar, so named for their fierce and savage inhabitants (P2;14).

Ungo (*Ape*) The jackal (T17;3).

Ungo "Jackal" (*Ape*). A king great ape of Northern Rhodesia who carried Magra off from the Gregory safari in 1936 to use as a sacrifice for a Dum-dum. Tarzan defeated him and rescued the girl, then led the tribe of Ungo to take the place of the safari's porters and askaris, who had been "stolen" by Atan Thome. Ungo and his tribe later wandered down into Tuen-baka in search of Tarzan, causing a bit of chaos among the minions of Chon in the process (T20;11–12,24,30–32).
Ungo was apparently greatly impressed by Tarzan, because almost two years later and quite some distance away he saved Tarzan (after the latter had been shot by Tom Crump) by carrying him off to where he could be given food and water; he later led his tribe to fight for Tarzan against the Galla enemies of Alemtejo (T23;6–8,15,18,22).

Unis One of the most powerful nation-states of the planet Poloda, and practically only one to escape being completely destroyed or dominated by the aggressive Kapars. The Unisans are a brave and efficient people who have undergone one of the most stringent programs of self-control ever devised in order to save manpower and material for their century-long war with the Kapars. For instance, each Unisan has only two or three suits of clothes of a particular uniform design so that energy and material will not be wasted on frivolous fashions. Tangor was adopted by the Unisan people after appearing there in September of 1939 (after his death over Germany in World War II) and fell in love with the country despite the hardships of life there; he found the Unisans the bravest and most amazing people he had ever met, and quickly swore to help them in any way he could (B1; 2–3).

Unisan language The language of the country of Unis on the planet Poloda sounded like "a Japanese broadcast combined with a symphony concert" (B1;1).

United Teivos of America The Kalkar-run reorganization of the North American continent, ruled by a Kalkar jemadar from Washington, D.C. (MM2;2).

unk (*Ape*) Go (T22;9).

unk-nala "Go up" (*Ape*). Climb (TC).

Unter den Linden "Under the Lindens" (*Ger*). A famous boulevard of Berlin which ran from the Brandenberg Gate east for about a mile; it was at one time lined with palaces and museums, but these were mostly destroyed in World War II. Its route was followed by the main street of the 22nd-century city of New Gondar (LC;8).

Upindi A small river of central Africa (T23;6).

Ur (Niocene) The cave bear (E2;2).

Ur Jan The head of the assassin's guild of Zodanga on Barsoom. He was an enemy of Fal Sivas' because the scientist had employed a non-guild assassin to do his killing for him. Ur Jan was a large, well-built man who hated Rapas the Ulsio but accepted him into the guild in return for information about "Vandor" (the disguised John Carter). Ur Jan suspected "Vandor's" actual identity and decided to curtail his anti-guild activities by kidnapping Dejah Thoris and taking her to Thuria on Gar Nal's interplanetary flier, then holding her there to extract a promise of immunity from prosecution for the Assassin's Guild. On Thuria, however, he and Gar Nal were captured by the invisible Tarids and were forced to cooperate with John Carter to escape. During this period he became very impressed by Carter's nobility, courage and charisma, and after Gar Nal betrayed him by leaving Thuria without him, John Carter rescued Ur Jan, who then threw his sword at Carter's feet. Upon their return to Barsoom, he killed Gar Nal almost immediately (M8; 2–4,10–11,18–24).

Ur Raj A red Barsoomian man of Hastor, a padwar in the navy of Helium, who was imprisoned next to Vor Daj/Tor-dur-bar in the menagerie of Jal Had, Prince of Amhor. Ur Raj became very friendly with Vor Daj (not knowing, of course, who he actually was, nor that they had already met while Vor Daj was in his own body). They escaped the menagerie together and released all the other creatures as well. Ur Raj had invented a device that could identify makes of fliers by the sound of their motors, and was perfecting it when he was captured by Jal Had's men (M9;24–26).

Urambi Black Africans of Bantu origin whom Dr. von Harben worked among in east Africa (T12;3).

Urdu One of the languages of India, which many Barsoomian savants have succeeded in learning by monitoring Earthly radio broadcasts (M6;9).

Ursus Spelaeus The gigantic cave bear of the Pleistocene. See also ryth; ur.

usa A Barsoomian fruit tree which grows easily and bears a great deal of fruit with very little irrigation. This fruit is almost tasteless but very nutritious, and when cooked and highly spiced is one of the staples of both the poor and the military. It very roughly corresponds to the Earthly potato in its uses, but not its quality or character (M5;3).

Usanga The Negro sergeant of a group of German native troops of German East Africa who, early in 1915, deserted and headed for the interior, abducting Fraulein Bertha Kircher along the way. She escaped from him but was recaptured along with Lt. Smith-Oldwick, a downed British aviator whose plane Usanga had found. Usanga then forced Smith-Oldwick to teach him to fly, hoping to carry Kircher off and win tribute from all of the superstitious native tribes of the area through the use of the plane. He was eventually thrown to his death from the airborne plane by Tarzan, who had stowed away (T7;8,11–13).

Usen (*Apa*) God (A1;2).

Usha (*Ape*) The wind (T11;6).

Usher's Hotel A famous inn of Sydney, Australia (T22;30).

Usula One of Tarzan's Waziri warriors who had travelled with him to London and could speak some English; it was he whom Esteban Miranda depended upon for translation while impersonating an amnesiac Tarzan. Usula torched the camp of the traitorous Luvini, head man of the Hawkes safari, in order to drive his men into the open and free Jane, whom he believed to be a prisoner there. He thought she died in the fire, but was proven wrong when he and the Waziri found her with Tarzan (T9;10,17,20).

ut (*Pal*) Corn (T8).

utan (*Bar*) A Barsoomian military division which consists of 100 men commanded by a dwar (M2;21).

Utan The Pellucidarian warrior of the Zurts tribe who in 1932 befriended O-aa after finding her in possession of his dead brother's canoe, weapons and jalok and realizing that the jalok would never have befriended anyone who had killed his master (P7:4;6).

Utaw An iron-age civilization in the post-Kalkar 25th century American West. They provided iron for non-weapon uses (and other goods as well) to the Western tribes, but their metal was not as good as that of the Kolrado (MM3;1).

Utenga A Negro tribe of the Congo region whose villages were ravaged by the bloodthirsty Leopard Men until Tarzan defeated that cult in 1931 (T8;1–2).

Utengi The region inhabited by the Utenga people of central Africa (T18;1–2).

Uthia Tara of Helium's red Barsoomian slave girl, who was her mistress' closest friend and confidante (M5;1).

utor (*Ape*) Fear (TC).

Uvala A planet of the star Omos which lies almost directly opposite Poloda in its weird shared orbit. The Polodans once believed Uvala to be the land of the dead (B1;11).

Uxmal An ancient Mayan city of the Yucatan, founded in A.D. 1004 by Ah Cuitok Tutul Xiu and ruled until 1451 by his descendants. When those descendants were overthrown, they sailed off into the Pacific and settled a remote island, which they also named Uxmal, in 1453. The city on the island was named Chichen Itza after another Mayan city (T24;1,12).

Uziri The land of the Waziri tribe in Northern Rhodesia; it was the site of Tarzan's first African estates (T3;1)(T5).

V.C. Abbreviation for the Victoria Cross, a British medal for heroism (C1;2).

Va-gas The humanoid quadrupeds of Vanah. The males are as large as small horses and are superbly muscled; they have very wide, though humanoid, heads and cruel-looking features. They are lavender in color, shading to almost purple in some (especially big males). Females are smaller and less muscular than the males and have udders with four or six teats; they bear young in litters of up to six. Va-gas have three digits on each limb and go upon all fours, galloping at great speeds and making tremendous leaps. They can also go on two legs if they please, and do so while fighting, holding their weapons in their hands. Va-gas are primitive and nomadic but fairly intelligent. They wear a jumpsuit-like garment which ends above the knees and a harness on which they carry weapons or a burden; they are so strong as to be able to carry another of their own kind with ease. They use a special hooked spear (with which they can hook prey) in one hand and a dagger as large as an Earthly short sword in the other.

The Va-gas are carnivorous, but all higher forms of life in Va-nah have become extinct except for themselves and the U-gas, and the lower animals of Va-nah have poisonous flesh and cannot be eaten. Because of this the Va-gas constantly war among themselves to capture males of other tribes to eat; they even slit the throats of their own incapacitated wounded in order to ensure a supply of meat. They take females back to their own tribe to mate with, and a male can have as many females as he can capture from the enemy — the social status of a male is determined largely by the number of females he has. Because of their reproductive uses, females are not purposely killed to be eaten, but of course they sometimes die in childbirth, fights with other females, and raids by the U-gas, who eat both male and female Va-gas. In turn, Va-gas eat both male and female U-gas and supplement their diet with fruits and vegetables, though they cannot subsist solely on these foods. This situation determines sex distribution among the Va-gas, for although two-thirds of the young are born male, only one-seventh of all adult Va-gas are male — the rest have been killed and eaten by other tribes of Va-gas, abducted and eaten by U-gas, or wounded by enemies, then killed and eaten by their own people. When the No-vans tribe captured Julian 5th and Orthis, they did not eat them right away because they feared these strange creatures might be poisonous, an idea which Julian encouraged.

Va-ga children are unbelievably fiendish and wantonly cruel, habitually playing tricks on one another that might ultimately lead to death. As adults they are still cruel, though less chaotic, and they grow up quickly after being weaned. Children of a defeated tribe are inducted into the conquering tribe on an equal footing with the children born into it, as are the women of the defeated tribe. The creatures then give their loyalty to the new tribe, because it is obviously better able to provide meat and protection for them than their old tribe was (MM1;4–6).

The Kalkars and Laytheans (like the ancient U-gas) kept Va-gas as cattle, feeding them almost entirely with fruits and vegetables supplemented by the flesh of captured enemies and slaves, so that these Va-gas act as scavengers as well as food cattle. The Kalkars even went so far as to feed their own dead to the Va-gas, but the Laytheans did not do this. The Laytheans, however, have selectively bred their domestic Va-gas for stupidity and lack of imagination, with the result that they were little brighter than beasts (MM1;10–11).

A thousand Va-gas were brought to Earth by the Kalkars in 2050, but they must have been killed off or interbred with the Kalkars because they vanished as a separate species and are not mentioned later. This is possibly the reason that later Kalkars became so large (MM2;1)(MM3;7).

Va-nah The name given by its inhabitants to the interior world of the Earth's moon. Like Pellucidar in the Earth, it occupies the inner side of the 250-mile-thick lunar crust, so that its horizons curve upward. It is lit by a combination of the diffused glow of phosphorescent rocks and sunlight shining through the craters, many of which penetrate into the interior, where they are called **hoos**. Va-nah is heated by the same means, but since the craters are not evenly distributed the atmospheric heating is uneven, leading to powerful and violent windstorms accompanied by incredibly powerful lightning displays which include ball lightning. Though these storms utterly terrify the inhabitants, the light remains constant throughout them; there is no night within Va-nah.

The atmospheric pressure of Va-nah is low, but bearable, and the atmosphere is shallow and rarefies quickly with altitude; above 50 miles, there is no air to speak of. Because of the thinness and coldness of the air at high altitudes every mountaintop in Va-nah is snow-clad and glaciers are extremely common; these glaciers pour down into rivers and the three warm seas of Va-nah. The terrain is extremely rough, mountainous and well-watered, and strange, unearthly forests cover most of it. The only higher animals left in the world are the humanoid Va-gas and U-gas; all other types above amphibians died out long ago. This has led to the necessity of the Va-gas and U-gas eating each other.

In prehistoric times the exterior of Luna was apparently habitable by life-forms like our own who were forced to find their way into the interior when the atmosphere left, following the track of the plants and perhaps even lower animals that had already found their way in. The U-ga race eventually developed a high technology and conquered all of Va-nah, but that was many eons after their migration to it. They in turn were later overthrown by the Kalkars, who utterly destroyed the U-ga civilization and plunged Va-nah into almost complete barbarism (MM1;2, 4–5,10,12).

Vabaru   A member of the Praetorian Guard of 1st century Rome who was a friend of Tibur's (I;9).

Vac, Sir Jules de   The fencing master of the kings of England from the time of King John to that of his son Henry III. He was a Parisian who hated England and the English but loved King John, and he stayed on after John's death because of that love. He was the greatest swordsman in England of the day, and when he was insulted by King Henry one day in 1243 he swore revenge against him and England, a revenge he enacted by abducting the king's young son Richard and raising him as his own son. He raised the boy to hate the English (especially the king) and to become a famous outlaw called Norman of Torn, who preyed upon the barons and rich of England throughout the 1250s and 1260s from his base in the old castle Torn, which de Vac had bought in 1246 from someone who wished to be rid of it. De Vac had to fight constantly for many years to keep the boy in the path he had planned for him, from which Norman's good nature and the teaching of the kindly Father Claude were diverting him. In order to fulfill his plan he also had to commit at least five murders over the years and help Peter of Colfax to abduct Bertrade de Montfort, another good influence on Norman. When de Vac finally betrayed Norman to the king (so Henry would unknowingly order his own son hanged), his revenge backfired — the only swordsman good enough to kill Norman was de Vac, who was himself killed by Norman in

the fight. As the old man died, he told his story to those present — ironically, just in time to save the life of Norman, who had not yet died from his wounds (OT).

Vad Varo   Ulysses Paxton's Barsoomian name; it was given to him by Ras Thavas, who insisted that Paxton's Earthly name was "meaningless and impractical" (M6;2).

vadja   (*Amt*) Female (V2;9).

vadjong   (*Amt*) Queen (V2;9).

Vaja   The beloved of U Dan, a padwar of Zor on Barsoom. She was a cousin of Multis Par, Prince of Zor, who kidnapped her and used her to force U Dan into tricking John Carter into a Morgor trap by threatening to rape, torture and mutilate her until U Dan acquiesced (M11B;2).

Val Dor   A dwar in the army of Helium on Barsoom, a warrior of great repute who became enslaved in Manator. Gahan of Gathol met him there and chose him as his odwar for the game of jetan in which he hoped to win back Tara of Helium. Val Dor escaped with Gahan's men to the camp of U-Thor, from which he was led by Ghek to Tara's damaged flier. After he succeeded in repairing the machine, he flew to Gathol for help (M5;16,22).

Valentina   (1904–) A Hollywood clothing designer of the 1930s and 1940s (B1;5).

Valentino, Rudolph   (1895–1926) The screen name of Rodolpho d'Antonguolla, a silent movie actor who was famous for highly romanticized roles such as *The Sheik* (1921); his female followers could only be described as fanatical (T17;2).

Validus Augustus   The Emperor of the East at Castrum Mare when Tarzan and Erich von Harben came there in 1923. He was a paranoid tyrant who believed whatever stories of treachery were whispered into his ears, and thus condemned von Harben and Mallius Lepus to death after making the sycophant Fulvus Fupus his heir. He was killed by von Harben's servant Gabula during the games that August, after Tarzan started a slave revolt (T12;8,13,21).

Valla Dia   The Princess of Duhor on Barsoom who was captured by Phundahl (in a raid on the Amhorian ship which had abducted her from her father's palace) and sold to Ras Thavas as a slave. He in turn sold her body to Xaxa, the hideous Jeddara of Phundahl, and transplanted their brains while Ulysses Paxton watched. The latter began to fall in love with her after seeing her great beauty, and speaking to her while she inhabited the body of the hideous old woman completed the process. Paxton eventually succeeded in abducting Xaxa and restoring Valla Dia to her own body, after which he married her and brought her back home, where he was declared a noble. He had to do this without help from Ras Thavas, to whom Valla Dia was merely case # 4296-E-2631-H (M6;3,13–14).

Valley Dor see **Dor, Valley of**

Valley of Diamonds The valley believed by the writers at **B.O. Pictures** to be mythical when they sent a film crew to its supposed location in 1932; the crew found that it was indeed real and inhabited by advanced, English-speaking gorillas who were the product of a several-generations-old genetic engineering project conducted by a 100-year-old English biologist known only as **God**. He had implanted human genes in the gametes of gorillas he shot with tranquilizer darts, repeating the experiments constantly from generation to generation, and slowly the children of the gorillas became more intelligent and developed the capacity to speak and understand human language. At this point he began to teach them the English language, culture and technology, and by 1932 there was in the valley a thriving city which the gorillas called **London**. Unfortunately, whenever a child was born with visible human characteristics it would usually be killed by the parents, so the gorillas continued to look like gorillas. Those few that were not killed would eventually be driven out and went to live in the valley's south end (see **Mutants, Londonian**) (T17; 2–3,17,24–28). See also **Valley of the Palace of Diamonds**.

Valley of Lost Souls The name given by the **First-Born** of Barsoom to the valley between the **Mountains of Otz** to the south and the icy border mountains to the north. It is cut in half by the canyon of the **Iss**, several thousand feet deep, which crosses it from north to south and proves an effective barrier to most. The valley is grassy and has several small forests which are watered by the small

rivers formed by the melting ice. It is populated by those who, changing their minds at almost the last minute, forsake the **Pilgrimage** and climb the steep canyon walls up to the valley. There they inhabit several villages of mixed populations which are always warring against one another. Slaves of the **Therns** occasionally escape to the valley, but they are not pursued because there is no way past the ice barrier and anyone who escaped to the outer world would be killed anyway. The First-Born leave them alone because they have nothing worth stealing and are too few in number for an interesting fight (M2;8).

Valley of Or-tis A gorgeous, park-like valley near **Santa Monica, California**, in which the pure human **Or-tis** descendants lived in **Kalkar**-controlled 25th century California. The palace of the true Or-tis (**Or-tis 15th**) was there, but the usurper **Or-tis 16th** abandoned it and moved to the Kalkar capital at Los Angeles, leaving the palace to be inhabited by **Raban** the giant, who then began to prey upon the pure human Or-tis as well as upon the Kalkars (MM3;8).

Valley of the First-Born What the Rift of Kamtol is called by its inhabitants, a colony of the **Black Pirates of Barsoom**. Their city there is called **Kamtol** (M10:1;7).

Valley of the Jukans see **Jukans** (P6;4–5)

Valley of the Kalkars The San Fernando Valley of California, last foothold of the **Kalkars** in North America, which they held for the entire 24th and a third of the 25th century after being driven back into it by **Julian 15th** in 2309. **Julian 20th** succeeded in getting a foothold in it in 2430, and drove the last Kalkars into the sea two years later (MM3;1,3,10).

Valley of the Palace of Diamonds A heavily forested, bowl-shaped valley surrounded by towering cliffs and located to the east of **Opar**, from which the only pass into the valley leads. The valley was ruled for millennia by the **Bolgani**, a race of gorillas with a great deal of **great ape** and human (Oparian) blood. They were about 1100 in number and, unlike the Oparians, were not a race in decline; they carried out new construction projects and tried to expand their reach, though they were limited by the presence of Opar in the way of the only pass out of their valley. The valley is also inhabited by a race of subhuman **Gomangani** (about 5000 in number) with sloping foreheads and long arms; they are as meek as cattle and were used as slaves by the Bolgani, who walk upright and are very intelligent. The eastern mountains of the valley are diamond-rich and are the source of the stones for which the valley was named.

Into this valley Tarzan fled with **La of Opar** in the summer of 1917, only to find that there was no other way out of it. He was forced to enter the **Palace of Diamonds** itself to save La, who had been taken by the Bolgani when Tarzan went to explore. He eventually saved her and found out about another exit from the valley — a mine shaft that completely penetrated one of the eastern mountains. While in the valley, Tarzan also began a revolution among the Gomangani that resulted in their conquering the valley and driving out the Bolgani, but one would imagine that the subhuman creatures could not really run a country, and would soon fall back into barbarism and perhaps even come under the domination of the surviving Bolgani again (T9;11–16).

Valley of the Sepulcher A hidden valley in southern Abyssinia which could only be reached from the south through a long tunnel after ascending a long and winding trail from the edge of the mountains the valley lay in; the only distinguishing mark of this outer trail was a 60-foot-tall limestone cross with faded inscriptions at its base. There was also a winding pass into the valley from the north. The valley is forested and lovely and is the site of the fabled lost city of **Nimmr**, which is inhabited by the descendants of a lost group of crusaders (who had been shipwrecked in Africa in 1191) and their black **Galla** peasants. At the north end of the valley lies the rival **City of the Sepulcher**, which has the same kind of inhabitants. All the Gallas of the nearby tribes knew how to get into the valley, but none who had gone there had ever returned because they had been enslaved or killed by the valley people (T11;7,9,12).

Valley People An aboriginal tribe of Amtor's northern hemisphere who were enemies of the **Timal** people (V4;20).

Valois, Eugenie Marie Celeste de la, Countess of Crecy The young and beautiful wife of Henri de la Valois, Count of Crecy, who was marooned on a South Pacific island with him after their yacht was wrecked on their honeymoon cruise about 1892. They died of exposure, hunger and thirst soon afterward, but she gave birth before she died and their baby daughter **Nadara** was raised by the savages of the island. Nadara had no knowledge of her origin until her mother's jewels were given to her by her adoptive father and their significance explained by him and by **Captain Burlinghame** of the *Priscilla* (CG1;11)(CG2;2,13).

Valois, Henri de la, Count of Crecy A French nobleman who on his honeymoon trip around the world about 1892 was shipwrecked with his beautiful young wife on a South Pacific island inhabited only by savages. Their daughter **Nadara** was raised by one of the tribes and had no knowledge of her real parents after they died of exposure, but her adoptive father told her the truth (as far as he knew it) as he was dying (CG1;11)(CG2;2).

Valois, Nadara de la *see* Nadara (CG2;13)

Valparaiso The principal seaport of Chile (LC;4).

Valthor A young noble of **Athne** whom Tarzan saved from a band of **shiftas** in September of 1930; he then led Tarzan back to his country, which Tarzan wished to see, but they became separated in crossing a flooded river and met a few weeks later in **Cathne**, where Tarzan again saved Valthor, this time from a lion pit (T16;3–4,12). A few years later, there was a revolution in Athne and many of the nobles were killed. Valthor, however, was such a likable man that the revolutionaries only imprisoned him at hard labor — they did not dare kill him, because the people loved him too much. He was freed from prison when the Cathneans came to replace **Zygo** on the throne (T21;20–25).

Vama The subofficer in charge of the expedition from **Lodidhapura** to find the escaped **Fou-tan** in the mid–1920s. He later came to know and befriend **Gordon King** (HM;4–7,13).

Van (*Ape*) Well (TC).

Van der Bos, Tak A Dutch reserve officer of **Sumatra** who fell into the hands of a group of criminal refugees who were hiding from both the **Japanese** and the Dutch guerrillas in the hills of Sumatra; he helped Tarzan escape the criminals when he also fell into their hands in the spring of 1944. He and his wife were old friends of Corrie van der Meer, and he joined Tarzan's "Foreign Legion" after they escaped the criminals, but he was killed when a Japanese ship sunk the proa in which the group had hoped to reach Australia (T22;12,21,29–30).

Van der Meer, Corrie The only daughter of Hendrik van der Meer and the former Elsje Verschoor, who fled into the Sumatran jungle with her servant Sing Tai after her mother died and her father was killed by the occupying Japanese troops in January of 1942. She hid successfully for two years, but was then discovered and imprisoned by Lt. Sokabe, from whom she was rescued by Tarzan and the crew of the downed bomber *Lovely Lady*, with whom he had come to Sumatra. She and Captain Jerry Lucas soon found themselves falling in love with one another despite (or perhaps because of) the harrowing conditions. After months of fighting and privation, they made their way to the coast (during which time the girl proved her survival abilities again and again), where they set out in a native proa for Australia and were saved en route by a British submarine. She and Lucas were married by the sub's commander before they got to Sydney (T22).

Van der Meer, Hendrik A rubber planter of pre–World War II Sumatra who refused to evacuate his family in the face of the Japanese threat until it was too late. He was forced to flee to the hills to escape the Japanese in January of 1942, but was caught and killed. His daughter Corrie, however, escaped with Sing Tai (T22;1).

Van Eyk, Robert An American millionaire and a friend of Stanley Wood's who occasionally backed his expeditions, including his 1935 one to the Kaji country. He decided to go along on that particular expedition and was captured by the Kaji along with Wood; he was rescued six months later by Tarzan, who had met and befriended the escaped Wood (T21;2–3,9–11).

Van Horn, Doctor Carl A former American naval surgeon who was recruited by Professor Arthur Maxon in Singapore to assist him in his artificial life experiments. He soon became attracted to Virginia Maxon, and her beauty (not to mention the fortune she was heir to) caused him to want to marry her but she consistently refused, even under threat. He tried on several occasions to get rid of Professor Maxon, who of course would have opposed his plan; failing that, he lied to him and told him that Number Thirteen had abducted Virginia so the professor would turn against the creature he had wanted for her to marry. He also continued his efforts to secure the professor's "treasure," only to be killed in the attempt by Dyak head-hunters he had double-crossed. In the end his evil saved the day, because the U.S.S. *New Mexico* came to Maxon's island in search of him for his previous crimes and so arrived in Borneo in time to save the rest of the party and return them to civilization (Q).

Van Nuys The California home town of Staff Sergeant Carter Douglas of the *Lovely Lady* (T22;26).

Van Prins, Captain Kervyn The commanding officer of the band of Dutch guerrillas to whom Tarzan went to ask for information in Japanese-held Sumatra during the spring of 1944; he afterward cooperated with Tarzan against the invaders (T22;15–27).

Van-Tija The principal wife of Nastor, a dator of the First-Born of Kamtol on Barsoom. She bought Llana of Gathol as a slave and refused to let her husband have the girl, even though he threatened and bribed her (M10:2;11).

Vanada One of the eleven co-orbital planets of the star Omos. Vanada lies between Rovos and Sanada, three planets away from Poloda (B1).

Vanaja The beautiful daughter of Tovar of Pandar in the medieval Amtorian country of Gavo. The "wizard" Morgas "turned her into a zaldar" because she would not mate with him, but she was rescued, deprogrammed and restored to her parents by Carson Napier and Ero Shan (V5;4,7–10).

Vanator The Barsoomian cruiser that carried Gahan, Jed of Gathol to visit Helium the day before the great hurricane of 1915; it also carried him out in the hurricane in search of Tara of Helium, who was lost in her personal flier (M5;3).

Vanda An orang-utan of Sumatra who befriended Tarzan after he saved her **balu** from a python (T22;11).

vando (*Ape*) Good (T24;11).

Vandor The alias used by John Carter while posing as an assassin in Zodanga (M8;1).

Vantor The commander of the **Falsan** neolantar of Amtor who captured **Carson Napier, Duare** and **Ero Shan** when they blundered too close to the Falsan fleet in their anotar late in 1931 and were shot down. He tried to molest Duare, for which she killed him and escaped from the ship during the night (V4; 44–45,51).

Vanuma The eldest wife of **Jal Had,** Prince of **Amhor** on Barsoom. She tried to hire **Gantun Gur** to kill **Janai** so her husband could not add yet another wife to his harem, especially one as beautiful as Janai. Of course, she did not realize that Gantun Gur's body was at the time inhabited by **Tun-gan's** brain, or that he was a friend of Janai's. Poor Vanuma was soon afterward poisoned by order of Jal Had, for which he was afterward overthrown by her family (M9;25–26).

vaquero (*Sp*) Cowboy (K2;9).

Varo A great general of the Amtorian nation of **Korva** who remained loyal to his **jong** after the Zani takeover of the 1920s (V3;13).

Vas Kor A **Dusarian** nobleman in the service of **Astok** who entered **Carthoris'** household posing as a slave in order to sabotage his **destination compass** and bring him to **Aanthor,** where he was to have been ambushed. Astok later recruited Vas Kor to assassinate **Thuvia of Ptarth** so she could place no blame for her abduction, thus leaving all Barsoom to believe Carthoris to be the abductor. Carthoris foiled the plan by killing Vas Kor (M4;2–3,14).

vat room number four The **culture vat** of **Morbus** in which something had gone terribly wrong; instead of individual **hormads** a huge mass of body parts connected by tissue was growing out of control. It could not be reached to be destroyed, and since **Ras Thavas** had left with John Carter, no one knew how to stop the growth until Ras Thavas returned and had the navy of **Helium** destroy the whole mess with incendiary bombs (M9;13,31).

Vatinius The captain of the **Praetorian Guard** at the time of Emperor **Caligula's** assassination in January of A.D. 41 (I;21).

Vauxhall A British automotive manufacturer of the early 20th century (T7;20).

Vay Thon The high priest of Siva in the lost Cambodian city of **Lodidhapura.** He was an old man who often became so lost in meditation that he became oblivious to his surroundings and would wander off into the jungle. He was a good and kind man, though, and well-loved by his people. **Gordon King's** first act upon reaching Lodidhapura was to shoot a tiger which was stalking the old man, an act which won Vay Thon's gratitude and prompted him to come and give comfort and warning to King while he was a prisoner of **Lodivarman** on two separate occasions (HM; 3–4,7,14).

ved (*Ape*) Mountain; this is probably a mistake (see next entry) (T22;15).

ved (*Pal*) Mountain (T8;2).

vedette A mounted scout (T10;7).

vegetation, Barsoomian Most Barsoomian vegetation is scarlet, purple or yellow, but some of the trees of the **Valley Dor** are of stranger colors. Some of the vegetation of the planet flourishes with almost no water (see **mantalia; moss; usa**), and others with very little (see **gloresta**), but most of the other plants need irrigation to flourish, such as those along the **canals** or rare **rivers** or lakes (M2;1,9).

vegetation, Euroban The vegetation of Jupiter, existing as it does with only the reddish light of that planet's immense volcanoes, is pallid in color and mostly carnivorous. These plants actually have a sluggish nervous system and are animal-like in some characteristics, even to the point of having muscular tissue. The smallest plants catch only insects, but the very largest can eat even humans or larger animals. See also **trees, Euroban** (M11B;8).

vegetation, Lunarian Most of the vegetation of **Va-nah** is of pale colors, especially lavender, pink, violet and yellow. The grasses are pink when young and become flesh-colored at maturity. The flowers are very complex in form, very pale in color, very large, and very beautiful. The vegetation of the outer moon is like a giant **fungus** which lives and dies within a single month, growing quickly and vanishing just as quickly. See also **trees, Va-nah** (MM1;1,3).

vegetation, Pellucidarian Pellucidarian vegetation is a mix of outer Earthly types with prehistoric forms like giant **cycads** and club mosses (P1;2).

Vejara One of the ladies-in-waiting to **Duare** of Vepaja; she helped **Carson Napier** rescue Duare from her death sentence late in 1930 (V3;20).

Veltopishago A king of the **Minunian** city of **Veltopismakus** a long time ago. He was the enemy of King **Klamataamorosal** of **Trohanadalmakus** (T10;6).

Veltopismakus The ancient **Minunian** city that was rival to **Trohanadalmakus**; each of them stole most of its slaves from the other, even into the present day (T10;6).

Vendome, the The restaurant in which Burroughs had lunch with **Pat Morgan** and so got the story of **Jimber-Jaw** (J;1).

vental In the **Minunian** military, an officer in charge of an **ental** of ten men (T10; 11,13).

ventex In the **Minunian** military, an officer in charge of an **entex** of 50 men (T10; 13).

Vepaja The land of giant **trees** on Amtor, inhabited by the last colonies of that world's former ruling race, which was overthrown by the communistic **Thorists** and forced into seclusion on the distant continent. Vepaja was once a vast empire of millions, but is today only a small, mostly democratic and classless society which inhabits cities carved from the upper levels of the giant trees in order to hide from Thorist spies; its inhabitants seldom descend to the surface except for occasional trade or **basto** hunting. The Vepajans are an extremely traditional and honor-bound society to whom their beliefs are more important than even life. Their ancestors were fairly scientifically advanced in some areas (particularly medicine and chemistry), but were woefully backward in others (most notably geology and physics); the modern Vepajans keep the knowledge of these ancestors alive, but no longer have the facilities for more scientific advancement. It was among the

Vepajans that **Carson Napier** originally threw his lot after landing upon Amtor, but he was forced to flee the country when he and **Duare**, the Janjong of Vepaja, dared to express their forbidden love to one another (V1;5-7).

Vercingetorix (?-46 B.C.) A Gallic chieftain who rebelled against Roman rule and was defeated by Julius Caesar. He was taken back to Rome and displayed in Caesar's triumph, then put to death (I;4).

vere A huge and hideous predatory lizard of Amtor which grows to a length of about 20 feet. It has a vaguely crocodilian head but no teeth, being equipped instead with a row of upcurving white horns along its upper jaw. It also has a sticky tongue which it can shoot out as a frog or chameleon can, and it uses this tongue to encircle prey and drag it to its mouth, where it is swallowed whole. The vere is beautifully colored in red, black and yellow and has a single, huge compound eye which covers the whole top of its head. Its breath is poisonous and causes faintness, and it whistles shrilly when attacking. It inhabits very steep cliffs, which it can climb with ease (V2;8).

Vernon A Hollywood nightclub and restaurant of the 1920s (GH;5).

Verschoor, Elsje The maiden name of Mrs. Hendrik van der Meer. She died of exhaustion while fleeing the Japanese in February of 1942 (T22;1).

Vestako The chief of the royal dome of **Elkomoelhago**, king of the **Minunian** city of **Veltopismakus**, while Tarzan was imprisoned there; he was an unabashed bribe-taker who would betray anyone for money (T10;10).

Veza The mayor of the lost city of **Xuja**; he was killed by **Lt. Smith-Oldwick** while the latter was escaping the lion's den in which he had been imprisoned (T7;21-23).

Via Cunigulo "Tunnel Road" (Lat). The road from the only tunnel through the **Wiramwazi Mountains** to the lost Roman city of **Castra Sanguinarius** (T12).

Via Flaminia "Flaminian Way" (Lat). A Roman road along which criminal slaves were crucified (I;2).

Via Mare "Sea Road" (Lat). The road from the lost Roman city of **Castra Sanguinarius** to **Castrum Mare**, some 25 miles away (T12;22).

Via Principalis "Main Street" (*Lat*). The main avenue of **Castra Sanguinarius**; it bisects the city from the Palace of Caesar to the Colosseum (T12;14).

Vibiu A member of Rome's Praetorian Guard who helped **Britannicus** to find his friend **Tibur** one day in A.D. 17 (I;2).

Victor One of the Filipino cabin boys of the O-220 expedition to Pellucidar in 1927 (P4;3).

Victor Emmanuel III (1869–1947) The king of Italy from 1900 to 1946. In 1922 he allowed **Mussolini** to reconstruct the Italian government (after the Fascist leader threatened to destroy Rome), and he became largely a figurehead thereafter until 1943, when he dismissed Mussolini and signed an armistice with the Allied powers (LL;15).

Victoria Falls The name given by the God of the gorillas of the Valley of Diamonds to **Omwamwi Falls** south of the valley (T17; 21).

Victorio The name given by the Mexicans to an **Apache** chief of the Chi-hen-ne tribe of the mid–19th century. He died in battle around 1881 and was succeeded as chief by **Loco** (A1;2,20).

Victory, Queen Queen of Grabritin as of July 6, 2137, when **Buckingham** killed her mother. He then took her as his own woman so he might be king. The date is known exactly because it was the same day that Lt. **Jefferson Turck** arrived and saved Victory from abduction by the **Elephant Country** people, only to have her fall into the clutches of Buckingham. She escaped, however, and returned Turck's favor by saving him from the lions Buckingham had thrown him to by bringing him his rifle and pistol. They then escaped together, fighting lions along the way, until they met up with Turck's men. The party then travelled to the European mainland, but on the way she was turned against Turck by the lies of **Snider**, who eventually abducted her. She killed him when he tried to have his way with her, then was captured by Abyssinians and taken as a slave for their Emperor **Menelek** to include in his harem. She was freed by Turck, who explained Snider's lies to her and, after they were saved from Abyssinia by the **Chinese**, they were married. After their return to **Pan-America**, she

returned to Grabritin with Turck and an expeditionary force to reclaim it from barbarism (LC;4–9).

Victory Day April 10, 1967; the last day of World War III, after which the entire Earth was at peace until the Lunarian invasion of 2050. In the next few years, all of the Earth's munitions were destroyed and severe weapons control laws enacted, with the result that the Lunarians were easily able to conquer the totally unprepared Earth people (MM1) (MM2;1).

Vicus Tuscus "Tuscany Street" (*Lat*). A street of ancient Rome inhabited largely by prostitutes and low people (I;12).

vik (*Amt*) The number nine (V1;8).

vik-ro "Nine-three" (*Amt*). The chemical element of atomic number 93, known on Earth as **neptunium**. It is used on Amtor as a trigger for atomic chain reactions (V1;8).

Vik-vik-vik "Nine Nine Nine" (*Amt*). The number always given to the Jong of **Voo-ad**, a city of the **Vooyorgan** of Amtor (V4;31–32).

Vik-yor "Nine Hundred" (*Amt*). A Vooyorgan of Amtor when **Carson Napier** and **Duare** were their prisoners in 1931. It was one of those mutants who were unable to divide (it had originally been the left half of Vik-vik-vik) and consequently was depressive and did not enjoy the pastimes of the others, eating and dancing and singing. Perhaps because of these differences, it fell in love with Duare as she hung paralyzed on the wall of the **Voo-ad Museum of Natural History** and helped her escape by giving her the antidote to the paralysis. It then abducted her, and they passed through several harrowing adventures after escaping Voo-ad, but it died of convulsions after glutting itself on nuts and water after a period of starvation; its body tried to divide and tore itself apart from within (V4; 33–41).

Villa, Francisco (Pancho) (1877–1923) A Mexican revolutionary who declared himself the enemy of **Venustiano Carranza** when the latter made himself president of Mexico in 1914. Villa began a revolution against him, and since Carranza was backed by the United States, Villa actually went so far as to occasionally cross the border and attack American towns, which brought the U.S. military into the affair (K2;6).

villosa A medieval garment made of long, fine hairs (OT;3).

Vilor A Thoran spy sent to Vepaja in 1929 to steal the formula for the **serum of longevity** and captured by **Klangan** in a raid by mistake. Once aboard **Carson Napier's** pirate ship *Sofal*, he made plans with fellow prisoner **Moosko** the **Ongyan**, and together they abducted **Duare** to **Noobol** (which the ship was passing at the time) with the help of the **Klangan** (V1;12–14).

Vinicianus, Annius (?–A.D. 66) A Roman senator who was involved in the plot to assassinate **Caligula** (I;21).

Violet Lady **Barbara Ramsgate's** maid, who accompanied her on her 1939 safari to **Northern Rhodesia** (T24B;5).

vir (*Amt*) An Amtorian unit of time, just barely over four minutes long. See also **te** (V2;16).

Virginia John Carter's home state, which he served as an army captain in the American Civil War (M1).

viscount Tarzan's rank as a British lord (T11;19).

Vishnu The Preserver; second person of the Hindu trinity of Godhead (HM;14).

visiscreen An imaginary Barsoomian telecommunications device which appears only in **"John Carter and the Giant of Mars"** (M11A;1).

Vista del Paso A residential street of Hollywood (GH;5).

Vitza The site of the favorite palace of **Alexis III** of **Margoth**; it lies some 20 miles by road from **Demia** (R;7).

Vivier, Comte de A nobleman of 18th century France (during the reign of Louis XIV) from whom **Colonel Joseph Vivier** was descended (LL;16).

Vivier, Colonel Joseph The French army officer to whose north African camp the amnesiac **Prince Michael** came for six weeks after rescuing Vivier's daughter **Marie** from abduction by treacherous **Arab** servants (LL;16).

Vivier, Marie The daughter of a French army officer of 1920s **Algeria** who was saved by the amnesiac **Prince Michael** from abduction. She afterward taught him to speak, read and write French (LL;14–16).

vo (*Ape*) Muscle (TC).

Vobis Kan The Jeddak of **Toonol** on **Barsoom** who had **Gor Hajus** executed on suspicion that the noted assassin was planning to assassinate him. Vobis Kan was a cruel tyrant, but even in logical Toonol the people felt that they could not overthrow him because he was the rightful ruler. Vobis Kan later occupied the **Tower of Thavas** because his paranoid mind had conceived of the idea that **Ras Thavas** had raised **Gor Hajus** from the dead and was conspiring with the assassin to eliminate him (M6;6,9,13–14).

Vodaro An Amtorian land mass which lies south of **Anlap**, partially in **Trabol** but mostly in **Karbol**. Because very little is known of it even in the surrounding countries, **Carson Napier** claimed to be from there while spying in **Amlot** in 1930 (V3;7).

Vodo The alias taken by **Carson Napier** while in **Amlot** in 1930; he claimed to be the **Tanjong** of **Vodaro** and there for adventure (V3;7).

Vogt, Ernie Rhonda Terry's riding instructor at the Los Angeles Riding School (T17;12).

Vogue A high fashion magazine first founded in 1892 (D;1).

vol A **Myposan** unit of currency equal to about 59 cents (1930 American money) (V4;7).

volcanoes, Euroban There is a chain of immense volcanoes along the equator of **Eurobus**; these huge torches are a hundred miles wide each and their flames shoot up many thousands of feet into the air, heating and lighting a world that would have been cold and dark beneath its impenetrable cloudcover without them. Besides the equatorial chain, other volcanoes dot the surface of the planet (M11B;3).

volcanoes, Pellucidarian The Pellucidarians think of volcanoes as proof of the existence of **Molop Az**, the flaming sea upon which flat Pellucidar is believed to float (P1; 10).

volcanoes, Va-nah The volcanoes of Va-nah all became extinct millions of years ago, and many of the **hoos** are actually volcanic pits that once led into the planet. Extinct volcanic calderas were used by the **U-gas** and **Kalkars** to build their cities in (MM1;10–11).

Voldan Ocean One of the four oceans of **Poloda**; it lies between **Karis** and **Auris** in the northern hemisphere (B2;2).

Vomer The **Myposan** officer in charge of the slaves at the **jong**'s palace when **Carson Napier** came there in 1930. Napier made an enemy of Vomer almost immediately (V4;4).

Von Coblich *see* **Coblich** (MK2;3)

Von der Tann, Princess Emma The daughter of **Prince Ludwig von der Tann**; she was the childhood sweetheart of **Leopold II** of **Lutha**. **Barney Custer** saved her from a runaway horse only a short time after entering Lutha, then later rescued her from **Blentz** Castle, where they were both imprisoned. She fell in love with the handsome, brave American whom she thought was her betrothed, and was heartbroken when she learned the truth. Even then, she continued to swear love to him and spurn Leopold, which made the king furious enough to attempt to execute Custer, who had saved his life (MK1;1–5,12). She held out for the next two years and decided to run away to America with Custer when he returned to Lutha in September of 1914, but instead married him in full view of everyone when he was officially made the King of Lutha after Leopold's death (MK2;7–9,15–16).

Von der Tann, Prince Ludwig The most popular nobleman of early 20th century **Lutha**, a loyal soldier from a long line of loyal soldiers who had a great deal of mistrust (and rightfully so) for his distant cousin, **Prince Peter of Blentz**. He was the chancellor of Lutha until Peter's regency, in protest of which he resigned. He later supported **Barney Custer** in his claim to the throne because he thought him to be **Leopold II**, and when Custer later rescued the real Leopold and revealed his true identity, von der Tann said that Custer would have made a better king than the thankless coward who had been born to the post (MK1;8–12).

He became chancellor again under Leopold in 1912, only to find all of his advice ignored while the king followed a path to ruin. When Barney Custer showed up again in September of 1914, von der Tann assisted him in running the Luthanian defense against **Austria** while the American was again disguised as Leopold, and he was the first to insist that Custer (who was after all the son of Leopold's aunt) take the throne after the useless monarch's death (MK2;5,10–11,15–16).

Von Goss, Underlieutenant The German officer under **Hauptmann Fritz Schneider** when he destroyed Tarzan's estate in 1914. Tarzan later encountered him while fighting in the German trenches and killed him with his bare hands (T7;1,4).

Von Harben, Erich The son of Tarzan's friend **Karl von Harben**. Erich was born in 1900 and graduated the university at 19 with a joint degree in archeology and dead languages. He was also an accomplished mountain climber, so it was only natural that he would set out to investigate the persistent legend of a lost tribe of white men who inhabited the **Wiramwazi Mountains**. He discovered in the center of the range a deep valley in which two cities of ancient Rome still existed and fell in with the inhabitants of the eastern city, **Castrum Mare**. He there fell in love with **Favonia**, the daughter of a patrician, thus making an enemy in the person of **Fulvus Fupus** (a favorite of the emperor), who managed to get von Harben sentenced to the games. Von Harben escaped, however, and was rescued by Tarzan soon afterward, bringing Favonia with him out of the valley (T12;1,6–8,13,21–23). Von Harben remained interested in the area, though, and in 1925 he discovered lake-dwelling natives there using a metal as light as cork but stronger than steel; he refined this metal and named it **harbenite** (T13;1).

Von Harben, Gretchen The young daughter of **Dr. Karl von Harben**, who was taken from her father's mission in the **Urambi** country by a band of **Oparian** renegades in the spring of 1920, and carried about with them for two months as their high priestess (whom they named "**Kla**") until she was rescued by the "**Tarzan Twins**" and returned to her father by Tarzan (TT2;8,12–13).

Von Harben, Doctor Karl A German missionary of east central Africa who befriended Tarzan after the ape-man helped rescue his daughter Gretchen from the clutches of a band of renegade Oparians in 1920 (TT2;11-13). He again went to Tarzan for help when his son Erich was lost in the Wiramwazi Mountains in 1923 (T12;1).

Von Horst, Lieutenant Wilhelm (Full name Friedrich Wilhelm Erich von Mendeldorf und von Horst) An extremely likable young German air force officer who was one of Captain Zuppner's lieutenants on the dirigible O-220 on its expedition to Pellucidar in 1927. He was lost soon after the expedition's arrival when a huge group of tarags herded a mixed group of herbivores together for a mass killing, scattering the explorers in the process and convincing them that von Horst had been killed (P4;2-3). He had actually only become lost and wandered across the countryside for quite some time, becoming a prisoner of (successively) a trodon, the cannibalistic Bastians, the Gorbuses of the Forest of Death, the Mammoth Men of Ja-ru, and the Ganaks. He escaped from each and was finally reunited with La-ja (the cave girl with whom he had fallen in love) after killing the mighty Gaz, who wanted her as his mate. A few weeks later he was found by David Innes, who had headed an expedition to search for him at the request of Jason Gridley (P5).

Von Kelter A German army officer stationed in the Pare Mountains in the first part of World War I (T7;5).

Von Schoenvorts, Baron Friedrich The German naval officer of World War I who commanded the U-33 and ordered the sinking of the American liner on which Bowen Tyler and Lys La Rue were passengers. Miss La Rue was von Schoenvorts' fiancée, but he did not know that she was aboard the ship. She was understandably upset about the affair when she discovered that it was his submarine that had sunk her ship, and after it was captured by the crew of the British tug which rescued her and Tyler from the English Channel, she broke off their engagement. Von Schoenvorts was a prisoner on his own ship for a while, but regained control for long enough to get the already-lost submarine into the South Pacific before the "allies" again took over and put him in irons. After they reached Caspak, Tyler suggested a truce which von Schoenvorts accepted, but he double-crossed Tyler

by stealing the U-33 after they had found and refined a crude oil source and succeeded in refueling the submarine; he even shelled the fort they had constructed as a parting gesture (C1;2-7).

Months later (early in 1917) he returned for more oil after getting lost and using up all of the U-boat's fuel. He tried to force the English to work for him, but was killed by Plesser, one of his own men, who was sick of the captain's mindless brutality (C3;5).

Vonbulen A farmer of the teivos of Chicago in Kalkar-occupied 22nd century America who was given Julian 8th's pen in the marketplace by Soor. When he refused to leave, Julian 9th threw him out, for which offense he was court-martialed; he could not be convicted, however, because Soor had no right under Kalkar law to give the pen to Vonbulen in the first place (MM2;5-6).

vong (*Amt*) Defend (V1;12).

voo (*Amt*) The article "the" or "a," number one, or the word "first" (V1;8).

Voo-ad "First City" (*Amt*). The wheel-shaped city of the Vooyorgan of Northern Anlap. It was a beautiful city, but unimaginatively designed and executed like everything else the Vooyorgan created. After Carson Napier and Duare released the warriors from the Museum of Natural History in 1931, they sacked and burned the city (V4;31,42).

voo-dum (*Ape*) Dance (TC).

voo-voo (*Ape*) Sing (TC).

vookor "One dagger" (*Amt*). The Amtorian military rank corresponding to an Earthly captain; he is in charge of either a small ship or 100 men (V1;9)(V4;25).

vootogan "First High Man" (*Amt*). An Amtorian togan (baron) who has a son mature enough to hold the title himself (V5;4).

vootoganja "First High Woman" (*Amt*). The consort of a vootogan; thus, the mother of a klootogan (V5;4).

Vooyorgan "First People" (*Amt*). The Amoeba People of Amtor, who live in the city of Voo-ad in Northern Anlap. They are all plump and soft looking, with no discernable gender and a well-defined reddish line running exactly down the center of the face and body, front and back — it is along this line that they fission to reproduce, each half then growing a new partner in a period of a few months. They eat and drink to excess (it makes them reproduce faster) and are always laughing and smiling for no reason. After fission, the right half retains the personality and number-name of the original, and eventually (after dividing about nine times) the older half grows rapidly old and dies, usually right after a division but sometimes during the day-to-day process of life; when this happens the dead half falls off and the other side goes on to grow a new partner. Occasionally, one half grows another half with no line of demarcation; these mutants cannot divide and must be careful not to consume too much food, lest the process of division begin and kill them in the process. They usually occur within the royal or noble castes.

The Vooyorgan are able to copy artistic creations perfectly, but they have no imagination whatsoever and cannot truly create. They carry sword and dagger, but are not good at fighting because they are great cowards; poison and hypocrisy are their chief weapons. Their only clothing is a skirt-like garment which is actually a series of long pouches sewn together and worn about the waist (V4; 31–41).

Vor Daj A padwar of the personal guard of John Carter who accompanied the Warlord on a mission to locate Ras Thavas when Dejah Thoris was severely injured and in dire need of the great physician's skill. On their mission, they were (fortunately) captured by Ras Thavas' **hormads** and taken directly to him. He and John Carter then helped Ras Thavas plan escape, but Vor Daj had Ras Thavas transfer his brain to the body of the hormad **Tor-dur-bar** so he might spy on the hormads and locate **Janai**, an Amhorian girl he had fallen in love with. He thereafter went by Tor-dur-bar's name until he was finally restored to his own body. As a hormad, he succeeded in becoming a guard for the third **Jed** of **Morbus**, locating Janai, rescuing her, and hiding her in a storeroom. Meanwhile, because of his great combat ability and major role in the conquest of Morbus by the third Jed (who had proclaimed himself **Jeddak** and changed his name to **Ay-mad**) he was made a **dwar**, giving him greater freedom of movement and greater powers in Morbus. When his suggestion for conquering the city

itself succeeded, he was made an **odwar** and promised Janai when she was found. This, however, made Ay-mad jealous, so Vor Daj/ Tor-dur-bar fled Morbus with Janai, **Sytor**, **Pandar**, **Tun-gan** and **Gan Had**. Sytor and Pandar betrayed him and abducted Janai, then got recaptured by the hormads; when he proposed the others return to Morbus in pursuit, Tun-gan and Gan Had ran away. Vor Daj/Tor-dur-bar finally succeeded in rescuing Janai anyway, but they were captured by Amhorians and he was locked up as an exhibit in the **menagerie** of **Jal Had**, Prince of Amhor. He eventually escaped, rescued Janai, and was restored to his own body, later realizing that she had known his secret for some time (M9). They were soon married and lived in **Helium** (M10:2;5).

Vorion A **Morgor** who struck John Carter to force him to respond more quickly during his language training. Carter knocked him flat in response, and he lay as one dead for a long time. He later insulted one of **Bandolian's** toadies and was sentenced to death for it, locked in the same cell as John Carter, **U Dan** and **Zan Dar** to await the next **graduation exercises**. He helped them escape after they promised to take him along with them, as he could only expect death among his fellow Morgors (M11B;2,5–6).

Vosar A cargo flier owned by Ras Thavas, aboard which Ulysses Paxton and his confederates stowed away to escape the **Tower of Thavas** (M6;7).

Vulhan The brother of **Allara**, the mother of **Stellara**. He was at first suspicious of his niece when she arrived on **Amiocap** in 1926, until her true paternity by Allara's husband **Fedol** was proven by a birthmark (P3;3).

vulp (*Ape*) Full (TC).

The Vulture The younger brother of **Julian 20th** who, in 2430, was 18 and already a great warrior. He was the hound chief of his tribe, whose responsibility it was to keep and train the sheep and guard dogs of the tribe. He accepted the offer of friendship of the true **Or-tis 16th** (the man who befriended Julian 20th, not the usurper with that title) in Julian's absence, a decision which allowed the Julians to drive the **Kalkars** from their capital; the decision was later upheld by Julian (MM3;2,9).

Vulture, the   A rich and powerful pirate of the 1920s East Indies on whose island Johnny Lafitte finally came to land after drifting in a derelict dirigible for two weeks. Lafitte joined the pirate's band, soon becoming his second in command, and worked with him for two years thereafter, but when the Vulture caught Lafitte making love to his consort **La Diablesa**, he tried to kill him. Lafitte barely escaped with his life to the island of the Vulture's enemy the **Portuguese**, and later returned with him to take the Vulture's island by force. They succeeded, but the Vulture would have killed Lafitte in the process had La Diablesa not shot him in the back first (PB;7–13).

Vyla   One of the two **Samary** men who shared a cave with **Lula** when **Carson Napier** came there in search of **Duare** in 1930 (V3;3).

wa   (*Ape*) Green (TC).

wa-usha   "Green wind" (*Ape*). Leaf (TC).

Wabi Shebele   A river of Ethiopia, possibly related in some way to the **Neubari** (T21;1).

Waco   The McLennan County, **Texas**, hometown of S.Sgt. **Bill Davis** of the **B-24** *Lovely Lady* (T22;26).

Wagambi   A tribe of black Africans of the west coast who lived in an area they called **Ugambi**. Some Wagambi came to **Jungle Island** on an exploratory mission in 1912 while Tarzan was marooned there; they tried to attack him, but were destroyed by Tarzan, **Sheeta** and the apes of **Akut** (T3;5).

Waganwazam   The tribe of African cannibals of the upper Ugambi River to whom Nikolas Rokoff planned to bring the infant Jack Clayton to be raised as a cannibal, because the tribe feared white men enough that they would not eat them (**Jane Clayton** was in the village unmolested for several days, as was Rokoff). Rokoff happened to catch up with the fleeing Jane just as she reached their village and retook her as a prisoner, but not Jack; he had actually had the wrong baby all along, and the baby he thought was Jack died in the village of a fever. Tarzan later came to the village in pursuit of Rokoff and would have been killed by the natives in order to get a reward from Rokoff, but he was warned by **Tambudza** (the wife of Chief **M'ganwazam**), to whom he had shown kindness, and so escaped (T3;11–14).

Wagon Mountain   The Arizona mountain which overlooks Hell's Bend Pass near Hendersville (HB;15).

wahine   (Hawaiian) Woman (B1).

Wainright, Jefferson, Jr.   The handsome, suave young son of Jefferson Wainright, Sr., who was about 21 at the time his father tried to swindle Diana Henders. The younger Wainright wooed Henders and almost won her hand until he showed his cowardice by running out on her during an Apache attack, thus contributing to her father's death in the attack. He later introduced his father to **Maurice Corson** (a classmate of his) and helped them plot against Diana; he was thus kicked out of town with the others when the scheme collapsed (HB;4–10,19).

Wainright, Jefferson, Sr.   The Massachusetts businessman who owned the territory north of the hills from the **Bar-Y Ranch** in 1880s Arizona. Because there was little good grazing land and water on his ranch, he wanted to buy out the Bar-Y, but **Elias Henders** would not sell. After his death, Wainright tried to trick **Diana Henders** into selling the ranch to him for a tiny fraction of its worth. She was too smart for him, however, and he vowed revenge, which he planned to gain by plotting with Maurice Corson to steal the ranch from her by legalistic trickery. They were foiled by **Bull**, who found documents to prove that the mine belonged solely to Diana. Wainright, his son and their accomplices were eventually run out of town at gunpoint (HB; 4–7,14–19).

Waja, Chief of the Waji   An imaginary character young **Jack Clayton** pretended to be when he bound and gagged Mr. **Harold Moore**, who was trying to stop Jack from going to see **Ajax**, the trained ape (T4;2).

Waji   A mythical African tribe invented by the young Jack Clayton (T4;2).

Wakandas   A tribe of warlike savages of the **Belgian Congo** who revolted against the Belgians around the turn of the century, killing most of the inhabitants of the **Morton** mission in the process (ME).

wala   (*Ape*) A nest. This could mean a bird's nest, an ape's nest, a hut, a cottage, or any other habitation (T19;22).

walmak (*Min*) A word that could be roughly translated as "wizard," though "a scientist who works miracles" would be a closer definition (T8;12).

Walumbe The Bansuto god of death (T17;14).

Wamabo A savage tribe of east Africa who captured Lt. Smith-Oldwick when he made a forced landing in their territory in the winter of 1915. They also captured Tarzan and would have eaten both of them had not Zutag come to the rescue (T7;9–10).

Wamala Zora Drinov's black servant boy on the Zveri expedition to east Africa in 1928 (T14;2).

Wamboli A fierce African tribe. Tarzan was rescued from one of its warriors in the fall of 1912 by his wolfhound Terkoz, who killed the man (E1;8).

wang (*Ape*) Arm (TC).

Wang Mang (45 B.C.–A.D. 23) Posthumous name of the Chinese Emperor Shih Huang-Ti, founder of the short-lived Hsin Dynasty. He ruled from A.D. 9–23 and first made contact with Sumatra "just prior to A.D. 23" (T22;27).

Wappi (*Ape*) The antelope; this presumably means any of the larger antelopes, as opposed to the smaller Bara (T6;8).

The War Chief The first novel of the two-volume Apache series, abbreviated A1. It chronicles the adventures of Shoz-dijiji, a white youth raised as an Apache (the adopted son of Geronimo) since infancy. He must battle not only the white race from which he sprang, but also certain enemies among the Apaches who resent his background, to make a place for himself as a war chief. The events took place in the years 1863 to 1881.

"War on Venus" The fourth novelette comprising *Escape on Venus*, in which Carson Napier finds himself caught in a war between two countries of Middle Anlap that fight with huge, tank-tread-supported landships, and again loses Duare.

war paint Shoz-dijiji, the Apache Devil, wore very distinctive war paint — a band of white across the eyes with blue above and below (A2;2).

Waranji A Waziri warrior who accompanied Stanley Wood on his 1935 search for the abducted Gonfala. He went all the way to Thenar with him, then returned for reinforcements at his behest (T21;18).

Ward One of Gum Smith's men (HB;17).

Ward, Bender The first mate of the *Halfmoon*; he shanghaied Billy Byrne from 1913 San Francisco and was later almost killed by Byrne for the deed (K1;1–2).

Warhoon One of the most vicious and bloodthirsty tribes of green men of Barsoom; they were far worse than their mortal enemies, the Tharks. The city of Warhoon, an ancient ruin from which the horde derives its name, is a few hundred miles northwest of Thark. Probably because of the almost insanely vicious behavior of its members, the horde is much smaller than that of Thark, numbering only about 20,000 members (M1;18).

Warlord of Barsoom The title granted to John Carter in 1888 by a jury of jeds and jeddaks, including Kulan Tith, Jeddak of Kaol; Thuvan Dihn, Jeddak of Ptarth; Mors Kajak, Jed of Lesser Helium; Tardos Mors, Jeddak of Helium; Talu, Jeddak of Jeddaks of Okar; Xodar, Jeddak of the First-Born; Tars Tarkas, Jeddak of Thark; the Jed of the reformed Therns; and 23 others. It is not simply an honorary title, but it is a very special one; it gives Carter the powers of a jeddak of all Barsoom in matters of war (M3;16).

The Warlord of Mars The third book in the Mars series, abbreviated M3, which was originally published in *All-Story* magazine as a four-part serial from December 1913 to March 1914. The original events took place in 1888 and were written down by John Carter while visiting the Earth during the summer of 1898. In it, John Carter had to track down Matai Shang, leader of the demystified Therns, after he abducted Dejah Thoris and Thuvia of Ptarth from the Temple of the Sun in the land of the First-Born. Carter pursued him north to Kaol, a backward country which still believed in the discredited Thern religion, then to Okar, the frozen north polar land of the yellow men of Barsoom.

warrior All Barsoomian men who are able to bear arms at all are considered warriors. The word also applies to a jetan piece which can move two squares straight in any direction or combination (M5).

Warriors' Corridor   The western entrance corridor of the four entering the royal dome of Veltopismakus in Minuni (T10;13).

Waruturi   A tribe of Ethiopian cannibals who could (unlike most of their kind) be dealt with if properly approached by a very strong party (T23;2,9,17).

Washington, D.C.   The capital city of the United States of America, one of the dual capitals of the world from 1967 to 2050, after which the Earth was conquered by the Kalkars and Washington made capital of the United Teivos of America (MM1)(MM2;1–2).

Wasimbu   The son of Muviro of the Waziri. He was Jane Clayton's personal bodyguard until the invasion of the Greystoke estate by the regiment of Fritz Schneider, during which the horrible Schneider had him crucified on the wall of the bungalow (T7;1).

Watenga   A variant of Utengi (T18;2).

water, bodies of   The following is a partial list of the many bodies of water on several worlds which have appeared in the works of Burroughs. See individual entries.

Aedis Flumen	Niger
Bandar Az	Noellat-Gerloo
Chinnereth	Omean
Congo	Omwamwi Falls
Darel Az	Palus Meridien
Ganale Dorya	Palus Septentrionium
Gerlat kum Rov	Pangani
Gulf of Torquas	Rela Am
Hudson	Restless Sea
Iss	Rio Mimbres
Jad-bal-lul	Rivers, Barsoomian
Jad-ben-lul	Ru
Jad-in-lul	Rupes Flumen
Japal, Great Lake	Sojar Az
Joram	Solent
Korsar Az	Syl
Korus	Tann
Lake Horus	Thames
Lake Rudolph	Throxeus
Lake Tana	Tiberis Flumen
Limosis Flumen	Toonolian Marshes
Lural Az	Trent
Mafa	Ugambi
Malacca Strait	Ugogo
Mare Orientis	Upindi
Mississippi	Wabi Shebelle
Nameless Strait	Zambezi
Neubari	

water tree   A tree of Vepaja which grows straight up without a branch all the way to the inner cloud envelope of Amtor more than six thousand feet up, where all of their foliage grows in one enormous tuft. These trees absorb water from the clouds and carry it down a porous core to the roots; the pressure of this water forces the sap up to the top of the tree. By tapping the trunk of this tree a supply of cool water may be obtained (V1;7).

Watson, Jed   An Iowa farmer who gave Billy Byrne food in exchange for his chopping wood when he was on the lam for the supposed murder of Old Man Schneider (K2;3).

Wayne, Cyril   An adagio dancer who was hired by Prominent Pictures to play Tarzan in their 1933 movie, *Tarzan of the Apes* (T17;33).

waz   (*Pal*) Black (T8;2).

Waz-don   "Black man" (*Pal*). The black-skinned, shaggy-haired, tailed humans of Pal-ul-don; they look much like a human Negro but have slightly more bestial features, heavy black hair all over their bodies, a prehensile tail, long thumbs and opposable big toes. They are arboreal and are intellectually equal to the Ho-don, but have a lower technology than the latter. They do, however, share the Ho-don's language, both spoken and written. They live in trees and caves (T8;2).

Waz-ho-don   "Black-White man" (*Pal*). A mixed race of Pal-ul-don (half Waz-don and half Ho-don) who live in primitive cave dwellings and huts in a village they call Bu-lur, which lies in the crevasse through which the valley's principal river passes into the great morass to the south. Lt. Obergatz fell in with the Waz-ho-don while in Pal-ul-don, and from them he learned the language (T8;19).

Waziri   An African tribe of fierce warriors who were encountered by Tarzan after his involuntary return to Africa late in 1910, when they lived in a palisaded village about 100 miles southeast of Tarzan's cottage in present-day Angola. After saving their warrior Busuli from a lion, Tarzan was adopted into the tribe by these noble, handsome black people who were so unlike the cannibalistic savages with whom Tarzan was familiar. After he led them to victory over the **Arabs**, who had come for ivory and slaves and killed many Waziri (including their chief), Tarzan was himself made chief of the tribe. The Waziri were the first African tribe Tarzan had ever encountered who owned gold jewelry, and they told him that it had been taken by their fathers from a great ruin inhabited by beastmen; this was the city of **Opar**, to which the Waziri led Tarzan after he became their chief, though their superstitious fear kept even the brave Waziri from going far within it. They helped Tarzan steal the gold from it, though, and were very sad when he announced that he was going back to England (T2;15–19,22, 25–26). He eventually returned, however, and they became his loyal followers and helpers ever after. Over time, Tarzan's example and guidance helped them to become less superstitious, and by 1928 they even dared to enter the "haunted" city of Opar (T14;16–17).

Waziri The chief of the African tribe whose name he bore. He was a wise old warrior who told Tarzan about the city of **Opar** and the **Waziri** expedition there many years before, which he had accompanied as a young man. Waziri was killed by a force of **Arabs** with **Manyuema** troops who had come for ivory and slaves a couple of months after Tarzan joined the tribe, and for his victory over these enemies Tarzan was made their new chief and took the name Waziri as well (T2;15–17).

Weapons A great plethora of weapons appears in the works of Burroughs. Each weapon listed below has its own entry.

acid
Arad
arrows, poisoned
axe, battle
axe, hand
bomb, time
bow, long
bow, short
bow, Tarzan's
cannon, T-ray
club, pal-ul-don
Colt .45
cutlass
dagger
disintegration rifle
Enfield
Flying Death
gladius hispanus
harquebus
honda
hook
javelin
khusa
knife, hunting
knife, Wieroo
knob stick
kris
lance
lasso
Luger
matchlock
parang
pike, Roman
pistol, Barsoomian
pistol, R-ray
radio bomb
ray gun
rifle, Barsoomian
rifle, electronic
rifle, Express
sabre
scimitar, Wieroo
sling, Zertalacolol
spear, Barsoomian
spear, Va-ga
Springfield
sumpitan
sword, hooked
sword, long
sword, Mayan
sword, short
30-30
Thompson submachine gun
torpedo, wheeled
trident
trident, wooden

weapons, Abyssinian The weapons of the Abyssinian army of the early 22nd century of *The Lost Continent* were of the same level of development as those of the early 20th (LC;8).

weapons, Barsoomian On Barsoom no adult, male or female, "is ever voluntarily without a weapon of destruction" (M1;4). All Barsoomian weapons are made of non-corrosive metal (M7;7).

weather, Amtorian Amtor has a strange double cloud envelope which keeps heat in check. Even though the planet is humid fogs and haze are a rarity, possibly due to the planet's natural radioactivity. This radiation results in a faint night illumination (even though no stars are visible through the double envelope) and is the result of a high preponderance of naturally occurring superheavy elements (see vik-ro; yor-san) in the planet's crust (V1;3–4,12). Whenever a rift occurs in both cloud envelopes simultaneously, the tremendous heat of the sun cuts through and causes fantastic storms (comparable to our hurricanes but on a much larger scale) from the uneven heating of atmosphere and ocean (V4;2).

weather, Barsoomian All Barsoomian mornings are clear and hot, except for six weeks when the ice at the poles melts; then it is cloudy. The nights are very cold (M1). The windstorm of 1915 which blew **Tara of Helium** away in her flier was a rare fluke. It was extremely powerful, lasting for two days and doing a great deal of damage, including the destruction of the yellow tower of Lesser Helium (M5;2).

weather, Va-nah The weather of the lunar interior is wholly governed by uneven heating and cooling produced by the scattered crater openings. Lunar storms are absolutely horrible; they feature hurricane-force winds, literally ear-splitting peals of thunder, and enormous lightning balls which roll down the mountains burning up everything in their paths and eventually exploding in earth-shaking thunderclaps (MM1;5).

Webster The California high school against which **Glenora** was playing when **Johnny Lafitte** made the fatal error which kept him second to **Frank Adams** in football all through college (PB).

wedding, Athnean The Athnean wedding is a brief, simple ceremony which includes among its vows a sentence of death to anyone who would cause one of the couple to be unfaithful to the other (T21;23).

wedding, Barsoomian *see* **marriage, Barsoomian**

wedding, Luthanian In **Lutha**, the bride walks up the aisle alone (MK2;14).

week, Unisan The week in the **Polodan** country of **Unis** is ten days long — nine work days and one day off (B1;4).

Weismuller, Johnny (1904–1984) An olympic swimmer (winner of 5 gold medals in 1924 and 1928) who became a movie actor in the 1930s and played **Tarzan** in numerous bad films which gave the American public the idea that Tarzan was a pidgin-speaking halfwit who lived in a tree with his common-law wife and had an adopted son called "Boy" (T22;7).

Welch, Eddie The mucker whom six-year-old **Billy Byrne** most admired; he was a common thief and a murderer (K1;1).

Well of Sounding Water A natural well of the island of **Amiocap** in Pellucidar which leads into the underground land of the **Coripies**. It was into this well that **Tanar the Fleet One** fell and became a prisoner of the Buried People (P3;7).

Wellah (*Ara*) By God (T11;1).

Weller, Jim One of the ranch hands of the Bar-Y Ranch of 1880s **Arizona**. He saw **Bull** associating with the outlaw **Gregorio** after Bull saved Gregorio from **Apaches**; by this innocent observation he unwittingly set up Bull to be framed as an outlaw (HB;2).

Welles, Sophia The fiancée of **Ogden Secor**; she was a rich young woman through

whom Secor knew the **Reverend Pursen**. She eventually married Pursen rather than Secor (and good riddance) thanks to Pursen's similar interests and Secor's lost fortune (GF;6, 9–10).

Welsh, Jimmy The American engineer who assisted **Carson Napier** in building his **rocket torpedo** in the late 1920s (V1;2).

Werper, Lieutenant Albert A Belgian officer who was transferred to an outpost in the **Belgian Congo** as a disciplinary action for some transgression and was driven mad by the conditions. In 1913 he shot his captain dead in a paranoid fit, then ran away after recovering his wits enough to realize the consequences his action would produce. He joined up with the **Arab** raiders of **Achmet Zek** and eventually helped Zek to abduct **Jane Clayton** by infiltrating Tarzan's estate in the guise of a French hunter named **Frecoult**. He then followed Tarzan's safari to **Opar** (after leaving Zek to abduct Jane) and so discovered the lost city's location, but was captured by the Oparians as a sacrifice, rescued by the amnesiac Tarzan, and escaped from the city and valley with the sacrificial knife of **La** in his hand. He later stole the pouch of jewels that Tarzan had taken from Opar and made his way back to Achmet Zek's camp, only to flee again when he realized that the Arab had seen his jewels as he examined them. He was pursued by Tarzan, but a strange coincidence caused the ape-man to lose the trail and Werper eventually met up with a force of **Abyssinian** soldiers on an expedition to punish Achmet Zek, who had conducted a raid in Abyssinia a few months before. By leading the troops to the place where he had seen the **Waziri** bury Tarzan's Oparian gold, Werper succeeded in playing the Arabs (who had also come in search of the gold) and the Abyssinians against one another and escaped in the fracas, but also lost the jewels along the way. He rescued and again lost Jane Clayton, then was found by Tarzan and succeeded in restoring his memory, but both were captured by a force of Belgian soldiers who were looking for Werper. Tarzan called the **great apes** and they were rescued, which allowed Werper to regain the jewels from **Chulk**, who had stolen them from **Mugambi**, who had stolen them from Werper in the Abyssinian camp. Werper then fled Tarzan, but was killed by some predator in the jungle, and Tarzan later recovered the jewels from his corpse (T5).

Wesl, William A bookkeeper of the early 20th century who married the cobbler's daughter who was a good friend of Hilda de Groot's. Wesl was a sort of timid revolutionary at whose home Prince Ferdinand met secretly with Hilda after King Otto had forbidden them to see each other; it was through him and his wife that the first contact between Andresy and Prince Ferdinand was made. Later, it was the hapless Wesl who was set up as the fall guy in King Otto's assassination; he was sent to the palace gardens at the proper time and shot dead by Carlyn while attempting to flee after hearing the shots fired by the true assassin (LL;9,17).

West A lieutenant aboard the *Barsoom* who was assigned a stateroom with Lt. Commander Orthis but preferred to be with his classmate Jay. Orthis later allowed the switch because he had developed a liking for Norton, the ship's ensign, with whom Jay was quartered. This change allowed Orthis to impart much of his knowledge to Norton, which later saved the ship (MM1;1–2,14).

West, Bill Chief cameraman for B.O. Pictures' *The Lion Man*, shot on location in the Ituri Forest of Africa in 1932. He was in love with Rhonda Terry and insisted on accompanying Tom Orman on his search for her and Naomi Madison even after they became completely lost. He apparently had a falling out with her later, because she married Tom Orman rather than West (T17;2–4,9–16,33).

West Camp One of the two "camps" (villages) found by Lt. Jefferson Turck on the Isle of Wight in 2137 (LC;3).

West Castle The castle of Sir Malud of Nimmr, which lies some nine miles west of the city proper (T11;12).

west coast trade language The pidgin tongue spoken by the west African natives to communicate with the Europeans; it was one of the many languages Tarzan spoke (T2;20).

West Lake Street The site of the 28th precinct police station in turn-of-the-century Chicago (K1;1).

West 145th Street The site of James Kelley's New York apartment (ME;2–3).

West Ranch A branch division of the Bar-Y Ranch of 1880s Arizona (HB;3).

Westminster Palace The London palace of the kings of England from the time of Edward the Confessor (who built it) to the time when it was taken over by Parliament as its home in the late 1200s. It burned down in 1834 and its site is now occupied by the present houses of Parliament (OT;2).

Westmore, Perc (1904–1970) A famous cosmetician of the 1930s and 1940s. He was one of the innovators of screen makeup and had his own line of cosmetics (B1;5).

Wettin The king of early 22nd century Grabritin; he was the father of Victory and was killed by Buckingham so he could marry Victory and thus become king (LC;4).

whale, Pellucidarian Some of the freshwater rivers and ponds of Pellucidar are inhabited by very small (five pound) purple whales which often eat vegetation overhanging the streams in which they live (P1;7).

Whimsey A British town famous for the fine whiskey produced there under the supervision of the town's first earl beginning in the late 19th century (T15;1).

Whimsey, First Earl of A British nobleman who won his peerage by large donations to the Liberal Party when it was in power around the turn of the century. His daughter was the aviatrix Lady Barbara Collis (T15;1).

Whiskers The nickname given by his students to the dour president of James Torrance, Jr.'s university (EE;1).

White The secretary of commerce of post–World War III America who died on March 15, 1969, and was replaced by Burroughs (MM2;1).

White, John A California rancher, the father of Kay White; he was a big, likable, middle-aged man who took an instant liking to "Bruce Marvel." Cory Blaine expected to collect a huge reward from him for his daughter's safe return, and after "Marvel" saved her White gave his blessings to her relationship with "Marvel" (D;13–15,20–23).

White, Kay A blond from California who was a guest at Cory Blaine's dude ranch. She was a simple girl who put on no airs and whom both Cory Blaine and "Bruce Marvel" fell in love with, the latter after saving her from a runaway horse. She also fell for him in spite of herself and he later saved her from Blaine's kidnapping plot, a rescue she facilitated by her extreme cleverness. In the end, they became lovers (and we may assume mates) after "Marvel" was revealed as Buck Mason and told his whole story (D;3–8, 12–23).

White, Major A famous big-game hunter who was the technical advisor to B.O. Pictures when they filmed *The Lion Man* on location in the Ituri Forest of Africa in 1932. He was killed by a poisoned Bansuto arrow on the safari's second day of passing through the Bansuto country (T17;1,5).

white eyes *see* pindah-lickoyee

White Horse The brother of Geronimo (A2;1).

white men of Barsoom *see* Lothar; Orovars; Therns

White Mountains A mountain range in Arizona in which John Carter and James Powell went prospecting in 1866. They were there attacked by Apaches, setting in motion the events that would take Carter to Mars (M1;1). During a camping trip in these same mountains (near the headwaters of the Little Colorado) nearly 70 years later, Burroughs was visited by John Carter and told the story that would later appear as *Swords of Mars* (M8).

White Plains A city of New York state, not far north of New York City (ME;2).

White Stables One of the four officially sanctioned racehorse syndicates of 1st century Rome (I;8).

Whitely One of the English crew of the captured U-33 (C1;5).

Whitewater Canyon A canyon of the Chiricahua Mountains of southern Arizona which empties into the Animas Valley south of the mountains (A1;20).

Whitman Publishing The publishing company which produced the Big Little Books, for which Burroughs wrote many adaptations of Tarzan stories, and also "John Carter and the Giant of Mars."

Whoa The white man's mispronunciation of the Apache name Juh (A1;15).

whuff (*Ape*) Smoke (TC).

wier (*Cpk*) A word whose exact meaning is unknown; "powerful" or "great" or "mighty" are probably good guesses (C3;4).

Wieroo "Great Bird" (*Cpk*). The most advanced race of Caspak; they are an evolutionary branch beyond modern humans. A Wieroo stands about human height, but the joints of its huge, bat-like wings reach a foot over its head. Wieroos are entirely hairless (lacking even eyebrows and lashes) and have extremely pale skin, blunt features, large heads, and huge, grey eyes with which they can see in the dark. Wieroos have powerful arms (with claw-like hands) and torsos, but very skinny legs, and they are very powerful fliers. They wear only a long, thin white robe which is open to the knees, but the robes of higher-caste Wieroos are marked in front with red, blue or yellow (see colors, Wieroo).

All Wieroos are male, and for this reason they capture and mate with cos-ata-lo Galus in hope of producing Wieroo females and thus ensuring themselves of supremacy in Caspak. They have a well-organized city, religion, government and legal system which stretches back through eons of time. They have the ability to make paper, and a written language. Wieroos follow a very strict and brutal philosophy called Tas-ad, which controls their lives entirely to the point where most Wieroos think alike, and are most unhappy about their endless quest for reproductive isolation and "world" (i.e., Caspak) conquest (C2;2–3,5)(C3;2–4).

Wiggs, Peter One of the Negro guards at the entrance to the hidden Valley of the Sepulcher when James Hunter Blake blundered into it in 1921 (T11;7).

Wild Bill *see* Willie (HB;11)

Wildcat Bob A little old gunslinger of 1880s Hendersville, Arizona, who had a terribly foul mouth and a great respect for women — he was very meek and gentle in any woman's presence, and was a persistent suitor of Mary Donovan's. He was also a staunch supporter of Bull, whom he refused to believe was the Black Coyote, and hated the crooked, cowardly Gum Smith, whom he opposed at every turn. Bob was shot in the back by Smith while guarding the real Black Coyote (Hal Colby) after he had been captured by Bull, but survived to marry Mary Donovan the next day when she realized that she liked the old man in spite of herself (HB;2–3,10,13, 17–19).

Wildred, Sir A Knight of the Sepulcher who met James Hunter Blake in the last event of the Great Tourney for 1921; they mutually unhorsed each other and were thus removed from combat. He later helped free Blake from the dungeon of the evil King Bohun of the City of the Sepulcher (T11;18,22).

Wilhelmstal A small hill town of German East Africa which was the summer seat of government for that colony (T7;5).

Willie The young, lanky, pimply-faced chore boy of the Bar-Y Ranch of 1880s Arizona. His own nickname for himself was "Wild Bill" (HB;11).

Wilson One of the sailors of the *Lady Alice* who was in the same lifeboat as William Clayton, Jane Porter and "Mr. Thuran" after the wreck of the yacht. After a week without food and the death of Tompkins, Wilson went crazy and attacked Clayton, then leaped into the ocean after being subdued by the others (T2;18).

Another Wilson was one of the crew of the British tug who saved Bowen Tyler and Lys La Rue from the English Channel and captured the submarine U-33 on June 4, 1916. He was an intelligent fellow of the British middle class (C1;3).

Winchelsea A small British town of east Sussex; it was a major seaport in the 13th century (OT;15).

wine, Barsoomian The most prized Barsoomian wine is that of Ptarth (M7;16).

Winter Garden A Hollywood restaurant of the 1920s (GH;27).

Wiramwazi Mountains A small but treacherous African mountain range which is said to be inhabited by a lost tribe of white men. This was only a legend until Erich von Harben found the lost Roman outposts of Castra Sanguinarius and Castrum Mare there in 1923. The deep valley in which these cities are hidden is as large or larger than the Grand Canyon and splits the Wiramwazi

plateau from a point about a mile in. This valley is about a mile deep, with a maximum north-south width of 17.5 miles and a maximum east-west length of 33.5 miles. It is forested, and its east end contains a shallow lake (9 miles north to south and 15 miles east to west) surrounded by papyrus marshes (T12;2). The mountains are the world's only known source of harbenite (T13;1).

Wisconsin An American state, location of the farm which Jane Porter's mother had left to her. She went to live there in the summer of 1909 to get away from Robert Canler for awhile, but he eventually showed up with the intent to force her to marry him. His plans were foiled by the arrival of Tarzan with Professor Porter's treasure, with which Canler could be repaid the money Porter owed him (T1;27–28).

Wison A crewman of the *Halfmoon* who was ordered by Skipper Simms to "go get" Billy Byrne after the latter beat up the ship's second mate; Wison wisely refused (K1;6).

"The Witch-Doctor Seeks Vengeance" The sixth story in the collection *Jungle Tales of Tarzan*, in which Bukawai came seeking payment from Momaya for the spell he never cast to get Momaya's son Tibo back from Tarzan (T6;5); when the woman would not pay, he stole the boy, and Tarzan had to go to his rescue. The story took place around 1908 and is abbreviated T6:6.

Withe, Miss A stenographer at the International Machine Company of 1910s Chicago whom Little Eva replaced after Jimmy Torrance started there as an efficiency expert (EE;18–19).

The Wizard of Venus The fifth Venus story (actually a novella), abbreviated P5. The events of the story took place in 1932 (soon after those of V4) but were not sent to Burroughs until 1941 (at the same time as those of V4). He wrote the story that year, but it was never published during his life; it was included in *Tales of Three Planets* in 1964, and later in a volume of its own with *Pirate Blood*. In the story, Carson Napier uses his telepathic powers to combat a self-proclaimed wizard who is controlling the people of Donuk with a combination of hypnosis, chicanery and fear.

Wlala The Betete woman to whom **Kali Bwana** was given to keep for Chief **Bobolo** after he took her from the **Leopard Men** in 1931. Wlala was a hateful little creature who was killed by Tarzan when she tried to eat Kali Bwana three days later (T18;15,18).

wo (Ape) This (TC).

woad see paint, body

wob (Ape) That (TC).

Woden The king of the gods in Germanic mythology; an all-seeing, all-wise warrior god who was very concerned with the affairs of his Earthly descendants (OT;7).

Wolak A slave of **Fal Sivas'** whom the Barsoomian inventor sent to kill John Carter; it was essentially an order to commit suicide (M8;13).

Wolf A chief of the federated clans that made up the **Tribe of Julian** in the post-**Kalkar** 25th century American West. In 2430, he was a strong, intelligent warrior of 50 (MM3;1).

The Wolf was also the name by which the early 20th century **Karlovan** bandit known as The Rider was called in the city (R;4).

Wolff The original guide of the **Gregory** expedition of 1936, who was replaced in that capacity by Tarzan. He still went along as a hunter and succeeded in stealing the map to **Ashair** and selling it to **Atan Thome**, his real employer. When the expedition finally reached the area of **Tuen-baka**, Wolff deserted, taking the willing porters and the unwilling **Magra** with him, but he made the mistake of trying to force the girl and she shot him dead with his own pistol (T20; 1-4,15-16).

Wolsey, Cardinal One of the privy-councilors of the gorilla-king **Henry VIII**. Wolsey threatened the king with excommunication unless he took the captured **Rhonda Terry** to God (T17;18).

Wolsey, Thomas (1475-1530) An English cardinal and privy-councillor to **Henry VIII** who wielded great religious and secular power and helped bring Henry to the peak of his power. He began to fall, however, when he failed to secure an annulment of Henry's marriage to Catherine of Aragon, and he died of a fever on his way to a trial on trumped-up

charges some of his noble enemies had brought against him (T17;18).

Women's Corridor The eastern entrance corridor to the royal dome of **Veltopismakus** in **Minuni** (T10;19).

Wong The Chinese cook of the **Bar-Y Ranch** (HB;11).

Wong Feng A Chinese shopkeeper and herbalist of **Loango**; one of the confederates of **Atan Thome** (T20;2).

Wood, Stanley An American travel writer who came to Africa in 1935 to look for the lost **Lord Mountford** and found him just as he was dying. Wood was afterward drawn by the power of the **Gonfal** into the **Kaji** country, where he spent six months and fell in love with their queen, **Gonfala**. She also fell in love with him and so helped him escape, but he was discovered by **Mafka** and drawn back to Kaji with Tarzan (who had since met and befriended him) in hot pursuit. Tarzan eventually rescued Wood from the **Castle of Mafka**, took the Gonfal, and gave Mafka over to the Kaji to deal with as they saw fit. Wood and Gonfala then headed for Europe, but Gonfala was abducted by **Spike** and **Troll** to "work" the Gonfal, which they had also stolen. Wood pursued their trail to the valley of **Thenar**, where he was captured by the revolutionary government of **Athne** and enslaved until he was rescued by Tarzan and sent back to civilization with Gonfala (T21;1-3,9-14, 18-25).

Wood of the Leopards A forest of the **Valley of the Sepulcher** which is inhabited by large, fierce leopards with little fear of man (T11;19).

Woola The great Barsoomian **calot** that was John Carter's pet "hound." It was at first assigned to him as a watchdog while he was a prisoner of the **Tharks**, but when he saved it from being killed by **white apes** and nursed it back to health, it became his lifelong friend. The fiercely loyal and protective creature followed Carter on all of his early adventures across the length and breadth of Barsoom. Of Woola, Carter said "[it] held in its poor ugly carcass more love, more loyalty, more gratitude than could have been found in the entire five million green Martians who rove the deserted cities and dead sea bottoms of Mars" (M1;6)(M2)(M3).

Woora The identical twin brother of **Mafka**, who was with him a wizard of the **Kaji** until he became jealous of him and stole the **Great Emerald**, companion stone to the **Gonfal**, and fled with his followers, who became the **Zuli**. He was a hideous, ancient man with yellow skin (but not Oriental features) and was extremely bony with age, except for a pot-belly. He was killed by the Englishman **Lord** in 1935 after Tarzan cleared the way (T21;3–6).

Worchester The British city in whose cathedral **King John** was buried in 1216 (OT;1).

World War I The name later applied to what at the time was called "The Great War," a local European conflict between **Serbia** and **Austria-Hungary** that eventually blossomed into an international war involving 32 countries. It began on July 28, 1914, and did not end until November 11, 1918 (Armistice Day). Tarzan actively fought in the African campaigns as a lone guerrilla after the Germans destroyed his estate (T7), and **Korak** enlisted as a regular and was sent to the **Argonne**, later learning to fly an airplane (T8)(T10;1). **Barney Custer** had to defend **Lutha** from Austrian incursions in the first few months of the war (MK2). **Bowen Tyler, Jr.**, was on the way to enlist in the American ambulance corps when his ship was sunk by a German U-boat in June of 1916 (C1;1), and **Julian 1st** died in the Argonne on Armistice Day (M1). In the time-line of *The Lost Continent*, the United States never entered World War I, deciding instead to allow the Europeans to fight it out among themselves and establishing a ban on contact with the entire eastern hemisphere (LC;1).

World War II A global war which began on September 1, 1939, with the invasion of Poland by Nazi Germany, eventually blossomed into a worldwide conflict involving 67 countries, and did not end until 1945, leaving the world a far different place than when it began. Tarzan fought in the Second World War as a uniformed regular in the RAF (T22), and **Tangor** fought in its early days as an RAF volunteer before the United States officially entered the war (B1;1).

World War III The conflict which lasted from 1959 to 1967 and resulted in the domination of America and its allies over the whole world. In a way this turned out to be a tragedy, for it meant that modern Western ideas of disarmament and gun control would now prevail, leaving the world defenseless for the Lunarian invasion of 2050 (MM1) (MM2;1).

Worth, Betty The woman of **Dennis Corrigan**, the man who was sent to the mines for reading in **Kalkar**-occupied 22nd century America. Betty was a member of the secret church to which **Julian 8th** and his family belonged, and was reunited with Corrigan for a short while at the beginning of the revolution, until he was killed (MM2;7,11).

Wright, Andrew A farmer of the teivos of Chicago in Kalkar-occupied 22nd century America. He was a friend of the Julian family's whose woman killed all of her female babies, as many women of the time did (MM2;4).

Wright-Smith, Algernon A young English aristocrat who was captured with the crew of the *Naiad* in 1938 by **Wilhelm Schmidt** and his pirate crew of the *Saigon* (T24;6).

writing, secret, Kaparan The secret writing of the **Kapars** of **Poloda** is invisible unless viewed under a special light (B2;2).

Wunos One of the 11 co-orbital planets of the star **Omos**. Wunos lies between **Banos** and **Zandar**, four planets away from **Poloda** (B1).

Xanator A dead city of ancient Barsoom located on the western shores of the ancient Gulf of Torquas and frequented by the green men of the horde of Torquas. Tavia was taken there by the warriors who captured her, and was saved by **Tan Hadron**, who had seen her from his vantage point in an ancient lighthouse (M7;4).

Xanila The Queen of **Xuja** from around 1855 to 1915. She was an Englishwoman (the daughter of a missionary) who was captured by **Arab** slave raiders at the age of 20; the party became lost in central Africa and eventually stumbled upon the desert of western Tanganyika, where the few party members who survived were captured by the Xujans. The maniacs made the beautiful Xanila their queen, passing her from king to king until she was quite an old woman when

Bertha Kircher was captured by the Xujans (T7;19).

Xanthus A noble house of **Athne** which was next in power to the royal house. Tarzan's friend **Valthor** was the son of the head of the house (T16;12).

Xarator A large active volcano at the north end of the valley of **Onthar** in the **Ethiopian Highlands**. It was used by the people of **Cathne** both to dispose of their dead and to execute political criminals (T16;3,11,17–18).

xat (*Bar*) The Barsoomian "minute," which equals about 2 minutes, 57 seconds. There are 50 xats in a **zode** (or Barsoomian hour) and each xat is divided into 200 **tals**, or Barsoomian seconds (M2;16).

Xatl Din A noble of the lost **Mayan** colony of **Uxmal** when Tarzan and the passengers and crew of the steamer *Saigon* was shipwrecked there late in 1938 (T24;11).

Xavarian The flagship of the fleet sent out by **Zat Arrras** from **Helium** to find **Dejah Thoris**, who had fled his advances during John Carter's long absence (M2;16).

Xax The chief of the **Coripi** tribe of Pellucidar who captured **Tanar the Fleet One** in 1925 and planned to save him with other prisoners to have one huge feast when there were enough captives. Xax was a huge, extra-hideous Coripi with purple mottling in his skin, suggesting putrefaction (P3;7).

Xaxa The **Jeddara** of **Phundahl** and High Priestess of **Tur**; she was a hideous and disfigured old woman who was as ugly spiritually as she was physically. She paid **Ras Thavas** an enormous sum to transfer her brain to the body of the gorgeous **Valla Dia**, but was later abducted by **Ulysses Paxton** and replaced in her own hideous carcass. By command of the Great Tur she was then deposed as jeddara and **Dar Tarus** was made jeddak; this so enraged her that she died in a fit of apoplexy (M6;1,13–14).

Xaxak A dator of the **First-Born** of the city of **Kamtol** on Barsoom who bought John Carter as a slave, and after seeing his skill with a sword decided to have him fight for stakes in the lesser **games**. After the **Jeddak Doxus** saw Carter's skill, Xaxak was forced to "give" him to the jeddak (M10:2;6–9).

Xerstle A **Cathnean** noble of the early 20th century, the son of a mine foreman who was raised to the nobility thanks to his friend **Erot**, another recently created noble. Xerstle tried to kill Tarzan at the instigation of Erot, but failed miserably (T16;10,14–15).

Xexots The yellow men of Pellucidar, who dwell south of the **Nameless Strait** in walled cities. The Xexots are much more highly developed than the other human races of Pellucidar (discounting the **Korsars** and the artificially-advanced **Empire of Pellucidar**) and have reached the bronze age. They have a monetary system and an advanced government and religion, but no writing or knowledge of ships (P7:2;4–7/3;1–7).

Xodar A dator of the **First-Born** of Barsoom whom John Carter defeated after killing his entire crew; he then bound him with his own **harness**. For this failure **Issus** made him the slave of John Carter, who himself had been enslaved by the First-Born. Carter befriended Xodar, however, convinced him of the falsity of Issus and her religion, and escaped the First-Born with his help. After the conquest of the blacks by the forces of **Helium** and **Thark**, Xodar was made **Jeddak** of the First-Born and promised to turn them into a worthwhile and productive nation (M2;9)(M3).

xot (*Pal*) The number 1,000 (T8; 21).

Xuja A lost city of Africa which lies at the bottom of a deep, forested valley in a high-altitude desert of western **Tanganyika**. It is a very ancient city, rectangular and walled, with narrow, crooked streets and two-story buildings, the second stories of which jut out over the sidewalks and are supported by columns. The public buildings are larger and more ornate and are topped by domes and minarets; statues, bas-reliefs and paintings of parrots (and to a lesser extent, monkeys and lions) decorate these buildings. All around the city are cultivated, irrigated fields.

The Xujan race, however, is made up of what could only be called "sane maniacs," a people who have the appearance of maniacs and the tendency toward violent, insane outbursts, yet on the whole can cooperate peacefully and sanely together. They have yellowish, dry, tough skin and black hair which grows out very stiffly from their scalps and down the forehead to some extent. Their pupils and irises are small (resulting in a great deal of white eyeball showing), and their canine teeth are very prominent. Otherwise, they have a somewhat Mongoloid appearance. Male Xujans wear pants and short tunics with soft sandals and leggings, and carry **sabres**; the women wear sari-like garments which leave their breasts uncovered.

The race settled in the valley ages ago and slowly changed over time, becoming inbred and imbecilic. This may be partly due to their bizarre religious rituals in which they worship **parrots**, especially one very old one which is their chief deity. These parrots are very intelligent and can repeat almost word for word what the monkeys of the forest tell them, thus warning the Xujans of the presence of intruders in their valley because the monkeys can speak the Xujan language (or else some Xujans speak the ape tongue, which is more likely). This language is weird but has some elements which are familiar to European languages, and its alphabet seems to be derived from Greek.

The Xujans originally ate lion meat as a religious ritual, but in modern times eat it exclusively, even going so far as to raise some lions as cattle; these lions are fed on deer and swine which are kept for the purpose and never eaten by the Xujans. They keep other lions as guard animals, especially the huge **black lion** of the forest without. Goats are kept for milk (T7;15–19).

Yacovarman (?–900) A great, near-legendary king of the **Khmers** of ancient **Cambodia**, who ruled from 889 to 900 and founded **Angkor**. Tradition holds that he was a leper (HM;7).

yad (*Ape*) Ear (TC).

yah (*Apa*) He (A1).

yah-ik-tee (*Apa*) "He is not here" (said of a dead friend) (A1;3).

yah-tats-an (*Apa*) "It is dead" (said of an animal) (A1;2).

Yale A prestigious Ivy League university attended by **David Innes** right around the turn of the century (P1;3).

Yamdor A huge red Barsoomian man, the loyal personal slave to **Ras Thavas**, who kept Yamdor's loyalty through gifts and endless favors. It was rumored among Ras Thavas'

other slaves that Yamdor was actually a woman's brain in a man's body, and indeed the hulking warrior acted like a woman in both positive and negative characteristics. Yamdor hated Ulysses **Paxton** and would have been only too happy to carry out Ras Thavas' order to destroy **Valla Dia**, had not Paxton hidden her first (M6;5).

Yan A Thoran armed merchantman of Amtor which was the first real prize taken by **Carson Napier's** pirate ship *Sofal* in 1929. Aboard the *Yan* was a Thorist Ongyan named Moosko (V1;12–13).

yan-des-tan (*Apa*) The sky (A1;4).

yang (*Ape*) Swing (TC).

Yanks The name given by the **Kalkar** rulers of 22nd century America to American nationalists; it was a name the Americans accepted as a title of honor (MM2;4–5).

yano A Barsoomian game of chance which is played by rolling tiny numbered spheres at a group of numbered holes. It is an ancient game, the Barsoomian equivalent of dice (M7;12).

Yaqui An Indian tribe of **Sonora** who at first strongly resisted the Spanish invaders, then gradually became settled, but rebelled against the Mexican government in the early 19th century in a series of uprisings that were not completely put down until 1887 (A1;5).

yat (*Ape*) Eye (T17;30).

Yat The chief of the **Timal** aborigines of the northern hemisphere of Amtor. He was the friend of **Jantor**, the **Jong** of **Japal** (V4;19).

yato (*Ape*) Look or see (TC).

yauger An iron rod used as a hunting club (A1;1).

Ydeni The **Kavuru** warrior whom Tarzan saved from a lion in 1934. Out of gratitude, he later told Tarzan of the secret passage from the **Temple of Kavandavanda** to the outside forest (T19;8,31).

yeacks Horrible invisible ogres of Hindu mythology who only appear when they are about to devour a human victim (HM;4).

year, Amtorian How it is arrived at when there are no observable astronomical phenomena on Amtor is unknown, or at least never mentioned by Carson Napier. For comparison purposes, one must assume he translated all measurements of Amtorian time into Earthly units for the reader's convenience (V1;4).

year, Barsoomian *see* **Ord**

year, Polodan The year of Poloda is about 300 days long; its day is roughly equal in length to that of the Earth (B1;5).

yegg *see* **yeggman**

yeggman (American slang) A thief who travels as a hobo (K2;3).

yel (*Ape*) Here (TC).

yeland (*Ape*) There (TC).

Yellow Franz A large, blond bandit chief of the Black Mountains of Lutha who captured Barney Custer after his escape from Blentz in October of 1912, intending to hold him for ransom as Leopold of Lutha, whom Franz (like everyone else) thought he was. Franz was shot dead by his servant Rudolph to save Custer, whom he also believed was his king (MK1;6).

yellow men of Barsoom The members of the ancient yellow race of Barsoom have black hair and beards and skins the color of ripe lemons. They were probably the most technologically advanced of the ancient races, and the red race is descended from a mixture of the yellow race with the ancient black and white races. While the oceans were drying up, the yellow race fled north to escape the green men and defeated the latter at the Battle of the Carrion Caves. The north polar land they built after the battle is called Okar, and is a frozen waste with a few cities built in huge domes that act as greenhouses, warming their interiors.

Although the Okarians were until recently reclusive, they did not have a superiority complex as did most of the other remnants of ancient races (see First-Born; Therns). As a matter of fact, many Okarians believed in the Thern religion, although it is doubtful that any ever took the Pilgrimage, because the existence of the yellow race was merely a legend until John Carter and Thuvan Dihn penetrated their country in pursuit of Matai Shang. Through careful monitoring of the outer world, the Okarians kept abreast with

developments in the rest of Barsoom, even though they remained apart from it (M3;8–9).

"Yellow Men of Mars" The original title of "Escape on Mars" when it appeared as a novelette in *Amazing Stories* magazine in August of 1941.

yellow men of Pellucidar *see* **Xexots**

Yellowstone A major river of Wyoming and Montana (J;3).

Yemeny An Arab sentry of the tribe el-Harb who was killed by Tantor when he came to save Tarzan from the tribe (T11;2).

Yersted The commander of the submarine that went between Omean and the Temple of Issus on Barsoom (M2;12).

yeti The name given by the natives of Tibet to the creature called the Abominable Snowman by Europeans. The yeti is closely related to the great apes of Africa (T6:10).

yo (*Ape*) Friend; this is probably an error — see next entry (T17;14).

yo (*Pal*) Friend (T8;4).

Yo Seno The keeper of the keys in the palace of Haj Osis, Jed of Tjanath on Barsoom. He was a coarse and bestial man who was accustomed to taking liberties with female prisoners and slaves in the palace, but was eventually killed by Tan Hadron (M7; 6,11).

Yoka The Pacific island (not far from Taiwan) to which a daimyo of the Japanese shogun house of Ashikaga fled around 1550 after his dynasty collapsed. His loyal samurai accompanied him and they intermixed with the natives until their descendants became a band of half-savages with only distorted traditions of Japan. Onto this island came the brigantine *Halfmoon* carrying Barbara Harding and the cutthroats who had abducted her, including Billy Byrne (K1;9–10).

Yonda The Klootoganja of Pandar, consort of Endar, when Carson Napier came to their country in 1932. She was a Tolan by blood and tried to warn Napier of the trap her mother-in-law had in store for him (V5;4).

Yonda One of the 11 co-orbital planets of the star Omos. It lies between Tonos and Banos, two planets away from Poloda (B1).

Yongi A river of Sonora which lies some 300 miles south of the American border (A2; 13).

yor (*Amt*) The number 100 (V1;8).

yor-san "Hundred five" (*Amt*). The Amtorian name for the radioactive and highly unstable element hahnium (atomic number 105), of which they apparently know a more stable form, because it is the primary constituent of lor, an Amtorian fuel which (when exposed to the radiations of vik-ro) undergoes an atomic chain reaction, releasing huge amounts of energy (V1;8).

yorgan "Hundred man" (*Amt*). The Amtorian word for a common person; it is the title given to the common citizens of Havatoo, who are still more intelligent and well-educated than most Amtorians. It is also the name of the area of Havatoo in which they live (V2;14).

Yorgan Lat "Commoner Avenue" (*Amt*). The broad avenue which runs parallel to the Klootag Lat about a third of a mile inside the outer wall of the Amtorian city of Havatoo. It is the outer boundary of the Yorgan section of the city, and many of its businesses and factories face the street (V2;15).

Yorimoto, Oda The ruler of Yoka, who was the descendant of a daimyo of the Ashikaga Dynasty who fled to the island from Japan around 1550 when his house fell from power. Yorimoto and his people were the degenerate products of the Ashikaga, mixing with the Malaysian savages who originally inhabited the island. He was killed by Barbara Harding with his own short sword when he tried to rape her and neglected to remove his weapons first (K1;9–10).

yorko (*Amt*) The number 1,000 (V4;25).

yorkokor "One thousand daggers" (*Amt*). An officer who commands one thousand men; the equivalent of a colonel in Amtorian armies (V4;25).

Yron The Myposan noble who bought Kandar and Carson Napier from the slave market when they were captured by the Myposans late in 1930 (V4;7).

Yucatan The large peninsula of the east coast of southern Mexico, which marks the southern end of the Gulf of Mexico. It is

covered in lush tropical jungle and was the home of the Maya people of the first millennium A.D .(T24;1).

yud (*Ape*) Come (T22;9).

Yuma Any of several Indian tribes of the lower Colorado River, western Arizona, or Sonora (A1;3).

Yuma Bill A Yuma Indian scout killed by the Apaches in the spring of 1879 (A1;20).

yut (*Ape*) "Stab" or "gore" (TC).

yuto (*Ape*) Cut (TC).

Za "Girl" (*Pal*). The name given by Tarzan to the bitch he got from Umanga to nurse Jad-bal-ja on. This was no easy feat at first, but eventually the two natural enemies became attached to one another (T9;1).

Zabo The green-uniformed secret police of the Polodan nation of Kapara. They were much like the Gestapo of Nazi Germany (B2;2).

Zad A green Barsoomian warrior of Thark who challenged John Carter to a fight at the instigation of Sarkoja. With the help of the latter, a mirror and the sun, he almost won (M1;14).

Zaire, Republic of The present-day name of the Congo Free State, where many of Tarzan's adventures took place, and where Mbonga's tribe of cannibals originally hailed from (T1;21).

zaldar Another of the peculiar-looking Amtorian herbivora; the zaldar is the Amtorian beef cow. Burroughs' description is choice: "A zaldar is a most amazing appearing animal. It has a large, foolish-looking head, with big, oval eyes, and two long, pointed ears that stand perpetually upright as though the creature were always listening. It has no neck and its body is all rounded curves. Its hind legs resemble in shape those of a bear; its front legs are similar to an elephant's, though of course, on a much smaller [and narrower] scale. Along its spine rises a single row of bristles. It has no tail and no neck, and from its snout depends a long tassel of hair. Its upper jaw is equipped with broad, shovel-like teeth, which always protrude beyond its short, tiny lower jaw. Its skin is covered with short hair and is a neutral mauve color, with large patches of violet, which, especially when it is lying down, make it almost invisible against the pastel shades of Amtorian scenery. When it feeds it drops down on its knees and scrapes up the turf with its shovel-like teeth, and then draws it into its mouth with a broad tongue. It also has to kneel down when it drinks, for, as I have said before, it has no neck. Notwithstanding its strange and clumsy appearance, it is very fast."

The normal zaldar is about the size of a Hereford cow; there is also a smaller breed, the pig-sized **neozaldar** (V4;54)(V5;3).

Zamak The captain of the prison guards of the castle of the **Tarids** of **Ladan** (M8; 18).

Zambezi The African river near whose headwaters **Opar** was built. The river flows south through **Angola** and **Zambia**, then east along the latter's border with Zimbabwe, then through Mozambique to the Indian Ocean. It is into its waters that the sacred river leaving **Tuen-baka** eventually flows (T2;19)(T20; 12).

Zambia The modern name of **Northern Rhodesia** (T5).

zan (*Amt*) Beast (V2;13).

zan (*Ape*) Skin (T1;5).

Zan Dar The **Savator** who was imprisoned with John Carter and U Dan on **Eurobus**. He told them a little about the **Morgors** and the politics of his planet, helped John Carter rescue **Dejah Thoris**, and took her to safety in his homeland of **Zanor** (M11B; 4-6).

Zanda A slave girl belonging to **Fal Sivas** of **Zodanga**, one of those on which he wished to experiment to develop his **mechanical brain**; she escaped, however, and ran for protection to the disguised John Carter, who was working for Fal Sivas. She acquainted Carter with Fal Sivas' experiments, and he hid her in his room; he later let her sneak back to her own quarters and chose her as his personal slave the next day. She did not know that her protector, whom she knew as "Vandor," was actually John Carter, whom she hated because he had arranged the sack of Zodanga, in which her father had died; his death later drove her mother to take the Pilgrimage in grief.

While Carter was later away in **Helium**, **Fal Sivas** again took her for experiment and Carter had to rescue her again upon his return, thus incurring Fal Sivas' wrath. She accompanied him to **Thuria** (though he did not tell her why they were going) and she was imprisoned with the others by the **Tarids**. She eventually escaped with the others, forgave her vendetta against Carter, and became romantically attached to **Jat Or** (M8;2-3,8, 12-13,24).

Zandar One of the 11 co-orbital planets of the star **Omos**. It lies between **Uvala** and **Wunos**, almost directly opposite **Poloda** (B1).

zangan "Beastman" (*Amt*). A ferocious Amtorian predator. Kloozangan are like men who go on all fours with short rear legs, the rear feet of which are tilted up so the zangan walks upon its rear toes — its hands, however, are more human. They are white-skinned and nearly hairless (except on head and jowls) and have small, savage eyes and heavy, undershot jaws with broad mouths armed with large, strong teeth. Kloozangan have flat noses and are omnivorous, but hunt in packs for nearly any prey, including man (V2;13).

Zani A Fascist political party of the nation of **Korva** on **Amtor** which came to power in the 1920s and displaced **Kord**, the rightful **Jong** of Korva, in favor of their leader **Mephis**, a common soldier. They arrived in power riding on a wave of unrest which followed a disastrous war in which Korva was economically debilitated, and like most revolutionary groups quickly established a totalitarian state. Zanis marked themselves by a **mohawk** haircut. After the death of Mephis by poisoning (at the hand of **Zerka**) the counter-revolutionaries struck and Zanism was overthrown, especially since many of those who claimed to be Zanis were actually sick of its ideas and practices and wanted their jong back (V3;6, 15-17).

Zanor A small and remote island of **Eurobus** which is thickly forested and covered with rough and treacherous mountains. It was of no economic or military value to the **Morgors**, who did not bother conquering it because of its lack of worth and the difficulty of assaulting it from the air. It is inhabited by a small nation of **Savators** who retained their independence from the Morgors, protecting themselves from attack by the inaccessibility of their mountain haunts; the largest mountain of Zanor is 20 miles high. To this island Dejah Thoris escaped with the help of U Dan, Zan Dar and Vorion; John Carter had to steal a Morgor ship to follow (M11B;4,9).

Zanzibar An island off the east coast of Africa, originally settled by Arabs, which became an important and powerful center of the slave and ivory trades. It became an English possession in 1890, and is today part of the nation of Tanzania (T7).

Zapata, Emiliano (1877–1919) A Mexican Indian revolutionary leader who proposed agrarian reforms and fought against almost all of Mexico's early revolutionary governments for their lack of those reforms. In 1914 he teamed up with Pancho Villa to fight Carranza and was subsequently assassinated by Carranza's agents (K2;6).

Zar The Vepajan noble house to which Duran belonged (V1;5).

zarith The Pellucidarian Tyrannosaurus, which is found on the continent the dirigible O-220 first arrived on, but not the one on which the Empire of Pellucidar lies (P5;9).

Zat Arrras A Zodangan nobleman who was made Jed of Zodanga after its reduction by Helium. With John Carter and Carthoris missing, Tardos Mors and Mors Kajak missing while searching for them, and Dejah Thoris missing while fleeing from Zat Arrras, the latter was the acting Jeddak of Helium. He used his influence to have John Carter tried and convicted of conspiracy and of returning from the Pilgrimage and locked him in the pits for almost an Earthly year, after which Carter was rescued by Carthoris. Zat Arrras committed suicide by leaping from his ship above the Lost Sea of Korus when Carter boarded it (M2;16–20).

zecchin (Also sequin) A gold trade coin of medieval times, also known as the Ducat, which was struck in Venice and used throughout Europe (OT;3).

zee (*Ape*) Leg (TC).

Zellerndorf, Count The Austrian ambassador to Lutha just before World War I, who persuaded Leopold of Lutha to pardon Prince Peter of Blentz, Coblich and Captain Maenck by convincing him that Prince

Ludwig von der Tann was his enemy. This was done to ensure that Austria have her way in Lutha, since Peter had made a deal with the Austrian Emperor through Zellerndorf (MK2;1).

zeppelin A form of rigid airship or dirigible which was widely used in the early part of the 20th century but largely abandoned after the *Hindenburg* disaster in May of 1937. The zeppelin was named for its German inventor, Graf Ferdinand von Zeppelin (P4;1).

Zerka A toganja of Amlot when Carson Napier came there in 1930. She liked his looks and befriended him, saving him from the fate at Zani hands that he would most certainly have blundered into otherwise. She was a powerful Zani and a powerful underground leader who originated many of the Zani excesses in the hopes that these would make the people hate the Zanis more and thus be more receptive to counter-revolution. She was eventually found out and would have been executed had Napier not come to save her with his anotar and many bombs (V3; 7–16).

Zero Popular name of the Mitsubishi A6M, the most common Japanese combat plane of World War II; it was one of the most versatile and maneuverable propeller-driven craft ever built (T22;2).

Zertalacolol The Minunian name for the subhuman alalus creatures that dwelt among the hills around their land. The females of the species are built largely, but not excessively tall, and have a huge musculature — they are easily able to move the huge blocks of sandstone with which they build their corrals. These females are about as hairy as most human males, are entirely mute, and are very vicious and hostile; their only cooperative venture is the building of the stone corrals in which captured males and their own children are kept. The creatures have small brains and very large, movable ears and are of a very primitive level of tool use — they have fire and chipped stone weapons. Males do not live among the females, but rather in the forest nearby, and are about five feet tall, slenderly built, and very effeminate in appearance and behavior. During mating season a female would sally forth whenever she felt the need, capture a male, keep him a few weeks to mate with, then let him go so as not to have to feed him for the rest of the year. Their own children they also kept corralled up, feeding them until they were old enough to fend for themselves, then letting them go. There was no love between the sexes or between parent and child, which Burroughs believed was a natural consequence of their perverse gender relationship.

Upon his crash-landing in Minuni on his first solo airplane flight, Tarzan was captured (while stunned from the crash) by a Zertala-colol woman and taken to her corral, but he later escaped with one of her male children, whom he taught to make superior weapons. The boy then taught this skill to the other men, who began the struggle to establish the "normal" order of gender roles (T10;2–5,9, 14,21).

zertol (*Min*) Prince (T10;13).

zertolosto (*Min*) Crown prince (T10; 16).

Zeyd A young Arab of the tribe el-Harb who was enamored of Ateja, the daughter of Sheik Ibn-jad. In 1921 he was framed by his rival Fahd for the attempted murder of Ibn-jad, but with Ateja's help he escaped the camp and certain execution. In his flight he encountered Tarzan, whom he told of Ibn-jad's plan to sack Nimmr. He later came with the Waziri to rescue Tarzan and was reunited with Ateja (T11;2,8,10,23–24).

Zithad The dator of the personal guards of Issus on Barsoom. He and John Carter met while the latter was a prisoner of the First-Born of Dor, and again when Carter was a prisoner among the First-Born of Kamtol while Zithad was visiting there. Carter killed him before he could reveal the Warlord's true identity (M2;12)(M10:2;12).

zitidar "Mastadonian draft animals" of Barsoom used by the green men to draw their chariots. They are also used for various purposes by the red men, especially as a source of leather. No clear description of a zitidar is ever given, except that they are very large and sometimes go mad (M5).

Zo-al The god or devil of the Va-gas, conceived of as a great beast who lives in the hoos and causes storms and other calamities when he is angry (MM1;5).

Zoanthrohago The Minunian walmak of Veltopismakus who discovered a process for temporarily shrinking organic matter which he used on Tarzan when the latter was captured by the Veltopismakusians; Tarzan was thus reduced to the size of a Minunian and enslaved. Zoanthrohago developed his machine while attempting to perfect a device for enlarging creatures, and its results were unpredictable — the shrinkage lasted for 3 to 39 lunar months and the return to normal size could take anywhere from two minutes to seven days. He was later condemned to death by Elkomoelhago in a fit of pique and imprisoned, but he helped Tarzan and his party to escape, and he and the Princess Janzara (who loved each other) escaped with them to Trohanadalmakus, where he was received as befitted a man of his intelligence and skill (T10;9,14,20–21).

Zodanga A powerful city-state of Barsoom (30 degrees south latitude, 172 degrees east longitude) which was once chief among the enemies of Helium. It is a modern and advanced city with walls 75 feet high and 50 feet thick which are built of enormous blocks of carborundum. The Zodangans are not evil people, but have a history of bad leadership. Shortly after Dejah Thoris' escape from the Tharks she was captured by the Zodangan prince Sab Than, who attempted to force her into marriage by threatening the destruction of Helium, which his father Than Kosis had attacked in the absence of Helium's fleet, which was still out searching for Dejah Thoris. John Carter and Kantos Kan entered the city and joined the Zodangan navy in order to rescue the princess, and eventually succeeded in doing so by accomplishing the sack of Zodanga by several hordes of green men united under Tars Tarkas. The city was then reduced to part of the Heliumetic Empire (M1).

In later times Zodanga became a Mecca for political malcontents from all over the Empire because many of its people lacked any love of their Heliumetic rulers. The city was also the home of the most powerful of the Barsoomian assassin's guilds, so John Carter was forced to travel there to fight his secret war against that guild (M8;1).

zode (*Bar*) The Barsoomian "hour," of which there are ten in a Barsoomian day; the first zode begins at dawn on the winter solstice. Each zode is 2 hours, 27 minutes, 42 seconds long and is divided into 50 shorter units called **xats** (M2;16).

Zog A big, good-natured **Thoran** sailor of Amtor who had been a slave before the revolution but preferred that to "freedom" under the **Thorists**, because then he had only one master, but now everyone above him in rank was his master. He joined **Carson Napier's** 1929 mutiny aboard the *Sofal* (V1;9).

zombie A creature of West Indian folklore; a human corpse returned to a semblance of life to do the bidding of a practitioner of voodoo. The creatures of **Skor**, **Jong** of **Kormor**, were very like zombies, but they were animated by scientific rather than magical means and controlled by Skor telepathically (V2;10).

Zopinga A **mugalla** of the **Bagalla** tribe who captured the "**Tarzan Twins**" after they became lost in the summer of 1920 (TT1;3–4).

zor (*Ape*) In (TC).

Zor (Niocene) The cave lion (E1;1).

Zor The Pellucidarian warrior of **Zoram** who was enslaved in **Oog** with **David Innes** in 1929. They escaped together into the Valley of the **Jukans**, where they were again imprisoned, but they escaped again and headed back towards **Sari**. Zor later married **Kleeto**, whom he saved from the Jukans, and they had a son (P6;3–15,28).

Zor A Barsoomian city-state 380 miles southeast of **Helium** that was conquered in the late 1930s after the disappearance of **Multis Par**, Prince of Zor, a thoroughly hated person who had been fomenting rebellion against Helium for a long time. After his disappearance, the trouble stopped, because the people of Zor wanted to be a part of the rich and powerful Heliumetic Empire (M11B;1–2).

Zoram A Pellucidarian tribe which inhabits the **Mountains of the Thipdars**. It was famed for the beauty of its women (P4;6,11).

zorat A peculiar-looking saddle animal of **Noobol** on Amtor. It is about the size of a small horse and has long, slender legs supported by almost horizontal femurs which act as shock absorbers for the rider. The zorat has round, nailless, heavily-calloused feet and a soft "natural saddle" in its back. It has a short, broad head with two large, saucer-like

eyes and floppy ears, and is herbivorous (V2;9).

zu (*Ape*) Big (T7;10).

zu-gor "Big growl" (*Ape*). Roar (TC).

zu-kut "Big hole" (*Ape*). Cave (TC).

zu-ro (*Ape*) Strong (TC).

Zu-tag "Big Neck" (*Ape*). A young bull ape of the tribe of **Go-lat** who (with the help of **Bertha Kircher** and eight of his fellow apes) saved Tarzan and **Lt. Smith-Oldwick** from being killed and eaten by the **Wamabo** tribe in the winter of 1915 (T7;10).

Zu-tho "Big Mouth" (*Ape*). A great ape of the tribe of **Ungo** who was with those who stumbled upon the **Temple of Chon** while waiting for Tarzan to return from **Ashair** in 1936. The agitated Zu-tho would have killed **Magra** had not Tarzan intervened (T20; 31–32).

Zu Tith The **Jed** of **Zor**, a cruel tyrant whom his people were glad to see defeated. His son, **Multis Par**, was just like him (M11B;2).

Zuanthrol "Giant" (*Min*). The name given to Tarzan by the people of **Veltopismakus** (T10;11).

Zubanev A Russian expatriate who met **Joseph Campbell** in London in 1939 and helped him to steal the plans for **Horace Brown's ignition disruptor** and take them to Rome to sell to the Fascists. When the plans were re-stolen by the Englishman **Lt. Cecil Giles-Burton**, they pursued in an Italian plane and shot him down over **Northern Rhodesia**, but were shot down themselves in the process. They joined the **Ramsgate** safari under assumed names to get to **Bangali**, but the safari was joined en route by Giles-Burton, who unfortunately did not recognize the villains. They recognized him, however, and murdered him for the plans. Campbell then murdered Zubanev so he would not have to split the proceeds from the sale of the documents with him (T24B;1–2,5–7).

Zugash "Big Tooth" (*Ape*). A king baboon of the **Ghenzi** region whose tribe Tarzan befriended while there in 1929 (T15;8).

Zuki The **Goolian** warrior of Barsoom who was selected to fight with **Vor Daj/**

Tor-dur-bar— helped, of course, by ten assistants, as is the cowardly Goolians' fashion (M9;21).

Zuli The enemies of the **Kaji**. Once, the Kaji had two wizards, **Mafka** and **Woora**, but the latter became jealous of the former's power, stole the **Great Emerald**, and went to live on the far side of the plateau with his loyal followers, who became the Zuli. Since the power of either the **Gonfal** or Great Emerald alone is less than that of the combination, the Kaji and Zuli continually war to steal the other stone. After the deaths of Mafka and Woora, the two tribes mended their rift and rejoined (T21;3–10).

Zuppner, Captain The captain of the dirigible **O-220** on its expedition to Pellucidar in June of 1927. Zuppner was a German military engineer who had designed airships before, during and since **World War I**, and so was a perfect choice for captain of the ship. He helped design and construct it as well (P4;2).

Zural The chief of the village of **Lar** on the island of **Amiocap** in Pellucidar. **Tanar the Fleet One** and **Stellara** were taken to him upon their arrival at the island, but he refused to believe that they were not **Korsars** and ordered them burned at the stake (P3;3–4).

Zurk The son of **Jalu**, chief of the **Zurts** of Pellucidar. Zurk wanted **O-aa** for a mate when she came to their country in 1932 but she repulsed him, thus making an enemy of him. She later wounded him with an arrow when he tried to attack her in the forest while she was hunting (P7;4;7–9).

Zuro An Amtorian girl of **Vepaja**, the woman of **Duran**, when **Carson Napier** first arrived there in 1929 (V1;4).

Zurts A neolithic tribe of Pellucidar which dwells on the shores of the **Korsar Az** south of **Korsar** and southwest of **Sari**. The Zurts have bows, agriculture, domesticated animals, huts and sails, and are not universally hostile to strangers (P7:4;6).

zut (*Ape*) Out (TC).

Zutho "Big Mouth" (*Ape*). A great bull ape of the tribe of **Toyat** who refused to kill Tarzan at Toyat's command because the ape-man had once nursed Zutho back to health when he was sick (T11;3). They later met again in the arena of the lost Roman city of **Castra Sanguinarius**, and Zutho helped Tarzan escape (T12;17). By 1931 Zutho had become the king of a tribe in the **Congo** region, where he saved Tarzan from a tribe of **pygmies** (T18;17–19).

Zveri, Peter A Russian communist who led an expedition to Africa in 1928 to foment rebellion among the natives and start a war between France and Italy through their African colonies. He was an arrogant, hateful man with dreams of an African empire, but was also a bully and a coward. He twice attempted to rob **Opar**, but his native followers refused to enter the city on both occasions. His attempts to start a war also failed, thanks both to his own poor planning and to Tarzan, and he was eventually shot in the back by **Zora Drinov**, whose family he had murdered during the Russian Revolution (T14;1,5–9,14–17).

Zygo The King of **Athne** who was overthrown by a revolution in the mid–1930s and escaped into the mountains with many of his loyal followers. He was replaced on the throne by the **Cathneans**, who wanted a worthy opponent to fight (T21;20–25).

Zytheb One of the priests of **Brulor** in **Ashair**; he was the keeper of the keys for the temple's cages, where would-be profaners were indefinitely imprisoned. **Helen Gregory** was given to him as a wife when she was brought to Ashair in November of 1936, but she hit him over the head with a heavy vase, killing him; she then stole his keys and let **Paul d'Arnot** and her brother **Brian** out of their cages (T20;18–20).

APPENDICES

A. Chronology of Events in Burrough's Fiction

Year	Book or events
23,000,000 B.C.	Mythical Tree of Life on Barsoom
13,000,000 B.C.	Pliocene epoch begins on Earth
3,000,000 B.C.	Primitive Kaldanes & rykors on Barsoom
2,000,000 B.C.	Kaldanes telepathically control rykors
1,500,000 B.C.	Paleolithic Barsoom; microcephalic rykors
1,000,000 B.C.	Quaternary period on Earth; Neolithic Barsoom
900,000 B.C.	Founding of Horz by Orovars
800,000 B.C.	Orovar shipping; founding of Aanthor, Thark, etc.
700,000 B.C.	Black and yellow races gain civilization
600,000 B.C.	Barsoomian lifespan exceeds 1000 years; Peking Man
500,000 B.C.	Barsoomian seas begin to recede; green men multiply; Tongue of Barsoom; Gathol founded
400,000 B.C.	Orovars in decline, colony at Otz; red Barsoomians
300,000 B.C.	Orovar cities abandoned; last alliance vs. green men
200,000 B.C.	Founding of Okar; atmosphere plant; first canals; great marshes of Barsoom; black race settles Dor & Omean; Therns
150,000 B.C.	City of Bantoom, modern rykors; Lothar founded; black race becomes a bandit race; Toonolian marshes; Manator, Morbus, Invak founded; Neanderthal Man on Earth
100,000 B.C.	Supposed date of the creation of the universe by Tur; the Niocene period in Africa; Barsoomian seas entirely gone; Kaolian forest; Phundahl, Jahar, Tjanath, Pankor founded; cult of Issus and the Pilgrimage; cult of Tur
75,000 B.C.	Kaol, Ptarth, Amhor, Duhor founded; canals complete
50,000 B.C.	Helium founded; on Earth, Neanderthal Man dies out; humans enter Pellucidar (probable)
40,000 B.C.	Toonol, Zodanga, Hastor founded; North America settled
21,000 B.C.	Tower of Thavas
10,000 B.C.	Approximate date of sinking of Atlantis; Neolithic revolution on Earth; radium power on Barsoom
6000 B.C.	Mechanics, modern weapons on Barsoom; Neolithic Earth

387

Year	Book or events
4000 B.C.	Radium motors, aircraft, radio on Barsoom; Black Pirates of Barsoom establish their legend; twin towers of Helium; Copper Age on Earth; Egyptian and Sumerian civilizations
3000 B.C.	Birth of the last Issus; advanced medicine, optics, and electronics; Bronze Age on Earth
2000 B.C.	Therns convinced of Issus' divinity; Middle Kingdom of Egypt, Babylonian Empire, Achaean Greece, Hsia Dynasty
1500 B.C.	Iron Age begins on Earth
1000 B.C.	Klufar's theory of Relativity of Distance (Amtor); Okarians isolate 8th ray; Egyptian decline, Assyria
500 B.C.	Red Barsoomians develop wireless to an art, isolate 8th ray; oldest Barsoomians of 20th century born; Persian Empire, Golden Age Greece, Roman Republic
100 B.C.	Approximate date of first large Barsoomian fliers
A.D. 1	Probable birthtime of Ras Thavas, Xaxa; formal psionics, advanced electronics on Barsoom; Roman Empire, Han Dynasty China
A.D. 16	I begins
A.D. 41	I ends
A.D. 100	Castra Sanguinarius founded
A.D. 200	Castrum Mare founded (from Castra Sanguinarius)
500	Nerve index machine of Kamtol; Fall of Rome; Buddhism; Dark Ages of Europe
900	Amtorian Serum of Longevity perfected; Red Barsoomians perfect Earth observation, pneumatic subways; Holy Roman, Mongol Empires on Earth
1191	An army on the 3rd crusade shipwrecked, lost in Africa
1200	Ras Thavas perfects transplants, Tardos Mors born
1243	O begins
1264	O ends
1400	Approximate time of Thor, founder of Thorism (Amtor)
1452	Uxmal founded by Mayan explorers
1500	Alemtejo founded (approx.); destination compass on Barsoom
1550	The Korsars enter Pellucidar (latest probable date)
1600	Mors Kajak (approximate birthdate)
1750	Ras Thavas perfects brain transplant on Barsoom
1800	Dejah Thoris (approximate birthdate)
1845	The *Dolly Dorcas* wrecked in the Arctic Ocean
1855	Birth of the "literary" Burroughs
1858	First genetic engineering by an eccentric Oxford biologist
1861	The American Civil War begins
1863	A1 begins
1865	End of the American Civil War
1866	M1; Green Tharks join Heliumetic alliance
1871	German Empire
1876	Failure of the atmosphere plant(Barsoom); John Carter returns to Earth
1881	A1 ends
1884	A2 begins
1886	A2 ends; M2 begins
1887	M2 ends; overthrow of Issus and the Therns
1888	M3
1889	Birth of Tarzan; M4 begins

Year	Book or events
1890	M4 ends
1896	Birth of Julian 1st
1898	Radium discovered on Earth
1903	P1 begins; powered flight on Earth
1906	T6 begins
1908	T6 ends
1909	T1 begins (main action)
1910	T1 ends; T2 begins
1911	CG1&2; T2 ends
1912	MK1; T3
1913	P1 ends, P2 begins; E1&2; T5; R
1914	MK2; World War I begins; K1; T7 begins
1915	K2 begins; M5; P2, T7 end; T8; T9 begins
1916	C1, C3; K2 ends
1917	K3; C2; T9 ends; Russian revolution
1918	Battle of the Argonne/World War I ends; M6 begins; T10
1920	M6 ends; TT1&2
1921	T11
1922	GH; Stalin becomes secretary-general of Soviet Union
1923	T12
1924	Discovery of the Gridley Wave
1925	P3 begins; improved flier motors, invisibility (Barsoom)
1926	M7; P3 ends; P4 begins; guided missiles, disintegration (Barsoom)
1927	P4 ends; P5 begins
1928	P5 ends; T14
1929	V1; V2, P6 begin; T15; Stalin dictator of the USSR
1930	P6, V2 end; V3 begins; M8; T16; approx. birthdate of the Burroughs who narrates MM1-3; first interplanetary flier, mechanical brain on Barsoom
1931	V3 ends; V4; P7; T18
1932	T17; V5
1933	Adolf Hitler dictator of Germany
1934	T19
1935	M9 begins; T21
1936	M9 ends; T20
1938	T23; T24
1939	B1; M10; World War II begins
1940	B2; M11A
1942	The first nuclear chain reaction
1944	T22
1945	World War II ends; official radio contact with Barsoom; the Atomic Bomb on Earth
1959	World War III begins
1967	World War III ends; Earth/Barsoom technological cooperation
2000	Birth of Julian 5th
2015	First Mars-Earth flier lost in space
2016	Julian 5th graduates from Air School
2024	First Earth-Mars ship launched (MM1 begins)
2036	MM1 ends; complete disarmament of Earth, breaking off of contact with Barsoom
2050	Kalkar conquest of Earth

Year	Book or events
2100	Birth of Julian 9th
2120	MM2
2137	(LC)
2309	Kalkars pushed completely out of American west
2409	Birth of Julian 20th
2430	MM3
2432	Birth of Julian 21st

B. Selected Words
from Featured Languages

Amtorian

ad	gerloo	lap	ortij	togan
al	gyan	lat	pol	toganja
ambad	hita	lo	ra	tokordogan
an	ho	lor	raj	tong
anotar	jan	loto	ro	tonglantar
ata	janjong	lotokor	rokor	tra
ath	jodades	maltu	rotik	vadjong
athgan	jong	med	rov	vik
ax	joram	mistal	san	vik-ro
bar	kalto	neo	sentar	vir
basto	kantum	neolantar	sera	vol
bol	kar	neozaldar	so	vong
dan	kloo	no	sofal	voo
du	klookor	nobar	sovong	vookor
el	klootogan	nobargan	tag	vootogan
ellat	klootoganja	noellat	tan	vootoganja
fal	ko	not	tanjong	yor
faltar	kob	notar	tarel	yor-san
faltargan	kolantar	o	tartum	yorgan
gan	kor	od	te	yorko
ganfal	kordogan	ong	ted	yorkokor
ganja	korgan	ongvoo	tharban	zaldar
gantor	kum	oolja	tik	zan
gap	kung	ooljagan	to	
gerlat	lantar	ooljaganja	tob	

Apache

chigo-na-ay	ink-tah	kan	pesh	tsoch
chil-jilt	intchi	kle-go-na-ay	pesh-litzogue	tzi-daltai
dahl	inzayu	klij	pindah	tzi-ditinde
dijiji	ish-kay-nay	kunh-gan-hay	shee-dah	Usen
duklij	ittindi	lekay	shoz	yah
es-a-da-ded	itza-chu	litzogue	si-chi-zi	yah-ik-tee
gun-ju-le	izze	metate	tapida	yan-des-tan
hogan	junh-gan-hay	nejeunee	tats-an	
ijan-ale	ka-chu	on	tizwin	

Ape

abu	Duro	Kudu	Sheeta	unk
Ara	ga	malb	Ska	Usha
Argo	gash	Manu	Skree	vando
balu	Gimla	Meetah	so	ved
Bara	go	mu	sord	yat
blat	Gorgo	nala	tag	yo
Bolgani	Histah	Numa	tand	yud
bu	Horta	Pacco	Tantor	zan
Buto	huh	Pamba	tar	zu
dako-zan	ka-goda	Pand	tarmangani	
dan-do	Kota	Pisah	Tongani	
Dango	kreegh-ah	Sabor	Ungo	

Arabic

afrit	billah	ghrol	jinn	rahla
am'dan	bint	gluck	khusa	sahar
aud	douar	hareem	menzil	sheik
aziz	el adrea	hejra	moghreby	sheytan
beduw	el fil	hijab	mukaad	simm
beled	fendy	houri	nargily	wellah
beyt	ghrazzu	jetta	nasrany	

Barsoomian

ad	dur	kadar	sak	than
ay	dwar	kaor	Sassoom	thoat
aytan	forandus	karad	silian	tor
banth	gorthan	mad	sof	ulsio
bar	haad	odwar	sofad	umak
calot	hekkador	ov	sorak	usa
corphal	Jasoom	padwar	tal	utan
Cosoom	jed	panthan	tanpi	xat
dator	jeddak	pi	tee	zitidar
dar	jedwar	polodona	teedwar	zode
darseen	jetan	Rasoom	teepi	

Caspak

a	cor	jo	lu	tas-ad
ata	cos	jo-oo	lua	wier
atis	ecca	ju	oo	
band	ga	kazor	pak	
batu	ho	kro	sto	
bo	jaal	lo	sva	

Latin

apodyterium	centurion	imperator	servilia	toga
atrium	flumen	lupanar	sinus	trireme
basilica	frigidarium	mare	subura	
caligae	gustatio	palla	tablinum	
carpentum	habet	palus	talent	

Minunian

amak	diadetax	hual	novand	walmak
aoponato	ee-ah	jetak	tuano	zertol
aopontando	ental	kamak	vental	zertolosto
diadet	entex	makus	ventex	zuanthrol

Pal-ul-don

a	don	ja	od	son
ab	dor	jad	og	ta
ad	e	jar	om	tan
adad	ed	jato	on	to
adaden	el	ko	otho	ton
aden	en	kor	pal	tor
adenaden	enen	lav	pal-e-don-so	tu
adenen	es	lee	pan	ul
an	et	lo	pastar	un
as	fur	lot	pele	ut
at	ged	lu	ro	ved
bal	go	lul	sad	waz
bar	gund	lur	san	xot
ben	guru	ma	sar	yo
bu	het	mo	sat	za
dak	ho	mu	so	
dan	id	no	sod	
den	in	o	sog	

Pellucidarian

ah	darel	karoo	rah	ta-ho
am	dyryth	ma	rahna	tandor
androde	gilak	maj	rela	thag
ara	go-sha	molop	ryth	trag
az	gyor	orthopi	sadok	
cors	karana	padang	sojar	

Polodan

da	el	jan	pom

Swahili

baba	kali	Mulungu	sahib
boma	memsahib	nyanza	simba

Va-nah

gu-e-ho	jemadav	keld	rympth
hoo	kalkar	nonovar	teivos
javadar	kamadar	ola	tor-ho
jemadar	kash	paladar	ula

[And see Appendix C on the next page]

C. Story Map for
Burroughs' Fiction Works

Stories related by cross-referencing

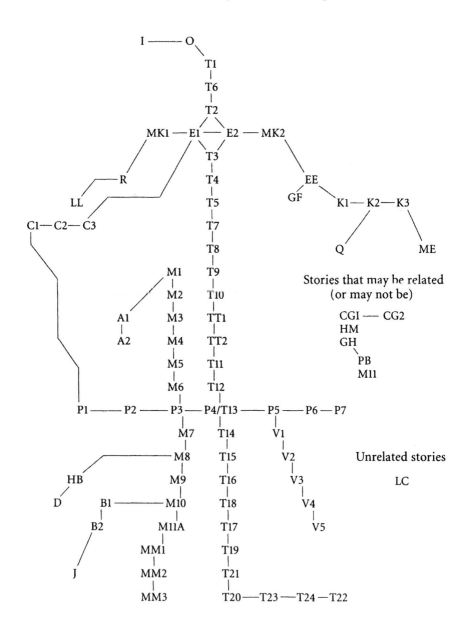

BIBLIOGRAPHY

American Library Directory 1992-93. New Providence, NJ: R. R. Bowker, 1992.

Behler, John L., and King, F. Wayne. *The Audubon Society Field Guide to North American Reptiles and Amphibians.* New York: Knopf, 1991.

Brown, Lauren. *Grasslands.* New York: Knopf, 1985.

The Cambridge Encyclopedia of Astronomy. New York: Crown, 1977.

Cassell's Spanish Dictionary. New York: Macmillan, 1978.

Chambers World Gazetteer. Cambridge: Chambers, 1988.

Current Biography Yearbook. (Several editions.) New York: H. W. Wilson.

Dictionary of American Biography. New York: Scribner, 1964.

Dictionary of American History. New York: Scribner, 1976.

Dictionary of Scientific Biography. New York: Scribner, 1970.

Dictionary of the Middle Ages. New York: Scribner, 1982.

Dixon, Dougal, et al. *The Macmillan Illustrated Encyclopedia of Dinosaurs and Prehistoric Animals.* New York: Macmillan, 1988.

Doty, Richard G. *The Macmillan Encyclopedic Dictionary of Numismatics.* New York: Macmillan, 1982.

Encyclopaedia Britannica. Fifteenth edition, 1988.

Ewen, David. *American Popular Songs.* New York: Random House, 1966.

Felleman, Hazel. *The Best Loved Poems of the American People.* New York: Doubleday, 1980.

Funk & Wagnalls New Encyclopedia. 1983 edition.

Gowlett, John A. J. *Ascent to Civilization.* New York: Knopf, 1984.

Guinagh, Kevin. *Dictionary of Foreign Phrases and Abbreviations.* Third edition. New York: H. W. Wilson, 1983.

Guns of the World. New York: Bonanza Books, 1977.

Hammond Gold Medallion World Atlas. Maplewood, NJ: Hammond, 1987.

The Harper Atlas of World History. New York: Harper & Row, 1987.

Havlice, Patricia Pate. *Popular Song Index.* Metuchen, NJ: Scarecrow Press, 1984.

Held, Robert. *The Age of Firearms.* Northfield, IL: Gun Digest, 1970.

Hirschfelder, Arlene, and Molin, Paulette. *The Encyclopedia of Native American Religions.* New York: Facts on File, 1992.

Hollingsworth, J. B. *The History of American Railroads.* New York: Exeter, 1983.

Leitch, Barbara. *A Concise Dictionary of Indian Tribes of North America.* Algonac, MI: Reference Publications, 1979.

Lewis, Charlton T., and Short, Charles. *A Latin Dictionary.* Oxford, 1966.

Lloyd, Ann, and Fuller, Graham. *The Illustrated Who's Who of the Cinema.* New York: Macmillan, 1983.

MacMahon, James A. *Deserts.* New York: Knopf, 1985.

McWhorter, George T. *Burroughs Dictionary.* Lanham, MD: University Press of America, 1987.

Marshall Cavendish Illustrated Encyclopedia of Plants and Earth Sciences. New York: Marshall Cavendish, 1990.

Marshall Cavendish International Wildlife Encyclopedia. New York: Marshall Cavendish, 1990.

Nash, Jay Robert, and Ross, Stanley Ralph. *The Motion Picture Guide*. Chicago: Cinebooks, 1985.

National Geographic Atlas of the World. Fifth edition, 1981.

New Century Cyclopedia of Names. New York: Appleton-Century-Crofts, 1954.

New Larousse Encyclopedia of Mythology. London: Hamlyn, 1981.

The Oxford English Dictionary.

Porges, Irwin. *Edgar Rice Burroughs: The Man Who Created Tarzan*. Provo, UT: Brigham Young University Press, 1975.

Random House Webster's College Dictionary. New York: Random House, 1991.

Reader's Digest Guide to Places of the World. London, 1987.

Reedstrom, Ernest Lisle. *Apache Wars: An Illustrated Battle History*. New York: Sterling, 1990.

Roy, John Flint. *A Guide to Barsoom*. New York: Ballantine Books, 1976.

Ruben, Samuel. *Handbook of the Elements*. La Salle, IL: Open Court, 1990.

Schlesinger, Arthur. *The Disuniting of America*. New York: Norton, 1992.

Shepherd, William R. *Historical Atlas*. Ninth edition. New York: Barnes & Noble, 1969.

Tapsell, R. F. *Monarchs, Rulers, Dynasties and Kingdoms of the World*. New York: Facts on File, 1983.

Ulrich's International Periodicals Directory. Thirty-first edition. New Providence, NJ: R. R. Bowker, 1992.

Webster's Biographical Dictionary. Springfield, MA: G. & C. Merriam, 1966.

Webster's New Geographical Dictionary. Springfield, MA: G. & C. Merriam, 1980.

Webster's Third New International Dictionary. Springfield, MA: G. & C. Merriam, 1971.

Wentworth, Harold, and Flexner, Stuart Berg. *Dictionary of American Slang*. Second edition. New York: Thomas Y. Crowell, 1975.

Who Was Who in America. Chicago: Marquis, 1989.

World Almanac. 1992 edition.

World Book Encyclopedia. 1991 edition.

INDEX